STATEMENT	DESCRIPTION (Page in Text)	EXAMPLE OF USAGE
ENTRY	Specifies entry point in a subprogram (784)	ENTRY POLY (X)
EQUIVALENCE	Establishes sharing of memory locations by different variables in same program unit (779)	EQUIVALENCE(X,Y), (ALPHA,A,T(3))
EXTERNAL	Specifies externally defined subprograms that may be used as arguments (369)	EXTERNAL F, QUAD
FORMAT	Defines a list of descriptors (257)	20 FORMAT (1X, 'ROOTS ARE', 2F8.3)
FUNCTION	Heading for a function subprogram (318)	FUNCTION AVE(X, N)
GO TO	Unconditionally transfers control to a specified statement (201)	GO TO 100
IMPLICIT	Used to establish a naming convention (771)	IMPLICIT REAL (L, N-Z), INTEGER (A-K)
INQUIRE	Determines properties of a file or of its connection to a unit number (722)	INQUIRE (EXIST = FLAG, NAME = FNAME)
INTEGER	Specifies integer type (46)	INTEGER X, CLASS, TABLE(10,20)
INTRINSIC	Specifies intrinsic functions that may be used as arguments (373)	INTRINSIC SIN, DSQRT
LOGICAL	Specifies logical type (160)	LOGICAL P, Q, TABLE(4,6)
Logical IF	Executes or bypasses a statement, depending on the truth or falsity of a logical expression (129)	IF (DISC .GT. 0) DISC = SQRT(DISC)
OPEN	Opens a file (287, 718)	OPEN(UNIT = 12, FILE = FNAME, STATUS = 'OLD')
PARAMETER	Defines parameters (48)	PARAMETER (LIM = 100, RATE = 1.5)
PAUSE	Interrupts program execution, program may be restarted (771)	PAUSE PAUSE 'PROGRAM PAUSE'
PRINT	Output statement (67–68, 256)	PRINT *, 'X = ',X PRINT * PRINT '(1X, 3I7)', M, N, M + N
PROGRAM	Program heading (72)	PROGRAM WAGES
READ	Input statement (68, 271, 284, 724)	READ *, ALPHA, BETA READ '(15, F7.2)', NUM, Z READ (12, *, END = 20) HOURS, RATE
REAL	Specifies real type (46)	REAL NUM, GAMMA, MAT(10,10)
RETURN	Returns control from subprogram to calling program unit (319, 786)	RETURN RETURN 2
REWIND	Positions file at initial point (290, 728)	REWIND 12
SAVE	Saves values of local variables in a subprogram for later references (421)	SAVE X, Y, NUM SAVE
Statement function	Function defined within a program unit by a single statement (330)	F(X,Y) = X**2 + Y**2
STOP	Terminates execution (770)	STOP STOP 'PROGRAM HALTS'
SUBROUTINE	Heading for subroutine subprogram (394)	SUBROUTINE CONVER (U, V, RHO, PHI)

WHILE, DO WHILE	First statement of a WHILE loop; not in standard FORTRAN 77 (204)	WHILE X > 0 DO DO WHILE X > 0
		   PRINT *, X PRINT *, X
		   X = X − .1 X = X − .1
		END WHILE END DO

WRITE	Output statement (67–68, 282, 729)	WRITE (*,*) A, B, C WRITE (12, '(1X, 3I6)') N1, N2, N3

Fortran 90
for Engineers
and Scientists

Larry Nyhoff
CALVIN COLLEGE

Sanford Leestma
CALVIN COLLEGE

Prentice Hall, Upper Saddle River, New Jersey 07458

Library of Congress Cataloging-in-Publication Data

Nyhoff, Larry R.
   FORTRAN 90 for engineers and scientists / Larry Nyhoff, Sanford
Leestma.
     p. cm.
   Includes index.
   ISBN 0-13-519729-5
    1. FORTRAN 90 (Computer program language) I. Leestma, Sanford.
II. Title.
QA76.73.F25N92   1997
005.13'3—dc20   96–17843
                                                CIP

Acquisitions Editor: Alan Apt
Developmental Editor: Sondra Chavez
Managing Editor: Laura Steele
Creative Director: Paula Maylahn
Art Director: Amy Rosen
Assistant to Art Director: Rod Hernandez
Production Manager: Bayani DeLeon
Production Editor: Judy Winthrop
Interior Designer: Sheree Goodman
Cover Designer: Heather Scott
Cover Photo: Science Museum/Science and Society Picture Library
Manufacturing Buyer: Donna Sullivan
Copy Editor: Kristen Cassereau

© 1997 by Prentice Hall, Inc.
Upper Saddle River, NJ 07458

Printed in the United States of America

10 9 8 7 6 5

ISBN 0-13-519729-5

Prentice-Hall International (UK) Limited, *London*
Prentice-Hall of Australia Pty. Limited, *Sydney*
Prentice-Hall of Canada, Inc., *Toronto*
Prentice-Hall Hispanoamericana, S. A., *Mexico*
Prentice-Hall of India Private Limited, *New Delhi*
Prentice-Hall of Japan, Inc., *Tokyo*
Prentice-Hall Asia Pte. Ltd., *Singapore*
Editora Prentice-Hall do Brasil, Ltda., *Rio de Janeiro*

Brief Table
of Contents

Contents

2   BASIC FORTRAN   42

2.1   Data Types + Algorithms = Programs   44

2.2   Data Types, Constants, and Variables   45

2.3   Arithmetic Operations and Functions   56

2.4   The Assignment Statement   62

2.5   Input/Output   69

2.6   Program Composition and Format   74

4   REPETITIVE EXECUTION   188

6   PROGRAMMING WITH FUNCTIONS   322

12   FILE PROCESSING   826

13   POINTERS AND LINKED STRUCTURES   876

APPENDICES

Preface

*F*ORTRAN, now more than 40 years old, is a language used throughout the world to write programs for solving problems in science and engineering. Indeed, thousands of programs and routines in standard libraries such as IMSL (International Mathematics and Statistics Library) and NAG (Numerical Algorithms Group) used by scientists and engineers are written in Fortran. Since its creation in the mid 1950s, it has undergone a number of modifications that have made it a very powerful yet easy-to-use language. These modifications, however, led to a proliferation of different dialects of FORTRAN, which hindered program portablity. Since some uniformity was desirable, the American National Standards Institute (ANSI) published the first FORTRAN standard in 1966. In the years following, extensions to this standard version of FORTRAN were developed, some of which came into common use. It became apparent that many of these features should be incorporated into a new standard. The resulting updated ANSI FORTRAN standard (ANSI X3.9-1978) is known popularly as FORTRAN 77. As more modern programming languages were developed, it became clear that some of the new concepts and techniques introduced in these languages should be supported in Fortran as well. Consequently, a new Fortran standard was prepared and eventually approved. This latest version of Fortran, called Fortran 90, includes all of the major features of earlier versions so that the large investment made in Fortran software is protected because these millions of lines of code will continue to execute properly in Fortran 90. Equally important, however, are the many new features added to the language to bring it up-to-date. These include the following:

- Replacement of the old fixed format for programs with a free form
- Longer names for objects, making programs easier to read
- New control constructs for selective and repetitive execution
- New kinds of subprograms to facilitate modular programming
- Powerful new array-processing mechanisms
- Programmer-defined data types
- Dynamic memory allocation and pointers for constructing complex data structures

Key Features

This book gives a complete and accurate presentation of Fortran 90 , but it is more than a programming manual. It reflects the fact that the main reason for learning a programming language is to use the computer to solve problems. A key emphasis of this text is problem solving. The book contains

- 64 complete programming examples
- 34 of these are special applications that illustrate problem-solving methodology. Applications include
    - Beam deflection
    - Quality control
    - Computer graphics
    - Electrical networks
    - Road construction
    - Searching a chemistry database
    - Internet addresses
    - Data compression

In addition, we have concentrated on making this text an effective learning tool. Some of the pedagogical features are:

- 365 quick quiz questions
- 700 written exercises
- 300 programming problems relevant to engineering and science
- Chapter summaries at the end of each chapter that include a description of the Fortran features introduced and used in that chapter
- Boxed displays that make it easy to find descriptions of the basic Fortran statements and constructs
- A design that makes the text attractive and readable

The text emphasizes the importance of good structure and style in programs. In addition to describing these concepts in general, each of the examples and applications demonstrates good algorithm design and programming style. At the end of each chapter, a Programming Pointers section summarizes the important points regarding structure and style. These sections also emphasize language features and warn against some problems that beginning programmers may experience.

This text is intended for a first course in computing and assumes no previous experience with computers. It provides a comprehensive description of Fortran 90, and most of the material presented can be covered in a one-semester course. Each chapter progresses from the simpler features to the more complex ones; the more difficult material thus appears in the last sections of the chapters.

Supplements

- An instructor's manual containing solutions to exercises and most of the programming problems.
- Sample programs and subprograms marked in the text with a disk icon and data files used in examples can be downloaded from our ftp site as follows:

  ftp to `ftp.prenhall.com`

  login as `anonymous`

  use your e-mail address as the password

  cd to `pub/esm/nyhoff/fortran.90`

Acknowledgments

We express our sincere appreciation to all who helped in any way in the preparation of this text, especially our acquistions editor Alan Apt, managing editor Laura Steele, development editor Sondra Chavez, and production editor Judy Winthrop. We also thank Larry Genalo and Ferenc Szidarovszky for suggesting several new examples and exercises and to Erin Fulp for the Internet address application in Chapter 13. We also appreciate the thoughtful reviews that were provided by Tom Walker, Ramzi Bualuan, Thomas Casavant, Sharad Laxpati, Bart Childs, and Larry Genalo. Their suggestions were most helpful. And, of course, we must once again thank our wives, Shar and Marge, whose love and understanding have kept us going through another year of textbook writing, and to our kids and grandkids, Jeff and Dawn, Jim, Greg and Julie, Tom and Joan, Rebecca, Megan and Joshua, Michelle, Sandy and Lori, and Michael, for not complaining about the times that their needs and wants were slighted because of our busy schedules. Above all, we give thanks to God for giving us the opportunity, ability, and strength to complete this text.

LARRY NYHOFF
SANFORD LEESTMA

Fortran 90
for Engineers
and Scientists

1

Introduction to Computing

I wish these calculations had been executed by steam.

CHARLES BABBAGE

One machine can do the work of fifty ordinary men. No machine can do the work of one extraordinary man.

ELBERT HUBBARD

If we really understand the problem, the answer will come out of it, because the answer is not separate from the problem.

KRISHNAMURTI

It's the only job I can think of where I get to be both an engineer and an artist. There's an incredible, rigorous, technical element to it, which I like because you have to do very precise thinking. On the other hand, it has a wildly creative side where the boundaries of imagination are the only real limitation.

ANDY HERTZFELD

*T*he modern electronic computer is one of the most important products of the twentieth century. It is an essential tool in many areas, including business, industry, government, science, and education; indeed, it has touched nearly every aspect of our lives. The impact of the twentieth-century information revolution brought about by the development of high-speed computing systems has been nearly as widespread as the impact of the nineteenth-century industrial revolution.

Early computers were very difficult to program. In fact, programming some of the earliest computers consisted of designing and building circuits to carry out the computations required to solve each new problem. Later, computer instructions could be coded in a language that the machine could understand. But these codes were very cryptic and programming was therefore very tedious and error-prone. Computers would not have gained widespread use if it had not been for the development of high-level programming languages such as Fortran. These languages made it possible to enter instructions using an English-like syntax.

Since its beginnings in the mid 1950s, Fortran has been refined and extended so that today it is one of the most widely used programming languages in engineering and science. Indeed, thousands of programs and routines in standard libraries such as IMSL (International Mathematics and Statistics Library) and NAG (Numerical Algorithms Group) used by scientists and engineers are written in Fortran.

Fortran 90 is the latest version of this programming language. It includes all of the major features of earlier versions so that the large investment made in Fortran software is protected because these millions of lines of code will continue to execute properly in Fortran 90. Equally important, however, are the many new features added to the language to bring it up-to-date. These include the following:

- Replacement of the old fixed format for programs, which dates back to the use of punched cards, with the free form allowed in Fortran 90

- Longer names for objects, making programs easier to read
- New control constructs for selective and repetitive execution (see Chapters 3 and 4)
- New kinds of subprograms to facilitate modular programming (see Chapters 6 and 7)
- Powerful new array-processing mechanisms (see Chapters 8 and 9)
- Programmer-defined data types (see Chapter 10)
- Dynamic memory allocation and pointers for constructing complex data structures (see Chapter 13)

All of these features combine with the continuing emphasis on efficient execution and ease of use to make Fortran 90 a powerful modern programming language for solving problems in science and engineering and to ensure that it will remain one of the dominant languages for scientific computing into the twenty-first century. It is this version of Fortran on which this text is based.

In this chapter we first provide some background by describing computing systems, their main components, and how information is stored in them. This is followed by a brief summary of how Fortran has developed. We also begin our study of programming and problem solving by developing a Fortran 90 program to solve a simple problem.

1.1 COMPUTING SYSTEMS

Two important concepts led to computers as we know them today: the **mechanization of arithmetic** and the **stored program** for the automatic control of computations. We will briefly describe some devices that have implemented these concepts.

Early Computing Devices

One of the earliest mechanical devices used in ancient civilizations to assist in computation is the abacus. Although its exact origin is unknown, it was used by the Chinese perhaps 3000 to 4000 years ago. In the early 1600s, the English mathematician William Oughtred invented the slide rule (Figure 1.1(a)), which used logarithms for rapid approximate computations. In 1642, the young French mathematician Blaise Pascal invented one of the first mechanical adding machines, a device that used a series of ten-toothed wheels connected so that numbers could be added or subtracted by moving the wheels. In the 1670s, the German mathematician Gottfried Wilhelm von Leibniz improved on the design of Pascal's machine so that it could also perform multiplication and division (Figure 1.1(b)). A number of other mechanical calculators followed that further refined Pascal's and Leibniz's designs. By the end of the nineteenth century, these calculators had become important tools in science, business, and commerce.

The second fundamental idea in the development of computers is that of a stored program to control the calculations. One early example of an automatically controlled

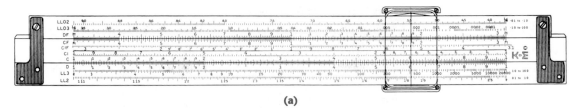

(a)

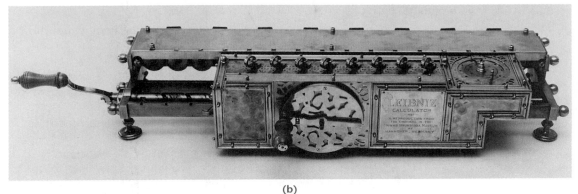

(b)

Figure 1.1

(a) A slide rule. (b) Leibniz's calculator. (Courtesy of IBM)

device is the loom invented by the Frenchman Joseph Marie Jacquard. This automatic loom used punched cards to position threads for the weaving process. A collection of these cards made up a program that directed the loom.

The two fundamental concepts of mechanical calculation and stored-program control were combined by the English mathematician Charles Babbage, who began work in 1822 on a machine called the Difference Engine (Figure 1.2(a)). This machine was designed to compute polynomials for the preparation of mathematical tables. With the assistance of his associate, Ada Augusta, considered by some to be the first programmer, Babbage later designed a more sophisticated machine called the Analytical Engine (Figure 1.2(b)). This machine had several special-purpose components that were intended to work together: a "mill" to carry out the arithmetic computations; a "store" for storing data and intermediate results; and other components for input and output of information. The operation of this machine was to be fully automatic, controlled by programs stored on punched cards, an idea based on Jacquard's earlier work. Although Babbage's machines could not be built during his lifetime because technology was not sufficiently advanced, they are the forerunners of the modern computer.

A related development in the United States was the census bureau's use of punched-card systems designed by Herman Hollerith to help compile the 1890 census. These systems used electrical sensors to interpret the information stored on the punched cards. In 1896, Hollerith left the census bureau and formed his own tabu-

Figure 1.2

(a) Babbage's
Difference
Engine. (b)
Babbage's
Analytical
Engine.
(Courtesy of
IBM)

(a)

(b)

lating company, which in 1924 became the International Business Machines Corporation (IBM).

The development of computing devices continued at a rapid pace in the United States. Some of the pioneers in this effort were Howard Aiken, John Atanasoff, J. P. Eckert, J. W. Mauchly, and John von Neumann. Repeating much of Babbage's work, Aiken designed a system consisting of several mechanical calculators working together. This work, which IBM supported, led to the invention in 1944 of the electromechanical Mark I computer. This machine is the best-known computer built before 1945 and may be regarded as the first realization of Babbage's Analytical Engine.

Electronic Computers

The first fully electronic computer was developed by John Atanasoff at Iowa State University. With the help of his assistant, Clifford Berry, he built a prototype in 1939 and completed the first working model in 1942. The best known of the early electronic computers was the ENIAC (Electronic Numerical Integrator and Computer), constructed in 1946 by J. P. Eckert and J. W. Mauchly at the Moore School of Electrical Engineering of the University of Pennsylvania (Figure 1.3). This extremely large machine contained over 18,000 vacuum tubes and 1500 relays and nearly filled a room 20 feet by 40 feet in size. It could multiply numbers approximately one thousand times faster than the Mark I could, but it was quite limited in its applications and was used primarily by the Army Ordnance Department to calculate firing tables and trajectories for various types of shells. Eckert and Mauchly later left the University of Pennsylvania to form the Eckert-Mauchly Computer Corporation,

Figure 1.3

ENIAC.
(Courtesy of
Sperry
Corporation)

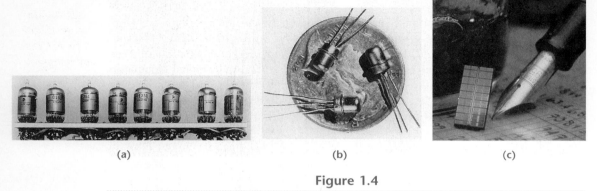

(a)   (b)   (c)

Figure 1.4

(a) Vacuum tubes. (b) Transistors. (c) A 4 million bit chip. (Photos courtesy of (a) IBM, (b) Bettmann, (c) IBM.)

which built the UNIVAC (Universal Automatic Computer), the first commercially available computer designed for both scientific and business applications.

The instructions, or program, that controlled the ENIAC's operation were entered into the machine by rewiring some parts of the computer's circuits. This complicated process was very time-consuming, sometimes taking several people several days, and during this time, the computer was idle. In other early computers, the instructions were stored outside the machine on punched cards or some other medium and were transferred into the machine one at a time for interpretation and execution. A new scheme, developed by Princeton mathematician John von Neumann and others, used internally stored commands. The advantages of this stored-program concept are that internally stored instructions can be processed more rapidly and, more important, that they can be modified by the computer itself while computations are taking place.

The actual physical components used in constructing a computer system are its **hardware**. Several generations of computers can be identified by the type of hardware used. The ENIAC and UNIVAC are examples of **first-generation** computers, which are characterized by their extensive use of vacuum tubes (Figure 1.4(a)). Advances in electronics brought changes in computing systems, and in 1958 IBM introduced the first of the **second-generation** computers, the IBM 7090. These computers were built between 1959 and 1965 and used transistors in place of vacuum tubes (Figure 1.4(b)). Consequently, these computers were smaller, required less power, generated far less heat, and were more reliable than their predecessors. They were also less expensive, as illustrated by the introduction of the first **minicomputer** in 1963, the PDP-8, which sold for $18,000, in contrast with earlier computers, whose six-digit price tags limited their sales to large companies only. The **third-generation** computers that followed used integrated circuits and introduced new techniques for better system utilization, such as multiprogramming and time-sharing. The IBM System/360 introduced in 1964 is commonly accepted as the first of this generation of computers. Computers of the 1980s and 1990s, called **fourth-generation** computers, use very large-scale integrated circuits (VLSI) on silicon chips and other

(a) (b)

Figure 1.5

(a) A Sun workstation. (b) A Cray supercomputer.

microelectronic advances to shrink their size and cost still more while enlarging their capability (Figure 1.4(c)). One of the pioneers in the development of transistors was Robert Noyce, a cofounder of the Intel Corporation, which introduced the 4004 microprocessor in 1971.

Microprocessors like the Intel 4004 made possible the development of the personal computers that are so common today. One of the most popular personal computers in the 1980s was the Apple II, constructed in a makeshift facility in a garage and introduced in 1977 by Steven Jobs and Steve Wozniak, then 21 and 26 years old, respectively. Jobs and Wozniak founded the Apple Computer Company, one of the major manufacturers of microcomputers today. This was followed in 1981 by the first of IBM's PCs, which have become the microcomputer standard in business and industry.

Continued advances in technology have produced a wide array of computer systems, ranging from portable laptop computers to powerful desktop machines such as workstations, to supercomputers capable of performing billions of operations each second, and to massively parallel computers that use a large number of microprocessors working together in parallel to solve large problems (Figure 1.5). Someone once noted that if progress in the automotive industry had been as rapid as in computer technology since 1960, today's automobile would have an engine that is less than 0.1 inch in length, would get 120,000 miles to a gallon of gas, would have a top speed of 240,000 miles per hour, and would cost $4.00.

System Software

The stored-program concept was a significant improvement over manual programming methods, but early computers still were difficult to use because of the complex coding schemes required for representing programs and data. Consequently, in addition to improved hardware, computer manufacturers began to develop collections of programs known as **system software**, which make computers easier to use. One of the more important advances in this area was the development of **operating systems**, which allocate storage for programs and data and carry out many other supervisory functions. In particular, an operating system acts as an interface between the user and the machine. It interprets commands given by the user and then directs the appropriate system software and hardware to carry them out. One of the most commonly used operating systems is UNIX, developed in 1971 by Ken Thompson and Dennis Ritchie at AT&T's Bell Laboratories. It is the only operating system that has been implemented on computers ranging from microcomputers to supercomputers. The most popular operating system for personal computers has for many years been MS-DOS, which was developed in 1981 by Bill Gates, founder of the Microsoft Corporation. More recently, **graphical user interfaces (GUI)**, such as MIT's X Window System for UNIX-based machines, Microsoft's Windows for personal computers, and Apple's Macintosh interface, have been devised to provide a simpler and more intuitive interface between humans and computers.

As we noted in the introduction to this chapter, one of the most important advances in system software was the development of **high-level languages**, which allow users to write programs in a language similar to natural language. A program written in a high-level language is known as a **source program**. For most high-level languages, the instructions that make up a source program must be translated into **machine language**, that is, the language used directly by a particular computer for all its calculations and processing. This machine-language program is called an **object program**. The programs that translate source programs into object programs are called **compilers**.

A Brief History of Fortran

One of the first high-level languages to gain widespread acceptance was **FORTRAN** (**FOR**mula **TRAN**slation), which was developed for the IBM 704 computer by **John Backus** and a team of 13 other programmers at IBM over a 3-year period (1954–1957). The group's first report on the completed language included the following comments:

> The programmer attended a one-day course on FORTRAN and spent some more time referring to the manual. He then programmed the job in four hours, using 47 FORTRAN statements. These were compiled by the 704 in six minutes, producing about 1000 instructions. He ran the program and found the output incorrect. He studied the output and was able to localize his error in a FORTRAN statement he had written. He rewrote the offending statement, recompiled, and found that the resulting program was correct. He estimated that it might have taken three days to code the job by hand, plus an unknown time to debug it, and that no appreciable increase in speed of execution would have been achieved thereby.

In the years that followed, other computer manufacturers developed FORTRAN compilers for their machines. Several of these provided extensions and variations of FORTRAN that were specific to their particular computers. Consequently, programs written for one machine could not be used on a different machine without modification. Over time, users developed large collections of FORTRAN programs, and the cost of converting all these programs whenever a new computer was installed became prohibitive.

To remedy these problems, efforts were made to standardize FORTRAN so that programs were **portable**, which means they can be processed on several different machines with little or no alteration. One of the earliest standard versions appeared in 1966, and in 1977 another revision appeared, known as FORTRAN 77. While the changes introduced in FORTRAN 77 were significant, it did not solve all of the problems in earlier versions, nor did it include many of the new features that were appearing in newer programming languages. Consequently, work began almost immediately on a new standard version; in 1991, an extensive revision known as Fortran 90 appeared, and compilers to support this new version of Fortran have been developed.[1] The American National Standards Institute (ANSI), which establishes standards for programming languages, decided that during the transition period there should be two American standards for Fortran, FORTRAN 77 and Fortran 90, while International Standards Organization (ISO) groups decided that Fortran 90 will be the only international Fortran standard.

Fortran 90 has standardized earlier versions of Fortran and provides a base from which newer versions of the language will be developed. In fact, another ANSI committee is already at work preparing a new version that will make it possible to design Fortran programs that will execute efficiently on massively parallel computers and that incorporate modern programming techniques such as object-oriented programming.

Applications

As the development of system software made computers increasingly easier to use, applications were developed in many areas, in particular, in science and engineering. These applications are far too many to enumerate, and those pictured in Figure 1.6 are intended only to show their diversity. In this text we will describe problems in many such areas and develop computer programs to solve these problems.

1.2 COMPUTER ORGANIZATION

In the preceding section, we noted that Babbage designed his Analytical Engine as a system of several separate components, each with its own particular function. This general scheme was incorporated in many later computers and is, in fact, a common feature of most modern computers. In this section we briefly describe the major components of a modern computing system and how program instructions and data are stored and processed.

Computing Systems

The heart of any computing system is its **central processing unit**, or **CPU**. The CPU controls the operation of the entire system, performs the arithmetic and logic

---

[1] "FORTRAN" has traditionally been written in all upper case. The new ANSI standard, however, specifies "Fortran" as the official spelling for Fortran 90.

operations, and stores and retrieves instructions and data. The instructions and data are stored in a high-speed **memory unit**. The **control unit** fetches these instructions from memory, decodes them, and directs the system to execute the operations indicated by the instructions. Those operations that are arithmetical or logical in nature are carried out using the circuits of the **arithmetic-logic unit** (**ALU**) of the CPU.

The memory unit typically consists of several components. One of these components is used to store the instructions and data of the programs being executed and has many names, including **internal**, **main**, **primary**, and **random access memory** (**RAM**). A second component is a set of special high-speed memory locations within the CPU, called **registers**. Values that are stored in registers can typically be accessed thousands of times faster than values stored in RAM.

One problem with both RAM and registers is that they are **volatile** memory components, that is, information stored in these components is lost if the power to the computing system is shut off (either intentionally or accidentally). **Read-only memory** (**ROM**) is **nonvolatile** memory used to store critical information such as start-up instructions which is too important to lose.

To provide long-term storage of programs and data, most computing systems also include memory components called **external** or **auxiliary** or **secondary memory**. Common forms of this type of memory are magnetic disks (such as hard disks and floppy disks) and magnetic tapes. These **peripheral devices** provide long-term storage for large collections of data, even if power is lost. However, the time required to access data stored on such devices can be thousands of times greater than the access time for data stored in RAM.

Other peripherals are used to transmit instructions, data, and computed results between the user and the CPU. These are the **input/output devices**, which have a variety of forms, such as terminals, scanners, voice input devices, printers, and plotters. Their function is to convert information from an external form understandable to the user to a form that can be processed by the computer system, and vice versa.

Figure 1.7 shows the relationship between the components in a computer system.

Memory Organization

The devices that comprise the memory unit of a computer are two-state devices. If one of the states is interpreted as 0 and the other as 1, then it is natural to use a **binary scheme**, using only the two binary digits (**bits**) 0 and 1 to represent information in a computer. These two-state devices are organized into groups of eight called **bytes**. Memory is commonly measured in bytes, and a block of $2^{10} = 1024$ bytes is called **1 K** of memory. Thus, one **megabyte** (= 1024 K) of memory consists of

Figure 1.6 (see next page)

(a) CAD design of an atomobile. (Courtesy of Ford Motor Company) (b) Automated insertion of components on electronic engine modules. (Courtesy of Ford Motor Company) (c) Robot-controlled Chrysler automobile assembly plant. (Courtesy of Cincinnati Milacron) (d) National Weather Service satellite imagery. (Lawrence Migdale/Tony Stone Images) (e) Oil-drilling computerized tracking model. (Chris Jones/The Stock Market) (f) Northern Arizona University observatory. (Don B. Stevenson/Uniphoto Picture Agency) (g) Flight deck of the Space Shuttle Columbia. (Uniphoto Picture Agency)

Figure 1.7

Major
components of
a computing
system.

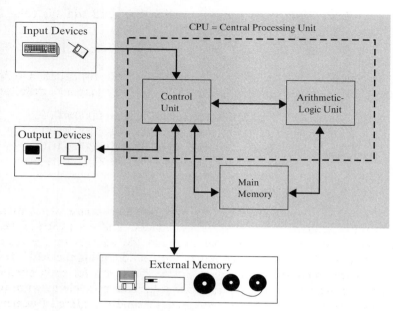

$1024 \times 2^{10} = 2^{10} \times 2^{10} = 2^{20} = 1,048,576$ bytes, or, equivalently, $2^{20} \times 2^3 = 2^{23}$ $= 8,384,608$ bits.

Bytes are typically grouped together into **words**. The number of bits in a word is equal to the number of bits in a CPU register. The word size thus varies from one computer to another, but common word sizes are 16 bits (= 2 bytes) and 32 bits (= 4 bytes). Associated with each word or byte is an **address** that can be used to directly access that word or byte. This makes it possible for the control unit to store information in a specific memory location and then to retrieve it later. The details of how various types of data are represented in a binary form and stored in a computer's memory are described in Appendix F.

Program instructions for processing data must also be stored in memory. They must be instructions that the machine can execute and they must be expressed in a form that the machine can understand, that is, they must be written in the machine language for that machine. These instructions consists of two parts: (1) a numeric **opcode**, which represents a basic machine operation such as load, multiply, add, and store; and (2) the address of the **operand**. Like all information stored in memory, these instructions must be represented in a binary form.

As an example, suppose that values have been stored in three memory locations with addresses 1024, 1025, and 1026 and that we want to multiply the first two values, add the third, and store the result in a fourth memory location 1027. To perform this computation, the following instructions must be executed:

1. Fetch the contents of memory location 1024 and load it into a register in the ALU.

2. Fetch the contents of memory location 1025 and compute the product of this value and the value in the register.

3. Fetch the contents of memory location 1026 and add this value to the value in the register.

4. Store the contents of the register in memory location 1027.

If the opcodes for load, store, add, and multiply are 16, 17, 35, and 36, respectively, these four instructions might be written in machine language as follows:

1. 00010000000000000000010000000000
2. 00100100000000000000010000000001
3. 00100011000000000000010000000010
4. 00010001000000000000010000000011

    opcode   operand

These instructions can then be stored in four (consecutive) memory locations. When the program is executed, the control unit will fetch each of these instructions, decode it to determine the operation and the address of the operand, fetch the operand, and then perform the required operation, using the ALU if necessary.

As we noted in the preceding section, programs for early computers had to be written in machine language and later it became possible to write programs in **assembly language**, which uses mnemonics (names) in place of numeric opcodes and variable names in place of numeric addresses. For example, the preceding sequence of instructions might be written in assembly language as

```
1. MOV  A,  ACC
2. MUL  B,  ACC
3. ADD  C,  ACC
4. STO  ACC, X
```

An **assembler**, which is part of the system software, translates such assembly-language instructions into machine language.

Today, most programs are written in a high-level language such as Fortran, and a compiler translates each statement in the program into a sequence of basic machine- (or assembly-) language instructions.

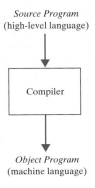

Source Program
(high-level language)

Compiler

Object Program
(machine language)

For example, for the preceding problem, the programmer could write the Fortran statement

$$X = A * B + C$$

which instructs the computer to multiply the values of A and B, add the value of C, and assign the value to X. The compiler then translates this statement into the sequence of four machine- (or assembly-) language instructions considered earlier.

Quick Quiz 1.2

1. What are two important concepts in the early history of computation?
2. Match each item in the first column with the associated item in the second column.

_____ John von Neumann	A. early high-level language
_____ Charles Babbage	B. first commercially available computer
_____ Blaise Pascal	C. graphical user interface
_____ Herman Hollerith	D. stored-program concept
_____ input/output device	E. Difference Engine
_____ first generation	F. designer of FORTRAN language
_____ bit	G. central processing unit
_____ compiler	H. language translator
_____ object program	I. binary digit
_____ Joseph Jacquard	J. electronic computer
_____ Ada Augusta	K. 1024
_____ source program	L. random access memory
_____ John Backus	M. written in high-level language
_____ byte	N. read-only memory
_____ UNIVAC	O. punched card
_____ UNIX	P. automatic loom
_____ CPU	Q. vacuum tubes
_____ FORTRAN	R. adding machine
_____ ENIAC	S. operating system
_____ K	T. written in machine language
_____ GUI	U. group of binary digits
_____ RAM	V. terminals, readers, printers
_____ ROM	W. first programmer

Exercises 1.2

For Exercises 1–12, describe the importance of the person to the history of computing:

1. Charles Babbage

2. Blaise Pascal

3. John von Neumann
4. Herman Hollerith
5. Joseph Jacquard
6. Gottfried Wilhelm von Leibniz
7. John Atanasoff
8. Steven Jobs
9. Robert Noyce
10. J. P. Eckert
11. John Backus
12. Steve Wozniak

For Exercises 13–17, describe the importance of the device to the history of computing:

13. ENIAC
14. Analytical Engine
15. Jacquard loom
16. UNIVAC
17. Mark I
18. Distinguish the four different generations of computers.

Briefly define each of the terms in Exercises 19–31:

19. stored-program concept
20. FORTRAN
21. UNIX
22. MS-DOS
23. source program
24. object program
25. machine language
26. assembly language
27. bit
28. byte
29. word
30. K
31. megabyte
32. What are the main functions of an operating system?
33. What are the main functions of a compiler?
34. What are the main functions of an assembler?

1.3 PROGRAMMING AND PROBLEM SOLVING—AN EXAMPLE

A computer **program** is a sequence of instructions that must be followed to solve a particular problem, and the main reason that people learn programming is so that they can use the computer as a problem-solving tool. At least four steps or stages can be identified in the program-development process:

1. Problem analysis and specification
2. Data organization and algorithm design
3. Program coding
4. Execution and testing

In this section we illustrate these steps with an example. This example is very simple so that we can emphasize the main ideas at each stage without getting lost in a maze of details.

PROBLEM: RADIOACTIVE DECAY

Problem:
Radioactive Decay

Nick Nuke is a nuclear physicist at Dispatch University and is conducting research with the radioactive element polonium. The half-life of polonium is 140 days, which means that because of radioactive decay, the amount of polonium that remains after 140 days is one-half of the original amount. Nick would like to know how much polonium will remain after running his experiment for 180 days if 10 milligrams are present initially.

Step 1:
Problem Analysis and Specification

The first stage in solving this problem is to analyze the problem and formulate a precise **specification** of it. This specification must include a description of the problem's **input**—what information is given and which items are important in solving the problem—and its **output**—what information must be produced to solve the problem. Input and output are two major parts of the problem's specification. Formulating the specification for this problem is easy:

Input	Output
Initial amount: 10 mg	Amount remaining
Half-life: 140 days	
Time period: 180 days	

The other items of information—the physicist's name, the name of the university, the name of the particular radioactive element—are not relevant (at least not to this problem) and can be ignored.

Determining the amount of polonium remaining can be done by hand or by using a calculator and does not warrant the development of a computer program for its solution. A program written to solve this particular problem would probably be used just once; because if the experiment runs longer, or if there is a different initial amount of polonium, or if a radioactive element with a different half-life is used, we have a new problem requiring a new program. This is obviously a waste of effort, since it is clear that each such problem is a special case of the more general problem of finding the residual amount of a radioactive element at any time, given any initial amount and the half-life for that element. Thus a program that solves the general problem can be used in a variety of situations and is consequently more useful than one designed for solving only the original special problem.

Generalization is therefore an important aspect of problem analysis. The effort involved in later phases of the problem-solving process demands that the program eventually developed be sufficiently flexible, that it solve not only the given specific problem but also related problems of the same kind with little, if any, modification required. In this example, therefore, the specification of the problem would be better formulated in general terms:

Input	Output
Initial amount	Amount remaining
Half-life	
Time period	

Step 2:
Data Organization and Algorithm Design

Now that we have a precise specification of the problem, we are ready to begin designing a plan for its solution. This plan has two parts:

1. Determine how to organize and store the data in the problem.
2. Develop procedures to process the data and produce the required output. These procedures are called **algorithms**.

Data Organization. As we noted, the input for this problem consists of the initial amount of some radioactive element, its half-life, and a time period. The output to be produced is the amount of the substance that remains at the end of the specified time period. We will use the variables *InitialAmount*, *HalfLife*, *Time*, and *AmountRemaining* to represent these quantities.

Algorithm Design. The first step in an algorithm for solving this problem is to obtain the values for the input items—initial amount, half-life, and time period. Next we must determine how to use this information to calculate the amount of the substance remaining after the given time period. Finally, the amount remaining must be displayed. Thus, our initial description of an algorithm for solving the problem is

1. Get values for *InitialAmount*, *HalfLife*, and *Time*.
2. Compute the value of *AmountRemaining* for the given *Time*.
3. Display *AmountRemaining*.

Algorithm Refinement. The next step in developing an algorithm to solve the problem is the **refinement** of any steps in the algorithm that require additional details. For example, in step 2 of the preceding algorithm, a formula is needed to compute the amount of polonium that remains after a given time period. The half-life of polonium is 140 days, and if we assume that the initial amount of polonium is 10 mg, then after 140 days, or one half-life,

$$10 \times 0.5$$

milligrams remain. At the end of 280 days, or two half-lives, the amount of polonium remaining is one half of this amount,

$$(10 \times 0.5) \times 0.5$$

which can also be written

$$10 \times (0.5)^2$$

Similarly, the amount of polonium at the end of 420 days, or three half-lives, is

$$10 \times (0.5)^3$$

The general formula for the amount of the substance remaining is

$$\text{amount remaining} = \text{initial amount} \times (0.5)^{\text{time/half-life}}$$

Thus, the second step in our algorithm is to perform this calculation for the data entered in step 1.

This rather lengthy description of the algorithm can be expressed more concisely as follows:

ALGORITHM FOR RADIOACTIVE-DECAY PROBLEM

This algorithm calculates the amount of a radioactive substance that remains after a specified time for a given initial amount and a given half-life.

Input: An *InitialAmount* of a radioactive substance, its
          HalfLife, and a *Time* period in days
Output: The *AmountRemaining*

1. Enter *InitialAmount*, *HalfLife*, and *Time*.
2. Calculate

   $$AmountRemaining = InitialAmount * (0.5) ** (Time \,/\, HalfLife)$$

3. Display *AmountRemaining*.

Note that the symbols *, /, and ** indicate multiplication, division, and exponentiation, respectively. Also note that we have included a brief specification of the problem that the algorithm solves at the beginning of the algorithm. Such **documentation** is important and should be included in every algorithm.

The steps in this algorithm might also be displayed graphically:

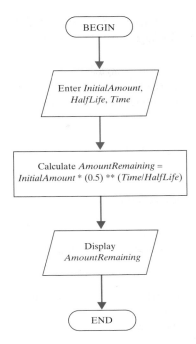

Here, parallelograms are used to indicate input/output operations, and rectangles represent assignments of values to variables.

Once we have finished the algorithm, we are ready to proceed to the coding stage.

Step 3:
Program Coding

The third step in developing a program to solve a problem is to implement the algorithm for solving the problem in some programming language. Figure 1.8 shows a Fortran 90 program for this example.

Figure 1.8 Radioactive decay.

```
PROGRAM Radioactive_Decay
!------------------------------------------------------------------------
! This program calculates the amount of a radioactive substance that
! remains after a specified time, given an initial amount and its
! half-life.  Variables used are:
!   InitialAmount    : initial amount of substance (mg)
!   HalfLife         : half-life of substance (days)
!   Time             : time at which the amount remaining is calculated (days)
!   AmountRemaining  : amount of substance remaining (mg)
!
! Input:   InitialAmount, HalfLife, Time
! Output:  AmountRemaining
!------------------------------------------------------------------------
```

Figure 1.8 *(cont.)*

```
IMPLICIT NONE

REAL :: InitialAmount, HalfLife, Time, AmountRemaining

! Get values for InitialAmount, HalfLife, and Time.

PRINT *, "Enter initial amount (mg) of substance,  its half-life (days)"
PRINT *, "and time (days) at which to find amount remaining:"
READ *, InitialAmount, HalfLife, Time

! Compute the amount remaining at the specified time.
AmountRemaining = InitialAmount * 0.5 ** (Time / HalfLife)

! Display AmountRemaining.
PRINT *, "Amount remaining =", AmountRemaining, "mg"

END PROGRAM Radioactive_Decay
```

The program begins with the PROGRAM statement

```
PROGRAM Radioactive_Decay
```

which marks the beginning of the program and associates the name Radioactive_Decay with it.

The PROGRAM statement is followed by **opening documentation** in the form of comments that describe the program. These comments summarize the purpose of the program and give the specification of the problem the program is to solve. An exclamation mark (!) indicates the beginning of a comment.

The statement

```
IMPLICIT NONE
```

that follows the opening documentation specifies that all variables to be used in this program must be declared explicitly. Thus, the next statement

```
REAL :: InitialAmount, HalfLife, Time, AmountRemaining
```

declares that variables InitialAmount, HalfLife, Time, and AmountRemaining will be used in the program and that their values will be real numbers.

The first step in the algorithm is an input instruction to enter values for the variables *InitialAmount, HalfLife,* and *Time:*

1. Enter *InitialAmount, HalfLife,* and *Time.*

This is translated into three statements in the program:

```
PRINT *, "Enter initial amount (mg) of substance, its half-life (days)"
PRINT *, "and time (days) at which to find amount remaining:"
READ *, InitialAmount, HalfLife, Time
```

The PRINT statements are used to prompt the user that the input values are to be entered. The READ statement actually assigns the three values entered by the user to the three variables InitialAmount, HalfLife, and Time. Thus, if the user enters

```
2, 140, 180
```

the value 2 will be assigned to InitialAmount, 140 to HalfLife, and 180 to Time.

The next step in the algorithm

2. Calculate

$$AmountRemaining = InitialAmount * (0.5) ** (Time / HalfLife).$$

translates into the Fortran assignment statement

```
AmountRemaining = InitialAmount * 0.5 ** (Time / HalfLife)
```

The output instruction

3. Display *AmountRemaining.*

is translated into the Fortran statement

```
PRINT *, "Amount remaining =", AmountRemaining, "mg"
```

The end of the program is indicated by the Fortran statement

```
END PROGRAM Radioactive_Decay
```

This statement terminates execution of the program.

Step 4:
Execution and Testing

Once an algorithm has been coded, the fourth step in the development process is to check that the algorithm and program are *correct*. One way to do this is to execute the program with input values for which the correct output values are already known (or are easily calculated). The procedure for submitting a program to a computer and executing it varies from one system to another; the details regarding your particular system can be obtained from your instructor, computer center personnel, or user manuals supplied by the manufacturer.

First you must gain access to the computer system. In the case of a personal computer, this may only mean turning on the machine and inserting the appropriate disk into the disk drive. For a larger system, some **login** procedure may be required to establish contact between a remote terminal and the computer. When you have gained access, you must enter the program, often by using an **editor** provided as part of the system software.

Once the Fortran source program has been entered, it must be compiled to produce an object file by giving appropriate system commands.[2] The resulting object file

---

[2] On some systems it may also be necessary to link the object file with certain system files.

can then be executed with test data to check its correctness. For example, the program in Figure 1.8 might be compiled on a UNIX system with the command

```
f90 fig1-8.f90 -o fig1-8
```

Giving the command

```
fig1-8
```

then causes the program to execute:

```
Enter initial amount (mg) of substance, its half-life (days)
and time (days) at which to find amount remaining:
2, 140, 140
Amount remaining = 1.0000000 mg
```

The program displays a message prompting the user for three input values, and after these values (highlighted in color) are entered, the desired output value is calculated and displayed.

Here we have entered the values 2, 140, and 140 since it is easy to check that the correct answer for these inputs is 1.0. Similarly, the correct results for simple input values like 4, 140, 280 and 4, 140, 420 are easily calculated and can be used as a quick check of the answers produced by the program.

Once we are confident that the program its correct, we can use it to solve the original problem of finding the amount of polonium remaining after 180 days if there are 10 mg present initially:

```
Enter initial amount (mg) of substance, its half-life (days)
and time (days) at which to find amount remaining:
10, 140, 180
Amount remaining = 4.1016769 mg
```

This example illustrates the **interactive mode** of processing, in which the user enters data values during program execution (from the keyboard), and the output produced by the program is displayed directly to the user (usually on a video screen). Another mode of operation is **batch processing**, in which the user prepares a file containing the program, the data, and certain command lines and submits it to the system. Execution then proceeds without any user interaction.

1.4 PROGRAMMING AND PROBLEM SOLVING—AN OVERVIEW

Programming and problem solving is an art in that it requires a good deal of imagination, ingenuity, and creativity. But it is also a science in that it uses certain techniques and methodologies. The term **software engineering** has come to be applied to the study and use of these techniques.

In the preceding section, we identified four steps in the program-development process:

1. Problem analysis and specification
2. Data organization and algorithm design
3. Program coding
4. Execution and testing

We illustrated these steps using the simple radioactive-decay problem. It must be realized, however, that in more substantial problems, these stages will be considerably more complex. In this section we will describe some of the additional questions and complications that arise, together with some of the software engineering techniques used to deal with them. We will also briefly describe an additional step that is particularly important in the **life cycle** of programs developed in real-world applications:

5. Program maintenance

Step 1:
Problem Analysis and Specification

As we have seen, the first step in developing a program to solve a problem is to analyze the problem and specify precisely what a solution to the problem requires. This specification must include

- A description of the problem's **input**: what information is given and which items are important in solving the problem
- A description of the problem's **output**: what information must be produced to solve the problem

Input and output are the two major parts of the problem's specification, and for a problem that appears in a programming text, they are usually not too difficult to identify.

The specifications of more complex problems often include other items, and considerable effort may be required to formulate them completely. These problems are sometimes stated vaguely and imprecisely, because even the person posing the problem may not fully understand it. For example, the manager of a large engineering firm might request a programmer to "develop a program to estimate costs for constructing a new engineering lab."

In these situations, many questions must be answered to formulate the problem's specification. Some of these answers are required to describe more completely the problem's input and output. What information is available regarding the construction project? How is the program to access this data? Has the information been validated, or must the program provide error checking? In what format should the output be displayed? Must reports be generated for company executives, zoning boards, environmental agencies, and/or other governmental agencies?

Other questions deal more directly with the required processing. What materials are required? What equipment will be needed? Are employees paid on an hourly or a salaried basis, or are there some of each? What premium, if any, is paid for overtime? What items must be withheld—for federal, state, and city income taxes, retirement plans, insurance, and the like—and how are they to be computed?

In some situations, still other questions concern how the program will be used. Will the users of the program be technically sophisticated, or must the program be made very user-friendly to accommodate novice users? How often will the program be used? What are the response-time requirements? What is the expected life of the program; that is, how long will it be used, and what changes can be expected in the future? What hardware and software are available?

Although this list is by no means exhaustive, it does indicate the wide range of information that may be required in analyzing and specifying a problem.

Step 2:
Data Organization and Algorithm Design

Once the specification of a problem is complete, the next step is to select appropriate structures to organize and store the problem's data and design algorithms to process the data. For the problems considered in the first several chapters of this text, the data items will be processed and stored using simple variables much like those used in mathematics to name quantities in algebraic formulas and equations; more complex structures will be discussed in later chapters.

Because the computer is a machine possessing no inherent problem-solving capabilities, the algorithms developed to solve a problem must be expressed as a sequence of simple steps. Programs to implement algorithms must be written in a language that the computer can understand. It is natural, therefore, to describe algorithms in a language that resembles those used to write computer programs, that is, in a "pseudoprogramming language" or, as it is more commonly called, **pseudocode**.

Unlike the definitions of high-level programming languages such as Fortran, there is no set of rules that precisely define pseudocode. It varies from one programmer to another. Pseudocode is a mixture of natural language and symbols, terms, and other features commonly used in high-level programming languages. Typically one finds the following features in various pseudocodes:

1. The usual computer symbols are used for arithmetic operations: + for addition, − for subtraction, * for multiplication, / for division, and ** for exponentiation.
2. Symbolic names (variables) are used to represent the quantities being processed by the algorithm.
3. Certain key words that are common in high-level languages may be used: for example, *Read* or *Enter* to indicate input operations, and *Display, Print,* or *Write* for output operations.
4. Indentation is used to indicate key blocks of instructions.

Some programmers use graphical representations of algorithms in addition to or in place of pseudocode descriptions. A number of such representations have been developed over the years, but probably the most common one is the **flowchart**, a diagram that uses symbols like those shown in Figure 1.9. Each step of the algorithm is placed in a box of the appropriate shape, and the order in which these steps are to be carried out is indicated by connecting them with arrows called **flow lines**. Although the use of flowcharts has diminished considerably, their two-dimensional nature, as opposed to the one-dimensional nature of a pseudocode description, makes it easier to visualize and understand the structure of some algorithms. For this reason, although most of the algorithms in this book will be given in pseudocode, we will use flowcharts for a few algorithms or parts of algorithms.

The steps that comprise an algorithm must be organized in a logical and clear manner so that the program that implements the algorithm will be similarly well structured. **Structured algorithms** and **programs** are designed using three basic methods of control:

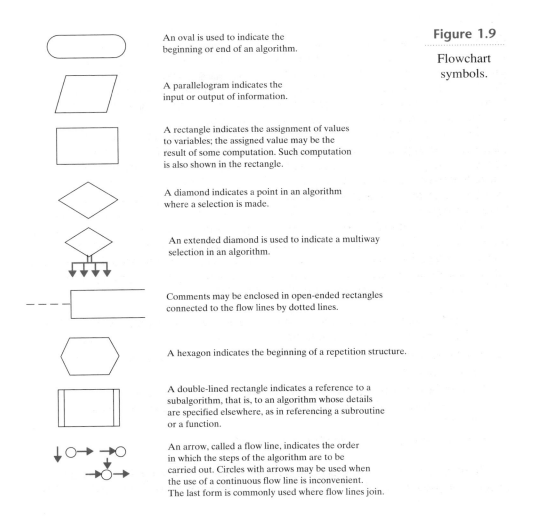

Figure 1.9

Flowchart symbols.

An oval is used to indicate the beginning or end of an algorithm.

A parallelogram indicates the input or output of information.

A rectangle indicates the assignment of values to variables; the assigned value may be the result of some computation. Such computation is also shown in the rectangle.

A diamond indicates a point in an algorithm where a selection is made.

An extended diamond is used to indicate a multiway selection in an algorithm.

Comments may be enclosed in open-ended rectangles connected to the flow lines by dotted lines.

A hexagon indicates the beginning of a repetition structure.

A double-lined rectangle indicates a reference to a subalgorithm, that is, to an algorithm whose details are specified elsewhere, as in referencing a subroutine or a function.

An arrow, called a flow line, indicates the order in which the steps of the algorithm are to be carried out. Circles with arrows may be used when the use of a continuous flow line is inconvenient. The last form is commonly used where flow lines join.

1. Sequential: Steps are performed in a strictly sequential manner, each step being executed exactly once.

2. Selection: One of a number of alternative actions is selected and executed.

3. Repetition: One or more steps are performed repeatedly.

These three control structures are individually quite simple, but in fact they are sufficiently powerful that any algorithm can be constructed using combinations of these structures.

Sequential execution is the default control mechanism—if the programmer does not stipulate selection or repetition, the statements in a program are executed in sequence from beginning to end. Our solution to the radioactive-decay problem used only sequential control; the steps are simply executed in order, from beginning to end, with each step being performed exactly once. The flowchart representation of the algorithm clearly displays its sequential nature.

For other problems, however, the solution may require that some of the steps be performed in some situations and bypassed in others. Such problems are considered in Chapter 3. Still other problems require that a step or a collection of steps be repeated; such problems are considered in Chapter 4.

As we have noted, two important parts of the plan for solving a problem are choosing structures to organize and store the data and designing algorithms to process the data. For example, in the construction problem we considered earlier, a file of personnel records containing names, social security numbers, number of dependents, and so on contains permanent information that must be stored in some structure so that it can be accessed and processed. Other information such as hours worked will be entered during program execution and can perhaps be stored in simple variables, as in the example we considered in the previous section.

A problem may be so complex that it is difficult to visualize or anticipate at the outset all the details of a complete solution to the problem. To solve such problems, a **divide-and-conquer** strategy is used, in which the original problem is partitioned into simpler subproblems, each of which can be considered independently. We begin by identifying the major tasks to be performed to solve the problem and arranging them in the order in which they are to be carried out. These tasks and their relation to one another can be displayed in a **structure diagram**. For example, a first structure diagram for the problem might be

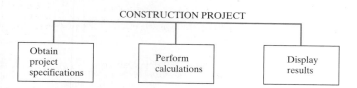

Usually one or more of these first-level tasks are still quite complex and must be divided into subtasks. For example, in the construction problem, some of the input data pertains to personnel requirements. Other data items refer to material requirements, and still others to equipment needs. Consequently, the task "Obtain project specifications" can be subdivided into three subtasks:

1. Obtain personnel requirements.
2. Obtain equipment requirements.
3. Obtain materials requirements.

Similarly, the task "Perform calculations" may be split into three subtasks:

1. Calculate personnel cost.
2. Calculate equipment cost.
3. Calculate materials cost.

In a structure diagram, these subtasks are placed on a second level below the corresponding main task, as pictured in Figure 1.10. These subtasks may require further division into still smaller subtasks, resulting in additional levels, as illustrated in Figure 1.11. This **successive refinement** continues until each subtask is sufficiently simple that the design of an algorithm for that subtask is straightforward.

This **top-down** approach to software development allows the programmer to design and test an algorithm and the corresponding program **module** for each subprob-

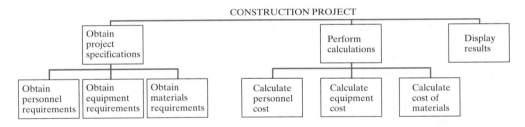

Figure 1.10

Second structure diagram.

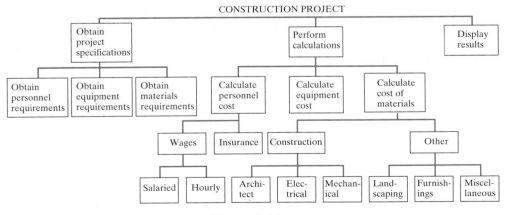

Figure 1.11

Third structure diagram.

lem independently of the others. For very large projects, a team approach might be used in which the low-level subtasks are assigned to different programmers. The individual program modules they develop are eventually combined into one complete program that solves the original problem.

Step 3:
Program Coding

The first two steps of the program-development process are extremely important, because the remaining phases will be much more difficult if the first two steps are skipped or are not done carefully. On the other hand, if the problem has been carefully analyzed and specified and if an effective plan has been designed, the program-coding step is usually straightforward.

Coding is the process of implementing data objects and algorithms in some programming language. In the second step of the problem-solving process, algorithms may be described in a natural language or pseudocode, but a program that implements an algorithm must be written in the vocabulary of a programming language and must conform to the **syntax**, or grammatical rules, of that language. This text is concerned with the vocabulary and syntax of Fortran, some features of which we now describe in the context of the example in the preceding section.

Variables. **Variables** are names used to identify various quantities. In the radioactive-decay problem, the variables *InitialAmount, HalfLife,* and *Time* represent the initial amount of a radioactive substance, its half-life, and time, respectively. The output in this example is the amount of the substance remaining after the specified time and is represented by the variable *AmountRemaining.*

In Fortran 90, variable names must begin with a letter, which may be followed by up to 30 letters, digits, or underscores. Thus, `InitialAmount`, `HalfLife`, `Time`, and `AmountRemaining` are valid variable names, and each name suggests what the variable represents. *Meaningful variable names should always be used because they make programs easier to read and understand.*

Types. The types of values that each variable may have must be declared. Variables whose values are real numbers—numbers that have a fractional part—are declared by placing a statement of the form

```
REAL :: list
```

at the beginning of the program, where *list* is a list of the variable names of real type. Thus, the statement

```
REAL :: InitialAmount, HalfLife, Time, AmountRemaining
```

in the program in Figure 1.8 declares that the variables `InitialAmount`, `HalfLife`, `Time`, and `AmountRemaining` are real variables. Variables whose values are integers are declared using a statement of the form

```
INTEGER :: list
```

Other types will be considered later.

Operations. Addition and subtraction are denoted in Fortran by the usual + and − symbols. Multiplication is denoted by * and division by /. Exponentiation is denoted by **.

Assignment. Assignment of a value to a variable is denoted by = in Fortran programs. For example, the assignment statement

```
AmountRemaining = InitialAmount * 0.5 ** (Time / HalfLife)
```

assigns the value of the expression

```
InitialAmount * 0.5 ** (Time / HalfLife)
```

to the variable AmountRemaining.

Input/Output. In the pseudocode description of an algorithm, the words *Read* and *Enter* are used for input operations, and *Display, Print,* and *Write* are used for output operations. The Fortran statement used for input is the READ statement. A simple form of this statement is

```
READ *, list
```

where list is a list of variables for which values are to be read. For example, the statement

```
READ *, InitialAmount, HalfLife, Time
```

reads values for the variables InitialAmount, HalfLife, and Time.
Simple output statements in Fortran are the PRINT statement of the form

```
PRINT *, list
```

and the WRITE statement of the form

```
WRITE (*, *) list
```

where list is a list of items to be displayed. For example, the statement

```
PRINT *, "Amount remaining = ", AmountRemaining
```

displays the label

```
Amount remaining =
```

followed by the value of the variable `AmountRemaining`.

Comments. Comment lines can also be incorporated into Fortran programs. They are preceded by an exclamation mark (!) and run to the end of the line.

Programming Style. Programs must be *correct, readable, and understandable*, and there are three principles for developing such programs. We conclude this section with a brief discussion of these principles.

1. *Programs should be well structured.* Two helpful guidelines in this regard are as follows:
   - *Use a top-down approach when developing a program for a complex problem.* Divide the problem into simpler and simpler subproblems until the solution of these subproblems is clear.
   - *Strive for simplicity and clarity.* Avoid clever programming tricks intended only to demonstrate the programmer's ingenuity or to produce code that executes only slightly faster.
2. The second principle is that *each program unit should be documented*. In particular:
   - *Each program should include opening documentation.* Comments should be included to explain what the program does, how it works, any special algorithms it uses, a summary of the problem's specification, assumptions, and so on; they may also include such items of information as the name of the programmer, the date the program was written and when it was last modified, and references to books and manuals that give additional information about the program. In addition, it is good practice to explain the variables used in the program.
   - *Comments should also be used to explain key program segments and/or segments whose purpose or design is not obvious.* However, too many detailed or unnecessary comments clutter the program and only make it more difficult to read and understand.
   - *Meaningful identifiers should be used.* For example, the statement

   ```
   Distance = Rate * Time
   ```

   is more meaningful than

   ```
   D = R * T
   ```

   or

   ```
   X7 = R * Zeke
   ```

Don't use "skimpy" abbreviations just to save a few keystrokes. Also, avoid "cute" identifiers, as in

```
HowFar = GoGo * Squeal
```

3. *A program should be formatted in a style that enhances its readability.* The following are some guidelines for good program style:
   - *Use spaces between the items in a statement to make it more readable.* For example, before and after each operator (+, −, =, etc.).
   - *Insert a blank line between sections of a program and wherever appropriate in a sequence of statements to set off blocks of statements.*
   - *Adhere rigorously to alignment and indentation guidelines to emphasize the relationship between various parts of the program.*

It is often difficult for beginning programmers to appreciate the importance of learning good programming habits that lead to the design of readable and understandable programs. The reason is that programs written in an academic environment are often quite different from those developed in real-world situations, in which program style and form are critical. Student programs are usually quite small (usually less than a few hundred lines of code); are executed and modified only a few times (almost never, once they have been handed in); are rarely examined in detail by anyone other than the student and the instructor; and are not developed within the context of budget constraints. Real-world programs, on the other hand, may be very large (several thousand lines of code); may be developed by teams of programmers; are commonly used for long periods of time and thus require maintenance if they are to be kept current and correct; and are often maintained by someone other than the original programmer.

As we discuss features of the Fortran language in the following chapters, additional principles for program design will be given. It is important for beginning programmers to follow these guidelines, even in early simple programs, so that good habits are established and carried on into the design of more complex programs.

Step 4:
Execution and Testing

Obviously, the most important characteristic of any program is that it be *correct*. No matter how well structured, how well documented, or how nice the program looks, if it does not produce correct results, it is worthless. The fact that a program executes without producing any error messages is no guarantee that it is correct. The results produced may be erroneous because of logic errors that the computer system cannot detect. It is the responsibility of the programmer to test each program in order to ensure that it is correct. (See Section 4.5 for more about program testing.)

Errors may occur in any of the phases of the program-development process. For example, the specifications may not accurately reflect information given in the problem; the algorithms may contain logic errors; and the program may not be coded correctly. The detection and correction of errors is an important part of software development and is known as validation and verification. **Validation** is concerned with checking that the algorithms and the program meet the problem's specification. **Verification** refers to checking that they are correct and complete. Validation is sometimes described as answering the question, Are we solving the correct problem? and verification as answering the question, Are we solving the problem correctly?

The program in Figure 1.8 was entered, compiled, and executed without error. Usually, however, a programmer will make some errors when designing the program or when attempting to enter and execute it. Errors may be detected at various stages of program processing and may cause the processing to be terminated. For example, an incorrect system command will be detected early in the processing and will usually prevent compilation and execution of the program. Errors in the program's syntax, such as incorrect punctuation or misspelled key words, will be detected during compilation. (On some systems, syntax errors may be detected while the program is being entered.) Such errors are called **syntax errors** or **compile-time errors** and usually make it impossible to complete the compilation and execution of the program. For example, if the output statement that displays the residual amount of radioactive substance were mistakenly written as

```
PRINT *, "Amount remaining =, AmountRemaining, "mg"
```

without a quotation mark after the equal sign, an attempt to compile and execute the program might result in a message like the following, signaling a "fatal" error:

```
Error: Unterminated character literal at line 27
Error: syntax error at line 27
***Malformed statement
[f90 terminated - errors found by pass 1]
```

Less severe errors may generate "warning" messages but the compilation will continue.

Other errors, such as an attempt to divide by zero in an arithmetic expression, may not be detected until execution of the program has begun. Such errors are called **run-time errors**. Explanations of the error messages displayed by your particular system can be found in the user manuals supplied by the manufacturer. In any case, the errors must be corrected by replacing the erroneous statements with correct ones, and the modified program must be recompiled and reexecuted.

Errors that are detected by the computer system are relatively easy to identify and correct. There are, however, other errors that are more subtle and difficult to identify. These are **logic errors** that arise in the design of the algorithm or in the coding of the program that implements the algorithm. For example, if the statement

```
AmountRemaining = InitialAmount * 0.5 ** (Time / HalfLife)
```

in the program of Figure 1.8 were mistakenly entered as

```
AmountRemaining = InitialAmount * 0.5 * (Time / HalfLife)
```

with the exponentiation symbol (**) replaced by the symbol for multiplication (*), the program would still be syntactically correct. No error would occur during the compilation or execution of the program. But the results produced by the program would be incorrect because an incorrect formula would have been used to calculate the residual amount of the substance. If the values 2, 140, and 140 were entered for the variables `InitialAmount`, `HalfLife`, and `Time`, respectively, the output produced by the program would be

```
Amount remaining = 1.0000000 mg
```

which is correct, even though the formula is not. However, for the test data 4, 140, 280, the output is

```
Amount remaining = 4.0000000 mg
```

which is obviously incorrect (since the initial and remaining amounts cannot be the same).

As this example demonstrates, *it is important to execute a program with several different sets of input data for which the correct results are known in advance.* This process of **program testing** is extremely important, as a *program cannot be considered to be correct until it has been checked with several sets of test data.* The test data should be carefully selected so that each part of the program is tested.

Thorough testing of a program will increase one's confidence in its correctness, but it must be realized that is almost never possible to test a program with every possible set of test data. No matter how much testing has been done, more can always be done. Testing is never finished; it is only stopped. Consequently, there is no guarantee that all the errors in a program have been found and corrected. Testing can only show the presence of errors, not their absence. It cannot prove that the program is correct; it can only show that it is incorrect.

Step 5:
Maintenance

The life cycle of a program written by a student programmer normally ends with the fourth step; that is, once the program has been written, executed, and tested, the assignment is complete. Programs in real-world applications, however, are often used for several years and are likely to require some modification. Software systems, especially large ones developed for complex projects, may have obscure bugs that were not detected during testing and that surface after the software has been placed in use. One important aspect of software maintenance is fixing such flaws in the software.

It may also be necessary to modify software to improve its performance, to add new features, and so on. Other modifications may be required because of changes in the computer hardware and/or the system software such as the operating system. External factors may also force program modification; for example, changes in building codes may mean revising part of a construction cost program. It is easier to make such changes in a well-structured program than in one that is poorly designed.

Quick Quiz 1.4

1. Name the five steps in the program-development process.

2. What are two important parts of a problem's specification?

3. What are the three basic methods of control used in designing structured algorithms?

4. Pseudocode is a high-level programming language (true or false).

5. A _____ is a graphical display of an algorithm.

6. The grammatical rules of a language are called its _____ .

7. The approach to a problem of identifying the major tasks to be performed, arranging them in the order in which they are to be carried out, and refining them into simpler subtasks, perhaps several times, until they are simple enough to be solved is called _____ .

8. What are the three types of errors that can occur in developing a program?

9. For the following temperature-conversion problem:

    (a) Identify both the information that must be produced to solve the problem and the given information that will be useful in obtaining the solution. Then design an algorithm to solve the problem.

    (b) Using the program in Figure 1.8 as a guide, write a Fortran program to solve the problem.

    Problem: The boiling point of water is 212° on the Fahrenheit scale and 100° on the Celsius scale. The freezing point of water is 32° on the Fahrenheit scale and 0° on the Celsius scale. Assuming a linear relationship ($F = a \cdot C + b$) between these two temperature scales, convert a temperature of C degrees on the Celsius scale to the corresponding Fahrenheit temperature, and display the Fahrenheit temperature.

Exercises 1.4

For each of the problems described in Exercises 1 and 2, identify both the information that must be produced to solve the problem and the given information that will be useful in obtaining the solution. Then design an algorithm to solve the problem.

1. Calculate and display the radius, circumference, and area of a circle with a given diameter.

2. Three resistors are arranged in parallel in the following circuit:

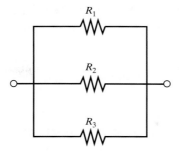

Calculate and display the combined resistance

$$\frac{1}{\dfrac{1}{R_1} + \dfrac{1}{R_2} + \dfrac{1}{R_3}}$$

for given values of R_1, R_2, and R_3.

3. Enter and execute the following Fortran 90 program on your computer system, but with the name, course name, and date replaced with your name and course name and the current date.

```
PROGRAM Arithmetic
!-----------------------------------------------------------------
! John Doe                   CPSC 141C              MonthName dd, yyyy
!                        ASSIGNMENT #1
!
! Program to add two real numbers. Variables used are:
!   X, Y : the two real numbers
!   Sum  : the sum of X and Y
!
! Output: X, Y, and Sum
!-----------------------------------------------------------------

   IMPLICIT NONE
   REAL :: X, Y, Sum

   X = 3.14
   Y = 2.057
   Sum = X + Y
   PRINT *, "Sum of", X, " and", Y, " is", Sum

END PROGRAM Arithmetic
```

4. For the program in Exercise 3, make the following changes and execute the modified program:

(a) Change `3.14` to `17.2375` in the statement that assigns a value to X.

(b) Change the variable names X and Y to `Alpha` and `Beta` throughout.

(c) Insert the comment

```
! Calculate the sum
```

before the statement that assigns a value to Sum.

(d) Insert the following comment and statement before the PRINT statement:

```
! Now calculate the difference
 Difference = Alpha - Beta
```

add the variable `Difference` to the list of variables in the REAL statement, and add another PRINT statement to display the value of `Difference`. Also, change the comments in the opening documentation appropriately.

5. Using the program in Figure 1.8 as a guide, write a Fortran program for the circle problem in Exercise 1.

6. Proceed as in Exercise 5, but for the resistance problem in Exercise 2.

CHAPTER REVIEW

Summary

In this chapter we have discussed the fundamental concepts of computing systems. We began with a brief history, focusing on the mechanization of arithmetic and the stored-program concept and on how these were implemented in various machines. We described the four generations of computers developed since the 1940s. We also reviewed the development of system software including operating systems and compilers. The main components of computing systems were described in Section 1.2, which included a description of machine-language and assembly-language programming and the compilation process. Section 1.3 contains an example that illustrates the four steps of the programming and problem-solving process:

1. Problem analysis and specification
2. Data organization and algorithm design
3. Program coding
4. Execution and testing

These steps are described more generally in the overview of the program-development process given in the last section of the chapter. These sections also contain a brief introduction to the Fortran 90 programming language.

FORTRAN 90 SUMMARY

Identifiers

Identifiers such as program names and variable names must begin with a letter, which may be followed by up to thirty letters, digits, or underscores.

Comments

A blank or a line that contains an exclamation mark (!) as the first non-blank character on the line is a comment line.

PROGRAM Statement

```
PROGRAM program-name
```

Example:

```
PROGRAM Radioactive_Decay
```

Purpose:
The PROGRAM statement names the program.

Types

```
REAL :: list-of-variable-names
INTEGER :: list-of-variable-names
```

Example:

```
REAL :: InitialAmount, HalfLife, Time, AmountRemaining
INTEGER :: Number_of_Points
```

Purpose:
Type statements declare the type of values that variables will have.

Operations

Operator	Operation
+	addition
−	subtraction
*	multiplication
/	division
**	exponentiation

Assignment Statement

```
variable = expression
```

Example:

```
AmountRemaining = InitialAmount * 0.5 ** (Time / HalfLife)
Number_of_Points = 0
```

Purpose:
Assign the value of the *expression* to the specified *variable*.

Input Statement

```
READ *, input-list-of-variables
```

Example:

```
READ *, InitialAmount, HalfLife, Time
READ *, Number_of_Points
```

Purpose:
The READ statement reads values for the variables in the input list.

Output Statements

```
PRINT *, output-list-of-expressions
WRITE (*, *) output-list-of-expressions
```

Examples:

```
PRINT *, "Amount remaining = ", AmountRemaining
WRITE (*, *) "Number of points = ", Number_of_Points -- 1
```

Purpose:
The PRINT and WRITE statements display the values of the expressions in the output list.

END PROGRAM Statement

```
END PROGRAM program-name
```

Purpose:

The END PROGRAM statement marks the end of a program and stops execution.

2

Basic Fortran

Kindly enter them in your note-book. And, in order to refer to them conveniently, let's call them A, B, and Z.

The tortoise in LEWIS CARROLL'S
What the Tortoise Said to Achilles.

In language, clarity is everything.

CONFUCIUS

Arithmetic is being able to count up to twenty without taking off your shoes.

MICKEY MOUSE

All the news that's fit to print.

ADOLPH S. OCHS

*O*ne important part of using the computer to solve a problem is implementing the algorithm for solving that problem as a program. We noted in the preceding chapter that while algorithms can be described somewhat informally in a pseudoprogramming language, the corresponding program must be written in strict compliance with the rules of some programming language. The program we wrote to solve the radioactive-decay problem introduced several features of the Fortran language.

We also noted that Fortran was developed in the mid 1950s by a team of programmers at IBM. In the years that followed, a number of versions of Fortran were developed by different computer companies, and in an attempt to minimize the differences among these versions, the American National Standards Institute (ANSI) established standards for the Fortran language. The two most recent standards are FOR-TRAN 77, which has been the most commonly used version of Fortran for the past several years, and Fortran 90, which is the basis for this text. Fortran 90 retains all of the features of FORTRAN 77, but it has also added many new features that make it a modern programming language, more powerful and easier to use than its predecessors. In this chapter we begin our study of Fortran 90 by considering some of its basic features and we illustrate their use with several examples and applications.

2.1   DATA TYPES + ALGORITHMS = PROGRAMS

We have seen in the preceding chapter that organizing a problem's data is an important part of developing a program to solve that problem. This may be numeric data representing times or temperatures, or character data representing names, or logical data used in designing a circuit, and so on. Consequently, a program for solving a problem must be written in a language that can store and process various types of data.

Fortran provides five basic data types:

integer

real

complex

character

logical

The first three are numeric types used to store and process various kinds of numbers; the character type is used to store and process strings of characters; and the logical type is used to store and process logical data values (.FALSE. and .TRUE.). In this chapter we will restrict our attention to integer, real, and character types; we will consider the logical data type in Chapter 3 and the complex type in Chapter 11.

Another important aspect of solving a problem is the development of algorithms to process the input data and produce the required output. A program for solving a problem must be written in a language that provides operations for processing data and instructions that carry out the steps of the algorithm. For example, Fortran provides basic arithmetic operations for numeric computations, input and output instructions for entering and displaying data, instructions for implementing the basic control structures, and so on.

Since these two basic aspects of problem solving—data types and algorithms—cannot be separated, a program for solving a problem must incorporate both; that is, some part of the program must specify the data to be processed, and another part must contain the instructions to do the processing. A Fortran program contains a **specification part** in which the names and types of constants and variables used to store input and output values as well as intermediate results are declared. This is followed by an **execution part**, which contains the statements that carry out the steps of the algorithm.

The general form of a program in Fortran is

FORTRAN Program

heading
specification part
execution part
subprogram part
END PROGRAM statement

The first statement of a Fortran program is its **heading**. This statement marks the beginning of the program and gives it a name. The heading is normally followed by **opening documentation** in the form of comments about the program's input, output, and purpose and may include other relevant information such as special algorithms that it implements, the date the program was written, when it was last modified, the name of the programmer, and so on. The other parts of a program are described in the following sections.

2.2 DATA TYPES, CONSTANTS, AND VARIABLES

We noted in the preceding section that organizing the data in a problem is an important part of program development and that a problem may involve several different types of data. In this section we describe the most commonly used forms of the Fortran integer, real, and character data types and how to declare constants and variables of these types. (Other forms that may be used to specify the range of integer values and the precision of real values are described in Chapter 11.)

Integers

An **integer** is a whole number (positive, negative, or zero) and may be represented in Fortran by a string of digits *that does not contain commas or a decimal point;* negative integer constants must be preceded by a minus sign, but a plus sign is optional for nonnegative integers. Thus

```
     0
   137
 -2516
+17745
```

are valid integer constants, whereas the following are invalid for the reasons indicated:

9,999	(Commas are not allowed in numeric constants.)
16.0	(Integer constants may not contain decimal points.)
--5	(Only one algebraic sign is allowed.)
7-	(The algebraic sign must precede the string of digits.)

Reals

Another numeric data type is the **real** type. Constants of this type may be represented as ordinary decimal numbers or in exponential notation. *In the decimal representation of real constants, a decimal point must be present, but no commas are allowed.* Negative real constants must be preceded by a minus sign, but the plus sign is optional for nonnegative reals. Thus

```
  1.234
 -0.01536
 +56473.
```

are valid real constants, whereas the following are invalid for the reasons indicated:

```
12,345       (Commas are not allowed in numeric constants.)
   63        (Real constants must contain a decimal point.)
```

The exponential representation of a real constant consists of an integer or decimal number, representing the mantissa or fractional part, followed by an exponent written as the letter E *with an integer constant following.* For example, the real constant 337.456 may also be written as

```
3.37456E2
```

which means 3.37456×10^2, or it may be written in a variety of other forms, such as

```
0.337456E3
337.456E0
33745.6E-2
337456E-3
```

Character Strings

Character constants, also called **strings,** are sequences of symbols from the Fortran character set. The ANSI standard character set for Fortran is given in Table 2.1.

The sequence of characters that comprise a character constant must be enclosed between double quotes or between apostrophes (single quotes), as long as the same character is used at the beginning and the end. The number of such characters is the **length** of the constant. For example,

```
"PDQ123-A"
```

is a character constant of length 8;

```
"John Q. Doe"
```

is a character constant of length 11, because blanks are characters and are included

Table 2.1 Fortran Character Set

Character	Meaning	Character	Meaning
0, ..., 9	digits	:	colon
A, ..., Z	uppercase letters	=	equal sign
a, ..., z	lowercase letters	!	exclamation mark
'	apostrophe	&	ampersand
"	double quote	$	dollar sign
(	left parenthesis	;	semicolon
)	right parenthesis	<	less than
*	asterisk	>	greater than
+	plus sign	%	percent symbol
−	minus sign	?	question mark
/	slash	,	comma
blank	blank or space	.	period

in the character count. Apostrophes could also be used to enclose the characters; for example,

```
'John Q. Doe'
```

but neither of the following is allowed:

```
"John Q. Doe'    (not allowed)
'John Q. Doe"    (not allowed)
```

If an apostrophe is to be one of the characters in a constant, double quotes should be used to enclose the string; for example,

```
"Don't"
```

Alternatively, apostrophes may be used to enclose the string, provided the apostrophe within the string is entered as a pair of apostrophes:

```
'Don''t'
```

In either case, this represents a character constant consisting of the five characters D, o, n, ', and t. Similarly, if a character constant contains a double quote, it can be enclosed between apostrophes; or it can be enclosed between double quotes, provided the double quote within the string is entered as a pair of double quotes.

Identifiers

Identifiers are names used to identify programs, constants, variables, and other entities in a program. In standard Fortran, *identifiers must begin with a letter, which may be followed by up to 30 letters, digits, or underscores.* **Thus**

```
Mass
Rate
Velocity
Speed_of_Light
```

are valid Fortran identifiers, but the following are invalid for the reasons indicated:

`R2-D2`	(Only letters, digits, and underscores are allowed in identifiers.)
`6Feet`	(Identifiers must begin with a letter.)

One should always use meaningful identifiers that suggest what they represent.

Fortran 90 makes no distinction between upper case and lower case (except in character constants). For example, `Velocity` is a valid identifier and will not be distinguished from `VELOCITY`, or `vELocITy`, even if one form is used in one place in the program and another is used somewhere else. A common practice—and one that we use in the sample programs in this text—is to write all Fortran key words (e.g., `READ` and `PRINT`) in upper case and all programmer-defined identifiers in lower case, usually capitalizing the first letter. If an identifier is made up of several words, we usually capitalize the first letter of each and sometimes separate the words by underscores.

Variables

In mathematics, a symbolic name is often used to refer to a quantity. For example, the formula

$$A = l \cdot w$$

is used to calculate the area (denoted by A) of a rectangle with a given length (denoted by l) and a given width (denoted by w). These symbolic names, A, l, and w, are called **variables**. If values are assigned to l and w, this formula can be used to calculate the value of A, which is then the area of a particular rectangle.

Variables were used in Chapter 1 in the discussion of algorithms and programs. When a variable is used in a Fortran program, the compiler associates it with a memory location. The value of a variable at any time is the value stored in the associated memory location at that time. Variable names are identifiers and thus must follow the rules for forming valid identifiers.

The type of a Fortran variable determines the type of value that may be assigned to that variable. It is therefore necessary to declare the type of each variable in a Fortran program. This can be done using **type statements**:

Declarations of Variables

Form:

```
type-specifier :: list
```

where

    type-specifier is usually one of the following:

```
INTEGER
REAL
COMPLEX
CHARACTER(length-specifier)
LOGICAL
```

    list is a list of identifiers, separated by commas. (See Chapters 10 and 11 for other forms of the type specifier).

Purpose:
Declares that the identifiers in *list* have the specified type. *Type statements must appear in the specification part of the program.*

Basic forms of the type statements used to declare integer variables and real variables are

```
REAL :: list
INTEGER :: list
```

respectively. Thus, the statements

```
INTEGER :: NumValues, Factorial, Sum
REAL :: Mass, Velocity
```

declare `NumValues`, `Factorial`, and `Sum` to be integer variables and `Mass` and `Velocity` to be real variables.

One form of the type statement used to declare character variables is

```
CHARACTER(LEN = n) :: list
```

or simply

```
CHARACTER(n) :: list
```

where *n* is an integer constant specifying the length of character constants to be assigned to the variables in the list. The names in the list must be separated by commas. The length specifier may be omitted, in which case the length of the values for the variables in the list is 1. For example, the type statement

```
CHARACTER(LEN = 15) :: FirstName, LastName
```

or

```
CHARACTER(15) :: FirstName, LastName
```

declares `FirstName` and `LastName` to be character variables and specifies that the length of any character value assigned to one of these variables is 15. The statement

```
CHARACTER :: Initial
```

declares `Initial` to be a character variable with values of length 1.

A length specifier of the form `*n` may also be attached to any of the individual variables in the list of a `CHARACTER` statement. In this case, this length specification for that variable overrides the length specification given for the list. The statement

```
CHARACTER(15) :: FirstName, LastName*20, Initial*1, Street, City
```

declares that `FirstName`, `LastName`, `Initial`, `Street`, and `City` are character variables and that the length of values for `FirstName`, `Street`, and `City` is 15, the length of values for `LastName` is 20, and the length of values for `Initial` is 1.

Variables of a given type must be used in a manner that is appropriate to that data type, since the program may fail to execute correctly otherwise. *It is therefore important to specify the correct type of each variable used in a program.* One must think carefully about each variable, what it represents, what type of values it will have, what operations will be performed on it, and so on. This will avoid (or at least lessen) the mixed-mode errors described in Potential Problem 11 of the Programming Pointers at the end of this chapter.

The IMPLICIT NONE Statement

Most programming languages require that the types of all variables be specified explicitly. In Fortran, however, any variable whose type is not *explicitly* declared in a type statement will be assigned a type according to an **implicit naming convention:** any undeclared identifier whose name begins with I, J, K, L, M, or N or their lowercase equivalents will be typed as integer, and all others will be typed as real.

An unfortunate consequence of this naming convention is that failing to declare the type of a variable is not an error, because the variables will be implicitly typed. Fortran 90 provides the `IMPLICIT NONE` statement, which cancels the naming convention:

IMPLICIT NONE *Statement*

Form:

```
IMPLICIT NONE
```

Purpose:
Cancels the naming convention. *This statement must appear at the beginning of the specification part of the program.*

It should be used in every program (and module) to guard against errors like those described in Potential Problem 13 in the Programming Pointers at the end of this chapter. Placing `IMPLICIT NONE` at the beginning of the specification part requires that the types of all named constants and variables (and functions) *must be* specified explicitly in type statements. Using any named constant or variable (or function) without declaring it explicitly in a type statement will be treated as an error by the compiler.

Variable Initialization

It is important to note that in Fortran, *all variables are initially undefined.* Although some compilers may initialize a variable with a particular value (e.g., 0 for numeric variables), this is not always true. It should be assumed that all variables are initially undefined, and they therefore should be initialized in the program.

Initial values can be assigned to variables (at compile time) in their declarations:

Initialization in Declarations

Form:

```
type-specifier :: list
```

where
> *type-specifier* is as described earlier,
> and *list* is a list of assignments of the form

```
Variable = ConstantExpression
```

separated by commas.

Purpose:
Declares each *Variable* to have the specified type and initializes it with the given *ConstantExpression* at compile time.

For example, to initialize the values of variables W, X, Y, and Z to `1.0`, `2.5`, `7.73`, and `-2.956`, respectively, we could use the statements

```
REAL :: W = 1.0, X = 2.5, Y = 7.73, Z = -2.956
```

Named Constants: The **PARAMETER** Attribute

Certain constants occur so often that they are given names. For example, the name "pi" is commonly given to the constant 3.14159... and the name "*e*" to the base 2.71828... of natural logarithms. Fortran allows the programmer to specify that an identifier names a constant by including a **PARAMETER attribute** in the declaration of that identifier:

Declaration of Named Constants

Form:

> *type-specifier*, PARAMETER :: *list*

where
> *type-specifier* is as described earlier,
> and *list* is a list of constant definitions of the form

> *identifier* = *constant-expression*

separated by commas.

Purpose:
Associates each *identifier* with the specified constant value *constant-expression*. The value of a named constant cannot be changed; any attempt to do so will cause a compile-time error.

For example, the declarations

```
INTEGER, PARAMETER :: Limit = 50
REAL, PARAMETER :: Pi = 3.141593, TwoPi = 2.0 * Pi
CHARACTER(2), PARAMETER :: Units = "cm"
```

associate the names `Limit` with the integer `50`, `Pi` and `TwoPi` with the real constants `3.141593` and `6.283186`, respectively, and `Units` with the character string `"cm"`. The last declaration can also be written

```
CHARACTER(*), PARAMETER :: Units = "cm"
```

Here the asterisk (*) is an **assumed length specifier** indicating that the length of the named constant (`Units`) being declared is to be the length (2) of the string constant (`"cm"`) with which it is being associated.

The names `Limit`, `Pi`, `TwoPi`, and `Units` can be used anywhere in the program that the corresponding constant value can be used (except as noted later in the text). For example, a statement such as

```
XCoordinate = Rate * COS(TwoPi * Time)
```

is equivalent to

```
XCoordinate = Rate * COS(6.283186 * Time)
```

but the first form is preferable because it is more readable and does not require modification if a different value with more or fewer significant digits is required for `Pi`.

Another way that named constants can make programs easier to read and to modify is by using them to avoid "magic numbers." To illustrate, suppose that the statements

```
Change = (0.1758 - 0.1257) * Population
Population = Population + Change
```

appear at one point in a program and that the statements

```
PopulationIncrease = 0.1758 * Population
PopulationDecrease = 0.1257 * Population
```

appear later. In these statements, the constants 0.1758 and 0.1257 magically appear, without explanation. If they must be changed, it will be necessary for someone to search through the program to locate all the places where they appear and to determine what they represent and which are the appropriate ones to change. To make the program more understandable and to minimize the number of statements that must be changed when other values are required, it is better to associate these constants with names, as in

```
REAL, PARAMETER :: BirthRate = 0.1758, DeathRate = 0.1257
```

(or to assign them to variables) and then use these names in place of the magic numbers:

```
Change = (BirthRate - DeathRate) * Population
Population = Population + Change
    ⋮
PopulationIncrease = BirthRate * Population
PopulationDecrease = DeathRate * Population
```

Readability is improved and the flexibility of the program is increased, because if these constants must be changed, one need only change their declarations.

Quick Quiz 2.2

1. Name the five basic Fortran data types.

2. Name the five parts of a Fortran program.

3. Character constants must be enclosed in _____ or _____ .

4. Identifiers must begin with _____ .

5. The maximum number of characters in a Fortran identifier is _____ .

For Questions 6–13, tell whether the string of characters forms a legal identifier. If it is not legal, indicate the reason.

6. Calorie   7. Type-A   8. 55MPH   9. MilesPerHour
10. Miles_Per_Hour   11. PS.175   12. N/4   13. M$

For Questions 14–28, tell whether the string of characters forms an integer, real, or character constant. If it is none of these, indicate the reason.

14. 1234   15. 1,234   16. -1.234
17. -1.   18. 0.123E+04   19. 'one'
20. one   21. 'Ohm's law'   22. "1234"
23. $12.34   24. 123E4   25. E4
26. +1234   27. 12+34   28. "12+34"

29. Write type statements to declare Mu to be an integer variable.

30. Write type statements to declare Time and Distance to be real variables.

31. Write type statements to declare Name1 and Name2 to be character variables with values of length 20 and Name3 a character variable with values of length 10.

For Questions 32–34, write declarations to name the constants with the specified names.

32. 32 with Gravity

33. 1.2E12 with Mars and 1.5E10 with Earth

34. "CHEM" with Department and 141 with CourseNumber

For Questions 35–37, write initialization declarations for each variable.

35. Rate1 and Rate2 to be real variables with initial values 1.25 and 2.33, respectively

36. Department to be a character variable with initial value "ENGR" and Course1, Course2 to be integer variables with initial values 141 and 142, respectively

37. Limit_1, Limit_2, Limit_3, and Limit_4 to be integer variables with initial values 10, 20, 20, and 30, respectively

Exercises 2.2

For Exercises 1–16, tell whether the string of characters forms a legal identifier. If it is not legal, indicate the reason.

1. X Axis	2. X-Axis	3. XAxis	4. X_A_X_I_S
5. Carbon14	6. 3M	7. Angle	8. Agnle
9. angel	10. R2D2	11. R2-D2	12. R2 D2
13. Two	14. A+	15. Z0000Z	16. ZZZZZZ

For Exercises 17–34, tell whether the string of characters forms an integer constant or a real constant. If it is neither of these, indicate the reason.

17. 5,280	18. 5280	19. "5280"
20. 528.0	21. 5280E0	22. -5280
23. --5280	24. +5280	25. 52+80
26. $52.80	27. 52E80	28. E5280
29. eighty	30. 0.528E0	31. .00005280
32. 0528	33. -52.80	34. +52E+80

For Exercises 35–42, tell whether the string of characters forms a legal character constant. If it is not legal, indicate the reason.

35. "Resultant force:'	36. "isn't"
37. "$5,280.00"	38. 'ABC
39. 'E = M * C ** 2'	40. 'A''B"C'
41. 'PRINT *, '	42. "'s Law"

43. Write type statements to declare `Temperature`, `Pressure`, and `Volume` to be real variables.

44. Write type statements to declare `Code` and `Count` to be integer variables and `XCoordinate` and `YCoordinate` to be real variables.

45. Write type statements to declare `Formula` and `Name` to be character variables with values of length 10 and `Amount` to be a real variable.

46. Write type statements to declare `Name`, `Street_Address`, `City`, and `State` to be character variables with values of length 20, 30, 15, and 2, respectively.

For Exercises 47–51, write declarations to name the constants with the specified names.

47. `1.25` with `Rate`

48. `100` with `Celsius_Boiling_Point` and `212` with `Fahrenheit_Boiling_Point`

49. `1.0E 5` with `Tolerance`, `0.001` with `Delta_X`, `500` with `Number_of_Intervals`

50. `"Fe2O3"` with `Formula`, `"Ferric Oxide"` with `Name`, and `.182` with `SpecificHeat`

51. `12713` with `IdNumber`, `"J. Smith"` with `Student_Name`, and `12.75` with `Rate`

For Exercises 52–56, write initialization declarations for each variable.

52. `Number_1` and `Number_2` to be integer variables with initial values 10 and 20, respectively

53. `Distance_1`, `Distance_2`, and `Distance_3` to be real variables, each with the initial value of 0.0

54. `Sum_1` and `Sum_2` to be real variables, each with an initial value of 0.0; and `Size_1`, `Size_2`, and `Size_3` to be integer variables with initial values 100, 200, and 300, respectively

55. `Char_1` and `Char_2` to be character variables of length 1, each with the initial value `"X"`

56. `Units_1`, `Units_2`, and `Units_3` to be character variables with initial values `"feet"`, `"inches"`, and `"centimeters"`, respectively; `Num_1`, `Num_2`, and `Num_3` to be integer variables with initial values 0, 0, and 1, respectively; and `Rate_1` and `Rate_2` to be real variables with initial values 0.25 and 1.5, respectively

2.3   ARITHMETIC OPERATIONS AND FUNCTIONS

In the preceding section we considered variables and constants of various types. These variables and constants can be processed by using operations and functions appropriate to their types. In this section we discuss the arithmetic operations and functions that are used with numeric data.

Operations

In Fortran, addition and subtraction are denoted by the usual plus (+) and minus (−) signs. Multiplication is denoted by an asterisk (*). This symbol must be used to denote every multiplication; thus, to multiply N by 2, we must use 2 * N or N * 2, not 2N. Division is denoted by a slash (/), and exponentiation is denoted by a pair of asterisks (**). For example, the quantity $B^2 - 4AC$ is written as

$$B \text{ ** } 2 - 4 \text{ * } A \text{ * } C$$

in a Fortran program. Table 2.2 summarizes these arithmetic operations.

When two constants or variables of the same type are combined using one of the four basic arithmetic operations (+, −, *, /), the result has the same type as the operands. For example, the sum of the integers 3 and 4 is the integer 7, whereas the sum of the real numbers 3.0 and 4.0 is the real number 7.0. This distinction may seem unimportant until one considers the division operation. Division of the real constant 9.0 by the real constant 4.0,

$$9.0 \text{ / } 4.0$$

TABLE 2.2   Operations

Operator	Operation
+	addition, unary plus
−	subtraction, unary minus
*	multiplication
/	division
**	exponentiation

produces the real quotient 2.25, whereas dividing the integer 9 by the integer 4,

$$9 \;/\; 4$$

produces the integer quotient 2, which is the integer part of the real quotient 2.25. Similarly, if the integer variable N has the value 2 and the real variable X has the value 2.0, the real division

$$1.0 \;/\; X$$

yields 0.5, whereas the integer division

$$1 \;/\; N$$

yields 0.

   Mixed-Mode Expressions. It is possible to combine integer and real quantities using arithmetic operations. Expressions involving different types of numeric operands are called **mixed-mode expressions**. When an integer quantity is combined with a real one, the integer quantity is converted to its real equivalent, and the result is of real type.
   The following examples illustrate the evaluation of some mixed-mode expressions; note that type conversion does not take place until necessary:

```
1.0 / 4 → 1.0 / 4.0 → 0.25
3.0 + 8 / 5 → 3.0 + 1 → 3.0 + 1.0 → 4.0
3 + 8.0 / 5 → 3 + 8.0 / 5.0 → 3 + 1.6 → 3.0 + 1.6 → 4.6
```

The last two examples show why *using mixed-mode expressions is usually considered poor programming practice*. The two expressions 3.0 + 8 / 5 and 3 + 8.0 / 5 are algebraically equal but are in fact not equal because of the differences in real and integer arithmetic.
   The only expressions in which operands of different types should be used are those in which a real value is raised to an integer power. For such expressions, exponentiation is carried out using repeated multiplication, as the following examples illustrate:

```
2.0 ** 3 → 2.0 * 2.0 * 2.0 → 8.0
(-4.0) ** 2 → (-4.0) * (-4.0) → 16.0
```

If, however, the exponent is a real quantity, exponentiation is performed using logarithms. For example,

$$2.0 \text{ ** } 3.0$$

is evaluated as

$$e^{3.0 \ln (2.0)}$$

which will not be exactly 8.0 because of roundoff errors that arise in storing real numbers and because the exponentiation and logarithm functions produce only approximate values. Another consequence of this method of performing exponentiation is that a negative quantity raised to a real power is undefined because the logarithms of negative values are not defined. Consequently, (-4.0) ** 2.0 is undefined, even though (-4.0) ** 2 is evaluated as (-4.0) * (-4.0) = 16.0. These examples show why *a real exponent should never be used in place of an integer exponent.*

There are, however, computations in which real exponents are appropriate. For example, in mathematics, $7^{1/2}$ denotes $\sqrt{7}$, the square root of 7. In Fortran, this operation of extracting roots can be performed using exponentiation with real exponents. Thus, to compute the square root of 7.0, we could write 7.0 ** 0.5 or 7.0 ** (1.0 / 2.0). (Note, however, that 7.0 ** (1 / 2) yields 7.0 ** 0 = 1.0.) Similarly, the cube root of a real variable X can be computed using X ** (1.0 / 3.0).

Priority Rules. Arithmetic expressions are evaluated in accordance with the following **priority rules:**

1. *All exponentiations are performed first; consecutive exponentiations are performed from right to left.*
2. *All multiplications and divisions are performed next, in the order in which they appear from left to right.*
3. *The additions and subtractions are performed last, in the order in which they appear from left to right.*

The following examples illustrate this order of evaluation:

```
2 ** 3 ** 2 = 2 ** 9 = 512
10 - 8 - 2 = 2 - 2 = 0
10 / 5 * 2 = 2 * 2 = 4
2 + 4 / 2 = 2 + 2 = 4
2 + 4 ** 2 / 2 = 2 + 16 / 2 = 2 + 8 = 10
```

The standard order of evaluation can be modified by using parentheses to enclose subexpressions within an expression. These subexpressions are evaluated first in the standard manner, and the results are then combined to evaluate the complete expression. If the parentheses are "nested," that is, if one set of parentheses is contained within another, the computations in the innermost parentheses are performed first.

For example, consider the expression

$$(5 \ * \ (11 \ - \ 5) \ ** \ 2) \ * \ 4 \ + \ 9$$

The subexpression 11 - 5 is evaluated first, producing

$$(5 \ * \ 6 \ ** \ 2) \ * \ 4 \ + \ 9$$

Next, the subexpression 5 * 6 ** 2 is evaluated in the standard order, giving

$$180 \ * \ 4 \ + \ 9$$

Now the multiplication is performed, giving

$$720 \ + \ 9$$

and the addition produces the final result

$$729$$

Expressions containing two or more operations must be written carefully to ensure that they will be evaluated in the order intended. Even though parentheses may not be necessary, they should be used freely to clarify the intended order of evaluation and to write complicated expressions in terms of simpler subexpressions. However, parentheses must balance (i.e., each left parenthesis must match a right parenthesis that appears later in the expression), since an unpaired parenthesis will result in an error.

The symbols + and - can also be used as **unary operators;** for example, +X and - (A + B) are allowed. But unary operators must be used carefully, because Fortran *does not allow two operators to follow in succession.* (Note that ** is interpreted as a single operator rather than two operators in succession.) For example, the expression N * -2 is not allowed; rather, it must be written as N * (-2). The unary operations have the same low priority as the corresponding binary operations.

Functions

Fortran provides library functions for many of the common mathematical operations and functions. For example, many computations involve the square root of a quantity. Consequently, Fortran provides a special **function** to implement this operation. This function is denoted by SQRT and is used by writing

```
SQRT(argument)
```

where `argument` is a *real-valued* constant, variable, or expression. For example, to calculate the square root of 7, we would write

```
SQRT(7.0)
```

but not `SQRT(7)`. If `B ** 2 - 4.0 * A * C` is a nonnegative, real-valued expression, its square root can be calculated by writing

```
SQRT(B ** 2 - 4.0 * A * C)
```

If the value of the expression `B ** 2 - 4.0 * A * C` is negative, an error will result because the square root of a negative number is not defined. To calculate the square root of an integer variable `Number`, it is necessary to convert its value to a real value using the type conversion function `REAL` before using `SQRT`:

```
SQRT(REAL(Number))
```

The Nth root of a real variable `X` can be computed by using

```
X ** (1.0 / REAL(N))
```

and the Nth root of an integer variable `NUM` by using

TABLE 2.3 Some Fortran Functions

Type of Function	Description	Argument(s)[*]	Type of Value
ABS(x)	Absolute value of x	Integer or real	Same as argument
COS(x)	Cosine of x radians	Real	Real
EXP(x)	Exponential function	Real	Real
INT(x)	Integer part of x	Real	Integer
FLOOR(x)	Greatest integer $\leq x$	Real	Integer
FRACTION(x)	Fractional part (mantissa) of x	Real	Real
LOG(x)	Natural logarithm of x	Real	Real
MAX($x_1, \ldots, x_n$)	Maximum of $x_1, \ldots, x_n$	Integer or real	Same as arguments
MIN($x_1, \ldots, x_n$)	Minimum of $x_1, \ldots, x_n$	Integer or real	Same as arguments
MOD(x, y)	x (mod y); $x - \text{INT}(x/y) * y$	Integer or real	Same as arguments
NINT(x)	x rounded to nearest integer	Real	Integer
REAL(x)	Conversion of x to real type	Integer	Real
SIN(x)	Sine of x radians	Real	Real
SQRT(x)	Square root of x	Real	Real
TAN(x)	Tangent of x radians	Real	Real

[*]In several cases, the arguments (and values) may be of extended precision or complex types. See Chapter 11.

```
REAL(NUM) ** (1.0 / REAL(N))
```

There are many other functions provided in Fortran; some of the more commonly used functions are listed in Table 2.3. Other functions, including the inverse trigonometric functions (ACOS, ASIN, ATAN, ATAN2) and the hyperbolic functions (COSH, SINH, TANH), are described in Table 6.1 and in Appendix D. To use any of these functions, we simply give the function name followed by the argument(s) enclosed in parentheses. In each case, the argument(s) must be of the type specified for that function in the table.

Quick Quiz 2.3

Find the value of each of the expressions in Questions 1–10.

1. `9 - 5 - 3`   2. `2.0 + 3.0 / 5.0`
3. `2 + 3 / 5`   4. `5 / 2 + 3`
5. `2 + 3 ** 2`   6. `(2 + 3) ** 2`
7. `25.0 ** 1 / 2`   8. `12.0 / 1.0 * 3.0`
9. `(2 + 3 * 4) / (8 - 2 + 1)`   10. `SQRT(6.0 + 3.0)`

Given that Two = 2.0, Three = 3.0, Four = 4.0, IntEight = 8, and IntFive = 5, find the value of each of the expressions in Questions 11–17.

11. `Two + Three * Three`   12. `IntFive / 3`
13. `(Three + Two / Four) ** 2`   14. `IntEight / IntFive * 5.1`
15. `Four ** 2 / Two ** 2`   16. `IntFive ** 2 / Two ** 2`
17. `SQRT(Two + Three + Four)`

18. Write a Fortran expression equivalent to $10 + 5B - 4AC$.

19. Write a Fortran expression equivalent to the square root of $A + 3B^2$.

Exercises 2.3

Find the value of each of the expressions in Exercises 1-17.

1. `12 - 5 + 3`   2. `2 ** 3 + 3 / 5`
3. `2.0 / 4`   4. `3 + 4 ** 2`
5. `(3 + 4) ** 2`   6. `3 ** 2 ** 3`
7. `(3 ** 2) ** 3`   8. `3 ** (2 ** 3)`

9. `(3 ** 2 ** 3)`   10. `25 ** 1 / 2`

11. `-3.0 ** 2`   12. `ABS(1 - 2 - 3)`

13. `EXP(3.0 - 2.0 - 1.0)`   14. `INT(5.0 + 4.0 / 3.0)`

15. `((2 + 3) ** 2) / (8 - (2 + 1))`

16. `(2 + 3 ** 2) / (8 - 2 + 1)`

17. `(2.0 + 3 ** 2) / (8 - 2 + 1)`

18. Write a Fortran expression equivalent to three times the difference $4 - N$ divided by twice the quantity $M^2 + N^2$.

19. Write a Fortran expression equivalent to the cube root of X (calculated as X to the one-third power).

20. Write a Fortran expression equivalent to $A^2 + B^2 - 2AB \cos T$.

21. Write a Fortran expression equivalent to the natural logarithm of the absolute value of $\dfrac{X - Y}{X + Y}$.

2.4   THE ASSIGNMENT STATEMENT

The **assignment statement** is used to assign values to variables and has the form

Assignment Statement

Form:

```
variable = expression
```

where
> *variable* is a valid Fortran identifier and
> *expression* may be a constant, another variable to which a value has previously been assigned, or a formula to be evaluated.

Purpose:
Assigns the value of *expression* to *variable*.

For example, suppose that `XCoordinate` and `YCoordinate` are real variables and `Number` and `Term` are integer variables, as declared by the following statements:

```
REAL :: XCoordinate, YCoordinate
INTEGER :: Number, Term
```

These declarations associate memory locations with these variables. This might be pictured as follows, with the question marks indicating that these variables are initially undefined.

XCOORD	?
YCOORD	?
NUMBER	?
TERM	?

Now consider the following assignment statements:

```
XCoordinate = 5.23
YCoordinate = SQRT(25.0)
Number = 17
Term = Number / 3 + 2
XCoordinate = 2.0 * XCoordinate
```

The first assignment statement assigns the real constant 5.23 to the real variable XCoordinate, and the second assigns the real constant 5.0 to the real variable YCoordinate. The next assignment statement assigns the integer constant 17 to the integer variable Number; the variable Term is still undefined, and the content of the memory location associated with it is uncertain.

XCOORD	5.23
YCOORD	5.0
NUMBER	17
TERM	?

This means that until the contents of these memory locations are changed, these values are substituted for the variable names in any subsequent expression containing these variables. Thus, in the fourth assignment statement, the value 17 is substituted for the variable Number; the expression Number / 3 + 2 is evaluated, yielding 7; and this value is then assigned to the integer variable Term; the value of Number is unchanged.

XCOORD	5.23
YCOORD	5.0
NUMBER	17
TERM	7

In the last assignment statement, the variable XCoordinate appears on both sides of the assignment operator (=). In this case, the current value 5.23 for XCoordinate is used in evaluating the expression 2.0 * XCoordinate, yielding the value 10.46; this value is then assigned to XCoordinate. The old value 5.23 is lost because it has been replaced with the new value 10.46.

XCOORD	10.46
YCOORD	5.0
NUMBER	17
TERM	7

Because there are different types of numeric variables and constants, it is possible to have not only mixed-mode arithmetic, as described in the preceding section, but also mixed-mode assignment. This occurs when the type of the value being assigned to a variable is different from the type of the variable.

If an integer-valued expression is assigned to a real variable, the integer value is converted to a real constant and then assigned to the variable. Thus, if the integer variable N has the value 9, and Alpha and Beta are real variables, the statements

```
Alpha = 3
Beta = (N + 3) / 5
```

assign the real value 3.0 to Alpha and the real value 2.0 to Beta.

In the case of a real-valued expression assigned to an integer variable, the fractional part of the real value is truncated, and the integer part is assigned to the variable. For example, if the real variable X has the value 5.75, and I, Kappa, and Mu are integer variables, the statements

```
I = 3.14159
Kappa = X / 2.0
Mu = 1.0 / X
```

assign the integer values 3, 2, and 0 to the variables I, Kappa, and Mu, respectively. As this example shows, *mixed-mode assignments are dangerous and should usually be avoided.* If it is necessary to truncate the fractional part of a real-valued expression and assign only the integer part, it would be better to indicate this explicitly by writing, for example,

```
Kappa = INT(X / 2.0)
```

An assignment statement may also be used to assign a value to a character variable. To illustrate, suppose that the character variables String, Truncated, and Padded are declared by the type statement

```
CHARACTER(5) :: String, Truncated, Padded*10
```

The assignment statement

```
String = "alpha"
```

assigns the value "alpha" to String. In this example, the declared length of the variable is equal to the length of the value assigned to this variable. *If, however, the lengths do not match, the values are padded with blanks or truncated as necessary.* If the declared length of the variable is greater than the length of the value being assigned, trailing blanks are added to the value; thus the statement

```
Padded = "particle"
```

assigns the value "particleƀƀ" to the variable Padded (where ƀ denotes a blank character). If the declared length of the variable is less than the length of the value being assigned, the value is truncated to the size of the variable, and the leftmost characters are assigned; thus the statement

```
Truncated = "temperature"
```

assigns the value "tempe" to the variable Truncated.

It is important to remember that *the assignment statement is not a statement of algebraic equality; rather, it is a* replacement *statement.* Some beginning programmers forget this and write the assignment statement

```
A = B
```

when the statement

```
B = A
```

is intended. These two statements produce very different results, as the first assigns the value of B to A, leaving B unchanged,

A   8.5   A = B   A   9.37
B   9.37   ───────▶   B   9.37

and the second assigns the value of A to B, leaving A unchanged.

A   8.5   B = A   A   8.5
B   9.37   ───────▶   B   8.5

To illustrate further that an assignment statement is a replacement statement, suppose that Delta and Rho are integer variables with the values 357 and 59, respectively. The following statements interchange the values of Delta and Rho, using the auxiliary variable Temp:

```
INTEGER Delta, Rho, Temp
        ⋮
Temp = Delta
Delta = Rho
Rho = Temp
```

As another example, consider the statement

```
Sum = Sum + X
```

Such a statement, in which the same variable appears on both sides of the assignment operator, often confuses beginning programmers. Execution of this statement causes the values of Sum and X to be substituted for these variables to evaluate the expression Sum + X, and the resulting value is then assigned to Sum. The following diagram illustrates this statement for the case in which the real variables Sum and X have the values 132.5 and 8.4, respectively.

Note that the old value of the variable Sum is lost because it was replaced with a new value.

Quick Quiz 2.4

Questions 1–8 assume that the following declarations have been made:

```
INTEGER :: M, N
REAL :: Pi, Alpha
```

Tell whether each is a valid Fortran assignment statement. If it is not valid, explain why it is not.

1. `Pi = 3.141593`

2. `3 = N`

3. `N      = N+   1`

4. `N+1 = N`

5. `Alpha = 1`

6. `Alpha = "1"`

7. `Alpha = Alpha`

8. `M = N = 1`

For Questions 9–14, assume that the following declarations have been made:

```
INTEGER :: IntEight = 8, IntFive = 5, JobId
REAL :: Two = 2.0, Three = 3.0, Four = 4.0, XValue
```

Find the value assigned to the given variable or indicate why the statement is not valid.

9. `XValue = (Three + Two / Four) ** 2`
10. `XValue = IntEight / IntFive + 5.1`
11. `JobId = IntEight / IntFive + 5.1`
12. `IntEight = IntEight + 2`
13. `XValue = SQRT(Three ** 2 + Four ** 2)`
14. `IntEight = ABS(Three - 4.5)`

For Questions 15–18, assume that the following declarations have been made:

```
CHARACTER(4) :: Alpha, Beta*1
```

Find the value assigned to the given variable, or indicate why the statement is not valid.

15. `Beta = 1`
16. `Beta = "1"`
17. `Alpha = "OneTwo"`
18. `Alpha = "12"`

For each of Questions 19–21, write a Fortran assignment statement that calculates the given expression and assigns the result to the specified variable.

19. *Rate* times *Time* to *Distance*
20. $\sqrt{A^2 + B^2}$ to C
21. Increments *Count* by 1.

Exercises 2.4

For Exercises 1–10, assume that the following declarations have been made:

```
INTEGER :: Number = 2, Mix = 5, JobId
INTEGER, PARAMETER :: Limit = 10
REAL :: Three = 3.0, Four = 4.0, XValue
REAL, PARAMETER :: Two = 2.0
```

Describe what the assignment statement does, or indicate why it is not valid.

1. `XValue = (Three + 5.0 / Four) ** 2`
2. `JobId = Mix ** 2 / Limit ** 2`
3. `Limit = Mix ** 2 / Number ** 2`
4. `XValue = Mix ** 2 / Limit ** 2`
5. `XValue = Mix ** 2 / Number ** 2`
6. `XValue = Mix ** 2 / Four ** 2 + Two`
7. `JobId = Mix ** 2 / Four ** 2 + Limit`
8. `Mix = Mix + Mix`
9. `XValue = SQRT(ABS(Two - Three))`
10. `JobId = MAX(INT(Four / 3), Mix)`

For Exercises 11–20, assume that the following declarations have been made:

```
CHARACTER(10) :: Alpha, Beta*5, Gamma*1, Delta*4
```

and that `Delta = "four"`. Find the value assigned to the given variable, or indicate why the statement is not valid.

11. `Gamma = 17`
12. `Gamma = "17"`
13. `Alpha = "OneTwoThreeFour"`
14. `Alpha = "1234"`
15. `Beta = 'don't'`
16. `Beta = "don't"`
17. `Beta = "ABCDEFGHIJKLMNOPQRSTUVWXYZ"`
18. `Beta = "123,456,789"`
19. `Alpha = Delta`
20. `Gamma = Delta`

For each of Exercises 21–25, write a Fortran assignment statement that calculates the given expression and assigns the result to the specified variable.

21. $\dfrac{1}{\dfrac{1}{R1} + \dfrac{1}{R2} + \dfrac{1}{R3}}$ to *Resistance*

22. P times $(1 + R)^N$ to *Accumulated_Value*

23. Area of triangle (one-half base times height) of base B and height H to *Area*

24. 5/9 of the difference $F - 32$ to C (conversion of Fahrenheit to Celsius)

25. $\dfrac{2V^2 \sin A \cos A}{G}$ to *Range*

For Exercises 26–28, give values for the integer variables I, J, and K and the real variable X for which the two expressions are not equal.

26. I * (J / K) and I * J / K
27. X * I / J and X * (I / J)
28. (I + J) / K and I / K + J / K

2.5 INPUT/OUTPUT

In the preceding section we considered the assignment statement, which enables us to calculate the values of expressions and store the results of these computations by assigning them to variables. For example, if a projectile is launched from an initial height of *InitialHeight* meters with an initial vertical velocity of *InitialVelocity* m/sec and a vertical acceleration of *Acceleration* m/sec^2, then the equations

$$Height = 0.5 \cdot Acceleration \cdot Time^2 + InitialVelocity \cdot Time + InitialHeight$$

and

$$Velocity = Acceleration \cdot Time + InitialVelocity$$

give the *Height* in meters and the vertical *Velocity* in meters per second (m/sec) at any *Time* in seconds after launch. Assignment statements to implement these equations are easy to write:

```
Height = 0.5 * Acceleration * Time ** 2 + &
         InitialVelocity * Time + InitialHeight
Velocity = Acceleration * Time + InitialVelocity
```

(The ampersand & at the end of the first line of the first assignment statement indicates that this statement is continued on the next line.)

Values must be assigned to the variables Acceleration, Time, InitialVelocity, and InitialHeight, however, before these statements can be used to compute values for Height and Velocity. The input statement that we consider in this section provides a convenient way to assign such values. Moreover, these assignment statements store the values of Height and Velocity, but they do not display them. The output statement also described in this section provides a method for easily displaying such information.

Fortran provides two types of input/output statements. In the first type, the programmer must explicitly specify the format in which the data is presented for input or, in the case of output, the precise format in which it is to be displayed. In the second type of input/output, certain predetermined standard formats that match the types of items in the input/output list are automatically provided by the compiler. It is this second type, known as **list-directed input/output,** that we consider in this section.

List-Directed Output

The simplest list-directed output statement has the following form:

List-Directed Output Statement

Forms:

```
PRINT *, output-list
```

or

```
WRITE (*, *) output-list
```

where
output-list is a single expression or a list of expressions separated by
   commas. Each of these expressions is a constant, a variable, or a formula.
These statements may also be used with no output list:

```
PRINT *
```

or

```
WRITE (*, *)
```

Purpose:
Displays the values of the items in the output list. Each output statement produces a new line of output. If the output list is omitted, a blank line is displayed.

For example, the PRINT statements

```
PRINT *, "At time", Time, "seconds"
PRINT *, "the vertical velocity is", Velocity, "m/sec"
PRINT *, "and the height is", Height, "meters"
```

could be used to display values of Time, Height, and Velocity. Execution of
these statements will produce output similar to the following:

```
At time 4.5000000 seconds
the vertical velocity is 45.8700752 m/sec
and the height is 4.0570767E+02 meters
```

Note that each PRINT statement produces a new line of output. The exact format and
spacing used to display these values are compiler-dependent, however; for example,

in some systems, all three real values might be displayed in exponential notation, and the number of spaces in an output line might be different from that shown.

List-Directed Input

The simplest form of the list-directed input statement is

List-Directed Input Statement

Form:

    READ *, input-list

or

    READ (*, *) input-list

where

input-list is a single variable or a list of variables separated by commas.

Purpose:
Obtains values (usually from the keyboard) and assigns them to the variables in the input list. The following rules apply:

1. A new line of data is processed each time a READ statement is executed.
2. If there are fewer entries in a line of input data than there are variables in the input list, successive lines of input are processed until values for all variables in the list have been obtained.
3. If there are more entries in a line of input data than there are variables in the input list, the first data values are used, and all remaining values are ignored.
4. The entries in each line of input data must be constants and of the same type as the variables to which they are assigned. (However, an integer value may be assigned to a real variable, with automatic conversion taking place.)
5. Consecutive entries in a line of input data must be separated by a comma or by one or more spaces.

For example, the statement

    READ *, InitialHeight, InitialVelocity, Time

can be used to obtain and assign values to the variables InitialHeight, InitialVelocity, and Time. These values will be entered during program execution. For example, to assign the values 100.0, 90.0, and 4.3 to the variables `InitialHeight`, `InitialVelocity`, and `Time`, respectively, the following line of input data could be used:

```
100.0, 90.0, 4.5
```

Spaces could be used as separators in place of the commas,

```
100.0 90.0 4.5
```

or more than one line of data could be used:

```
100.0 90.0
4.5
```

Character values can also be read using list-directed input, but they must be enclosed in single or double quotes if any of the following is true:

1. The character value extends over more than one line.
2. The character value contains blanks, commas, or slashes.
3. The character value begins with an apostrophe, a double quote, or a string of digits followed by an asterisk.

Truncation or blank padding is done when necessary, as described earlier for assignment statements. For example, if `Units_1` and `Units_2` have been declared by

```
CHARACTER(8) :: Units_1, Units_2
```

then entering the values

```
meter, centimeter
```

in response to the statement

```
READ *, Units_1, Units_2
```

assigns the value `"meterƁƁƁ"` to `Units_1` (where Ɓ denotes a blank) and the value `"centimet"` to `Units_2`.

In an interactive mode of operation, the values assigned to variables in an input list are entered during program execution. In this case, when a READ statement is encountered, program execution is suspended while the user enters values for all the variables in the input list. Program execution then automatically resumes. Because execution is interrupted by a READ statement, and because the correct number and types of values must be entered before execution can resume, *it is good practice to provide some message to prompt the user when it is necessary to enter data values.*

This is done by preceding each READ statement with a PRINT or WRITE statement that displays the appropriate prompts. The program in Figure 2.1 illustrates this by prompting the user when values for InitialHeight, InitialVelocity, and Time are to be entered.

Figure 2.1 Projectile problem.

```
PROGRAM Projectile
!-----------------------------------------------------------------
! This program calculates the velocity and height of a projectile
! given its initial height, initial velocity, and constant
! acceleration. Identifiers used are:
!
!    InitialHeight    : initial height of projectile (meters)
!    Height           : height at any time (meters)
!    InitialVelocity  : initial vertical velocity (m/sec)
!    Velocity         : vertical velocity at any time (m/sec)
!    Acceleration     : vertical acceleration (m/sec/sec)
!    Time             : time since launch (seconds)
!
! Input:  InitialHeight, InitialVelocity, Time
! Output: Velocity, Height
!-----------------------------------------------------------------

  IMPLICIT NONE
  REAL :: InitialHeight, Height, InitialVelocity, Velocity, &
          Acceleration = -9.80665, Time

  ! Obtain values for InitialHeight, InitialVeloc, and Time
  PRINT *, "Enter the initial height (m) and velocity (m/sec):"
  READ *, InitialHeight, InitialVelocity
  PRINT *, "Enter time in seconds at which to calculate height and velocity:"
  READ *, Time

  ! Calculate the height and velocity
  Height = 0.5 * Acceleration * Time ** 2 &
           + InitialVelocity * Time + InitialHeight
  Velocity = Acceleration * Time + InitialVelocity

  ! Display Velocity and Height
  PRINT *, "At time", Time, "seconds"
  PRINT *, "the vertical velocity is", Velocity, "m/sec"
  PRINT *, "and the height is", Height, "meters"

END PROGRAM Projectile
```

Figure 2.1 *(cont.)*

Sample runs:

```
Enter the initial height (m) and velocity (m/sec):
100.0 90.0
Enter time in seconds at which to calculate height and velocity:
4.5
At time    4.5000000 seconds
the vertical velocity  is 45.8700752 m/sec
and the height is   4.0570767E+02 meters


Enter the initial height (m) and velocity (m/sec):
150.0 100.0
Enter time in seconds at which to calculate height and velocity:
5.0
At time    5.0000000 seconds
the vertical velocity is  50.9667511 m/sec
and the height is   5.2741687E+02 meters


Enter the initial height (m) and velocity (m/sec):
150.0 100.0
Enter time in seconds at which to calculate height and velocity:
0
At time    0.0000000E+00 seconds
the vertical velocity is  1.0000000E+02 m/sec
and the height is   1.5000000E+02 meters


Enter the initial height (m) and velocity (m/sec):
150.0 100.0
Enter time in seconds at which to calculate height and velocity:
21.75
At time   21.7500000 seconds
the vertical velocity is  -1.1329465E+02 m/sec
and the height is   5.4208984 meters
```

2.6   PROGRAM COMPOSITION AND FORMAT

Program Composition

In Section 2.1 we noted that a Fortran program has the form

heading
specification part

execution part
subprogram part
END PROGRAM statement

The **program heading** has the form

PROGRAM *name*

where *name* is a legal Fortran identifier. This name must be distinct from all other names in the program and should be chosen to indicate the purpose of the program. Thus, the first statement in the program of Figure 2.1 to calculate the height and velocity of a projectile is

PROGRAM Projectile

Although the PROGRAM statement is optional, it should be used to identify the program and to distinguish it from other program units such as function subprograms, subroutine subprograms, and modules, which are described later.

Following the PROGRAM statement, there should be **opening documentation** like that in Figure 2.1 that explains the purpose of the program, clarifies the choice of variable names, and provides other pertinent information about the program. This documentation consists of comments, which are preceded by an exclamation mark (!) and run to the end of the line. Comments can be used to clarify the purpose and structure of key parts of the program. Program documentation is invaluable when revisions and modifications are made in the future, especially when they are made by persons other than the original programmer.

The **specification part** of a program must appear next. The first statement in this part should be

IMPLICIT NONE

to cancel the naming convention and ensure that all variables and constants are explicitly declared. These declarations are type statements such as

REAL :: InitialHeight, Height, InitialVelocity, Velocity, &
        Acceleration = -9.80665, Time

whose purpose is to specify the type of each of the variables used in the program. They also are placed in the specification part. The type statements we have considered thus far have the form

REAL :: *list*

for declaring real variables,

INTEGER :: *list*

for declaring integer variables, and

    CHARACTER(LEN = *n*) :: *list*

or

    CHARACTER(*n*) :: *list*

for declaring character variables. Others will be considered in later chapters.
Declarations of the form

    type-specifier :: *var*$_1$ = *const*$_1$, . . . , *var*$_n$ = *const*$_n$

may be included to initialize the values of variables at compile time. A declaration
may also contain the PARAMETER attribute to associate names with constants to be
used in the program. These declarations have the form

    type-specifier, PARAMETER :: *name*$_1$ = *const*$_1$, . . . , *name*$_n$ = *const*$_n$

Fortran statements are classified as either executable or nonexecutable. **Nonexecutable statements** provide information that is used during compilation of a program,
but they do not cause any specific action to be performed during execution. For example, the PROGRAM statement and type statements are nonexecutable statements.

Executable statements do specify actions to be performed during execution of
the program. Assignment statements and input/output statements are examples. Executable statements are placed in the third part of a Fortran program, its **execution
part**. These may be followed by a **subprogram section** that contains internal subprograms as described in Chapter 6.

The last statement in every program must be the **END PROGRAM statement**. This
statement indicates to the compiler the end of the program; it also halts execution of
the program.

Execution can also be terminated with a **STOP statement** of the form

    STOP

or

    STOP *constant*

where *constant* is an integer constant or a character constant. The constant will
be displayed when execution is terminated by a STOP statement of the second form,
but the precise form of the termination message depends on the compiler.[1]

---

[1] Some compilers require that a STOP statement be placed before the END statement to stop program
execution.

Program Format

Although earlier versions of Fortran have rather strict rules about where statements and comments can be placed, Fortran 90 allows considerably more flexibility in the program format. The main rules that must be followed are

- A line may have a maximum of 132 characters.
- A line may contain more than one statement, provided the statements are separated by semicolons. It is good practice, however, to put at most one statement per line.
- An ampersand (&) must be placed at the end of each line that is to be continued to the next line. At most 39 continuation lines are permitted.
- If a character string must be continued from one line to the next, an ampersand must be placed at the end of the line containing the first part of the string and another ampersand must be placed before the first character of the continuation of the string; for example,

```
PRINT *, "Enter the initial height (m) and &
         &the initial velocity (m/sec):"
```

- Any characters following an exclamation mark (!)—except within a string constant—and running to the end of the line form a comment. For example,

```
! This program displays a table of formulas
```

is a comment line. Comments may also be attached to statements; for example,

```
INTEGER :: Number ! Number of data values read
```

- If a statement requires a **statement label**, this label must precede the statement and be separated from it by at least one blank. Statement labels must be integers in the range 1 through 99999.

Quick Quiz 2.6

1. How are comments indicated?
2. Distinguish between executable and nonexecutable statements.
3. (True or false) Each execution of a PRINT statement produces output on a new line.
4. (True or false) Data values for a READ statement must be entered on the same line.
5. (True or false) Entries in a line of input data must be separated by commas.
6. (True or false) Every program must have a heading.

7. (True or false) Execution of an END statement halts program execution.

8. What output is produced by the statement PRINT *?

9. What output (if any) will be produced by the following program?

```
PROGRAM Demonstration

   IMPLICIT NONE
   INTEGER :: I, J
   REAL :: X, Y

   X = 37
   I = INT(X / 5)
   PRINT *, X, I
   READ *, X, I
   PRINT *, "X = ", X, " I = ", I
   READ *, Y
   READ *, J
   PRINT *, Y
   PRINT *, J

END PROGRAM Demonstration
```

Assume that the data values are entered as follows:

```
1.74 29
4.23 10
15
```

2.7   APPLICATION: TEMPERATURE CONVERSION

Problem

The boiling point of water is 212° on the Fahrenheit scale and 100° on the Celsius scale. The freezing point of water is 32° on the Fahrenheit scale and 0° on the Celsius scale. A program is to be developed that will convert a temperature on the Celsius scale to the corresponding Fahrenheit temperature.

Solution

Specification. Since the purpose of the program is to convert a Celsius temperature to the corresponding Fahrenheit temperature, it is clear that the input for this problem is a temperature on the Celsius scale and the output is a temperature on the Fahrenheit scale:

Input: A Celsius temperature

Output: A Fahrenheit temperature

Design. An initial description of an algorithm for solving this problem is straightforward:

1. Obtain the Celsius temperature.
2. Calculate the corresponding Fahrenheit temperature.
3. Display the Fahrenheit temperature.

Here, steps 1 and 3 are easy to implement using input and output statements. Step 2, however, requires some refinement, because we need a formula for converting a Celsius temperature into the equivalent Fahrenheit temperature. There is a linear relationship between the Celsius and Fahrenheit temperature scales; that is, $C°$ Celsius corresponds to $F°$ Fahrenheit, where

$$F = aC + b$$

for some constants a and b. We must first find the constants a and b. Because $0°$ Celsius corresponds to $32°$ Fahrenheit, we must have

$$32 = a \cdot 0 + b$$

so that $b = 32°$ F. This means that

$$F = aC + 32$$

Because $100°$ Celsius corresponds to $212°$ Fahrenheit, we must have

$$212 = a \cdot 100 + 32$$

which gives $a = 9/5$ °F/°C, so that our equation becomes

$$F = \frac{9}{5}C + 32$$

In a program to solve this problem, variables must be used to store two temperatures. We will use the following self-documenting names:

VARIABLES FOR TEMPERATURE PROBLEM

Celsius   Temperature on the Celsius scale

Fahrenheit   Temperature on the Fahrenheit scale

A final version of the algorithm in pseudocode can now be given:

ALGORITHM FOR TEMPERATURE PROBLEM

This algorithm converts a temperature of *Celsius* degrees on the Celsius scale to the corresponding *Fahrenheit* degrees on the Fahrenheit scale.

Input: A temperature in degrees Celsius

Output: A temperature in degrees Fahrenheit

1. Enter *Celsius*.
2. Calculate the Fahrenheit temperature:

$$Fahrenheit = \frac{9}{5} Celsius + 32$$

3. Display *Fahrenheit*.

Expressed in flowchart form, the algorithm is

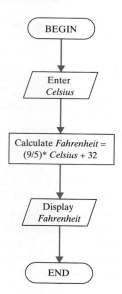

Program Coding. The program in Figure 2.2 is a first attempt to implement this algorithm. Note that the opening documentation contains a brief description of the program, a variable directory that explains what each variable represents, and the input/output specifications. Such documentation is important because it provides a brief summary of what the program does and makes it easier to read and understand the program itself.

Figure 2.2 Temperature conversion—a first attempt.

```
PROGRAM Temperature_Conversion_1
!-----------------------------------------------------------------
! Program to convert a temperature on the Celsius scale to the
! corresponding temperature on the Fahrenheit scale.
! Variables used are:
!    Celsius     : temperature on the Celsius scale
!    Fahrenheit : temperature on the Fahrenheit scale
!
! Input:  Celsius
! Output: Fahrenheit
!-----------------------------------------------------------------

  IMPLICIT NONE
  REAL :: Celsius, Fahrenheit

  ! Obtain Celsius temperature
  PRINT *, "Enter temperature in degrees Celsius:"
  READ *, Celsius

  ! Calculate corresponding Fahrenheit temperature
  Fahrenheit = (9/5) * Celsius + 32.0

  ! Display temperatures
  PRINT *, Celsius, "degrees Celsius =", &
           Fahrenheit, "degrees Fahrenheit"

END PROGRAM Temperature_Conversion_1
```

Execution and Testing. Beginning programmers are sometimes tempted to skip the testing phase of program development. Once a program has compiled without errors, they are content simply to execute the program using the input data given in the assignment and then hand in the output. For example, if the program is to be used to convert the three Celsius temperatures 11.193, −17.728, and 49.1 into Fahrenheit temperatures, a student might simply execute the program three times and hand in the output produced:

```
Enter temperature in degrees Celsius:
11.193
 11.1929998 degrees Celsius = 43.1930008 degrees Fahrenheit

Enter temperature in degrees Celsius:
-17.728
-17.7280006 degrees Celsius = 14.2719994 degrees Fahrenheit

Enter temperature in degrees Celsius:
49.1
 49.0999985 degrees Celsius = 81.0999985 degrees Fahrenheit
```

The fact that the program compiled without errors is no guarantee that it is correct, however, because it may contain logical errors. As we noted in Chapter 1, program testing is extremely important. Programs should be executed with test data for which the output produced can be verified by hand. For this program, we might first use an input value of 0 since it is easy to check that 0° C corresponds to 32° F.

Test run #1:

```
Enter temperature in degrees Celsius:
0
  0.0000000E+00 degrees Celsius = 32.0000000 degrees Fahrenheit
```

We see that the program has indeed produced the correct answer. However, we cannot be confident that a program is correct simply because it executes correctly for one set of test data.

Another natural test value to use for the temperature conversion program is 100° C, which corresponds to 212° F.

Test run #2:

```
Enter temperature in degrees Celsius:
100
  1.0000000E+02 degrees Celsius = 1.3200000E+02 degrees Fahrenheit
```

From this test run we see that the program is not correct. In fact, additional test runs will show that each output value is simply 32 plus the input value.

A review of the algorithm indicates that it is correct; thus the error apparently did not occur in the design stage. The error must therefore have occurred in the coding step. The statement that is suspect is the one that carries out the conversion:

```
Fahrenheit = (9/5) * Celsius + 32
```

The fact that each output value is simply 32 plus the input value suggests that the Celsius temperature Celsius is being multiplied by 1 instead of by 1.8 (= 9 / 5).

This is indeed the case since the integer division 9 / 5 in this expression produces the value 1.

Making this correction gives the program in Figure 2.3. (A version that uses repetition to process several temperatures is given in Section 4.3.)

Figure 2.3 Temperature conversion—final version.

```
PROGRAM Temperature_Conversion_2
!-----------------------------------------------------------------------
! Program to convert a temperature on the Celsius scale to the
! corresponding temperature on the Fahrenheit scale.
! Variables used are:
!    Celsius     : temperature on the Celsius scale
!    Fahrenheit : temperature on the Fahrenheit scale
!
! Input:  Celsius
! Output: Fahrenheit
!-----------------------------------------------------------------------

  IMPLICIT NONE
  REAL :: Celsius, Fahrenheit

  ! Obtain Celsius temperature
  PRINT *, "Enter temperature in degrees Celsius:"
  READ *, Celsius

  ! Calculate corresponding Fahrenheit temperature
  Fahrenheit = 1.8 * Celsius + 32.0

  ! Display temperatures
  PRINT *, Celsius, "degrees Celsius =", &
           Fahrenheit, "degrees Fahrenheit"

END PROGRAM Temperature_Conversion_2
```

The following test runs suggest that the program is correct:

Test run #1:

```
Enter temperature in degrees Celsius:
0
    0.0000000E+00 degrees Celsius = 32.0000000 degrees Fahrenheit
```

Test run #2:

```
Enter temperature in degrees Celsius:
100
   1.0000000E+02 degrees Celsius = 2.1200000E+02 degrees Fahrenheit
```

After several more test runs have been made so that we are confident the program is correct, we can execute the program with the given input values and be quite sure that the output values are correct:

```
Enter temperature in degrees Celsius:
11.193
   11.1929998 degrees Celsius = 52.1473999 degrees Fahrenheit

Enter temperature in degrees Celsius:
-17.728
-17.7280006 degrees Celsius =  8.9599609E-02 degrees Fahrenheit

Enter temperature in degrees Celsius:
49.1
   49.0999985 degrees Celsius =  1.2038000E+02 degrees Fahrenheit
```

2.8 APPLICATION: CIRCUITS WITH PARALLEL RESISTORS

Problem

In an electrical circuit, a current is generated if a voltage is applied across one or more resistances. Suppose that a circuit contains three resistors arranged in parallel:

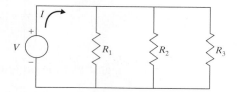

For such a circuit, the current depends on the voltage and the combined resistance of the three resistors. A program is needed to compute the current I in the circuit for a given voltage V and three given resistances R_1, R_2, and R_3.

Solution

Specification. The input and the output for this problem are easy to identify:

Input: Voltage (volts)
            Three resistances (ohms)

Output: Current (amperes)

Design. An initial description of an algorithm for solving this problem is

1. Obtain the voltage and the three resistances.
2. Calculate the current.
3. Display the current.

Here the second step requires refinement, since a formula is needed to calculate the current. By Ohm's law, the current I in a circuit is given by

$$I = \frac{V}{R}$$

where I is in amperes, the voltage V is in volts, and R is the total resistance in ohms. For three resistors connected in parallel, the total resistance is given by

$$R = \frac{1}{\dfrac{1}{R_1} + \dfrac{1}{R_2} + \dfrac{1}{R_3}}$$

It seems natural, therefore, to refine step 2 as follows:

2.1. Calculate the total resistance using the preceding formula.
2.2. Use Ohm's law to calculate the current.

Once again, variables must be used to store the values in this problem. We will use the following self-documenting names:

VARIABLES FOR CIRCUIT PROBLEM

Voltage	Voltage
Resistance_1, *Resistance_2*, *Resistance_3*	Three resistances
TotalResistance	Total resistance
Current	Current

A pseudocode description of the final algorithm is

ALGORITHM FOR CIRCUIT PROBLEM

This algorithm determines the current in a circuit containing three
resistors in parallel and in which a voltage is applied.

Input: *Resistance_1, Resistance_2, Resistance_3, Voltage*
Output: *Current*

1.   Enter *Resistance_1, Resistance_2, Resistance_3, Voltage.*
2.1. Calculate total resistance:

$$TotalResistance = \cfrac{1}{\cfrac{1}{Resistance\_1} + \cfrac{1}{Resistance\_2} + \cfrac{1}{Resistance\_3}}$$

2.2. Calculate the current:

$$Current = \frac{Voltage}{TotalResistance}$$

3.   Display *Current.*

Program Coding. The program in Figure 2.4 implements this algorithm. Note
again the brief description of the program, the variable directory explaining what each
variable represents, and the input/output specifications in the opening documentation.

Figure 2.4 Circuit problem.

```
PROGRAM Circuit_Analysis
!-------------------------------------------------------------------
! Program to determine the current in a circuit containing three
! resistors in parallel and in which a given voltage is applied.
! Variables used are:
!     Voltage           : voltage applied (volts)
!     Resistance_1,
!     Resistance_2,
!     Resistance_3      : three resistances (ohms)
!     TotalResistance   : total resistance
!     Current           : current (amperes)
!
! Input:   Resistance_1, Resistance_2, Resistance_3, Voltage
! Output:  Current
!-------------------------------------------------------------------
```

Figure 2.4 *(cont.)*

```
IMPLICIT NONE
REAL :: Resistance_1, Resistance_2, Resistance_3, &
        TotalResistance, Voltage, Current

! Obtain three resistances and voltage
PRINT *, "Enter three resistances (ohms):"
READ *, Resistance_1, Resistance_2, Resistance_3
PRINT *, "Enter the voltage applied (volts):"
READ *, Voltage

! Calculate total resistance and current
TotalResistance = 1.0 / &
        (1.0 / Resistance_1 + 1.0 / Resistance_2 + 1.0 / Resistance_3)
Current = Voltage / TotalResistance

! Display the current
PRINT *, "The current is", Current, "amps"

END PROGRAM Circuit_Analysis
```

Execution and Testing. As we saw in the preceding section, testing a program is extremely important. In the following sample runs, simple test data was selected so that the output can be verified by hand.

Test run #1:

```
Enter three resistances (ohms):
1.0, 1.0, 1.0
Enter the voltage applied (volts):
6.0
The current is 18.0000000 amps
```

Test run #2:

```
Enter three resistances (ohms):
0.5, 0.5, 0.5
Enter the voltage applied (ohms):
4.0
The current is 24.0000000 amps
```

Test run #3:

```
Enter three resistances (ohms):
0.3, 0.4, 0.5
Enter the voltage applied (volts):
5.0
The current is 39.1666679 amps
```

2.9   APPLICATION: CONCENTRATION OF AN ACID BATH

Problem

Suppose that the manufacturing process for castings at a certain plant includes cooling each casting in a water bath, followed by cleaning it by immersion in an acid bath. When the casting is transferred from the water bath to the acid bath, a certain amount of water accompanies it, thereby diluting the acid. When the casting is removed from the acid bath, the same amount of this diluted mixture is also removed; thus the volume of the liquid in the acid bath remains constant, but the acidity decreases each time a casting is immersed. We wish to design a program to (1) determine when the acidity falls below some lower limit at which the mixture becomes too diluted to clean castings; and (2) determine the acidity of the liquid in the acid bath after a given number of castings have been immersed.

Solution

Specification. From the preceding description of the problem, we can easily determine the problem's input and output.

Input: Initial amount of acid in the acid bath
         Amount of water that is mixed with the acid when a casting is
             transferred from the water bath
         Lower limit on the acidity
         Number of castings immersed

Output: Maximum number of castings that may be immersed before the
             acidity falls below the specified lower limit
         Measure of the acidity after the specified number of castings have
             been immersed

Design. A first version of an algorithm for solving this problem is as follows:

1. Get the initial amount of acid in the acid bath, the amount of water transferred with each casting, and the lower limit on the acidity.
2. Calculate the maximum number of castings that may be immersed before the acidity falls below this limit.
3. Display this number of castings.
4. Enter the number of castings to be cleaned.
5. Calculate the acidity of the mixture after cleaning the castings.
6. Display this acidity.

Here steps 2 and 5 must be refined. We observe that if A is the original amount of acid and W is the amount of water that is mixed in at each stage, the concentration of acid in the mixture when the first casting is immersed is

$$\frac{A}{A + W}$$

When this casting is removed from the acid bath, the amount of acid in the diluted mixture is

$$\left(\frac{A}{A + W}\right) \cdot A$$

This means that when the second casting is immersed, the concentration of the mixture becomes

$$\frac{\left(\dfrac{A}{A + W}\right) \cdot A}{A + W}$$

which can be written as

$$\left(\frac{A}{A + W}\right)^2$$

In general, the concentration of acid in the diluted mixture after n castings have been immersed is given by

$$\left(\frac{A}{A + W}\right)^n$$

This is the formula needed in step 5 of the problem.

For step 2, if L denotes the lower limit on acidity, we must determine the least value of n for which

$$\left(\frac{A}{A + W}\right)^n < L$$

Taking logarithms, we find that this inequality is equivalent to

$$n > \frac{\log L}{\log A - \log(A + W)}$$

so that the desired value of n is the least integer greater than the expression on the right side.

We will use the following variables to store the quantities involved:

Cast aluminum block for a V-8 engine at Ford's Romeo, Michigan, Engine Plant. (Photo courtesy of Ford Motor Company)

▼

VARIABLES FOR ACID DILUTION PROBLEM

Acidity	Amount of acid in the mixture
Water	Amount of water added with each immersion
Limit_on_Acidity	Lower limit on acidity
MaxCastings	Maximum number of castings that can be cleaned
NumCastings	Number of castings to be cleaned
Concentration	Proportion of acid in the mixture

▲

With the preceding refinements and using these variables, we can write the following pseudocode description of the final algorithm for solving the problem.

▼

ALGORITHM FOR ACID DILUTION PROBLEM

This algorithm determines how often a mixture of acid and water can be used before acidity falls below some lower limit. It also determines the acidity of the mixture after a given number of castings have been immersed in it.

Input: *Acidity, Water, Limit_on_Acidity, NumCastings*
Output: *MaxCastings, Concentration*

1. Enter *Acidity, Water,* and *Limit_on_Acidity.*

2. Calculate $MaxCastings = 1 + \dfrac{\log(Limit\_on\_Acidity)}{\log(Acidity) - \log(Acidity + Water)}$.

3. Display *MaxCastings.*

4. Enter *NumCastings.*

5. Calculate *Concentration* = (*Acidity* / (*Acidity* + *Water*)) ** *NumCastings.*

6. Display *Concentration.*

▲

Program Coding. The program in Figure 2.5 implements the preceding algorithm.

Figure 2.5 Acid dilution problem.

```
PROGRAM Acid_Dilution
!-------------------------------------------------------------------
! Program to determine how often a mixture of acid and water can be
! used before its acidity falls below some specified lower limit, and
! to determine the acidity of the diluted mixture after a given number
! of castings have been immersed in it. Variables used are:
!    Acidity           : amount of acid in the mixture
!    Water             : amount of water added with each casting immersion
!    Limit_on_Acidity  : lower limit on acidity
!    MaxCastings       : maximum number of castings that can be cleaned
!    NumCastings       : number of castings to be cleaned
!    Concentration     : proportion of acid in the mixture
!
! Input:   Acidity, Water, Limit_on_Acidity, NumCastings
! Output:  MaxCastings, Concentration
!-------------------------------------------------------------------

  IMPLICIT NONE
  INTEGER :: MaxCastings, NumCastings
  REAL :: Acidity, Water, Limit_on_Acidity, Concentration

  ! Enter original amount of acid, amount of water transferred,
  ! and lower limit on acidity

  PRINT *, "Enter original amount of acid (gal), amount of water added (gal),"
  PRINT *, "and the lower limit on the acidity:"
  READ *, Acidity, Water, Limit_on_Acidity

  ! Calculate and display the maximum number of castings that can
  ! be cleaned

  MaxCastings = 1 + INT(LOG(Limit_on_Acidity) / &
              (LOG(Acidity) - LOG(Acidity + Water)))
  PRINT *, "At most", MaxCastings, "castings can be immersed before "
  PRINT *, "acidity falls below", Limit_on_Acidity

  ! Enter number of castings to be cleaned

  PRINT *
  PRINT *, "How many castings are to be cleaned (at most", MaxCastings, ")?"
  READ *, NumCastings

  ! Calculate and display the acidity after this many castings have
  ! been immersed
```

Figure 2.5 *(cont.)*

```
Concentration = (Acidity / (Acidity + Water)) ** NumCastings
PRINT *, "The proportion of acid in the mixture after"
PRINT *, NumCastings, "immersions is", Concentration


END PROGRAM Acid_Dilution
```

Execution and Testing. The following sample runs use test data to verify that the program is correct.

Test run #1:

```
Enter original amount of acid (gal), amount of water added (gal),
and the lower limit on the acidity:
100, 100, 1
At most 1 castings can be immersed before
acidity falls below   1.0000000

How many castings are to be cleaned (at most 1 )?
1
The proportion of acid in the mixture after
1 immersions is   0.5000000
```

Test run #2:

```
Enter original amount of acid (gal), amount of water added (gal),
and the lower limit on the acidity:
100, 100, 0.1
At most 4 castings can be immersed before
acidity falls below   0.1000000

How many castings are to be cleaned (at most 4 )?
2
The proportion of acid in the mixture after
2 immersions is   0.2500000
```

Test run #3:

```
Enter original amount of acid (gal), amount of water added (gal),
and the lower limit on the acidity:
90, 10, 0.7
At most 4 castings can be immersed before
acidity falls below   0.7000000
```

```
How many castings are to be cleaned (at most 4 )?
2
The proportion of acid in the mixture after
2 immersions is    0.8099999
```

Test run #4:

```
Enter original amount of acid (gal), amount of water added (gal),
and the lower limit on the acidity:
400, 0.05, 0.75
At most 2302 castings can be immersed before
acidity falls below    0.7500000

How many castings are to be cleaned (at most 2302 )?
190
The proportion of acid in the mixture after
190 immersions is    0.9765394
```

*2.10   INTRODUCTION TO FILE INPUT/OUTPUT

Up to this point we have assumed that the data for the sample programs was entered from the keyboard during program execution and that the output was displayed on the screen. For some computer systems, such interactive input/output is not possible or may be clumsy. For these systems it may be necessary or convenient to store input data in a disk file and design the program to read data from this file; it may also be necessary or convenient to store a program's output in a disk file for later processing. In this section we briefly describe how such input and output using files can be carried out in Fortran. (A more detailed description is given in Section 5.5 and in Chapter 12.)

To illustrate these file-processing features, we will rewrite the projectile program in Figure 2.1 so that input values are read from a file named fig2-6.dat:

Listing of fig2-6.dat:

```
100.0, 90.0
4.5
```

The first line contains the initial height and the initial velocity, and the second line contains the time at which the height and velocity are to be calculated. We will also design the program so that the output will be written to a file named fig2-6.out:

Listing of fig2-6.out:

```
At time 4.5000000 seconds
the vertical velocity is 45.8700752 m/sec
and the height is 4.0570767E+02 meters
```

Opening Files

Before a file can be used for input or output in a Fortran program, it must be "opened." This can be accomplished using an **OPEN statement** of the form

```
OPEN (UNIT = unit-number, FILE = file-name, STATUS = status)
```

where *unit-number* is an integer that will be used to reference this file in a READ or WRITE statement, *file-name* is the name of the disk file, and *status* is the character string "OLD" if the file already exists, or the string "NEW" otherwise. Thus we might use the statement

```
OPEN(UNIT = 12, FILE = "fig2-6.dat", STATUS = "OLD")
```

to open the input file, and the statement

```
OPEN(UNIT = 13, FILE = "fig2-6.out", STATUS = "NEW")
```

to create and open an output file.

File I/O

Once a file has been given a unit number, data can be read from or written to that file using special forms of the READ and WRITE statements:

```
READ (unit-number, *) input-list
WRITE (unit-number, *) output-list
```

For example, the statement

```
READ (12, *) InitialHeight, InitialVelocity, Time
```

can be used to read values for InitialHeight, InitialVeloc, and Time from the file fig2-6.dat. The statements

```
WRITE (13, *) "At time", Time, "seconds"
WRITE (13, *) "the vertical velocity is", Velocity, "m/sec"
WRITE (13, *) "and the height is", Height, "meters"
```

can be used to produce output to the file fig2-6.out.

Example: The Projectile Program Revisited

Figure 2.6 shows the complete program for the projectile problem. It reads the initial height, the initial velocity, and the time from the disk file fig2-6.dat described earlier and writes output to the disk file fig2-6.out. Note that no output statements are used to prompt for input since all values are read from a file, but a

PRINT statement is used to display a message indicating that program execution is complete.

Figure 2.6 Projectile program with file I/O.

```
PROGRAM Projectile_2
!--------------------------------------------------------------------
! This program calculates the velocity and height of a projectile
! given its initial height, initial velocity, and constant
! acceleration. Identifiers used are:
!     InitialHeight    : initial height of projectile (meters)
!     Height           : height at any time (meters)
!     InitialVelocity  : initial vertical velocity (m/sec)
!     Velocity         : vertical velocity at any time (m/sec)
!     Acceleration     : constant vertical acceleration (m/sec/sec)
!     Time             : time since launch (seconds)
!
! Input (file):  InitialHeight, InitialVelocity, Time
! Output (file): Velocity, Height
!--------------------------------------------------------------------

  IMPLICIT NONE
  REAL :: InitialHeight, Height, InitialVelocity, Velocity, Time
  REAL, PARAMETER :: Acceleration = -9.80665

  ! Open disk files fig2-6.dat and fig2-6.out
  OPEN(UNIT = 12, FILE = "fig2-6.dat", STATUS = "OLD")
  OPEN(UNIT = 13, FILE = "fig2-6.out", STATUS = "NEW")

  ! Read values for InitialHeight, InitialVeloc, and Time
  READ (12, *) InitialHeight, InitialVelocity, Time

  ! Calculate the height and velocity
  Height = 0.5 * Acceleration * Time ** 2 &
           + InitialVelocity* Time + InitialHeight
  Velocity = Acceleration * Time + InitialVelocity

  ! Write values of Time, Velocity, and Height to fig2-6.out
  WRITE (13, *) "At time", Time, "seconds"
  WRITE (13, *) "the vertical velocity is", Velocity, "m/sec"
  WRITE (13, *) "and the height is", Height, "meters"

  ! Signal user that program is finished
  PRINT *, "*** Program is finished ***"

END PROGRAM Projectile_2
```

*2.11   ARITHMETIC ERRORS

In Chapter 1 we learned that all information stored in a computer must be represented in a binary form. One common representation of a real number is to express it in exponential binary form

$$f \times 2^e$$

with the mantissa (fractional part) f and the exponent e, and then use one part of a memory word or words to store the mantissa and another part to store the exponent (see Appendix F):

On many systems, real numbers are stored using twenty-four bits for the mantissa and eight for the exponent. It should be clear that

1. Because of the limited number of bits allotted to the exponent, only a finite range of real numbers can be stored.
2. Because of the limited number of bits allotted to the mantissa, most real numbers in this range cannot be stored exactly.

The limited range of reals that can be stored gives rise to two kinds of errors: **overflow errors** and **underflow errors**, and the limited number of bits allotted to the mantissa gives rise to **roundoff errors**.

Overflow/Underflow Errors

Overflow occurs when an exponent for a real value is too large to be stored. For real values, an 8-bit exponent restricts the range of values to approximately -10^{38} to 10^{38}, and overflow occurs for values outside this range:

Underflow occurs when an exponent for a real value is too small to be stored. Real values represented using an 8-bit exponent must be greater than approximately 10^{-38} or less than -10^{-38}, and underflow occurs between these values:

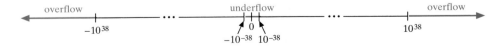

On some systems, execution of a program is terminated when an underflow or overflow error occurs and an appropriate error message is displayed. On others, execution may continue with the largest or smallest representable value used in the computation.

Roundoff Errors

Real numbers like $\pi = 3.141592653589\ldots$ and $1/3 = 0.33333333\ldots$, which do not have terminating decimal representations, do not have terminating binary representations either and thus cannot be stored exactly using a finite number of bits. Even such "nice" terminating decimals as 0.1 do not have terminating binary representations (see Appendix F). In fact, of all reals of the form $0.d$, where d is a digit, only 0.0 and 0.5 can be represented exactly; 0.1, 0.2, 0.3, 0.4, 0.6, 0.7, 0.8, and 0.9 cannot. Only 4 two-digit reals of the form $0.d_1 d_2$ can be represented exactly, namely, 0.00, 0.25, 0.50, and 0.75; the remaining 96 two-digit reals cannot. In general, the only real numbers that can be represented exactly in the computer's memory are those that can be written in the form $m/2^k$, where m and k are integers.

Roundoff errors may be compounded when real numbers are combined in arithmetic expressions. To illustrate, consider adding the three real numbers 0.4104, 1.0, and 0.2204; for simplicity, assume that the computations are done using decimal representation with four-digit precision. The exponential representations of these values are 0.4104×10^0, 0.1000×10^1, and 0.2204×10^0. The first step in the addition of two values is to "align the decimal point" by increasing the smaller of the two exponents and shifting the mantissa. Thus, the sum of the first two values is obtained by adding 0.0410×10^1 and 0.1000×10^1, which gives 0.1410×10^1. Adding the third number again requires adjusting the exponent and shifting the mantissa, 0.0220×10^1, and the final result is 0.1630×10^1, or 1.630. On the other hand, if the two smaller values are added first, giving 0.6308×10^0, and then the larger number is added, the result is 0.1631×10^1, or 1.631 (assuming rounding). In a long chain of such calculations, these small errors can accumulate so that the error in the final result may be very large. This example also illustrates that two real quantities that are algebraically equal, such as $(A + B) + C$ and $(A + C) + B$, may have computed values that are not equal. Consequently, care must be taken when comparing two real values to see whether they are equal.

Many other familiar algebraic equalities fail to hold for real data values; for example, values of the real variables A, B, and C can be found for which the values of the following real expressions are not equal:

```
(A + B) + C    and    A + (B + C)
(A * B) * C    and    A * (B * C)
A * (B + C)    and    (A * B) + (A * C)
```

As another example of the effect of roundoff error, consider the following short program:

```
PROGRAM Demo_1

    IMPLICIT NONE
    REAL :: A, B, C
```

```
READ *, A, B
C = ((A + B) ** 2 - 2 * A * B - B ** 2) / A ** 2
PRINT *, C

END PROGRAM Demo_1
```

The following table shows the output produced by one computer system for various values of A and B:

A	B	C
0.5	888.0	1.00000
0.1	888.0	-6.2499995
0.05	888.0	-24.9999981
0.03	888.0	69.4444427
0.01	888.0	0.0000000E+00

These results are rather startling, since the algebraic expression

$$\frac{(A + B)^2 - 2AB - B^2}{A^2}$$

can be written as

$$\frac{A^2 + 2AB + B^2 - 2AB - B^2}{A^2}$$

which simplifies to

$$\frac{A^2}{A^2}$$

and thus is identically 1 (provided $A \neq 0$).

CHAPTER REVIEW

Summary

This chapter begins a systematic study of the Fortran language. We started by considering the five basic Fortran data types,

integer
real
complex
character
logical

and we described how variables and constants are formed and declared using the INTEGER, REAL, and CHARACTER type statements and how values can be assigned to them using the PARAMETER attribute and initialization declarations. Sections 2.3 and 2.4 described how expressions are formed and how the assignment statement can be used to assign values of expressions to variables. Input and output were discussed in Section 2.5. Section 2.6 described the overall composition of a program. The three examples in the next sections illustrated the program-development process and the Fortran features considered in this chapter. The chapter ends with two optional sections. The first gives a brief introduction to file input/output and the second describes some of the arithmetic errors that may occur in computing with real numbers.

FORTRAN SUMMARY

Identifiers

Identifiers such as program names and variable names must begin with a letter, which may be followed by up to 30 letters, digits, or underscores.

Program Structure

program heading   (PROGRAM statement)
specification part (type declarations)
execution part   (executable statements)
subprogram part
END PROGRAM statement

Comments

Any characters following an exclamation mark (!)—except within a string constant—and running to the end of the line form a comment.

PROGRAM Statement

PROGRAM *program-name*

Example:

PROGRAM Projectile

Purpose:
The PROGRAM statement names the program.

Declarations of Variables

```
REAL :: list
INTEGER :: list
CHARACTER(LEN = n) :: list or CHARACTER(n) :: list
```

Examples:

```
REAL :: InitialHeight, Height, InitialVelocity, Velocity
INTEGER :: MaxCastings, NumCastings
CHARACTER(10) :: FirstName, LastName, Initial*1
```

Purpose:
Type statements declare the type of values that variables will have.

IMPLICIT NONE Statement

```
IMPLICIT NONE
```

Purpose:
Cancels the naming convention.

Initialization Declarations

```
type-specifier :: var₁ = const₁, . . . , varₙ= constₙ
```

where each var_i is a variable and each $const_i$ is a constant expression.

Example:

```
INTEGER :: Count = 1
REAL :: Sum_X = 0.0, Sum_Y = 0.0
CHARACTER(20) :: Name = "John Q. Doe"
```

Purpose:
Initializes each variable var_i with the corresponding constant value in $const_i$ at compile time.

PARAMETER Attribute

```
type-specifier, PARAMETER :: name₁ = const₁, . . . , nameₙ = constₙ
```

where each $name_i$ is an identifier and each $const_i$ is a constant expression.

Example:

```
INTEGER, PARAMETER :: Limit = 100
REAL, PARAMETER :: Pi = 3.141593
```

Purpose:
Associates each $name_i$ with the constant $const_i$.

Operations

Operator	Operation
+	addition
–	subtraction
*	multiplication
/	division
**	exponentiation

Functions

Function	Description
ABS(x)	Absolute value of x
COS(x)	Cosine of x radians
EXP(x)	Exponential function
FLOOR(x)	Greatest integer $\leq x$
FRACTION(x)	Fractional part (mantissa) of x
INT(x)	Integer part of x
LOG(x)	Natural logarithm of x
MAX($x_1, \ldots, x_n$)	Maximum of $x_1, \ldots, x_n$
MIN($x_1, \ldots, x_n$)	Minimum of $x_1, \ldots, x_n$
MOD(x, y)	$x \pmod y$; x - INT(x/y) * y
NINT(x)	x rounded to nearest integer
REAL(x)	Conversion of x to real type
SIN(x)	Sine of x radians
SQRT(x)	Square root of x
TAN(x)	Tangent of x radians

See Tables 2.3 and 6.1 and Appendix D for additional information about these and other functions provided in Fortran.

Assignment Statement

```
variable = expression
```

Examples:

```
Count = 0
Height = 0.5 * Acceleration * Time ** 2 &
         + InitialVelocity * Time + InitialHeight
Velocity = Acceleration * Time + InitialVelocity
Name = "John Q. Doe"
```

Purpose:
Assigns the value of the *expression* to the specified *variable*.

Input Statement

For interactive input:

```
READ *, input-list-of-variables
```

or

```
READ (*, *) input-list-of-variables
```

For input from a file:

```
READ (unit-number, *) input-list-of-variables
```

Example:

```
READ *, InitialHeight, InitialVelocity
READ *, NumCastings
READ (12, *) InitialHeight, InitialVelocity, Time
```

Purpose:
The READ statement reads values for the variables in the input list.

Output Statements

For interactive output:

```
PRINT *, output-list-of-expressions
WRITE (*, *) output-list-of-expressions
```

For output to a file:

```
WRITE (unit-number, *) output-list-of-expressions
```

Examples:

```
PRINT *, "Enter the initial height and velocity:"

PRINT *, "At time", Time, "seconds"
PRINT *, "the vertical velocity is", Velocity, "m/sec"
PRINT *, "and the height is", Height, "meters"

WRITE(13, *) "At time", Time, "seconds"
WRITE(13, *) "the vertical velocity is", Velocity, "m/sec"
WRITE(13, *) "and the height is", Height, "meters"
```

Purpose:
The PRINT and WRITE statements display the values of the expressions in the output list.

OPEN Statement

```
OPEN (UNIT = unit-number, FILE = file-name, STATUS = status)
```

Examples:

```
OPEN(UNIT = 12, FILE = "fig2-6.dat", STATUS = "OLD")
OPEN(UNIT = 13, FILE = "fig2-6.out", STATUS = "NEW")
```

Purpose:
The OPEN statement assigns a unit number to a disk file, which may already exist (status is OLD) or which will be created (status is NEW), and makes it accessible for input/output.

STOP Statement

```
STOP
```

or

```
STOP constant
```

where *constant* is an integer constant or a character constant.

Purpose:
Stops execution of the program. In the second form, the specified constant will be displayed.

END PROGRAM Statement

```
END PROGRAM program-name
```

Purpose:
The END PROGRAM statement marks the end of a program and stops execution.

Program Format

- A line may have a maximum of 132 characters.
- A line may contain more than one statement, provided the statements are separated by semicolons.
- An ampersand (&) must be placed at the end of each line that is to be continued to the next line. At most 39 continuation lines are permitted.
- If a character string must be continued from one line to the next, an ampersand must be placed at the end of the line containing the first part of the string and another ampersand must be placed before the first character of the continuation of the string.
- A statement label must be an integer with at most five digits and must precede the statement and be separated from it by at least one blank.

PROGRAMMING POINTERS

In this section we consider some aspects of program design and suggest guidelines for good programming style. We also point out some errors that may occur when writing Fortran programs.

Program Style and Design

1. In the examples in this text, we adopt certain style guidelines for Fortran programs, and you should write your programs in a similar style. The following standards are used (others are described in the Programming Pointers of subsequent chapters):
   - When a statement is continued from one line to another, indent the continuation line(s).
   - Document each program with comment lines at the beginning of the program to explain the purpose of the program and what the variables represent. You should also include in this documentation your name, date, course number, assignment number, and so on.
   - Break up long expressions into simpler subexpressions.
   - Insert a blank comment line between the opening documentation and the specification statements at the beginning of the program and between these statements and the rest of the program.

- To improve readability, insert a blank space between items in a Fortran statement such as before and after assignment operators and arithmetic operators.

2. *Programs cannot be considered correct until they have been validated using test data.* Test all programs with data for which the results are known or can be checked by hand calculation.

3. *Programs should be readable and understandable.*
   - *Use meaningful identifiers that suggest what each identifier represents.* For example,

   ```
   Distance = Rate * Time
   ```

   is more meaningful than

   ```
   D = R * T
   ```

   or

   ```
   Z7 = Alpha * X
   ```

   Also, avoid "cute" identifiers, as in

   ```
   HowFar = GoGo * Squeal
   ```

   - *Do not use "magic numbers" that suddenly appear without explanation,* as in the statement

   ```
   Output = 0.1758 * Amount + 1.34E-5
   ```

   If these numbers must be changed, someone must search through the program to determine what they represent and which ones should be changed and to locate all their occurrences. It is thus better to associate them with named constants, as in

   ```
   REAL, PARAMETER :: Rate = 0.1758, Error = 1.34E-5
   ```

   or assign them to variables, as in

   ```
   REAL :: Rate = 0.1758, Error = 1.34E-5
   ```

   - *Use comments to describe the purpose of a program, the meaning of variables, and the purpose of key program segments.* However, do not clutter the program with needless comments; for example, the comment in

   ```
   ! Add 1 to Count
   Count = Count + 1
   ```

is not helpful in explaining the statement that follows it and so should be omitted.

- *Label all output produced by a program.* For example,

```
PRINT *, "Rate =", Rate, " Time = ", Time
```

produces more informative output than does

```
PRINT *, Rate, Time
```

4. *Programs should be general and flexible.* They should solve a class of problems rather than one specific problem. It should be relatively easy to modify a program to solve a related problem without changing much of the program. Avoiding the use of magic numbers, as described in 3, is important in this regard.

Potential Problems

1. *Do not confuse* I *or* l *(lowercase "ell") and* 1 *or* 0 *(zero) and* O *(the letter "oh").* For example, the statement

```
PR0GRAM Dilute
```

produces an error, because the numeral 0 is used in place of the letter O. Many programmers distinguish between these in handwritten programs by writing the numeral 0 as ∅.

2. *String constants must be enclosed between double quotes or between apostrophes.* If the beginning quote and the ending quote are different or if either is missing, an error will result.

3. *If a string constant must be broken at the end of a line, an ampersand (&) must be placed after the last character on that line and another ampersand before the first character on the next line.*

4. *All multiplications must be indicated by* *. For example, 2 * N is valid, but 2N is not.

5. *Division of integers produces an integer.* For example, 1 / 2 has the value 0. Similarly, if N is an integer variable greater than 1, 1/N will have the value 0.

6. *Parentheses in expressions must be paired.* For each left parenthesis there must be a matching right parenthesis that appears later in the expression.

7. *The values of named constants may not be changed.* Any attempt to do so produces a compile-time error.

8. *All variables are initially undefined.* Although some compilers may initialize variables to specific values (e.g., 0 for numeric variables), it should be assumed that all variables are initially undefined. For example, the statement Y = X + 1

usually produces a "garbage" value for Y if X has not previously been assigned a value.

9. *Initializations in declarations are done only once, during compilation, before execution of the program begins.* In particular, this means that the variables are not reinitialized while the program is being executed. Potential Problem 6 in the Programming Pointers Section of Chapter 4 explains this problem in detail.

10. *A value assigned to a variable must be of a type that is appropriate to the type of the variable.* Thus, entering the value 2.7 for an integer variable Number in the statement

```
READ *, Number
```

may generate an error message. However, an integer value read for a real variable is automatically converted to real type.

11. *Mixed-mode assignment must be used with care.* For example, if A, B, and C are real variables but Number is an integer variable, the statement

```
Number = - B + SQRT(B ** 2 - 4.0 * A * C)
```

calculates the real value of the expression on the right side correctly but then assigns only the integer part to Number. This happens, for example, when the types of these variables are determined by Fortran's naming convention.

12. *In assignment statements and in list-directed input, if a character value being assigned or read has a length greater than that specified for the character variable, the rightmost characters are truncated. If the value has a length less than that specified for the variable, blanks are added at the right.* Thus, if String is declared by

```
CHARACTER(10) :: String
```

the statement

```
String = "ABCDEFGHIJKLMNO"
```

will assign the string "ABCDEFGHIJ" to String, and

```
String= "ABC"
```

will assign the string "ABCɃɃɃɃɃɃɃ" to String. An acronym sometimes used to remember this is

- **APT:** for **A**ssignment (and list-directed input), both blank-**P**adding and **T**runcation occur on the right.

13. *The types of all variables should be declared in type statements and the IM-PLICIT NONE statement should be used to ensure this.* If IMPLICIT NONE

is not used, any variable whose type is not explicitly specified will have its type determined by the Fortran naming convention. Thus, if the variable `Number` has not been declared to be of real type, the function reference `SQRT(Number)` causes an error, since `SQRT` requires a real argument and `Number` is of integer type according to the naming convention. If A, B, C, and `Number` have not been declared, execution of the statement

```
Number = - B + SQRT(B ** 2 - 4.0 * A * C)
```

produces the result described in Potential Problem 12. According to Fortran's naming conventions, A, B, and C are real variables, so the real value of the expression on the right side is calculated correctly, but only its integer part is assigned to `Number` because the naming convention specifies that it is an integer variable.

14. *A comma must precede the input/output list in input/output statements of the form*

```
READ *, input-list
PRINT *, output-list
```

PROGRAMMING PROBLEMS

1. For three resistors connected in series as in the following circuit,

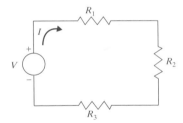

the total resistance is the sum of the individual resistances. Modify the program in Figure 2.4 by adding statements to calculate and display the current in a circuit in which the three resistors are connected in series.

2. For a circuit like that in Problem 1, the voltage across one of resistors R_1, R_2, R_3 is given by $R_i * I$, $i = 1, 2, 3$, where I is the current in the circuit. Extend the program of Problem 1 to calculate and display the voltages across each of the resistors.

3. Write a program to read the lengths of the two legs of a right triangle and to calculate and display the area of the triangle (one-half the product of legs) and the length of the hypotenuse (square root of the sum of the squares of the legs).

4. The Pythagorean theorem states that the sum of the squares of the sides of a right triangle is equal to the square of the hypotenuse. Thus, for a right triangle with

sides 3 and 4, the length of the hypotenuse is 5. Similarly, a right triangle with sides 5 and 12 has a hypotenuse of 13, and a right triangle with sides 8 and 15 has a hypotenuse of 17. Triples of integers such as 3, 4, 5, or 5, 12, 13, or 8, 15, 17, which represent the two sides and the hypotenuse of a right triangle, are called *Pythagorean triples*. There are infinitely many such triples, and they all can be generated by the formulas

$$side_1 = m^2 - n^2$$

$$side_2 = 2mn$$

$$hypotenuse = m^2 + n^2$$

where m and n are positive integers and $m > n$. Write a program that reads values for m and n and then calculates and displays the Pythagorean triple generated by these formulas.

5. Write a program to read values for the three sides a, b, and c of a triangle and then calculate its perimeter and its area. These should be displayed together with the values of a, b, and c using appropriate labels. (For the area, you might use Hero's formula for the area of a triangle:

$$area = \sqrt{s(s - a)(s - b)(s - c)}$$

where s is one-half the perimeter.)

6. The current in an alternating current circuit that contains resistance, capacitance, and inductance in series is given by

$$I = \frac{E}{\sqrt{R^2 + (2\pi f L - 1/(2\pi f C))^2}}$$

where I = current (amperes), E = voltage (volts), R = resistance (ohms), L = inductance (henrys), C = capacitance (farads), and f = frequency (hertz). Write a program that reads values for the voltage, resistance, capacitance, and frequency and then calculates and displays the current.

7. At t seconds after firing, the horizontal displacement x and the vertical displacement y (in feet) of a rocket are given by

$$x = v_0 t \cos \theta$$

$$y = v_0 t \sin \theta - 16t^2$$

where v_0 is the initial velocity (ft/sec) and θ is the angle (in radians) at which the rocket is fired. Write a program that reads values for v_0, θ, and t, calculates x and y using these formulas, and displays these values.

8. Boyle's law states that at constant temperature, the volume V of a sample of gas varies inversely with the pressure P under which it is measured. This gives the equation

$$P \cdot V = k$$

where k is a constant. Write a program that first reads known values for P and V and uses these values to determine k. The program should then read another pressure for this same gas at constant temperature and calculate and display the volume it will occupy.

9. A rocket is propelled by the ejection of part of its mass to the rear. The forward force on the rocket is the reaction to the backward force of the ejected mass, and as more material is ejected, the mass of the rocket decreases. For a vertically launched rocket under certain assumptions (no air resistance, constant g), it can be shown that the velocity V (m/sec) at time t seconds is given by

$$V = V_0 + V_r \ln\left(\frac{M_0}{M}\right) - gt$$

where M kg is the mass of the rocket at time t sec, V_0 m/sec and M_0 kg are the initial velocity and mass (at $t = 0$ sec), g is the gravitational constant (approximately 9.80665 m/sec^2), and V_r m/sec is the velocity of the rocket relative to the ejected fuel. Write a program to read values for V_0, V_r, M_0, M, and t and then calculate and display the velocity of the rocket.

10. The speed in miles per hour of a satellite moving in a circular orbit about a celestial body is given approximately by

$$\text{speed} = \sqrt{\frac{C}{D}}$$

where C is a constant depending on the celestial body and D is the distance from the center of the celestial body to the satellite (in miles). Write a program that reads the value of the constant C for a celestial body and a value for D and then calculates and displays the speed of the satellite. Run the program with the following values: (Earth) $C = 1.2E12$; (moon) $C = 1.5E10$; (Mars) $C = 1.3E11$.

11. One set of *polar coordinates* of a point in a plane is given by (r, θ), where r is the length of the ray from the origin to the point and θ is the measure of an angle from the positive x-axis to this ray.

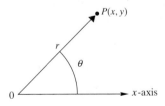

Write a program that reads polar coordinates for a point and calculates and displays its rectangular coordinates (x, y) obtained by using the formulas

$$x = r \cos \theta$$

$$y = r \sin \theta$$

12. The equation of the curve formed by a hanging cable weighing w pounds per foot of length can be described by

$$y = a \cosh \frac{x}{a}$$

where $a = H/w$, with H representing the horizontal tension pulling on the cable at its low point, and cosh is the hyperbolic cosine function defined by

$$\cosh u = \frac{e^u + e^{-u}}{2}$$

Write a program that reads values of w, H, and x and calculates and displays the corresponding value of y.

13. Write a program to convert a measurement given in feet to the equivalent number of **(a)** yards, **(b)** inches, **(c)** centimeters, and **(d)** meters (1 foot = 12 inches; 1 yard = 3 feet; 1 inch = 2.54 centimeters; 1 meter = 100 centimeters). Read the number of feet, and display, with appropriate labels, the number of yards, the number of feet, the number of inches, the number of centimeters, and the number of meters.

14. The formula for the volume of an oblate spheroid, such as the Earth, is

$$V = \frac{4}{3} \pi a^2 b$$

where a and b are the half-lengths of the major and minor axes, respectively. Write a program that reads values for a and b and then calculates and displays the volume. Use your program to find the volume of the Earth for which the values of a and b are 3963 miles and 3950 miles, respectively.

15. In order for a shaft with an allowable shear strength of S lb/in^2 to transmit a torque of T in-lbs, it must have a diameter of at least D inches, where D is given by

$$D = \sqrt[3]{\frac{16T}{S}}$$

If P horsepower is applied to the shaft at a rotational speed of N rpm, the torque is given by

$$T = 63000 \frac{P}{N}$$

Write a program that reads values for P, N, and S and then calculates and displays the torque developed and the required diameter to transmit that torque. Run your program with the following inputs:

P (HP)	N (rpm)	S (psi)
20	1500	5000
20	50	5000
270	40	6500

16. The period of a pendulum is given by the formula

$$P = 2\pi \sqrt{\frac{L}{g}} \left(1 + \frac{1}{4} \sin^2 \left(\frac{\alpha}{2} \right) \right)$$

where

g = 980 cm/sec^2

L = pendulum length (cm)

α = angle of displacement

Write a program to read values for L and α and then calculate and display the period of a pendulum having this length and angle of displacement. Run your program with the following inputs:

L (cm)	α (degrees)
120	15
90	20
60	5
74.6	10
83.6	12

17. A containing tank is to be constructed that will hold 500 cubic meters of oil when filled. The shape of the tank is to be a cylinder (including a base) surmounted by a cone, whose height is equal to its radius. The material and labor costs to construct the cylindrical portion of the tank are $300 per square meter, and the costs for the conical top are $400 per square meter. Write a program that calculates and displays the heights of the cylinder and the cone for a given radius that is input and that also calculates and displays the total cost of constructing the tank. Starting with a radius of 4.0 meters and incrementing by various (small) step sizes, run your program several times to determine the dimensions of the tank that will cost the least.

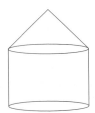

18. Write a program to read the thickness, density, and outside radius of a hollow ball and to calculate and display its volume and the mass. Starting with a value of 0.2 cm, run your program several times to find the largest wall thickness of a copper ball (density = 0.0089 kg/cm^3) with an outside radius of 50.0 cm that will float in water. (For the ball to float, its volume must be at least 1000 times its mass.)

19. The declining-balance formula for calculating depreciation is

$$V_N = V_0(1 - R)^N$$

where

V_N = the value after N years
V_0 = the initial value
R = the rate of depreciation
N = the number of years

Write a program to read values for V_0, R, and N and then calculate and display the depreciated value. Run the program several times to find the depreciated value of a new machine just purchased by Dispatch Die-Casting for $50,000 at the end of each year of its useful life. Assume that the rate of depreciation is 12 percent and that the usual life of the machine is 5 years.

20. The castings produced at Dispatch Die-Casting must be shipped in special containers that are available in four sizes—huge, large, medium, and small—that can hold 50, 20, 5, and 1 castings, respectively. Write a program that reads the number of castings to be shipped and displays the number of containers needed to send the shipment most efficiently. The output for input value 598 should be similar to the following:

```
CONTAINER    NUMBER
==================
  HUGE         11
  LARGE         2
  MEDIUM        1
  SMALL         3
```

21. The length of the line segment joining two points $P_1(x_1, y_1)$ and $P_2(x_2, y_2)$ is given by

$$\sqrt{(x_2 - x_1)^2 + (y_2 - y_1)^2}$$

and the midpoint of the segment has the coordinates

$$\left(\frac{x_1 + x_2}{2}, \frac{y_1 + y_2}{2} \right)$$

The slope of the line through P_1 and P_2 is given by

$$\frac{y_2 - y_1}{x_2 - x_1}$$

(provided $x_1 \neq x_2$), and the slope-intercept equation of this line is

$$y = mx + b$$

where m is the slope and b is the y-intercept; b can be calculated by

$$b = y_1 - mx_1$$

The perpendicular bisector of the line segment joining P_1 and P_2 is the line through the midpoint of this segment and having slope $-1/m$ (provided $m \neq 0$). Write a program that reads the coordinates of two points, P_1 and P_2, with distinct x-coordinates and distinct y-coordinates and calculates and displays the length of the segment P_1P_2, the midpoint of the segment, the slope of the line through P_1 and P_2, its y-intercept, its slope-intercept equation, and the equation of the perpendicular bisector of P_1P_2.

22. Write a program that will read a student's number, his or her old grade point average (GPA), and old number of course credits (e.g., 30179, 3.29, 19) and then display these with appropriate labels. Then read the course credit and grade for each of four courses; for example, C1 = 1.0, G1 = 3.7, C2 = 0.5, G2 = 4.0, and so on. Calculate

number of old honor points = (old # of course credits) $*$ (old GPA)

number of new honor points = C1 $*$ G1 + $\cdots$ + C4 $*$ G4

total # of new course credits = C1 + C2 + C3 + C4

$$\text{current GPA} = \frac{\text{\# of new honor points}}{\text{\# of new course credits}}$$

Display the current GPA with an appropriate label. Then calculate

$$\text{cumulative GPA} = \frac{(\text{\# of old honor points}) + (\text{\# of new honor points})}{(\text{\# of old course credits}) + (\text{\# of new course credits})}$$

and display this with a label.

FEATURES NEW TO FORTRAN 90

Several of the Fortran 90 features described in this chapter are not provided in FORTRAN 77. This section lists some of these.

Constants and Variables

- The separator : : may be used in type specification statements to separate the type identifier from the item being declared; for example,

```
INTEGER :: X, Y
```

In FORTRAN 77 this would be written

```
INTEGER X, Y
```

- Modified forms of type specification statements can be used to initialize variables; for example, the type statement

```
REAL :: Rate = 7.25
```

declares `Rate` to be a real variable with initial value 7.25. In FORTRAN 77 a `DATA` statement would be required:

```
REAL RATE
DATA RATE /7.25/
```

- Parameters can be declared and defined in a single type statement; for example,

```
REAL, PARAMETER :: Pi = 3.141593
```

In FORTRAN 77 this would be written

```
REAL PI
PARAMETER (PI = 3.141593)
```

- Integer values may have binary, octal, or hexadecimal representations in `DATA` statements.
- Strings may be enclosed in either apostrophes (`'`) or double quotes (`"`).
- Identifiers may consist of up to 31 letters, digits, or underscores (`_`).
- A modified form of the `IMPLICIT` statement, `IMPLICIT NONE`, cancels the naming convention, with the result that the types of all named constants and variables (and functions) *must be* specified explicitly in type statements.

Arithmetic Operations and Functions

- Several new arithmetic functions have been added.

Program Format and Composition

- Free-form source code is allowed and lines may extend up to 132 characters. FORTRAN 77 has rather strict rules that dictate where statements and comments are to be placed. These rules are summarized in the following diagram:

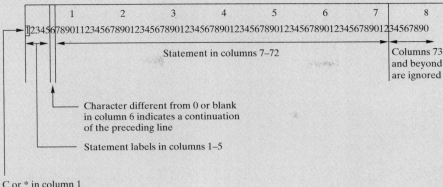

C or * in column 1
indicates a comment

- New characters, including lowercase letters, have been added to the Fortran character set.

- More than one statement may be placed on a line. A semicolon is used to separate such statements.

- In-line comments that begin with an exclamation point (!) and extend to the end of the line are allowed.

- Continuation of a statement can be indicated by using an ampersand (&) as the last non-blank character in the line being continued or the last non-blank character before the exclamation mark that marks the beginning of a comment.

- A program may have a subprogram section that immediately precedes the END statement.

- The END statement may have the form END PROGRAM *name*, where *name* is the name used in the program heading.

3

Selective Execution

When you get to the fork in the road, take it.

Yogi Berra

If you can keep your head, when all about are losing theirs . . .

Rudyard Kipling

"Would you tell me, please, which way I ought to go from here?"
"That depends a great deal on where you want to get to," said the
Cat.

Lewis Carroll

We are all special cases.

Albert Camus

Then Logic would take you by the throat, and force you to do it!

Achilles in Lewis Carroll's
What the Tortoise Said to Achilles

*I*n Chapter 2 we described several software engineering techniques that assist in the design of programs that are easy to understand and whose logical flow is easy to follow. Such programs are more likely to be correct when first written than poorly structured programs; and if they are not correct, the errors are easier to find and correct. Such programs are also easier to modify, which is especially important since such modifications may be required long after the program was originally written and are often made by someone other than the original programmer.

We noted that one important software engineering principle is that algorithms and programs should be structured. In a **structured program**, the logical flow is governed by three basic control structures: **sequence**, **selection**, and **repetition**. Sequential control, as illustrated in the following diagram, simply refers to the execution of a sequence of statements in the order in which they appear so that each statement is executed exactly once. All the sample programs in Chapter 2 are "straight-line" programs in which the only control used is sequential.

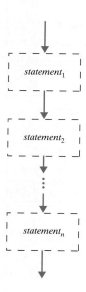

Sequence is a fundamental control mechanism, but it is not powerful enough to solve all problems. For some problems, the solution requires selecting one of several alternative actions. Two such problems will be described in detail and solved in this chapter.

Problem 1: Classifying a Pollution Index.

The pollution-index problem described in Section 3.3 requires calculating and classifying a pollution index. A value of 50 or greater for the index indicates a hazardous condition, whereas a value lower than 50 indicates a safe condition.

In this problem a selection must be made between displaying a message that indicates a hazardous condition and displaying a message that indicates a safe condition:

> If the pollution index is greater than 50
>   Display a "hazardous condition" message
> Else
>   Display a "safe condition" message

In this problem, one of two possible actions is selected, but in other problems there may be several alternative actions. The fluid-flow problem described and solved in Section 3.5 is such a problem.

Problem 2: Determining the Type of Fluid Flow in a Pipe.

Flow of a fluid through a pipe may be one of three types: laminar, turbulent, or unstable (switches between turbulent and laminar). The problem is to determine the type of flow for a particular pipe and fluid.

To solve this problem, the *Reynold's number* must be computed and compared with two cutoff values:

If the Reynold's number is less than the first cutoff value, the flow is laminar.

If the Reynold's number is greater than or equal to the first cutoff value but less than a second cutoff value, the flow is unstable.

If the Reynold's number is greater than or equal to the second cutoff value, the flow is turbulent.

There are thus three alternatives and exactly one of them must be selected.

In this chapter we show how the selection structures needed to solve such problems are implemented in Fortran.

3.1 LOGICAL EXPRESSIONS

Several of the Fortran statements that are used to implement selection and repetition structures involve logical expressions. Consequently, before we can describe these control structures, we must examine logical expressions in more detail.

Simple Logical Expressions

Logical expressions may be either **simple** or **compound**. Simple logical expressions are logical constants (.TRUE. and .FALSE.) or logical variables (see Section 3.8) or **relational expressions** of the form

$$expression_1 \; relational\text{-}operator \; expression_2$$

where both $expression_1$ and $expression_2$ are numeric or character (or logical) expressions, and the $relational\text{-}operator$ may be any of the following:

Symbol	Meaning
< or .LT.	Is less than
> or .GT.	Is greater than
== or .EQ.	Is equal to
<= or .LE.	Is less than or equal to
>= or .GE.	Is greater than or equal to
/= or .NE.	Is not equal to

Note that there are two forms for each of the relational operators: a symbolic form and an abbreviated form of the operator's name. Since it promotes program readability, we will use only the symbolic forms in this text.

The following are examples of simple logical expressions:

```
.TRUE.
X < 5.2
Number == -999
```

If X has the value 4.5, the logical expression X < 5.2 is true. If Number has the value 400, the logical expression Number == -999 is false. In logical expressions such as

```
B ** 2 >= 4.0 * A * C
```

which contain both arithmetic operators and relational operators, the arithmetic operations are performed first; that is, this logical expression is equivalent to

```
(B ** 2) >= (4.0 * A * C)
```

Thus, if A, B, and C have the values 2.0, 1.0, and 3.0, respectively, this logical expression is evaluated as

```
1.0 >= 24.0
```

which is clearly false.

When using the relational operators == and /=, it is important to remember that *many real values cannot be stored exactly* (see Section 2.11). *Consequently, logical expressions formed by comparing real quantities with == are often evaluated as false, even though these quantities are algebraically equal.* The program in Figure 3.3 illustrates this.

For character data, numeric codes are used to establish an ordering for the character set. Two standard coding schemes are ASCII and EBCDIC (see Appendix A). They differ in the codes assigned to characters, but in both schemes, the letters are in alphabetical order and the digits are in numerical order. Thus

```
"A" < "F"
"6" > "4"
```

are true logical expressions. Two strings are compared character by character using these numeric codes. For example, for a logical expression of the form

$$string_1 < string_2$$

if the first character of $string_1$ is less than the first character of $string_2$ (that is, precedes it in the coding sequence), then $string_1$ is less than $string_2$. Thus,

```
"cat" < "dog"
```

is true, since c is less than d. If the first characters of $string_1$ and $string_2$ are the same, the second characters are compared; if these characters are the same, the third characters are compared, and so on. Thus,

```
"cat" < "cow"
```

is true, since a is less than o. Similarly,

```
"June" > "July"
```

is true, since n is greater than l. Two strings with different lengths are compared as though blanks are appended to the shorter string, resulting in two strings of equal length to be compared. For example, the logical expression

```
"cat" < "cattle"
```

is evaluated as

```
"catɓɓɓ" < "cattle"
```

(where ɓ denotes a blank), which is true because a blank character precedes all letters.

Compound Logical Expressions

Compound logical expressions are formed by combining logical expressions by using the **logical operators**

```
.NOT.
.AND.
.OR.
.EQV.
.NEQV.
```

These operators are defined in the following table, where p and q represent logical expressions.

Logical Operator	Logical Expression	Definition
.NOT.	.NOT. p	.NOT. p is true if p is false and is false if p is true.
.AND.	p .AND. q	*Conjunction* of p and q: p .AND. q is true if both p and q are true; it is false otherwise.
.OR.	p .OR. q	*Disjunction* of p and q: p .OR. q is true if p or q or both are true; it is false otherwise.
.EQV.	p .EQV. q	*Equivalence* of p and q: p .EQV. q is true if both p and q are true or both are false; it is false otherwise.
.NEQV.	p .NEQV. q	*Nonequivalence* of p and q: p .NEQV. q is the negation of p .EQV. q; it is true if one of p or q is true and the other is false; it is false otherwise.

These definitions are summarized in the following **truth tables**, which display all the possible values for the logical expressions p and q and the corresponding values of the compound logical expression:

p	.NOT. p
.TRUE.	.FALSE.
.FALSE.	.TRUE.

p	q	p .AND. q	p .OR. q	p .EQV. q	p .NEQV. q
.TRUE.	.TRUE.	.TRUE.	.TRUE.	.TRUE.	.FALSE.
.TRUE.	.FALSE.	.FALSE.	.TRUE.	.FALSE.	.TRUE.
.FALSE.	.TRUE.	.FALSE.	.TRUE.	.FALSE.	.TRUE.
.FALSE.	.FALSE.	.FALSE.	.FALSE.	.TRUE.	.FALSE.

In a logical expression containing several of these operators, the operations are performed in the order .NOT., .AND., .OR., .EQV. (or .NEQV.). Parentheses may be used to indicate those subexpressions that should be evaluated first. For example, consider logical expressions of the form

```
.NOT. p .AND. q
p .AND. (q .OR. r)
```

In the first expression, the subexpression .NOT. p is evaluated first, and this result is then combined with the value of q, using the operator .AND.. The entire expression is therefore true only in the case that p is false and q is true. In the second example, the subexpression q .OR. r is evaluated first; the possible values it may have are displayed in the following truth table:

p	q	r	p .AND. (q .OR. r)
.TRUE.	.TRUE.	.TRUE.	.TRUE.
.TRUE.	.TRUE.	.FALSE.	.TRUE.
.TRUE.	.FALSE.	.TRUE.	.TRUE.
.TRUE.	.FALSE.	.FALSE.	.FALSE.
.FALSE.	.TRUE.	.TRUE.	.TRUE.
.FALSE.	.TRUE.	.FALSE.	.TRUE.
.FALSE.	.FALSE.	.TRUE.	.TRUE.
.FALSE.	.FALSE.	.FALSE.	.FALSE.

This value is then combined with the value of p using the operator .AND.:

p	q	r	p .AND.	(q .OR. r)
.TRUE.	.TRUE.	.TRUE.	.TRUE.	.TRUE.
.TRUE.	.TRUE.	.FALSE.	.TRUE.	.TRUE.
.TRUE.	.FALSE.	.TRUE.	.TRUE.	.TRUE.
.TRUE.	.FALSE.	.FALSE.	.FALSE.	.FALSE.
.FALSE.	.TRUE.	.TRUE.	.FALSE.	.TRUE.
.FALSE.	.TRUE.	.FALSE.	.FALSE.	.TRUE.
.FALSE.	.FALSE.	.TRUE.	.FALSE.	.TRUE.
.FALSE.	.FALSE.	.FALSE.	.FALSE.	.FALSE.

When a logical expression contains arithmetic operators, relational operators, and logical operators, the operations are performed in the following order:

1. Arithmetic operations (and functions)
2. Relational operations
3. Logical operations in the order .NOT., .AND., .OR., .EQV. (or .NEQV.)

For example, if the integer variable N has the value 4, the logical expression

```
N**2 + 1 > 10 .AND. .NOT. N < 3
```

or with parentheses inserted to improve readability,

```
(N**2 + 1 > 10) .AND. .NOT. (N < 3)
```

is true. The logical expression

```
N == 3 .OR. N == 4
```

is valid and is true, whereas

```
N == 1 .OR. 2
```

is not, since this would be evaluated as

```
(N == 1) .OR. 2
```

and 2 is not a logical expression to which .OR. can be applied.

Quick Quiz 3.1

1. The two logical constants are _____ and _____.
2. List the six relational operators.
3. List the five logical operators.

For Questions 4–8, assume that P, Q, and R are logical expressions with the values .TRUE., .TRUE., and .FALSE., respectively. Find the value of each logical expression.

4. P .AND. .NOT. Q 5. P .AND. Q .OR. .NOT. R

6. P .AND. .NOT. (Q .OR. R)   7. .NOT. P .AND. Q

8. P .OR. Q .AND. R

For Questions 9–13, assume that Number, Count, and Sum are integer variables with values 3, 4, and 5, respectively. Find the value of each logical expression, or indicate why it is not valid.

9. Sum - Number <= 4

10. Number**2 + Count**2 == Sum**2

11. Number < Count .OR. Count < Sum

12. 0 <= Count <= 5

13. (Number + 1 < Sum) .AND. .NOT. (Count + 1 < Sum)

14. Write a logical expression to express that X is nonzero.

15. Write a logical expression to express that X is strictly between -10 and 10.

16. Write a logical expression to express that both X and Y are positive or both X and Y are negative.

Exercises 3.1

For Exercises 1–10, assume that M and N are integer variables with the values -5 and 8, respectively, and that X, Y, and Z are real variables with the values -3.56, 0.0, and 44.7, respectively. Find the value of the logical expression.

1. M <= N

2. 2 * ABS(M) <= 8

3. X * X < SQRT(Z)

4. `NINT(Z)  ==  (6 * N - 3)`

5. `(X <= Y) .AND. (Y <= Z)`

6. `.NOT. (X < Y)`

7. `.NOT. ((M <= N) .AND. (X + Z > Y))`

8. `.NOT. (M <= N) .OR. .NOT. (X + Z > Y)`

9. `.NOT. ((M > N) .OR. (X < Z)) .EQV.  &`
   `      ((M <= N) .AND. (X >= Z))`

10. `.NOT. ((M > N) .AND. (X < Z)) .NEQV.  &`
    `      ((M <= N) .AND. (X >= Z))`

For Exercises 11–16, assume that A, B, and C are logical expressions. Use truth tables to display the value of the logical expression for all possible values of A, B, and C.

11. `A .OR. .NOT. B`

12. `.NOT. (A .AND. B)`

13. `.NOT. A .OR. .NOT. B`

14. `A .AND. .TRUE. .OR. (1 + 2 == 4)`

15. `A .AND. (B .OR. C)`

16. `(A .AND. B) .OR. (A .AND. C)`

For Exercises 17–25, write a logical expression to express the given condition.

17. X is greater than 3.

18. Y is strictly between 2 and 5.

19. R is negative and Z is positive.

20. Alpha and Beta are both positive.

21. Alpha and Beta have the same sign (both are negative or both are positive).

22. $-5 < X < 5$.

23. A is less than 6 or is greater than 10.

24. $P = Q = R$.

25. X is less than 3, or Y is less than 3, but not both.

For Exercises 26–28, assume that A, B, and C are logical expressions.

26. Write a logical expression that is true if and only if A and B are true and C is false.

27. Write a logical expression that is true if and only if A is true and at least one of B or C is true.

28. Write a logical expression that is true if and only if exactly one of A and B is true.

3.2 IF CONSTRUCTS

A **selection structure** selects one of several alternative sets of statements for execution. This selection is based on the value of a logical expression.

Simple IF Construct

In the simplest selection structure, a sequence of statements (also called a **block** of statements) is executed or bypassed depending on whether a given logical expression is true or false. This is pictured in the following diagram:

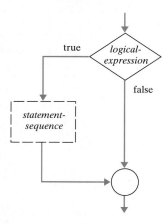

This selection structure is implemented in Fortran by using an **IF construct** (also called a **block IF construct**) of the form

> #### IF *Construct (Simple Form)*
>
> **Form:**
>
>   IF (logical-expression) THEN
>   statement-sequence
>   END IF
>
> where
>   *statement-sequence* is a sequence of Fortran statements.
>
> Note that the logical expression must be enclosed in parentheses.
>
> **Purpose:**
> If the logical expression is true, the specified sequence of statements is executed; otherwise it is bypassed. In either case, execution continues with the statement in the program following the END IF.

For example, in the IF construct

```
IF (X >= 0) THEN
   Y = X * X
   Z = SQRT(X)
END IF
```

the logical expression X >= 0 is evaluated, and if it is true, Y is set equal to the square of X and Z is set equal to the square root of X; otherwise, these assignment statements are not executed.

Fortran also provides a still simpler IF construct that can be used if the statement sequence consists of a single statement. It is called a **logical IF statement** and has the following form:

Logical IF Statement

Form:

```
IF (logical-expression) statement
```

where
   statement is a Fortran statement.

Note that the logical expression must be enclosed in parentheses.

Purpose:
If the logical expression is true, the specified statement is executed; otherwise it is bypassed. In either case, execution continues with the next statement in the program.

For example, in the logical IF statement

```
IF (1.5 <= X  .AND.  X <= 2.5) PRINT *, X
```

if $1.5 \le X \le 2.5$, the value of X is displayed; otherwise, the PRINT statement is bypassed. In either case, execution continues with the next statement in the program.

General Form of the IF Construct

In the preceding selection structure, the selection is made between (1) executing a given sequence of statements and (2) bypassing these statements. In the two-way selection pictured in the following diagram, the selection is made between (1) executing one sequence (block) of statements and (2) executing a different sequence (block) of statements.

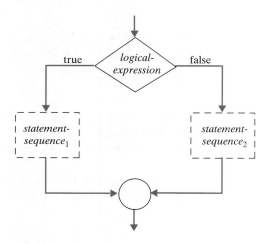

This selection structure is implemented in Fortran by an IF construct that allows the programmer not only to specify the sequence of statements to be executed when the logical expression is true but also to indicate an alternative statement sequence to be executed when it is false. This IF construct has the form

IF *Construct (General Form)*

Form:

```
IF (logical-expression) THEN
    statement-sequence₁
ELSE
    statement-sequence₂
END IF
```

where:
> *statement-sequence*$_1$ and *statement-sequence*$_2$ are sequences of Fortran statements; and the ELSE part is optional.

Note that the logical expression must be enclosed in parentheses.

Purpose:
If the logical expression is true:
> *statement-sequence*$_1$ is executed and
> *statement-sequence*$_2$ is bypassed.

If the logical expression is false:
> *statement-sequence*$_1$ is bypassed;
> if there is an ELSE part, *statement-sequence*$_2$ is executed;
> otherwise, execution will simply continue with the next statement following the END IF statement that terminates the IF construct.

In either case, execution continues with the next statement in the program (unless, of course, execution is terminated or control is transferred elsewhere by one of the statements in the statement sequence selected).

As an example of this form of an IF construct, consider the problem of calculating the values of the following piecewise continuous function:

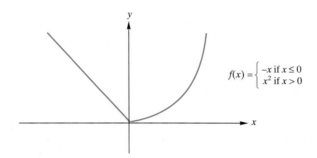

$$f(x) = \begin{cases} -x \text{ if } x \leq 0 \\ x^2 \text{ if } x > 0 \end{cases}$$

An IF construct containing an ELSE clause makes this easy:

```
IF (X <= 0) THEN
    F_Value = -X
ELSE
    F_Value = X ** 2
END IF
```

Example: Quadratic Equations

As another illustration of using an IF construct to implement a two-alternative selection structure, consider the problem of solving the quadratic equation

$$Ax^2 + Bx + C = 0$$

by using the quadratic formula to obtain the roots

$$\frac{-B \pm \sqrt{B^2 - 4AC}}{2A}$$

In this problem, the input values are the coefficients A, B, and C of the quadratic equation, and the output is the pair of real roots or a message indicating that there are no real roots (in case $B^2 - 4AC$ is negative). An algorithm for solving a quadratic equation is as follows:

Figure 3.1

Flowchart for
quadratic
equation
algorithm.

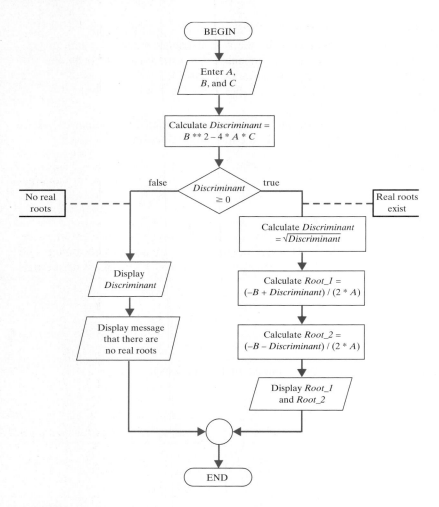

ALGORITHM FOR SOLVING QUADRATIC EQUATIONS

This algorithm solves a quadratic equation $Ax^2 + Bx + C = 0$ using
the quadratic formula. If the discriminant $Discriminant = B^2 - 4AC$
is nonnegative, the pair of real roots $Root\_1$ and $Root\_2$ is
calculated; otherwise, a message is displayed indicating that there
are no real roots.

Input: The coefficients A, B, and C
Output: The roots of the equation or the (negative) discriminant and
           a no-real-roots message

1. Enter A, B, and C.

2. Calculate $Discriminant = B ** 2 - 4 * A * C$.

3. If $Discriminant \geq 0$ then do the following:

    a. Calculate $Discriminant = \sqrt{Discriminant}$.

    b. Calculate $Root\_1 = (-B + Discriminant) / (2 * A)$.

    c. Calculate $Root\_2 = (-B - Discriminant) / (2 * A)$.

    d. Display $Root\_1$ and $Root\_2$.

Else do the following:

    a. Display $Discriminant$.

    b. Display a message that there are no real roots.

Figure 3.1 displays the structure of this algorithm in flowchart form.

    The program in Figure 3.2 implements this algorithm. Note the indentation of the statements in the IF construct. Although not required, it is good programming style to set off these statements in this manner to emphasize that they constitute a single block.

Figure 3.2 Quadratic equations.

```
PROGRAM QuadraticEquations_1
!--------------------------------------------------------------------
! Program to solve a quadratic equation using the quadratic formula.
! Variables used are:
!    A, B, C          : the coefficients of the quadratic equation
!    Discriminant   : the discriminant, B**2 - 4.0*A*C
!    Root_1, Root_2 : the two roots of the equation
!
! Input:  The coefficients A, B, and C
! Output: The two roots of the equation or the (negative) discriminant
!         and a message indicating that there are no real roots
!--------------------------------------------------------------------

  IMPLICIT NONE
  REAL :: A, B, C, Discriminant, Root_1, Root_2

  ! Get the coefficients
  PRINT *, "Enter the coefficients of the quadratic equation:"
  READ *, A, B, C

  ! Calculate the discriminant
  Discriminant = B**2 - 4.0*A*C
```

Figure 3.2 *(cont.)*

```
! Check if discriminant is nonnegative.  If it is, calculate and
! display the roots.  Otherwise display the value of the discriminant
! and a no-real-roots message.
IF (Discriminant >= 0) THEN
   Discriminant = SQRT(Discriminant)
   Root_1 = (-B + Discriminant) / (2.0 * A)
   Root_2 = (-B - Discriminant) / (2.0 * A)
   PRINT *, "The roots are", Root_1, Root_2
ELSE
   PRINT *, "Discriminant is", Discriminant
   PRINT *, "There are no real roots"
END IF


END PROGRAM QuadraticEquations_1
```

Sample runs:

```
Enter the coefficients of the quadratic equation:
1, -5, 6
The roots are    3.0000000    2.0000000

Enter the coefficients of the quadratic equation:
1, 0, -4
The roots are    2.0000000    -2.0000000

Enter the coefficients of the quadratic equation:
1, 0, 4
Discriminant is -16.0000000
There are no real roots

Enter the coefficients of the quadratic equation:
3.7, 16.5, 1.7
The roots are   -0.1055275    -4.3539319
```

The Effect of Roundoff Errors

We noted in Section 3.1 that it is important to remember that because real values cannot be stored exactly, logical expressions formed by comparing real quantities with == are often evaluated as false, even though these quantities are algebraically equal. The program in Figure 3.3 demonstrates this by showing that for some real values X, the value of Y computed by

```
Y = X * (1.0 / X)
```

is not 1. In this program, an IF construct uses the logical expression

    Y == 1.0

to check if the value of Y is equal to 1 and selects an appropriate message to be displayed based on the value of this logical expression.

 Figure 3.3 The effect of roundoff error.

```
PROGRAM Roundoff_Errors
!----------------------------------------------------------------------
! Program to show inexact representation of reals by showing that for
! some real values X, X * (1.0 / X) is not equal to 1.  Variables
! used are:
!    X:  a real number entered by the user
!    Y:  X * (1.0 / X)
!
! Input:   X
! Output:  The value of X, the value of Y = X * (1.0 / X), and a
!          message indicating whether Y is equal to 1
!----------------------------------------------------------------------

   IMPLICIT NONE
   REAL :: X, Y

   ! Get an arbitrary nonzero real number X
   PRINT *, "Enter nonzero real number:"
   READ *, X

   ! Calculate product of X and 1/X, display it and
   ! the difference between it and 1
   Y = X * (1.0 / X)
   PRINT *, "X =", X, "     Y = X * (1 / X) =", Y
   PRINT *, "1.0 - Y =", 1.0 - Y

   ! Check if product is 1 and display appropriate message
   IF (Y == 1.0) THEN
      PRINT *, "Y equals 1"
   ELSE
      PRINT *, "Due to roundoff error, Y does not equal 1"
   END IF

END PROGRAM Roundoff_Errors
```

Figure 3.3 *(cont.)*

Sample runs:

```
Enter nonzero real number:
0.1
X =    0.1000000      Y = X * (1 / X) =    1.0000000
1.0 - Y =   0.0000000E+00
Y equals 1

Enter nonzero real number:
3.1415
X =    3.1415000      Y = X * (1 / X) =    0.9999999
1.0 - Y =   5.9604645E-08
Due to roundoff error, Y does not equal 1

Enter nonzero real number:
15.7981
X =   15.7981005      Y = X * (1 / X) =    0.9999999
1.0 - Y =   5.9604645E-08
Due to roundoff error, Y does not equal 1
```

As this program demonstrates, if two real values are subject to error caused by inexact representation, it is not advisable to check whether they are equal. Rather, it is better to check whether the absolute value of their difference is small:

```
IF (ABS(real-value₁ - real-value₂) < Tolerance) THEN
   ⋮
```

where `Tolerance` is some small positive real value such as `1E-6`.

3.3 APPLICATION: POLLUTION INDEX

Problem

The level of air pollution in the city of Dogpatch is measured by a pollution index. Readings are made at 12:00 P.M. at three locations: at the Abner Coal Plant; downtown at the corner of Daisy Avenue and 5th Street; and at a randomly selected location in a residential area. The integer average of these three readings is the pollution index, and a value of 50 parts per million or greater for this index indicates a hazardous condition, whereas values lower than 50 parts per million indicate a safe condition. Because this index must be calculated daily, the Dogpatch environmental statistician would like a program that calculates the pollution index and then determines the appropriate condition, safe or hazardous.

Solution

Specification.   The relevant given information consists of three pollution readings and the cutoff value used to distinguish between safe and hazardous conditions. A solution to the problem consists of the pollution index and a message indicating the condition. Generalizing so that any cutoff value, not just 50, can be used, we can specify the problem as follows:

Input: Three pollution readings
Constant: Cutoff value to distinguish between safe and hazardous conditions
Output: Pollution index = integer average of the pollution readings
              Condition: safe or hazardous

Smog over Los Angeles, California. (Photo courtesy of Uniphoto Picture Agency)

Design.   The first step in an algorithm to solve this problem is to obtain values for the input items—the three pollution readings. The next step is to calculate the pollution index by averaging the three readings. An appropriate air-quality message must then be displayed. Thus, an initial description of an algorithm is

1. Obtain the three pollution readings.
2. Calculate the pollution index.
3. Display an appropriate air-quality message.

Coding step 1 is straightforward, but steps 2 and 3 require some refinement. For step 2, once the three pollution readings have been entered, we need only add them and divide the sum by 3 to obtain their average. We will use the following identifiers to store the input values, the cutoff value, and the pollution index:

IDENTIFIERS FOR POLLUTION-INDEX PROBLEM

Level_1, *Level_2*, *Level_3*	Three pollution readings
Cutoff	Cutoff value
Index	Pollution index

In step 3, one of two possible actions must be selected. Either a message indicating a safe condition or a message indicating a hazardous condition must be displayed. The appropriate action is selected by comparing the pollution index with the cutoff value. A refined version of step 3 might thus be written in pseudocode as

If *Index* < *Cutoff* then
　　Display "Safe condition"
Else
　　Display "Hazardous condition"

A final version of the algorithm can now be given:

ALGORITHM FOR POLLUTION-INDEX PROBLEM

This algorithm reads three pollution levels and then calculates a pollution index, which is the integer average of these three readings. If this index is less than a specified cutoff value, a message indicating a safe condition is displayed; otherwise, a message indicating a hazardous condition is displayed.

Input:　　*Level_1*, *Level_2*, *Level_3*
Constant:　*Cutoff*
Output:　　The pollution *Index* and a message indicating the air quality

1. Enter *Level_1*, *Level_2*, and *Level_3*.

2. Calculate $Index = \dfrac{Level\_1 + Level\_2 + Level\_3}{3}$.

3. If *Index* < *Cutoff* then
　　Display "Safe condition"
Else
　　Display "Hazardous condition"

The following flowchart representation of this algorithm shows that its basic overall structure is sequential but that one of the steps in this sequential execution is a selection. The highlighted region of the diagram clearly shows the two alternatives, one of which must be selected according to the truth or falsity of the condition *Index < Cutoff*; a diamond-shaped box like that shown is commonly used to indicate that a selection must be made.

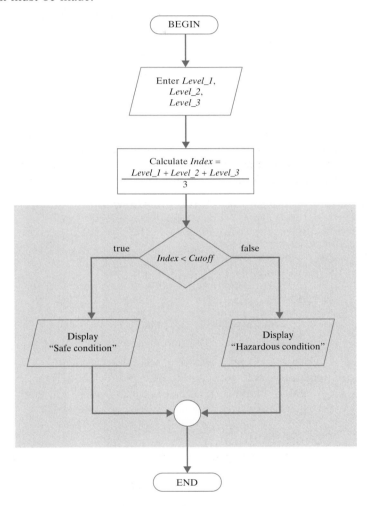

Coding. The Fortran program in Figure 3.4 implements the preceding algorithm. The cutoff point is stored as a named constant `Cutoff` so that it can be easily modified later if necessary. The selection structure

If *Index < Cutoff* then
    Display "Safe condition"
Else
    Display "Hazardous condition"

in the algorithm is implemented in the Fortran program by the following IF construct:

```fortran
IF (Index < Cutoff) THEN
    PRINT *,  "Safe condition"
ELSE
    PRINT *,  "Hazardous condition"
END IF
```

Figure 3.4 Pollution index.

```fortran
PROGRAM Pollution
!------------------------------------------------------------------
! Program that reads 3 pollution levels, calculates a pollution
! index as their integer average, and then displays an appropriate
! air-quality message.   Identifiers used are:
!    Level_1, Level_2, Level_3 : the three pollution levels
!    Cutoff : a cutoff value that distinguishes between hazardous
!              and safe conditions (constant)
!    Index  : the integer average of the pollution levels
!
! Input:    The three pollution levels
! Constant: The cutoff value (parts per million)
! Output:   The pollution index and a "safe condition" message if
!           this index is less than the cutoff value, otherwise a
!           "hazardous condition" message
!------------------------------------------------------------------

  IMPLICIT NONE
  INTEGER :: Level_1, Level_2, Level_3, Index
  INTEGER, PARAMETER ::  Cutoff = 50

  ! Get the 3 pollution readings
  PRINT *, "Enter 3 pollution readings (parts per million):"
  READ *, Level_1, Level_2, Level_3

  ! Calculate the pollution index
  Index = (Level_1 + Level_2 + Level_3) / 3

  ! Check if the pollution index is less than the cutoff and
  ! display an appropriate air-quality message
  IF (Index < Cutoff) THEN
     PRINT *, "Safe condition"
  ELSE
     PRINT *, "Hazardous condition"
  END IF

END PROGRAM Pollution
```

Execution and Testing.   Test runs with input data like the following indicate that the program is correct:

```
Enter 3 pollution readings (parts per million):
1, 2, 3
Safe condition

Enter 3 pollution readings (parts per million):
50, 60, 70
Hazardous condition
```

It can then be used to calculate pollution indices and conditions for other inputs such as

```
Enter 3 pollution readings (parts per million):
55, 39, 48
Safe condition

Enter 3 pollution readings (parts per million):
68, 49, 57
Hazardous condition
```

3.4 NESTED IFS AND IF-ELSE IF CONSTRUCTS

Nested IF Constructs

The sequence(s) of statements in an IF construct may themselves contain other IF constructs. In this case, the second IF construct is said to be **nested** within the first. For example, suppose the right branch of the earlier piecewise continuous function is modified so that the function becomes constant for $x \geq 1$:

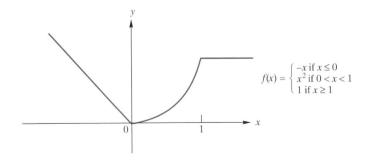

$$f(x) = \begin{cases} -x \text{ if } x \leq 0 \\ x^2 \text{ if } 0 < x < 1 \\ 1 \text{ if } x \geq 1 \end{cases}$$

The earlier IF construct for evaluating this function can be modified by inserting another IF construct within the ELSE block:

```
IF (X <= 0) THEN
   F_Value = -X
ELSE
   IF (X < 1.0) THEN
      F_Value = X ** 2
   ELSE
      F_Value = 1.0
   END IF
END IF
```

Example: Pay Calculation

As another example of a nested IF construct, consider the following problem of calculating wages. Suppose that some employees of a company are paid weekly an amount equal to their annual salaries divided by 52, whereas all other employees are paid on an hourly basis with all hours over 40 paid at one-and-a-half times the regular hourly rate. A program is to be written to calculate wages for either type of employee.

A first version of an algorithm for solving this problem is

1. Enter the employee type: S (salaried) or H (hourly).

2. Enter the appropriate pay information, annual salary or hourly rate and hours worked, and calculate the employee's pay.

3. Display the employee's pay.

Here, step 3 obviously needs refinement. If the employee is salaried, the annual salary must be entered and the pay calculated. Otherwise, the hourly rate and hours worked must be entered and the employee's pay calculated. We will use the following variables to store the input values and the employee's pay:

VARIABLES FOR PAY CALCULATION PROBLEM

EmployeeType	Type of employee ("S" or "H")
Salary	Annual salary for a salaried employee
HoursWorked	Hours worked for an hourly employee
HourlyRate	Hourly rate for an hourly employee
Pay	Employee's pay

The following algorithm solves this problem.

ALGORITHM FOR PAY CALCULATION PROBLEM

This algorithm calculates weekly pay for an employee. Some are salaried and others are paid on an hourly basis. For hourly employees, time and a half is paid for overtime.

Input: *EmployeeType*
              Salary for salaried employees
              HoursWorked and *HourlyRate* for hourly employees
Output: *Pay*

1. Enter *EmployeeType* (S or H).

2. If *EmployeeType* = "S" (salaried) do the following:

   a. Enter *Salary*.

   b. Calculate *Pay* = *Salary* / 52.

   Else do the following:

   a. Enter *HoursWorked* and *HourlyRate*.

   b. If (*HoursWorked* > 40)

       Calculate *Pay* = 40 * *HourlyRate*
                    + 1.5 * *HourlyRate* * (*HoursWorked* − 40)

     Else
       Calculate *Pay* = *HoursWorked* * *HourlyRate*

3. Display *Pay*.

The nesting of the IF construct based on the condition *HoursWorked* > 40 within the outer construct based on the condition *EmployeeType* = "S" is clearly seen in the flowchart in Figure 3.5, which shows the structure of this algorithm.

The program in Figure 3.6 implements this algorithm. Note again the indentation used to indicate the blocks in the IF constructs and the nesting of the IF constructs for calculating hourly wages within the ELSE part of the IF construct that checks the employee's type.

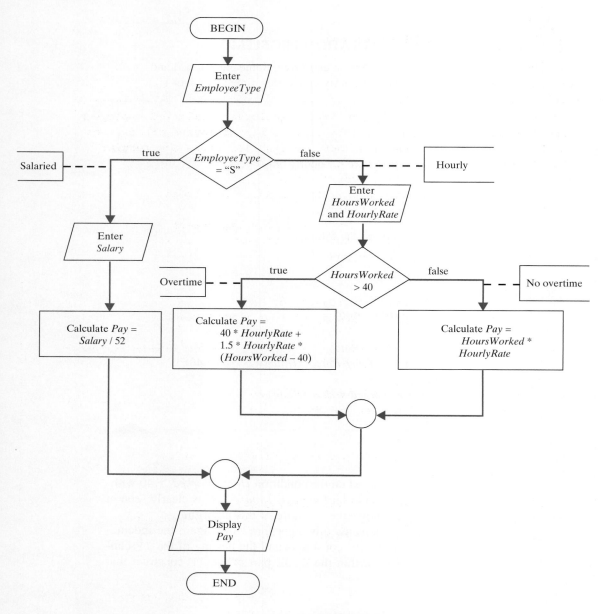

Figure 3.5

Flowchart for pay calculation algorithm.

Figure 3.6 Pay calculation.

```
PROGRAM Pay_Calculation
!-------------------------------------------------------------------
! Program to calculate weekly pay for an employee.  Salaried employees
! receive 1/52 of their annual salaries.  Other employees are paid on
! an hourly basis with overtime hours paid at 1.5 times the regular
! hourly rate.   Identifiers used are:
!     EmployeeType : employee type (S or H)
!     Salary       : annual salary (for salaried employees)
!     HoursWorked  : hours worked and
!     HourlyRate   :   hourly rate (for hourly employees)
!     Multiplier   : multiplier for overtime pay
!     Pay          : employee's pay
!
! Input:  EmployeeType
!         Salary for salaried employees, or
!         HoursWorked and HourlyRate for hourly employees
! Output: Pay
!-------------------------------------------------------------------

  CHARACTER(1) :: EmployeeType
  REAL :: Salary, HoursWorked, HourlyRate, Pay
  REAL, PARAMETER :: Multiplier = 1.5

  ! Get employee type (S or H)
  PRINT *, "Enter the type of employee (S or H):"
  READ *, EmployeeType

  ! Select appropriate method of calculating pay:
  IF (EmployeeType == "S") THEN                 ! Salaried employee
     PRINT *, "Enter employee's annual salary:"
     READ *, Salary
     Pay = Salary / 52

  ELSE                                          ! Hourly employee
     PRINT *, "Enter hours worked and hourly rate:"
     READ *, HoursWorked, HourlyRate
     IF (HoursWorked > 40.0) THEN
        Pay = 40.0 * HourlyRate &
            + Multiplier * HourlyRate * (HoursWorked - 40.0)
     ELSE
        Pay = HoursWorked * HourlyRate
     END IF
  END IF
```

Figure 3.6 *(cont.)*

```
  ! Display employee's pay
  PRINT *, "Employee's pay is", Pay

END PROGRAM Pay_Calculation
```

Sample runs:

```
Enter the type of employee (S or H):
S
Enter employee's annual salary:
52000
Employee's pay is    1.0000000E+03

Enter the type of employee (S or H):
H
Enter hours worked and hourly rate:
35.0, 9.50
Employee's pay is    3.3250000E+02

Enter the type of employee (S or H):
H
Enter hours worked and hourly rate:
50.0, 11.25
Employee's pay is    6.1875000E+02
```

IF-ELSE IF Construct

The selection structures considered thus far have involved selecting one of two alternatives. It is also possible to use the IF construct to design selection structures that contain more than two alternatives. For example, consider again the piecewise continuous function defined by

$$f(x) = \begin{cases} -x & \text{if } x \le 0 \\ x^2 & \text{if } 0 < x < 1 \\ 1 & \text{if } x \ge 1 \end{cases}$$

This definition really consists of three alternatives and was implemented earlier using an IF construct of the form

```
IF (logical-expression₁) THEN
    statement-sequence₁
ELSE
    IF (logical-expression₂) THEN
```

```
              statement-sequence₂
      ELSE
              statement-sequence₃
       END IF
  END IF
```

But compound `IF` constructs that implement selection structures with many alternatives can become quite complex, and the correspondence among the `IF`s, `ELSE`s, and `END IF`s may not be clear, especially if the statements are not indented properly. A better format that clarifies the correspondence between `IF`s and `ELSE`s and also emphasizes that the statement implements a **multialternative selection structure** is an **IF-ELSE IF construct:**

IF-ELSE IF *Construct*

Form:

```
   IF (logical-expression₁) THEN
       statement-sequence₁
   ELSE IF (logical-expression₂) THEN
       statement-sequence₂
   ELSE IF (logical-expression₃) THEN
       statement-sequence₃
          ⋮
   ELSE
       statement-sequenceₙ
   END IF
```

where
   each *statement-sequenceᵢ* is a sequence of Fortran statements;
   and the ELSE clause is optional.

Purpose:
When an `IF-ELSE IF` construct is executed, the logical expressions are evaluated to determine the first expression that is true; the associated sequence of statements is executed, and execution then continues with the next statement following the construct (unless one of these statements transfers control elsewhere or terminates execution). If none of the logical expressions is true, the statement sequence associated with the `ELSE` statement is executed, and execution then continues with the statement following the construct (unless it is terminated or transferred to some other point by a statement in this block). This `IF` construct thus implements an *n*-way selection structure in which exactly one of *statement-sequence₁, statement-sequence₂, …, statement-sequenceₙ* is executed.

Example: Modified Pollution-Index Problem

As an example of an IF-ELSE IF construct, suppose that in the pollution-index problem of the preceding section, three air-quality conditions—good, fair, and poor—are to be used instead of two—safe and hazardous. Two cutoff values will be used, *LowCutoff* and *HighCutoff*, both in parts per million. A pollution index less than *LowCutoff* indicates a good condition; an index between *LowCutoff* and *HighCutoff* a fair condition; and an index greater than *HighCutoff* a poor condition. The following algorithm solves this problem.

ALGORITHM FOR MODIFIED POLLUTION-INDEX PROBLEM

This algorithm reads three pollution levels and then calculates a pollution index, which is the integer average of these three readings. If this index is less than a specified cutoff value, a message indicating a good condition is displayed; if it is between this cutoff value and a larger one, a message indicating a fair condition is displayed; and if the index is greater than the larger cutoff value, a message indicating a poor condition is displayed.

Input: *Level_1*, *Level_2*, *Level_3*

Constants: *LowCutoff* and *HighCutoff*

Output: The pollution *Index* and a message indicating the air quality

1. Enter *Level_1*, *Level_2*, and *Level_3*.

2. Calculate $Index = \dfrac{Level\_1 + Level\_2 + Level\_3}{3}$.

3. If *Index* < *LowCutoff* then
      Display "Good condition"
   Else if *Index* < *HighCutoff* then
      Display "Fair condition"
   Else
      Display "Poor condition"

The flowchart in Figure 3.7 that displays the structure of this algorithm clearly shows the three-way selection structure in step 3. The program in Figure 3.8 uses an IF-ELSE IF construct to implement this three-way selection structure.

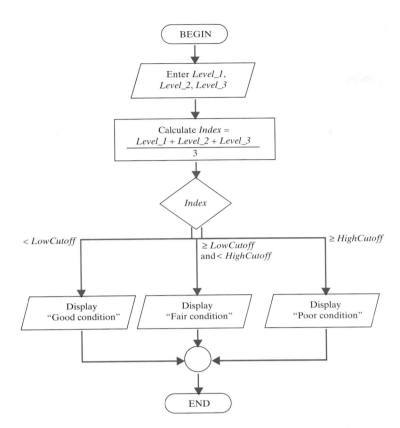

Figure 3.7

Flowchart for modified pollution-index problem.

Figure 3.8 Pollution index—version 2.

```
PROGRAM Pollution_2
!-------------------------------------------------------------------
! Program that reads 3 pollution levels, calculates a pollution
! index as their integer average, and then displays an appropriate
! air-quality message.   Identifiers used are:
!   Level_1, Level_2, Level_3 : the three pollution levels
!   LowCutoff, HighCutoff      : cutoff values that distinguish
!                                between good/fair, and fair/poor
!                                conditions, respectively
!   Index : the integer average of the pollution levels
!
! Input:      The three pollution levels
! Constants:  The two cutoff values
! Output:     The pollution index and a "good condition" message if
!             this index is less than LowCutoff, a "fair condition"
!             message if it is between LowCutoff and HighCutoff,
!             and a "poor condition" message otherwise
!-------------------------------------------------------------------
```

Figure 3.8 *(cont.)*

```
IMPLICIT NONE
INTEGER :: Level_1, Level_2, Level_3, Index
INTEGER, PARAMETER :: LowCutoff = 25, HighCutoff = 50

! Get the 3 pollution readings
PRINT *, "Enter 3 pollution readings (parts per million):"
READ *, Level_1, Level_2, Level_3

! Calculate the pollution index
Index = (Level_1 + Level_2 + Level_3) / 3

! Classify the pollution index and display an appropriate
! air-quality message
IF (Index < LowCutoff) THEN
   PRINT *, "Good condition"
ELSE IF (Index < HighCutoff) THEN
   PRINT *, "Fair condition"
ELSE
   PRINT *, "Poor condition"
END IF

END PROGRAM Pollution_2
```

Sample runs:

```
Enter 3 pollution readings (parts per million):
30, 40, 50
Fair condition

Enter 3 pollution readings (parts per million):
50, 60, 70
Poor condition

Enter 3 pollution readings (parts per million):
20, 21, 24
Good condition
```

Named Constructs

In Fortran 90, `IF` and `IF-ELSE IF` constructs may be named by attaching a label at the beginning and end of the construct so that it has the form

```
name: IF (logical-expression) THEN
        ⋮
      END IF name
```

for example,

```
Update: IF (X > Largest) THEN
   Largest = X
   Position = N
END IF Update
```

The purpose of this naming feature is to provide a way to clarify lengthy or complex constructs such as nested IFs in which there are several END IFs and it may not be clear which END IF corresponds to which IF. In this case it may be helpful to label corresponding IFs and END IFs; for example,

```
EmpType: IF (EmployeeType == "S") THEN    ! salaried employee
   PRINT *, "Enter employee's annual salary:"
   READ *, Salary
   Pay = Salary / 52
ELSE                                       ! hourly employee
   PRINT *, "Enter hours worked and hourly rate:"
   READ *, HoursWorked, HourlyRate
   Overtime: IF (HoursWorked > 40.0) THEN
      Pay = 40.0 * HourlyRate &
         + Multiplier * HourlyRate * (HoursWorked - 40.0)
      ELSE
         Pay = HoursWorked * HourlyRate
   END IF Overtime
END IF EmpType
```

The name used in an IF or IF-ELSE IF construct may also be attached following the keyword THEN in any ELSE IF part of the construct and following the keyword ELSE in an ELSE part; for example,

```
EmpType: IF (EmployeeType == "S") THEN    ! salaried employee
   PRINT *, "Enter employee's annual salary:"
   READ *, Salary
   Pay = Salary / 52
ELSE EmpType                               ! hourly employee
   PRINT *, "Enter hours worked and hourly rate:"
   READ *, HoursWorked, HourlyRate
   Overtime: IF (HoursWorked > 40.0) THEN
      Pay = 40.0 * HourlyRate &
         + Multiplier * HourlyRate * (HoursWorked - 40.0)
      ELSE Overtime
         Pay = HoursWorked * HourlyRate
   END IF Overtime
END IF EmpType
```

3.5   APPLICATION: FLUID FLOW IN A PIPE

Problem

The flow of fluid through a pipe is either laminar, turbulent, or unstable (switches between turbulent and laminar), depending on certain characteristics of the flow and the pipe. In laminar flow, the fluid travels the pipe in concentric layers, called *laminae*, with little mixing between the layers. Turbulent flow is much less structured, with considerable mixing.

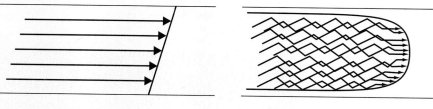

Laminar   Turbulent

Experiments have shown that a combination of four factors determines the type of flow. This dimensionless combination is referred to as the *Reynold's number*, N_R, and is given by

$$N_R = \frac{\rho \cdot V \cdot D}{\eta}$$

where

ρ is the density of the fluid

V is the average forward velocity for the fluid across the pipe

D is the diameter of the pipe

η is the viscosity

N_R is dimensionless and is therefore the same value in any consistent set of units. Since it is a ratio of density $\times$ velocity $\times$ diameter to viscosity, the less viscous the material (all other things being equal), the higher the Reynold's number and, therefore, the more turbulent the flow.

A program is needed to compute the Reynold's number and to determine whether the flow of a given fluid is laminar, turbulent, or unstable.

Solution

Specification. To solve the problem, we must know the density of the fluid, its average forward velocity, its viscosity, and the diameter of the pipe. The Reynold's number N_R can then be calculated. We must also know what cutoff values for N_R determine the type of flow; we will assume that these are constants for the problem. A solution to the problem consists of the Reynold's number and a message indicating the type of flow. This gives the following specification for the problem:

Input: The fluid's density, average forward velocity, and viscosity
            The diameter of the pipe

Constants: Cutoff values to distinguish between laminar, unstable, and turbulent flows

Output: Reynold's number
            Type of flow

The Great Alaska Pipeline near Delta, Alaska. (Photo courtesy of Charlie Ott/Photo Researchers, Inc.)

Design. An algorithm for this problem is very similar to that for the modified pollution-index problem in the preceding section. We will use the following identifiers:

IDENTIFIERS FOR FLOW PROBLEM

Density	Density of the fluid
Velocity	Average forward velocity of the fluid
Viscosity	Viscosity of the fluid
Diameter	Diameter of the pipe
ReynoldsNumber	Reynold's number
LowCutoff, HighCutoff	Cutoff values

ALGORITHM FOR FLOW PROBLEM

This algorithm reads the density, average forward velocity, and viscosity of a fluid and the diameter of the pipe through which it is flowing. The Reynold's number is calculated and the type of flow—laminar, unstable, turbulent—is then determined according to whether the Reynold's number is less than a lower cutoff value, is between two cutoff values, or is greater than the larger cutoff value.

Input: *Density, Velocity, Viscosity, Diameter*
Constants: *LowCutoff, HighCutoff*
Output: *ReynoldsNumber* and the type of flow

1. Enter *Density, Velocity, Viscosity,* and *Diameter*.

2. Calculate $ReynoldsNumber = \dfrac{Density \times Velocity \times Diameter}{Viscosity}$.

3. Display *ReynoldsNumber*.

4. If *ReynoldsNumber* < *LowCutoff* then
      Display "Flow is laminar"
   Else if *ReynoldsNumber* < *HighCutoff*
      Display "Flow is unstable"
   Else
      Display "Flow is turbulent"

Coding, Execution, and Testing. The program in Figure 3.9 implements the preceding algorithm. It was tested with several input values for which the results were easy to check. The sample run shown is for water at 20° C, where density is 1 g/cm^3 and viscosity is 0.01 dyne/cm^2.

Figure 3.9 Flow through a pipe.

```
PROGRAM Flow_Through_a_Pipe
!------------------------------------------------------------------
! Program that reads the density, average forward velocity, and
! viscosity of a fluid and the diameter of the pipe through which
! it is flowing.  The Reynold's number is calculated and the type
! of flow -- laminar, unstable, turbulent -- is then determined
! according to whether the Reynold's number is less than a lower
! cutoff value, is between two cutoff values, or is greater than
! the larger cutoff value. Identifiers used are:
!   Density, Viscosity    : density and viscosity of the fluid
!   Velocity              : average forward flow of the fluid
!   Diameter              : diameter of the pipe
!   LowCutoff, HighCutoff : cutoff values that distinguish between
!                                laminar/unstable and unstable/turbulent
!                                types of flow
!   ReynoldsNumber        : the Reynold's number
!
! Input:     Density, Viscosity, Velocity and  Diameter
! Constants: LowCutoff and HighCutoff
! Output:    ReynoldsNumber and a message indicating the type of flow
!------------------------------------------------------------------

  IMPLICIT NONE
  REAL :: Density, Viscosity, Velocity, Diameter, ReynoldsNumber
  REAL, PARAMETER :: LowCutoff = 2000.0, HighCutoff = 3000.0

  ! Get the density, velocity, viscosity, and diameter
  PRINT *, "Enter the density of the fluid:"
  READ *, Density
  PRINT *, "Enter the viscosity of the fluid:"
  READ *, Viscosity
  PRINT *, "Enter the average forward velocity of the fluid:"
  READ *, Velocity
  PRINT *, "Enter the diameter of the pipe:"
  READ *, Diameter

  ! Calculate the Reynold's number
  ReynoldsNumber = (Density * Velocity * Diameter) / Viscosity
```

Figure 3.9 *(cont.)*

```
! Display the input data, the Reynold's number, and a message
! indicating the type of flow
PRINT *, "For a fluid with density ", Density
PRINT *, "viscosity ", Viscosity
PRINT *, "and average forward velocity ", Velocity
PRINT *, "flowing through a pipe of diameter ", Diameter
PRINT *, "the Reynold's number is ", ReynoldsNumber
PRINT *

IF (ReynoldsNumber < LowCutoff) THEN
   PRINT *, "Flow is laminar"
ELSE IF (ReynoldsNumber < HighCutoff) THEN
   PRINT *, "Flow is unstable"
ELSE
   PRINT *, "Flow is turbulent"
END IF

END PROGRAM Flow_Through_a_Pipe
```

Sample Run:

```
Enter the density of the fluid:
1.0
Enter the viscosity of the fluid:
0.0125
Enter the average forward velocity of the fluid:
10.0
Enter the diameter of the pipe:
1.0
For a fluid with density     1.0000000
viscosity    1.2500000E-02
and average forward velocity   10.0000000
flowing through a pipe of diameter    1.0000000
the Reynold's number is     8.0000000E+02

Flow is laminar
```

Quick Quiz 3.5

For Questions 1–6, determine if each is a legal `IF` statement.

1. IF (A > B) PRINT *, A

2. IF B < C   N = N+1

3. IF (X <= Y) STOP

4. IF (A = X) READ *, Y

5. `IF (1 <= N <= 10) N = 10`   6. `IF (N > 1) PRINT *, "*"`

Questions 7–9 refer to the following `IF` construct:

```
IF (X >= Y) THEN
   PRINT *, X
ELSE
   PRINT *, Y
END IF
```

7. Describe the output produced if X = 5 and Y = 6.
8. Describe the output produced if X = 5 and Y = 5.
9. Describe the output produced if X = 6 and Y = 5.

Questions 10–12 refer to the following `IF` construct:

```
IF (X >= 0) THEN
   IF (Y >= 0) THEN
      PRINT *, X + Y
   ELSE
      PRINT *, X - Y
   END IF
ELSE
   PRINT *, Y - X
END IF
```

10. Describe the output produced if X = 5 and Y = 5.
11. Describe the output produced if X = 5 and Y = −5.
12. Describe the output produced if X = −5 and Y = 5.

Questions 13–17 refer to the following `IF` construct:

```
IF (N >= 90) THEN
   PRINT *, "Excellent"
ELSE IF (N >= 80)
   PRINT *, "Good"
ELSE IF (N >= 70)
   PRINT *, "Fair"
ELSE
   PRINT *, "Bad"
END IF
```

13. Describe the output produced if N = 100.
14. Describe the output produced if N = 90.

15. Describe the output produced if N = 89.

16. Describe the output produced if N = 70.

17. Describe the output produced if N = 0.

18. Write a statement that displays "Out of range" if Number is negative or greater than 100.

19. Write an efficient IF statement to assign N the value 1 if X ≤ 1.5, 2 if 1.5 < X < 2.5, and 3 otherwise.

Exercises 3.5

Exercises 1–4 refer to the following IF statement:

```
IF (X * Y >= 0) THEN
    PRINT *, "Yes"
ELSE
    PRINT *, "No"
END IF
```

1. Describe the output produced if X = 5 and Y = 6.

2. Describe the output produced if X = 5 and Y = −6.

3. Describe the output produced if X = −5 and Y = 6.

4. Describe the output produced if X = −5 and Y = −6.

Exercises 5–7 refer to the following IF statement:

```
IF (ABS(N) <= 4) THEN
    IF (N > 0) THEN
        PRINT *, 2*N + 1
    ELSE
        PRINT *, 2*N
    END IF
ELSE
    PRINT *,  N, "out of range"
END IF
```

5. Describe the output produced if N = 2.

6. Describe the output produced if N = −7.

7. Describe the output produced if N = 0.

For Exercises 8–11, write Fortran statements that will do what is required.

8. If Code = 1, read X and Y and calculate and print the sum of X and Y.

9. If A is strictly between 0 and 5, set B equal to $1/A^2$; otherwise set B equal to A^2.

10. Display the message "Leap year" if the integer variable Year is the number of a leap year. (A leap year is a multiple of 4; and if it is a multiple of 100, it must also be a multiple of 400.)

11. Assign a value to Cost corresponding to the value of Distance given in the following table:

Distance	Cost
0 through 100	5.00
More than 100 but not more than 500	8.00
More than 500 but less than 1000	10.00
1000 or more	12.00

For Exercises 12–15, write an IF construct to evaluate the given function.

12. The output of a simple d-c generator; the shape of the curve is the absolute value of the sine function. (100 V is the maximum voltage.)

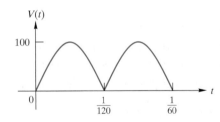

13. A rectified half-wave; the curve is a sine function for half the cycle and zero for the other half. (Maximum current is 5 amp.)

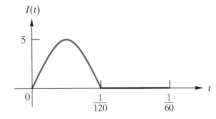

14. Sawtooth; the graph consists of two straight lines. The maximum voltage of 100 V occurs at the middle of the cycle.

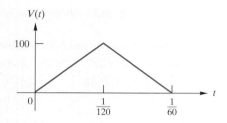

15. The excess pressure $p(t)$ in a sound wave whose graph is as follows:

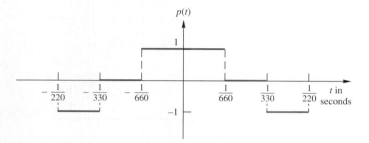

3.6   THE CASE CONSTRUCT

In the preceding sections we saw that an IF-ELSE IF construct can be used to implement a selection structure in which exactly one of several alternative actions is selected and performed. In this construct, the selection is made by evaluating one or more logical expressions, and because selection criteria can usually be formulated as logical expressions, an IF-ELSE IF construct can be used to implement almost any multialternative selection structure. In this section we describe the CASE construct, which, although it is not as general as the IF-ELSE IF construct, is useful for implementing some selection structures.

A CASE construct has the following form:

CASE *Construct*

Form:

```
SELECT CASE (selector)
   CASE (label-list₁)
      statement-sequence₁
   CASE (label-list₂)
      statement-sequence₂
      ⋮
   CASE (label-listₙ)
      statement-sequenceₙ
END SELECT
```

where
> the *selector* is an integer, character, or logical expression;
> each of the (*label-list_i*) is a list of one or more possible values of the selector, enclosed in parentheses, or is the word DEFAULT;
> the values in this list may have any of the forms

```
value
value₁ : value₂
value₁ :
      : value₂
```

> to denote a single *value*, the range of values from *value₁* through *value₂*, the set of all values greater than or equal to *value₁*, or the set of all values less than or equal to *value₂*, respectively.

Purpose:

When this CASE construct is executed, the selector is evaluated; if this value is in *label-list_i*, *statement-sequence_i* is executed, and execution continues with the statement following the END SELECT statement. If the value is not in any of the lists of values, the sequence of statements associated with DEFAULT is executed, if there is such a statement sequence, and continues with the statement following the CASE construct otherwise.

Examples of CASE Constructs

As an illustration of a CASE construct, consider the problem of displaying the class name (Freshman, Sophomore, Junior, Senior, Graduate) that corresponds to a numeric class code (1, 2, 3, 4, 5): The following CASE construct can be used to do this:

```
SELECT CASE (ClassCode)
    CASE (1)
        PRINT *, "Freshman"
    CASE (2)
        PRINT *, "Sophomore"
    CASE (3)
        PRINT *, "Junior"
    CASE (4)
        PRINT *, "Senior"
    CASE (5)
        PRINT *, "Graduate"
    CASE DEFAULT
        PRINT *, "Illegal class code", ClassCode
END SELECT
```

Note the use of the CASE DEFAULT statement to display an error message in case the value of the selector ClassCode is none of 1, 2, 3, 4, or 5. Although this CASE DEFAULT statement can be placed anywhere in the list of a CASE statement, it is customary to place it at the end.

The selector may also be a character or logical expression. For example, the following CASE construct performs the conversions of the preceding example in the reverse direction:

```
SELECT CASE (ClassName)
   CASE ("Freshman")
      ClassCode = 1
   CASE ("Sophomore")
      ClassCode = 2
   CASE ("Junior")
      ClassCode = 3
   CASE ("Senior")
      ClassCode = 4
   CASE ("Graduate")
      ClassCode = 5
   CASE DEFAULT
      PRINT *, "Illegal class name: ", ClassName
END SELECT
```

Ranges of values may also be used in the CASE label lists. For example, suppose we want to assign a letter grade to a student's average, as specified in the following table:

Average	Letter Grade
Average $\geq$ 90	A
80 $\leq$ average $<$ 90	B
70 $\leq$ average $<$ 80	C
60 $\leq$ average $<$ 70	D
Average $<$ 60	F

If Average is a real value, we can use the following CASE construct to implement this five-way selection structure:

```
SELECT CASE (INT(Average))
   CASE (90:)
      Grade = "A"
   CASE (80:89)
      Grade = "B"
   CASE (70:79)
      Grade = "C"
```

```
      CASE (60:69)
         Grade = "D"
      CASE (:59)
         Grade = "F"
   END SELECT
```

Note that the real quantity `Average` is converted to integer type by using the `INT` function so that it can be used as a selector in a `CASE` construct. Also note the use of `90:` to indicate values of 90 and above for the selector expression `INT(Average)` and `:59` to indicate values of 59 and below.

Named CASE Constructs

Like `IF` and `IF-ELSE IF` constructs, a name may be attached to a `CASE` construct:

```
name: SELECT CASE (selector)
         ⋮
END SELECT name
```

For example,

```
Class: SELECT CASE (ClassCode)
    CASE (1)
       PRINT *, "Freshman"
    CASE (2)
       PRINT *, "Sophomore"
    CASE (3)
       PRINT *, "Junior"
    CASE (4)
       PRINT *, "Senior"
    CASE (5)
       PRINT *, "Graduate"
     CASE DEFAULT
        PRINT *, "Illegal class code", Class code
END SELECT Class
```

3.7 APPLICATION: POLLUTION INDICES REVISITED

In Sections 3.3 and 3.4 we considered the problem of classifying a pollution index, computed as the integer average of three pollution readings. The program in Figure 3.8 used the following `IF-ELSE IF` construct to select the appropriate pollution condition (good, fair, poor) determined by the pollution `Index`:

```
                        IF (Index < LowCutoff) THEN
                            PRINT *, "Good condition"
                        ELSE IF (Index < HighCutoff) THEN
                            PRINT *, "Fair condition"
                        ELSE
                            PRINT *, "Poor condition"
                        END IF
```

A CASE construct can also be used to carry out this classification, as shown in
the program in Figure 3.10. This program is a modification of that in Figure 3.8 that
results from replacing the preceding IF–ELSE IF construct by a CASE construct.

Figure 3.10 Pollution indices—version 3.

```
PROGRAM Pollution_3
!-----------------------------------------------------------------
! Program that reads 3 pollution levels, calculates a pollution
! index as their integer average, and then displays an appropriate
! air-quality message.    Identifiers used are:
!    Level_1, Level_2, Level_3 : the three pollution levels
!    LowCutoff, HighCutoff      : cutoff values that distinguish
!                                 between good/fair, and fair/poor
!                                 conditions, respectively
!    Index : the integer average of the pollution levels
!
! Input:      The three pollution levels
! Constants:  The two cutoff values
! Output:     The pollution index and a "good condition" message if
!             this index is less than LowCutoff, a "fair condition"
!             message if it is between LowCutoff and HighCutoff,
!             and a "poor condition" message otherwise
!-----------------------------------------------------------------

  IMPLICIT NONE
  INTEGER :: Level_1, Level_2, Level_3, Index
  INTEGER, PARAMETER :: LowCutoff = 25, HighCutoff = 50

  ! Get the 3 pollution readings
  PRINT *, "Enter 3 pollution readings (parts per million):"
  READ *, Level_1, Level_2, Level_3

  ! Calculate the pollution index
  Index = (Level_1 + Level_2 + Level_3) / 3
```

Figure 3.10 *(cont.)*

```
! Classify the pollution index and display an appropriate
! air-quality message
SELECT CASE (Index )
   CASE (:LowCutoff - 1)
      PRINT *, "Good condition"
   CASE (LowCutoff : HighCutoff - 1)
      PRINT *, "Fair condition"
   CASE (HighCutoff:)
      PRINT *, "Poor condition"
END SELECT

END PROGRAM Pollution_3
```

Quick Quiz 3.7

Assume that Code is an integer variable, Name is a character variable, and X is a real variable.

1. If Number has the value 99, tell what output is produced by the following CASE construct, or indicate why an error occurs:

   ```
   SELECT CASE(Number)
     CASE DEFAULT
       PRINT *, "default"
     CASE (99)
       PRINT *, Number + 99
     CASE (-1)
       PRINT *, Number - 1
   END SELECT
   ```

2. As in 1, but for Number $= -1$.

3. As in 1, but for Number $= 50$.

4. If the value of Code is the letter B, tell what output is produced by the following CASE construct, or indicate why an error occurs:

   ```
   SELECT CASE (Code)
     CASE ("A", "B")
       PRINT *, 123
     CASE ("P" : "Z")
       PRINT *, 456
   END SELECT
   ```

5. As in 4, but suppose the value of Code is the letter Q.

6. As in 4, but suppose the value of Code is the letter M.

7. If the value of X is 2.0, tell what output is produced by the following CASE construct, or indicate why an error occurs:

```
SELECT CASE (X)
   CASE (1.0)
      PRINT *, X + 1.0
   CASE (2.0)
      PRINT *, X + 2.0
END SELECT
```

Exercises 3.7

1. Write a CASE construct that increases Balance by adding Amount to it if the value of the character variable TransCode is D; decrease Balance by subtracting Amount from it if TransCode is W; display the value of Balance if TransCode is P; and display an illegal-transaction message otherwise.

2. Write a CASE construct to assign a value to Cost corresponding to the value of Distance given in the following table:

Distance	Cost
0 through 100	5.00
More than 100 but not more than 500	8.00
More than 500 but less than 1000	10.00
1000 or more	12.00

3. Write a CASE construct to display the name of a month or an error message for a given value of the integer variable Month. Display an error message if the value of Month is less than 1 or greater than 12.

4. Proceed as in 3, but display the number of days in a month. (See Exercise 10 of Section 3.5 regarding the determination of leap years.)

5. Proceed as in 4, but assume that Month is a character variable whose value is the name of month.

3.8 THE LOGICAL DATA TYPE

Recall that there are two **logical constants** in Fortran,

```
.TRUE.
```

and

```
.FALSE.
```

(Note the periods that must appear as part of these logical constants.) A **logical variable** is declared using a LOGICAL type statement of the form

```
LOGICAL :: list
```

where `list` is a list of variables being typed as logical. Like all type statements, this type statement must appear in the specification part of the program. For example,

```
LOGICAL :: RootExists, End_of_Data
```

declares that RootExists and End_of_Data are logical variables.

An assignment statement of the form

```
logical-variable = logical-expression
```

can be used to assign a value to a logical variable. Thus,

```
End_of_Data = .TRUE.
```

is a valid assignment statement; it assigns the value .TRUE. to End_of_Data. Likewise,

```
RootExists = Discriminant >= 0
```

is a valid assignment statement and assigns .TRUE. to RootExists if Discriminant is nonnegative and assigns .FALSE. otherwise.

Logical values can be displayed using list-directed output. A logical value is displayed as only a T or an F, usually preceded by a space. For example, if A, B, and C are logical variables that are true, false, and false, respectively, the statement

```
PRINT *, A, B, C, .TRUE., .FALSE.
```

produces

```
T F F T F
```

as output.

Logical values can also be read using list-directed input. In this case, the input values consist of optional blanks followed by an optional period followed by T or F, which may be followed by other characters. The value .TRUE. or .FALSE. is assigned to the corresponding variable according to whether the first letter encountered is T or F. For example, for the statements

```
LOGICAL :: A, B, C
READ *, A, B, C
```

the following data could be entered:

```
.T., F, .FALSE
```

The values assigned to A, B, and C would be .TRUE., .FALSE., and .FALSE., respectively. This would also be the case if the following data were entered:

```
.T., FALL, .FLASE
```

In the next section we consider the design of logical circuits. The program in Figure 3.10 that models a circuit for a binary half-adder uses logical variables A and B to represent inputs to the circuit and logical variables Sum and Carry to represent the outputs produced by the circuit.

3.9 APPLICATION: LOGICAL CIRCUITS

Problem

Addition of binary digits is defined by the following table:

+	0	1
0	0	1
1	1	10

We wish to design a program to model a logical circuit, called a **binary half-adder,** that implements this operation.

Solution

Specification.   The input in this problem consists of two binary digits. Adding two bits produces a sum bit and a carry bit whose values are given by

Inputs	Carry bit	Sum bit
0 0	0	0
0 1	0	1
1 0	0	1
1 1	1	0

Thus the input/output specification for this problem is as follows:

Input: Two binary digits to be added

Output: A sum bit and a carry bit that result from adding the inputs

Design.   Arithmetic operations are implemented in computer hardware by logical circuits. The following circuit is a binary half-adder that adds two binary digits:

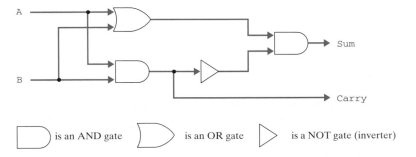

It contains four basic electronic components called **gates**: two AND gates, one OR gate, and one NOT gate (also called an *inverter*). The inputs to these gates are pulses of current applied to the lines leading into the gates, and the outputs are pulses of current on the lines emanating from the gates. In the case of an AND gate, an output pulse is produced only if there are pulses on both input lines. An OR gate produces an output pulse only if there is an input pulse on at least one of the input lines. A NOT gate is designed to produce an output pulse only when there is no incoming pulse.

If we associate the logical expression "a pulse is present" with each line, that is, if we interpret true as the presence of a pulse and false as the absence of a pulse, then logical expressions can be used to represent the outputs produced by a logical circuit. In circuit design, $+$ is used to denote OR, $\cdot$ to denote AND, and an overbar to denote NOT. Using this notation, we can represent the output *Sum* in the circuit for a binary half-adder by

$$Sum = (A + B) \cdot \overline{(A \cdot B)}$$

and the output *Carry* by

$$Carry = A \cdot B$$

The values of these logical expressions are displayed in the following truth table:

A	B	Carry	Sum
true	true	true	false
true	false	false	true
false	true	false	true
false	false	false	false

If we interpret false as the binary digit 0 and true as the binary digit 1, we see that this truth table corresponds to the table for the sum and carry bits given earlier in the problem's specification.

For this problem we will use the following variable names:

VARIABLES FOR THE LOGICAL CIRCUIT PROBLEM

A, B   Input bits

Sum, Carry   The sum and carry bits produced when *A* and *B* are added

An algorithm for solving the problem is simple:

ALGORITHM FOR LOGICAL CIRCUIT PROBLEM

This algorithm determines the sum and carry bits produced by a binary half-adder.

Input: *A, B*
Output: *Sum, Carry*

1. Enter *A* and *B*.
2. Calculate *Sum* = $(A + B) \cdot \overline{(A \cdot B)}$.
3. Calculate *Carry* = $A \cdot B$.
4. Display *Sum* and *Carry*.

Coding. The program in Figure 3.11 implements the preceding algorithm, using logical variables A, B, Sum, and Carry. The logical expressions for Sum and Carry,

$$Sum = (A + B) \cdot \overline{(A \cdot B)}$$

$$Carry = A \cdot B$$

are implemented by the Fortran logical expressions

```
Sum = (A .OR. B) .AND. .NOT. (A .AND. B)
Carry = A .AND. B
```

Figure 3.11 A binary half-adder.

```
PROGRAM Half_Adder
!------------------------------------------------------------------
! Program to calculate the outputs from a logical circuit that
! represents a binary half-adder.  Variables used are:
!    A, B        : the two logical inputs to the circuit
!    Sum, Carry : the two logical outputs
!
! Input:    The two logical inputs A and B
! Output:   The two logical outputs Sum and Carry, which represent the
!           sum and carry that result when the input values are added
!------------------------------------------------------------------

  IMPLICIT NONE
  LOGICAL :: A, B, Sum, Carry

  PRINT *, "Enter logical inputs A and B:"
  READ *, A, B
  Sum = (A .OR. B) .AND. .NOT. (A .AND. B)
  Carry = A .AND. B
  PRINT *, "Carry, Sum =", Carry, Sum

END PROGRAM Half_Adder
```

Execution and Testing. The following sample runs show the outputs produced for each possible combination of logical values for the two inputs:

```
Enter logical inputs A and B:
T T
Carry, Sum = T F
```

```
Enter logical inputs A and B:
T F
Carry, Sum = F T

Enter logical inputs A and B:
F T
Carry, Sum = F T

Enter logical inputs A and B:
F F
Carry, Sum = F F
```

Note that if we identify the binary digits 0 and 1 with false and true, respectively, the program's output can be interpreted as a demonstration that $1 + 1 = 10$ ($\text{Sum} = 0$, $\text{Carry} = 1$), $1 + 0 = 01$, $0 + 1 = 01$, and $0 + 0 = 00$. This program, therefore, correctly implements binary addition of one-bit numbers.

Quick Quiz 3.9

True or false:

1. If Okay is a logical variable, the statement Okay = FALSE will set it to false.

2. If Okay is a logical variable and Code has the value 6128, then the statement Okay = (Code = 6128) will set Okay to true.

3. If Okay is a logical variable and Alpha has the value 5, then the statement Okay = 1 < Alpha < 7 will set Okay to true.

4. If Okay is a logical variable and the character variable Logic has the value ".TRUE.", then the statement Okay = Logic will set Okay to true.

For Questions 5–7, assume that Okay, Here, and There are logical variables and that Here and There have been set to true.

5. Okay = .NOT. Here .AND. .NOT. There will set Okay to true.

6. Okay = .NOT. (Here .OR. There) will set Okay to true.

7. Okay = Here .AND. .NOT. .NOT. There will set Okay to true.

8. If the logical variable Okay has been set to true, then the statement PRINT *, Okay will display .TRUE..

9. FALSE, .FALSE., and FALLS are all legal input values for a logical variable in a READ statement.

10. If Fred T. Tarantula is input for the statement READ *, P, Q, R, the logical variables P, Q, and R will become false, true, and true, respectively.

11. Write statements to declare `Larger` to be a logical variable and to set it to true if the value of A is greater than the value of B and to false otherwise.

12. Write statements to declare logical variables `FreshPerson` and `UpperclassPerson`, to set `FreshPerson` to true if the value of `Class` is 1 and to false otherwise, and to set `UpperclassPerson` to false if the value of `Class` is 1 and to true otherwise.

Exercises 3.9

In Exercises 1–9, assume that M and N are integer variables with the values −2 and 5, respectively, and that X, Y, and Z are real variables with the values −1.99, 5.5, and 9.99, respectively. Find the value assigned to the logical variable Okay, or indicate why an error occurs.

1. `Okay = M <= N`

2. `Okay = 2 * ABS(M) <= 8`

3. `Okay = X * X < SQRT(Z)`

4. `Okay = NINT(Z) == (6 * N - 3)`

5. `Okay = Okay .AND. (N == 6)`

6. `Okay = .NOT. (X < Y)`

7. `Okay = .NOT. ((M <= N) .AND. (X + Z > Y))`

8. `Okay = .NOT. (M <= N) .OR. .NOT. (X + Z > Y)`

9. `Okay = .NOT. ((M > N) .OR. (X < Z)) .EQV. &`
   `((M <= N) .AND. (X >= Z))`

For Exercises 10–17, write an assignment statement that will set the logical variable Okay to true if the condition is true and to false otherwise.

10. X is strictly between 0 and 10.

11. X and Y are both positive.

12. X and Y are both negative, or both are positive.

13. $-1 \leq X < 1$.

14. X is neither less than 0 nor greater than 100.

15. W, X, Y, and Z are all equal to each other.

16. W, X, Y, and Z are in increasing order.

17. X is greater than 10, or Y is greater than 10, but not both.

18. A *binary full-adder* has three inputs: the two bits A and B being added and a "carry-in" bit C_In (representing the carry bit that results from adding the bits

to the right of A and B in two binary numbers). It can be constructed from two binary half-adders and an OR gate:

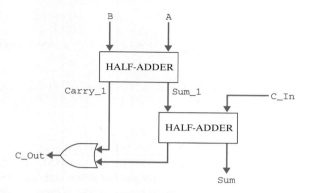

Assuming that Sum_1, Carry_1, Sum, and C_Out have been declared to be logical variables, and that values have been assigned to the inputs A, B, and C_In, write assignment statements to assign values to

(a) Sum_1 and Carry_1

(b) Sum and C_Out (assuming that values have already been assigned to Sum_1 and Carry_1)

19. An *adder* to calculate binary sums of two-bit numbers

```
       A2  A1
    +  B2  B1
   ──────────────
 C_Out  S2  S1
```

where S1 and S2 are the sum bits and C_Out is the carry-out bit, can be constructed from a binary half-adder and a binary full-adder:

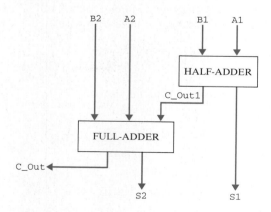

Assuming that S1, S2, C_Out1, and C_Out have been declared to be logical variables, and that values have been assigned to the inputs A1, A2, B1, and B2, write statements to assign values to

(a) S1 and C_Out1

(b) S2 and C_Out (assuming that values have already been assigned to S1 and C_Out1)

CHAPTER REVIEW

Summary

This focus of this chapter was selective execution, the second of the three basic control structures used in writing programs. In selective execution, the action selected is determined by the value of a logical expression; thus the chapter began with a study of logical expressions, both simple and compound. Simple logical expressions are formed using the relational operators <, >, ==, /=, <=, and >=, and compound expressions are formed by using the logical operators .NOT., .AND., .OR., .EQV., and .NEQV.. Selective execution is implemented in Fortran using IF constructs and CASE constructs, the various forms of which are described in detail and illustrated in this chapter. In the last two sections we describe the LOGICAL data type and illustrate its use in the design of logical circuits.

FORTRAN SUMMARY

Relational Operators

Symbol	Meaning
< or .LT.	Is less than
> or .GT.	Is greater than
== or .EQ.	Is equal to
<= or .LE.	Is less than or equal to
>= or .GE.	Is greater than or equal to
/= or .NE.	Is not equal to

Logical Operators

.NOT.
.AND.
.OR.
.EQV.
.NEQV.

Logical Expressions

Logical constants (.TRUE. and .FALSE.)
Logical variables
Simple logical expressions of the form

```
expression₁  relational-operator  expression₂
```

where the expressions are both numeric or character or logical expressions
Compound logical expressions of the form

```
.NOT. logical-expr
```

or

```
logical-expr₁ logical-operator logical-expr₂
```

where *logical-expr₁* and *logical-expr₂* are logical expressions and the *logical-operator* is a binary logical operator (.AND., .OR., .EQV., .NEQV.)

Block IF Statement

```
IF (logical-expression) THEN
    statement-sequence₁
ELSE
    statement-sequence₂
END IF
```

where the ELSE part is optional.

Examples:

```
IF (X > 0) THEN
   PRINT *, X
   Y = SQRT(X)
   PRINT *, Y
ELSE
   PRINT *, "X is negative or zero"
END IF


IF (Count == 0) THEN
   PRINT *, "No data values were processed"
END IF
```

Purpose:

If the logical expression is true, *statement-sequence*$_1$ is executed and *statement-sequence*$_2$ is bypassed; otherwise *statement-sequence*$_1$ is bypassed and *statement-sequence*$_2$ is executed, unless the ELSE part is omitted. In either case, execution continues with the next statement in the program (unless it is terminated or control is transferred elsewhere by one of the statements in the statement sequence selected).

Logical IF Statement

```
IF (logical-expression) statement
```

Example:

```
IF (Count == 0) PRINT *, "No data values were processed"
```

Purpose:

If the logical expression is true, *statement* is executed; otherwise, it is bypassed.

IF-ELSE IF Construct

```
IF (logical-expression₁) THEN
    statement-sequence₁
ELSE IF (logical-expression₂) THEN
    statement-sequence₂
ELSE IF (logical-expression₃) THEN
    statement-sequence₃
        ⋮
ELSE
    statement-sequenceₙ
END IF
```

Example:

```
IF (Index < LowCutoff) THEN
    PRINT *, "Good condition"
ELSE IF (Index < HighCutoff) THEN
    PRINT *, "Fair condition"
ELSE
    PRINT *, "Poor condition"
END IF
```

Purpose:

The logical expressions are evaluated to determine the first expression that is true; the associated sequence of statements is executed; if none of the logical expressions is true, the statement sequence in the ELSE statement is executed. Execution then continues with the next statement following the construct (unless one of these statements transfers control elsewhere or terminates execution).

CASE Construct

```
SELECT CASE (selector)
    CASE (label-list₁)
        statement-sequence₁
    CASE (label-list₂)
        statement-sequence₂
        ⋮
    CASE (label-listₙ)
        statement-sequenceₙ
END SELECT
```

where $selector$ is an integer, character, or logical expression; each $label$-$list_i$ is a list of one or more possible values of the selector having one of the following forms,

```
value
value₁ : value₂
value₁ :
: value₂
```

or is the word DEFAULT. These forms denote a single $value$, the range of values from $value_1$ through $value_2$, all values greater than or equal to $value_1$, and all values less than or equal to $value_2$, respectively.

Example:

```
SELECT CASE (Index)
    CASE (:LowCutoff - 1)
        PRINT *, "Good condition"
    CASE (LowCutoff : HighCutoff - 1)
        PRINT *, "Fair condition"
    CASE (HighCutoff:)
        PRINT *, "Bad condition"
END SELECT
```

Purpose:
If the value of $selector$ is in $label$-$list_i$, $statement$-$sequence_i$ is executed, and execution continues with the statement following the END SELECT statement. If the value is not in any $label$-$list_i$, the sequence of statements as-

sociated with DEFAULT is executed, if there is such a statement sequence, and continues with the statement following the CASE construct otherwise.

LOGICAL Type Statement

```
LOGICAL :: list-of-variable-names
```

Example:

```
LOGICAL :: End_of_Data, Sorted
```

Purpose:
Declares identifiers to be of LOGICAL type.

PROGRAMMING POINTERS

Program Style and Design

1. *All programs can be written using the three basic control structures: sequential, selection, and repetition.*
2. *The statement sequence(s) within IF and CASE constructs should be indented; for example,*

```
IF (logical-expression)
    statement₁
       ⋮
    statementₙ
ELSE
    statementₙ₊₁
       ⋮
    statementₘ
END IF
```

3. *Multialternative selection structures can be implemented more efficiently with an IF-ELSE IF construct than with a sequence of IF statements.* For example, using the statements

```
IF (Score >= 90) Grade = "A"
IF ((Score >= 80) .AND. (Score < 90)) Grade = "B"
IF ((Score >= 70) .AND. (Score < 80)) Grade = "C"
IF ((Score >= 60) .AND. (Score < 70)) Grade = "D"
IF (Score < 60) Grade = "F"
```

is less efficient than using

```
IF (Score >= 90) THEN
    Grade = "A"
ELSE IF (Score >= 80) THEN
    Grade = "B"
ELSE IF (Score >= 70) THEN
    Grade = "C"
ELSE IF (Score >= 60) THEN
    Grade = "D"
ELSE
    Grade = "F"
END IF
```

In the first case, all of the IF statements are executed for each score processed, and three of the logical expressions are compound expressions. In the second case, each logical expression is simple, and not all of the expressions are evaluated for each score; for example, for a score of 85, only the logical expressions Score >= 90 and Score >= 80 are evaluated.

4. *Multialternative selection statements of the form*

```
IF (variable == constant₁)
    statement-sequence₁
ELSE IF (variable == constant₂)
    statement-sequence₂
         ⋮
ELSE IF (variable == constantₙ)
    statement-sequenceₙ
ELSE
    statement-sequenceₙ₊₁
```

in which each variable$_i$ *and* constant$_i$ *is of integer, character, or logical type, are usually implemented more efficiently using a* CASE *construct:*

```
SELECT CASE(variable)
{
    CASE (constant₁)
        statement-sequence₁
    CASE (constant₂)
        statement-sequence₂
             ⋮
    CASE (constantₙ)
        statement-sequenceₙ
    CASE DEFAULT
        statement-sequenceₙ₊₁
}
```

For example, we might write the code segment in 3 even more efficiently as follows:

```
SELECT CASE (Score)
    CASE (90:)
        Grade = "A"
    CASE (80:89)
        Grade = "B"
    CASE (70:79)
        Grade = "C"
    CASE (60:69)
        Grade = "D"
    CASE (:59)
        Grade = "F"
END SELECT
```

Potential Problems

1. *Periods must be used in the logical operators* .NOT., .AND., .OR., .EQV., *and* .NEQV..

2. *Parentheses must enclose the logical expression in an* IF *construct or in a logical* IF *statement.*

3. *Parentheses must enclose the selector and each label-list in a* CASE *construct.*

4. *Real quantities that are algebraically equal may yield a false logical expression when compared with* == *because most real values are not stored exactly.* For example, even though the two real expressions X * (1.0 / X) and 1.0 are algebraically equal, the logical expression X * (1.0 / X) == 1.0 is usually false. Thus, if two real values RealNumber_1 and RealNumber_2 are subject to roundoff error, it is usually not advisable to check whether they are equal. It is better to check whether the absolute value of their difference is small:

```
IF (ABS(RealNumber_1 - RealNumber_2) < Tolerance) THEN
                        ⋮
```

where Tolerance is some small positive real value such as 1E-6.

5. *Each* IF *construct (but not logical* IF *statements) must be closed with an* END IF *statement.*

6. *Each* CASE *construct must be closed with an* END SELECT *statement.*

7. *It should be assumed that all subexpressions are evaluated when determining the value of a compound logical expression.* Suppose, for example, that we write an IF construct of the form

```
IF ((X >= 0) .AND. (SQRT(X) < 5.0)) THEN
    PRINT *, "Square root is less than 5"
                    ⋮
END IF
```

in which the subexpression X >= 0 is intended to prevent an attempt to calculate the square root of a negative number when X is negative. Some compilers may evaluate the subexpression X >= 0 and, if it is false, not evaluate the second subexpression, SQRT(X) < 5.0. Other compilers evaluate both parts, and thus an error results when X is negative. This error can be avoided by rewriting the construct as

```
IF (X >= 0) THEN
    IF (SQRT(X) < 5.0) THEN
        PRINT *, "Square root is less than 5"
            ⋮

    END IF
END IF
```

PROGRAMMING PROBLEMS

Section 3.4

1. Write a program to read one of the codes "C" for circle, "S" for square, or "T" for equilateral triangle, and a number representing the radius of the circle, the side of the square, or the side of the triangle, respectively. Then calculate and display the area and the perimeter of that geometric figure with appropriate labels. (See Programming Problems 3 and 5 in Chapter 2.)

2. Modify the program in Figure 3.2 for solving quadratic equations so that when the discriminant is negative, the complex roots of the equation are displayed. If the discriminant D is negative, these roots are given by

$$\frac{-B \pm \sqrt{-D}\, i}{2A}$$

where $i^2 = -1$.

3. Write a program that reads values for the coefficients A, B, C, D, E, and F of the equations

$$Ax + By = C$$

$$Dx + Ey = F$$

of two straight lines. Then determine whether the lines are parallel (their slopes are equal) or the lines intersect. If they intersect, determine whether the lines are perpendicular (the product of their slopes is equal to -1).

4. Write a program that reads the coordinates of three points and then determines whether they are collinear.

5. Suppose the following formulas give the safe loading L in pounds per square inch for a column with slimness ratio S:

$$
L = \begin{cases}
16500 - .475S^2 & \text{if } S < 100 \\[2mm]
\dfrac{17900}{2 + (S^2/17900)} & \text{if } S \geq 100
\end{cases}
$$

Write a program that reads a slimness ratio and then calculates the safe loading.

6. Suppose that a gas company bases its charges on consumption according to the following table:

Gas Used	Rate
First 70 cubic meters	$5.00 minimum cost
Next 100 cubic meters	5.0¢ per cubic meter
Next 230 cubic meters	2.5¢ per cubic meter
Above 400 cubic meters	1.5¢ per cubic meter

Meters readings are four-digit numbers that represent cubic meters. Write a program in which the meter reading for the previous month and the current meter reading are entered and then the amount of the bill is calculated. *Note*: The current reading may be less than the previous one; for example, the previous reading may have been 9897, and the current one is 0103.

Section 3.5

7. Write a program that reads a cutoff value and then finds the average forward velocity for water at 20° C (density = 1 g/cm^3 and viscosity = 0.01 dyne/cm^2) flowing in a 1 cm pipe so that N_R is equal to this cutoff value. Execute the program with the following values:
   (a) 2000.0, the cutoff between laminar and unstable flow in Figure 3.9.
   (b) 3000.0, the cutoff between unstable and turbulent flow in Figure 3.9.

Section 3.7

8. Proceed as in Problem 6 but use a CASE construct to determine the applicable rate.

9. Write a program that reads numbers representing TV channels and then uses a CASE construct to determine the call letters of the station that correspond to each number or some message indicating that the channel is not used. Use the following channel numbers and call letters (or use those that are available in your locale):

   2: WCBS
   4: WNBC
   5: WNEW
   7: WABC

9: WOR
11: WPIX
13: WNET

10. A computer supply company discounts the price of each of its products depending on the number of units bought and the price per unit. The discount increases as the numbers of units bought and/or the unit price increases. These discounts are given in the following table:

Number Bought	Unit Price (dollars)		
	0–10.00	10.01–100.00	100.01–
1–9	0%	2%	5%
10–19	5%	7%	9%
20–49	9%	15%	21%
50–99	14%	23%	32%
100–	21%	32%	43%

Write a program that reads the number of units bought and the unit price and then calculates and prints the total full cost, the total amount of the discount, and the total discounted cost.

11. Locating avenues' addresses in mid-Manhattan is not easy; for example, the nearest cross street to 866 Third Avenue is 53rd Street, whereas the nearest cross street to 866 Second Avenue is 46th Street. To locate approximately the nearest numbered cross street for a given avenue address, the following algorithm can be used:

Cancel the last digit of the address, divide by 2, and add or subtract the number given in the following (abbreviated) table:

1st Ave.	Add 3
2nd Ave.	Add 3
3rd Ave.	Add 10
4th Ave.	Add 8
5th Ave. up to 200	Add 13
5th Ave. 200 up to 400	Add 16
6th Ave. (Ave. of the Americas)	Subtract 12
7th Ave.	Add 12
8th Ave.	Add 10
10th Ave.	Add 14

Write a program that reads an avenue address and then uses a CASE construct to determine the number of the nearest cross street, according to the preceding algorithm.

12. An airline vice president in charge of operations needs to determine whether or not the current estimates of flight times are accurate. Since there is a larger possibility of variations due to weather and air traffic in the longer flights, he allows a larger error in the time estimates for them. He compares an actual flight time with the estimated flight time and considers the estimate to be too large, acceptable, or too small, depending on the following table of acceptable error margins:

Estimated Flight Time in Minutes	Acceptable Error Margin in Minutes
0–29	1
30–59	2
60–89	3
90–119	4
120–179	6
180–239	8
240–359	13
360–	17

For example, if an estimated flight time is 106 minutes, the acceptable error margin is 4 minutes. Thus, the estimated flight time is too large if the actual flight time is less than 102 minutes, or the estimated flight time is too small if the actual flight time is greater than 110 minutes; otherwise, the estimate is acceptable. Write a program that reads an estimated flight time and an actual flight time, uses a CASE construct to determine the acceptable error according to this table, and then prints whether the estimated time is too large, acceptable, or too small. If the estimated flight time is either too large or too small, the program should also print the amount of the overestimate or underestimate.

Section 3.8

13. In a certain region, pesticide can be sprayed from an airplane only if the temperature is at least 70° F, the relative humidity is between 15 and 35 percent, and the wind speed is at most 10 miles per hour. Write a program that accepts three numbers representing temperature, relative humidity, and wind speed; assigns the value true or false to the logical variable OkToSpray according to these criteria; and displays this value.

14. Write a program that reads triples of real numbers and assigns the appropriate value of true or false to the following logical variables:

Triangle: True if the real numbers can represent lengths of the sides of a triangle and false otherwise (the sum of any two of the numbers must be greater than the third)

Equilateral: True if `Triangle` is true and the triangle is equilateral (the three sides are equal)

Isosceles: True if `Triangle` is true and the triangle is isosceles (at least two sides are equal)

Scalene: True if `Triangle` is true and the triangle is scalene (no two sides are equal)

The output from your program should have a format like the following:

```
Enter 3 lengths:
2, 3, 3
Triangle is:   T
Equilateral is:   F
Isosceles is:   T
Scalene is:   F
```

15. Write a program to implement a binary full-adder as described in Exercise 18 of Section 3.9, and use it to verify the results shown in the following table:

A	B	C_In	Sum	C_Out
0	0	0	0	0
0	0	1	1	0
0	1	0	1	0
0	1	1	0	1
1	0	0	1	0
1	0	1	0	1
1	1	0	0	1
1	1	1	1	1

16. Write a program to implement an adder as described in Exercise 19 of Section 3.9, and use it to demonstrate that $00 + 00 = 000$, $01 + 00 = 001$, $01 + 01 = 010$, $10 + 01 = 011$, $10 + 10 = 100$, $11 + 10 = 101$, and $11 + 11 = 110$.

FEATURES NEW TO FORTRAN 90

The selection structures described in this chapter have several features that were not present in FORTRAN 77:

- Symbolic forms of the relational operators ($<$, $>$, $==$, $<=$, $>=$, and $/=$)
- Named IF constructs
- The CASE construct

4

Repetitive Execution

Progress might be a circle, rather than a straight line.

EBERHARD ZEIDLER

But what has been said once can always be repeated.

ZENO OF ELEA

It's déjà vu all over again.

YOGI BERRA

A rose is a rose is a rose.

GERTRUDE STEIN

*I*n earlier chapters we noted that programs can be designed using three basic control structures: sequence, selection, and repetition. In the preceding chapters we described sequence and selection, and in this chapter we consider the third basic control structure, repetition. A **repetition structure** or **loop** makes possible the repeated execution of one or more statements, called the **body of the loop**.

There are two basic types of repetition:

1. *Repetition controlled by a counter*, in which the body of the loop is executed once for each value of some control variable in a specified range of values

2. *Repetition controlled by a logical expression*, in which the decision to continue or to terminate repetition is determined by the value of some logical expression

We will consider both types of loops in this chapter and illustrate how they are used in solving several problems, including the following.

Problem 1: Calculating Depreciation Tables. The depreciation-table problem described in Section 4.2 requires calculating and displaying a table showing how much a product has depreciated in each year of its useful life.

Displaying a depreciation table requires a loop that varies a year counter over the specified number of years:

For each year ranging from 1 to the useful life of the product do the following:
1. Calculate the depreciation for that year.
2. Display the year and the amount of depreciation.

In this problem the number of times that steps 1 and 2 must be repeated is known before repetition begins. In other problems like the following, the number of repetitions is not known in advance.

Problem 2: Calculating Mean Time to Failure.   In the mean-time-to-failure problem described in Section 4.4, a collection of data values must be read and processed. The number of data values is not known in advance and must be determined as the program executes.

In the solution of this problem, repetition continues until a special end-of-data value is entered:

> Repeat the following:
> 1. Read the next data value.
> 2. If the end-of-data value was read, terminate repetition.
>   Else process the data value.

In this chapter we will show how DO loops can be used to implement both counter-controlled loops and other kinds of loops.

4.1   COUNTER-CONTROLLED DO LOOPS

Fortran 90 provides one basic loop construct, the **DO construct**. There are two basic forms of this construct, one to implement counter-controlled loops and another to implement loops controlled by a logical expression. In this section we consider the first form; the second type of loop is considered in Section 4.3.

DO constructs for counter-controlled loops have the following form:

DO *Construct for Counter-Controlled Loops*

Form:

```
DO control-variable = initial-value, limit, step-size
   statement-sequence
END DO
```

where
   control-variable is an integer variable;
   initial-value, *limit*, and *step-size* are integer expressions;
   step-size must be nonzero; it may be omitted, in which case the value
      of *step-size* is taken to be 1.

Purpose:
Implements the repetition structures shown in Figure 4.1. When this loop is executed:

1. The control variable is assigned the initial value.
2. The control variable is compared with the limit to see if it is
   - less than or equal to the limit, for a positive step size.
   - greater than or equal to the limit, for a negative step size.
3. If so, the sequence of statements, called the **body of the loop,** is executed, the step size is added to the control variable, and step 2 is repeated. Otherwise, repetition terminates.

Note that if the termination test in step 2 is satisfied initially, the body of the loop is never executed.

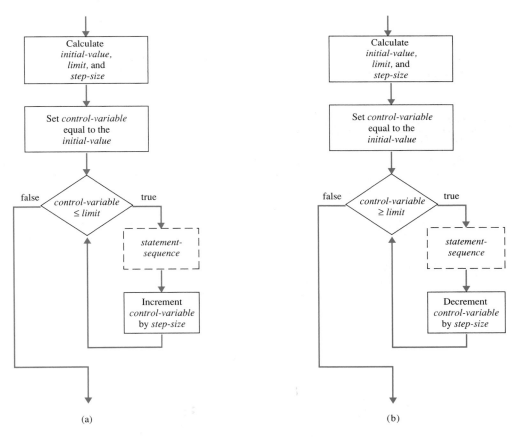

(a)   (b)

Figure 4.1

DO loop with (a) positive step size, (b) negative step size.

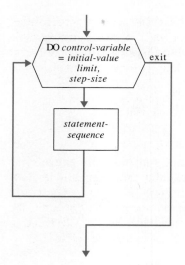

Figure 4.2

Counter-controlled DO loops in flowcharts.

DO loops will be represented in flowcharts as shown in Figure 4.2 to emphasize that they are repetition structures. The hexagon at the beginning of the loop is intended to include the initialization, testing, and incrementing, which are shown explicitly in Figure 4.1.

To illustrate, consider the DO loop

```
DO Number = 1, 9
    PRINT *, Number, Number**2
END DO
```

where Number is an integer variable. In this example, Number is the control variable, the initial value is 1, the limit is 9, and the step size is 1. When this DO loop is executed, the initial value 1 is assigned to Number, and the PRINT statement is executed. The value of Number is then increased by 1, and because this new value 2 is less than the limit 9, the PRINT statement is executed again. This repetition continues as long as the value of the control variable Number is less than or equal to the limit 9. Thus, the output produced by this DO loop is

```
1    1
2    4
3    9
4    16
5    25
6    36
7    49
8    64
9    81
```

If the step size in a DO loop is negative, the control variable is decremented rather than incremented, and repetition continues as long as the value of the control variable is greater than or equal to the limit. This is illustrated in Figure 4.1(b). Note that if the initial value is less than the limit, the body of the loop is never executed.

For example, consider the DO loop

```
DO Number = 9, 1, -1
    PRINT *, Number, Number**2
END DO
```

The control variable `Number` is assigned the initial value 9, and because this value is greater than the limit 1, the `PRINT` statement is executed. The value of `Number` is then decremented to 8, and because this new value is greater than the limit, the `PRINT` statement is executed again. This process continues as long as the value of `Number` is greater than or equal to the limit 1. Thus the output produced is

```
9  81
8  64
7  49
6  36
5  25
4  16
3  9
2  4
1  1
```

The initial values of the control variable, the limit, and the step size are determined before repetition begins and cannot be changed during execution of the DO *loop.* Within the body of the DO loop, the values of variables that specify the initial value, the limit, and the step size may change, but this does not affect the number of repetitions.[1] Also, the statements within a DO loop may use the value of the control variable, but *they must not modify the value of the control variable.* (See Potential Problem 1 in the Programming Pointers at the end of this chapter.)

Example: Summation

The initial value, the limit, and the step size in a DO construct may be variables or expressions. To illustrate, consider the declaration

```
INTEGER :: Number, I, Sum
```

---

[1] The number of repetitions is calculated as the larger of the value 0 and the integer part of

$$\frac{limit\ -\ initial\text{-}value\ +\ step\text{-}size}{step\text{-}size}$$

and the statements

```
READ *, Number
DO I = 1, Number
   Sum = Sum + I
END DO
```

The value read for Number is the limit for the DO loop. The program in Figure 4.3 uses these statements to compute the sum $1 + 2 + \cdots + Number$.

Figure 4.3 Summation.

```
PROGRAM Sum_of_Integers
!-----------------------------------------------------------------------
! Program to compute the sum of the first Number integers.
! Variables used are:
!   Number : the last integer
!   Sum    : the sum  1 + 2 + . . . + Number
!   I      : DO loop control variable
!
! Input:  Number
! Output: Number and Sum
!-----------------------------------------------------------------------

  IMPLICIT NONE
  INTEGER :: Number, I, Sum = 0

  PRINT *, "This program computes the sum 1 + 2 + ... + Number."
  PRINT *, "Enter Number:"
  READ *, Number

  DO I = 1, Number
     Sum = Sum + I
  END DO

  PRINT *, "1 + 2 + ... +", Number, "=", Sum

END PROGRAM Sum_of_Integers
```

Sample run:

```
This program computes the sum 1 + 2 + ... + Number.
Enter Number:
10
1 + 2 + ... + 10 = 55
```

Example: A Multiplication Table

The body of a DO loop may contain another DO loop. In this case, the second DO loop is said to be **nested** within the first DO loop. As an example, consider the program in Figure 4.4, which calculates and displays products of the form M * N for M ranging from 1 through Last_M and N ranging from 1 through Last_N for integer variables M, N, Last_M, and Last_N. The table of products is generated by the DO loop

```
DO M = 1, Last_M
   DO N = 1, Last_N
      Product = M * N
      PRINT *, M, " ", N, "  ", Product
   END DO
END DO
```

In the sample run, both Last_M and Last_N are assigned the value 4. The control variable M is assigned its initial value 1, and the internal DO loop

```
   DO N = 1, Last_N
      Product = M * N
      PRINT *, M, " ", N, "  ", Product
   END DO
```

is executed with M = 1. This calculates and displays the first four products, 1 * 1, 1 * 2, 1 * 3, and 1 * 4. The value of M is then incremented by 1, and the preceding DO loop is executed again with M = 2. This calculates and displays the next four products, 2 * 1, 2 * 2, 2 * 3, and 2 * 4. The control variable M is then incremented to 3, producing the next four products, 3 * 1, 3 * 2, 3 * 3, and 3 * 4. Finally, M is incremented to 4, giving the last four products, 4 * 1, 4 * 2, 4 * 3, and 4 * 4.

Figure 4.4 Printing a multiplication table.

```
PROGRAM Multiplication_Table
!------------------------------------------------------------------------
! Program to calculate and display a list of products of two numbers.
! Variables used are:
!   M, N            : the two numbers being multiplied
!   Product         : their product
!   Last_M, Last_N  : the last values of M and N
!
! Input:  Last_M and Last_N, the largest numbers to be multiplied
! Output: List of products M * N
!------------------------------------------------------------------------
```

Figure 4.4 *(cont.)*

```fortran
    IMPLICIT NONE
    INTEGER :: M, N, Last_M, Last_N, Product

    PRINT *, "Enter the last values of the two numbers:"
    READ *, Last_M, Last_N
    PRINT *, "M    N  M * N"
    PRINT *, "============="

  DO M = 1, Last_M
     DO N = 1, Last_N
        Product = M * N
        PRINT *, M, " ", N, "   ", Product
     END DO
  END DO

END PROGRAM Multiplication_Table
```

Sample run:

```
Enter the last values of the two numbers:
4, 4
M    N  M * N
=============
1    1    1
1    2    2
1    3    3
1    4    4
2    1    2
2    2    4
2    3    6
2    4    8
3    1    3
3    2    6
3    3    9
3    4    12
4    1    4
4    2    8
4    3    12
4    4    16
```

Quick Quiz 4.1

1. Name and briefly describe the two basic types of repetition structures.

For Questions 2–7, describe the output produced.

2.
```
DO I = 1, 5
    PRINT *, "Hello"
END DO
```

3.
```
DO I = 1, 5, 2
    PRINT *, "Hello"
END DO
```

4.
```
DO I = 1, 6
    PRINT *, I, I + 1
END DO
```

5.
```
DO I = 6, 1, -1
    PRINT *, I
    PRINT *
    PRINT *, I**2
END DO
```

6.
```
DO I = 6, 6
    PRINT *, "Hello"
END DO
```

7.
```
DO I = 6, 5
    PRINT *, "Hello"
END DO
```

8. What, if anything, is wrong with the following DO loop?

```
DO I = 1, 10
    PRINT *, I
    I = I + 1
END DO
```

9. How many lines of output are produced by the following?

```
DO I = 1, 5
    PRINT *, I
    DO J = 1, 4
        PRINT *, I + J
    END DO
END DO
```

Exercises 4.1

For Exercises 1–5, assume that I, J, and K are integer variables. Describe the output produced by the given program segment.

1.
```
DO I = -2, 3
    PRINT *, I, " squared = ", I * I
END DO
```

```
2. DO I = 1, 5
      PRINT *, I
      DO J = I, 1, -1
         PRINT *, J
      END DO
   END DO
```

```
3. K = 5
   DO I = -2, 3
      PRINT *, I + K
      K = 1
   END DO
```

```
4. DO I = 1, 3
      DO J = 1, 3
         DO K = 1, J
            PRINT *, I, J, K
         END DO
      END DO
   END DO
```

```
5. DO I = 1, 3
      DO J = 1, 3
         DO K = I, J
            PRINT *, I + J + K
         END DO
      END DO
   END DO
```

In Exercises 6–8, assume that I, J, and Limit are integer variables and that Alpha and DeltaX are real variables. Describe the output produced, or explain why an error occurs.

```
6. Alpha = -5.0
   DeltaX = 0.5
   DO I = 1, 5
      PRINT *, Alpha
      Alpha = Alpha + DeltaX
   END DO
```

```
7. PRINT *, "Values:"
   DO I = 0, 2
      DO J = 1, I
         PRINT *, I, J
      END DO
   END DO
   PRINT *, "The end"
```

```
8. Limit = 3
   DO I = 1, Limit
      Limit = 1
      PRINT *, I, Limit
   END DO
```

9. Write statements to print the first 100 positive integers.

10. Write statements to print the first 100 even positive integers.

11. Write statements to read a value for the integer variable N and then print the first N positive even integers.

12. Write statements to print all positive integers having at most three digits, the last of which is 0.

13. Write statements to read a value for the integer variable N and then print all integers from 1 through 1000 that are multiples of N.

14. Write statements to read a value for the integer variable N, and then read and find the sum of N real numbers.

15. Write statements to print the square roots of the first 25 odd positive integers.

4.2 APPLICATION: DEPRECIATION TABLES

Problem

Depreciation is the decrease in the value over time of some asset due to wear and tear, decay, declining price, and so on. For example, suppose that a company purchases a new robot for $20,000 that will be used on its assembly line for 5 years. After that time, called the *useful life* of the robot, it can be sold at an estimated price of $5,000, which is the robot's *salvage value*. Thus, the value of the robot will have depreciated $15,000 over the 5-year period. A program is needed to calculate depreciation tables that display the depreciation in each year of an item's useful life.

A robotic arm. (Photo courtesy of John Madere/The Stock Market)

Solution

Specification. The input for this problem is the purchase price of an item, its useful life, and its salvage value. The output is a depreciation table. However, there are several ways to calculate depreciation, and thus another input is an indicator of which method to use. A specification for this problem is therefore as follows:

Input: The purchase price of an item
            The item's useful life (in years)
            The item's salvage value
            An indicator of which method of depreciation to use

Output: A depreciation table

Design. A first version of an algorithm for solving this problem is:

1. Get the purchase price, useful life, and salvage value of the item.
2. Calculate the amount to depreciate: purchase price − salvage value.
3. Determine which method of depreciation is to be used.
4. Generate a depreciation table.

Coding steps 1 and 2 is straightforward, as is coding step 3, once we know how many different methods of calculating depreciation to provide. There are many methods, but we will consider only two here: the *straight-line* method and the *sum-of-the-years'-digits* method. Thus we might refine step 3 as:

3. Enter an indicator to select the method for calculating depreciation to be used: 1 for the straight-line method and 2 for the sum-of-the-years'-digits method.

Step 4 also obviously needs refinement. Generating a table requires a loop, and a counter-controlled loop is appropriate here. We can rewrite step 4 as

4. Repeat the following for each year from 1 to the end of the useful life: Display the year number and the depreciation for that year, calculated using the method selected in step 3.

To complete the algorithm, we must describe the two methods of calculating depreciation. We will use the following variables:

VARIABLES FOR DEPRECIATION PROBLEM

Price	Purchase price of item
SalvageValue	Its salvage value
Amount	Amount to be depreciated
UsefulLife	Useful life in years

Method	Method of depreciation to use
Year	Year in which depreciation is being calculated
Depreciation	Depreciation for that year

In the **straight-line method** for calculating depreciation, the amount to be depreciated is divided evenly over the specified number of years. For example, straight-line depreciation of $15,000 over a 5-year period gives an annual depreciation of $15,000 / 5 = $3,000. Thus, to calculate depreciation using this method, we simply calculate *Depreciation = Amount / UsefulLife*.

To illustrate the **sum-of-the-years'-digits method** for calculating depreciation, consider again depreciating $15,000 over a 5-year period. To use this method, we first calculate the "sum of the years," 1 + 2 + 3 + 4 + 5 = 15. In the first year, 5/15 of $15,000 ($5,000) is depreciated; in the second year, 4/15 of $15,000 ($4,000) is depreciated; and so on, giving the following depreciation table:

Year	Depreciation
1	$5,000
2	$4,000
3	$3,000
4	$2,000
5	$1,000

Thus, to use this method, we must add another variable to our list of identifiers:

ANOTHER VARIABLE FOR DEPRECIATION PROBLEM

Sum: $1 + 2 + \cdots + UsefulLife$

Once this sum has been calculated, we can calculate depreciation for a given *Year* as *Depreciation = (UsefulLife − Year + 1) * Amount / Sum.*

We are now ready to give a complete algorithm for solving this problem. We must add statements to calculate *Sum*. These should be placed before the loop for generating the depreciation table, since it would be inefficient to calculate this sum over and over again for each year. Our final algorithm is as follows:

ALGORITHM FOR DEPRECIATION PROBLEM

Algorithm to generate depreciation tables using either the straight-line method or the sum-of-the-years'-digits method.

| Input: | *Price, UsefulLife, SalvageValue,* and *Method* |
| Output: | A depreciation table showing the year number and the amount to be depreciated in that year |

1. Enter *Price*, *UsefulLife*, and *SalvageValue*.
2. Calculate *Amount = Price − SalvageValue*.
3. Enter *Method*.
4. If *Method = 1*

   Calculate *Depreciation = Amount / UsefulLife*.

   Else:
   a. Set *Sum* to 0.
   b. Repeat the following for *Year* ranging from 1 to *UsefulLife*:

   Add *Year* to *Sum*.

5. Repeat the following for *Year* ranging from 1 to *UsefulLife*:
   a. If *Method = 2*

   Calculate *Depreciation = (UsefulLife − Year + 1) ∗ Amount / Sum*.

   b. Display *Year* and *Depreciation*.

Coding. The program in Figure 4.5 implements this algorithm. It uses DO loops to carry out the repetitions required in steps 4 and 5.

Figure 4.5 Calculating depreciation.

```
PROGRAM Depreciation_Table
!------------------------------------------------------------------
! Program to calculate and display a depreciation table using one of
! two methods of depreciation:
!      (1) straight-line
!      (2) sum-of-the-years'-digits
! Variables used are:
!     Price         :   purchase price of item
!     SalvageValue  :   and its salvage value
!     Amount        :   amount to be depreciated (Price - SalvageValue)
!     UsefulLife    :   its useful life
!     Method        :   method of depreciation (1 or 2)
!     Depreciation  :   amount of depreciation
!     Year          :   number of year in depreciation table
!     Sum           :   1 + 2 + ... + UsefulLife
!                          (for sum-of-the-years'-digits method)
!
! Input:  Price, SalvageValue, UsefulLife, and Method
! Output: Table showing year number and depreciation for that year
!------------------------------------------------------------------
```

Figure 4.5 *(cont.)*

```
IMPLICIT NONE
REAL :: Price, SalvageValue, Amount, Depreciation
INTEGER :: UsefulLife, Method, Year, Sum

! Get the information about the item
PRINT *, "Enter purchase price, useful life, and salvage value:"
READ *, Price, UsefulLife, SalvageValue

! Calculate amount to be depreciated
Amount = Price - SalvageValue

! Get method of depreciation to be used
PRINT *, "Enter:"
PRINT *, "   1 for straight-line depreciation"
PRINT *, "   2 for sum-of-the-years'-digits method"
READ *, Method

! Determine which type of depreciation method to use
IF (Method == 1) THEN            ! straight-line method
   Depreciation = Amount / UsefulLife
ELSE                             ! sum-of-the-years'-digits method
   Sum = 0
   DO Year = 1, UsefulLife
      Sum = Sum + Year
   END DO
END IF

! Generate the depreciation table
PRINT *
PRINT *, "Year    Depreciation"
PRINT *, "==================="
DO Year = 1, UsefulLife
   IF (Method == 2) THEN
      Depreciation = (UsefulLife - Year + 1) * Amount / REAL(Sum)
   END IF
   PRINT *, " ", Year, Depreciation
END DO

END PROGRAM Depreciation_Table
```

Execution and Testing. This program was executed several times using test data for which the results were easy to check. It was then run with the data given in the problem.

Run #1 of program:

```
Enter purchase price, useful life, and salvage value:
20000, 5, 5000
Enter:
   1 for straight-line depreciation
   2 for sum-of-the-years'-digits method
1

Year    Depreciation
===================
   1   3.0000000E+03
   2   3.0000000E+03
   3   3.0000000E+03
   4   3.0000000E+03
   5   3.0000000E+03
```

Run #2 of program:

```
Enter purchase price, useful life, and salvage value:
20000, 5, 5000
Enter:
   1 for straight-line depreciation
   2 for sum-of-the-years'-digits method
2

Year    Depreciation
===================
   1   5.0000000E+03
   2   4.0000000E+03
   3   3.0000000E+03
   4   2.0000000E+03
   5   1.0000000E+03
```

4.3 GENERAL DO LOOPS: DO-EXIT CONSTRUCT

The counter-controlled DO loop described in Section 4.1 is used to implement a repetition structure in which the number of iterations is determined before execution of the loop begins. For some problems, however, the number of iterations cannot be determined in advance and a more general repetition structure is required. Repetition in such loops is usually controlled by some logical expression, as pictured in Figure 4.6(a).

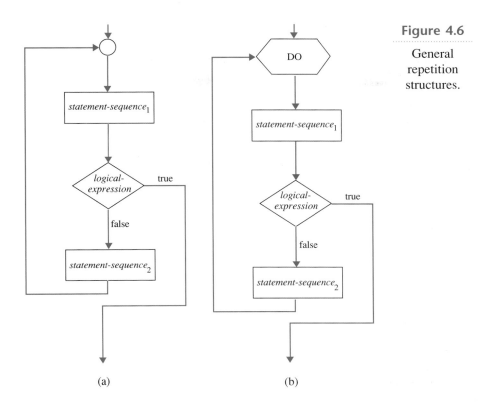

Figure 4.6

General repetition structures.

(a)   (b)

Fortran 90 provides a DO-EXIT construct that can be used to implement such repetition structures. For consistency with the flowchart representation of counter-controlled DO loops in Figure 4.2, we will picture such loops in flowcharts as shown in Figure 4.6(b).

DO-EXIT *Construct*

Form:

```
DO
    statement-sequence₁
    IF (logical-expression) EXIT
    statement-sequence₂
END DO
```

where
    either *statement-sequence₁* or *statement-sequence₂* may be omitted.

Purpose:

Implements a repetition structure in which repetition is controlled by a logical expression, as pictured in Figure 4.6. The statements that make up the body of the loop are executed repeatedly until the *logical-expression* in the IF statement becomes true. Repetition is then terminated, and execution continues with the statement following the END DO.

Warning: If the *logical-expression* never becomes true, an **infinite loop** results.

Example: Summation

To illustrate the use of a loop controlled by a logical expression, consider the following variation of the summation problem considered in Section 4.1:

For a given value of *Limit*, what is the smallest positive integer *Number* for which the sum

$$1 + 2 + \cdots + Number$$

is greater than *Limit*, and what is the value of this sum?

To solve this problem we use three variables:

Number: A positive integer added to the sum
Sum: $1 + 2 + \cdots + Number$
Limit: The specified limit for the sum

We begin with *Number* and *Sum* initialized to 0. If this value of *Sum* exceeds the value of *Limit*, the problem is solved. Otherwise we increment *Number* by 1, add it to *Sum*, and then check to see if this value of *Sum* exceeds *Limit*. Once again, if it does, the problem is solved; and if not, *Number* must be incremented again and added to *Sum*. This process is continued as long as the value of *Sum* is less than or equal to *Limit*. Eventually, the value of *Sum* will exceed *Limit* and the problem is solved. This leads to the following algorithm.

ALGORITHM FOR SUMMATION PROBLEM

Algorithm to find the smallest positive *Number* for which the sum $1 + 2 + \cdots + Number$ is greater than some specified value *Limit*.

Input: An integer *Limit*
Output: *Number* and *Sum*

1. Enter *Limit*.

2. Set *Number* equal to 0.

3. Set *Sum* equal to 0.

4. Repeat the following:
   a. If *Sum* > *Limit*, terminate repetition; otherwise continue with the following.
   b. Increment *Number* by 1.
   c. Add *Number* to *Sum*.

5. Display *Number* and *Sum*.

Figure 4.7 displays the structure of this algorithm in flowchart form.

As the flowchart in Figure 4.7 clearly indicates, the logical expression that controls repetition of the loop is evaluated at the top of the loop, and thus this loop is sometimes called a **pretest loop** or a "test-at-the-top" loop. If this logical expression is false initially, the statements that follow it will not be executed; such a loop is thus said to have **zero-trip** behavior. In the preceding summation algorithm, therefore, if the value −1 is entered for *Limit*, the loop will be exited immediately and execution will continue with the display instruction that follows the loop; the value 0 will be displayed for both *Number* and *Sum*.

A pretest loop can be implemented by a DO-EXIT construct of the form

```
DO
    IF (logical-expression) EXIT
    statement-sequence
END DO
```

For example, the program in Figure 4.8 uses the DO-EXIT construct

```
DO
    IF (Sum > Limit) EXIT   ! terminate repetition
    ! otherwise continue with the following:
    Number = Number + 1
    Sum = Sum + Number
END DO
```

to implement the loop

Repeat the following:
   a. If *Sum* > *Limit*, terminate repetition; otherwise continue with the following.
   b. Increment *Number* by 1.
   c. Add *Number* to *Sum*.

in the summation algorithm given earlier.

Because the logical expression in a pretest loop is evaluated before the repetition begins, the statements that comprise the body of the loop are not executed if this expression is initially false. Note how the last sample run demonstrates the zero-trip behavior of a pretest loop; when the value −1 is entered for Limit, the IF statement causes an immediate transfer of control to the last PRINT statement that displays the value 0 for both Number and Sum.

Figure 4.7

Flowchart for summation algorithm.

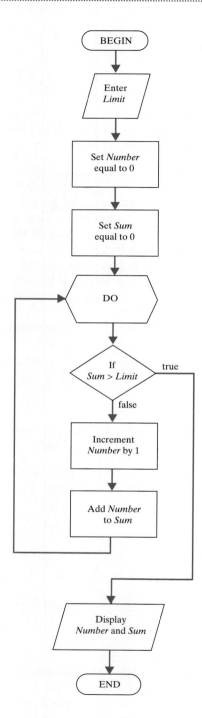

Figure 4.8 Calculating sums.

```fortran
PROGRAM Summation
!-----------------------------------------------------------------------
! Program to find the smallest positive integer Number for which the
! sum 1 + 2 + ... + Number is greater than some specified value Limit.
! Variables used are:
!    Number : the current number being added
!    Sum    : the sum 1 + 2 + ... + Number
!    Limit  : the value that Sum is to exceed
!
! Input:  An integer Limit
! Output: Number and the value of Sum
!-----------------------------------------------------------------------

  IMPLICIT NONE
  INTEGER :: Number, Sum, Limit

  ! Read Limit and initialize Number and Sum
  PRINT *, "Enter value that 1 + 2 + ... + ? is to exceed:"
  READ *, Limit
  Number = 0
  Sum = 0

  ! Repeat--terminate when Sum exceeds Limit
  DO
     IF (Sum > Limit) EXIT    ! terminate repetition
     ! otherwise continue with the following:
     Number = Number + 1
     Sum = Sum + Number
  END DO

  ! Print the results
  PRINT *, "1 + ... +", Number, "=", Sum, ">", Limit

END PROGRAM Summation
```

Sample runs:

```
Enter value that 1 + 2 + ... + ? is to exceed:
10
1 + ... + 5 = 15 > 10
```

Figure 4.8 *(cont.)*

```
Enter value that 1 + 2 + ... + ? is to exceed:
10000
1 + ... + 141 = 10011 > 10000

Enter value that 1 + 2 + ... + ? is to exceed:
-1
1 + ... + 0 = 0 > -1
```

In the first sample run of Figure 4.8, in which the value 10 is entered for Limit, the body of the loop is executed five times, as indicated in the following table,
which traces its execution:

Number	Sum	Sum < Limit	Action
0	0	.TRUE.	Execute body of loop
1	1	.TRUE.	Execute body of loop
2	3	.TRUE.	Execute body of loop
3	6	.TRUE.	Execute body of loop
4	10	.TRUE.	Execute body of loop
5	15	.FALSE.	Terminate repetition

A similar trace table for the second sample run would show that the loop body
is executed 141 times. A trace table for the third sample run shows that the loop body
is not executed, because the logical expression Sum < Limit that controls repetition is initially false:

Number	Sum	Sum < Limit	Action
0	0	.FALSE.	Terminate repetition; that is, bypass loop body

Input Loops

One common use of loops is to read and process a set of data values. Because it
may not be possible or practical to determine beforehand how many data values must
be processed, a general loop should be used rather than a counter-controlled DO loop.

One of the easiest ways to implement input loops is by using a **test-in-the-
middle loop** of the form

Repeat the following:
  1. Read a data value.
  2. If the end of data was encountered, terminate repetition; otherwise
     continue with the following.
  3. Process the data value.

In step 2, it must be possible to detect when the end of data occurred. One method is to use an `IOSTAT =` clause as described in the next chapter. For interactive input, another common method is to append to the data set an artificial data value called an **end-of-data flag** or **sentinel**, which is distinct from any possible data item. As each data item is read, it is checked to determine whether it is this end-of-data flag. If it is, repetition is terminated; otherwise it is processed as a regular data value. This technique for reading and processing data values is used in solving the mean-time-to-failure problem of the next section.

In the summation problem we used a *pretest loop* in which the logical expression that controls repetition is evaluated *before* the body of the loop is executed, and in the preceding discussion of input loops, we showed how a *test-in-the-middle loop* can be used to read and process data values. Sometimes, however, it is appropriate to use a **posttest** or "test-at-the-bottom" loop, in which the termination test is made *after* the body of the loop is executed. Such a structure can be implemented in Fortran with a program segment of the form

```
DO
    statement-sequence
    IF (logical-expression) EXIT
END DO
```

Such loops can be used to implement input loops in which the user is asked at the end of each repetition whether there is more data to process. Such loops are sometimes called **query-controlled input loops**.

To illustrate a query-controlled input loop, we reconsider the problem of converting Celsius temperatures to Fahrenheit temperatures described in Section 2.7. The program developed there to solve this problem was designed to process only one temperature at a time. To process several temperatures, the program must be executed for each one.

This program can be easily modified to process several temperatures by "wrapping" the statement within a loop that reads and processes a temperature and then asks the user if there is more data to be processed. Using such a query-controlled input loop, we can modify the algorithm given earlier as follows:

ALGORITHM FOR TEMPERATURE CONVERSION PROBLEM

This algorithm converts temperatures on the Celsius scale to the corresponding temperatures on the Fahrenheit scale. Values are processed until the user indicates that there is no more data.

Input: Temperatures in degrees Celsius
            User responses
Output: Temperatures in degrees Fahrenheit

Repeat the following:

1. Enter *Celsius*.
2. Calculate *Fahrenheit* = 1.8 * *Celsius* + 32.
3. Display *Fahrenheit*.
4. Ask the user if there are more temperatures to process.
5. Read the user's *Response* (Y or N).
6. If *Response* = "N", terminate repetition.

The program in Figure 4.9 implements this algorithm; the query-controlled input loop is highlighted in color.

Figure 4.9 Temperature conversion—repetitive version.

```
PROGRAM Temperature_Conversion_3
!-------------------------------------------------------------------
! Program to convert temperatures on the Celsius scale to the
! corresponding temperatures on the Fahrenheit scale.  A query-
! controlled input loop is used to process several temperatures.
! Variables used are:
!   Celsius     : temperature on the Celsius scale
!   Fahrenheit  : temperature on the Fahrenheit scale
!   Response    : user's response to the more-data query
!
! Input:  Celsius, Response
! Output: Fahrenheit
!-------------------------------------------------------------------

  IMPLICIT NONE
  REAL :: Celsius, Fahrenheit
  CHARACTER(1) :: Response

  ! Query-controlled loop to process temperatures
  DO
     ! Obtain Celsius temperature
     PRINT *, "Enter temperature in degrees Celsius:"
     READ *, Celsius

     ! Calculate corresponding Fahrenheit temperature
     Fahrenheit = 1.8 * Celsius + 32.0

     ! Display temperatures
     PRINT *, Celsius, "degrees Celsius =", &
              Fahrenheit, "degrees Fahrenheit"
```

Figure 4.9 *(cont.)*

```
     ! Ask user if there is more data
     PRINT *
     PRINT *, "More temperatures to convert (Y or N)?"
     READ *, Response
     IF (Response == "N") EXIT
  END DO

END PROGRAM Temperature_Conversion_3
```

Sample run:

```
Enter temperature in degrees Celsius:
0
  0.0000000E+00 degrees Celsius =  32.0000000 degrees Fahrenheit

More temperatures to convert (Y or N)?
Y
Enter temperature in degrees Celsius:
11.193
 11.1929998 degrees Celsius =  52.1473999 degrees Fahrenheit

More temperatures to convert (Y or N)?
Y
Enter temperature in degrees Celsius:
-17.728
-17.7280006 degrees Celsius =   8.9599609E-02 degrees Fahrenheit

More temperatures to convert (Y or N)?
N
```

The DO-CYCLE Construct

The EXIT statement causes repetition of a loop to terminate by transferring control to the statement following the END DO statement. Sometimes it is necessary to terminate only the current repetition and jump ahead to the next one. Fortran 90 provides the **CYCLE statement** for this purpose.

CYCLE *Statement*

Form:

```
     CYCLE
```

Purpose:
To terminate the current pass through a loop and proceed to the next iteration. It may be used with both counter-controlled and general DO loops.

To illustrate the use of CYCLE, suppose that in the temperature-conversion program in Figure 4.9, we wanted to process only temperatures of 0° C or above. For this, we need only add the statement

```
IF (Celsius < 0.0)
    PRINT *, "*** Temperature must be 0 or above ***"
    CYCLE
END IF
```

after the READ *, Celsius statement in the query-controlled input loop:

```
! Query-controlled loop to process temperatures
  DO
      ! Obtain Celsius temperature
      PRINT *, "Enter temperature in degrees Celsius:"
      READ *, Celsius

      IF (Celsius < 0.0)
          PRINT *, "*** Temperature must be 0 or above ***"
          CYCLE
      END IF

      ! Calculate corresponding Fahrenheit temperature
      Fahrenheit = 1.8 * Celsius + 32.0

      ! Display temperatures
      PRINT *, Celsius, "degrees Celsius =", &
               Fahrenheit, "degrees Fahrenheit"

      ! Ask user if there is more data
      PRINT *
      PRINT *, "More temperatures to convert (Y or N)?"
      READ *, Response
      IF (Response == "N") EXIT
  END DO
```

If a negative value is entered for Celsius, a message will be displayed and the CYCLE statement will cause the rest of the loop body to be skipped. A new pass through the loop will begin so that a new value for Celsius will be entered.

Named DO Constructs

We noted in Section 3.4 that Fortran 90 permits naming IF and IF-ELSE IF constructs by attaching a label at the beginning and end of the construct. DO constructs can also be named in this way:

```
name: DO . . .
        ⋮
END DO name
```

This is especially useful in the case of nested DO loops. It helps with determining which END DO is matched with which DO. Thus, the nested loops in the summation example of Section 4.1 could perhaps better be written as

```
Outer: DO M = 1, Last_M
    Inner: DO N = 1, Last_N
        Product = M * N
        PRINT *, M, " ", N, "  ", Product
    END DO Inner
END DO Outer
```

The name attached to a DO construct can also be attached to an EXIT or CYCLE statement within that construct. This causes control to transfer to the END DO having the same name. For example, suppose that a problem requires calculating A^N for several values of A and for several values of N for each A value. Suppose that entering 0 for A and N signals the end of input. Nested DO constructs of the following form could be used:

```
A_Loop: DO
    PRINT *, "Enter A:"
    READ *, A
    N_Loop: DO
        PRINT *, "Enter N:"
        READ *, N
        IF (N == 0) THEN
            IF (A == 0) EXIT A_Loop
            EXIT N_Loop
            PRINT *, A ** N
        END IF
    END DO N_Loop
END DO A_Loop
```

4.4 APPLICATION: MEAN TIME TO FAILURE

Problem

One important statistic used in measuring the reliability of a component in a circuit is the *mean time to failure*, which can be used to predict the circuit's lifetime. This is especially important in situations in which repair is difficult or even impossible, such as for a computer circuit in a space satellite. Suppose that NASA has awarded an engineering laboratory a contract to evaluate the reliability of a particular component for a future space probe to Mars. As part of this evaluation, an engineer at this laboratory has tested several of these circuits and recorded the time at which each failed; now she would like a program to process this data and determine the mean time to failure.

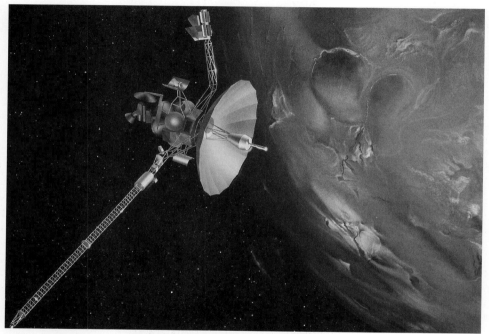

Space probe. (Photo courtesy of Kazuaki Iwasaki/The Stock Market)

Solution

Specification. The input for this problem is obviously a collection of failure times for the component being tested, and the output is clearly the average or mean of these times. To calculate this mean, we must know how many tests were conducted, but this information is not given in the statement of the problem. We cannot assume, therefore, that it is part of the input, and so the program will have to be flexible enough to process any number of data values. A specification of the input and output for this problem thus might be

Input: A collection of numeric values (number unknown)
Output: The number of values
            The mean of the values

Design. In developing algorithms to solve problems like this, one useful method is to begin by considering how the problem could be solved without using a computer, perhaps instead using pencil and paper and/or a calculator. To solve the problem in this manner, we enter the values one at a time, counting each value as it is entered and adding it to the sum of the preceding values. This procedure involves two quantities:

1. A counter that is incremented by 1 each time a data value is entered
2. A running sum of the data values

Data Value	Counter	Sum
	0	0.0
3.4	1	3.4
4.2	2	7.6
6.0	3	13.6
5.5	4	19.1
$\vdots$	$\vdots$	$\vdots$

The procedure begins with 0 as the value of the counter and 0.0 as the initial value of the sum. At each stage, a data value is entered, the value of the counter is incremented by 1, and the data value is added to the sum, producing a new sum. These steps are repeated until eventually all the data values have been processed, and the sum is then divided by the counter to obtain the mean value. An initial algorithm for solving the problem thus is

1. Initialize a counter and a running sum to zero.
2. Repeatedly read a new data value, count it, and add it to the running sum.
3. After all the data has been processed, calculate the mean value and display the counter and the mean value.

Here, coding step 1 is straightforward and only steps 2 and 3 require some refinement. Clearly, step 2 requires an input loop as described in the preceding section:

2. Repeat the following:
    a. Attempt to read a failure time.
    b. If the end of data is encountered, terminate repetition; otherwise, continue with the following.
    c. Increment the counter by 1.
    d. Add the failure time to the running sum.

After all of the data has been entered, the mean failure time is computed by dividing the final sum by the counter. If, however, there were no data values at all, steps c and d would be bypassed and both the counter and the sum would be 0. The division operation required in step 3 to compute the mean failure time cannot be performed because division by zero is not permitted. To guard against this error, we will check that the counter is nonzero before performing this division:

3. If the counter is nonzero do the following:
   a. Divide the sum by the count to obtain the mean failure time.
   b. Display the count and the mean failure time.
   Else
       Display a "no data" message.

We can now write a complete algorithm for solving this problem. We will use the following variables:

VARIABLES FOR MEAN-TIME-TO-FAILURE PROBLEM

FailureTime	Current failure time read
NumTimes	Number of failure-time readings
Sum	Sum of failure times
MeanFailureTime	Mean time to failure

A pseudocode description of this algorithm then is

ALGORITHM FOR MEAN-TIME-TO-FAILURE PROBLEM

Algorithm to read failure times, count them, and find the mean time to failure. Values are read until an end-of-data flag is encountered.

Input: A collection of failure times
Output: The mean time to failure and the number of failure times

1. Initialize *NumTimes* to 0 and *Sum* to 0.0.
2. Repeat the following:
   a. Attempt to read *FailureTime*.
   b. If the end of data is encountered, terminate repetition; otherwise, continue with the following.
   c. Increment *NumTimes* by 1.
   d. Add *FailureTime* to the running *Sum*.
3. If *NumTimes* $\neq$ 0 do the following:
   a. Calculate *MeanFailureTime* = *Sum* / *NumTimes*.
   b. Display *NumTimes* and *MeanFailureTime*.
   Else
       Display a "no data" message.

The flowchart in Figure 4.10 gives a graphical representation of the structure of this algorithm. Note that all three control structures—sequence, selection, and repe-

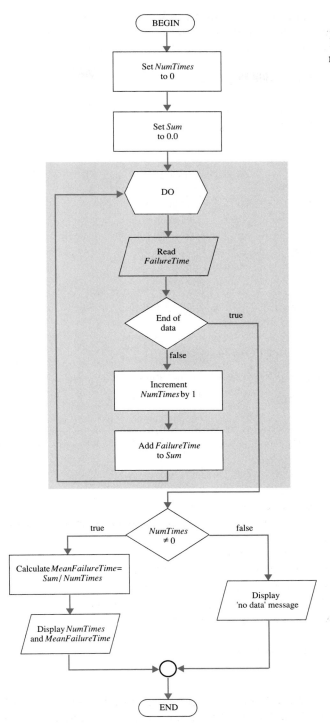

Figure 4.10

Flowchart for mean-time-to-failure algorithm.

tition—are used in this algorithm. The highlighted region shows the input loop used to read and process failure times.

Coding. The program in Figure 4.11 implements the algorithm for solving this problem. It uses the following sentinel-controlled loop implemented as a DO-EXIT construct for the input loop in step 2:

```
DO
    PRINT *, "Enter failure time:"
    READ *, FailureTime

    ! If end-of-data, terminate repetition
    IF (FailureTime == EndDataFlag) EXIT

    ! Otherwise, continue with the following:
    NumTimes = NumTimes + 1
    Sum = Sum + FailureTime
END DO
```

Figure 4.11 Mean time to failure.

```
PROGRAM Mean_Time_to_Failure

!-------------------------------------------------------------------
! Program to read a list of failure times, count them, and find the
! mean time to failure.  Values are read until an end-of-data flag
! is read.  Identifiers used are:
!   FailureTime      : the current failure time read
!   EndDataFlag      : a constant -- the end-of-data flag
!   NumTimes         : the number of failure-time readings
!   Sum              : sum of failure times
!   MeanFailureTime  : the mean time to failure
!
! Input:  A list of failure times
! Output: Number of failure times read and their mean or a message
!         indicating that no failure times were entered
!-------------------------------------------------------------------

  IMPLICIT NONE
  INTEGER :: NumTimes
  REAL :: FailureTime, Sum, MeanFailureTime
  REAL, PARAMETER :: EndDataFlag = -1.0
```

Figure 4.11 *(cont.)*

```fortran
! Initialize Sum and NumTimes and give instructions to user
Sum = 0.0
NumTimes = 0
PRINT *, "Enter failure time of", EndDataFlag, "to stop."

! Repeat the following
DO
    PRINT *, "Enter failure time:"
    READ *, FailureTime

    ! If end-of-data, terminate repetition
    IF (FailureTime == EndDataFlag) EXIT

    ! Otherwise, continue with the following:
    NumTimes = NumTimes + 1
    Sum = Sum + FailureTime
END DO

! Calculate and display mean time to failure
IF (NumTimes /= 0) THEN
    MeanFailureTime = Sum / NumTimes
    PRINT *
    PRINT *, "Number of failure time readings:", NumTimes
    PRINT *, "Mean time to failure:", MeanFailureTime
ELSE
    PRINT *, "No failure times were entered."
END IF

END PROGRAM Mean_Time_to_Failure
```

Execution and Testing. Test runs with input data like the following indicate that the program is correct:

Test run #1:

```
Enter failure time of  -1.0000000 to stop.
Enter failure time:
-1.0
No failure times were entered.
```

Test run #2:

```
Enter failure time of  -1.0000000 to stop.
Enter failure time:
25.5
Enter failure time:
-1.0

Number of failure time readings: 1
Mean time to failure:   25.5000000
```

Test run #3:

```
Enter failure time of  -1.0000000 to stop.
Enter failure time:
3.0
Enter failure time:
4.0
Enter failure time:
5.0
Enter failure time:
-1.0

Number of failure time readings: 3
Mean time to failure:    4.0000000
```

It can then be used to calculate mean failure times for other data sets such as

```
Enter failure time of  -1.0000000 to stop.
Enter failure time:
127
Enter failure time:
123.5
Enter failure time:
155.4
Enter failure time:
99
Enter failure time:
117.3
Enter failure time:
201.5
Enter failure time:
-1.0

Number of failure time readings: 6
Mean time to failure:    1.3728334E+02
```

4.5 PROGRAM TESTING AND DEBUGGING TECHNIQUES: AN EXAMPLE

In Section 1.4 we noted that three types of errors may occur when developing a program to solve a problem: syntax or compile-time errors, run-time errors, and logic errors. **Syntax errors** such as incorrect punctuation, unbalanced parentheses, and misspelled key words are detected during the program's compilation, and an appropriate error message is usually displayed. **Run-time errors** such as division by zero and integer overflow are detected during the program's execution, and again, a suitable error message is often displayed. These two types of errors are, for the most part, relatively easy to correct, since the system error messages often indicate the type of error and where it occurred. **Logic errors**, on the other hand, are usually more difficult to detect, since they arise in the design of the algorithm or in coding the algorithm as a program, and in most cases, no error messages are displayed to assist the programmer in identifying such errors.

The Programming Pointers at the ends of the chapters in this book include warnings about some of the more common errors. As programs become increasingly complex, however, the logic errors that may occur are more subtle and consequently more difficult to identify and correct. In this section we consider an example of a program that contains logic errors and we describe techniques that are useful in detecting them.

Example: Range of Noise Levels

Suppose that as a programming exercise, students were asked to write a program to read a list of positive integers representing noise levels (in decibels) in an automobile under various conditions and to determine the range, that is, the difference between the largest and the smallest values. The following program heading, opening documentation, and variable declarations were given, and the students were asked to write the rest of the program:

```
PROGRAM Range_of_Noise_Levels

!-----------------------------------------------------------------
! Program to read a list of noise levels in decibels and determine
! the range of values.  A negative noise level is used to signal
! the end of data.  Variables used are:
!   NoiseLevel    :   the current noise level being processed
!   LargestLevel  :   the largest value read so far
!   SmallestLevel :   " smallest "    "   "   "
! Input:  A list of noise levels in decibels
! Output: The range of noise levels
!-----------------------------------------------------------------

   IMPLICIT NONE
   INTEGER :: NoiseLevel, LargestLevel, SmallestLevel
```

One attempted solution was the following (in which the statements have been numbered for easy reference):

```
(1)     PRINT *, "Enter noise levels in decibels (integers)."
(2)     PRINT *, "Enter zero or a negative value to stop."

        ! Initialize largest noise level with a small value
        ! and smallest with a very large value

(3)     LargestLevel = 0
(4)     SmallestLevel = 999

        ! Repeat the following

(5)     DO
(6)        PRINT *, "Noise level?"
(7)        READ *, NoiseLevel
(8)        IF (NoiseLevel > LargestLevel) THEN
(9)           LargestLevel = NoiseLevel
(10)       ELSE IF (NoiseLevel < SmallestLevel) THEN
(11)          SmallestLevel = NoiseLevel
(12)       END IF
(13)       IF (NoiseLevel < 0) EXIT
(14)    END DO

(15)    PRINT *, "Range of noise levels =", &
                    LargestLevel - SmallestLevel, "decibels"
(16) END PROGRAM Range_of_Noise_Levels
```

Execution of the program produced

```
Enter noise levels in decibels (integers).
Enter zero or a negative value to stop.
Noise level? 94
Noise level? 102
Noise level? 88
Noise level? -1
Range of noise levels = 103 decibels
```

Data values were read and processed, terminating when the end-of-data flag -1 was read. The correct range for this set of noise levels is 14, however, and not 103 as computed by the program.

Trace Tables

One common approach to finding logic errors in a program is manually constructing a **trace table** of the segment of the program that is suspect. This technique, also known as **desk checking**, consists of recording in a table, step by step, the values of all or certain key variables in the program segment. In this example, the following trace table for the loop in statements 5 through 14 might be obtained:

Statements	NoiseLevel	LargestLevel	SmallestLevel
First pass through the loop:			
5–7	94	0	999
8–9	94	94	999
Second pass through the loop:			
5–7	102	94	999
8–9	102	102	999
Third pass through the loop:			
5–7	88	102	999
10–11	88	102	88
Fourth pass through the loop:			
5–7	−1	102	88
10–11	−1	102	−1

The last line in this trace table shows why the range is incorrect: the value of SmallestLevel became −1 on the last pass through the loop because the value −1 used to signal the end of data was read and processed as a noise level.

Debugging

The execution of a program segment can also be traced automatically by inserting temporary output statements or by using special system-debugging software to display the values of key variables at selected stages of program execution. For example, we might insert the statement

```
PRINT *, "Noise level", NoiseLevel
```

after the READ statement to echo the data values as they are entered, and the statements

```
PRINT *, "Largest", LargestLevel, "  Smallest", SmallestLevel
PRINT *
```

after the IF construct to display the values of these variables on each pass through the loop. The resulting output then is

```
Enter noise levels in decibels (integers).
Enter zero or a negative value to stop.
Noise level? 94
Noise level 94
Largest 94   Smallest 999
```

```
Noise level? 102
Noise level 102
Largest 102    Smallest 999

Noise level? 88
Noise level 88
Largest 102    Smallest 88

Noise level? -1
Noise level -1
Largest 102    Smallest -1

Range of noise levels = 103 decibels
```

This technique must not be used indiscriminately, however, since incorrect placement of such temporary debugging statements may display output that is not helpful in locating the source of the error. Also, if too many such statements are used, so much output may be produced that it will be difficult to isolate the error.

Modifying and Testing the Program

Either manual or automatic tracing of this program reveals that the error is that the value -1 used to signal the end of data was processed as a noise level. A first reaction might be to fix this error by using an IF statement to keep this from happening:

```
IF (NoiseLevel > 0) THEN
   IF (NoiseLevel > LargestLevel) THEN
      LargestLevel = NoiseLevel
   ELSE IF (NoiseLevel < SmallestLevel) THEN
      SmallestLevel = NoiseLevel
   END IF
END IF
```

"Quick and dirty" patches like this one are not recommended, however, because they often fail to address the real source of the problem and they make the program unnecessarily complicated and messy.

The real source of difficulty in the preceding example is that the student did not use the correct technique for reading and processing data. As we noted in Section 4.3, when an end-of-data flag is used to signal the end of data, the correct approach is to test for termination immediately after each data value is read.

Using this standard technique for reading and processing data, the student rewrote his program as follows:

```
(1)      PRINT *, "Enter noise levels in decibels (integers)."
(2)      PRINT *, "Enter zero or a negative value to stop."

         ! Initialize largest noise level with a small value
         ! and smallest with a very large value

(3)      LargestLevel = 0
(4)      SmallestLevel = 999

         ! Repeat the following

(5)      DO
(6)         PRINT *, "Noise level?"
(7)         READ *, NoiseLevel
(8)         IF (NoiseLevel < 0) EXIT
(9)         IF (NoiseLevel > LargestLevel) THEN
(10)           LargestLevel = NoiseLevel
(11)        ELSE IF (NoiseLevel < SmallestLevel) THEN
(12)           SmallestLevel = NoiseLevel
(13)        END IF
(14)     END DO

(15)     PRINT *, "Range of noise levels =", &
                     LargestLevel - SmallestLevel, "decibels"
(16) END PROGRAM Range_of_Noise_Levels
```

A sample run with the same data values now produces the correct output:

```
Enter noise levels in decibels (integers).
Enter zero or a negative value to stop.
Noise level? 94
Noise level? 102
Noise level? 88
Noise level? -1
Range of noise levels = 14 decibels
```

The student may now be tempted to conclude that the program is correct. However, to establish confidence in the correctness of a program, it is necessary to test it with several sets of data. For example, the following sample run reveals that the program still contains a logic error:

```
Enter noise levels in decibels (integers).
Enter zero or a negative value to stop.
Noise level? 88
Noise level? 94
Noise level? 102
Noise level? -1
Range of noise levels = -897 decibels
```

Tracing the execution of the loop produces the following:

Statements	NoiseLevel	LargestLevel	SmallestLevel
First pass through the loop:			
5–8	88	0	999
9–10	88	88	999
Second pass through the loop:			
5–8	94	88	999
9–10	94	94	999
Third pass through the loop:			
5–8	102	94	999
9–10	102	102	999
Fourth pass through the loop:			
5–7	−1	102	999

This trace table reveals that the value of SmallestLevel never changes, suggesting that the statement

```
SmallestLevel = NoiseLevel
```

is never executed. The reason is that the logical expression NoiseLevel > LargestLevel is true for each data value because these values are entered in increasing order; consequently, the ELSE IF statement is never executed. This error can be corrected by using two IF constructs in place of the single IF-ELSE IF construct,

```
IF (NoiseLevel > LargestLevel) THEN
   LargestLevel = NoiseLevel
END IF
IF (NoiseLevel < SmallestLevel) THEN
   SmallestLevel = NoiseLevel
END IF
```

or using logical IF statements,

```
IF (NoiseLevel > LargestLevel) LargestLevel = NoiseLevel
IF (NoiseLevel < SmallestLevel) SmallestLevel = NoiseLevel
```

The resulting program is then correct but is not as efficient as it could be, because the logical expressions in both of these IF statements must be evaluated on each pass through the loop. A more efficient alternative is described in the exercises.

Summary

Logic errors may be very difficult to detect, especially in more complex programs, and it is very important that test data be carefully selected so that each part of the program is thoroughly tested. The program should be executed with data values entered in several different orders, with large data sets and small data sets, with extreme values, and with "bad" data. For example, entering the noise levels in increasing order revealed the existence of a logic error in the program. Also, even though the last version of the program will produce correct output if legitimate data values are read, the output

```
Range of noise levels = -999 decibels
```

would be produced if a negative value were entered immediately. Although it may not be necessary to guard against invalid data input in student programs, those written for the public domain—especially programs used by computer novices—should be as **robust** as possible and should not "crash" or produce "garbage" results when unexpected data values are read.

When a logic error is detected, a trace table is an effective tool for locating the source of the error. Once it has been found, the program must be corrected and then tested again. It may be necessary to repeat this cycle of testing, tracing, and correcting many times before the program produces correct results for a wide range of test data.

Thorough testing of a program will increase one's confidence in its correctness, but it must be realized that is almost never possible to test a program with every possible set of test data. No matter how much testing has been done, more can always be done. Testing is never finished; it is only stopped. Consequently, there is no guarantee that all the errors in a program have been found and corrected. Testing can only show the presence of errors, not their absence. It cannot prove that the program is correct; it can only show that it is incorrect. In some applications, the fact that a program might still contain some obscure bugs may not be critical, but in others, for example, in programs used to guide a space shuttle, errors cannot be tolerated. Certain formal techniques have been developed for proving that a program is correct and will always execute correctly (assuming no system malfunction), but a study of these techniques is beyond the scope of this introductory text.

Quick Quiz 4.5

1. What is the difference between a pretest and a posttest loop?
2. (True or false) A pretest loop is always executed at least once.
3. (True or false) A posttest loop is always executed at least once.
4. Name the three types of errors that may occur in developing a program to solve a problem.

5. Division by zero is an example of a _____ error.

6. A missing quote is an example of a _____ error.

7. Omitting a step in the design of an algorithm is an example of a _____ error.

8. Assuming that Number is an integer variable, describe the output produced by the following loop:

```
Number = 1
DO
    IF (Number > 100) EXIT
    PRINT *, Number
    NUM = 2 * Number
END DO
```

9. Assume that Number and Limit are integer variables, and consider the following program segment:

```
READ *, Limit
Number  = 0
DO
    IF (Number > Limit) EXIT
    PRINT *, Number
    Number = Number + 1
END DO
```

Describe the output produced for the following inputs:

(a) 4   (b) -2

10. Assume that Number and Limit are integer variables, and consider the following program segment:

```
READ *, Limit
Number  = 0
DO
    PRINT *, Number
    Number = Number + 1
    IF (Number > Limit) EXIT
END DO
```

Describe the output produced for the following inputs:

(a) 4   (b) -2

Exercises 4.5

1. Consider the following algorithm:

   1. Initialize X to 0, Y to 5, Z to 25.
   2. Repeat the following:
       a. If $X > 4$ terminate repetition; otherwise continue with the following.
       b. Set $Y = Z - Y$, $A = X + 1$, and then increment X by 1.
       c. If $A > 1$ then
           Set $Z = Z - 5$, $A = A^2$, and then set $B = Z - Y$.
   3. Display A, B, X, Y, and Z.

   Complete the following trace table for this algorithm, which displays the labels of the statements in the order in which they are executed and the values of the variables at each stage:

Statement	A	B	X	Y	Z	
1	?	?	0	5	25	
2	"	"	"	"	"	
2a	1	"	1	20	"	(? = undefined)
2b	"	"	"	"	"	
2a	2	"	2	5	"	
⋮	⋮	⋮	⋮	⋮	⋮	
3	"	"	"	"	"	

   Exercises 2–4 use the following algorithm:

   1. Enter A.
   2. Repeat the following:
       a. If $A > 0.3$ terminate repetition; otherwise, continue with the following.
       b. Increment A by 0.1.
       c. If $A \neq 0.3$ then do the following:
           i.   Set S and X to 0, T to 1.
           ii. While $T \leq 6$ do the following:
               (a) Add T to X and then increment T by 2.
       d. Else do the following:
           i.   Set T to 0, X to 1, and $S = 3 * S$.
           ii. While $T \leq 5$ do the following:
               (a) Increment T by 1 and then set $X = X * T$.
       e. Display A, S, and X.

Construct a trace table similar to that in Exercise 1 for the given algorithm, assuming that the given value is entered for A.

2. 0.   3. 0.3   4. 1.0

5. Given the following algorithm:

1. Initialize I, A, and X to 0.

2. Repeat the following:

a. If I $\geq$ 4 terminate repetition; otherwise, continue with the following.

b. Increment I by 1.

c. Enter b, h, k.

d. If k $\geq$ 1 then do the following:

i.   Set $A = \dfrac{bh}{2}$.

ii. If k $\geq$ 2 then do the following:

(a) Set $X = \dfrac{bh^3}{36}$.

e. Display I, b, h, A, and X.

Construct a trace table similar to that in Exercise 1 for the given algorithm, assuming that the following values are entered for b, h, and k:

b	h	k
3	6	1
4	3	2
5	2	0
2	6	6

6. Write a loop to print the first 100 positive integers.

7. Write a loop to print the value of X and decrease X by 0.5 as long as X is positive.

8. Write a loop to read values for A, B, and C and print their sum, repeating this procedure while none of A, B, or C is negative.

9. Write a loop to print the square roots of the first 25 odd positive integers.

10. Write a loop to calculate and print the squares of consecutive positive integers until the difference between a square and the preceding one is greater than 50.

11. Write a loop to print a list of points (X, Y) on the graph of the equation $Y = X^3 - 3X + 1$ for X ranging from -2 to 2 in steps of 0.1.

12. Design an algorithm that uses a loop to count the number of digits in a given integer.

13. Write Fortran statements to implement the algorithm in Exercise 12.

14. Develop an algorithm to approximate the value of e^x using the infinite series

$$e^x = \sum_{n=0}^{\infty} \frac{x^n}{n!}$$

15. Construct a trace table for the algorithm in Exercise 14, and trace the value of n, x^n, $n!$, each term $x^n/n!$, and the value of the sum of all terms up through the current one for $n = 0, 1, \ldots, 10$, and $x = 0.8$.

For each of the problems described in Exercises 16–19, specify the input and output for the problem, make a list of variables you will use in describing a solution to the problem, and then design an algorithm to solve the problem.

16. Suppose that a professor gave a quiz to her class and compiled a list of scores ranging from 50 through 100. She intends to use only three grades: A if the score is 90 or above, B if it is below 90 but above or equal to 75, and C if it is below 75. She would like a program to assign the appropriate letter grades to the numeric scores.

17. A car manufacturer wants to determine average noise levels for the 10 different models of cars the company produces. Each can be purchased with one of five different engines. Design an algorithm to enter the noise levels (in decibels) that were recorded for each possible model and engine configuration and to calculate the average noise level for each model as well as the average noise level over all models and engines.

18. The "divide-and-average" method for approximating the square root of any positive number A is as follows: for any initial approximation X that is positive, find a new approximation by calculating the average of X and A/X, that is,

$$\frac{X + A/X}{2}$$

Repeat this procedure with X replaced by this new approximation, stopping when X and A/X differ in absolute value by some specified error allowance, such as .00001.

19. Dispatch Die-Casting currently produces 200 castings per month and realizes a profit of $300 per casting. The company now spends $2000 per month on research and development and has a fixed operating cost of $20,000 per month that does not depend on the amount of production. If the company doubles the amount spent on research and development, it is estimated that production will increase by 20 percent. The company president would like to know, beginning with the current status and successively doubling the amount spent on research and development, at what point the net profit will begin to decline.

20. Consider a cylindrical reservoir with a radius of 30.0 feet and a height of 30.0 feet that is filled and emptied by a 12-inch diameter pipe. The pipe has a 1000.0-foot-long run and discharges at an elevation 20.0 feet lower than the bottom of the reservoir. The pipe has been tested and has a roughness factor of 0.0130.

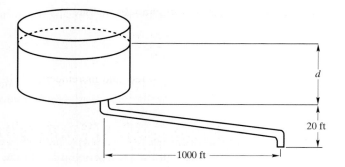

Several formulas have been developed experimentally to determine the velocity at which fluids flow through such pipes. One of these, the *Manning formula*, is

$$V = \frac{1.486}{N} R^{2/3} S^{1/2}$$

where

V = velocity in feet per second

N = roughness coefficient

R = hydraulic radius = $\dfrac{\text{cross-sectional area}}{\text{wetted perimeter}}$

S = slope of the energy gradient $\left(= \dfrac{d + 20}{1000} \text{ for this problem} \right)$

The rate of fluid flow is equal to the cross-sectional area of the pipe multiplied by the velocity.

Design an algorithm to estimate the time required to empty the reservoir, given the reservoir's height, roughness coefficient, hydraulic radius, and pipe radius. Do this by assuming a constant flow rate for 5-minute segments.

21. A 100.0-pound sign is hung from the end of a horizontal pole of negligible mass. The pole is attached to the building by a pin and is supported by a cable, as shown. The pole and cable are each 6.0 feet long.

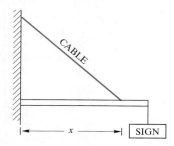

Design an algorithm to find the appropriate place (indicated by x in the diagram) to attach the cable to the pole so that the tension in the cable will be minimized.

The equation governing static equilibrium tells us that

$$\text{tension} = \frac{100 \cdot 6 \cdot 6}{x\sqrt{36 - x^2}}$$

Calculate the tension for x starting at 1.0 feet and incrementing it by 0.1 feet until the approximate minimum value is located.

4.6 APPLICATION: LEAST-SQUARES LINE

Problem

Suppose the following data was collected in an experiment to measure the effect of temperature on resistance:

Temperature (°C)	Resistance (ohms)
20.0	761
31.5	817
50.0	874
71.8	917
91.3	1018

The plot of this data in Figure 4.12 indicates a linear relationship between temperature and resistance.

In general, whenever the relation between two quantities x and y appears to be roughly linear, that is, when a set of points (x, y) tends to fall along a straight line, one can ask for the equation

$$y = mx + b$$

of a best-fitting line for these points. We wish to develop a program that finds the equation of the line that "best fits" such a data set. This equation (called a **regression equation**) can then be used to predict the value of y by evaluating the equation for a given value of x.

Solution

Specification:

Input: A set of data points
Output: Equation of a line that best fits the data

Figure 4.12

Least-squares line.

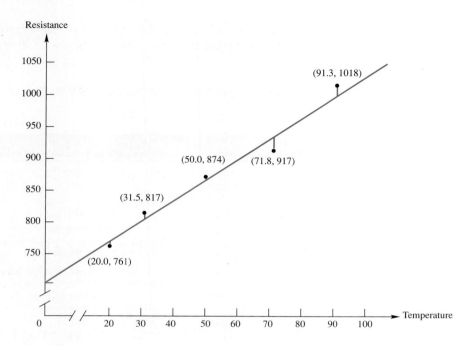

Design. A standard method for finding the **regression coefficients** m and b of the line that best fits a given data set is the **method of least squares**, so named because it produces the line $y = mx + b$, for which the sum of the squares of the deviations of the observed y-values from the predicted y-values (using the equation) is as small as possible (see Figure 4.12); that is, values of m and b are found to minimize the sum

$$\sum_{i=1}^{n} [y_i - (mx_i + b)]^2$$

$$= [y_1 - (mx_1 + b)]^2 + [y_2 - (mx_2 + b)]^2 + \cdots + [y_n - (mx_n + b)]^2$$

Using the methods of calculus for minimizing a function of two variables, one obtains the following formulas for the slope m and the y-intercept b:

$$\text{slope} = m = \frac{(\Sigma xy) - (\Sigma x)\,\bar{y}}{(\Sigma x^2) - (\Sigma x)\,\bar{x}}$$

$$y\text{-intercept} = b = \bar{y} - m\bar{x}$$

where

Σx is the sum of the x-values

Σx^2 is the sum of the squares of the x-values

Σxy is the sum of the products xy of corresponding x- and y-values

$\bar{x}$ and $\bar{y}$ are the means of the x- and y-values, respectively

From these formulas we see that a program to find a least-squares line must count the data points and compute several sums. The variables we will use are as follows:

VARIABLES FOR LEAST-SQUARES LINE PROBLEM

X, Y	Coordinates of data point
$EndDataFlag$	End-of-data flag
$NumPoints$	Number of data points
Sum_of_X	Sum of the X-values
Sum_of_Y	Sum of the Y-values
$Sum\_of\_X\_squared$	Sum of the squares of the X-values
Sum_of_XY	Sum of the products $X * Y$
X_Mean, Y_Mean	Mean of the Xs and mean of the Ys
$Slope, Y\_Intercept$	Slope and y-intercept of least-squares line

ALGORITHM FOR LEAST-SQUARES LINE PROBLEM

Algorithm to find the equation of the least-squares line for a set of data points (X, Y).

Input: A collection of data points
Output: The equation of the least-squares line

1. Initialize $NumPoints$, Sum_of_X, Sum_of_Y, $Sum\_of\_X\_squared$, and Sum_of_XY all to 0.
2. Repeat the following:
   a. Attempt to read a data point X, Y.
   b. If the end of data is encountered, terminate repetition; otherwise continue with the following.
   c. Increment $NumPoints$ by 1.
   d. Add X to Sum_of_X.
   e. Add X^2 to $Sum\_of\_X\_squared$.
   f. Add Y to Sum_of_Y.
   g. Add $X * Y$ to Sum_of_XY.
3. Calculate $X\_Mean = \dfrac{Sum\_of\_X}{NumPoints}$ and $Y\_Mean = \dfrac{Sum\_of\_Y}{NumPoints}$.

4. Calculate $Slope = \dfrac{Sum\_of\_XY - Sum\_of\_X * Y\_Mean}{Sum\_of\_X\_squared - Sum\_of\_X * X\_Mean}$

   and $Y\_Intercept = Y\_Mean - Slope * X\_Mean$.
5. Display $Slope$ and $Y\_Intercept$.

Coding. The program in Figure 4.13 implements the preceding algorithm for finding the equation of the least-squares line for a given set of data points.

Figure 4.13 Least-squares line.

```fortran
PROGRAM Least_Squares_Line
!-----------------------------------------------------------------------
! Program to find the equation of the least-squares line for a set
! of data points.  Identifiers used are:
!   X, Y                : (X,Y) is the observed data point
!   EndDataFlag         : end-of-data flag (constant)
!   NumPoints           : number of data points
!   Sum_of_X            : sum of the Xs
!   Sum_of_X_squared    : sum of the squares of the Xs
!   Sum_of_Y            : sum of the Ys
!   Sum_of_XY           : sum of the products X*Y
!   X_Mean              : mean of the Xs
!   Y_Mean              : mean of the Ys
!   Slope               : slope of least-squares line
!   Y_Intercept         : y-intercept of the line
!
! Input:  A collection of data points
! Output: The equation of the least-squares line
!-----------------------------------------------------------------------

  IMPLICIT NONE
  INTEGER :: NumPoints
  REAL :: X, Y, Sum_of_X, Sum_of_X_squared, Sum_of_Y, Sum_of_XY,&
          X_Mean, Y_Mean, Slope, Y_Intercept
  REAL, PARAMETER :: EndDataFlag = -99.0

  ! Initialize counter and the sums to 0 and read first data point

  NumPoints = 0
  Sum_of_X = 0.0
  Sum_of_X_squared = 0.0
  Sum_of_Y = 0.0
  Sum_of_XY = 0.0
  PRINT *, "To stop, enter", EndDataFlag, " for coordinates of point."

  ! Repeat the following:
  DO
     PRINT *, "Enter point:"
     READ *, X, Y

     ! If end of data, terminate repetition
     IF ((X == EndDataFlag) .OR. (Y == EndDataFlag)) EXIT
```

Figure 4.13 *(cont.)*

```
    ! Otherwise continue with the following
    NumPoints = NumPoints + 1
    Sum_of_X = Sum_of_X + X
    Sum_of_X_squared = Sum_of_X_squared + X ** 2
    Sum_of_Y = Sum_of_Y + Y
    Sum_of_XY = Sum_of_XY + X * Y
  END DO

  ! Find equation of least-squares line

  X_Mean = Sum_of_X / NumPoints
  Y_Mean = Sum_of_Y / NumPoints
  Slope = (Sum_of_XY - Sum_of_X * Y_Mean) / &
          (Sum_of_X_squared - Sum_of_X * X_Mean)
  Y_Intercept = Y_Mean - Slope * X_Mean
  PRINT *
  PRINT *, "Equation of least-squares line is y =", &
           Slope, "x +", Y_Intercept

END PROGRAM Least_Squares_Line
```

Execution and Testing. After the program has been tested with several simple data sets to check its correctness, it can be run with the given data to find the equation of the least-squares line:

Sample run:

```
To stop, enter -99.0000000  for coordinates of point.
Enter point: 20.0, 761
Enter point: 31.5, 817
Enter point: 50.0, 874
Enter point: 71.8, 917
Enter point: 91.3, 1018
Enter point: -99, -99

Equation of least-squares line is y = 10.6731482 x + 1.6189899E+02
```

Exercises 4.6

1. Display in a flowchart the structure of the algorithm for calculating a least-squares line.

2. The density ρ (g/ml) of water is given in the following table for various temperatures $T\,^\circ$ C:

$T°C$	$\rho(T)$ (g/ml)
0	0.99987
10	0.99973
20	0.99823
30	0.99568
40	0.99225
50	0.98807
60	0.98324

Find the least-squares line for this data, and use it to estimate the density at 5° C, 15° C, 25° C, 35° C, 45° C, and 55° C. Compare the computed values with the actual values given in the following table:

$T°C$	$\rho(T)$ (g/ml)
5	0.99999
15	0.99913
25	0.99707
35	0.99406
45	0.99024
55	0.98573

3. An oxyacetylene torch was used to cut a 1-inch piece of metal. The relationship between the metal thickness and cutting time is shown in the following table:

Thickness (in)	Cutting Time (min)
0.25	0.036
0.375	0.037
0.5	0.039
0.75	0.042
1.0	0.046
1.25	0.050
1.5	0.053
2.0	0.058
2.5	0.065
3.0	0.073
3.5	0.078
4.0	0.085
4.5	0.093
5.0	0.102

Find the least-squares line for this data, and use it to estimate the cutting time for thicknesses of 1.75 inches, 3.25 inches, and 4.75 inches.

CHAPTER REVIEW

Summary

The focus of this chapter was repetitive execution, the third of the three basic control structures used in writing programs. There are two basic types of repetition structures: loops controlled by a counter and general loops, which are controlled by logical expressions. A counter-controlled loop is implemented in Fortran using a counter-controlled DO loop. Section 4.1 describes these loops in detail, and Section 4.2 applies them to the problem of computing depreciation tables. General loops are implemented in Fortran 90 using a general DO loop and a DO-EXIT construct to terminate repetition. Sections 4.3 and 4.4 describe three major kinds of general loops—pretest, posttest, and test-in-the-middle—and illustrate how these are implemented in Fortran by considering three different problems. One important use of pretest loops is to read and process a collection of data values, and common types of input loops such as sentinel-controlled input loops and query-controlled input loops are described and illustrated.

Section 4.5 describes the three types of errors that can occur in program development: syntax or compile-time errors, run-time errors, and logic errors. In general, logic errors are more difficult to find and correct than are syntax and run-time errors, and this section illustrates several program testing and debugging techniques. The last section of the chapter describes the use of loops in computing the equation of a least-squares line.

FORTRAN SUMMARY

Counter-Controlled DO Loop

```
DO control-variable = initial-value, limit, step-size
   statement-sequence
END DO
```

Examples:

```
DO Number = 1, 10
   PRINT *, Number, Number**2
END DO
```

```
DO Number = 10, 1, -1
   PRINT *, Number, Number**2
END DO
```

Purpose:

When a counter-controlled DO loop is executed:

1. The control variable is assigned the initial value.

2. The control variable is compared with the limit to see if it is:
   - less than or equal to the limit, for a positive step size
   - greater than or equal to the limit, for a negative step size

3. If so, the sequence of statements, called the *body of the loop*, is executed, the step size is added to the control variable, and step 2 is repeated. Otherwise, repetition terminates.

General DO Loop—DO-EXIT Construct

```
DO
    statement-sequence₁
    IF (logical-expression) EXIT
    statement-sequence₂
END DO
```

where *statement-sequence₁* or *statement-sequence₂* may be omitted (giving a *posttest loop* and a *pretest loop*, respectively).

Examples:

```
! Pretest loop
DO
    IF (Sum > Limit) EXIT
    Number = Number + 1
    Sum = Sum + Number
END DO


! Posttest loop:  a query-controlled input loop
DO
    PRINT *, "Enter data value:"
    READ *, Value
    Sum = Sum + Value
    PRINT *, "More (Y or N)?"
    READ *, Response
    IF (Response == "N") EXIT
END DO


! Test-in-the-middle loop:  a sentinel-controlled input loop
DO
    PRINT *, "Enter data value:"
    READ *, Value
    IF (Value == EndOfDataFlag) EXIT
    NumValues = NumValues + 1
    Sum = Sum + Value
END DO
```

Purpose:

The statements that make up the body of the loop are executed repeatedly until the *logical-expression* in the IF statement becomes true. Repetition is then terminated and execution will continue with the statement following the END DO.

PROGRAMMING POINTERS

Program Style and Design

1. *The body of a loop should be indented.*

```
DO variable = init, limit, step
    statement₁
       ⋮
    statementₙ
END DO


DO
    statement₁
       ⋮
    statementₙ
    IF (logical-condition) EXIT
    statementₙ₊₁
       ⋮
    statementₘ

END DO
```

2. *All programs can be written using the three control structures considered thus far: sequence, selection, and repetition.*

Potential Problems

1. *The control variable in a* DO *loop may not be modified within the loop. Modifying the initial value, limit, or step size does not affect the number of repetitions.* For example, the statements

```
K = 5
DO I = 1, K
    PRINT *, K
    K = K - 1
END DO
```

produce the output

```
5
4
3
2
1
```

Modifying the control variable I, as in the following DO loop,

```
DO I = 1, 5
   PRINT *, K
   I = I - 1
END DO
```

is an error and produces a message such as

```
Error: Assignment to DO variable I at line 3
       detected at I@=
```

One consequence is that nested DO loops must have different control variables.

2. *The statements within a general* DO *loop controlled by a logical expression must eventually cause the logical expression to become true, because otherwise an infinite loop will result.* For example, if X is a real variable, the statements

```
X = 0.0
DO
   IF (X == 1.0) EXIT
   PRINT *, X
   X = X + 0.3
END DO
```

will produce an infinite loop.

Output:

```
0.0000000E+00
0.3000000
0.6000000
0.9000000
1.2000000
1.5000000
1.8000000
    ⋮
```

Since the value of X is never equal to 1.0, repetition is not terminated. In view of Potential Problem 5, the statements

```
X = 0.0
DO
   IF (X == 1.0) EXIT
   PRINT *, X
   X = X + 0.1
END DO
```

may also produce an infinite loop.

Output:

```
0.0000000E+00
0.1000000
0.2000000
0.3000000
0.4000000
0.5000000
0.6000000
0.7000000
0.8000001
0.9000001
1.0000001
1.1000001
1.2000002
    ⋮
```

Since X is initialized to 0 and 0.1 is added to X 10 times, X should have the value 1. However, the logical expression X == 1.0 may remain false because most real values are not stored exactly.

3. *Parentheses must enclose the logical expression in* IF *statements.*

4. *Periods must be used in the logical operators* .NOT., .AND., .OR., .EQV., *and* .NEQV..

5. *Real quantities that are algebraically equal may yield a false logical expression when compared with* == *because most real values are not stored exactly.*

6. *Declarations initialize variables at compile time, not during execution.* This is important to remember when a program processes several sets of data and uses variables that must be initialized to certain values before processing each data set. To illustrate, consider the following program:

```
INTEGER :: Number, Sum = 0
CHARACTER(1) :: Response

DO ! query-controlled input loop

   DO  ! sentinel-controlled input loop for current data set
      READ *, Number

      ! If end of current data set, terminate repetition.
      IF (Number == -999) EXIT
```

```
           ! Otherwise continue with the following.
      Sum = Sum + Number
   END DO

   PRINT *, "Sum =", Sum
   PRINT *
   PRINT *, "More data (Y or N)?"
   READ *, Response
   IF (Response == "N") EXIT
END DO
```

In the following sample run,

```
10
20
30
-999
Sum = 60

More data (Y or N)?
Y
15
125
-999
Sum = 200

More data (Y or N)?
N
```

the sum of the first data set is correctly displayed as 60, but the sum of the second data set is 140, and not 200 as shown. The error is caused by the fact that when the second set of numbers is processed, Sum is not reset to 0, because the initialization is done at compile time, not during execution. The obvious solution is to insert the statement

```
Sum = 0
```

between the two DO statements.

PROGRAMMING PROBLEMS

Sections 4.1 and 4.2

1. A certain product is to sell for Price dollars per item. Write a program that reads values for Price and the Number of items sold and then produces a table showing the total price of from 1 through TotalNumber units.

2. A ship with a total displacement of M metric tons starts from rest in still water under a constant propeller thrust of T kilonewtons. The ship develops a total resistance to motion through water that is given by $R = 4.50\,V^2$, where R is in kilonewtons and V is in meters per second. The acceleration of the ship is $A = (T - R)/M$. From these equations, an equation for the velocity of the ship can be derived:

$$V = \sqrt{\frac{T}{4.50}}\,(1 - e^{-9.00\,S/M})$$

where S is the distance in meters. Write a program that will read values for M, T, and S and will display a table of values of V in knots for S ranging from 0 to 20 nautical miles in steps of 0.5 nautical miles (1 nautical mile = 1.852 km, 1 knot = 1 nautical mile per hour). Deduce from your table the maximum possible speed for the ship.

3. The mechanism shown is part of a machine that a company is designing:

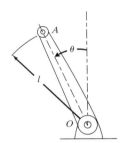

During operation, the rod OA will oscillate according to $\theta = \theta_0 \sin(2\pi t/\tau)$, where θ is measured in radians, θ_0 is the maximum angular displacement, τ is the period of motion, t = time in seconds measured from $t = 0$ when OA is vertical. If l is the length OA, the magnitude of the acceleration of point A is given by

$$|a_A| = \frac{4\pi^2 l\theta_0}{\tau^2}\sqrt{\theta_0^2 \cos^4\left(\frac{2\pi t}{\tau}\right) + \sin^2\left(\frac{2\pi t}{\tau}\right)}$$

Write a program that will read values for θ_0, l, and τ and that will then calculate a table of values of t, θ, and $|a_A|$ for $t = 0.0$ to 0.5 in steps of 0.05 (in seconds). Execute the program with $\tau = 2$ sec, $\theta_0 = \pi/2$, and $l = 0.1$ m.

4. Suppose that at a given time, genotypes AA, AB, and BB appear in the proportions x, y, and z, respectively, where $x = 0.25$, $y = 0.5$, and $z = 0.25$. If individuals of type AA cannot reproduce, the probability that one parent will donate gene A to an offspring is

$$p = \frac{1}{2}\left(\frac{y}{y + z}\right)$$

since $y/(y + z)$ is the probability that the parent is of type AB and the probability that such a parent will donate gene A is $1/2$. Then the proportions x', y', and z' of AA, AB, and BB, respectively, in each succeeding generation are given by

$$x' = p^2, \qquad y' = 2p(1 - p), \qquad z' = (1 - p)^2$$

and the new probability is given by

$$p' = \frac{1}{2}\left(\frac{y'}{y' + z'}\right)$$

Write a program to calculate and print the generation number and the proportions of AA, AB, and BB under appropriate headings until the proportions of both AA and AB are less than some small positive value.

5. The sequence of **Fibonacci numbers** begins with the integers

$$1, 1, 2, 3, 5, 8, 13, 21, \ldots$$

where each number after the first two is the sum of the two preceding numbers. Write a program that reads a positive integer n and then displays the first n Fibonacci numbers.

6. One property of the Fibonacci sequence (see Problem 5) is that the ratios of consecutive Fibonacci numbers (1/1, 1/2, 2/3, 3/5, ...) approach the "golden ratio"

$$\frac{\sqrt{5} - 1}{2}$$

Modify the program in Problem 5 to display Fibonacci numbers and the decimal values of the ratios of consecutive Fibonacci numbers.

7. The infinite series

$$\sum_{k=0}^{\infty} \frac{1}{k!}$$

converges to the number e. (For a positive integer k, $k!$, read "k factorial," is the product of the integers from 1 through k; 0! is defined to be 1.) The nth *partial sum* of such a series is the sum of the first n terms of the series; for example,

$$\frac{1}{0!} + \frac{1}{1!} + \frac{1}{2!} + \frac{1}{3!}$$

is the fourth partial sum. Write a program to calculate and print the first 10 partial sums of this series.

8. If a loan of A dollars, which carries a monthly interest rate of R (expressed as a decimal), is to be paid off in N months, then the monthly payment P will be

$$P = A\left[\frac{R(1 + R)^N}{(1 + R)^N - 1}\right]$$

During this time period, some of each monthly payment will be used to repay that month's accrued interest, and the rest will be used to reduce the balance owed.

Write a program to print an *amortization table* that displays the payment number, the amount of the monthly payment, the interest for that month, the amount of the payment applied to the principal, and the new balance. Use your program to produce an amortization table for a loan of $50,000 to be repaid in 36 months at 1 percent per month.

9. Another method of calculating depreciation is the **double-declining-balance method**. In this method, if an amount is to be depreciated over n years, $2/n$ times the undepreciated balance is depreciated annually. For example, using this method to depreciate $150,000 over a 5-year period, we would depreciate 2/5 of $150,000 ($60,000) the first year, leaving an undepreciated balance of $90,000. In the second year, 2/5 of $90,000 ($36,000) would be depreciated, leaving an undepreciated balance of $54,000. Since only a fraction of the remaining balance is depreciated in each year, the entire amount will never be depreciated. Consequently, it is permissible to switch to the straight-line method at any time.

   (a) Develop an algorithm for this method of calculating depreciation.

   (b) Modify the program in Figure 4.5 so that it includes this third method of calculating depreciation as one of the options. Also, modify the output so that the year numbers in depreciation tables begin with the current year rather than with year number 1.

Section 4.3–4.5

10. (a) Write a program that solves the noise-level range problem discussed in Section 4.5 but is more efficient than those described in the text. (*Hint*: Initialize `LargestLevel` and `SmallestLevel` to the first data value.)

    (b) For each of the following data sets, construct a trace table for the repetition structure used in your program, and determine the range of noise levels that will be computed by your program:

    (i)   88, 109, 94, -1
    (ii)   88, 94, 102, -1
    (iii) 102, 94, 88, -1
    (iv)   88, -1
    (v) -1

$$P = 50000 * ((.01 * ((1+.01)^{**}$$
$$36)$$

11. Write a program to implement the algorithm displayed in the flowchart of Figure 4.14.

12. Write a program to calculate all the Fibonacci numbers less than 5000 and the decimal values of the ratios of consecutive Fibonacci numbers (see Problem 5).

13. Write a program to read the data values shown in the following table, calculate the miles per gallon in each case, and print the values with appropriate labels:

Miles Traveled	Gallons of Gasoline Used
231	14.8
248	15.1
302	12.8
147	9.25
88	7
265	13.3

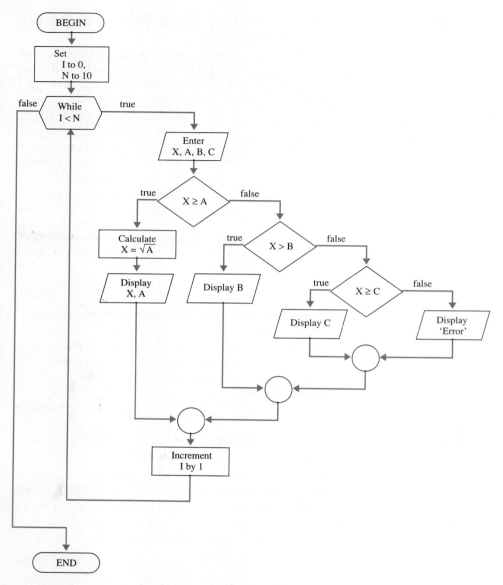

Figure 4.14

14. Write a program to read a set of numbers, count them, and find and print the largest and smallest numbers in the list and their positions in the list.

15. Suppose that a ball dropped from a building bounces off the pavement and that on each bounce it returns to a certain constant percentage of its previous height. Write a program to read the height from which the ball was dropped and the percentage of rebound. Then let the ball bounce repeatedly and print the height of the ball at the top of each bounce, the distance traveled during that bounce, and

the total distance traveled thus far, terminating when the height of the ball is almost zero (less than some small positive value).

16. Write a program to implement the divide-and-average algorithm in Exercise 18 of Section 4.5. Execute the program with $A = 3$ and error allowance $= 0.00001$, and use the following initial approximations: 1, 10, 0.01, and 100. Also execute the program with $A = 4$, error allowance $= 0.00001$, and initial approximations 1 and 2.

17. Write a program to read a set of numbers, count them, and calculate the mean, variance, and standard deviation of the set of numbers. The *mean* and *variance* of numbers $x_1, x_2, \ldots, x_n$ can be calculated using the following formulas:

$$\text{mean} = \frac{1}{n} \sum_{i=1}^{n} x_i \qquad \text{variance} = \frac{1}{n} \sum_{i=1}^{n} x_i^2 - \frac{1}{n^2} \left(\sum_{i=1}^{n} x_i \right)^2$$

The *standard deviation* is the square root of the variance.

18. Two measures of central tendency other than the (arithmetic) mean (defined in Problem 17) are the *geometric mean* and the *harmonic mean* defined for a list of positive numbers $x_1, x_2, \ldots, x_n$ as follows:

$$\text{geometric mean} = \sqrt[n]{x_1 \cdot x_2 \cdots x_n}$$

$$= \text{the } n\text{th root of the product of the numbers}$$

$$\text{harmonic mean} = \frac{n}{\dfrac{1}{x_1} + \dfrac{1}{x_2} + \cdots + \dfrac{1}{x_n}}$$

Write a program that reads a list of numbers, counts them, and calculates their arithmetic mean, geometric mean, and harmonic mean. These values should be printed with appropriate labels.

19. Write a program to implement the algorithm for estimating the time required to empty the reservoir described in Exercise 20 of Section 4.5.

20. Suppose that two hallways, one 8 feet wide and the other 10 feet wide, meet at a right angle and that a ladder is to be carried around the corner from the narrower hallway into the wider one. Using the similar triangles in the following diagram, we see that

$$L = x + \frac{10x}{\sqrt{x^2 - 64}}$$

Write a program that initializes x to 8.1 and then increments it by 0.1 to find to the nearest 0.1 foot the length of the longest ladder that can be carried around the corner. (*Note*: This length is the same as the minimum value of the distance L.)

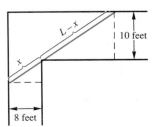

Section 4.6

21. In some situations, an exponential function

$$y = ae^{bx}$$

gives a better fit to a set of data points than does a straight line. One common method to determine the constants a and b is to take logarithms

$$\ln y = \ln a + bx$$

and then use the method of least squares to find values of the constants b and $\ln a$. Write a program that uses this method to fit an exponential curve to a set of data points. Run it for the values in the following table, which gives the barometric pressure readings, in millimeters of mercury, at various altitudes.

Altitude (meters) x	Barometric Pressure (millimeters) y
0	760
500	714
1000	673
1500	631
2000	594
2500	563

22. Related to the least-squares method is the problem of determining whether there is a linear relationship between two quantities x and y. One statistical measure used in this connection is the *correlation coefficient*. It is equal to 1 if there is a perfect positive linear relationship between x and y, that is, if y increases linearly as x increases. If there is a perfect negative linear relationship between x and y, that is, if y decreases linearly as x increases, then the correlation coefficient has the value -1. A value of 0 for the correlation coefficient indicates that there is no linear relationship between x and y, and nonzero values between -1 and 1 indicate a partial linear relationship between the two quantities. The correlation coefficient for a set of n pairs of x- and y-values is calculated by

$$\frac{n(\Sigma xy) - (\Sigma x)(\Sigma y)}{\sqrt{(n\Sigma x^2 - (\Sigma x)^2)(n\Sigma y^2 - (\Sigma y)^2)}}$$

where

Σx is the sum of the x-values

Σy is the sum of the y-values

Σx^2 is the sum of the squares of the x-values

$\sum y^2$ is the sum of the squares of the y-values

$\sum xy$ is the sum of the products xy of corresponding x- and y-values

Write a program to calculate the correlation coefficient of a set of data points. Run it for the data points used in the sample run for Figure 4.15 and for several data sets of your own.

FEATURES NEW TO FORTRAN 90

The repetition structures described in this chapter have several features that were not present in FORTRAN 77:

- Counter-controlled DO loops of the forms

  ```
  DO control-variable = initial-value, limit, step-size
     statement-sequence
  END DO
  ```

  The only form provided in FORTRAN 77 is

  ```
      DO n, control-variable = initial-value, limit, step-size
         statement-sequence
  n   CONTINUE
  ```

- DO constructs of the form

  ```
  DO WHILE (logical-expression)
     statement-sequence
  END DO
  ```

  used to implement while loops (see Appendix F)
- DO constructs of the form

  ```
  DO
     statement-sequence
  END DO
  ```

  or

  ```
  DO n
     statement-sequence
  n   CONTINUE
  ```

  to implement loop-forever repetition structures
- Named DO constructs
- EXIT and CYCLE statements

5

Input/Output

The moving finger writes; and having writ
Moves on: not all your piety nor wit
Shall lure it back to cancel half a line,
Nor all your tears wash out a word of it.

When I read some of the rules for speaking and writing the English
language correctly . . . I think
        Any fool can make a rule
        And every fool will mind it.

HENRY THOREAU

I can only assume that a "Do Not File" document is filed in a "Do
Not File" file.

SENATOR FRANK CHURCH

*I*n Chapter 2 we noted that there are two types of input/output statements in Fortran, **list-directed** and **formatted** (or more precisely, programmer-formatted). In our discussion thus far, we have restricted our attention to list-directed input/output. This method is particularly easy to use because the format for the input or output of data is automatically supplied by the compiler. It does not, however, permit the programmer to control the precise format of the output. For example, using list-directed output, one cannot specify that real values are to be displayed with only two digits to the right of the decimal point, even though this might be appropriate in some applications. The precise form of the output can be specified, however, using the formatted output statement introduced in this chapter.

Sometimes input data has a predetermined form, and the programmer must design the program to read this data. This can be accomplished by using the formatted input statement, which is also introduced in this chapter.

If the volume of input data is large, a data file is usually prepared, and data is read from it rather than entered from the keyboard. Data may also be output to a file rather than to the screen or to a printer. In this chapter we consider some of the statements provided in Fortran for processing files.

In the last section we describe some special input/output features. These include some less commonly used format descriptors, some features of list-directed input/output not presented in Chapter 2, and NAMELIST input/output.

5.1   FORMATTED OUTPUT

There are two output statements in Fortran, the PRINT statement and the WRITE statement. The **PRINT statement** is the simpler of the two and has the following form:

PRINT *Statement*

Form:

```
PRINT format-specifier, output-list
```

where
  format-specifier is one of the following:
  1. * (an asterisk);
  2. a character constant or a character variable (or expression or array) whose value specifies the format for the output;
  3. the label of a FORMAT statement;

  output-list is a single expression or a list of expressions separated by commas; it may also be empty, in which case the comma preceding the list is omitted.

Purpose:
Displays the values of the items in the *output-list*. Each execution of a PRINT statement produces a new line of output. If the output list is omitted, a blank line is displayed. The *format-specifier* specifies the format in which values of the expressions in the output list are to be displayed.

As we saw in Chapter 2, an asterisk (*) indicates list-directed output whose format is determined by the types of expressions in the output list. This is adequate when the precise form of the output is not important. However, for reports and other kinds of output in which results must appear in a precise form, list-directed formatting is not adequate, and format specifiers of type 2 or 3 must be used. A large part of this section is devoted to the design of these format specifiers.

In the second type of format specifier, the formatting information is given as a character string of the form

```
'(list of format descriptors)'
```

or

```
"(list of format descriptors)"
```

that is, a character string that consists of format descriptors, separated by commas and enclosed in parentheses. (We will usually use the first form, since the list of format descriptors may include character strings, and we have been using double quotes to enclose them.)

In the third type of format specifier, the formatting information is supplied by a **FORMAT statement** whose statement number is specified. This statement has the form

---

FORMAT *Statement*

Form:

> *label* FORMAT(*list of format descriptors*)

where
   label is an integer in the range 1 through 99999.

Purpose:
Specifies output format.

The format descriptors specify precisely the format in which the items in the output list are to be displayed. For example, any of the following output statements

```
PRINT *, Number, Temperature

PRINT '(1X, I5, F8.2)', Number, Temperature

PRINT 20, Number, Temperature
```

where statement 20 is the statement

```
20 FORMAT(1X, I4, F8.2)
```

could be used to display the values of the integer variable Number and the real variable Temperature. In these statements, 1X, I4, and F8.2 are format descriptors that specify the format in which the values of Number and Temperature are to be displayed. If Number and Temperature have the values 17 and 10.25, respectively, then we know that list-directed output produced by the first statement is compiler-dependent but might appear as follows:

```
  17   10.25000
--------------
```

The output produced by the second and third forms is not compiler-dependent and appears as follows:

```
    17    10.25
-------------
```

(If control characters are in effect, there will be one less space at the beginning of this output line.)

There are many format descriptors that may be used in format specifiers. A list of the most useful descriptors is given in Table 5.1. In this section we consider those most commonly used, deferring the others until Section 5.7.

Table 5.1　Format Descriptors

Forms		Use
Iw	I$w.m$	Integer data
Bw	B$w.m$	Integer data in binary form
Ow	O$w.m$	Integer data in octal form
Zw	Z$w.m$	Integer data in hexadecimal form
F$w.d$		Real data in decimal notation
E$w.d$	E$w.d$Ee	Real data in exponential notation
ES$w.d$	ES$w.d$Ee	Real data in scientific notation
EN$w.d$	EN$w.d$Ee	Real data in engineering notation
G$w.d$	G$w.d$Ee	General i/o descriptor
A	Aw	Character data
"x... x"	'x... x'	Character strings
Lw		Logical data
Tc　　TLn	TRn	Tab descriptors
nX		Horizontal spacing
/		Vertical spacing
:		Format scanning control

w: a positive integer constant specifying the field width

m: a nonnegative integer constant specifying the minimum number of digits to be read/displayed

d: a nonnegative integer constant specifying the number of digits to the right of the decimal point

e: a nonnegative integer constant specifying the number of digits in an exponent

x: a character

c: a positive integer constant representing a character position

n: a positive integer constant specifying the number of character positions

Control Characters

Some Fortran compilers use the first character of each line of output directed to a printer to control vertical spacing. If this character is a **control character**, it is removed from the output line and is used to effect the appropriate printer control. The standard control characters with their effects are as follows:

Control Characters

Control Character	Effect
blank	Normal spacing: advance to the next line before printing
0	Double spacing: skip one line before printing
1	Advance to top of next page before printing
+	Overprint the last line printed

The details regarding how your particular system uses control characters (and whether it uses any others) can be obtained from system manuals, your instructor, or computer center personnel.

When control characters are in effect, it is important to pay attention to printer control, because otherwise the output may not be what was intended. To illustrate, consider the following statement:

```
PRINT '(I3)', N
```

The format descriptor I3 specifies that the value to be printed is an integer and is to be printed in the first three positions of a line. If the value of N is 15, the three positions are filled with b15 (where b denotes a blank). If control characters are in effect, the blank in the first position is removed and is interpreted as a control character. This produces normal spacing and displays the value 15 in the first two positions of a new line:

```
 15
 --
```

If, however, the value of N is 150, the first three positions are to be filled with 150. The character 1 in the first position is removed and interpreted as a control character. It is not printed, but instead the value 50 is printed at the top of a new page:

```
 50
 --
```

When control characters are in effect, it is a good practice to use the first print position of each output line to indicate explicitly what printer control is desired. This can be done by making the first descriptor of each format specifier one of the following:

1X or "   " for normal spacing

"0" for double spacing

"1" for advancing to a new page

"+" for overprinting

For list-directed output, a blank will automatically be inserted at the beginning of each output line as a control character and produce normal spacing.

The default output device for many systems is the screen and control characters are not normally in effect. We will assume that this is the case in this text:

> In the examples of this text, control characters are *not* assumed. However, so that these examples do not need modification for systems in which control characters are in effect, we will use an appropriate format descriptor (e.g., 1X) at the beginning of each output format specifier.

Integer Output—The I Descriptor

The I descriptor used to describe the format in which integer data is to be displayed has the form

$$rIw \qquad \text{or} \qquad rIw.m$$

where

Mol ozord
m=1 2 263.
not m=0

I   denotes integer data

w   is an integer constant indicating the width of the field in which the data is to be displayed, that is, the number of spaces to be used in displaying it

r   is an integer constant called a *repetition indicator*, indicating the number of such fields; for example, 4I3 is the same as I3, I3, I3, I3; if there is only one such field, the number 1 need not be given

m   is the minimum number of digits to be displayed

Integer values are *right-justified* in fields of the specified sizes; that is, each value is displayed so that its last digit appears in the rightmost position of the field. For example, if the values of the integer variables Number, L, and Kappa are given by

```
INTEGER :: Number = 3, L = 5378, Kappa = -12345
```

then the statement

```
PRINT '(1X, 2I5, I7, I10)', Number, Number - 3, L, Kappa
```

or

```
PRINT 30, Number, Number - 3, L, Kappa
30 FORMAT(1X, 2I5, I7, I10)
```

produce the following output:

```
      3     0    5378      -12345
```

The statements

```
PRINT '(1X, 2I5.2, I7, I10.7)', Number, Number - 3, L, Kappa
PRINT '(1X, 2I5.0, I7, I10)', Number, Number - 3, L, Kappa
```

or

```
PRINT 31, Number, Number - 3, L, Kappa
PRINT 32, Number, Number - 3, L, Kappa
31 FORMAT(1X, 2I5.2, I7, I10.7)
32 FORMAT(1X, 2I5.0, I7, I10)
```

produce

```
   03    00     5378   -0012345
    3          5378     -12345
```

If an integer value (including a minus sign if the number is negative) requires more spaces than specified by a descriptor, the field is filled with asterisks. Thus, the statement

```
PRINT '(1X, 4I3)', Number, Number - 3, L, Kappa
```

will produce

```
  3   0******
```

Real Output—The F Descriptor

One of the descriptors used to format real (floating-point) data has the form

$$rFw.d$$

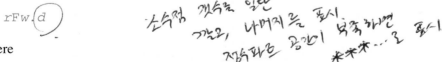

where

- F   denotes real (floating-point) data
- *w*   is an integer constant indicating the *total width of the field* in which the data is to be displayed
- *d*   is an integer constant indicating the number of digits to the right of the decimal point

r is the repetition indicator, an integer constant indicating the number of such fields; again, if there is to be only one such field, the number 1 is not required

Real values are *right-justified* in the specified fields. For a descriptor $Fw.d$, if the corresponding real value has more than d digits to the right of the decimal point, it is *rounded to d digits.* If it has fewer than d digits, the remaining positions are filled with zeros. In most systems, values less than 1 in magnitude are displayed with a zero to the left of the decimal point (for example, 0.123 rather than .123).

For example, to display the values of the integer variables In and Out and the values of the real variables A, B, and C as given by

```
INTEGER :: In = 625, Out = -19
REAL :: A = 7.5, B = .182, C = 625.327
```

we can use the statements

```
PRINT '(1X, 2I4, 2F6.3, F8.3)', In, Out, A, B, C
```

or

```
PRINT 50, In, Out, A, B, C
50 FORMAT(1X, 2I4, 2F6.3, F8.3)
```

The resulting output is

```
 625 -19 7.500 0.182 625.327
---------------------------------
```

To provide more space between the numbers and to round each of the real values to two decimal places, we can use the format specification

```
(1X, 2I10, 3F10.2)
```

This displays the numbers right-justified in fields containing 10 spaces, as follows:

```
        625        -19      7.50      0.18    625.33
----------------------------------------------------
```

As with the I descriptor, if the real number being output requires more spaces than specified by the descriptor, the entire field is *filled with asterisks.* For example,

```
REAL :: Beta = -567.89

PRINT 55, 123.4
PRINT 55, Beta
55 FORMAT(1X, F5.2)
```

produces

```
  * * * * *
 - - - - - -
  * * * * *
 - - - - - -
```

It should be noted that for a descriptor F*w.d*, one should have

$$w \geq d + 3$$

to allow for the sign of the number, the first digit, and the decimal point.

Real Output—The E, ES, and EN Descriptors

Real data may also be output using E, ES, and EN descriptors. The E descriptor has the form

$rEw.d$ or $rEw.dEe$

[handwritten: E±00 e) default : 2. E±02]

where

E indicates that the data is to be output in exponential notation

w is an integer constant that indicates the total width of the field in which the data is to be displayed

d is an integer constant indicating the number of decimal digits to be displayed

r is the repetition indicator, an integer constant indicating the number of such fields; it need not be used if there is only one field

e is the number of positions to be used in displaying the exponent

Although some details of the output are compiler-dependent, real values are usually displayed in *normalized form*—a minus sign, if necessary, followed by one leading zero, then a decimal point followed by *d* significant digits, and E with an appropriate exponent in the next four spaces for the first form or *e* spaces for the second form. For example, if values of real variables A, B, C, and D are given by

```
REAL :: A = .12345E8, B = .0237, C = 4.6E-12, D = -76.1684E12
```

the statement

```
PRINT '(1X, 2E15.5, E15.4, E14.4)', A, B, C, D
```

produces output like the following:

```
     0.12345E+08      0.23700E-01      0.4600E-11    -0.7617E+14
 - - - - - - - - - - - - - - - - - - - - - - - - - - - - - - - - - - - - -
```

As with the F descriptor, a field is *asterisk-filled* if it is not large enough for the value. It should also be noted that for a descriptor E$w.d$ one should have

$$w \geq d + 7$$

or for the second form E$w.d$Ee,

$$w \geq d + e + 5$$

to allow space for the sign of the number, a leading zero, a decimal point, and E with the exponent.

The ES descriptor has the form

rES$w.d$ or rES$w.d$Ee

where r, w, d, and e have the same meaning as for the E descriptor. This **scientific** descriptor ES is used in the same manner as the E descriptor, except that values are normalized so that the mantissa is at least 1 but less than 10 (unless the value is zero). For example, for the preceding real variables A, B, C, and D, the output produced by the statement

```
PRINT '(1X, 2ES15.5, ES15.4, ES14.4)', A, B, C, D
```

is

```
      1.23450E+07     2.37000E-02      4.6000E-12    -7.6168E+13
------------------------------------------------------------------
```

The EN descriptor is an **engineering** descriptor and has the form

rEN$w.d$ or rE$w.d$Ee

where r, w, d, and e have the same meaning as for the E descriptor. It also is used in the same manner as the E descriptor, except that the exponent is constrained to be a multiple of 3 so that a nonzero mantissa is greater than or equal to 1 and less than 1000. For example, if the preceding output statement is changed to

```
PRINT '(1X, 2EN15.5, EN15.4, EN14.4)', A, B, C, D
```

the output produced is

```
     12.34500E+06   23.70000E-03      4.6000E-12   -76.1684E+12
------------------------------------------------------------------
```

Character Output

Character constants may be displayed by including them in the list of descriptors of a format specifier. For example, if X and Y have the values 0.3 and 7.9, respectively, the statements

```
    PRINT '(1X, "X =", F6.2, " Y =", F6.2)', X, Y
```

or

```
    PRINT 70, X, Y
70 FORMAT(1X, "X =", F6.2, " Y =", F6.2)
```

produce as output

```
X =   0.30 Y =   7.90
--------------------
```

Character data may also be displayed by using an A format descriptor of the form

rA or rAw

where

w (if used) is an integer constant specifying the field width

r is the repetition indicator, an integer constant indicating the number of such fields; it may be omitted if there is only one field

In the first form, the field width is determined by the length of the character value being displayed. In the second form, if the field width exceeds the length of the character value, that value is *right-justified* in the field. In contrast with numeric output, however, if the length of the character value exceeds the specified field width, the output consists of the *leftmost w* characters. For example, the preceding output would also be produced if the labels were included in the output list, as follows:

```
    PRINT '(1X, A, F6.2, A, F6.2)', "X =", X, " Y =", Y
```

or

```
    PRINT 71, "X =", X, " Y =", Y
71 FORMAT(1X, A, F6.2, A, F6.2)
```

Placing labels in the output list rather than in the format specifier allows the format specifier to be reused to display other labels and values, as in

```
    PRINT 71, "Mean is", X_Mean, &
              " with standard deviation", Std_Dev
```

Positional Descriptors—x and T

Two format descriptors can be used to provide spacing in an output line. An X descriptor can be used to insert blanks in an output line. It has the form *nX*   ~~insert~~

where *n* is a positive integer constant that specifies the number of blanks to be inserted.

The T descriptor has the form

T*c*

where *c* is an integer constant denoting the number of the space on a line at which a field is to begin. This descriptor functions much like a tab key on a typewriter and causes the next output field to begin at the specified position on the current line. One difference is that the value of *c* may be less than the current position; that is, "tabbing backward" is possible.[1]

As an illustration of these descriptors, suppose that Number is an integer variable, and consider the output statement

```
PRINT 75, "John Q. Doe", "CPSC", Number
```

together with either of the following FORMAT statements:

```
75 FORMAT(1X, A11, 3X, A4, 2X, I3)
```

→ *I5*   남은공간 앞 blank.

or

```
75 FORMAT(1X, A11, T16, A4, 2X, I3)
```

If Number has the value 141, the output produced is

```
| John Q. Doe    CPSC  141
```

Note that the descriptor 2X in either FORMAT statement can be replaced by T22 and that the pair of descriptors 2X, I3 can be replaced by the single descriptor I5. This same output is produced by the statements

```
PRINT 75, "John Q. Doe", Number, "CPSC"
75 FORMAT(1X, A11, T22, I3, T16, A4)
```

which use the backward-tabbing feature of the T descriptor.

Repeating Groups of Format Descriptors

As we have seen, it is possible to repeat some format descriptors by preceding them with a *repetition indicator*. For example,

---

[1] In some systems, a run-time error will occur if *c* is less than the current position.

```
3F10.2
```

is equivalent to

```
F10.2, F10.2, F10.2
```

It is also possible to repeat a group of descriptors by enclosing the group in parentheses and then placing a repetition indicator before the left parenthesis. For example, the format specifier

```
'(1X, A, F6.2, A, F6.2)'
```

can be written more compactly as

```
'(1X, 2(A, F6.2))'
```

Similarly, the format specifier

```
'(1X, I10, F10.2, I10, F10.2, I10, F10.2, E15.8)'
```

can be shortened to

```
'(1X, 3(I10, F10.2), E15.8)'
```

Additional levels of groups are permitted. For example, the format specifier

```
'(1X, E18.2, I3, A, I3, A, E18.2, I3, A, I3, A, F8.4)'
```

can be written more compactly as

```
'(1X, 2(E18.2, 2(I3, A)), F8.4)'
```

The Slash (/) Descriptor

By using a slash (/) descriptor, a single output statement can be used to display values on more than one line, with different formats. The slash causes output to begin on a new line. It can also be used with a repetition indicator to skip several lines. It is not necessary to use a comma to separate a slash descriptor from other descriptors. For example, the statements

```
PRINT 85, "Values"
PRINT *
PRINT *
PRINT 86, N, A, M, B
PRINT *
PRINT 87, C, D
```

```
85 FORMAT(1X, A)
86 FORMAT(1X, 2(I10, F10.2))
87 FORMAT(1X, 2E15.7)
```

can be combined in the pair of statements

```
PRINT 88, "Values", N, A, M, B, C, D
88 FORMAT(1X, A, 3/ 1X, 2(I10, F10.2) // 1X, 2E15.7)
```

If the values of N, A, M, B, C, and D are given by

```
N = 5173
A = 617.2
M = 7623
B = 29.25
C = 37.555
D = 5.2813
```

then in both cases the resulting output is

```
Values
---------------------------------------------
---------------------------------------------
---------------------------------------------
        5173      617.20         7623      29.25
---------------------------------------------

  0.3755500E+02  0.5281300E+01
---------------------------------------------
```

Scanning the Format

When a formatted output statement is executed, the corresponding format specifier is scanned from left to right in parallel with the output list to locate the appropriate descriptors for the output items. The types of the descriptors should match the types of the values being displayed; for example, a real value should not be displayed with an I descriptor. If the values of all the items in the output list have been displayed before all the descriptors have been used, scanning of the format specifier continues. Values of character constants are displayed, and the positioning specified by slash, X, and T descriptors continues until one of the following is encountered:

1. The right parenthesis signaling the end of the list of format descriptors
2. An I, F, E, ES, EN, A, L, G, B, O, or Z descriptor
3. A colon

In cases 2 and 3, all remaining descriptors in the format specifier are ignored.
To illustrate, consider the statements

```
PRINT '(1X, I5, 3I6)', I; J
PRINT '(1X, F5.1, F7.0, F10.5)', X, Y
PRINT '(1X, 5(" Item is", A10))', "Bumper", "Headlight"
PRINT '(1X, 5(:)" Item is", A10))', "Bumper", "Headlight"
```

If I and J are integer variables with values I = 1 and J = 2 and X and Y are real variables with values given by X = 5.6 and Y = 7.8, these statements produce the output

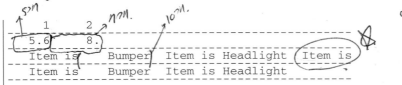

(handwritten notes: descriptor 끝? , output 끝? / descriptor 갖고, output 밀등 끝.*)*

Note that like the slash, the colon descriptor need not be separated from other descriptors by a comma.

If the list of descriptors is exhausted before the output list is, a new line of output is begun, and the format specifier or part of it is rescanned. If there are no internal parentheses within the format specifier, the rescanning begins with the first descriptor. For example, the statements

```
INTEGER :: M1 = 1, M2 = 2, M3 = 3, M4 = 4, M5 = 5
PRINT '(1X, 2I3)', M1, M2, M3, M4, M5
```

produce the output

```
    1  2
 ----------
    3  4
 ----------
    5
 ----------
```

If the format specifier does contain internal parentheses, rescanning begins at the left parenthesis that matches the next-to-last right parenthesis; any repetition counter preceding this format group is in effect. Thus, if integer variables K, L1, L2, and L3 have values

(handwritten note: (o o ((o o))) rescanned.*)*

```
K = 3
L1 = 21; L2 = 22; L3 = 23
```

and real variables X, Y1, Y2, and Y3 have values

```
X = 4.0
Y1 = 5.5; Y2 = 6.66; Y3 = 7.77
```

the statements

```
PRINT 125, K, X, L1, Y1, L2, Y2, L3, Y3
125 FORMAT(1X, I5, F10.3 / (1X, I10, F12.2))
```

읽으며 다시돌.

produce the output

```
     3      4.000
----------------------
            21        5.50
----------------------
            22        6.66
----------------------
            23        7.77
----------------------
```

Thus, it is possible to specify a special format for the first output items and a different format for subsequent items by enclosing the last format descriptors in parentheses. In this example, when the right parenthesis of the FORMAT statement is encountered after displaying the value of Y1, a new line is begun, and the descriptors following the second left parenthesis are reused to display the values of L2 and Y2 and then again on a new line to display the values of L3 and Y3.

5.2 EXAMPLE: PRINTING TABLES OF COMPUTED VALUES

In some of the sample programs of Chapter 4, the output was displayed in a table format. For example, the output produced in the sample run of the depreciation-table program in Figure 4.5 was

```
Year    Depreciation
====================
  1     5.0000000E+03
  2     4.0000000E+03
  3     3.0000000E+03
  4     2.0000000E+03
  5     1.0000000E+03
```

One unpleasant feature of this table is that the values in the second column are displayed in exponential notation, even though decimal format would be more appropriate for these monetary values. Note also that all the values are displayed with seven digits to the right of the decimal point, even though two would be better for this program. With list-directed output, however, the format of the output cannot be controlled by the programmer.

Positioning headings for the columns of a table above the values in the columns can also be rather difficult, because the programmer cannot control the format or the spacing of these values. It may be necessary to change the output statements and re-execute the modified program several times before the appearance of the output is satisfactory.

The format descriptors in this section make it quite easy to control the format of the output, and correct placement of items such as table headings is also considerably easier than with list-directed output. The program in Figure 5.1 demonstrates this. It reads a value for an integer LastNumber and then outputs a table of values of N, the square and the cube of N, and its square root for N = 1, 2, . . . , LastNumber.

Figure 5.1 Table of squares, cubes, and square roots—version 1.

```
PROGRAM Table_of_Values
!-------------------------------------------------------------------
! Program demonstrating the use of formatted output to print a table
! of values of N, the square and cube of N, and the square root of N
! for N = 1, 2, ..., LastNumber, where the value of LastNumber is read
! during execution.  Variables used are:
!    N           : counter
!    LastNumber : last value of N
!
! Input:  LastNumber
! Output: Table of values of N, N**2, N**3, and square root of N
!-------------------------------------------------------------------

   INTEGER :: N, LastNumber

   PRINT *, "Enter last number to be used:"
   READ *, LastNumber

   ! Print headings

   PRINT '(// 1X, A8, T12, A8, T22, A8, T32, A9 / 1X, 40("="))', &
         "Number", "Square", "  Cube", "Sq. root"

   ! Print the table

   DO N = 1, LastNumber
      PRINT '(1X, I6, 2I10, 2X, F10.4)', &
            N, N**2, N**3, SQRT(REAL(N))
   END DO

END PROGRAM Table_of_Values
```

Sample run:

```
Enter last number to be used:
10
```

Figure 5.1 *(cont.)*

Number	Square	Cube	Sq. root
1	1	1	1.0000
2	4	8	1.4142
3	9	27	1.7321
4	16	64	2.0000
5	25	125	2.2361
6	36	216	2.4495
7	49	343	2.6458
8	64	512	2.8284
9	81	729	3.0000
10	100	1000	3.1623

5.3   FORMATTED INPUT

We have seen that input is accomplished in Fortran by a **READ statement**. This statement has two forms, the simpler of which is the following:

READ *Statement*

Form:

```
READ format-specifier, input-list
```

where
input-list is a single variable or a list of variables separated by commas; and
format-specifier specifies the format in which the values for the items in the input list are to be entered. As in the case of output, the format specifier may be

1. * (an asterisk),
2. a character constant or a character variable (or expression or array), whose value specifies the format for the output,
3. the label of a FORMAT statement.

Effect:
Reads values for the variables in the *input-list* using the formats given in the *format-specifier*.

The most commonly used form of the READ statement is the one in which the format specifier is an asterisk. As we saw in Chapter 3, this form indicates list-directed input in which the format is determined by the types of variables in the input list. In all situations except those in which the data has a specific predetermined form, list-directed input should be adequate. When the data items are of a predetermined form, it may be necessary to use a format specifier of type 2 or 3 to read them.

As in the case of output, the format specifier may be a character constant or variable (or expression or array) whose value has the form

```
'(list of format descriptors)'
```

or

```
"(list of format descriptors)"
```

or the label of a FORMAT statement of the form

```
label FORMAT(list of format descriptors)
```

The format descriptors are essentially the same as those discussed for output in the preceding section. Character constants, however, may not appear in the list of format descriptors, and the colon separator is not relevant to input.

Integer Input

Integer data can be read using the I descriptor of the form

```
rIw
```

where w indicates the width of the field, that is, the number of characters to be read, and r is the repetition indicator specifying the number of such fields. To illustrate, consider the following example:

```
INTEGER :: I, J, K

READ '(I6, I4, I7)', I, J, K
```

or

```
READ 5, I, J, K
5 FORMAT(I6, I4, I7)
```

For the values of I, J, and K to be read correctly, the numbers should be entered as follows: the value for I in the first six positions, the value for J in the next four positions, and the value for K in the next seven positions. Thus, if the values to be read are

```
I:   -123
J:   45
K:   6789
```

the data may be entered as follows:

```
 -123    45     6789
 --------------------
```

Had the data been entered as

```
 -123     45      6789
 ---------------------
```

the same values would be assigned since *blanks within numeric fields are ignored* (unless specified using the BZ descriptor described in Section 5.7). If the format specification were changed to

```
(I4,  I2,  I4)
```

the data should be entered as

```
 -123456789
 ----------
```

with no intervening blanks. Here the first four characters are read for I, the next two characters for J, and the next four characters for K.

Real Input

One of the descriptors used to input real data is the F descriptor of the form

$$rFw.d$$

where w indicates the width of the field to be read, d is the number of digits to the right of the decimal point, and r is the repetition indicator.

There are two ways that real data may be entered:

1. The numbers may be entered without decimal points.
2. The decimal point may be entered as part of the input value.

In the first case, the d specification in the format descriptor $Fw.d$ automatically positions the decimal point so that there are d digits to its right. For example, if we wish to enter the following values for real variables A, B, C, D, and E,

```
A:    6.25
B:   -1.9
C:    75.0
D:    .182
E:    625.327
```

we can use the statement

```
READ '(F3.2, 2F3.1, F3.3, F6.3)', A, B, C, D, E
```

or

```
READ 10, A, B, C, D, E
10 FORMAT(F3.2, 2F3.1, F3.3, F6.3)
```

and enter the data in the following form:

```
625-19750182625327
```

Of course, we can use wider fields, for example,

```
(F4.2, 2F4.1, 2F8.3)
```

and enter the data in the form

```
 625 -19 750       182   625327
```

In the second method of entering real data, the position of the decimal point in the value entered overrides the position specified by the descriptor. Thus, if the number to be read is 9423.68, an appropriate descriptor is F6.2 if the number is entered without a decimal point and F7.2, or F7.1, or F7.0, and so on, if the number is entered with a decimal point. For example, the preceding values for A, B, C, D, and E can be read using the statement

```
READ '(4F5.0, F8.0)', A, B, C, D, E
```

with the data entered in the following form:

```
 6.25 -1.9   75. .182 625.327
```

Note that each field width must be large enough to accommodate the number entered, including the decimal point and the sign.

Real values entered in E notation can also be read using an F descriptor. Thus for the format specification

```
(3F6.0, 2F10.0)
```

the data of the preceding example could also have been entered as

```
.625E1  -1.9   75.0    18.2E-2 6.25327E2
```

In this case, the E need not be entered if the exponent is preceded by a sign. The following would therefore be an alternative method for entering the preceding data:

```
.625+1   -1.9   75.0     18.2-2 6.25327+2
```

The E, ES, and EN descriptors may also be used in a manner similar to that for the F descriptor.

Character Input

Character data can be read using an A descriptor of the form

rA or rAw

where r is a repetition indicator, and in the second form w is the width of the field to be read. In the first form, the width of the field read for a particular variable in the input list is the length specified for that variable in the CHARACTER statement.

When a READ statement whose input list contains a character variable is executed, *all* characters in the field associated with the corresponding A descriptor are read. For example, if the line of data

```
Fourscore and seven years ago
```

is read by the statements

```
CHARACTER(6) :: Speech1, Speech2

READ '(2A)', Speech1, Speech2
```

the values assigned to Speech1 and Speech2 are

```
Speech1:   Foursc
Speech2:   ore an
```

Note that six characters were read for each of Speech1 and Speech2, as this is their declared length. If the following line of data

```
AB1''34;an,apple a day
```

were entered, the values assigned would be

```
Speech1:   AB1''3
Speech2:   4;an,a
```

If the format specifier

'(2A6)'

were used, the same values would be assigned to Speech1 and Speech2. If, however, the format specifier

'(A2, A12)'

were used, the values assigned would be

Speech1:   ABØØØØ   (where Ø denotes a blank)
Speech2:   an,app

Note that in the case of Speech2, a field of size 12 was read but the *rightmost* 6 characters were assigned. (See Potential Problem 3 in the Programming Pointers at the end of this chapter.)

Skipping Input Characters

The positional descriptors X and T may be used in the format specifier of a READ statement to skip over certain input characters. For example, if we wish to assign the following values to the integer variables I, J, and K:

I: 4
J: 56
K: 137

by entering data in the form

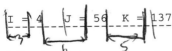

the following statements may be used:

```
READ '(3X, I2, 6X, I3, 5X, I4)', I, J, K
```

or

```
READ '(T4, I2, T12, I3, T20, I4)', I, J, K
```

Input characters are also skipped if the end of the input list is encountered before the end of the data line has been reached. To illustrate, if the statements

```
READ 25, Number1, X
READ 25, Number2, Y
25 FORMAT(I5, F7.0)
```

are used to read values for the integer variables `Number1` and `Number2` and real variables `X` and `Y` from the data lines

```
   17    3.56    34    13.4
 9064 570550 3199 47
```

the values assigned to `Number1` and `X` are

```
Number1:  17
      X:  3.56
```

and the values assigned to `Number2` and `Y` are

```
Number2:  9064
      Y:  570550.
```

All other information on these two lines is ignored.

Multiple Input Lines

Recall that a new line of data is required each time a `READ` statement is executed. A new line of data is also required whenever a slash (`/`) is encountered in the format specifier for the `READ` statement. This may be used in case some of the data entries are separated by blank lines, remarks, and the like, which are to be skipped over by the `READ` statement. For example, the following data

```
Amount to be produced
585.00
Reaction rate
(This assumes constant temperature)
5.75
```

can be read by a single `READ` statement, and the values 585.00 and 5.75 assigned to `Amount` and `Rate`, respectively, as follows:

```
REAL :: Amount, Rate

READ '(/ F6.0 3/ F4.0)', Amount, Rate
```

or

```
READ 30, Amount, Rate
30 FORMAT(/ F6.0 3/ F4.0)
```

The first slash causes the first line to be skipped, so that the value 585.00 is read for `Amount`; the three slashes then cause an advance of three lines, so that 5.75 is read for `Rate`.

A new line is also required if all descriptors have been used and the input list still contains variables for which values must be read. In this case, the format specifier is rescanned, as in the case of output. Thus, the statements

```
INTEGER :: I, J, K, L, M

READ '(3I8)', I, J, K/ L, M
```

require two lines of input, the first containing the values of I, J, and K and the second, the values of L and M.

Quick Quiz 5.3

1. (True or false) The control character 0 causes the printer to advance to a new page.

2. (True or false) The format descriptor 3I2 is the same as I2, I2, I2.

3. (True or false) In the format descriptor F10.3, 10 refers to the number of digits to the left of the decimal point, and 3 refers to the number of digits to the right of the decimal point.

4. (True or false) For the format descriptor I2, if the integer to be output requires more than 2 spaces, the entire field will be blank.

5. (True or false) The format descriptor T is used to truncate values.

6. (True or false) If there are fewer descriptors than values in the output list, then the remaining values will be output using the last descriptor in the format identifier.

7. (True or false) For an F descriptor, real values are rounded to the number of decimal places specified.

8. The _____ descriptor causes output to begin on a new line.

9. Integers are _____ (left- or right-) justified in the fields specified in the I descriptor.

10. If N has the value 100, the statement PRINT '(1X, 4I3)', N will display the value 100 _____ times.

For Questions 11–13, assume the following declarations have been made:

```
REAL :: X = 234.56, Y = -1.0
INTEGER :: I = 987, J = -44
CHARACTER(20) :: Form = '(1X, I5, F10.1)'
```

Describe the output produced by each statement. Clearly indicate the spacing of characters within each line as well as the spacing between lines. (Assume that printer control characters are not in effect.)

```
11. PRINT 5, I, X
    5 FORMAT(1X, "I =", I3, 2X, "X =", F8.3, "THE END")
```

```
12. PRINT Form, I, X, J, Y
13. PRINT '(1X, F10.0 / 1X, I3, T11, I5)', X, I, J
```

For each of the READ statements in Questions 14–18, show how the data must be entered so that X is assigned the value 123.45, Y the value 6.0, I the value 99, and J the value 876. Assume that Form is declared by:

```
CHARACTER(20) :: Form = '(2I3, F5.2, F1.0)'
```

```
14. READ *, I, J, X, Y
15. READ '(2I3, 2F6.0)', I, J, X, Y
16. READ '(I3, F7.0, 2X, I5, T20, F5.0)', I, X, J, Y
17. READ FORM, I, J, X, Y
18. READ 9, I, X, J, Y
    9 FORMAT(I2, F5.2 / I3, F2.1)
```

Exercises 5.3

Assuming that the following declarations

```
INTEGER :: Number = 12345
REAL :: Alpha = 87.6543
CHARACTER(25) :: Form_1 = '(1X, I10, F10.2, "---")', &
                 Form_2 = '(1X, I10, F10.2 : "---")', &
                 Title*8 = "Exercise"
```

have been made, describe the output that will be produced by the statements in Exercises 1–26. For Exercises 1–20, assume that control characters *are not in effect*.

```
1. PRINT *, "Computer science -- ", Title, " 5.3"
2. PRINT *, Number, Number + 1
3. PRINT *, "Alpha =", Alpha, " Number =", Number
4. PRINT *
5. PRINT '(" Computer science -- Exercise", F4.1)', &
         3 * 2.1 - 1.0
6. PRINT 10, Title, 5.3
   10 FORMAT(" Computer science -- ", A, F5.2)
7. PRINT '(1X, A, F4.1)', "Computer science", 5.3
```

8. PRINT '(" Computer science --", A10, F6.3)', &
       Title, 5.3

9. PRINT 20, Title, 5.3
   20 FORMAT(" Computer science --", A2, F3.1)

10. PRINT 30, Number, Number + 1, Alpha, Alpha + 1, &
        Alpha + 2
    30 FORMAT(1X, 2I7, F10.5, F10.3, F10.0)

11. PRINT '(1X, I5, 4X, I4, T20, I6)', Number, &
        Number + 1, Number + 2

12. PRINT 40, Number, Alpha, Number + 1, Alpha + 1
    40 FORMAT(1X, I5, F7.4 / 1X, I5, E12.5)

13. PRINT '(1X, I10, F10.3)', Number, Alpha, &
        Number + 1, Alpha + 1

14. PRINT Form_1, Number, Alpha, Number + 1, Alpha + 1

15. PRINT Form_2, Number, Alpha, Number + 1, Alpha + 1

16. PRINT '(1X, I5, A2, I6, / 1X, 13("="))', &
        Number, "=", 12345

17. PRINT 50, Number, Alpha, Number, Alpha
    50 FORMAT(3/ 2(1X, I6 // 1X, F6.2) 3/ " ******")

18. PRINT 60, Number, Alpha, Number, Alpha, Number, &
        Alpha
    60 FORMAT(1X, I6, F7.2, 1X, I5, F6.1)

19. PRINT 70, Number, Alpha, Number, Alpha, Number, &
        Alpha
    70 FORMAT(1X, I6, F7.2, (1X, I5, F6.1))

20. PRINT '(1X, 10("*"), A, 10("*"))', "THE END"

For Exercises 21–26, assume that control characters *are in effect.*

21. PRINT '("Computer science -- ", A, F5.2)', Title, &
        5.3

22. PRINT '(1X, A, F4.1)', "Computer science", 5.3

23. PRINT 80, Number, Number + 1, Alpha, Alpha + 1, &
        Alpha + 2
    80 FORMAT("0", 2I7, F10.5, F10.3, F10.0)

24. PRINT '(1X, I5, 4X, I4, T20, I6)', Number, &
        Number + 1, Number + 2

25. PRINT '(1X, I5, F7.4 / I5, E12.5)', &
        Number, Alpha, Number + 1, Alpha + 1

26. PRINT '(1X, I5, F7.4)', Number, Alpha
    PRINT '("+", TI5, I5, E12.5)', Number + 1, Alpha + 1

For the `READ` statements in Exercises 27–39, assuming the declarations

```
INTEGER :: I, J
REAL :: X, Y
CHARACTER(20) :: Form_1 = '(2I3, F5.2, F1.0)', &
                 Form_2 = '(I5, F6.0)', &
                 C*8
```

show how the data should be entered so that X, Y, I, J, and C are assigned the values 123.77, 6.0, 77, 550, and "Fortran", respectively:

27. `READ *, I, J, X, Y`

28. `READ '(2I3, 2F6.0)', I, J, X, Y`

29. `READ '(I3, F7.0, 2X, I5, T20, F5.0)', I, J, X, Y`

30. `READ Form_1, I, J, X, Y`

31. `READ Form_2, I, X, J, Y`

32. `READ 200, I, X, J, Y`
    `200 FORMAT(I2, F5.2 / I3, F2.1)`

33. `READ 210, X, Y, I, J`
    `210 FORMAT(F5.2, 1X, F1.0, T4, I2, T9, I3)`

34. `READ 220, X, I, Y, J`
    `220 FORMAT(2(F5.2, I3))`

35. `READ 230, X, I, Y, J, C`
    `230 FORMAT(F6.2 / I5 // F6.0, I6 / A)`

36. `READ *, C, J`

37. `READ '(A, I2, F5.2)', C, I, X`

38. `READ '(A7, I3, F6.2)', C, I, X`

39. `READ '(A10, I10, F10.0)', C, I, X`

40. Describe the output that will be produced if the following program is executed with the specified input data:

```
PROGRAM Column

  INTEGER :: N, I
  REAL :: R, Delta_R, R1, S1
  CHARACTER(30) :: Output_Format

  Output_Format = '(1X, 2X, I2, 2(5X, F10.3))'
  100 FORMAT(T3, "Index", T14, "S Ratio", T30, "Load")

  READ '(/ I5, 2F10.4)', N, R, Delta_R
  PRINT 100
```

```
   DO I = 1, N
      R1 = R + Delta_R * (I - 1)
      IF (R1 < 120.0) THEN
         S1 = 17000.0 - 0.485*R1**2
      ELSE
         S1 = 18000.0 / (1.0 + R1**2/18000.0)
      END IF

      IF (MOD(I, 2) == 0) THEN
         PRINT Output_Format, I, R1, S1
      END IF
   END DO

END PROGRAM Column
```

Input data:

```
123456789012345678901234567890  ← Character positions
    4       100.0     100000
```

5.4 THE WRITE STATEMENT AND THE GENERAL READ STATEMENT

The PRINT and READ statements used thus far are simple Fortran input/output statements. However, in Sections 2.5 and 2.10 we saw that there is a more general output statement, the WRITE statement, and a more general form of the READ statement. In this section we will describe these more general forms, and in the next section we will show how they are used for file input/output.

The WRITE Statement

The **WRITE statement** has a more complicated syntax than the PRINT statement, but it is a more general output statement. It has the following form:

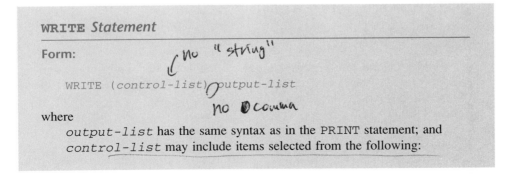

WRITE *Statement*

Form:

WRITE (*control-list*) *output-list*   [handwritten: "no "string"" ; "no ① comma"]

where

    output-list has the same syntax as in the PRINT statement; and
    control-list may include items selected from the following:

1. a unit specifier indicating the output device,
2. a format specifier,
3. an `ADVANCE` = clause,
4. other items that are especially useful in file processing.

Purpose:

Displays the values of the items in the *output-list* as directed by the specifications in the *control-list*, which must include a unit specifier and (except for the more advanced applications described in Chapter 12) a format specifier as well.

The **unit specifier** is an integer expression whose value designates the output device, or it may be an asterisk, indicating the standard output device (usually a monitor screen or a printer). The unit specifier may be given in the form

    UNIT = unit-specifier

or simply

    unit-specifier

If the second form is used, the unit specifier must be the first item in the control list.

The **format specifier** may be given in the form

    FMT = format-specifier

or simply

    format-specifier

where *format-specifier* may be of any of the forms allowed in the `PRINT` statement. If the second form is used, the format specifier must be the second item in the control list and the unit specifier (without "`UNIT` =") must be the first item.

The **ADVANCE = clause** has the form

    ADVANCE = character-expression

where the value of *character-expression* (after removing any trailing blanks and converting lower case to upper case) is one of the strings "`NO`" or "`YES`". It may be used only with formatted output.

To illustrate the `WRITE` statement, suppose that the values of `Gravity` and `Weight` are to be displayed on an output device having unit number 6. The statement

```
WRITE (6, *) Gravity, Weight
```

or any of the following equivalent forms

```
WRITE (6, FMT = *) Gravity, Weight

WRITE (UNIT = 6, FMT = *) Gravity, Weight

WRITE (Output_Unit, *) Gravity, Weight

WRITE (UNIT = Output_Unit, FMT = *) Gravity, Weight
```

where Output_Unit is an integer variable with value 6, produce list-directed output to this device. If this device is the system's standard output device, the unit number 6 may be replaced by an asterisk in any of the preceding statements; for example,

```
WRITE (*, *) Gravity, Weight
```

and each of these is equivalent to the short form

```
PRINT *, Gravity, Weight
```

Formatted output of these values can be produced by statements like the following:

```
WRITE (6, '(1X, 2F10.2)') Gravity, Weight

WRITE (6, FMT = '(1X, 2F10.2)') Gravity, Weight

WRITE (6, 30) Gravity, Weight
30 FORMAT(1X, 2F10.2)

WRITE (UNIT = 6, FMT = 30) Gravity, Weight
30 FORMAT(1X, 2F10.2)
```

The ADVANCE = clause is used to specify whether output should advance to a new line after the current output has been completed. ADVANCE = "NO" causes nonadvancing output, whereas ADVANCE = "YES" is the default condition and causes an advance to a new line of output after the WRITE statement has been executed.

Nonadvancing output is useful in displaying prompts for interactive input. For example, the statements

```
PRINT *, "Enter last number to be used:"
READ *, LastNumber
```

in the program of Figure 5.1 might be replaced by

```
WRITE (*, '(A)', ADVANCE = "NO") "Enter last number to be used: "
READ *, LastNumber
```

When the program is executed, the prompt will be displayed, but there will be no advance to a new line, and so the input value can be entered on the same line as the prompt:

```
Enter last number to be used: 10
```

Note that the ADVANCE = *clause may not be used* with list-directed output.

The General READ Statement

The general form of the READ statement is

READ *Statement*

Form:

```
READ (control-list) input-list
```

where
   input-list is a variable or a list of variables separated by commas; and
   control-list may include items selected from the following:
   1. a unit specifier indicating the input device,
   2. a format specifier,
   3. an ADVANCE = clause,
   4. an IOSTAT = clause or an END = clause to detect an input error or an end-of-file condition, as described in the next section,
   5. other items that are particularly useful in processing files.

Purpose:
Reads values for the variables in the *input-list* as directed by the specifications in the *control-list*. The unit specifier, the format specifier, and the ADVANCE = clause have the same forms as described for the WRITE statement.

As an illustration of the general form of the READ statement, suppose that values for Code, Time, and Rate are to be read using the input device 5. The statement

```
READ (5, *) Code, Time, Rate
```

or any of the following equivalent forms

```
READ (5, FMT = *) Code, Time, Rate

READ (UNIT = 5, FMT = *) Code, Time, Rate

READ (In, *) Code, Time, Rate

READ (UNIT = In, FMT = *) Code, Time, Rate
```

where `In` has the value 5, can be used. If this device is the system's standard input device, an asterisk may be used in place of the device number in any of the preceding unit specifications; for example,

```
READ (*, *) Code, Time, Rate
```

Formatted input is also possible with the general `READ` statement; for example,

```
READ (5, '(I6, 2F6.2)') Code, Time, Rate
```

or

```
READ (UNIT = 5, FMT = '(I6, 2F6.2)') Code, Time, Rate
```

or

```
READ (UNIT = 5, FMT = 10) Code, Time, Rate
```

or

```
READ (5, 10) Code, Time, Rate
```

where `10` is the number of the following `FORMAT` statement:

```
10 FORMAT(I6, 2F6.2)
```

5.5 FILE PROCESSING

Up to this point we have assumed that the data for the sample programs was entered from the keyboard during program execution and that the output was displayed on the screen. This is usually adequate if the amounts of input/output data are relatively small. However, applications involving large data sets can be processed more conveniently if the data is stored in a file. Files are usually stored on disks or on some other form of external (secondary) memory. In this section we consider the characteristics of files and some of the Fortran statements for processing them. (Others are described in Chapter 12.)

The data values in a file to be used as an input file must be arranged in a form suitable for reading by a READ statement. These values are read during program execution, just like data entered by the user from the keyboard. For example, if the variables Code, Temperature, and Pressure are declared by

```
INTEGER :: Code
REAL :: Temperature, Pressure
```

and the values for these variables are to be read from a file using a list-directed READ statement, this data file might have the following form:

```
37, 77.5, 30.39
22, 85.3, 30.72
1, 100.0, 29.95
78, 99.5, 29.01
        ⋮
```

If the values are to be read using the format specifier

```
(I2, 2F6.0)
```

the file might have the form

```
37   77.5 30.39
22   85.3 30.72
 1  100.0 29.95
78   99.5 29.01
        ⋮
```

whereas the format specifier

```
(I2, F4.1, F4.2)
```

would be appropriate for the file

```
37 7753039
22 8533072
  110002995
78 9952901
        ⋮
```

Opening Files

Before a file can be used in a Fortran program, a number, called a *unit number*, must be connected to it and several items of information about the file must be supplied. This process is called *opening* the file and is accomplished using an **OPEN statement** of the following form:

OPEN *Statement*

Form:

```
OPEN (open-list)
```

where
> *open-list* includes
> 1. a unit specifier indicating a unit number connected to the file being opened,
> 2. a FILE = clause giving the name of the file being opened,
> 3. a STATUS = clause specifying the status of the file,
> 4. an ACTION = clause specifying whether the file is to be opened for reading only, for writing only, or for both,
> 5. a POSITION = clause that positions the file,
> 6. an IOSTAT = clause indicating whether the file was successfully opened.

(Other items that may be included are described in Chapter 12.)

Purpose:

Opens the file associated with the specified unit number so that input/output can take place. The unit specifier has the form described for the WRITE statement. Reference to this file by a READ or WRITE statement is by means of this unit number.

The FILE = clause has the form

```
FILE = character-expression
```

where the value of *character-expression* (ignoring trailing blanks) is the name of the file to be connected to the specified unit number.

The STATUS = clause has the form

```
STATUS = character-expression
```

where the value of *character-expression* (ignoring trailing blanks and with lowercase letters converted to upper case) is one of

```
"OLD"
"NEW"
"REPLACE"
```

(or another value described in Chapter 12). OLD means that the file already exists in the system. NEW means that the file does not yet exist and is being created by the program; execution of the OPEN statement creates an empty file with the specified name and changes its status to OLD. REPLACE creates a new file, replacing the old one if one already exists, and changes its status to OLD.

The ACTION = clause has the form

```
ACTION = i-o-action
```

where *i-o-action* is a character expression whose value (ignoring trailing blanks and with lowercase letters converted to upper case) is one of

```
"READ"
"WRITE"
"READWRITE"
```

The file will be opened for reading only, for writing only, or for both reading and writing, respectively.

The POSITION = clause has the form

```
POSITION = character-expression
```

where the value of *character-expression* (ignoring trailing blanks and with lowercase letters converted to upper case) is one of

```
"REWIND"
"APPEND"
"ASIS"
```

These specifiers position the file at its initial point, at the end of the file, or leave its position unchanged, respectively.

An IOSTAT = clause has the form

```
IOSTAT = status-variable
```

where *status-variable* is an integer variable to which the value zero is assigned if the file is opened successfully and a positive value is assigned otherwise. A positive value usually represents the number of an appropriate error message in a list found in system manuals.

For example, to open a file named INFO.DAT from which data values are to be read, we might use the the statement

```
OPEN (UNIT = 12, FILE = "INFO.DAT", STATUS = "OLD", &
      ACTION = "READ", POSITION = "REWIND", &
      IOSTAT = OpenStatus)
```

where `OpenStatus` is an integer variable. If the program containing this statement is to be used with various data files, it is better not to "hard wire" the file's name into the program. Instead we can declare a character variable to store the file's name, have the user input the name,

```
CHARACTER(12) :: FileName

WRITE (*, '(1X, A)', ADVANCE = "NO") &
      "Enter name of data file: "
READ *, FileName
```

and then use the following OPEN statement:

```
OPEN (UNIT = 12, FILE = FileName, STATUS = "OLD", &
      ACTION = "READ", POSITION = "REWIND", &
      IOSTAT = OpenStatus)
```

If the file is successfully opened, the status variable `OpenStatus` will be set to 0. If the file cannot be opened—for example, if `INFO.DAT` does not exist—`OpenStatus` will be assigned some positive value. In this case, an appropriate message can be displayed and program execution terminated:

```
IF (OpenStatus > 0) STOP "*** Cannot open file ***"
```

To open a new file named `REPORT` to which values are to be written we might use the OPEN statement

```
OPEN (UNIT = 13, FILE = "REPORT", STATUS = "NEW", &
      ACTION = "WRITE", IOSTAT = OpenStatus)
```

to create the file.   A WRITE statement such as

```
WRITE (13, '(1X, I3, F7.0, F10.2)') Code, Temperature, Pressure
```

might then be used to write the values of `Code`, `Temperature`, and `Pressure` to this file.

Closing Files

The **CLOSE statement** has a function opposite that of the OPEN statement and is used to disconnect a file from its unit number. This statement has the form

CLOSE *Statement*

Form:

```
CLOSE (close-list)
```

where
  close-list must include a unit specifier and may include other items
    as described in Chapter 12.

Purpose:
Closes the file associated with the specifed unit number.

After a CLOSE statement is executed, the closed file may be reopened by using an OPEN statement; the same unit number may be connected to it or a different one may be used. All files that are not explicitly closed by means of a CLOSE statement are automatically closed when an END statement or a STOP statement is executed.

File Input/Output

Once a file has been connected to a unit number, data can be read from or written to that file using the general forms of the READ and WRITE statements in which the unit number appearing in the control list is the same as the unit number connected to the file. To illustrate, suppose that the file INFO.DAT has been opened successfully for reading and we wish to read and process values for Code, Temperature, and Pressure from this file.

In the preceding section, we noted that the control list of a general READ statement may contain an **IOSTAT = clause** to detect an end-of-file condition or an input error. This clause has the following form:

IOSTAT = *Clause*

Form:

```
IOSTAT = status-variable
```

where
  status-variable is an integer variable.

Purpose:
When a READ statement containing an IOSTAT = clause is executed, the *status-variable* is assigned:

1. a positive value if an input error occurs (usually the number of an error message in a list found in the system manuals),

2. a negative value if the end of data is encountered but no input error occurs,

3. zero if neither an input error nor the end of data occurs.

For example, if `InputStatus` is an integer variable, an input loop of the following form can be used to read and process values for `Code`, `Temperature`, and `Pressure` from a file with unit number 12, terminating repetition when the end of the file is reached:

```
DO
    ! Read next data value
    READ (12, *, IOSTAT = InputStatus) Code, Temperature, Pressure

    IF (InputStatus > 0) STOP "*** Input error ***"
    IF (InputStatus < 0) EXIT  ! end of file

    ! Otherwise continue processing data
    Count = Count + 1
        ⋮
    SumOfPressures = SumOfPressures + Pressure
END DO
```

An alternative method of detecting an end-of-file condition is to use an **END =** **clause** in the control list of a general `READ` statement. This clause has the form

END = *Clause*

Form:

```
END = statement-number
```

where
   statement-number is the number of an executable statement.

Purpose:
When a `READ` statement containing an END = clause is executed, if the end of data is encountered, the statement with the specified *statement-number* is the next statement to be executed. Often a **CONTINUE statement** is used to mark the point to which control is to transfer.

To illustrate, consider the following program segment to read values for `Code`, `Temperature`, and `Pressure` from a file:

```
DO
   ! Read next data value; exit loop if end of data
     READ (12, *, END = 20) Code, Temperature, Pressure

   ! Otherwise continue processing data
     Count = Count + 1
        ⋮
     SumOfPressures = SumOfPressures + Pressure
END DO
20 CONTINUE
        ⋮
```

When the end of this file is reached, the `DO` loop is exited and execution continues with the `CONTINUE` statement.

File-Positioning Statements

There are several Fortran statements that may be used to position a file. One of these is the **REWIND statement**, a simple form of which is

---

REWIND *Statement*

Form:

```
    REWIND unit
```

where
      unit is the unit number connected to a file.

Purpose:
Positions the file at its beginning.

Another file-positioning statement is the **BACKSPACE statement**. The following is a simple form of this statement:

BACKSPACE *Statement*

Form:

```
    BACKSPACE unit
```

where
> $unit$ is the unit number connected to a file.

Purpose:
Positions the file at the beginning of the preceding line.

If the file is at its initial point, these statements have no effect.

Quick Quiz 5.5

1. In the statement WRITE (10, 20) X, Y, 10 is the _____ of some output device.
2. In the statement WRITE (10, 20) X, Y, 20 is the number of a _____ statement.
3. Write a WRITE statement that is equivalent to the statement PRINT *, Answer.
4. (True or false) The clause FILE = "NEW" in an OPEN statement indicates that the file does not yet exist and is being created by the program.
5. Write a statement to open an existing file QUIZ with unit number 15.
6. Write a statement to read a value for an integer variable Score from positions 6–8 of the file in Question 5.
7. (True or false) The clause IOSTAT = Var will assign a negative value to Var if the end of data is encountered but no input error occurs.
8. (True or false) In the statement READ (5, 10, END = 15) Score, program execution will continue at statement 15 when there are no more values to be read.
9. (True or false) The BACKSPACE statement can be used to output a value to the left of the current position.
10. The _____ statement can be used to position a file at its beginning.

5.6 APPLICATION: TEMPERATURE AND VOLUME READINGS

Problem

Suppose that a device monitoring a process records time, temperature, pressure, and volume and stores this data in a file. Each record in this file contains

Time in positions 1–4

Temperature in positions 5–8

Pressure in positions 9–12

Volume in positions 13–16

The value for time is an integer representing the time at which the measurements were taken. The values for temperature, pressure, and volume are real numbers but are recorded with no decimal point. Each must be interpreted as a real value having a decimal point between the third and fourth digits.

A program is to be designed to read the values for the temperature and volume, display these values in tabular form, and display the equation of the least-squares line determined by these values (see Section 4.6).

Monitoring temperature with a digital thermometer. (Photo courtesy of Adam Hart Davis/Science Photo Library/Photo Researchers, Inc.)

Solution

Specification:

Input (entered by the user): Name of the data file
Input (from the data file):   Temperature and volume readings
Output (to the screen):   Table of temperature and volume readings
                              Equation of least-squares line

Design. The main part of an algorithm for solving this problem is calculating the least-squares line that best fits the given data. Using the algorithm given in Section 4.6 for finding this least-squares line, we can easily design an algorithm for solving this problem.

ALGORITHM FOR TEMPERATURE–VOLUME PROBLEM

1. Get the name of the file and open the file for input; if this fails, terminate execution.
2. Display headings for the table.
3. Initialize the counts and sums needed in calculating the least-squares line to 0.
4. Do the following:
   a. Attempt to read a pair of temperature and volume readings from the file.
   b. If an input error occurred, terminate execution.
      If the end of the file was encountered, terminate repetition.
      Otherwise proceed with the following.
   c. Display the temperature and the volume.
   d. Compute the quantities needed to calculate the least-squares line as described in the algorithm of Section 4.6.
5. Compute and display the equation of the least-squares line.

Coding. The program in Figure 5.2 implements the preceding algorithm.

Figure 5.2 Temperature and volume readings.

```
PROGRAM Temperature_Volume_Readings
!------------------------------------------------------------------
! Program to read temperatures and volumes from a file containing
! time, temperature, pressure, and volume readings made by some
! monitoring device.  The temperature and volume measurements are
! displayed in tabular form, and the equation of the least-squares
! line y = mx + b (x = temperature, y = volume) is calculated.
! Variables used are:
```

Figure 5.2 *(cont.)*

```
!    FileName          : name of data file
!    OpenStatus        : status variable for OPEN statement
!    InputStatus       : status variable for READ statement
!    Temperature       : temperature recorded
!    Volume            : volume recorded
!    Count             : count of (Temperature, Volume) pairs
!    SumOfTemps        : sum of temperatures
!    SumOfTemps2       : sum of squares of temperatures
!    SumOfVols         : sum of volumes
!    SumOfProds        : sum of the products Temperature * Volume
!    MeanTemperature   : mean temperature
!    MeanVolume        : mean volume
!    Slope             : slope of the least-squares line
!    Y_Intercept       : y-intercept of the line
!
! Input (file):    Collection of temperature and volume readings
! Output (screen): Table of readings and equation of least-squares
!                  line
!-----------------------------------------------------------------------

  IMPLICIT NONE
  INTEGER :: Count = 0, OpenStatus, InputStatus
  CHARACTER(20) :: FileName
  REAL :: Temperature, Volume, SumOfTemps = 0.0 , SumOfTemps2 = 0.0, &
          SumOfVols = 0.0, SumOfProds = 0.0, MeanTemperature, &
          MeanVolume, Slope, Y_Intercept

  ! Open the file as unit 15, set up the input and output
  ! formats, and display the table heading

  WRITE (*, '(1X, A)', ADVANCE = "NO") "Enter name of data file: "
  READ *, FileName
  OPEN (UNIT = 15, FILE = FileName, STATUS = "OLD", IOSTAT = OpenStatus)
  IF (OpenStatus > 0) STOP "*** Cannot open the file ***"

  100 FORMAT(4X, F4.1, T13, F4.1)
  110 FORMAT(1X, A11, A10)
  120 FORMAT(1X, F8.1, F12.1)
  PRINT *
  PRINT 110, "Temperature", "Volume"
  PRINT 110, "===========", "======"

  ! While there is more data, read temperatures and volumes,
  ! display each in the table, and calculate the necessary sums
```

Figure 5.2 *(cont.)*

```
DO
   READ (UNIT = 15, FMT = 100, IOSTAT = InputStatus) Temperature, Volume
   IF (InputStatus > 0) STOP "*** Input error ***"
   IF (InputStatus < 0) EXIT  ! end of file

   PRINT 120, Temperature, Volume
   Count = Count + 1
   SumOfTemps = SumOfTemps + Temperature
   SumOfTemps2 = SumOfTemps2 + Temperature ** 2
   SumOfVols = SumOfVols + Volume
   SumOfProds = SumOfProds + Temperature * Volume
END DO

! Find equation of least-squares line

MeanTemperature = SumOfTemps / REAL(Count)
MeanVolume = SumOfVols / REAL(Count)
Slope = (SumOfProds - SumOfTemps * MeanVolume) / &
        (SumOfTemps2 - SumOfTemps * MeanTemperature)
Y_Intercept = MeanVolume - Slope * MeanTemperature

PRINT 130, Slope, Y_Intercept
130 FORMAT(//1X, "Equation of least-squares line is"  &
           /1X, "      y =", F5.1, "x + ", F5.1,  &
           /1X, "where x is temperature and y is volume")

CLOSE (15)

END PROGRAM Temperature_Volume_Readings
```

Execution and Testing. This program should be tested with several small data files to check its correctness. It can then be run with the data file described in the statement of the problem:

Listing of file `fil5-2.dat`:

```
1200034203221015
1300038803221121
1400044803241425
1500051303201520
1600055503181665
1700061303191865
1800067503232080
1900072103282262
2000076803252564
2100083503272869
2200088903303186
```

Execution of the program using this file produced the following output:

Sample run

```
Enter name of data file: fil5-2.dat

Temperature    Volume
===========    ======
      34.2     101.5
      38.8     112.1
      44.8     142.5
      51.3     152.0
      55.5     166.5
      61.3     186.5
      67.5     208.0
      72.1     226.2
      76.8     256.4
      83.5     286.9
      88.9     318.6

Equation of least-squares line is
    y =   3.8x + -39.8
where x is temperature and y is volume
```

A Refinement Using Run-Time Formatting

For formatted input/output in the preceding program we used a FORMAT statement. As we have seen, however, a format specifier may also be a character expression whose value is the list of format descriptors. For example, the statement

```
PRINT '(1X, F8.1, F12.1)', Temperature, Volume
```

is equivalent to the pair of statements

```
PRINT 120, Temperature, Volume
120 FORMAT(1X, F8.1, F12.1)
```

A character variable could also be used:

```
CHARACTER(40) :: Form
            ⋮
Form = '(1X, F8.1, F12.1)'
PRINT Form, Temperature, Volume
```

A list of format descriptors can also be read at run time and assigned to a character variable like Form which can then be used as a format specifier. This makes it possible to change the format used for input or output each time a program is run without having to modify the program itself. This is illustrated in the program in Figure 5.3, which is like that in Figure 5.2 except that the user enters the input format during execution and the least-squares line is not calculated.

Two sample runs are shown. The first uses the data file given earlier,

```
1200034203221015
1300038803221121
1400044803241425
1500051303201520
1600055503181665
1700061303191865
1800067503232080
1900072103282262
2000076803252564
2100083503272869
2200088903303186
```

in which the fifth through eighth digits constitute the temperatures and the last four digits are the volumes. A decimal point must be positioned in each value so there is one digit to its right. Thus, an appropriate format specifier is

```
(4X, F4.1, T13, F4.1)
```

The second data file is

```
12:00PM
34.2 32.2 101.5
1:00PM
38.8 32.2 112.1
2:00PM
44.8 32.4 142.5
3:00PM
51.3 32.0 152.0
4:00PM
55.5 31.8 166.5
5:00PM
61.3 31.9 186.5
6:00PM
67.5 32.3 208.0
7:00PM
72.1 32.8 226.2
8:00PM
76.8 32.5 256.4
```

```
9:00PM
83.5 32.7 286.9
10:00PM
88.9 33.0 318.6
```

for which an appropriate format specifier is

```
(/ F4.0, 5X, F6.0)
```

When the program is executed, the user enters the name of the file (FileName) and the appropriate format specifier Form for that file.

Figure 5.3 Temperature and volume readings—version 2.

```
PROGRAM Temperature_Volume_Readings_2
!-----------------------------------------------------------------------
! Program to read temperatures and volumes from a file containing
! time, temperature, pressure, and volume readings made by some
! monitoring device.  The temperature and volume measurements are
! displayed in tabular form.  Format specifiers for these files
! are entered during execution.  Variables used are:
!   FileName     : name of data file
!   OpenStatus   : status variable for OPEN statement
!   InputStatus  : status variable for READ statement
!   Form         : input format specifier
!   Temperature  : temperature recorded
!   Volume       : volume recorded
!
! Input (file):     Collection of temperature and volume readings
! Input (keyboard): Format specifiers
! Output (screen):  Table of readings
!-----------------------------------------------------------------------

  IMPLICIT NONE
  CHARACTER(50) :: Form, FileName*20
  INTEGER :: OpenStatus, InputStatus
  REAL :: Temperature, Volume

  ! Open the file as unit 15.  If successful, set up the
  ! input and output formats, and display the table heading

  WRITE (*, '(1X, A)', ADVANCE = "NO") "Enter name of data file: "
  READ *, FileName
  OPEN (UNIT = 15, FILE = FileName, STATUS = "OLD", IOSTAT = OpenStatus)
  IF (OpenStatus > 0) STOP "*** Cannot open the file ***"
```

Figure 5.3 *(cont.)*

```
PRINT *, "Enter input format for ", FileName
READ '(A)', Form

110 FORMAT(1X, A11, A10)
120 FORMAT(1X, F8.1, F12.1)
PRINT *
PRINT 110, "Temperature", "Volume"
PRINT 110, "===========", "======"

! While there is more data, read temperatures and volumes
! and display each in the table

DO
   READ (UNIT = 15, FMT = Form, IOSTAT = InputStatus) Temperature, Volume
   IF (InputStatus > 0) STOP "*** Input error ***"
   IF (InputStatus < 0) EXIT  ! end of file

   PRINT 120, Temperature, Volume
END DO

CLOSE (15)

END PROGRAM Temperature_Volume_Readings_2
```

Sample runs:

```
Enter name of data file: fil5-3a.dat
Enter input format for fil5-3a.dat
(4X, F4.1, T13, F4.1)

Temperature    Volume
===========    ======
     34.2      101.5
     38.8      112.1
     44.8      142.5
     51.3      152.0
     55.5      166.5
     61.3      186.5
     67.5      208.0
     72.1      226.2
     76.8      256.4
     83.5      286.9
     88.9      318.6
```

Figure 5.3 *(cont.)*

```
Enter name of data file: fil5-3b.dat
Enter input format for fil5-3b.dat
(/ F5.0, 5X, F6.0)

Temperature       Volume
===========       ======
       34.2        101.5
       33.8        112.1
       44.8        142.5
       51.3        152.0
       55.5        166.5
       61.3        186.5
       67.5        208.0
       72.1        226.2
       76.8        256.4
       83.5        286.9
       88.9        318.6
```

5.7   MISCELLANEOUS INPUT/OUTPUT TOPICS

In this chapter we have described several of the more commonly used format descriptors. These descriptors are used to specify the precise format of output produced by a formatted PRINT or WRITE statement and to specify the format of values to be read by a formatted READ statement. In this section we describe a number of less commonly used format descriptors, some additional features of list-directed input that were not mentioned in Chapter 2, and NAMELIST input/output.

The G Descriptor

A G (general) descriptor of the form

$$rGw.d \qquad \text{or} \qquad rGw.dEe$$

where

- w is an integer constant that indicates the total width of the field in which the data is to be displayed
- d is an integer constant indicating the number of significant digits to be displayed
- r is the repetition indicator, an integer constant indicating the number of such fields; it is not required if there is only one field
- e is the number of positions to be used in displaying the exponent

may be used for input/output of values of any type. For integer, logical, and character data, this descriptor acts in the same manner as rIw, rLw, and rAw, respectively. A real value that is output using a G descriptor is displayed using an F or E descriptor, depending on the magnitude (absolute value) of the real number.

Intuitively, the G descriptor functions like an F descriptor for values that are neither very large nor very small, but like an E descriptor otherwise. More precisely, suppose that a real quantity has a value that if expressed in normalized scientific notation would have the form

$$\pm 0.d_1 d_2 \cdots d_n \times 10^k$$

and this value is to be displayed using a $Gw.d$ descriptor. If $0 \le k \le d$, this value is output in "F form" with a field width of $w - 4$ followed by four blanks. If, however, k is negative or greater than d, it is output using an $Ew.d$ descriptor. In either case, d significant digits are displayed. The following examples illustrate:

Value	G Descriptor	Output Produced
0.123456	G12.6	0.123456 -----------
0.123456E1	G11.6	1.23456 ----------
0.123456E5	G11.6	12345.6 ----------
0.123456E6	G11.6	123456. ----------
0.123456E7	G12.6	0.123456E+07 -----------

The G descriptor may also be used for real input. In this case it functions much like the F descriptor.

The B, O, and Z Descriptors

The B, O, and Z descriptors are used to display integers in binary, octal, and hexadecimal form, respectively. They have the forms

rBw	or	$rBw.m$
rOw	or	$rOw.m$
rZw	or	$rZw.m$

where

w is an integer constant indicating the width of the field in which the data is to be displayed, that is, the number of spaces to be used in displaying it

r is the repetition indicator, an integer constant indicating the number of such fields; if there is to be only one such field, the number 1 is not required

m is the minimum number of digits to be displayed

For example, to display the values of the integer variables In and Out as given by

```
INTEGER :: In = 15, Out = 256
```

in binary, octal, and hexadecimal, we can use the statements

```
PRINT '(1X, A13, 2B10)', "Binary:", In, Out
PRINT '(1X, A13, 2O10)', "Octal:", In, Out
PRINT '(1X, A13, 2Z10)', "Hexadecimal:", In, Out
```

The resulting output is

```
     Binary:      1111 100000000
      Octal:        17       400
Hexadecimal:         F       100
```

The L Descriptor

An L descriptor is used for formatted input/output of logical values. This format descriptor has the form

```
rLw
```

where

w   is an integer constant specifying the field width

r   is the repetition indicator, an integer constant specifying the number of such fields. It may be omitted if there is only one field.

For output, the field consists of $w - 1$ spaces followed by a T or an F. For example, if A, B, and C are logical variables given by

```
LOGICAL :: A = .TRUE., B = .FALSE., C = .FALSE.
```

the statement

```
PRINT '(1X, L4, L2, 2L5)', A, B, C, A .OR. C
```

produces

```
   T F    F    T
```

Logical data can also be read using an L descriptor. The input value consists of optional blanks followed by an optional period followed by a T for true or an F for false; any characters following T or F are ignored. For example, if the line of data

```
 .TRUE   TWO.F FT
 ------------------
```

is read by the statements

```
LOGICAL :: A, B, C, D, E
READ '(2L6, 3L2)', A, B, C, D, E
```

then A, B, and E are assigned the value true, and C and D the value false.

The BN and BZ Descriptors

Blanks within a numeric input field may be interpreted as zeros, or they may be ignored. The programmer may specify which interpretation is to be used by including a BN or BZ descriptor in the format specifier. If a BN ("Blank Null") or BZ ("Blank Zero") descriptor is encountered during a scan of the list of descriptors, all blanks in fields determined by subsequent numeric descriptors in that format specifier are ignored or interpreted as zero, respectively. In all cases, a numeric field consisting entirely of blanks is interpreted as the value 0. If neither descriptor is used, blanks are ignored.

To illustrate, consider the following data line:

```
537  6.258E3
 -------------
```

If Number is an integer variable and Alpha is a real variable, the statement

```
READ '(BZ, I5, F8.0)', Number, Alpha
```

assigns the following values to Number and Alpha:

```
Number:   53700
Alpha:    6.258E30
```

since the BZ descriptor causes the two blanks in the field corresponding to the I5 descriptor and the single blank in the field corresponding to the F8.0 descriptor to be interpreted as zeros. On the other hand,

```
READ '(BN, I5, F8.0)', Number, Alpha
```

assigns the values

```
Number:   537
Alpha:    6.258E3
```

since the BN descriptor causes these same blanks to be ignored. The statement

```
READ '(BZ, I5, BN, F8.0)', Number, Alpha
```

assigns the values

```
Number:    53700
Alpha:     6.258E3
```

The S, SP, and SS Descriptors

The S, SP, and SS descriptors may be used to control the output of plus (+) signs in a numeric output field. If the SP ("Sign Positive") descriptor appears in a format specifier, all positive numeric values output by the statement are preceded by a + sign. On the other hand, the SS ("Sign Suppress") descriptor suppresses the output of all such + signs. An S descriptor may be used to restore control to the computer system, which has the option of displaying or suppressing a + sign.

The TL and TR Descriptors

The TL and TR descriptors are positional descriptors of the form

```
TLn      and      TRn
```

where n is a positive integer constant. They indicate that input or output of the next data value is to occur n positions to the left or right, respectively, of the current position. Thus a descriptor of the form TLn causes a backspace of n positions. In the case of input, this makes it possible to read the same input value several times. For example, for the data line

```
123
---
```

the statements

```
INTEGER :: Number
REAL :: Alpha, Beta
READ '(I3, TL3, F3.1, TL3, F3.2)', Number, Alpha, Beta
```

assign the integer value 123 to NUM, the real value 12.3 to Alpha, and the real value 1.23 to Beta:

```
Number:    123
Alpha:     12.3
Beta:      1.23
```

In the case of output, a descriptor of the form TLn causes a backspace of n positions on the current output line. However, subsequent descriptors may cause characters in these n positions to be replaced rather than overprinted. For both input and output, a descriptor of the form TRn functions in exactly the same manner as nX.

List-Directed Input

In a data line, consecutive commas with no intervening characters except blanks represent **null values,** which leave unchanged the corresponding variables in the input list of a list-directed READ statement. If the variables have previously been assigned values, the values are not changed; if they have not been assigned values, the variables remain undefined. A slash in a data line terminates the input and leaves unchanged the values of the remaining variables in the input list.

If the same value is to be read for r consecutive variables in the input list, this common value may be entered in the corresponding data line in the form

```
r*value
```

A repeated null value may be indicated by

```
r*
```

In this case, the corresponding r consecutive items in the input list are unchanged.

The following examples illustrate these conventions for list-directed input. They are not used in list-directed output, except that a given processor has the option of displaying

```
r*value
```

for successive output items that have the same value.

Statement	Data Entered	Result
READ *, J, K, A, B	1,,,2.3	J = 1 K and A are unchanged B = 2.3
READ *, J, K, A, B	,,,,	J, K, A, and B all are unchanged
READ *, J, K, A, B	1,2/	J = 1 K = 2 A and B are unchanged
READ *, J, K, A, B	/	J, K, A, and B all are unchanged
READ *, J, K, A, B	2*1, 2*2.3	J = 1 and K = 1 A = 2.3 and B = 2.3
READ *, J, K, A ,B	1, 2*, 2.3	J = 1 K and A are unchanged B = 2.3

In the third and fourth examples, any values following the slash would be ignored.

NAMELIST Input/Output

A NAMELIST feature can be used to read or display a group of values of variables by referring to a single name. This is acccomplished by grouping the variable names together in a **NAMELIST declaration** of the form

```
NAMELIST /group-name/ variable-list
```

in the specification part of a program unit. Several such declarations may be made in the same NAMELIST statement and may be separated by commas. Note that each group name must be enclosed between slashes.

To illustrate, suppose we wish to process several time values in a program. The declarations

```
INTEGER :: Hours, Minutes, Seconds
CHARACTER(2) :: AM_or_PM
NAMELIST /Time/ Hours, Minutes, Seconds, AM_or_PM
```

could be used to declare the variables Hours, Minutes, Seconds, and AM_or_PM and associate them with the group name Time.

To read values for the variables in a namelist group, a general READ statement is used that contains no input/ouput list and in which the format specifer is replaced by the namelist *group-name* or by a clause of the form NML = *group-name*:

```
READ (unit-specifier, NML = group-name)
```

or

```
READ (unit-specifier, group-name)
```

Data for namelist input must have a special form:

```
&group-name variable₁ = value₁, variable₂ = value₂, . . . /
```

Note that an ampersand (&) attached to the group name must be placed at the beginning of the input list and a slash (/) at the end. For example, to assign the values 12, 30, 00, "PM" to Hours, Minutes, Seconds, AM_or_PM, respectively, we could use the READ statement

```
READ (*, NML = Time)
```

and enter the data

```
&Time Hours = 12, Minutes = 30, Seconds = 00, AM_or_PM = "PM" /
```

or perhaps

```
&Time Hours = 12
      Minutes = 30
      Seconds = 00
      AM_or_PM = "PM"/
```

To display the values of the variables in a namelist group, a general WRITE statement is used that contains no input/ouput list and in which the format specifer is replaced by the namelist *group-name* or by a clause of the form NML = *group-name*:

```
WRITE (unit-specifier, NML = group-name)
```

or

```
WRITE (unit-specifier, group-name)
```

Namelist output will have a form similar to that used for namelist input. For example, the statement

```
WRITE (*, Time)
```

might produce as output

```
&TIME HOURS = 12, MINUTES = 30, SECONDS = 0, AM_OR_PM = PM/
```

CHAPTER REVIEW

Summary

This chapter gives a detailed look at input/output. The first three sections deal with formatted input/output of integer, real, and character values together with format descriptors that control spacing. Section 5.4 describes the WRITE statement and the general form of the READ statement, both of which are used for file input/output. Sections 5.5 and 5.6 describe and illustrate the most commonly used file-processing features of Fortran. The last section describes a number of less commonly used format descriptors, some additional features of list-directed input, and NAMELIST input/output.

FORTRAN SUMMARY

PRINT Statement

```
PRINT format-specifier, output-list
```

where *format-specifier* is one of the following:

1. * (an asterisk) for list-directed output
2. a character constant or a character variable (or expression or array) whose value specifies the format for the output
3. the label of a FORMAT statement

Examples:

```
PRINT *, "At time", Time, " velocity is", Velocity

PRINT '(1X, A, F6.2, A, F6.3)', &
      "At time", Time, " velocity is", Velocity

PRINT 10, Time, Velocity
10 FORMAT(1X, "At time", F6.2, " velocity is", F6.3)
```

Purpose:

The PRINT statement displays the values of the expressions in the output list in the format prescribed by the format specifier.

FORMAT Statement

```
FORMAT(list of format descriptors)
```

where each *format descriptor* has one of the following forms:

Iw or Iw.m	for integer data
Bw or Bw.m	for integer data in binary form
Ow or Ow.m	for integer data in octal form
Zw or Zw.m	for integer data in hexadecimal form
Fw.d	for real data in decimal notation
Ew.d or Ew.dEe	for real data in exponential notation
ESw.d or ESw.dEe	for real data in scientific notation
ENw.d or ENw.dEe	for real data in engineering notation
Gw.d	general i/o descriptor
A or Aw	for character data
"x... x" or 'x... x'	for character strings
Lw	for logical data
Tc, TLn, or TRn	tab descriptors
nX	for horizontal spacing
/	for vertical spacing
:	for format scanning control
S, SP, or SS	sign descriptors
BN or BZ	blank interpretation

Example:

```
10 FORMAT(1X, "At time", F6.2, " velocity is", F6.3)
```

Purpose:

Specify input or output format.

WRITE Statement

```
WRITE (control-list) output-list
```

where *output-list* has the same syntax as in the PRINT statement; and *control-list* may include items selected from the following:

1. a unit specifier indicating the output device:

```
UNIT = unit-specifier
```

or simply

```
unit-specifier
```

2. a format specifier:

```
FMT = format-specifier
```

or simply

```
format-specifier
```

3. other items that are especially useful in file processing

Examples:

```
WRITE (*, *) "At time", Time, " velocity is", Velocity

WRITE (6, '(1X, A, F6.2, A, F6.3)') &
      "At time", Time, " velocity is", Velocity

WRITE (*, 10), Time, Velocity
WRITE (6, 10), Time, Velocity
10 FORMAT(1X, "At time", F6.2, " velocity is", F6.3)
```

Purpose:

The WRITE statement displays the values of the expressions in the output list on the specified output device, using the format determined by the format specifier.

Control Characters

In some systems, the first character of each line of output is used to control vertical spacing:

Control Character	Effect
blank	Normal spacing: advance to the next line before printing
0	Double spacing: skip one line before printing
1	Advance to top of next page before printing
+	Overprint the last line printed

READ Statement

```
READ format-specifier, input-list
```

or

```
READ (control-list) input-list
```

where *input-list* is a list of variables; and *control-list* may include items selected from the following:

1. a unit specifier (as described earlier for the WRITE statement) indicating the input device
2. a format specifier (as described earlier for the WRITE statement)
3. an IOSTAT = clause or an END = clause
4. other items that are especially useful in file processing

Examples:

```
READ *, Code, Time, Rate
READ (*, *) Code, Time, Rate
READ (5, *) Code, Time, Rate
READ (UNIT = 5, FMT = *) Code, Time, Rate
READ (UNIT = 5, FMT = '(I6, 2F6.2)') Code, Time, Rate
READ (UNIT = 5, FMT = 10) Code, Time, Rate
10 FORMAT(I6, 2F6.2)
```

Purpose:

The READ statement reads values for the variables in the input list from the specified input device, using the format prescribed by the format specifier.

IOSTAT = Clause

```
IOSTAT = integer-variable
```

Example:

```
READ (12, *, IOSTAT = InputStatus) Code, Temperature, Pressure
```

Purpose:
When used in a READ statement, this clause assigns a value to the specified integer variable, indicating the following:

A positive value: An input error has occurred
A negative value: End of data was encountered, but no input error occurred
Zero: No input error nor the end of data occurred

END = Clause

```
END = statement-number
```

Example:

```
READ (12, *, END = 20) Code, Temperature, Pressure
```

Purpose:
When used in a READ statement, this clause causes the statement with the specified number to be executed next if the end of data is encountered.

OPEN Statement

```
OPEN(open-list)
```

where *open-list* includes (among other things):

1. a unit specifier (as described earlier for the WRITE statement) indicating the input/output device
2. a clause of the form FILE = *name-of-file-being-opened*
3. a STATUS = clause specifying the status of the file
4. a POSITION = clause that positions the file
5. an IOSTAT = clause that indicates if the file was opened successfully

Examples:

```
OPEN(UNIT = 12, FILE = "fil5-3.dat", &
     STATUS = "OLD", IOSTAT = OpenStatus)
OPEN(UNIT = 13, FILE = "fig5-3.out", &
     STATUS = "NEW", IOSTAT = OpenStatus)
OPEN(UNIT = 14, FILE = "fig5-3.out", STATUS = "OLD", &
     POSITION = "APPEND", IOSTAT = OpenStatus)
```

Purpose:

The OPEN statement assigns a unit number to a disk file and makes it accessible for input/output. A status of OLD means that the file already exists; a status of NEW means that the file does not exist but will be created; a status of REPLACE means that a new file will be created and will replace the old one if one already exists. Specifying a position of APPEND positions the file at its end so that subsequent output will be appended to the file. If the file is opened successfully, 0 is assigned to the status variable in the IOSTAT = clause; otherwise a positive value is assigned.

CLOSE Statement

```
CLOSE(close-list)
```

where *close-list* must include a unit specifier (and may include other items).

Examples:

```
CLOSE(UNIT = 12)
CLOSE(13)
```

Purpose:

The CLOSE statement closes the file associated with the specifed unit number.

REWIND Statement

```
REWIND unit
```

where *unit* is the unit number connected to a file.

Example:

```
REWIND 12
```

Purpose:

The REWIND statement positions the file at its beginning.

BACKSPACE Statement

```
BACKSPACE unit
```

where *unit* is the unit number connected to a file.

Example:

```
BACKSPACE 12
```

Purpose:
The BACKSPACE statement positions the file at the beginning of the preceding line.

PROGRAMMING POINTERS

Program Style and Design

1. *Label all output produced by a program.* For example,

```
PRINT '(1X, "Rate =", 8.2, "  Time =", F8.2)', Rate, Time
```

produces more informative output than

```
PRINT '(1X, 2F8.2)', Rate, Time
```

2. *Echo input values.* Input values, especially those read from a file, should be echoed; that is, they should be displayed as they are read (at least during program testing).

Potential Problems

1. *For some systems, the first position of each output line indicates explicitly what printer control is desired.* In some cases, control characters are always in effect; in others, they are not in effect unless a specific system command or compiler option is used.

2. *Formatted output of a numeric value produces a field filled with asterisks if the output requires more spaces than allowed by the specified field width.* For formatted output of real numbers with a descriptor of the form $Fw.d$, one should always have

$$w \geq d + 3$$

For descriptors of the form $Ew.d$, $ESw.d$, and $ENw.d$, one should have

$$w \geq d + 7$$

and for descriptors of the form $Ew.dEe$, $ESw.dEe$, and $ENw.dEe$,

$$w \geq d + e + 5$$

3. *For formatted input with some compilers, blanks within a numeric field may be interpreted as zeros by some systems and ignored by others.* (The BZ and BN descriptors described in Section 5.7 may be used to specify explicitly which interpretation is to be used.)

4. *For formatted input/output, characters are truncated or blanks are added, depending on whether the field width is too small or too large. For input, trunca-*

tion occurs on the left, and blank padding on the right; for output, truncation occurs on the right, and blank padding on the left. The acronyms sometimes used to remember this are

- **POT:** **P**adding on the left with blanks occurs for formatted **O**utput, or **T**runcation of rightmost characters occurs.
- **TIP:** **T**runcation of leftmost characters occurs for formatted **I**nput, or **P**adding with blanks on the right occurs.

These are analogous to the acronym given in Potential Problem 12 in the Programming Pointers of Chapter 2 for assignment of character values:

- **APT:** For **A**ssignment (and list-directed input), both blank **P**adding and **T**runcation occur on the right.

To illustrate, suppose `String` is declared by

```
CHARACTER(10) :: String
```

If `String = "ABCDEFGHIJ"` then the output produced by the statements

```
PRINT '(1X, A5)', String
PRINT '(1X, A15)', String
```

is

```
ABCDE
ƀƀƀƀƀABCDEFGHIJ
```

For the formatted input statement

```
READ '(A5)', String
```

if the value entered is

```
ABCDE
```

(which might be followed by any other characters), the value assigned to `String` is ABCDEƀƀƀƀƀ. For the statement

```
READ '(A15)', String
```

entering the data

```
ABCDEFGHIJKLMNO
```

assigns the value FGHIJKLMNO to `String`.

PROGRAMMING PROBLEMS

Section 5.1

1. Write a program that reads two three-digit integers and then calculates and displays their sum and their difference. The output should be formatted to appear as follows:

```
    456              456
+   123          -   123
-----            -----
    579              333
```

2. Write a program that reads two three-digit integers and then calculates and displays their product and the quotient and the remainder that result when the first is divided by the second. The output should be formatted to appear as follows:

```
    739                    61   R    7
X    12                   ----
------           12 )  739
   8868
```

3. Write a program that reads two three-digit integers and then displays their product in the following format:

```
       749
X      381
    ------
       749
     5992
   2247
   ------
   285369
```

   Execute the program with the following values: 749 and 381; −749 and 381; 749 and −381; −749 and −381; 999 and 999.

4. Suppose that a certain culture of bacteria has a constant growth rate r, so that if there are n bacteria present, the next generation will have $n + r \cdot n$ bacteria. Write a program that reads the original number of bacteria, the growth rate, and an upper limit on the number of bacteria and then displays a table with appropriate headings that shows the generation number, the increase in the number of bacteria from the previous generation, and the total number of bacteria in that generation, for the initial generation number through the first generation for which the number of bacteria exceeds the specified upper limit.

Section 5.2

5. Angles are commonly measured in degrees, minutes ('), and seconds ("). There are 360 degrees in one complete revolution, 60 minutes in 1 degree, and 60 sec-

onds in 1 minute. Write a program that reads two angular measurements, each in the form

$$dddDmm'ss"$$

where *ddd*, *mm*, and *ss* are the number of degrees, minutes, and seconds, respectively, and then calculates and displays their sum. Use this program to verify each of the following:

```
74D29'13" + 105D8'16" = 179D37'29"
7D14'55" + 5D24'55" = 12D39'50"
20D31'19" + 0D31'30" = 21D2'49"
122D17'48" + 237D42'12" = 0D0'0"
```

6. Write a program that will read a student's number, his or her old GPA, and old number of course credits, followed by the course credit and grade for each of four courses. Calculate and display the current and cumulative GPAs with appropriate labels. (See Programing Problem 22 of Chapter 2 for details of the calculations.) Design the program so that it will accept data entered in the form

```
SNUMB 24179  GPA 3.25 CREDITS 19.0
CREDITS/GRADES 1.0 3.7 0.5 4.0 1.0 2.7 1.0 3.3
```

Section 5.6

7. Write a program that reads the time, temperature, pressure, and volume measurements from a data file like that described in Section 5.6; converts the time from military to ordinary time (e.g., 0900 is 9:00 A.M., 1500 is 3:00 P.M.); calculates the average temperature, average pressure, and average volume; and displays a table like the following:

TIME	TEMPERATURE	PRESSURE	VOLUME
12:00 PM	34.2	32.2	101.5
⋮	⋮	⋮	⋮
10:00 PM	88.9	33.0	318.6
AVERAGES	?	?	?

(with the ?s replaced by the appropriate averages).

For the following exercises, see Appendix B for a description of the files USERS.DAT, STUDENT.DAT, and INVENTOR.DAT.

8. Write a program to search the file USERS.DAT to find and display the resource limit for a specified user's identification number.

9. Write a program to read the file STUDENT.DAT and produce a report for all freshmen with GPAs below 2.0. This report should include the student's number and cumulative GPA, with appropriate headings.

10. Write a program to search the file `INVENTOR.DAT` to find an item with a specified stock number. If a match is found, display the unit price, the item name, and the number currently in stock; otherwise, display a message indicating that the item was not found.

11. At the end of each month, a report is produced that shows the status of each user's account in the file `USERS.DAT`. Write a program to accept the current date and produce a report of the following form, in which the three asterisks (`***`) indicate that the user has already used 90 percent or more of the resources available to him or her, and *mm/dd/yy* is the current date.

```
            USER ACCOUNTS--mm/dd/yy


                RESOURCE   RESOURCES
     USER-ID     LIMIT       USED
     -------     -----       ----
      10101      $750     $380.81
      1010       $650     $598.84***
                   ⋮
```

12. Write a program to read the file `STUDENT.DAT` and calculate
    (a) the average cumulative GPA for all male students
    (b) the average cumulative GPA for all female students

FEATURES NEW TO FORTRAN 90

- Additional format descriptors have been added. For example, integer descriptors of the form B*w*, B*w.m*, O*w*, O*w.m*, Z*w*, and Z*w.m* can be used to display integers in binary, octal, and hexadecimal form, respectively. A *scientific* descriptor ES can be used in the same manner as the E descriptor to display real values in scientific notation. An *engineering* descriptor EN is used in the same manner as the E descriptor, except that the exponent is constrained to be a multiple of 3 so that a nonzero mantissa is greater than or equal to 1 and less than 1000. The G descriptor can also be used with integer, logical, and character types, and in these cases, it follows the rules of the I, L, and A descriptors.

- A repetition indicator may be used with the slash descriptor; for example, 3/ is equivalent to /// in a format specifier.

- An ADVANCE = clause may appear in the control list of a general formatted READ or WRITE statement; ADVANCE = "NO" causes nonadvancing input/output, whereas ADVANCE = "YES" is the default condition and causes an advance to a new line of input or output after the input/output statement has been executed.

- The NAMELIST feature can be used to read or display an annotated list of values.

6

Programming with Functions

On two occasions I have been asked [by members of Parliament], 'Pray, Mr. Babbage, if you put into the machine wrong figures, will the right answers come out?' I am not able rightly to apprehend the kind of confusion of ideas that could provoke such a question.

CHARLES BABBAGE

Fudd's Law states: 'What goes in must come out.' Aside from being patently untrue, Fudd's Law neglects to mention that what comes out need not bear any resemblance to what went in.

V. OREHCK III (fictitious)

All the best work is done the way ants do things—by tiny but untiring and regular additions.

LAFCADIO HEARN

*T*he problems we have considered thus far have been simple enough that algorithms for their complete solution are quite straightforward. For more complex problems, it may not be possible to anticipate at the outset all the steps needed to solve the problem. In this case, it is helpful to divide the problem into a number of simpler problems. Each of these subproblems is then considered individually and algorithms designed to solve them. The complete algorithm for the original problem is then described in terms of these subalgorithms. **Subprograms** can be written to implement each of these subalgorithms, and these subprograms can be combined to give a complete program that solves the original problem. In Fortran these subprograms are **functions** and **subroutines** whose execution is controlled by some other **program unit**, either the main program or some other subprogram. In this chapter we will consider how functions are written and used in this modular style of programming. In the next chapter, subroutines will be considered.

6.1 FUNCTIONS

Intrinsic Functions

The Fortran language provides many **intrinsic,** or **library, functions.** These intrinsic functions include not only the numeric functions introduced in Chapter 2 but also a number of other numeric functions, as well as character and logical functions. Table 6.1 gives a list of the most commonly used numeric intrinsic functions.

Table 6.1 Fortran Numeric Intrinsic Functions

Fortran Function	Description	Type of Arguments*	Type of Value
ABS(x)	Absolute value of x	I, R	Same as argument
		C	R
ACOS(x)	Arccosine (in radians) of x	R	Same as argument
AIMAG(x)	Imaginary part of x	C	R
AINT(x)	Value resulting from truncation of fractional part of x	R	Same as argument
ANINT(x)	x rounded to the nearest integer INT(x + .5) if $x \geq 0$ INT(x - .5) if $x < 0$	R	Same as argument
ASIN(x)	Arcsine (in radians) of x	R	Same as argument
ATAN(x)	Arctangent (in radians) of x	R	Same as argument
ATAN2(x, y)	Arctangent (in radians) of x / y	R	Same as argument
CEILING(x)	Least integer greater than or equal to x	R	I
CMPLX(x)	Conversion of x to complex type $(x + 0i)$	I, R, C	C
CMPLX(x, y)	Conversion of x, y to complex type $(x + yi)$	I, R, C	C
CONJG(x)	Conjugate of x	C	C
COS(x)	Cosine of x (in radians)	R, C	Same as argument
COSH(x)	Hyperbolic cosine of x	R	Same as argument
DBLE(x)	Conversion of x to double precision	I, R	D
DIM(x, y)	x - y if $x \geq y$ 0 if $x < y$	I, R	Same as argument
DPROD(x, y)	Double-precision product of x and y	I, R	D
EXP(x)	Exponential function e^x	R, C	Same as argument
FLOOR(x)	Greatest integer less than or equal to x	R	I
FRACTION(x)	Fractional part of x	R	I
INT(x)	Conversion of x to integer type; sign of x or real part of x times the greatest integer $\leq$ ABS(x)	I, R, C	I
LOG(x)	Natural logarithm of x	R, C	Same as argument
LOG10(x)	Common (base 10) logarithm of x	R	Same as argument

Table 6.1 *(cont.)*

Fortran Function	Description	Type of Arguments*	Type of Value
MAX(x_1, ..., x_n)	Maximum of x_1, ..., x_n	I, R	Same as arguments
MIN(x_1, ..., x_n)	Minimum of x_1, ..., x_n	I, R	Same as arguments
MOD(x, y)	x - INT(x /y) * y	I, R	Same as arguments
MODULO(x, y)	x (mod y)	I, R	Same as arguments
NINT(x)	x rounded to the nearest integer [see ANINT(x)]	R	I
REAL(x)	Conversion of x to real type	I, R, C	R
SIGN(x, y)	Transfer of sign: ABS(x) if $y \geq 0$ -ABS(x) if $y < 0$	I, R	Same as arguments
SIN(x)	Sine of x (in radians)	R, C	Same as argument
SINH(x)	Hyperbolic sine of x	R	Same as argument
SQRT(x)	Square root of x	R, C	Same as argument
TAN(x)	Tangent of x (in radians)	R	Same as argument
TANH(x)	Hyperbolic tangent of x	R	Same as argument

* I = integer, R = real, D = double-precision real, C = complex. Types of arguments in a given function reference must be the same.

As we have seen, any of these functions may be used in an expression by giving its name followed by the actual arguments, enclosed in parentheses. For example, if Number_1, Number_2, Small, Alpha, Beta, and X are declared by

```
INTEGER :: Number_1, Number_2, Small
REAL :: Alpha, Beta, X
```

then the statements

```
PRINT *, ABS(X)
Alpha = ANINT(100.0 * Beta) / 100.0
Small = MIN(0, Number_1, Number_2)
```

display the absolute value of X, assign to Alpha the value of Beta rounded to the nearest hundredth, and assign to Small the smallest of the three integers 0, Number_1, and Number_2.

Function Subprograms

In some programs it is convenient for the user to define additional functions. Such **programmer-defined functions** are possible in Fortran. Once defined, they are used in the same way as library functions. They are written as **function subpro-**

grams, which are separate program units whose syntax is similar to that of a Fortran (main) program:

Function Subprogram

function heading
specification part
execution part
END FUNCTION statement

The **function heading** is a **FUNCTION statement** of the following form:

Function Heading (simplified)

Form:

    FUNCTION *function-name(formal-argument-list)*

or

    type-identifier FUNCTION *function-name(formal-argument-list)*

where   *real, Integer . . -*

  function-name may be any legal Fortran identifier;
  formal-argument-list is an identifier or a list (possibly empty) of identifiers separated by commas;
  type-identifier is an optional type identifier (INTEGER, REAL, COMPLEX, LOGICAL, CHARACTER, or a programmed-defined data type described in Chapter 10).

Purpose:
Names the function and declares its arguments. In the second form, *type-identifier* is the type of the value returned by the function. In the first form, the type of the function value must be specified in the specification part of the function. The variables in the *formal-argument-list* are called **formal** or **dummy arguments** and are used to pass information to the function subprogram.

Note that in the second form of the function heading, double colons are *not* used to separate the *type-identifier* from the keyword FUNCTION.

The specification part of a function subprogram has the same form as the specification part of a Fortran program with the additional stipulations that

1. It must declare the type of the function value if this has not been included in the function heading.
2. It must declare the types of each of the function's formal arguments. These declarations should also contain an **INTENT specifier** that tells how the arguments are to transfer information.

Similarly, the execution part of a function subprogram has the same form as the execution part of a Fortran program with the additional stipulation that it should include at least one statement that assigns a value to the identifier that names the function. Normally, this is done with an assignment statement of the form

```
function-name = expression
```

where *expression* may be any expression involving constants, the formal arguments of the function, other variables already assigned values in this subprogram, as well as references to other functions. The last statement of the subprogram must be

```
END FUNCTION function-name
```

(For external functions this statement can be shortened to END.) The value of the function will be returned to the program unit that references it when this END FUNCTION statement is encountered or when a **RETURN statement** of the form

```
RETURN
```

is executed.

Example: Temperature Conversion

The formula for converting temperature measured in Fahrenheit to Celsius is

$$C = (F - 32) / 1.8$$

where F is the Fahrenheit temperature to be converted and C is the corresponding Celsius temperature. Suppose we wish to define a function that performs this conversion.

A function subprogram to implement this function will have one formal argument representing a Fahrenheit temperature, and so an appropriate heading is

```
FUNCTION Fahr_to_Celsius(Temperature)
```

Since this function returns a real value, its name must be declared to be of type REAL in the function's specification part,

```
REAL :: Fahr_to_Celsius
```

or in the function's heading:

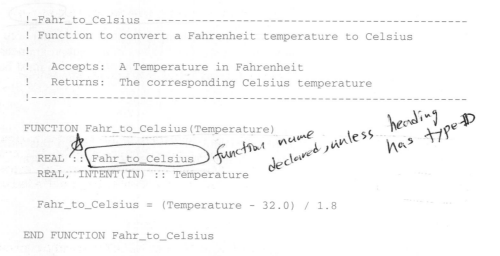

```
    REAL  FUNCTION Fahr_to_Celsius(Temperature)
```

(Note that double colons : : are not used in this case.) Since the formal argument `Temperature` must be of type `REAL` and will be used only to transfer information into the function, the specification part of this function subprogram must also contain the declaration

```
    REAL, INTENT(IN) :: Temperature
```

The complete function subprogram is

```
!-Fahr_to_Celsius ------------------------------------------------
! Function to convert a Fahrenheit temperature to Celsius
!
!    Accepts:   A Temperature in Fahrenheit
!    Returns:   The corresponding Celsius temperature
!----------------------------------------------------------------

FUNCTION Fahr_to_Celsius(Temperature)
    REAL :: Fahr_to_Celsius
    REAL, INTENT(IN) :: Temperature

    Fahr_to_Celsius = (Temperature - 32.0) / 1.8

END FUNCTION Fahr_to_Celsius
```

(handwritten annotation: function name declared, unless heading has type ID)

This subprogram can be made accessible to a program, called the **main program**, in three ways:

1. It is placed in a subprogram section in the main program just before the END PROGRAM statement (as described later); in this case it is called an **internal subprogram**.

2. It is placed in a module (as described later) from which it can be imported into the program; in this case it is called a **module subprogram**.

3. It is placed after the END   PROGRAM statement of the main program, in which case it is called an **external subprogram**.

In this section we will use only internal subprograms. Module subprograms are described in Section 6.5 and external subprograms in Section 6.6.

Internal subprograms are placed in a subprogram section at the end of the main program (or at the end of an external subprogram). The program unit (main program or subprogram) that contains an internal subprogram is called a **host** for that subprogram. This subprogram section has the form

Subprogram Section

Form:

```
CONTAINS
    subprogram₁
    subprogram₂
        ⋮
    subprogramₙ
```

where

each *subprogramᵢ* is a function or subroutine subprogram that does not contain a subprogram section.

Purpose:

Makes it possible to include within a program unit subprograms that will be referenced only by that program unit.

Figure 6.1 illustrates the use of an internal subprogram. In this example, program `Temperature_Conversion_1` is the main program (because its heading contains the keyword `PROGRAM`), and the function subprogram is named `Fahr_to_Celsius`. The main program uses the function `Fahr_to_Celsius` in the statement

```
CelsiusTemp = Fahr_to_Celsius(FahrenheitTemp)
```

to find the Celsius temperature corresponding to `FahrenheitTemp` and assign this value to `CelsiusTemp`.

Figure 6.1 Temperature conversions.

```
PROGRAM Temperature_Conversion_1
!-----------------------------------------------------------------------
! Program to convert several Fahrenheit temperatures to the
! corresponding Celsius temperatures.  The function Fahr_to_Celsius
! is used to perform the conversions.  Identifiers used are:
!   Fahr_to_Celsius : internal function subprogram that converts
!                     Fahrenheit temperatures to Celsius
!   FahrenheitTemp  : a Fahrenheit temperature to be converted
!   CelsiusTemp     : the corresponding Celsius temperature
!   Response        : user response to "More data?" query
!
! Input:   FahrenheitTemp, Response
! Output:  CelsiusTemp
!-----------------------------------------------------------------------
```

Figure 6.1 *(cont.)*

```fortran
IMPLICIT NONE
REAL :: FahrenheitTemp, CelsiusTemp
CHARACTER(1) :: Response

DO
   ! Get a Fahrenheit temperature
   WRITE (*, '(1X, A)', ADVANCE = "NO") "Enter a Fahrenheit temperature: "
   READ *, FahrenheitTemp

   ! Use the function Fahr_to_Celsius to convert it to Celsius
   CelsiusTemp = Fahr_to_Celsius(FahrenheitTemp)

   ! Output the result
   PRINT '(1X, 2(F6.2, A))', FahrenheitTemp, &
         " in Fahrenheit is equivalent to ", CelsiusTemp, " in Celsius"

   ! Check if more temperatures are to be converted
   WRITE (*, '(/ 1X, A)', ADVANCE = "NO") &
         "More temperatures to convert (Y or N)? "
   READ *, Response
   IF (Response /= "Y") EXIT
END DO

CONTAINS

   !- Fahr_To_Celsius ---------------------------------------
   ! Function to convert a Fahrenheit temperature to Celsius
   !
   !   Accepts:  A Temperature in Fahrenheit
   !   Returns:  The corresponding Celsius temperature
   !---------------------------------------------------------

   FUNCTION Fahr_to_Celsius(Temperature)

      REAL:: Fahr_to_Celsius
      REAL, INTENT(IN) :: Temperature

      Fahr_to_Celsius = (Temperature - 32.0) / 1.8

   END FUNCTION Fahr_to_Celsius

END PROGRAM Temperature_Conversion_1
```

Figure 6.1 *(cont.)*

Sample run:

```
Enter a Fahrenheit temperature: 32
 32.00 in Fahrenheit is equivalent to   0.00 in Celsius

More temperatures to convert (Y or N)? Y
Enter a Fahrenheit temperature: 212
212.00 in Fahrenheit is equivalent to 100.00 in Celsius

More temperatures to convert (Y or N)? Y
Enter a Fahrenheit temperature: -22.5
-22.50 in Fahrenheit is equivalent to -30.28 in Celsius

More temperatures to convert (Y or N)? N
```

Argument Association

A **reference** to a function has the form

```
function-name(actual-argument-list)
```

The values of the **actual arguments** become the values of the function's formal arguments, the function subprogram is executed, and when its END FUNCTION statement or a RETURN statement is encountered, the value of the function is passed back to the program unit that contains the reference.

To illustrate, consider the following diagram, which pictures the flow of control in the program in Figure 6.1:

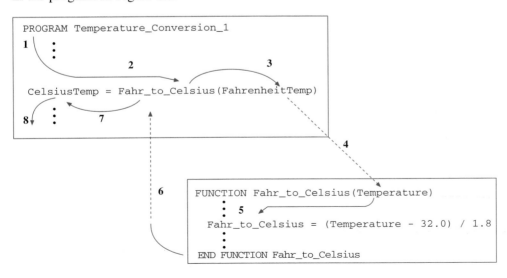

When the program is run, execution proceeds from the beginning of the main program in the usual manner (1) until the assignment statement containing the reference to function `Fahr_to_Celsius` is reached (2). At that time, the actual argument `FahrenheitTemp` (3) in this reference is evaluated and copied to the formal argument `Temperature` of `Fahr_to_Celsius` (4). Control is transferred from the main program to the function subprogram `Fahr_to_Celsius`, which begins execution (5). The statement

```
Fahr_to_Celsius = (Temperature - 32.0) / 1.8
```

is evaluated, and since `Temperature` contains a copy of the value of `FahrenheitTemp`, the resulting value is the Celsius equivalent of `FahrenheitTemp`. When execution reaches the end of the function, control transfers back to the main program (6) and the value computed by the preceding expression is returned as the value of the function. In the main program this value is then assigned to `CelsiusTemp` (7), and execution continues on through the remainder of the main program (8).

When a function is referenced, the intent is that the values of the actual arguments are passed to the formal arguments and these values are then used in computing the value of the function, but these values should not change while the function executes.

Including the `INTENT(IN)` specification in a formal argument's declaration ensures that

1. the value of the corresponding actual argument is passed to the formal argument, and

2. the value of the formal argument cannot be changed while the function is being executed. [1]

Any attempt to change the value of the formal argument will result in a compile-time error. For example, if we added the statement `Temperature = 0.0` to the function `Fahr_to_Celsius` in Figure 6.1, an attempt to compile the resulting program would produce an error message like

```
Error: Attempt to set the value of INTENT(IN) dummy argument
Temperature at line 52 detected at Temperature =
```

It is important to note that *if the `INTENT(IN)` clause is not used in the declaration of a formal argument, the value of the formal argument may be changed in the function and the value of the corresponding actual argument will also change.* For example, if the `INTENT(IN)` specification was not included in the declaration of the formal argument `Temperature` of function subprogram `Fahr_to_Celsius` and this function contained the statement

```
Temperature = 0.0
```

---

[1] The `INTENT` attribute may also be used to specify other kinds of argument association, as described in Section 7.1.

a function reference such as

```
CelsiusTemp = Fahr_to_Celsius(FahrenheitTemp)
```

would change the value of the actual argument FahrenheitTemp to zero.
Another consequence of this association between actual arguments and formal arguments is that *the number and type of the actual arguments must agree with the number and type of the formal arguments* (except when keyword or optional arguments are used, as described in Section 7.7). For example, the function reference in

```
CelsiusTemp = Fahr_to_Celsius(2.5, 1)
```

is not allowed because the number of actual arguments does not match the number of formal arguments.

Example: Function of Several Variables

In the preceding example, the function subprogram Fahr_to_Celsius had a single argument. Functions may, however, have any number of arguments, and they need not all be of the same type. To illustrate, suppose we wish to use the function

$$f(x, y, n) = \begin{cases} x^n + y^n & \text{if } x \geq y \\ 0 & \text{otherwise} \end{cases}$$

where x and y are real numbers and n is an integer. A function subprogram to implement this function will have three formal arguments, X, Y, and N, and so an appropriate function heading is

```
FUNCTION F(X, Y, N)
```

Since the function returns a real value and since X and Y must be of type REAL and N of type INTEGER, the specification part of this function subprogram is

```
REAL :: F
REAL, INTENT(IN) :: X, Y
INTEGER, INTENT(IN) :: N
```

The complete function subprogram is

```
FUNCTION F(X, Y, N)

  REAL :: F
  REAL, INTENT(IN) :: X, Y
  INTEGER, INTENT(IN) ::  N
```

```
          IF (X >= Y) THEN
             F = X ** N + Y ** N
          ELSE
             F = 0.0
          END IF

       END FUNCTION F
```

If A, B, and C are real variables, then for the function reference in the statement

```
       PRINT *, F(A, B + C, 2)
```

the value of the variable A is passed to the formal argument X, the value of the expression B + C is passed to the formal argument Y, and the integer 2 is passed to the formal argument N. The INTENT(IN) specified in the declarations of X, Y, and N ensures that the values of X, Y, and N may not be changed in the function F.

Example: Pollution Index

In the preceding example, the argument types and the result types of the functions all were numeric. This need not be the case, however. The arguments and the function values may be of any type. To illustrate, consider again the pollution-index problem described in Section 3.3 in which air quality is determined by the value of a pollution index. The air quality is judged to be safe if this index is less than some cutoff value; otherwise, it is considered hazardous. A function that accepts this pollution index and returns the appropriate air-quality indicator will have an integer argument, and the function values will be character strings.

```
!- AirQuality ----------------------------------------------
! Determines the air quality for a given pollution index.
! It is "safe" if the index is less than some Cutoff value
! and is "hazardous" otherwise.
!
! Accepts: An integer PollutionIndex
! Returns: Character string AirQuality
!
! Note:  Cutoff is a local constant
!-----------------------------------------------------------

FUNCTION AirQuality(PollutionIndex)

   CHARACTER(9) :: AirQuality
   INTEGER, INTENT(IN) :: PollutionIndex
   INTEGER, PARAMETER :: Cutoff = 50      ! parts per million
```

```
    IF (PollutionIndex < Cutoff) THEN
        AirQuality = "safe"
    ELSE
        AirQuality = "hazardous"
    END IF

END FUNCTION AirQuality
```

We could also specify the type and length of values of the function `AirQual-ity` using the **assumed length specifier (*)**:

```
    CHARACTER(*) :: AirQuality
```

In this case, a declaration that specifies the length of values of `AirQuality` must appear in any program unit (main program or subprogram) that references `AirQuality`. The assumed length specifer may also be used in the specification part of a subprogram to declare the types of formal character arguments.

Local Identifiers—The Factorial Function

Some function subprograms like that in the preceding example require the use of constants and/or variables in addition to the formal arguments. As illustrated in the function subprogram `AirQuality`, these **local identifiers** are declared in the specification part of the subprogram.

As an example of a function subprogram that uses local variables, we consider the *factorial function*. The factorial of a nonnegative integer n is denoted by $n!$ and is defined by

$$n! = \begin{cases} 1 & \text{if } n = 0 \\ 1 \times 2 \times 3 \times \cdots \times n & \text{if } n > 0 \end{cases}$$

A function subprogram to define this integer-valued function will have one integer argument N, but it will also use a local variable I as a control variable in a DO loop that computes N!. The complete function subprogram is

```
!- Factorial -----------------------------------------------
! Function to calculate the factorial N! of N, which is
! 1 if N = 0, 1 * 2 * · · · * N if N > 0.
!
! Accepts:   Integer N
! Returns:   The integer N!
!
! Note:  I is a local integer variable used as a counter.
!-----------------------------------------------------------
```

```
FUNCTION Factorial(N)

   INTEGER :: Factorial
   INTEGER, INTENT(IN) :: N
   INTEGER :: I

   Factorial = 1
   DO I = 2, N
      Factorial = Factorial * I
   END DO

END FUNCTION Factorial
```

Example: Poisson Probability Function

The program in Figure 6.2 uses the function subprogram `Factorial` in calculating values of the **Poisson probability function**, which is the probability function of a random variable, such as the number of radioactive particles striking a target in a given period of time, the number of flaws in a given length of magnetic tape, or the number of failures in an electronic device during a given time period. This function is defined by

$$P(n) = \frac{\lambda^n \cdot e^{-\lambda}}{n!}$$

where

λ = the average number of occurrences of the phenomenon per time period

n = the number of occurrences in that time period

For example, if the average number of particles passing through a counter during 1 millisecond in a laboratory experiment is 3 ($\lambda = 3$), then the probability that exactly 5 particles enter the counter ($n = 5$) in a given millisecond will be

$$P(5) = \frac{3^5 \cdot e^{-3}}{5!} = 0.1008$$

The program in Figure 6.2 reads values for `NumOccurs` and `AveOccurs`, uses the statement

```
Probability = Poisson(AveOccurs, NumOccurs)
```

to calculate the Poisson probability, and then displays this probability. The value of N! is obtained by the function `Poisson` from the function subprogram `Factorial`.

Figure 6.2 Poisson probability distribution.

```fortran
PROGRAM Poisson_Probability
!-------------------------------------------------------------------
! Program to calculate the Poisson probability function using the
! function subprogram Poisson.  Identifiers used are:
!   AveOccurs    : average # of occurrences of phenomenon per
!                  time period
!   NumOccurs    : number of occurrences in a time period
!   Probability  : Poisson probability
!   NumProbs     : number of probabilities to calculate
!   I            : DO-loop control variable
!   Poisson      : internal function subprogram to calculate Poisson
!                  probability
!   Factorial    : internal function subprogram to calculate factorials
!
! Input:   NumProbs and values for AveOccurs and NumOccurs
! Output:  Poisson probabilities
!-------------------------------------------------------------------

  IMPLICIT NONE
  REAL :: AveOccurs, Probability
  INTEGER :: NumProbs, I, NumOccurs

  PRINT *, "This program calculates Poisson probabilities."
  WRITE (*, '(1X, A)', ADVANCE = "NO") &
        "How many probabilities do you wish to calculate? "
  READ *, NumProbs

  DO I = 1, NumProbs
     WRITE (*, '(1X, A)', ADVANCE = "NO") &
           "Enter average # of occurrences per time period: "
     READ *, AveOccurs
     WRITE (*, '(1X, A)', ADVANCE = "NO") &
           "Enter # of occurrences for which to find probability: "
     READ *, NumOccurs
     Probability = Poisson(AveOccurs, NumOccurs)
     PRINT 10, Probability
     10 FORMAT(1X, "Poisson probability = ", F6.4 /)
  END DO

CONTAINS
```

Figure 6.2 *(cont.)*

```
!-Poisson -----------------------------------------------------------
! Function to calculate the Poisson probability
!                               N     -Lambda
!                      Lambda * e
!           Poisson(N) =   -----------------
!                               N!
! Function Factorial is called to calculate N!
!
! Accepts:  Real number Lambda and integer N
! Returns:  The poisson probability given by the formula above
!-------------------------------------------------------------------

FUNCTION Poisson(Lambda, N)

  REAL :: Poisson
  REAL, INTENT(IN) :: Lambda
  INTEGER, INTENT(IN) :: N

  Poisson = (Lambda ** N * EXP(-Lambda)) / REAL(Factorial(N))

END FUNCTION Poisson

!- Factorial -------------------------------------------------------
! Function to calculate the factorial N! of N, which is 1 if N = 0,
! 1 * 2 * . . . * N if N > 0.
!
! Accepts:  Integer N
! Returns:  The integer N!
!
! Note:  I is a local integer variable used as a counter.
!-------------------------------------------------------------------

FUNCTION Factorial(N)

  INTEGER, INTENT(IN) ::  N
  INTEGER :: Factorial, I

  Factorial = 1
  DO I = 2, N
     Factorial = Factorial * I
  END DO

END FUNCTION Factorial

END PROGRAM Poisson_Probability
```

Figure 6.2 *(cont.)*

Sample run:

```
This program calculates Poisson probabilities.
How many probabilities do you wish to calculate? 2
Enter average # of occurrences per time period: 3
Enter # of occurrences for which to find probability: 5
Poisson probability = 0.1008

Enter average # of occurrences per time period: 4
Enter # of occurrences for which to find probability: 6
Poisson probability = 0.1042
```

The order in which subprograms are arranged is not important. Thus, in Figure 6.2, the subprogram `Factorial` could just as well precede the subprogram `Poisson`.

Scope

In a program that contains subprograms, there may be several points at which entities (variables, constants, subprograms, types) are declared—in the main program, in subprograms, or as described later, in modules. The portion of the program in which any of these items is *visible*, that is, where it is accessible and can be used, is called its **scope**.

There is one general scope principle:

Fundamental Scope Principle

The scope of an entity is the program or subprogram in which it is declared.

One scope rule that follows from the fundamental principle applies to items that are declared within a subprogram, that is, to the formal arguments of the subprogram and to the constants and variables declared in its specification part (and type identifiers, described in Chapter 10):

Scope Rule 1

An item declared within a subprogram is not accessible outside that subprogram.

Such items are therefore said to be **local** to that subprogram. For example, the scope of local variables `I` and `N` in function `Factorial` is this function subprogram; they cannot be accessed outside it.

Any item declared in the main program is called a **global entity** because it is accessible throughout the entire program, except within internal subprograms in which a local entity has the same name.

Scope Rule 2

A global entity is accessible throughout the main program and in any internal subprogram in which no local entity has the same name as the global item.

For example, in Figure 6.2, the variables AveOccurs, NumOccurs, Probability, NumProbs, and I are global variables. All of them are accessible to the main program, and all but I are accessible to the function Factorial. The global variable I is not accessible within Factorial, because I is the name of a local variable within Factorial. A reference to the variable I within Factorial yields the value of the local variable I, whereas a reference to I outside the function gives the value of the global variable I. Thus the same identifier I names two different variables that are associated with two different memory locations.

Scope rule 2 also applies to internal subprograms. For example, Factorial is global and thus can be referenced in either the main program or by Poisson. The function Poisson also is global and can thus be referenced in the main program. (It cannot be referenced within Factorial, however, because Poisson references Factorial, and thus Factorial would indirectly be referencing itself.)

Although global variables can be used to share data between the main program and internal subprograms or between internal subprograms, it is usually unwise to do so, since this practice reduces the independence of the various subprograms and thus makes modular programming more difficult. Changing the value of a global variable in one part of the program has the dangerous **side effect** of changing the value of that variable throughout the entire program, including all internal subprograms. Consequently, it is difficult to determine the value of that variable at any particular point in the program.

Statement labels are not governed by Scope rule 2. Thus the FORMAT statement in the main program in Figure 6.2 cannot be used within Poisson or Factorial, because its statement label is not accessible to these subprograms.

The naming convention established by an IMPLICIT statement in the main program is also global. Thus, in Figure 6.2, the IMPLICIT NONE statement in the main program applies to both Poisson and Factorial so that it is not necessary to include it in these subprograms.

Saving the Values of Local Variables

The values of local variables in a subprogram are not retained from one execution of the subprogram to the next unless either

1. They are initialized in their declarations, or
2. They are declared to have the **SAVE attribute**.

Thus, for example, if we wish to count the number of times a function subprogam is executed, we could add the following statements:

```
FUNCTION F(. . .)

   INTEGER :: Count = 0
      . . .
   Count = Count + 1
      . . .
END FUNCTION F(. . .)
```

Because `Count` is initialized within this subprogram, its value will be preserved from one function reference to the next.

To ensure that values of local uninitialized variables are saved from one execution of a subprogram to the next, we can specify that these variables have the SAVE attribute in their declarations

```
type, SAVE :: list-of-local-variables
```

or by using a **SAVE statement** of the form

```
SAVE list-of-local-variables
```

If the list is omitted, the values of all variables in the subprogram will be saved.

Declaring a Function's Type

The declaration of the type of a function can be made in two ways. The first method, and the one that we use in our examples, is to declare the function's result type in the specification part of the subprogram, as illustrated in the following examples.

```
FUNCTION Atomic_Number(X, Y)
   INTEGER :: Atomic_Number
   REAL, INTENT(IN) :: X, Y
      ⋮
END FUNCTION Atomic_Number

FUNCTION Element(Name, N)
   CHARACTER(10) :: Element
   CHARACTER(15), INTENT(IN) :: Name
   INTEGER, INTENT(IN) :: N
      ⋮
END FUNCTION Element
```

In the last example, we could specify the type and length of the function `Element` and/or the formal argument `Name` using the assumed length specifier (*) as follows:

```
FUNCTION Element(Name, N)
   CHARACTER(*) :: Element
   CHARACTER(*), INTENT(IN) :: Name
   INTEGER, INTENT(IN) :: N
```

In this case, the length of `Element` is the length specified in the program unit referencing the function, and the length of `Name` is the length of the corresponding actual argument.

The second method of declaring a function's type is to *attach it without colons* (`::`) at the beginning of the function heading. Thus, the preceding examples could also be written as follows:

```
INTEGER FUNCTION Atomic_Number(X, Y)
   REAL, INTENT(IN) :: X, Y
      ⋮
END FUNCTION Atomic_Number


CHARACTER(10) FUNCTION Element(Name, N)
   CHARACTER(15), INTENT(IN) :: Name
   INTEGER, INTENT(IN) :: N
      ⋮
END FUNCTION Element
```

or using the assumed length specifier in the last example,

```
CHARACTER(*) FUNCTION Element(Name, N)
   CHARACTER(*), INTENT(IN) :: Name
   INTEGER, INTENT(IN) :: N
      ⋮
END FUNCTION Element
```

Quick Quiz 6.1

1. What are the two kinds of Fortran subprograms?

2. List the four parts of a function subprogram.

3. In the function heading FUNCTION Sum(A, B), A and B are called _____.

4. For a function whose heading is REAL FUNCTION Sum(A, B), the type of the value returned by the function is _____.

5. List the three ways that a subprogram can be made accessible to a program.

6. The part of a program in which a variable can be accessed is called the _____ of that variable.

7. (True or false) Function subprograms and the main program may use the same identifiers.

Questions 8–10 deal with the following internal function:

```
FUNCTION What(N)

    INTEGER :: What
    INTEGER, INTENT(IN) :: N
    What = (N * (N + 1)) / 2

END FUNCTION What
```

8. If the statement `Number1 = What(Number2)` appears in the main program, `Number2` is called a(n)_____ argument in this function reference.

9. If the statement `Number = What(3)` appears in the main program, the value assigned to `Number` will be _____.

10. (True or false) The value assigned to `Number` by the statement `Number = What(5)` in the main program will be 15.

11. (True or false) The statement `N = 1` may be inserted in the function `What`.

12. Write a function that calculates values of $x^2 \sin x$.

Exercises 6.1

1. Write a function `Range` that calculates the range between two integers, that is, the result of subtracting the smaller integer from the larger one.

2. Write a real-valued function `Round` that has a real argument `Amount` and an integer argument `N` and that returns the value of `Amount` rounded to N places. For example, the function references `Round(10.536, 0)`, `Round(10.536, 1)`, and `Round(10.536, 2)` should give the values 11.0, 10.5, and 10.54, respectively.

3. The number of bacteria in a culture can be estimated by

$$N \cdot e^{kt}$$

where N is the initial population, k is a rate constant, and t is time. Write a function to calculate the number of bacteria present at time t for given values of k and N.

4. Write functions to define the logical functions

$$\sim p \wedge \sim q \quad (\text{not } p \text{ and not } q)$$

and

$$\sim(p \vee q) \quad (\text{not } (p \text{ or } q))$$

5. Write a function that has as arguments the coordinates of two points $P_1(x_1, y_1)$ and $P_2(x_2, y_2)$ and returns the distance $\sqrt{(x_2 - x_1)^2 + (y_2 - y_1)^2}$ between P_1 and P_2.

6. Write a real-valued function `NumericGrade` that accepts a letter grade and returns the corresponding numeric value (A = 4.0, B = 3.0, C = 2.0, D = 1.0, F = 0.0).

7. Write a character-valued function `LetterGrade` that assigns a letter grade to an integer score using the following grading scale:

$$\begin{array}{rl}
90\text{–}100: & \text{A} \\
80\text{–}89: & \text{B} \\
70\text{–}79: & \text{C} \\
60\text{–}69: & \text{D} \\
\text{Below } 60: & \text{F}
\end{array}$$

8. Write a function that calculates the sum $m + (m + 1) + \cdots + n$, for two given integers m and n.

9. Write a function `Days_in_Month` that returns the number of days in a given month and year. (See Exercise 10 of Section 3.5, which describes which years are leap years.)

10. Write a logical-valued function that determines if an integer is a perfect square.

11. The *greatest common divisor* (GCD) of two integers a and b, not both of which are zero, is the largest positive integer that divides both a and b. The *Euclidean algorithm* for finding this greatest common divisor of a and b, GCD(a, b), is as follows: If $b = 0$, GCD(a, b) is a. Otherwise, divide a by b to obtain quotient q and remainder r, so that $a = bq + r$. Then GCD(a, b) = GCD(b, r). Replace a by b and b by r and repeat this procedure. Because the remainders are decreasing, a remainder of 0 will eventually result. The last nonzero remainder is then GCD(a, b). For example:

$$\begin{array}{ll}
1260 = 198 \cdot 6 + 72 & \text{GCD}(1260, 198) = \text{GCD}(198, 72) \\
198 = 72 \cdot 2 + 54 & \hphantom{\text{GCD}(1260, 198)} = \text{GCD}(72, 54) \\
72 = 54 \cdot 1 + 18 & \hphantom{\text{GCD}(1260, 198)} = \text{GCD}(54, 18) \\
54 = 18 \cdot 3 + 0 & \hphantom{\text{GCD}(1260, 198)} = 18
\end{array}$$

Note: If either a or b is negative, replace it with its absolute value.
Write a function subprogram to calculate the GCD of two integers.

12. A *prime number* is an integer $n > 1$ whose only positive divisors are 1 and n itself. Write a logical-valued function that determines whether n is a prime number.

6.2   APPLICATION: BEAM DEFLECTION

Modular Programming

In the introduction to this chapter, we claimed that one of the advantages of sub-programs is that they enable a programmer to develop programs in a **modular** fashion. This means that the major tasks to be performed by the program can be identified and then individual subprograms for these tasks can be designed and tested. Programs written in this manner are not only easier to develop and test and easier to understand, but they are also easier to modify, since individual subprograms can be added, deleted, or altered. In this section we illustrate this technique of modular programming by developing a *menu-driven* program for calculating beam deflections.

PROBLEM

Problem:

The analysis of beams is an important part of the structural analysis carried out before construction of a building begins. One frequently used type of beam is a *cantilever beam*, which has one end fixed and the other end free. The deflection at the free end of the beam depends on the beam's loading conditions. Three of the many possible loading cases are shown in the following diagrams. In these diagrams, W is the total load (Newtons), δ is the deflection (meters) caused by the load at any distance x in meters from the free end of the beam, l is the length of the beam in meters, a and b are the lengths in meters as shown, and w is the unit load (N/m) in the uniform loading cases.

1. end load, W

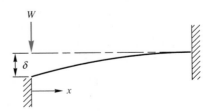

2. intermediate load, W

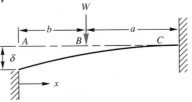

3. uniform load, $W = wl$

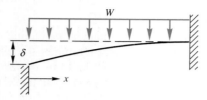

We wish to develop a program that will calculate the deflection of a cantilever beam for each of these three loading cases.

Solution

Specification.   We assume that all forces are coplanar, that the beam is in static equilibrium, and that the mass of the beam may be neglected. With these assumptions, the following equations can be used to calculate the deflections for the three load cases:

1. $\delta = [-W / (6EI)][x^3 - 3l^2x + 2l^3]$
2. $\delta = [-W / (6EI)][-a^3 + 3a^2l - 3a^2x]$ from A to B
   $\delta = [-W / (6EI)][(x - b)^3 - 3a^2(x - b) + 2a^3]$ from B to C
3. $\delta = [-W / (24EIl)][x^4 - 4l^3x + 3l^4]$

Here E is the modulus of elasticity (in pascals), which depends on the material the beam is made of, and I is the moment of inertia (m^4), which depends on the cross section of the beam. In this example we consider an I beam made of steel, where $I = 4.15 \times 10^{-8}$ m^4 and $E = 2.05 \times 10^{11}$ Pa.

We see from the description of the problem and the preceding equations that the problem's input and output include the following:

Input: Modulus of elasticity
          Moment of inertia
          Length of the beam
          Type of loading condition
          Distance from end of beam for an intermediate load

Output: Deflection of the beam

Design.   The program will read the beam information, including the modulus of elasticity, the moment of inertia, and the length of the beam, and also the number of points along the beam at which the deflection is to be calculated. The user will then indicate which types of loading conditions are to be used, and the deflection at the number of equally spaced points specified by the user will be calculated. A first version of an algorithm for solving this problem thus is

1. Read the beam information.

2. Repeat the following until user is ready to stop:
    a. Get an option from the user (0, 1, 2, or 3).
    b. If the option is not between 0 and 3
        Display an illegal option message.
       Else if option is 0
        Display a termination message.
       Else
        Output a table of deflections for a load type corresponding to the user-selected option.

Here, the else part of step 2b clearly requires refinement. We must specify the number of points at which the deflection is to be calculated. A loop is needed to range over these points, calculate the deflection at each point, using the formula appropriate for the case selected, and then display the deflection. We can now give a complete algorithm for solving this problem. We will use the following variables:

VARIABLES FOR BEAM DEFLECTION PROBLEM

Elasticity	Modulus of elasticity (Pa)
Inertia	Moment of inertia (m^4)
BeamLength	Length of the beam (m)
NumPoints	Number of points at which deflections are to be found
Delta_x	Distance between points (m)
Option	Option selected by the user
Load	Load on the beam (N)
x	Distance from the free end of the beam (m)
Deflection	Deflection of beam at distance x (m)
a	Distance along the beam (needed in case 2) (m)
I	Counts points along the beam

ALGORITHM FOR BEAM DEFLECTION PROBLEM

Algorithm to calculate deflections in a cantilever beam under a given load at equally spaced points along the beam. There are three types of load conditions:

1. single point load at the free end

2. single point load at an interior point

3. uniformly distributed load

Input: *Elasticity, Inertia, BeamLength, Option, Load, a, NumPoints*

Output: Table of deflections at points along the beam

1. Read *Elasticity, Inertia, BeamLength*.

2. Repeat the following:

    a. Enter *Option*.

    b. If *Option* is not between 0 and 3

       Display an illegal option message.

    Else if *Option* = 0

       Terminate repetition.

    Else do the following:

      i. Enter *Load*.

      ii. If *Option* = 2, enter *a*.

      iii. Enter *NumPoints*.

      iv. Calculate *Delta_x = BeamLength / NumPoints*.

      v. Set *x* to 0.

      vi. Do the following for *I* ranging from 1 to *NumPoints*:

         (1) Calculate *Deflection* at distance *x* using the appropriate formula as determined by *Option*.

         (2) Display *x* and *Deflection*.

         (3) Increment *x* by *Delta_x*.

Coding. The fact that the method of calculating the deflection is different in the three cases suggests that separate subprograms be used to do the calculations in each of the cases. Figure 6.3 shows three such function subprograms, `Case_1`, `Case_2`, and `Case_3`. The main program is **menu-driven**: it displays a menu of options; the user selects one of these options; and the appropriate function `Case_1`, `Case_2`, or `Case_3` is called to calculate the deflection.

Although the final program is given here, it could well be developed in a piece-wise manner by writing and testing only some of the subprograms before writing the others. For example, we might develop and test function `Case_1` before working on the other two functions. The undeveloped functions could simply have empty execution parts. Usually, however, they are **program stubs** that at least signal execution of these subprograms; for example,

```
PRINT *, "Executing case 2"
Case_2 = 0
END
```

In some cases they might also produce temporary printouts to assist in checking other subprograms. The example in Section 7.5 illustrates the use of such program stubs.

Figure 6.3 Beam deflection.

```fortran
PROGRAM Beam_Deflection
!-----------------------------------------------------------------------
! This program calculates deflections in a cantilever beam
! under a given load. Three different loading conditions are
! analyzed:
!   Case #1 : a single point load at the free end of the beam
!   Case #2 : a single point load at an interior point
!   Case #3 : load uniformly distributed along the beam
!
! Variables used are:
!   Elasticity : modulus of elasticity (Pa)
!   Inertia    : moment of inertia (m**4)
!   BeamLength : length of the beam (m)
!   NumPoints  : number of points at which deflections are found
!   Delta_x    : distance between points (m)
!   Option     : option selected by the user
!   Load       : load on the beam (N)
!   x          : distance from the free end of the beam (m)
!   a          : distance along the beam (m)
!   I          : control variable used in DO loop
!   Deflection : deflection at distance x (m)
!   Case_1     : internal function to compute deflection in case #1
!   Case_2     :      "        "     "      "         "       " case #2
!   Case_3     :      "        "     "      "         "       " case #3
!
! Input:  Elasticity, Inertia, BeamLength, NumPoints, Option, Load, a
! Output: A table of deflections at points along the beam
!-----------------------------------------------------------------------

  IMPLICIT NONE
  INTEGER :: NumPoints, Option, I
  REAL :: Elasticity, Inertia, BeamLength, Delta_x, Load, x, a, &
          Deflection

  ! Get beam information
  PRINT *, "Enter:"
  WRITE (*, '(6X, A)', ADVANCE = "NO") "Modulus of elasticity (Pa): "
  READ *, Elasticity
  WRITE (*, '(6X, A)', ADVANCE = "NO") "Moment of inertia (m**4): "
  READ *, Inertia
  WRITE (*, '(6X, A)', ADVANCE = "NO") "Length of the beam (m): "
  READ *, BeamLength
```

Figure 6.3 *(cont.)*

```
! Repeat the following until user selects option 0 to stop
DO
   PRINT *
   PRINT *, "The following options are available:"
   PRINT *, "   0 : Stop"
   PRINT *, "   1 : End Load"
   PRINT *, "   2 : Intermediate Load"
   PRINT *, "   3 : Uniform load"
   WRITE (*, '(1X, A)', ADVANCE = "NO") "Select one: "
   READ *, Option

   IF (Option < 0 .OR. Option > 3) THEN
      PRINT *, "Not a valid option"

   ELSE IF (Option == 0) THEN
      PRINT *, "Done processing for this beam"
      EXIT

   ELSE
      PRINT *,   "Enter total load for cases 1 and 2, unit load for case 3."
      WRITE (*, '(1X, A)', ADVANCE = "NO") "Load (N)? "
      READ *, Load
      IF (Option == 2) THEN
         WRITE (*, '(1X, A)', ADVANCE = "NO") "Enter the distance a (m):"
         READ *, a
      END IF

      WRITE (*, '(1X, A)', ADVANCE = "NO") "Enter number of points to use: "
      READ *, NumPoints
      Delta_x = BeamLength / REAL(NumPoints)

      PRINT *
      PRINT *, "Distance (m)    Deflection (m)"
      PRINT *, "=============================="

      x = 0.0
      DO I = 1, NumPoints
         SELECT CASE (Option)
            CASE (1)
               Deflection = &
                   Case_1(Elasticity, Inertia, BeamLength, Load, x)
            CASE (2)
               Deflection = &
                   Case_2(Elasticity, Inertia, BeamLength, Load, a, x)
            CASE (3)
               Deflection = &
                   Case_3(Elasticity, Inertia, BeamLength, Load, x)
         END SELECT
```

Figure 6.3 *(cont.)*

```
          PRINT '(1X, F7.2, E20.6)', x, Deflection

          x = x + Delta_x

      END DO

    END IF

  END DO

CONTAINS

  !- Case_1 -----------------------------------------------------------
  ! Computes deflections for a single point load at the free end
  ! of the beam.  Local variable used:
  !    Temp  : temporary variable used in calculating deflection
  !
  ! Accepts: Elasticity, Inertia, BeamLength, Load, x (see main program)
  ! Returns: Deflection
  !-------------------------------------------------------------------

  FUNCTION Case_1(Elasticity, Inertia, BeamLength, Load, x)

    REAL :: Case_1, Temp
    REAL, INTENT(IN) :: Elasticity, Inertia, BeamLength, Load, x

    Temp = x**3 - 3.0 * BeamLength**2 * x + 2.0 * BeamLength**3
    Case_1 = (-Load / (6.0 * Elasticity * Inertia)) * Temp

  END FUNCTION Case_1

  !- Case_2 -----------------------------------------------------------
  ! Computes deflections for a single point load at an interior
  ! point of the beam.  Local variables used:
  !    b    : distance along the beam
  !    Temp : temporary variable used in calculating deflection
  !
  ! Accepts: Elasticity, Inertia, BeamLength, Load, a, x (see main prog.)
  ! Returns: Deflection
  !-------------------------------------------------------------------

  FUNCTION Case_2(Elasticity, Inertia, BeamLength, Load, a, x)

    REAL :: Case_2, b, Temp
    REAL, INTENT(IN) :: Elasticity, Inertia, BeamLength, Load, a,  x
```

Figure 6.3 *(cont.)*

```
   b = BeamLength - a
   IF (x < b) THEN
      Temp = -a**3 + 3.0 * a**2 * BeamLength - 3.0 * a**2 * x
   ELSE
      Temp = (x - b)**3 - 3.0 * a**2 * (x - b) + 2.0 * a**3
   END IF
   Case_2 = (-Load / (6.0 * Elasticity * Inertia)) * Temp

END FUNCTION Case_2


!- Case_3 -------------------------------------------------------------
! Computes deflections for a load uniformly distributed along
! the beam.  Local variables used:
!   TotalLoad  : total load
!   Temp       : temporary variable used in calculating deflection
!
! Accepts: Elasticity, Inertia, BeamLength, Load, x (see main program)
! Returns: Deflection
!----------------------------------------------------------------------

FUNCTION Case_3(Elasticity, Inertia, BeamLength, Load, x)

   REAL :: Case_3, Temp, TotalLoad
   REAL, INTENT(IN) :: Elasticity, Inertia, BeamLength, Load, x

   TotalLoad = Load * BeamLength
   Temp = x**4 - 4.0 * BeamLength**3 * x + 3.0 * BeamLength**4
   Case_3 = (-TotalLoad / (24.0 * Elasticity * Inertia * BeamLength))&
            * Temp

END FUNCTION Case_3

END PROGRAM Beam_Deflection
```

Execution and Testing.   The program was tested with several sets of test data to verify its correctness. The following sample run shows the deflection tables obtained using the modulus of elasticity and moment of inertia given in the statement of the problem.

Sample run:

```
Enter
     Modulus of elasticity (Pa): 2.05E11
     Moment of inertia (m**4): 4.15E-8
     Length of the beam (m): 1.0
```

```
The following options are available:
    0 : Stop
    1 : End Load
    2 : Intermediate Load
    3 : Uniform load
Select one: 1
Enter total load for cases 1 and 2, unit load for case 3.
Load (N)? 125.0
Enter number of points to use: 10

Distance (m)    Deflection (m)
==============================
    0.00        -0.489764E-02
    0.10        -0.416544E-02
    0.20        -0.344794E-02
    0.30        -0.275982E-02
    0.40        -0.211578E-02
    0.50        -0.153051E-02
    0.60        -0.101871E-02
    0.70        -0.595063E-03
    0.80        -0.274268E-03
    0.90        -0.710156E-04

The following options are available:
    0 : Stop
    1 : End Load
    2 : Intermediate Load
    3 : Uniform load
Select one: 2
Enter total load for cases 1 and 2, unit load for case 3.
Load (N)? 125.0
Enter the distance a (m): 0.5
Enter number of points to use: 10

Distance (m)    Deflection (m)
==============================
    0.00        -0.153051E-02
    0.10        -0.134685E-02
    0.20        -0.116319E-02
    0.30        -0.979528E-03
    0.40        -0.795866E-03
    0.50        -0.612205E-03
    0.60        -0.430992E-03
    0.70        -0.264472E-03
    0.80        -0.127339E-03
    0.90        -0.342834E-04
```

```
     The following options are available:
        0 : Stop
        1 : End Load
        2 : Intermediate Load
        3 : Uniform load
  Select one: 3
  Enter total load for cases 1 and 2, unit load for case 3.
  Load (N)? 125.0
  Enter number of points to use: 10

  Distance (m)      Deflection (m)
  ================================
        0.00          -0.183661E-02
        0.10          -0.159179E-02
        0.20          -0.134783E-02
        0.30          -0.110693E-02
        0.40          -0.872759E-03
        0.50          -0.650468E-03
        0.60          -0.446665E-03
        0.70          -0.269431E-03
        0.80          -0.128318E-03
        0.90          -0.343446E-04

  The following options are available:
        0 : Stop
        1 : End Load
        2 : Intermediate Load
        3 : Uniform load
  Select one: 0
  Done processing for this beam
```

6.3 APPLICATION: ROOT FINDING, INTEGRATION, AND DIFFERENTIAL EQUATIONS

Mathematical models are used to solve problems in a wide variety of areas, including science, engineering, business, and the social sciences. Many of these models consist of ordinary algebraic equations, differential equations, systems of equations, and so on, and the solution of the problem is obtained by finding solutions of these equations. Methods for solving such equations that can be implemented in a computer program are called **numerical methods**, and the analysis and application of such numerical methods is an important area of scientific computing. In this section we consider three types of problems in which numerical methods are routinely used: root finding, integration, and solving differential equations.

Root Finding

In many applications, it is necessary to find a **zero** or **root** of a function f, that is, to solve the equation

$$f(x) = 0$$

For some functions f, it may be very difficult or even impossible to find this solution exactly. Examples include the function

$$f(v) = 50 \cdot 10^{-9}(e^{40v} - 1) + v - 20$$

which may arise in a problem of determining the d-c operating point in an electrical circuit, or a function of the form

$$f(x) = x \tan x - a$$

for which a zero must be found to solve some heat conduction problems.

For such functions, an iterative numerical method may be used to find an approximate zero. One method that is often used for differentiable functions is **Newton's method.** This method consists of taking an initial approximation x_1 to the root and constructing the tangent line to the graph of f at point $P_1(x_1, f(x_1))$. The point x_2 at which this tangent line crosses the x-axis is the second approximation to the root. Another tangent line may be constructed at point $P_2(x_2, f(x_2))$, and the point x_3 where this tangent line crosses the x-axis is the third approximation. For many functions, this sequence of approximations $x_1, x_2, x_3, \ldots$ converges to the root, provided that the first approximation is sufficiently close to the root. The following diagram illustrates Newton's method:

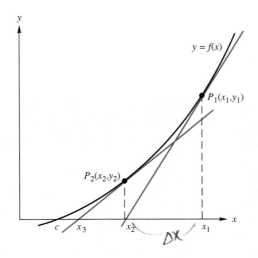

If x_n is an approximation to the zero of f, then the formula for obtaining the next approximation, x_{n+1}, by Newton's method is

$$x_{n+1} = x_n - \frac{f(x_n)}{f'(x_n)}$$

where f' is the derivative of f.

The following algorithm uses Newton's method to find a root of a function F. An initial approximation to a zero of F is read, and successive approximations using Newton's method are generated and displayed as long as

$$|F(X)| \ge Epsilon$$

for some small positive number *Epsilon*. If the number of iterations exceeds an upper limit *NumIterations* (in case of divergence), execution is terminated.

ALGORITHM FOR NEWTON'S METHOD

Algorithm to find an approximate root of a given function F. *FPrime* is the derivative of F.

Input: An error tolerance *Epsilon*, limit (*NumIterations*) on the number of iterations, and an initial approximation *OldApprox* to the root

Output: Iteration number N, the Nth approximation, and the value of F at that approximation

1. Read *Epsilon*, *NumIterations*, and *OldApprox*.
2. Set *F_Value* equal to $F(OldApprox)$.
3. Initialize N to 0.
4. Display N, *OldApprox*, and *F_Value*.
5. Repeat the following:
   a. If |*F_Value*| < *Epsilon* or N > *NumIterations*, terminate repetition. Otherwise continue with the following.
   b. Increment N by 1.
   c. Set *FDeriv_Old* equal to *FPrime*(*OldApprox*).
   d. If *FDeriv_Old* = 0 then do the following:
       i. Display a message that Newton's method fails.
       ii. Terminate repetition.
   Else do the following:

   i. Calculate *NewApprox* = *OldApprox* $- \dfrac{F\_Value}{FDeriv\_Old}$.

   ii. Set *F_Value* equal to $F(NewApprox)$.
   iii. Display N, *NewApprox*, and *F_Value*.
   iv. Set *OldApprox* equal to *NewApprox*.

The program in Figure 6.4 implements this algorithm and uses it to find an approximate root of the function

$$f(x) = x^3 + x - 5$$

Function subprograms are used to define this function and its derivative:

$$f'(x) = 3x^2 + 1$$

Figure 6.4 Newton's method.

```
PROGRAM Newtons_Method
!------------------------------------------------------------------------
! Program to find an approximate root of a function F using Newton's
! method.  Variables used are:
!   F, FPrime    : the function and its derivative (internal functions)
!   OldApprox    : previous approximation (initially the first one)
!   FDeriv_Old   : value of the derivative of F at OldApprox
!   NewApprox    : the new approximation
!   F_Value      : value of F at an approximation
!   Epsilon      : repetition stops when ABS(F_Value) is less than
!                  Epsilon
!   NumIterations : limit on number of iterations
!   N             : number of iterations
!
! Input:  Epsilon, NumIterations, and OldApprox
! Output: Iteration number N, the Nth approximation, and the value of
!         F at that approximation, or an error message indicating
!         that the method fails
!------------------------------------------------------------------------

  IMPLICIT NONE
  INTEGER :: NumIterations, N
  REAL :: OldApprox, FDeriv_Old, NewApprox, Epsilon, F_Value

  ! Get termination values Epsilon and NumIterations and
  ! initial approximation

  PRINT *, "Enter epsilon, limit on # of iterations,"
  PRINT *, " and the initial approximation:"
  READ *, Epsilon, NumIterations, OldApprox
  PRINT *
```

Figure 6.4 *(cont.)*

```
! Initialize F_Value and N; print headings and initial values

F_Value = F(OldApprox)
N = 0
PRINT *, "   N        X(N)         F(X(N))"
PRINT *, "==============================="
PRINT 10, 0, OldApprox, F_Value
10 FORMAT(1X, I3, F11.5, E14.5)

! Iterate using Newton's method while ABS(F_Value) is greater
! than or equal to Epsilon and N has not reached NumIterations

DO
   IF ((ABS(F_Value) < Epsilon) .OR. (N > NumIterations)) EXIT
   ! If a termination condition met, stop generating approximations

   ! Otherwise continue with the following
   N = N + 1
   FDeriv_Old = FPrime(OldApprox)

   ! Terminate if the derivative is 0 at some approximation
   IF (FDeriv_Old == 0) THEN
      PRINT *, "Newton's method fails -- derivative = 0"
      EXIT
   END IF

   ! Generate a new approximation
   NewApprox = OldApprox - (F_Value / FDeriv_Old)
   F_Value = F(NewApprox)
   PRINT 10, N, NewApprox, F_Value
   OldApprox = NewApprox

END DO

CONTAINS

!-F(X)---------------------------------------
! Function for which a root is being found
!-------------------------------------------

FUNCTION F(X)

   REAL :: F
   REAL, INTENT (IN) :: X

   F = X**3 + X - 5.0

END FUNCTION F
```

Figure 6.4 *(cont.)*

```
!-FPrime(X)---------------------------------
! The derivative of the function F
!-------------------------------------------

FUNCTION FPrime(X)

   REAL :: FPrime
   REAL, INTENT (IN) :: X

   FPRIME = 3.0*X**2 + 1.0

END FUNCTION FPrime

END PROGRAM Newtons_Method
```

Sample run:

```
Enter epsilon, limit on # of iterations,
and the initial approximation:
1E-4, 20, 1.0

  N        X(N)          F(X(N))
=================================
   0     1.00000    -0.30000E+01
   1     1.75000     0.21094E+01
   2     1.54294     0.21620E+00
   3     1.51639     0.32449E-02
   4     1.51598     0.14305E-05
```

Numerical Integration

Another problem in which numerical methods are often used is that of approximating the area under the graph of a nonnegative function $y = f(x)$ from $x = a$ to $x = b$, thus obtaining an approximate value for the integral

$$\int_a^b f(x)\,dx$$

One common method for approximating this integral is to divide the interval $[a, b]$ into n subintervals each of length $\Delta x = (b - a)/n$ using $n - 1$ equally spaced points $x_1, x_2, \ldots, x_{n-1}$. Locating the corresponding points on the curve and connecting consecutive points using line segments forms n trapezoids:

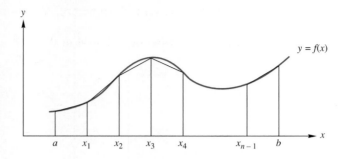

The sum of the areas of these trapezoids is approximately the area under the graph of f.

The bases of the first trapezoid are $y_0 = f(a)$ and $y_1 = f(x_1)$, and thus its area is

$$\frac{1}{2}\Delta x(y_0 + y_1)$$

Similarly, the area of the second trapezoid is

$$\frac{1}{2}\Delta x(y_1 + y_2)$$

where $y_2 = f(x_2)$, and so on. The sum of the areas of the n trapezoids is

$$\frac{1}{2}\Delta x(y_0 + y_1) + \frac{1}{2}\Delta x(y_1 + y_2) + \frac{1}{2}\Delta x(y_2 + y_3) + \cdots + \frac{1}{2}\Delta x(y_{n-1} + y_n)$$

where $y_0, y_1, \ldots, y_{n-1}, y_n$ are the values of the function f at $a, x_1, \ldots, x_{n-1}, b$, respectively. Combining terms, we can write this sum more simply as

$$\Delta x\left(\frac{y_0 + y_n}{2} + y_1 + y_2 + \cdots + y_{n-1}\right)$$

or, written more concisely using Σ (sigma) notation, as

$$\Delta x\left(\frac{y_0 + y_n}{2} + \sum_{i=1}^{n-1} y_i\right)$$

which is then an approximation of the area under the curve.

The following algorithm uses this **trapezoidal method** to approximate the integral of some given function F.

ALGORITHM FOR TRAPEZOIDAL APPROXIMATION OF AN INTEGRAL

Algorithm to approximate the integral of a function F over an interval $[A, B]$ using the trapezoidal method.

Input: The endpoints A, B of the interval and the number N of
            subintervals to use

Output: Approximate value of the integral of F from A to B

1. Read A, B, and N.

2. Calculate $DeltaX = \dfrac{B - A}{N}$.

3. Set X equal to A.

4. Set Sum equal to 0.

5. Do the following for I ranging from 1 to $N - 1$:
   a. Add $DeltaX$ to X.
   b. Calculate $Y = F(X)$.
   c. Add Y to Sum.

6. Calculate $Sum = DeltaX \cdot \left(\dfrac{F(A) + F(B)}{2} + Sum \right)$.

7. Display N and Sum.

The program in Figure 6.5 implements the preceding algorithm and uses it to approximate

$$\int_0^1 (x^2 + 1)\,dx$$

A function subprogram is used to define the integrand

$$f(x) = x^2 + 1$$

Figure 6.5 Trapezoidal approximation of an integral—version 1.

```
PROGRAM Approximate_Integration
!-------------------------------------------------------------------
! Program to approximate the integral of a function over the interval
! [A,B] using the trapezoidal method.  Identifiers used are:
!    A, B   : the endpoints of the interval of integration
!    N      : the number of subintervals
!    I      : counter
!    DeltaX : the length of the subintervals
!    X      : a point of subdivision
!    Y      : the value of the function at X
!    Sum    : the approximating sum
!    F      : the integrand (internal function)
!
! Input:  A, B, and N
! Output: Approximation to integral of F on [A, B]
!-------------------------------------------------------------------
```

Figure 6.5 *(cont.)*

```fortran
IMPLICIT NONE
REAL :: A, B, DeltaX, X, Y, Sum
INTEGER :: N, I

PRINT *, "Enter the interval endpoints and the # of subintervals:"
READ *, A, B, N

! Calculate subinterval length
! and initialize the approximating Sum and X

DeltaX = (B - A) / REAL(N)
X = A
Sum = 0.0

! Now calculate and display the sum

DO I = 1, N - 1
   X = X + DeltaX
   Y = F(X)
   Sum = Sum + Y
END DO

Sum = DeltaX * ((F(A) + F(B)) / 2.0 + Sum)

PRINT '(1X, "Approximate value using", I4, &
      " subintervals is", F10.5)', N, Sum

CONTAINS

   !-F(X)---------------
   ! The integrand
   !-------------------

   FUNCTION F(X)

     REAL :: F
     REAL, INTENT(IN) :: X

     F = X**2 + 1.0

   END FUNCTION F

END PROGRAM Approximate_Integration
```

Figure 6.4 *(cont.)*

Sample runs:

```
Enter the interval endpoints and the # of subintervals:
0, 1, 10
Approximate value using  10 subintervals is   1.33500


Enter the interval endpoints and the # of subintervals:
0, 1, 50
Approximate value using  50 subintervals is   1.33340


Enter the interval endpoints and the # of subintervals:
0, 1, 100
Approximate value using 100 subintervals is   1.33335
```

Numerical Solutions of Differential Equations

Equations that involve derivatives or differentials are called **differential equations.** These equations arise in a large number of problems in science and engineering. It is very difficult or even impossible to solve many differential equations exactly, but it may be possible to find an approximate solution using a numerical method. There are many such methods, and we describe two of the simpler ones here. We will assume that we wish to find an approximate solution to a **first-order differential equation**

$$y' = f(x, y)$$

that satisfies a given **initial condition**

$$y(x_0) = y_0$$

Euler's Method.   **Euler's method** for obtaining an approximate solution over some interval $[a, b]$, where $a = x_0$, is as follows:

EULER'S METHOD

1. Select an x-increment Δx.

2. For $n = 0, 1, 2, \ldots$, do the following:
   a. Set $x_{n+1} = x_n + \Delta x$.
   b. Find the point $P_{n+1}(x_{n+1}, y_{n+1})$ on the line through $P_n(x_n, y_n)$ with slope $f(x_n, y_n)$.
   c. Display y_{n+1}, which is the approximate value of y at x_{n+1}.

The following diagram illustrates Euler's method:

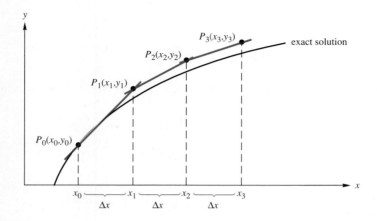

The program in Figure 6.6 uses Euler's method to obtain an approximate solution for

$$y' = 2xy$$

$$y(0) = 1$$

Sample runs with $a = 0$, $b = 1$, $\Delta x = 0.2$ and $a = 0$, $b = 0.5$, $\Delta x = 0.05$ are shown.

Figure 6.6 Euler's method.

```
PROGRAM Eulers_Method
!------------------------------------------------------------------------
! Program that uses Euler's method to obtain an approximate solution
! to a first-order differential equation of the form:
!                        Y' = F(X, Y)
! Variables used are:
!   X                 : current X-value
!   X_Next            : next X-value (X + DeltaX)
!   Y                 : approximate Y-value corresponding to X
!   DeltaX            : X-increment used
!   NumIterations     : number of iterations
!   N                 : counts iterations
!   F                 : function in the diff. equation (internal function)
!
! Input:  Initial values for X and Y, DeltaX, and NumIterations
! Output: A sequence of points (X, Y) that approximate the solution
!         curve
!------------------------------------------------------------------------
```

Figure 6.6 *(cont.)*

```
IMPLICIT NONE
REAL :: X, Y, X_Next, DeltaX
INTEGER :: N, NumIterations

! Get given information; print table headings and initial values

PRINT *, "Enter X0 and Y0, X-increment to use, and"
PRINT *, "the number of values to calculate:"
READ *, X, Y,  DeltaX, NumIterations
PRINT *
PRINT *, "        X              Y"
PRINT *, "===================="
PRINT '(1X, 2F10.5)',  X, Y

! Iterate with Euler's method

DO N = 1, NumIterations
   X_Next = X + DeltaX
   Y = Y + F(X,Y) * DeltaX
   X = X_Next
   PRINT '(1X, 2F10.5)', X, Y
END DO

CONTAINS

  !- F(X, Y) -------------------------------------------
  ! The function F in differential equation Y' = F(X, Y)
  !-----------------------------------------------------

  FUNCTION F(X, Y)

    REAL :: F
    REAL, INTENT(IN) :: X, Y

    F = 2.0 * X * Y

  END FUNCTION F

END PROGRAM Eulers_Method
```

Sample runs:

```
Enter X0 and Y0, X-increment to use, and
the number of values to calculate:
0, 1,  .2, 5
```

Figure 6.6 *(cont.)*

```
     X            Y
====================
  0.00000    1.00000
  0.20000    1.00000
  0.40000    1.08000
  0.60000    1.25280
  0.80000    1.55347
  1.00000    2.05058


Enter X0 and Y0, X-increment to use, and
the number of values to calculate:
0, 1, .05, 10


     X            Y
====================
  0.00000    1.00000
  0.05000    1.00000
  0.10000    1.00500
  0.15000    1.01505
  0.20000    1.03028
  0.25000    1.05088
  0.30000    1.07715
  0.35000    1.10947
  0.40000    1.14830
  0.45000    1.19423
  0.50000    1.24797
```

For the differential equation and initial condition considered in the preceding example, the exact solution is

$$y = e^{x^2}$$

In this case, therefore, we can compare the approximate *y*-values with the exact values to see how well Euler's method does.

x	$y = e^{x^2}$
0.0	1.00000
0.1	1.01005
0.2	1.04081
0.3	1.09417
0.4	1.17351
0.5	1.28401

Comparing these values with the approximate y-values in the sample runs of Figure 6.6, we note that the accuracy of Euler's method did improve when a smaller x-increment was used. However, if Euler's method is used over a larger range of x-values, the error in the y-values can grow rapidly; for example, if we had used 40 iterations in the second sample run, the approximate y-value for $x = 2$ would have been 39.0929, but the exact y-value is 54.5982.

Runge-Kutta Method. One of the most popular and most accurate numerical methods for solving a first-order differential equation is the following **Runge-Kutta method:**

RUNGE-KUTTA METHOD

1. Select an x-increment Δx.
2. The approximate solution y_{n+1} at $x_{n+1} = x_0 + (n + 1)\Delta x$ for $n = 0, 1, 2, \ldots$ is given by

$$y_{n+1} = y_n + \frac{1}{6}(K_1 + 2K_2 + 2K_3 + K_4)$$

where

$$K_1 = \Delta x \cdot f(x_n, y_n)$$

$$K_2 = \Delta x \cdot f\left(x_n + \frac{\Delta x}{2}, y_n + \frac{K_1}{2}\right)$$

$$K_3 = \Delta x \cdot f\left(x_n + \frac{\Delta x}{2}, y_n + \frac{K_2}{2}\right)$$

$$K_4 = \Delta x \cdot f(x_n + \Delta x, y_n + K_3)$$

A program implementing the Runge-Kutta method is left as an exercise.

6.4 APPLICATION: ROAD CONSTRUCTION

Problem:

The Cawker City Construction Company has contracted to build a highway for the state highway commission. Several sections of this highway must pass through hills from which large amounts of dirt must be excavated to provide a flat and level roadbed. For example, one section that is 1000 feet in length must pass through a hill whose height (in feet) above the roadbed has been measured at equally spaced distances and tabulated as follows:

Distance	Height
0	0
100	6
200	10
300	13
400	17
500	22
600	25
700	20
800	13
900	5
1000	0

1000 ft

75 ft

In estimating the construction costs, the company needs to know the volume of dirt that must be excavated from the hill.

Freeway construction (F3 Freeway, Oahu, HI). (Photo courtesy of Vince Streano/Tony Stone Images)

Solution

Specification. The input to this problem consists of the length of the section of road to be constructed, the width of the road, and the estimates of the hill's height at equally spaced points along this section. The output is the volume of dirt that must be removed. Thus, we have the following specification for the problem:

Input: The length of a section of road
            The width of the road
            A list of heights at equally spaced points along this section

Output: The volume of dirt to be removed

Design. To estimate the volume of dirt to be removed, we will assume that the height of the hill does not vary from one side of the road to the other. The volume can then be calculated as

Volume = (cross-sectional area of the hill) × (width of the road)

and the cross-sectional area of the hill can be calculated as an integral:

$$\text{Cross-sectional area of the hill} = \int_{0}^{1000} h(x)\,dx$$

where $h(x)$ is the height of the hill at a distance x feet along the section of road. Since the value of $h(x)$ is known at equally spaced points along the road, the trapezoidal method can be used to approximate this integral.

An algorithm for solving this problem is then straightforward.

ALGORITHM FOR HIGHWAY CONSTRUCTION PROBLEM

Algorithm to approximate the volume of dirt to be removed in constructing a section of highway through a hill.

Input: Length and width of the road section and heights of the hill at
            equally spaced points

Output: Volume of dirt to be removed

1. Obtain the length and width of the section of highway.

2. Use the trapezoidal method to approximate the integral for the cross-sectional area of the hill.

3. Compute the volume of dirt to be removed:

Volume = (cross-sectional area of the hill) × (width of the road)

Coding.   The program in Figure 6.7 implements this algorithm. The number of equally spaced points at which height measurements have been made and the heights themselves are read from a data file. The length and width of the section of highway are entered from the keyboard. Note that the coding of the trapezoidal method from Figure 6.5 has been modified so that function values are read from a file rather than computed using a function subprogram.

Figure 6.7 Road construction.

```
PROGRAM Road_Construction
!--------------------------------------------------------------------
! Program to approximate the volume of dirt to be removed in
! constructing a section of highway through a hill.  Identifiers
! used are:
!   Length    : length of the section of road
!   Width     : width of the road
!   FileName  : name of data file containing hill information
!   NumPoints : the number of points where height of hill was measured
!   DeltaX    : distance between points
!   I         : counter
!   Y         : the height of the hill
!   Sum       : sum approximating the integral for cross-sectional area
!               of the hill
!
! Input (keyboard): Length, Width
! Input (file):     NumPoints and values of Y (heights of hill)
! Output:           Volume of dirt to be removed
!--------------------------------------------------------------------

  IMPLICIT NONE
  REAL :: Length, Width, Delta_X, Y, Sum
  INTEGER :: NumPoints, I
  CHARACTER(20) :: FileName

  ! Get road information and name of data file containing hill information

  PRINT *, "Enter length and width of section of road (in feet):"
  READ *, Length, Width
  PRINT *, "Enter name of file containing hill information:"
  READ *, FileName
```

Figure 6.7 *(cont.)*

```
! Open the data file, read the number of points at which height of hill
! was measured, and compute the distance between these points

OPEN (UNIT = 10, FILE = FileName, STATUS = "OLD", &
      ACTION = "READ", POSITION = "REWIND")
READ (10, *) NumPoints
Delta_X = Length / REAL(NumPoints - 1)

! Initialize the approximating Sum
READ (10, *) Y
Sum = Y / 2.0

! Now calculate Sum, which approximates cross-sectional area of hill
DO I = 1, NumPoints - 2
   READ (10, *) Y
   Sum = Sum + Y
END DO

READ (10, *) Y
Sum = Sum + Y / 2.0
Sum = Delta_X * Sum

PRINT *, "Volume of dirt to be removed is approximately"
PRINT *, Sum * Width, "cubic feet."

END PROGRAM Road_Construction
```

Execution and Testing. The program was executed with several simple data files to verify its correctness. It was then executed using a file containing the data given in the statement of the problem:

Listing of file `fil6-7.dat`

```
11
0
6
10
13
17
22
25
20
13
5
0
```

Run of program:

```
Enter length and width of section of road (in feet): 1000, 75
Enter name of file containing hill information:  fil6-7.dat
Volume of dirt to be removed is approximately
   9.8250000E+05 cubic feet.
```

Exercises 6.4

Root Finding

1. The steady state of a certain circuit with a coil wound around an iron core is obtained by solving the equation $f(\Phi) = 0$ for the flux Φ, where

$$f(\Phi) = 20 - 2.5\Phi - 0.015\Phi^3$$

It is easy to check that the function f changes sign in the interval $[6, 7]$. Use Newton's method to find a solution to the equation in this interval.

2. The state of an imperfect gas is given by van der Waal's equation:

$$\left(p + \frac{\alpha}{v^2}\right)(v - \beta) = RT$$

where

p = pressure (atm)

v = molar volume (l/mole)

T = absolute temperature (°K)

R = gas constant (0.0820541 atm/mole °K)

For carbon dioxide, $\alpha = 3.592$ and $\beta = 0.04267$. Assume that $p = 0.9$ atm and $T = 300°$ K. Use Newton's method to solve the equivalent cubic equation

$$pv^3 - (\beta p + RT)v^2 + \alpha v - \alpha\beta = 0$$

for v.

3. The Cawker City Construction Company can purchase a new microcomputer for $4440 or by paying $141.19 per month for the next 36 months. You are to determine what annual interest rate is being charged in the monthly payment plan. The equation that governs this calculation is the *annuity formula*

$$A = P \cdot \left(\frac{(1 + R)^N - 1}{R(1 + R)^N}\right)$$

where A is the amount borrowed, P is the monthly payment, R is the monthly interest rate (annual rate/12), and N is the number of payments. Use Newton's method to solve this equation for R.

4. In level flight, the total drag on the Cawker City Construction Company jet is equal to the sum of parasite drag (D_P) and the drag due to lift (D_L), which are given by

$$D_P = \frac{\sigma f V^2}{391} \quad \text{and} \quad D_L = \frac{1245}{\sigma e} \left(\frac{W}{b}\right)^2 \frac{1}{V^2}$$

where V is velocity (mph), W is weight (15,000 lb), b is the span (40 ft), e is the wing efficiency rating (0.800), f = parasite drag area (4 ft^2), and σ = (air density at altitude)/(air density at sea level) = 0.533 at 20,000 ft (for standard atmosphere). Use Newton's method to find the constant velocity V needed to fly at minimum drag (level flight), which occurs when $D_P = D_L$.

5. The following figure shows a mass M attached to a slender steel rod of mass m:

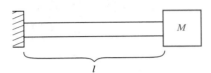

The frequency equation for the free undamped longitudinal vibration is

$$\beta \tan \beta = \frac{m}{M}$$

where

$$\beta = \frac{\omega l}{c}$$

Here

$$c = \sqrt{\frac{E}{\rho}}$$

l = length of the rod (115 in)
E = Young's modulus (= 3×10^7 psi)
ρ = mass per unit volume (= 7.2×10^{-4} lb $\times$ sec^2/in^4)

Use Newton's method to find the smallest positive root of the frequency equation if

$$m/M = 0.40.$$

6. Flexible cables have many applications in engineering, such as suspension bridges and transmission lines. Cables used as transmission lines carry their own uniformly distributed weight and assume the shape of a catenary shown in the following figure. These curves have equations of the form

$$y = a \cosh\left(\frac{x}{a}\right)$$

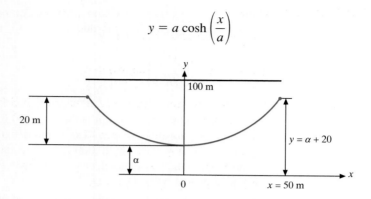

Assume that the cable has a span of 100 m and maximum deflection of 20 m and that the weight of the cable per unit length is $w = 50$ N/m. The minimum and maximum tensions occur in the middle (when $y = a$) and at the ends (when $y = a + 20$) and can be computed as

$$T_{min} = w \cdot a \qquad \text{and} \qquad T_{max} = w \cdot (a + 20)$$

Find these extreme tension values by first using Newton's method to solve the equation

$$a + 20 = a \cosh\left(\frac{50}{a}\right)$$

to find the value of a and then substituting this value into the equations for T_{min} and T_{max}.

7. The cross section of a trough with length L is a semicircle with radius $r = 1$ m. Assume that the trough is filled with water to within a distance h from the top. The volume V of the water is given by

$$V(h) = L\left(\frac{1}{2}\pi r^2 - r^2 \arcsin\left(\frac{h}{r}\right) - h\sqrt{r^2 - h^2}\right)$$

where the three terms represent the area of the semicircle and areas $2A_1$ and $2A_2$, respectively, as pictured in the following figure:

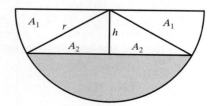

Assume that $L = 10$ m and $V = 10$ m^3. Find the depth of the water (which is $r - h = 1 - h$). Note that $V(0) = \pi L/2 \approx 15.7$, that $V(r) = 0$, and that V decreases as h increases; thus, there is a unique solution for h. Use Newton's method to find this solution.

Numerical Integration

8. The current i passing through a capacitor is given by

$$i(t) = 10 \sin^2 \left(\frac{t}{\pi} \right) \quad \text{(amps)}$$

where t denotes time in seconds. Assume that the capacitance C is 5 F (farads). The voltage across the capacitor is given by

$$v(T) = \frac{1}{C} \int_0^T i(t)\,dt \quad \text{(volts)}$$

Find the value of $v(T)$ for $T = 1, 2, 3, 4,$ and 5 seconds.

9. The circumference C of an ellipse with major axis $2a$ and minor axis $2b$ is given by

$$C = 4a \int_0^{\pi/2} \sqrt{1 - \left(\frac{a^2 - b^2}{a^2} \right) \sin^2 \Phi}\; d\Phi$$

Assume that a room has the shape of an ellipse with $a = 20$ m, $b = 10$ m, and height $h = 5$ m. Find the total area $A = hC$ of the wall.

10. The fraction f of certain fission neutrons having energies above a certain threshold energy E^* can be determined by the formula

$$f = 1 - 0.484 \int_0^{E^*} e^{-E} \sin(h \sqrt{2E})\, dE$$

Find the value of f for $E^* = 0.5, 1.0, 1.5, 2.0, 2.5,$ and 3.0.

11. A particle with mass $m = 20$ kg is moving through a fluid and is subjected to a viscous resistance

$$R(v) = -v^{3/2}$$

where v is its velocity. The relation between time t, velocity v, and resistance R is given by

$$t = \int_{v_0}^{v(t)} \frac{m}{R(v)}\, dv \quad \text{(seconds)}$$

where v_0 is the initial velocity. Assuming that $v_0 = 15$ m/sec, find the time T required for the particle to slow down to $v(T) = 7.5$ m/sec.

12. Suppose that a spring has been compressed a distance x_c:

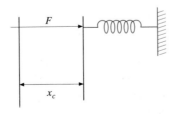

If $F(x)$ is the external force, then the absorbed energy can be expressed as

$$E = \int_0^{x_c} F(x)dx$$

Assume that

$$F(x) = \frac{1}{2} e^{x^2} \sin^2(3x^2) \qquad \text{(Newtons)}$$

and $x_c = 1$ cm. Compute the absorbed energy.

Numerical Solutions of Differential Equations

13. The linear-lag behavior of the components of control systems usually is modeled by the differential equation

$$y' + \frac{1}{\tau} y = \frac{Au(t)}{\tau}$$

where

y = time-dependent output of the component
A = gain factor
u = time-dependent input of the component
τ = time constant

Select $\tau = 1$, $A = 8$, and assume that $y(0) = 0$ and that the input is given by

$$u(t) = e^{t/2} \sin t$$

Use Euler's method with step size $\Delta t = 0.1$ to obtain an approximate solution to this initial-value problem for $y(t)$ in the interval $[0, 10]$.

14. Consider a spherical water tank with radius R drained through a circular orifice with radius r at the bottom of the tank:

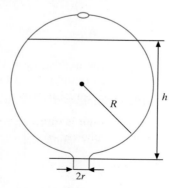

Since there is an air hole at the top of the tank, an atmospheric pressure can be found in the empty portion of the tank. In order to determine the time when the tank should be drained from any level to any other level, the water height h as a function of time should be determined. For any height, the volume of the tank is known to be

$$V = \frac{1}{3} \pi h^2 (3R - h)$$

If the area of the orifice is A and the velocity of the water flowing through the orifice is V, then

$$\frac{dV}{dt} = -\pi r^2 \sqrt{2gh}$$

where $g = 115.8$ ft/min^2 is the gravitation constant. Differentiation of the equation for V leads to the following:

$$\frac{dV}{dt} = (2\pi hR - \pi h^2) \frac{dh}{dt}$$

so

$$\frac{dh}{dt} = \frac{-r^2 \sqrt{2gh}}{2hR - h^2}$$

Assume that $R = 15$ ft and $r = 0.2$ ft and that the initial condition is $h(0) = 28$ ft. Use Euler's method to solve the initial-value problem for h. Select the step size $\Delta t = 1$ min, and continue the calculations until the water height becomes less than 0.2 ft.

15. A new gas well is estimated to contain 9000 tons of natural gas at a pressure of $p_0 = 900$ psia. The distribution system is connected to the well at the discharge pressure $p* = 400$ psia. The discharge Q in tons per day through the outlet pipe from the well is approximated by the equation

$$Q = \alpha(p^2 - p^{*2})^\beta$$

where

$\alpha = 1.115 \times 10^{-4}$

$\beta = 0.8$

$p =$ initial pressure of gas in the well in psia

It is also assumed that the gas pressure is directly proportional to the discharge Q, which is modeled by the differential equation

$$\frac{dp}{dt} = -kQ$$

with

$$k = \frac{900 \text{ psia}}{9000 \text{ tons}} = 0.1 \frac{\text{psia}}{\text{tons}}$$

Combining the two equations leads to the initial-value problem

$$\frac{dp}{dt} = -k\alpha(p^2 - p^{*2})^\beta$$

$$p(0) = p_0$$

Use Euler's method with step size $\Delta t = 0.01$ to solve this initial-value problem. Perform 10 steps.

16. The following figure shows a circuit consisting of a coil wound around an iron core, a resistance, a switch, and a voltage source:

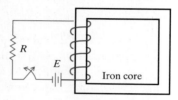

The magnetization curve is given by the equation

$$Ni = \frac{1}{2}\Phi + \frac{3}{1000}\Phi^3$$

where

N = number of turns of coil

i = current (amperes)

Φ = flux in core (kilolines)

Kirchoff's law gives the differential equation

$$E = Ri + L\frac{di}{dt} = Ri + 10^{-5}\frac{d\Phi}{dt}$$

where

L = self-inductance (henrys)

R = resistance (ohms)

t = time (sec)

Assume $N = 100$ and $R = 500$. Then

$$\frac{d\Phi}{dt} = E - 2.5\Phi - 0.015\Phi^3, \qquad \Phi(0) = 0$$

where t is now measured in milliseconds. Assume that $E = 20$ V. Use Euler's method with step size $\Delta t = 0.01$ to obtain a solution of this initial-value problem in the interval $[0, 2]$.

17. The number of individuals in a population is measured each year. Let $P(t)$ denote the population at year t. Let α denote the birthrate, and assume that the death rate is proportional to the size of the population, that is, the death rate is $\beta = \gamma P(t)$, where γ is a constant. Hence the growth rate of the population is given by the logistic equation

$$P'(t) = \alpha P(t) - \gamma [P(t)]^2$$

Assume that $P(0) = 50{,}000$, $\alpha = 3 \times 10^{-2}$, and $\gamma = 1.5 \times 10^{-7}$. Use Euler's method with step size $\Delta t = 0.01$ to find the population after 5 years.

6.5 INTRODUCTION TO MODULES

In the preceding sections, we have seen that subprograms are separate program units written to perform specific computations. Often these are computations that arise in a variety of applications, and it is convenient to be able to use them in different programs. Fortran 90 provides modules that can be used to package together related subprograms (and other items) and in this section we describe the composition of modules and how they can be used to build such libraries of subprograms.

Modules

A **module** is a program unit used to package together type declarations, subprograms, and definitions of new data types as described in Chapter 10. A simple form of a module that contains only subprograms is

---

Module (simplified)

Form:

```
MODULE module-name
CONTAINS
    subprogram₁
    subprogram₂
       ⋮
    subprogramₙ
END MODULE module-name
```

where

$subprogram_1, subprogram_2, \ldots, subprogram_n$ are function and/or subroutine subprograms. Such subprograms are called **module subprograms**.

> **Purpose:**
> Packages *subprogram*$_1$, *subprogram*$_2$, ..., *subprogram*$_n$ together into
> a **library** that can be used in any other program unit.

Example: A Temperature-Conversion Library

The temperature conversion performed by the function `Fahr_to_Celsius` in the program of Figure 6.1 is a conversion that may be useful in other applications. It is an integral part of the program, and copying it for use in another program is inconvenient. Putting this and related temperature-conversion subprograms in a module makes it possible to reuse them as needed. Figure 6.8 gives a partial listing of the contents of such a module.

Figure 6.8 A temperature-conversion module.

```
MODULE Temperature_Library
!-----------------------------------------------------------------
! Module that contains the following subprograms for processing
! temperatures on various scales:
!    Fahr_to_Celsius, a Fahrenheit-to-Celsius conversion function
!    Celsius_to_Fahr, a Celsius-to-Fahrenheit conversion function
!    . . .
!-----------------------------------------------------------------

  IMPLICIT NONE

CONTAINS

  !-Fahr_to_Celsius -----------------------------------------------
  ! Function to convert a Fahrenheit temperature to Celsius.
  !    Accepts:  A Temperature in Fahrenheit
  !    Returns:  The corresponding Celsius temperature
  !----------------------------------------------------------------

  FUNCTION Fahr_to_Celsius(Temperature)

    REAL :: Fahr_to_Celsius
    REAL, INTENT(IN) :: Temperature

    Fahr_to_Celsius = (Temperature - 32.0) / 1.8

  END FUNCTION Fahr_to_Celsius
```

Figure 6.8 *(cont.)*

```
!-Celsius_to_Fahr------------------------------------------------
! Function to convert a Celsius temperature to Fahrenheit.
!   Accepts:  A Temperature in Celsius
!   Returns:  The corresponding Fahrenheit temperature
!----------------------------------------------------------------

FUNCTION Celsius_to_Fahr(Temperature)

   REAL :: Celsius_to_Fahr
   REAL, INTENT(IN) :: Temperature

   Celsius_to_Fahr = 1.8 * Temperature + 32.0

 END FUNCTION Celsius_to_Fahr

 ! ... Other temperature-related subprograms can be added ...

END MODULE Temperature_Library
```

As noted earlier, a module can also contain type declarations and other items besides subprograms. For example, declarations of temperature-related constants such as

```
REAL, PARAMETER :: HeatOfFusion = 79.71, &
                   HeatOfVaporization = 539.55
```

could be added to the module `Temperature_Library`.

Using a Module

Once a module has been written, its contents can be made available to any other program unit by placing in that program unit a **USE statement** of the following form:

USE *Statement*

Forms:

```
   USE module-name

   USE module-name, ONLY: list

   USE module-name, rename-list
```

where
>   *module-name* is the name of a module;
>   *list* is a list of identifiers declared in that module and renamings of these
>   identifiers of the form

```
new-identifier => identifier
```

Purpose:
In the first form, all identifiers declared in the specified module are **imported**
into the program unit containing this USE statement and can be used throughout that program unit. In the second form, only the identifiers listed are imported. These identifiers or their new names can then be used in the program unit
containing this USE statement.

Note: The USE statement must be placed at the beginning of the specification
part of a program unit.

Figure 6.9 is a modification of the program in Figure 6.1 that imports the contents of the module `Temperature_Library` and uses the function
`Fahr_to_Celsius` to perform conversions of several Fahrenheit temperatures to
Celsius. Note that the USE statement could be replaced by

```
USE Temperature_Library, ONLY: Fahr_to_Celsius
```

Figure 6.9 Temperature conversions.

```
PROGRAM Temperature_Conversion_2
!-----------------------------------------------------------------------
! Program to convert several Fahrenheit temperatures to the
! corresponding Celsius temperatures.  The function Fahr_to_Celsius
! from module Temperature_Library is used to perform the conversions.
! Identifiers used are:
!   Fahr_to_Celsius : module function subprogram that converts
!                     Fahrenheit temperatures to Celsius
!   FahrenheitTemp  : a Fahrenheit temperature to be converted
!   CelsiusTemp     : the corresponding Celsius temperature
!   Response        : user response to "More data?" query
!
! Imported: Fahr_to_Celsius from module Temperature_Library
! Input:    FahrenheitTemp, Response
! Output:   CelsiusTemp
!-----------------------------------------------------------------------
```

Figure 6.9 *(cont.)*

```
USE Temperature_Library

IMPLICIT NONE
REAL :: FahrenheitTemp, CelsiusTemp
CHARACTER(1) :: Response

DO
    ! Get a Fahrenheit temperature
    WRITE (*, '(1X, A)', ADVANCE = "NO") "Enter a Fahrenheit temperature: "
    READ *, FahrenheitTemp

    ! Use the module function Fahr_to_Celsius to convert it to Celsius
    CelsiusTemp = Fahr_to_Celsius(FahrenheitTemp)

    ! Output the result
    PRINT '(1X, 2(F6.2, A))', FahrenheitTemp, &
            " in Fahrenheit is equivalent to ", CelsiusTemp, " in Celsius"

    ! Check if more temperatures are to be converted
    WRITE (*, '(/ 1X, A)', ADVANCE = "NO") &
            "More temperatures to convert (Y or N)? "
    READ *, Response
    IF (Response /= "Y") EXIT
END DO

END PROGRAM Temperature_Conversion_2
```

Compiling and Linking Programs and Modules

Translation of a source program to produce an executable program consists of two separate steps:

1. **Compilation**, in which the source program is translated to an equivalent machine-language program, called an *object program,* which is stored in an *object file*. (UNIX object files have the extension `.o`; DOS object files have the extension `.OBJ`.)

2. **Linking**, in which any references to functions contained in a module are linked to their definitions in that module, creating an *executable program,* which is stored in an *executable file*.

Since modules also need to be compiled, translation of a program that uses a module may require three separate actions:

1. Separate compilation of the program's source file, creating an object file
2. Separate compilation of the module, creating a different object file
3. Linking the function calls in the program's object file to the function definitions in the module's object file, creating an executable program

It makes no difference whether the source program or the module is compiled first, but *both source programs and modules must be compiled before linking can be performed.* The following diagram illustrates this process:

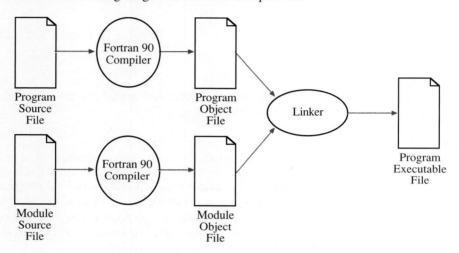

For some compilers, these three steps can be accomplished with a single command. For example, for the NAGware f90 Compiler (UNIX), the command

```
f90 fig6-8.f90 fig6-9.f90 -o fig6-9
```

will compile the module `fig6-8.f90`, the source program `fig6-9.f90`, and link the resulting object files together to form the executable file `fig6-9`. If the module has already been compiled separately using the command

```
f90 -c fig6-8.f90
```

to create object file `fig6-8.o`, then compiling the source program and linking the resulting object file with the module's object file can be accomplished using the command

```
f90 fig6-8.o fig6-9.f90 -o fig6-9
```

If both the module and the source program have been compiled separately,

```
f90 -c fig6-8.f90
f90 -c fig6-9.f90
```

the object files `fig6-8.o` and `fig6-9.o` can be linked using the command

```
f90 fig6-8.o fig6-9.o -o fig6-9
```

6.6 EXTERNAL FUNCTIONS

In Section 6.1 we noted that function subprograms can be classified in three ways:

1. Internal subprograms
2. Module subprograms
3. External subprograms

In the preceding sections we have described internal and module functions in detail, and in this section we consider external subprograms.

External Subprograms

A subprogram can be made accessible to a program unit by attaching it after the END statement of the program unit. In this case it is called an **external subprogram**. Figure 6.10 illustrates. The function subprogram `Fahr_to_Celsius` is an external subprogram attached to program `Temperature_Conversion_3`. Note that `Fahr_to_Celsius` is *declared in both the main program and the subprogram*.

Figure 6.10 Temperature conversions.

```
PROGRAM Temperature_Conversion_3
!-------------------------------------------------------------------
! Program to convert several Fahrenheit temperatures to the
! corresponding Celsius temperatures.  The function Fahr_to_Celsius
! is used to perform the conversions.  Identifiers used are:
!   Fahr_to_Celsius : external function subprogram that converts
!                     Fahrenheit temperatures to Celsius
!   FahrenheitTemp  : a Fahrenheit temperature to be converted
!   CelsiusTemp     : the corresponding Celsius temperature
!   Response        : user response to "More data?" query
!
! Input:   FahrenheitTemp, Response
! Output:  CelsiusTemp
!-------------------------------------------------------------------
```

Figure 6.10 *(cont.)*

```
REAL :: Fahr_to_Celsius
REAL :: FahrenheitTemp, CelsiusTemp
CHARACTER(1) :: Response

DO
   ! Get a Fahrenheit temperature
   WRITE (*, '(1X, A)', ADVANCE = "NO") "Enter a Fahrenheit temperature: "
   READ *, FahrenheitTemp

   ! Use the external function Fahr_to_Celsius to convert it to Celsius
   CelsiusTemp = Fahr_to_Celsius(FahrenheitTemp)

   ! Output the result
   PRINT '(1X, 2(F6.2, A))', FahrenheitTemp, &
         " in Fahrenheit is equivalent to ", CelsiusTemp, " in Celsius"

   ! Check if more temperatures are to be converted
   WRITE (*, '(/ 1X, A)', ADVANCE = "NO") &
         "More temperatures to convert (Y or N)? "
   READ *, Response
   IF (Response /= "Y") EXIT
END DO

END PROGRAM Temperature_Conversion_3

!- Fahr_to_Celsius -------------------------------------------
! Function to convert a Fahrenheit temperature to Celsius
!   Accepts:  A Temperature in Fahrenheit
!   Returns:  The corresponding Celsius temperature
!-----------------------------------------------------------

FUNCTION Fahr_to_Celsius(Temperature)

  IMPLICIT NONE
  REAL :: Fahr_to_Celsius
  REAL, INTENT(IN) :: Temperature

  Fahr_to_Celsius = (Temperature - 32.0) / 1.8

END FUNCTION Fahr_to_Celsius
```

Interfaces

A main program and external subprograms are separate, independent program units. Neither the main program nor any subprogram can access any of the items declared locally in any other subprogram, nor can an external subprogram access any of the items declared in the main program. The only way that information is passed from one program unit to another is by means of the arguments and the function name.

Since internal subprograms are contained within a host, the compiler can check each reference to the subprogram to determine if it has the correct number and types of arguments (and other properties) and for a function subprogram, whether the value returned is used correctly. Similarly, module subprograms are referenced in statements within that module or in statements that follow a USE statement for that module, and the compiler can check that the arguments and result returned are used correctly. In both cases, the subprogram has an **explicit interface**. An external subprogram is separate from the main program and from other program units, however, and the compiler may not be able to check whether references to it are correct. Consequently, external subprograms are said to have **implicit interfaces.**

To ensure that a compiler can perform the necessary consistency checks, it is desirable that external subprograms have explicit interfaces. Some compilers even require them for all external subprograms. (Explicit interfaces are necessary to use some of the new features of Fortran 90 such as optional arguments, described in Section 7.7, and pointer arguments, described in Section 13.2.)

Interface blocks can be used to provide these explicit interfaces. They have several different forms and uses, but the form needed for external subprograms is

```
INTERFACE
   interface-body
END INTERFACE
```

where *interface-body* consists of:

1. The subprogram heading (except that different names may be used for the formal arguments)

2. Declarations of the arguments and the result type in the case of a function

3. An END FUNCTION (or END SUBROUTINE) statement

Figure 6.11 illustrates the use of an interface block to provide an explicit interface for the function Fahr_to_Celsius.

Figure 6.11 Temperature conversions.

```
PROGRAM Temperature_Conversion_4
!----------------------------------------------------------------------
! Program to convert several Fahrenheit temperatures to the
! corresponding Celsius temperatures.  The function Fahr_to_Celsius
! is used to perform the conversions.  Identifiers used are:
!   Fahr_to_Celsius : external function subprogram that converts
!                       Fahrenheit temperatures to Celsius
!   FahrenheitTemp  : a Fahrenheit temperature to be converted
!   CelsiusTemp     : the corresponding Celsius temperature
!   Response        : user response to "More data?" query
!
! Input:   FahrenheitTemp, Response
! Output:  CelsiusTemp
!----------------------------------------------------------------------

  IMPLICIT NONE

  INTERFACE
    FUNCTION Fahr_to_Celsius(Temperature)
      REAL :: Fahr_to_Celsius
      REAL, INTENT(IN) :: Temperature
    END FUNCTION Fahr_to_Celsius
  END INTERFACE

  REAL :: FahrenheitTemp, CelsiusTemp
  CHARACTER(1) :: Response

  DO
     ! Get a Fahrenheit temperature
     WRITE (*, '(1X, A)', ADVANCE = "NO") "Enter a Fahrenheit temperature: "
     READ *, FahrenheitTemp

     ! Use the function Fahr_to_Celsius to convert it to Celsius
     CelsiusTemp = Fahr_to_Celsius(FahrenheitTemp)

     ! Output the result
     PRINT '(1X, 2(F6.2, A))', FahrenheitTemp, &
           " in Fahrenheit is equivalent to ", CelsiusTemp, " in Celsius"
```

Figure 6.11 *(cont.)*

```
      ! Check if more temperatures are to be converted
      WRITE (*, '(/ 1X, A)', ADVANCE = "NO") &
            "More temperatures to convert (Y or N)? "
      READ *, Response
      IF (Response /= "Y") EXIT
   END DO

END PROGRAM Temperature_Conversion_4

!- Fahr_to_Celsius -------------------------------------------
! Function to convert a Fahrenheit temperature to Celsius
!    Accepts:   A Temperature in Fahrenheit
!    Returns:   The corresponding Celsius temperature
!-------------------------------------------------------------

FUNCTION Fahr_to_Celsius(Temperature)

   IMPLICIT NONE
   REAL :: Fahr_to_Celsius
   REAL, INTENT(IN) :: Temperature

   Fahr_to_Celsius = (Temperature - 32.0) / 1.8

END FUNCTION Fahr_to_Celsius
```

6.7 INTRODUCTION TO RECURSION

All of the examples of function references considered thus far have involved a main program referencing a subprogram or one subprogram referencing another subprogram. In fact, a subprogram may even reference itself, a phenomenon known as **recursion**. In this section we show how recursion is implemented in Fortran 90.

To illustrate the basic idea of recursion, we consider the problem of calculating the factorial function. The first definition of the factorial $n!$ of a nonnegative integer n that one usually learns is

$$n! = 1 \times 2 \times \cdots \times n, \qquad \text{for } n > 0$$

and that $0!$ is 1. In calculating a sequence of consecutive factorials, however, it would be foolish to calculate each one using this definition, that is, to multiply together the numbers from 1 through n each time; for example,

$$0! = 1$$

$$1! = 1$$

$$2! = 1 \times 2 = 2$$

$$3! = 1 \times 2 \times 3 = 6$$

$$4! = 1 \times 2 \times 3 \times 4 = 24$$

$$5! = 1 \times 2 \times 3 \times 4 \times 5 = 120$$

It is clear that once one factorial has been calculated, it can be used to calculate the next one; for example, given the value 4! = 24, we can use this value to calculate 5! simply by multiplying the value of 4! by 5:

$$5! = 5 \times 4! = 5 \times 24 = 120$$

and this value can then be used to calculate 6!:

$$6! = 6 \times 5! = 6 \times 120 = 720$$

and so on. Indeed, to calculate $n!$ for any positive integer n, we need only know the value of 0!,

$$0! = 1$$

and the fundamental relation between one factorial and the next:

$$n! = n \times (n - 1)!$$

This approach to calculating factorials leads to the following recursive definition of $n!$:

$$0! = 1$$

$$\text{For } n > 0, n! = n \times (n - 1)!$$

Another classic example of a function that can be calculated recursively is the power function that calculates x^n, where x is a real value and n is a nonnegative integer. The first definition of x^n that one learns is usually an iterative (nonrecursive) one:

$$x^n = \underbrace{x \times x \times \cdots \times x}_{n \ x\text{'s}}$$

and later one learns that x^0 is defined to be 1. (For convenience, we assume here that x^0 is 1 also when x is 0, although in this case it is usually left undefined.)

In calculating a sequence of consecutive powers of some number, however, it would again be foolish to calculate each one using this definition, that is, to multiply the number by itself the required number of times; for example,

$$3.0^0 = 1$$

$$3.0^1 = 3.0$$

$$3.0^2 = 3.0 \times 3.0 = 9.0$$

$$3.0^3 = 3.0 \times 3.0 \times 3.0 = 27.0$$

$$3.0^4 = 3.0 \times 3.0 \times 3.0 \times 3.0 = 81.0$$

$$3.0^5 = 3.0 \times 3.0 \times 3.0 \times 3.0 \times 3.0 = 243.0$$

Once again, the value of this function for a given integer can be used to calculate the value of the function for the next integer. For example, to calculate 3.0^4, we can simply multiply the value of 3.0^3 by 3.0:

$$3.0^4 = 3.0 \times 3.0^3 = 3.0 \times 27.0 = 81.0$$

Similarly, we can use the value of 3.0^4 to calculate 3.0^5:

$$3.0^5 = 3.0 \times 3.0^4 = 3.0 \times 81.0 = 243.0$$

and so on. We need only know the value of 3.0^0,

$$3.0^0 = 1$$

and the fundamental relation between one power of 3.0 and the next:

$$3.0^n = 3.0 \times 3.0^{n-1}$$

This suggests the following recursive definition of x^n:

$$x^0 = 1$$

$$\text{For } n > 0, x^n = x \times x^{n-1}$$

In general, a function is said to be **defined recursively** if its definition consists of two parts:

1. An **anchor** or **base case**, in which the value of the function is specified for one or more values of the argument(s)
2. An **inductive** or **recursive step,** in which the function's value for the current value of the argument(s) is defined in terms of previously defined function values and/or argument values

We have seen two examples of such recursive definitions of functions, the factorial function

$0! = 1$	(the anchor or base case)
For $n > 0, n! = n \times (n-1)!$	(the inductive or recursive step)

and the power function

$x^0 = 1$	(the anchor or base case)
For $n > 0, x^n = x \times x^{n-1}$	(the inductive or recursive step)

In each definition, the first statement specifies a particular value of the function, and the second statement defines its value for n in terms of its value for $n - 1$.

As we noted in these examples, such recursive definitions are useful in calculating function values $f(n)$ for a sequence of consecutive values of n. Using them to calculate any one particular value, however, requires computing earlier values. For example, consider using the recursive definition of the factorial function to calculate 5!. We must first calculate 4!, because 5! is defined as the product of 5 and 4!. But to calculate 4! we must calculate 3! because 4! is defined as $4 \times 3!$. And to calculate 3!, we must apply the inductive step of the definition again, $3! = 3 \times 2!$, then again to find 2!, which is defined as $2! = 2 \times 1!$, and once again to find $1! = 1 \times 0!$. Now we have finally reached the anchor case:

$$5! = 5 \times 4!$$
$$\downarrow$$
$$4! = 4 \times 3!$$
$$\downarrow$$
$$3! = 3 \times 2!$$
$$\downarrow$$
$$2! = 2 \times 1!$$
$$\downarrow$$
$$1! = 1 \times 0!$$
$$\downarrow$$
$$0! = 1$$

Since the value of 0! is given, we can now backtrack to find the value of 1!,

$$5! = 5 \times 4!$$
$$\downarrow$$
$$4! = 4 \times 3!$$
$$\downarrow$$
$$3! = 3 \times 2!$$
$$\downarrow$$
$$2! = 2 \times 1!$$
$$\downarrow$$
$$1! = 1 \times 0! = 1 \times 1 = 1$$
$$\downarrow \quad \nearrow$$
$$0! = 1$$

then backtrack again to find the value of 2!,

$$5! = 5 \times 4!$$
$$\downarrow$$
$$4! = 4 \times 3!$$
$$\downarrow$$
$$3! = 3 \times 2!$$
$$\downarrow$$
$$2! = 2 \times 1! = 2 \times 1 = 2$$
$$\downarrow \quad \nwarrow$$
$$1! = 1 \times 0! = 1 \times 1 = 1$$
$$\downarrow \quad \nearrow$$
$$0! = 1$$

and so on until we eventually obtain the value 120 for 5!:

$$5! = 5 \times 4! = 5 \times 24 = 120$$
$$4! = 4 \times 3! = 4 \times 6 = 24$$
$$3! = 3 \times 2! = 3 \times 2 = 6$$
$$2! = 2 \times 1! = 2 \times 1 = 2$$
$$1! = 1 \times 0! = 1 \times 1 = 1$$
$$0! = 1$$

As this example demonstrates, calculating function values by hand using recursive definitions may require considerable bookkeeping to record information at the various levels of the recursive evaluation so that after the anchor case is reached, this information can be used to backtrack from one level to the preceding one. Fortunately, most modern high-level languages, including Fortran, support recursive subprograms, and the computer does all of the necessary bookkeeping and backtracking automatically.

Subprograms may be declared to be recursive by attaching the word **RECURSIVE** at the beginning of the subprogram heading. For a recursive function, a **RESULT clause** must also be attached at the end of the function heading to specify a variable that will be used to return the function result rather than the function name. *The type of the function is specified by declaring the type of this result variable* instead of the name of the function.

To illustrate, consider the factorial function again. The recursive definition of this function can be implemented as a recursive function in Fortran in a straightforward manner:

```
!-Factorial ---------------------------------------------
!   Function to calculate factorials (recursively).
!
!     Accepts:  integer n >= 0.
!     Returns:  n!
!-------------------------------------------------------

RECURSIVE FUNCTION Factorial(n) RESULT (Fact)

   INTEGER :: Fact              ! Result variable
   INTEGER, INTENT(IN) :: n

   IF (n == 0) THEN
      Fact = 1
   ELSE
      Fact = n * Factorial(n - 1)
   END IF

END FUNCTION Factorial
```

When this function is referenced, the inductive step

```
ELSE
    Fact = n * Factorial(n - 1)
```

causes the function to reference itself repeatedly, each time with a smaller argument, until the anchor case

```
IF (n == 0) THEN
    Fact = 1
```

is reached.

For example, consider the reference `Factorial(5)` to calculate 5!. Since the value of `n`, which is 5, is not 0, the inductive step generates another reference to `Factorial` with argument `n - 1 = 4`. Before execution of the original function reference is suspended, the current value 5 of the argument `n` is saved so that the value of `n` can be restored when execution resumes. This might be pictured as follows:

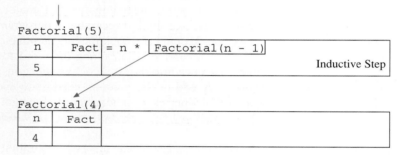

Since the value 4 of `n` in this function reference is not 0, the inductive step in this second reference to `Factorial` generates another reference to `Factorial` with argument 3. Once again, the value 4 of `n` is saved so that it can be restored later:

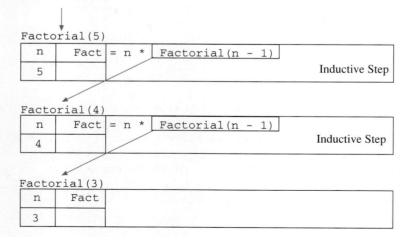

The inductive step in this function reference with argument n = 3 generates another reference to `Factorial` with argument 2, which in turn generates another reference with argument 1, which in turn generates another reference with argument 0.

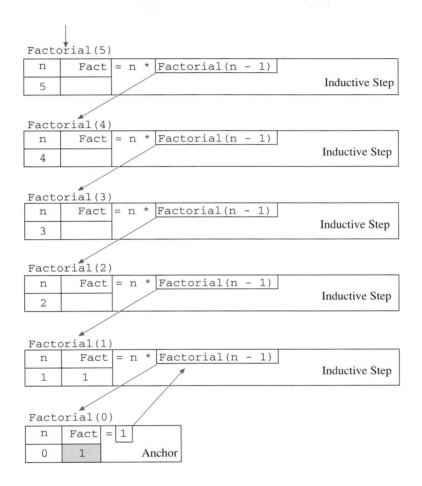

Because the anchor condition is now satisfied in this last function reference, no additional references are generated; instead the value 1 is assigned to `Fact`.

The function reference with argument 0 is thus completed, and the value 1 is returned as the value for `Factorial(0)`. Execution of the preceding function is resumed. The value of the argument n is restored, and the expression n * `Factorial(n - 1)` = 1 * `Factorial(0)` = 1 * 1 = 1 is calculated and returned as the value of `Factorial(1)`:

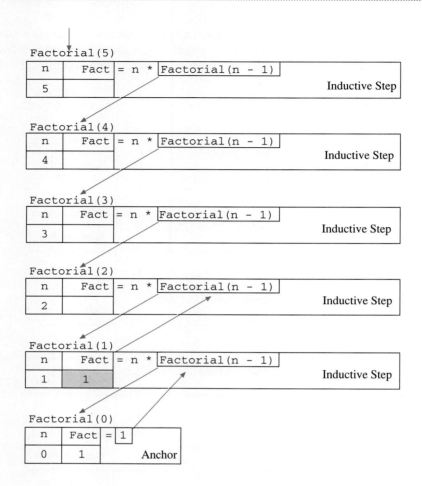

Execution of Factorial with argument 1 is thus complete, and execution of the preceding reference is resumed. The value of n is restored, and the value of n * Factorial(n - 1) = 2 * Factorial(1) = 2 * 1 = 2 is calculated for Factorial(2):

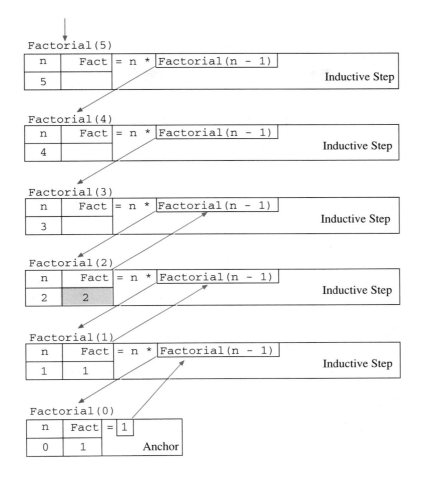

Execution of the preceding reference to `Factorial` is resumed; the value 3 of the argument n is restored; and the expression n * Factorial(n - 1) = 3 * Factorial(2) = 3 * 2 = 6 is computed for Factorial(3). This completes the reference to `Factorial` with argument 3, and execution of the preceding reference resumes. The value 4 is restored to the argument n, and the value n * Factorial(n - 1) = 4 * Factorial(3) = 4 * 6 = 24 is computed for Factorial(4). Since this completes the function reference with argument 4, execution of the original function reference resumes. The value 5 is restored to the argument n, and the value n * Factorial(n - 1) = 5 * Factorial(4) = 5 * 24 = 120 is computed for Factorial(5):

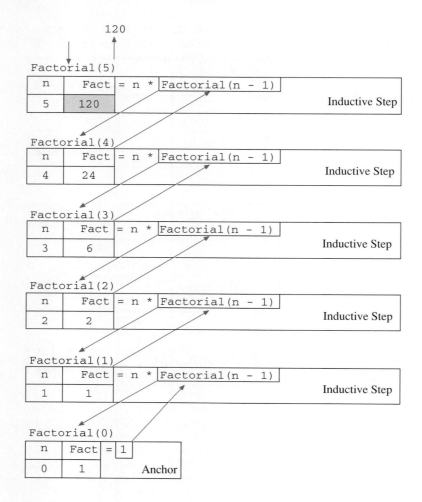

The value 120 is thus returned as the value for Factorial(5).

Many problems can be solved with equal ease using either a recursive or a nonrecursive algorithm. For example, the factorial function was implemented in this section as a recursive function, but this function can be written nonrecursively just as easily (see Figure 6.2). Nonrecursive subprograms may execute more rapidly and utilize memory more efficiently than the corresponding recursive subprograms. Thus, if an algorithm can be described either recursively or nonrecursively with little difference in effort, it is usually better to use the nonrecursive formulation.

For some problems, recursion is the most natural and straightforward technique. The following example is one such problem (as is the Towers of Hanoi problem described in the next chapter). For these problems, nonrecursive algorithms may not be obvious, may be more difficult to develop, and may be less readable than recursive ones. For such problems, the simplicity of the recursive algorithms compensates for any inefficiency. Unless the programs are to be executed many times, the extra effort required to develop nonrecursive solutions is not warranted.

Example: Street Network

Consider a network of streets laid out in a rectangular grid, for example,

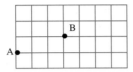

In a *northeast path* from one point in the grid to another, one may go only to the north (up) and to the east (right). For example, there are four northeast paths from A to B in the preceding grid:

To count the paths, we might proceed (recursively) as follows. To get from A to B, there are two ways to begin:

Case 1:   Go one block north (up); call this point A_1

Case 2:   Go one block east (right); call this point A_2

In either case we must count paths on a smaller grid. In the first case, there are the same number of columns separating A_1 and B, but there is one less row. In the second case, there are the same number of rows separating A_2 and B, but there is one less column. This suggests the following inductive step in a recursive solution to the problem:

Number of paths from A to B

= (Number of paths from A_1 to B) + (Number of paths from A_2 to B)

The function Number_of_Paths in Figure 6.12 uses this recursive approach to count the number of northeast paths from one point to another in a rectangular grid. The anchor case is that in which points A and B coincide.

Figure 6.12 Counting paths in a street network.

```
PROGRAM Path_Counter
!---------------------------------------------------------------------
! Program to count "northeasterly" paths from a given starting point
! in a network of streets to a specified ending point.  Identifiers
! used are:
!    StartRow, StartColumn : coordinates of starting point
!    EndRow, EndColumn     : coordinates of ending point
!    Number_of_Paths       : recursive function to count paths
!
! Input:  StartRow, StartColumn, EndRow, EndColumn
! Output: Number of northeast paths
!---------------------------------------------------------------------

  IMPLICIT NONE
  INTEGER :: StartRow, StartColumn, EndRow, EndColumn

  PRINT *, "Enter the starting coordinates (row then column):"
  READ *, StartRow, StartColumn
  PRINT *,  "Enter the ending coordinates (row then column):"
  READ *, EndRow, EndColumn

  PRINT *, "There are", &
           Number_of_Paths(EndRow - StartRow, &
                        EndColumn - StartColumn),  " paths"

CONTAINS

  ! Number_of_Paths ------------------------------------------------
  ! A recursive function to calculate the number of northeasterly paths
  ! in a network of streets. Identifiers used are:
  !    NumRows,  NumColumns : number of rows and columns from starting
  !                           position to ending position
  !    Num_Paths            : number of paths
  !
  ! Accepts:  Number_of_Rows, Number_of_Columns
  ! Returns:  Num_Paths
  !----------------------------------------------------------------

  RECURSIVE FUNCTION &
     Number_of_Paths(NumRows, NumColumns) RESULT (Num_Paths)
```

Figure 6.12 *(cont.)*

```
    INTEGER, INTENT(IN) :: NumRows, NumColumns
    INTEGER :: Num_Paths

    IF ((NumRows == 0) .OR. (NumColumns == 0)) THEN
       Num_Paths = 1
    ELSE
       Num_Paths = Number_of_Paths(NumRows - 1, NumColumns) &
                 + Number_of_Paths(NumRows, NumColumns - 1)
    END IF

  END FUNCTION Number_of_Paths

END PROGRAM Path_Counter
```

Sample runs:

```
Enter the starting coordinates (row then column): 0, 1
Enter the ending coordinates (row then column): 3, 2
There are 4  paths

Enter the starting coordinates (row then column): 1, 1
Enter the ending coordinates (row then column): 1, 1
There are 1  paths

Enter the starting coordinates (row then column): 0, 1
Enter the ending coordinates (row then column): 7, 4
There are 120  paths

Enter the starting coordinates (row then column): 0, 0
Enter the ending coordinates (row then column): 7, 4
There are 330  paths
```

Quick Quiz 6.7

1. _____ is the phenomenon of a subprogram referencing itself.

2. Describe what it means to say that a function is defined recursively.

3. A function subprogram is declared to be recursive by attaching the word _____ at the beginning of the function heading.

4. For a recursive function, a _____ clause must be attached at the end of the function heading to specify that an identifier other than the function name will be used for the function result.

5. (True or false)   A nonrecursive function for computing some value may execute more rapidly than a recursive function that computes the same value.

6. For the following recursive function, find `F(5)`.

```
RECURSIVE FUNCTION F(N) RESULT (F_Value)

    INTEGER :: F_Value
    INTEGER, INTENT(IN) :: N

    IF (N == 0) THEN
       F_Value = 0
    ELSE
       F_Value = N + F(N - 1)
    END IF

END FUNCTION F
```

7. For the function in Question 6, find `F(0)`.

8. For the function in Question 6, suppose + is changed to * in the inductive step. Find `F(5)`.

Exercises 6.7

For Exercises 1–4, determine what is calculated by the given recursive functions.

```
1. RECURSIVE FUNCTION F(X, N) RESULT (F_Value)

    REAL :: F_Value
    REAL, INTENT(IN) :: X
    INTEGER, INTENT(IN) :: N

    IF (N == 0) THEN
       F_Value = 0
    ELSE
       F_Value = X + F(X, N - 1)
    END IF

END FUNCTION F
```

2. RECURSIVE FUNCTION F(N) RESULT (F_Value)

```
   INTEGER :: F_Value
   INTEGER, INTENT(IN) :: N

   IF (N < 2) THEN
      F_Value = 0
   ELSE
      F_Value = 1 + F( N / 2)
   END IF

END FUNCTION F
```

3. RECURSIVE FUNCTION F(N) RESULT (F_Value)

```
   INTEGER :: F_Value
   INTEGER, INTENT(IN) :: N

   IF (N == 0) THEN
      F_Value = 0
   ELSE
      F_Value = F(N / 10) + MOD(N, 10)
   END IF

END FUNCTION F
```

4. RECURSIVE FUNCTION F(N) RESULT (F_Value)

```
   INTEGER :: F_Value
   INTEGER, INTENT(IN) :: N

   IF (N < 0) THEN
      F_Value = F(-N)
   ELSE IF (N < 10) THEN
      F_Value = N
   ELSE
      F_Value = F(N / 10)
   END IF

END FUNCTION F
```

5. Given the following function F, use the method illustrated in this section to trace the sequence of function calls and returns in evaluating F(1, 5) and F(8, 3).

```
   RECURSIVE FUNCTION F(Num1, Num2) RESULT (F_Value)

     INTEGER :: F_Value
     INTEGER, INTENT(IN) :: Num1, Num2
```

```
IF (Num1 > Num2) THEN
    F_Value = 0
ELSE IF (Num2 == Num1 + 1) THEN
    F_Value = 1
ELSE
    F_Value = F(Num1 + 1, Num2 - 1) + 2
END IF
```

```
END FUNCTION F
```

For Exercises 6–9, write a nonrecursive version of the function.

6. The function in Exercise 1.

7. The function in Exercise 2.

8. The function in Exercise 3.

9. The function in Exercise 4.

10. Write a recursive function that computes x^n for a real value x and a nonnegative integer n.

11. Write a recursive function that returns the number of digits in a nonnegative integer.

12. Write a recursive function that computes the greatest common divisor of two integers (see Exercise 11 of Section 6.1).

13. **Binomial coefficients** can be defined recursively as follows:

$$\left.\begin{array}{l} \dbinom{n}{0} = 1 \\[2mm] \dbinom{n}{n} = 1 \end{array}\right\} \quad \text{(anchor)}$$

$$\text{For } 0 < k < n, \dbinom{n}{k} = \dbinom{n-1}{k-1} + \dbinom{n-1}{k} \quad \text{(inductive step)}$$

Write a recursive function or procedure to calculate binomial coefficients.

CHAPTER REVIEW

Summary

Modular programming and top-down design are important problem-solving techniques, and most programming languages provide subprograms to support these approaches. In Fortran, subprograms may be functions or subroutines; this chapter considers functions. It begins by giving a list of commonly used Fortran numeric intrinsic functions (see Table 6.1). It then describes how programmers can design and use their own functions. These techniques are illustrated with several examples. The examples in Section 6.3 demonstrate the use of functions in programs for doing numeric processing such as root finding, approximating integrals, and solving differential equations. Section 6.4 illustrates integrating a function whose values are tabulated in a file. Section 6.5 describes how functions can be packaged together in a module, Section 6.6 describes external functions, and Section 6.7 describes recursive functions.

FORTRAN SUMMARY

Function Subprogram

function heading
specification part
execution part
END FUNCTION statement

Function Heading

```
FUNCTION name(formal-argument-list)
```

or

```
type-identifier FUNCTION name(formal-argument-list)
```

where the function `name` may be any legal Fortran identifier, `formal-argument-list` is a list of identifiers, and `type-identifier` is optional. For a recursive function, the first form of the heading must be modified as follows:

```
RECURSIVE FUNCTION name(formal-argument-list) RESULT (var)
```

where `var` is a variable whose value will be returned as the function value. The type of `var` (and not `name`) must be declared in the function's specification part.

Example:

```
FUNCTION Fahr_to_Celsius(Temperature)
REAL FUNCTION Fahr_to_Celsius(Temperature)
RECURSIVE FUNCTION Factorial(n) RESULT (Fact)
```

Purpose:
Names the function and declares its arguments. In the second form, the type of the value returned by the function is also declared in the function heading; in the first form, this must be done in the specification part of the function subprogram.

SAVE Attribute and Statement

```
type, SAVE :: list-of-local-variables
```

or

```
SAVE list-of-local-variables
```

where the list of variables may be omitted in the second form.

Examples:

```
REAL, SAVE :: Alpha, Beta, Gamma
```

```
SAVE
```

Purpose:
Saves the values of local variables from one subprogram reference to the next. If the list of variables is omitted in the statement form, all local variables will be saved.

Module (simple form)

```
MODULE module-name

CONTAINS
    subprogram₁
    subprogram₂
        ⋮
    subprogramₙ

END MODULE name
```

Example:

```
MODULE Temperature_Library

CONTAINS
  FUNCTION Fahr_to_Celsius
      ⋮
  END FUNCTION Fahr_to_Celsius

  FUNCTION Celsius_to_Fahr
      ⋮
  END FUNCTION Celsius_to_Fahr

END MODULE Temperature_Library
```

Purpose:
To package together subprograms (and other items).

USE Statement

```
USE module-name
```

or

```
USE module-name, ONLY: list
```

or

```
USE module-name, rename-list
```

where
  module-name is the name of a module;
  list is a list of identifiers declared in that module;
  rename-list is a list of renamings of identifiers in the module and has the
    form

```
    new-identifier => identifier
```

Example:

```
USE Temperature_Library

USE Temperature_Library ONLY: Fahr_to_Celsius, &
                              C_to_F => Celsius_to_Fahr
```

Purpose:
Imports the items from the specified module into a program unit. The USE statement must appear at the beginning of the specification part of the program unit. The first form imports all identifiers from the module; the second imports only those listed and can be used to rename some or all of these identifiers with new identifiers.

PROGRAMMING POINTERS

Program Style and Design

1. *Subprograms should be documented in the same way that the main program is.* The documentation should include a brief description of the processing carried out by the subprograms, the values passed to them, the values returned by them, and what the arguments and local variables represent.

2. *Subprograms are separate program units, and the program format should reflect this fact.* In this text, we
   - insert one or more blank lines before and after each subprogram to set it off from other program units
   - follow the stylistic standards described in earlier chapters when writing subprograms

3. *An* `INTENT(IN)` *clause should be used in the declaration of each argument of a function subprogram to specify that values will only be passed to that argument and not returned by it.* This protects the argument by ensuring that its value is not changed within the subprogram.

4. *Programs for solving complex problems should be designed in a modular fashion.* The problem should be divided into simpler subproblems so that subprograms can be written to solve each of them.

Potential Problems

1. *The number of actual arguments in a reference to a function must be the same as the number of formal arguments (unless some arguments have been declared to be optional, as described in Section 7.7); also, the type of each actual argument must agree with the type of the corresponding formal argument.* For example, consider a function

```
FUNCTION Pythagoras(Side_1, Side_2)

   INTEGER :: Pythagoras
   INTEGER, INTENT(IN) :: Side_1, Side_2

   Pythagoras = Side_1 ** 2 + Side_2 ** 2

END FUNCTION Pythagoras
```

The function references

```
Pythagoras(K, L, M)
```

and

```
Pythagoras(2, 3.5)
```

are not correct. In the first case, the number of actual arguments does not agree with the number of formal arguments; in the second, the real value 3.5 cannot be associated with the integer argument Num2.

2. *The argument checking described in Potential Problem 1 is done automatically by the compiler for module functions and internal functions. Interface blocks may be used to ensure that similar checking is done for external functions.*

3. *The type of an external function must be declared both in the function subprogram and in the program unit that references the function.*

4. *If a formal argument is not declared to have the* INTENT(IN) *attribute and its value is changed in a subprogram, the value of the corresponding actual argument also changes.* For example, if the function F is defined by the function subprogram

```
FUNCTION F(X, Y)

   REAL :: F, X, Y

   F = X ** 2 - 2.5 * Y + 3.7 * Y ** 2
   X = 0

END FUNCTION F
```

then when the function is referenced in the main program by a statement such as

```
Alpha = F(Beta, Gamma)
```

where Alpha, Beta, and Gamma are real variables, the value of the function is assigned to Alpha, but Beta is set equal to zero, since it corresponds to the formal argument X, whose value is changed in the subprogram.

PROGRAMMING PROBLEMS

Section 6.1

1. Write a program that inputs several pairs of integers, calls the function Range in Exercise 1 of Section 6.1 to calculate the range between each pair, and displays this range.

2. Write a program that inputs real numbers, calls the function Round in Exercise 2 of Section 6.1 to round each real value to a specified number of places, and displays the rounded value.

3. Write a program that reads values for an initial population of bacteria, a rate constant, and a time (e.g., 1000, 0.15, 100), calls the function from Exercise 3 of Section 6.1 to calculate the number of bacteria at that time, and displays this value.

4. Write a program that accepts both an angle measurement and the letter D or R, indicating that the angle is measured in degrees or radians, respectively, and that then uses an appropriate function to convert the measurement to the other units. (One of the conversion formulas is $R = (\pi/180)D$.)

5. Write a logical-valued function that determines whether a character is one of the digits 0 through 9. Use it in a program that reads several characters and checks to see whether each is a digit.

6. Write a program that reads the coordinates of several triples of points and determines whether they can be the vertices of a triangle. (The sum of the lengths of each pair of sides must be greater than the length of the third side.) Use the function from Exercise 5 of Section 6.1 to calculate distances between points.

7. If an amount of A dollars is borrowed at an annual interest rate r (expressed as a decimal) for y years, and n is the number of payments to be made per year, then the amount of each payment is given by

$$\frac{r \cdot A/n}{1 - \left(1 + \dfrac{r}{n}\right)^{-n \cdot y}}$$

Write a function to calculate these payments. Use it in a program that reads several values for the amount borrowed, the interest rate, the number of years, and the number of payments per year and displays the corresponding payment for each set of values.

8. Write a program that reads several test scores and displays for each the corresponding letter grade and the numeric value of that grade. Use the functions `NumericGrade` and `LetterGrade` from Exercises 6 and 7 of Section 6.1.

9. Write a program that reads several pairs of integers `Number_1` and `Number_2` and for each pair calls the function from Exercise 8 of Section 6.1 to calculate the sum of the integers from `Number_1` through `Number_2` and displays this sum.

10. Write a program to calculate *binomial coefficients*

$$\binom{n}{k} = \frac{n!}{k!\,(n-k)!}$$

using a function subprogram to calculate factorials. Let n run from 1 through 10, and for each such n, let k run from 0 through n.

11. Suppose that in an experiment the probability that a certain outcome will occur is p; then $1 - p$ is the probability that it will not occur. The probability that in n independent trials the desired outcome will occur exactly k times is given by

$$\binom{n}{k} p^k (1-p)^{n-k}$$

Write a program to calculate this probability for several values of n and k, using a function subprogram to calculate factorials.

12. The *power series*

$$1 + x + \frac{x^2}{2!} + \frac{x^3}{3!} + \cdots = \sum_{k=0}^{\infty} \frac{x^k}{k!}$$

converges to e^x for all values of x. Write a function subprogram that uses this series to calculate values for e^x to five-decimal-place accuracy (i.e., using terms up to the first one that is less than 10^{-5} in absolute value) and that uses a function subprogram to calculate factorials. Use these subprograms in a main program to calculate and print a table of values for the function

$$\cosh(x) = \frac{e^x + e^{-x}}{2}$$

and also the corresponding values of the library function COSH for $x = -1$ to 1 in increments of 0.1.

13. A more efficient procedure for evaluating the power series in Problem 12 is to observe that if $a_n = x^n/n!$ and $a_{n+1} = x^{n+1}/(n+1)!$ are two consecutive terms of the series, then

$$a_{n+1} = \frac{x}{n+1} a_n$$

Write a function subprogram to calculate e^x using the power series of Problem 12 and using this relationship between consecutive terms. Then use this in a main program to print a table of values for the function

$$\sinh(x) = \frac{e^x - e^{-x}}{2}$$

and the corresponding values of the library function SINH for $x = -2$ to 2 in increments of 0.1.

14. Write a program that reads several integers and, for each, displays a message indicating whether it is a perfect square. Use the function from Exercise 10 of Section 6.1 to determine if a number is a perfect square.

15. The Euclidean algorithm for finding the greatest common divisor of two integers was described in Exercise 11 of Section 6.1. Use the function developed there in a program that calculates the GCD of any finite set of integers using the following:

If $d = \text{GCD}(a_1, \ldots, a_n)$, then
$$\text{GCD}(a_1, \ldots, a_n, a_{n+1}) = \text{GCD}(d, a_{n+1})$$

For example:

$$\text{GCD}(1260, 198) = 18$$

$$\text{GCD}(1260, 198, 585) = \text{GCD}(18, 585) = 9$$

$$\text{GCD}(1260, 198, 585, 138) = \text{GCD}(9, 138) = 3$$

16. Write a program that reads several integers, uses the function from Exercise 12 of Section 6.1 to determine whether each is a prime, and displays each number with the appropriate label "is prime" or "is not prime."

17. (a) Write a function `DaysBetween` that returns the number of days between two given dates. Use the function from Exercise 9 of Section 6.1 to calculate the number of days in a month.

(b) A person's biorhythm index on a given day is the sum of the values of his or her physical, intellectual, and emotional cycles. Each of these cycles begins at birth and forms a sine curve having an amplitude of 1 and periods of 23, 33, and 28 days, respectively. Write a program that accepts the current date, a person's name, and his or her birthdate and then calculates the biorhythm index for that person. (See Exercise 10 of Section 3.5 regarding leap years.)

Section 6.2

18. Write a menu-driven program that allows the user to convert measurements either from miles to kilometers (1 mile = 1.60935 kilometers), from feet to meters (1 foot = 0.3048 meter), or from degrees Fahrenheit to degrees Celsius ($C = (5/9)(F - 32)$). Use functions to carry out the various conversions. A sample run of the program should proceed somewhat as follows:

```
Available options are:
0. Display this menu.
1. Convert miles to kilometers.
2. Convert feet to meters.
3. Convert degrees Fahrenheit to degrees Celsius.
4. Quit.

Enter an option (0 to see menu): 3
Enter degrees Fahrenheit: 212
This is equivalent to 100.00 degrees Celsius

Enter an option (0 to see menu): 0
Available options are:
0. Display this menu.
1. Convert miles to kilometers.
2. Convert feet to meters.
3. Convert degrees Fahrenheit to degrees Celsius.
4. Quit.

Enter an option (0 to see menu): 1
Enter miles: 10
This is equivalent to   16.10 kilometers

Enter an option (0 to see menu): 2
Enter number of feet: 1
This is equivalent to    0.31 meters.

Enter an option (0 to see menu): 4
```

Sections 6.3 and 6.4

Root Finding

19. Another method for finding an approximate zero of a function is the *bisection method.* In this method, we begin with two numbers a and b, where the function values $f(a)$ and $f(b)$ have opposite signs. If f is continuous between $x = a$ and $x = b$—that is, if there is no break in the graph of $y = f(x)$ between these two values—then the graph of f must cross the x-axis at least once between $x = a$ and $x = b$, and thus there must be at least one solution of the equation $f(x) = 0$ between a and b. To locate one of these solutions, we first bisect the interval $[a, b]$ and determine in which half f changes sign, thereby locating a smaller subinterval containing a solution of the equation. We bisect this subinterval and determine in which half f changes sign; this gives a still smaller subinterval containing a solution.

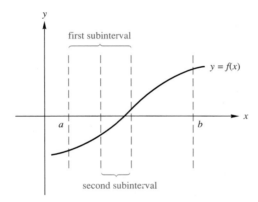

Repeating this process gives a sequence of subintervals, each of which contains a solution of the equation and whose length is one-half that of the preceding interval. Note that at each step, the midpoint of a subinterval of length L is within $L/2$ of the exact solution:

Write a program to implement the bisection method, and use it to find a solution of the equation $x^3 + x - 5 = 0$.

20. Proceed as in Exercise 1 of Section 6.4, but use the bisection method.

21. Proceed as in Exercise 2 of Section 6.4, but use the bisection method.

22. Proceed as in Exercise 3 of Section 6.4, but use the bisection method.

23. Proceed as in Exercise 4 of Section 6.4, but use the bisection method.

24. Proceed as in Exercise 5 of Section 6.4, but use the bisection method.

25. Proceed as in Exercise 6 of Section 6.4, but use the bisection method.

26. Proceed as in Exercise 7 of Section 6.4, but use the bisection method.

Numerical Integration

27. The familiar equation work = force × distance can be used to compute the work done by a force whose line of action is in the direction of displacement. However, if the force is applied at some angle θ to the direction of motion, the equation becomes

$$\text{work} = \text{force} \times \cos\theta \times \text{distance}$$

Write a program in which the user enters the force (newtons), the angle θ (radians), and the distance (meters) and returns the work done (joules). Run your program using a force of 9.32 N, an angle of 0.52 radians, and a path length of 30 m.

28. In Problem 27, if the angle between the force and the path of motion changes during the displacement, the work done by a force F (newtons) in moving an object from $s = a$ to $s = b$ (meters) along the line is given by

$$W = F \int_a^b \cos(\theta(s))ds \quad \text{(joules)}$$

where $\theta(s)$ is the angle at a distance s from the initial point a. Write a program that asks the user to enter values for a, b, and F, that reads a value for n and the value of $\theta(s)$ at n equally spaced points along the path of motion from a data file, and that then uses the trapezoidal method to approximate this integral. The program should then compute and display the work done. Run your program using a force of 10.38 N, $a = 0.0$ m, $b = 30.0$ m, and the following angles at points $a, a + \Delta s, a + 2\Delta s, \ldots, b$: 0.5, 1.4, 0.75, 0.9, 1.3, 1.48, 1.5, 1.6 (all in radians).

29. Proceed as in Problem 28, but suppose that the angle θ is fixed and the force varies. In this case, the work done is given by

$$W = \cos\theta \int_a^b F(s)ds$$

where $F(s)$ is the angle at a distance s from the initial point a. Write a program that asks the user to enter values for a, b, and θ, that reads a value for n and the value of $F(s)$ at n equally spaced points along the path of motion from a data file, and that then uses the trapezoidal method to approximate this integral. The program should then compute and display the work done. Run your program using an angle of $\theta = 0.35$ radians, $a = 10.0$ m, $b = 40.0$ m, and the following forces at points $a, a + \Delta s, a + 2\Delta s, \ldots, b$: 0.0, 4.5, 9.0, 13.0, 14.0, 10.5, 12.0, 7.8, 5.0 (all in newtons).

30. Proceed as in Problems 28 and 29, but suppose both the angle and the force vary. In this case, the work done is given by

$$W = \int_a^b F(s) \cos(\theta(s)) ds$$

where $F(s)$ is the angle at a distance s from the initial point a. Write a program that asks the user to enter values for a and b, that reads a value for n and the values of $F(s)$ and $\theta(s)$ at n equally spaced points along the path of motion from a data file, and that then uses the trapezoidal method to approximate this integral. The program should then compute and display the work done. Run your program using $a = 20.0$ m, $b = 50.0$ m, and the following pairs of values for $F(s)$ and $\theta(s)$ at points $a, a + \Delta s, a + 2\Delta s, \ldots, b$ (all in newtons and radians):

$F(s)$	$\theta(s)$
0.0	0.60
4.3	0.87
7.8	1.02
9.9	0.99
12.5	1.20
16.3	0.98
18.4	0.86
21.7	0.43
25.4	0.23
22.3	0.14
20.9	0.15
18.7	0.08

31. Another method of numerical integration that generally produces better approximations than the trapezoidal method is based on the use of parabolas and is known as *Simpson's rule*. In this method, the interval $[a, b]$ is divided into an even number n of subintervals, each of length Δx; and the sum

$$\frac{\Delta x}{3} [f(x_0) + 4f(x_1) + 2f(x_2) + 4f(x_3)$$

$$+ 2f(x_4) + \cdots + 2f(x_{n-2}) + 4f(x_{n-1}) + f(x_n)]$$

is used to approximate the integral of f over the interval $[a, b]$. Write a program to approximate an integral using Simpson's rule.

32. Proceed as in Figure 6.5, but use Simpson's rule. Compare the sample runs.

33. Proceed as in Problem 28, but use Simpson's rule.

34. Proceed as in Problem 29, but use Simpson's rule.

35. Proceed as in Problem 30, but use Simpson's rule.

36. Proceed as in Exercise 8 of Section 6.4, but use Simpson's rule with $n = 50$.

37. Proceed as in Exercise 9 of Section 6.4, but use Simpson's rule with $n = 20$.

38. Proceed as in Exercise 10 of Section 6.4, but use Simpson's rule with $n = 10$, 20, 30, and 40. Compare the results.

39. Proceed as in Exercise 11 of Section 6.4, but use Simpson's rule with $n = 100$ and compare your result with the true answer:

$$T = \int_{7.5}^{15} 20v^{-3/2}\, dv = \left. \frac{-40}{\sqrt{v}} \right|_{7.5}^{15} \approx 4.27797$$

40. Proceed as in Exercise 12 of Section 6.4, but use Simpson's rule with $n = 50$.

Numerical Solutions of Differential Equations

41. Write a program to implement the Runge-Kutta method for solving differential equations. Run the program using the differential equation given in the description of Euler's method:

$$y' = 2xy$$

$$y(0) = 1$$

42. Suppose that an object at a certain temperature T_0 (°C) is dropped into a liquid at a lower temperature T_s (°C). If the amount of liquid is quite large and is stirred, we can assume that the object's heat will spread quickly enough through the liquid so that the temperature of the liquid will not change appreciably. We can then assume that the object loses heat at a rate proportional to the difference between its temperature and the temperature of the liquid. Thus, the differential equation that models this problem is

$$T' = k(T - T_s)$$

where $T(t)$ (°C) is the temperature of the object at time t seconds, k is the constant of proportionality, and

$$T(0) = T_0$$

is the initial condition. The exact solution of this differential equation can be shown to be

$$T = T_s + (T_0 - T_s)e^{-kt}$$

Write a program that uses the Runge-Kutta method to obtain an approximate solution. Run the program with $T_s = 70°$ C, $T_0 = 300°$ C, and $k = .19$ for $t = 0$ seconds to $t = 20$ seconds with various t increments. Print a table of approximate T values, exact T values, and the differences between them.

43. Proceed as in Exercise 13 of Section 6.4, but use the Runge-Kutta method.
44. Proceed as in Exercise 14 of Section 6.4, but use the Runge-Kutta method.
45. Proceed as in Exercise 15 of Section 6.4, but use the Runge-Kutta method.
46. Proceed as in Exercise 16 of Section 6.4, but use the Runge-Kutta method.
47. Proceed as in Exercise 17 of Section 6.4, but use the Runge-Kutta method.

Section 6.5

48. Design a module for converting weights from the U.S. system to the metric system. Some useful conversion formulas are: 16 ounces = 1 pound, 2000 pounds = 1 ton, 1 ounce = 28.349523 grams, 1 kilogram = 1000 grams.

49. Design a module for converting lengths from the U.S. system to the metric system. Some useful conversion formulas are: 12 inches = 1 foot, 3 feet = 1 yard, 1 mile = 5280 feet, 1 inch = 2.540005 centimeters, 1 meter = 100 centimeters, 1 kilometer = 1000 meters.

50. Design a module for converting volumes from the U.S. system to the metric system. Some useful conversion formulas are: 2 pints = 1 quart, 4 quarts = 1 gallon, 1 pint = 0.4731631 liters, 1 kiloliter = 1000 liters.

Section 6.7

51. Write a program to test one of the recursive functions in Exercises 1–4 of Section 6.7; the function should be an internal function. Add output statements to the function to trace its actions as it executes. For example, the trace displayed for F(21) for the function F in Exercise 2 of Section 6.7 should have a form like

```
F(21) = 1 + F(10)
    F(10) = 1 + F(5)
        F(5) = 1 + F(2)
            F(2) = 1 + F(1)
                F(1) returns 0
            F(2) returns 1
        F(5) returns 2
    F(10) returns 3
F(21) returns 4
```

where the indentation level reflects the depth of the recursion. (*Hint*: This can be accomplished by using a variable Level declared and initialized in the main program that is incremented when the function is entered and decremented when it is exited.)

52. Write a program to test the recursive power function of Exercise 10 in Section 6.7.

53. Write a program to test the recursive digit-counter function of Exercise 11 in Section 6.7.

54. Write a program to test the recursive greatest common divisor function of Exercise 12 in Section 6.7.

55. Write a program to test the recursive binomial coefficient function of Exercise 13 in Section 6.7.

56. Consider a square grid, with some cells empty and others containing an asterisk. Define two asterisks to be *contiguous* if they are adjacent to each other in the same row or in the same column. Now suppose we define a *blob* as follows:

    (a) A blob contains at least one asterisk.
    (b) If an asterisk is in a blob, then so is any asterisk that is contiguous to it.
    (c) If a blob has more than two asterisks, then each asterisk in it is contiguous to at least one other asterisk in the blob.

    For example, there are four blobs in the partial grid

    seven blobs in

    and only one in

    Write a program that uses a recursive function to count the number of blobs in a square grid. Input to the program should consist of the locations of the asterisks in the grid, and the program should display the grid and the blob count.

FEATURES NEW TO FORTRAN 90

Fortran 90 has added a number of new features that facilitate modular programming, including the following:

- A number of new intrinsic functions have been added. Among the predefined numeric functions are

  CEILING(X): the least integer greater than or equal to the real value X
  FLOOR(X): the greatest integer less than or equal to the real value X

- Subprograms may be recursive.

- Program units may contain internal subprograms. A CONTAINS statement in a program unit signals that internal subprogram definitions follow.

- Explicit interfaces with a subprogram may be provided by means of an interface block.

- Modules can be used to package definitions and declarations of constants, variables, types, and subprograms so they can be used by other program units.

7

Programming with Subroutines

Anyone who considers arithmetical methods of producing random digits is, of course, in a state of sin.

JOHN VON NEUMANN

Great things can be reduced to small things, and small things can be reduced to nothing.

CHINESE PROVERB

From a little distance one can perceive an order in what at the time seemed confusion.

F. SCOTT FITZGERALD

There are two ways of constructing a software design: One way is to make it so simple that there are obviously no deficiencies, and the other way is to make it so complicated that there are no obvious deficiencies. The first method is far more difficult.

C. A. R. HOARE

*S*ubprograms in Fortran can be either functions or subroutines. In the preceding chapter, we considered only function subprograms. In this chapter we focus on subroutine subprograms, whose execution, like function subprograms, is controlled by some other program unit, either the main program or some other subprogram.

As we noted in Chapter 6, complex problems are best solved by dividing them into simpler subproblems and designing subprograms to solve these subproblems. In some cases it may be necessary to divide the subproblems still further until the resulting subproblems are simple enough that algorithms for their solution can be easily designed. This **top-down** approach that uses a **divide-and-conquer** strategy is also described and illustrated in this chapter.

In the last sections of this chapter, we describe how subprograms can be passed as arguments to other subprograms, how optional and keyword arguments are used, and how a recursive subroutine can be used to solve a problem in artificial intelligence.

7.1   SUBROUTINE SUBPROGRAMS

Subroutine subprograms have many features in common with function subprograms:

- They are program units designed to perform particular tasks under the control of some other program unit.
- They have the same basic form: each consists of a heading, a specification part, an execution part, and an END statement.
- They may be internal, module, or external subprograms.
- The scope rules described in Section 6.1 apply to both functions and subroutines.
- They may be used as arguments of other subprograms (see Section 7.6).
- They may have optional and keyword arguments (see Section 7.7).
- They may be recursive (see Section 7.8).

They differ, however, in the following respects:

- Functions are designed to return a single value to the program unit that references them. Subroutines often return more than one value, or they may return no value at all but simply perform some task such as displaying a list of instructions to the user.
- Functions return values via function names; subroutines return values via arguments.
- A function is referenced by using its name in an expression, whereas a subroutine is referenced by a CALL statement.

The form of a subroutine subprogram is

Subroutine Subprogram

subroutine heading
specification part
execution part
END SUBROUTINE statement

The **subroutine heading** is a **SUBROUTINE** statement of the following form:

Subroutine Heading

Forms:

    SUBROUTINE *subroutine-name(formal-argument-list)*

or for a recursive subroutine,

    RECURSIVE SUBROUTINE *subroutine-name(formal-argument-list)*

where
> *subroutine-name* may be any legal Fortran identifier;
> *formal-argument-list* is an identifier or a list (possibly empty) of identifiers separated by commas. If there are no formal arguments, the parentheses may be omitted.

Purpose:
Names the subroutine and declares its arguments. The variables in the *formal-argument-list* are called **formal** or **dummy arguments** and are used to pass information to and from the subroutine.

A subroutine is referenced by a **CALL statement** of the form:

CALL *Statement*

Form:

    CALL *subroutine-name(actual-argument-list)*

where
> *subroutine-name* is the subroutine being called;
> *actual-argument-list* contains the variables, constants, or expressions that are the actual arguments. The number of actual arguments must equal the number of formal arguments (except when the subroutine has optional arguments, as described in Section 7.7), and each actual argument must agree in type with the corresponding formal argument. If there are no actual arguments, the parentheses in the subroutine reference may be omitted.

Purpose:
Calls the named subroutine. Execution of the current program unit is suspended; the actual arguments are associated with the corresponding formal arguments; and execution of the subroutine begins. When execution of the subroutine is completed, execution of the original program unit resumes with the statement following the CALL statement.

Example: Displaying an Angle in Degrees

As a simple illustration, suppose we wish to develop a subroutine that accepts from the main program an angular measurement in degrees, minutes, and seconds and displays it as an equivalent number of degrees. For example, the value 100° 30′ 36″ is to be displayed as

```
100 degrees, 30 minutes, 36 seconds
is equivalent to
100.510 degrees
```

This subroutine will have three formal arguments, all of type INTEGER, the first representing the number of degrees, the second the number of minutes, and the third the number of seconds. Thus, an appropriate heading for this subroutine is

```
SUBROUTINE PrintDegrees(Degrees, Minutes, Seconds)
```

where Degrees, Minutes, and Seconds must be declared of type INTEGER in the specification part of the subroutine. The complete subroutine is

```
!-PrintDegrees-------------------------------------------
! Subroutine to display a measurement of Degrees, Minutes,
! Seconds as the equivalent degree measure.
!
! Accepts:  Degrees, Minutes, Seconds
! Output:   Values of Degrees, Minutes, and Seconds and the
!           equivalent degree measure
!--------------------------------------------------------


SUBROUTINE PrintDegrees(Degrees, Minutes, Seconds)

   INTEGER, INTENT(IN) :: Degrees, Minutes, Seconds

   PRINT 10, Degrees, Minutes, Seconds, &
             REAL(Degrees) + REAL(Minutes)/60.0 + &
             REAL(Seconds)/3600.0
   10 FORMAT (1X, I3, " degrees", I3, " minutes", &
             I3, " seconds" / 1X, "is equivalent to" / &
             1X, F7.3, " degrees")

END SUBROUTINE PrintDegrees
```

This subroutine is an internal subprogram in the program of Figure 7.1 and is referenced by the CALL statement

```
CALL PrintDegrees(NumDegrees, NumMinutes, NumSeconds)
```

This statement causes the values of the actual arguments NumDegrees, NumMinutes, and NumSeconds to be passed to the formal arguments Degrees, Minutes, and Seconds, respectively, and initiates execution of the subroutine. When

the end of the subroutine is reached, execution resumes with the statement following
this CALL statement in the main program.

Figure 7.1 Displaying an angle in degrees.

```fortran
PROGRAM Angles_1
!-------------------------------------------------------------------
! Program demonstrating the use of a subroutine PrintDegrees to
! display an angle in degrees.  Variables used are:
!  NumDegrees : degrees in the angle measurement
!  NumMinutes : minutes in the angle measurement
!  NumSeconds : seconds in the angle measurement
!  Response   : user response to more-data question
!
! Input:  NumDegrees, NumMinutes, NumSeconds, Response
! Output: Equivalent measure in degrees (displayed by PrintDegrees)
!-------------------------------------------------------------------

  IMPLICIT NONE
  INTEGER :: NumDegrees, NumMinutes, NumSeconds
  CHARACTER(1) :: Response

  ! Read and convert angles until user signals no more data
  DO
     WRITE (*, '(1X, A)', ADVANCE = "NO") &
           "Enter degrees, minutes, and seconds: "
     READ *, NumDegrees, NumMinutes, NumSeconds
     CALL PrintDegrees(NumDegrees, NumMinutes, NumSeconds)
     WRITE (*, '(/ 1X, A)', ADVANCE = "NO") "More angles (Y or N)? "
     READ *, Response
     IF (Response /= "Y") EXIT
  END DO

CONTAINS

  !-PrintDegrees--------------------------------------------------
  ! Subroutine to display a measurement of Degrees, Minutes, Seconds
  ! as the equivalent degree measure.
  !
  ! Accepts:  Degrees, Minutes, Seconds
  ! Output:   Values of Degrees, Minutes, and Seconds and the
  !           equivalent degree measure
  !--------------------------------------------------------------
```

Figure 7.1 *(cont.)*

```
SUBROUTINE PrintDegrees(Degrees, Minutes, Seconds)

   INTEGER, INTENT(IN) :: Degrees, Minutes, Seconds

   PRINT 10, Degrees, Minutes, Seconds, &
             REAL(Degrees) + REAL(Minutes)/60.0 + REAL(Seconds)/3600.0
   10 FORMAT (1X, I3, " degrees", I3, " minutes",  I3, " seconds" &
             / 1X, "is equivalent to" / 1X, F7.3, " degrees")

END SUBROUTINE PrintDegrees

END PROGRAM Angles_1
```

Sample run:

```
Enter degrees, minutes, and seconds: 100, 30, 36
100 degrees 30 minutes 36 seconds
is equivalent to
100.510 degrees

More angles (Y or N)? Y
Enter degrees, minutes, and seconds: 360, 0, 0
360 degrees  0 minutes  0 seconds
is equivalent to
360.000 degrees

More angles (Y or N)? Y
Enter degrees, minutes, and seconds: 1, 1, 1
  1 degrees  1 minutes  1 seconds
is equivalent to
  1.017 degrees

More angles (Y or N)? N
```

Example: Displaying an Angle in Degrees–Minutes–Seconds Format

The specification part of subroutine `PrintDegrees` contains only type statements that specify the types of the formal arguments. In general, however, a subroutine's specification part has the same structure as the specification part of a Fortran program and thus may include other declarations. For example, suppose we wish to develop a subroutine `Print_Degrees_Minutes_Seconds` to accept the measure of an angle in either radians or degrees and then display it in a degrees–minutes–seconds format. This subroutine will have two formal arguments: a real argument that is the measure of the angle and a character argument that indicates whether radian measure or degree measure has been used. An appropriate subroutine heading is

```
SUBROUTINE Print_Degrees_Minutes_Seconds (Angle, Measure)
```

where `Angle` will be declared to be of type `REAL` and `Measure` of type `CHARACTER(1)` in the subroutine's specification part. If `Angle` is measured in radians, it will be necessary to find its degree equivalent by multiplying `Angle` by $180/\pi$. Thus we define a real constant `Pi` within the subroutine and declare a real local variable `Angle_in_Degrees` to store this angle. The integer variables `Degrees`, `Minutes`, and `Seconds` are used to store degrees, minutes, and seconds, respectively. Thus the opening documentation, heading, and specification part of this subroutine are as follows; the comments indicate what processing must be done in the body of the subroutine:

```
!-Print_Degrees_Minutes_Seconds---------------------------
! Subroutine to display an angular measurement Angle in
! either radians or degrees in a degrees-minutes-seconds
! format.  Measure is "R" or "D" according to whether
! Angle is given in radians or degrees.  Local
! identifiers used are:
!   Pi                 : the constant pi
!   Angle_in_Degrees : the degree equivalent of Angle
!   Degrees            : the number of degrees
!   Minutes            : the number of minutes
!   Seconds            : the number of seconds
!
! Accepts:  Angle and Measure
! Output:   Value of Angle in degrees-minutes-seconds format
!-----------------------------------------------------------

SUBROUTINE Print_Degrees_Minutes_Seconds(Angle, Measure)

   REAL, INTENT(IN) :: Angle
   CHARACTER(1), INTENT(IN) :: Measure
   REAL :: Angle_in_Degrees
   REAL, PARAMETER :: Pi = 3.141593
   INTEGER :: Degrees, Minutes, Seconds


   ! First get the degree equivalent of the angle


   ! Now determine the number of degrees, minutes, and seconds

END SUBROUTINE Print_Degrees_Minutes_Seconds
```

The complete subroutine `Print_Degrees_Minutes_Seconds` is shown in Figure 7.2. The main program reads values for `Angle` and `Measure` and then passes these values to the formal arguments having the same names in subroutine `Print_Degrees_Minutes_Seconds` by means of the CALL statement

```
CALL Print_Degrees_Minutes_Seconds(Angle, Measure)
```

Note that although in the preceding example we used different names for the actual arguments and the corresponding formal arguments, it is not necessary, as this example illustrates.

Figure 7.2 Displaying an angle in degrees–minutes–seconds format.

```
PROGRAM Angles_2
!-------------------------------------------------------------------
! Program demonstrating the use of an internal subroutine
! Print_Degrees_Minutes_Seconds to display an angle measured in
! radians or degrees in degrees-minutes-seconds format.
! Variables used are:
!     Angle    : angle measurement
!     Measure  : "R" if radian measure, "D" if degree measure
!     Response : user response to more-data question
!
! Input:  Angle, Measure, and Response
! Output: Value in Angle in degrees-minutes-seconds format (displayed
!         by Print_Degrees_Minutes_Seconds)
!-------------------------------------------------------------------

  REAL :: Angle
  CHARACTER(1) :: Measure, Response

  ! Read and convert angles until user signals no more data
  DO
     WRITE (*, '(1X, A)', ADVANCE = "NO") &
           "Enter angle and R if in radians, D if in degrees: "
     READ *, Angle, Measure
     CALL Print_Degrees_Minutes_Seconds(Angle, Measure)
     WRITE (*, '(/ 1X, A)', ADVANCE = "NO") "More angles (Y or N)? "
     READ *, Response
     IF (Response /= "Y") EXIT
  END DO

CONTAINS
```

Figure 7.2 *(cont.)*

```fortran
!-Print_Degrees_Minutes_Seconds------------------------------------
! Subroutine to display an angular measurement Angle in either
! radians or degrees in a degrees-minutes-seconds format.
! Measure is "R" or "D" according to whether Angle is given
! in radians or degrees.  Local identifiers used are:
!   Pi                : the constant pi
!   Angle_in_Degrees : the degree equivalent of Angle
!   Degrees           : the number of degrees
!   Minutes           : the number of minutes
!   Seconds           : the number of seconds
!
! Accepts:  Angle and Measure
! Output:   Value of Angle in degrees-minutes-seconds format
!------------------------------------------------------------------

SUBROUTINE Print_Degrees_Minutes_Seconds(Angle, Measure)

  REAL, INTENT(IN) :: Angle
  CHARACTER(*), INTENT(IN) :: Measure
  REAL :: Angle_in_Degrees
  REAL, PARAMETER :: Pi = 3.141593
  INTEGER :: Degrees, Minutes, Seconds

  ! First get the degree equivalent of the angle

  IF (Measure == "R") THEN
     PRINT 10, Angle, "radians"
     Angle_in_Degrees = (180.0 / Pi) * Angle
  ELSE IF (Measure == "D") THEN
     PRINT 10, Angle, "degrees"
     Angle_in_Degrees = Angle
  ELSE
     PRINT *, Measure, " is an illegal type of measure"
     RETURN
  END IF
10 FORMAT (1X, F10.5, 1X, A / 1X, " is equivalent to")

  ! Now determine the number of degrees, minutes, and seconds

  Degrees = INT(Angle_in_Degrees)
  Angle_in_Degrees = Angle_in_Degrees - REAL(Degrees)
  Degrees = MOD(Degrees, 360)
  Angle_in_Degrees = 60.0 * Angle_in_Degrees
  Minutes = INT(Angle_in_Degrees)
  Angle_in_Degrees = Angle_in_Degrees - REAL(Minutes)
  Seconds = INT(Angle_in_Degrees * 60.0)
```

Figure 7.2 *(cont.)*

```
   PRINT 20, Degrees, Minutes, Seconds
   20 FORMAT (1X, I4, " degrees,", I3, " minutes,", I3, " seconds")

 END SUBROUTINE Print_Degrees_Minutes_Seconds

END PROGRAM Angles_2
```

Sample run:

```
Enter angle and R if in radians, D if in degrees: 3.141593 R
   3.14159 radians
 is equivalent to
 180 degrees,  0 minutes,  0 seconds

More angles (Y or N)? Y
Enter angle and R if in radians, D if in degrees: 555.55 D
 555.54999 degrees
 is equivalent to
 195 degrees, 32 minutes, 59 seconds

More angles (Y or N)? Y
Enter angle and R if in radians, D if in degrees: 1 R
   1.00000 radians
 is equivalent to
  57 degrees, 17 minutes, 44 seconds

More angles (Y or N)? N
```

Example of a Subroutine That Returns Values: Converting Coordinates

The subroutines in the preceding examples do not return values to the main program; they only display the information passed to them. As an illustration of a subroutine that does return values to the main program, consider the problem of converting the polar coordinates (r, θ) of a point P to rectangular coordinates (x, y). The first polar coordinate r is the distance from the origin to P, and the second polar coordinate θ is the angle from the positive x-axis to the ray joining the origin with P.

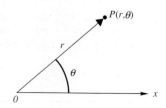

The formulas that relate the polar coordinates to the rectangular coordinates for a point are

$$x = r \cos \theta$$
$$y = r \sin \theta$$

Because the subprogram that performs this conversion must return *two* values (x and y), it is natural to use a subroutine like the following:

```
!-Convert_to_Rectangular------------------------------------
! Subroutine to convert polar coordinates (R, Theta) to
! rectangular coordinates (X, Y).
!
! Accepts:  Polar coordinates R and Theta (in radians)
! Returns:  Rectangular coordinates X and Y
!----------------------------------------------------------

SUBROUTINE Convert_to_Rectangular(R, Theta, X, Y)

   REAL, INTENT(IN) :: R, Theta
   REAL, INTENT(OUT) :: X, Y

   X = R * COS(Theta)
   Y = R * SIN(Theta)

END SUBROUTINE Convert_to_Rectangular
```

The program in Figure 7.3 uses this subroutine to convert polar coordinates to rectangular coordinates. It reads values for RCoord and TCoord, calls the subroutine Convert_to_Rectangular with the statement

```
CALL Convert_to_Rectangular(RCoord, TCoord, XCoord, YCoord)
```

to calculate the corresponding rectangular coordinates XCoord and YCoord, and then displays these coordinates.

Figure 7.3 Converting polar coordinates to rectangular coordinates.

```
PROGRAM Polar_to_Rectangular
!-------------------------------------------------------------------
! This program accepts the polar coordinates of a point and displays
! the corresponding rectangular coordinates.  The internal subroutine
! Convert_to_Rectangular is used to effect the conversion.
! Variables used are:
!   RCoord, TCoord : polar coordinates of a point
!   XCoord, YCoord : rectangular coordinates of a point
!   Response       : user response to more-data question
!
! Input:  RCoord, TCoord, and Response
! Output: XCoord and YCoord
!-------------------------------------------------------------------
```

Figure 7.3 *(cont.)*

```
IMPLICIT NONE
REAL :: RCoord, TCoord, XCoord, YCoord
CHARACTER(1) :: Response

! Read and convert coordinates until user signals no more data
DO
    WRITE (*, '(1X, A)', ADVANCE = "NO") &
          "Enter polar coordinates (in radians): "
    READ *, RCoord, TCoord
    CALL Convert_to_Rectangular(RCoord, TCoord, XCoord, YCoord)
    PRINT *, "Rectangular coordinates:", XCoord, YCoord
    WRITE (*, '(/ 1X, A)', ADVANCE = "NO") &
          "More points to convert (Y or N)? "
    READ *, Response
    IF (Response /= "Y") EXIT
END DO

CONTAINS

  !-Convert_to_Rectangular------------------------------------------
  ! Subroutine to convert polar coordinates (R, Theta) to rectangular
  ! coordinates (X, Y).
  !
  ! Accepts:  Polar coordinates R and Theta (in radians)
  ! Returns:  Rectangular coordinates X and Y
  !-----------------------------------------------------------------

  SUBROUTINE Convert_to_Rectangular(R, Theta, X, Y)

    REAL, INTENT(IN) :: R, Theta
    REAL, INTENT(OUT) :: X, Y

    X = R * COS(Theta)
    Y = R * SIN(Theta)

  END SUBROUTINE Convert_to_Rectangular

END PROGRAM Polar_to_Rectangular
```

Sample run:

```
Enter polar coordinates (in radians): 1.0, 0
Rectangular coordinates:    1.0000000    0.0000000E+00
```

Figure 7.3 *(cont.)*

```
More points to convert (Y or N)? Y
Enter polar coordinates (in radians): 0, 1.0
Rectangular coordinates:    0.0000000E+00    0.0000000E+00

More points to convert (Y or N)? Y
Enter polar coordinates (in radians): 1.0, 1.57
Rectangular coordinates:    7.9627428E-04    0.9999997

More points to convert (Y or N)? Y
Enter polar coordinates (in radians): 4.0, 3.14159
Rectangular coordinates:   -4.0000000    1.0140727E-05

More points to convert (Y or N)? N
```

Argument Association

When the CALL statement

```
CALL Convert_to_Rectangular(RCoord, TCoord, XCoord, YCoord)
```

in the program in Figure 7.3 is executed, the values of the actual arguments RCoord and TCoord are passed to the formal arguments R and Theta, respectively:

Actual Arguments	Formal Arguments
RCoord ⟶	R
TCoord ⟶	Theta
XCoord	X
YCoord	Y

R and Theta have been declared to be IN arguments because the intent is that values are only to be passed to them and used within the subroutine. They are not intended to return new values to the calling program unit, and thus no new values may be assigned to them within the subroutine.

The formal arguments X and Y are declared to have the **INTENT(OUT) attribute** because they are intended only to pass values back to the calling program unit. Thus, after values for X and Y are calculated and execution of the subroutine is complete, these values are passed back to the corresponding actual arguments XCoord and YCoord:

Actual Arguments		Formal Arguments
RCoord	$\longrightarrow$	R
TCoord	$\longrightarrow$	Theta
XCoord	$\longleftarrow$	X
YCoord	$\longleftarrow$	Y

A formal argument may also be declared to have the **INTENT(INOUT)** attribute. Such arguments can be used to pass information both to and from the subroutine:

$$actual\text{-}argument \longleftrightarrow formal\text{-}argument$$

Because both OUT *and* INOUT *arguments are intended to pass values back to the calling program unit, the corresponding actual arguments must be variables.*

For all subprograms, *the number and type of the actual arguments must agree with the number and type of the formal arguments* (except when keyword or optional arguments are used, as described in Section 7.7). Also, if the intent of a dummy argument is not specified, it is treated as though it is an INOUT argument. As we saw in Section 6.1, this may have undesirable consequences.

Quick Quiz 7.1

1. What are the two kinds of Fortran subprograms?

2. List the four parts of a subroutine subprogram.

3. In the subroutine heading SUBROUTINE Display(A, B), A and B are called _____ .

4. List three differences between subroutine subprograms and function subprograms.

Questions 5–10 refer to the following internal subroutine Calculate:

```
SUBROUTINE Calculate(Alpha, Number_1, Number_2)
   REAL, INTENT(IN) :: Alpha
   INTEGER, INTENT(OUT) :: Number_1
   INTEGER, INTENT (INOUT) :: Number_2
      ⋮
   END SUBROUTINE Calculate
```

Also, assume that the following declarations have been made in the main program:

```
          INTEGER :: Code, Id_Number
          REAL :: Rate
```

Tell if the given statement is a valid reference to Calculate.

5. `Rate = Calculate(2.45, Code, Id_Number)`
6. `CALL Calculate(Rate + 0.5, 0, Code 2 Id_Number)`
7. `CALL Calculate(Rate, Id_Number)`
8. `CALL Calculate(Rate, Code, Id_Number)`
9. `CALL Calculate`
10. `CALL Calculate(Rate, Rate, Rate)`
11. What output will the following program produce?

```
PROGRAM Question_11

   IMPLICIT NONE
   CHARACTER(3) :: Str_1 = "cat", Str_2 = "dog", Str_3 = "elk"

   CALL Change(2, Str_1, Str_2, Str_3)
   PRINT *, "String =", Str_1, Str_2, Str_3

CONTAINS
   SUBROUTINE Change(Number, A, B, C)

      INTEGER, INTENT(IN) :: Number
      CHARACTER(3), INTENT(INOUT) :: A, B, C
      CHARACTER(3) :: Bat = "bat"

      IF (Number < 3) THEN
         A = Bat
         B = Bat
      ELSE
         C = Bat
      END IF

   END SUBROUTINE Change

END PROGRAM Question_11
```

Exercises 7.1

1. Write a subroutine that displays the name of a month whose number (1–12) is passed to it.

2. Write a subroutine `Switch` that interchanges the values of two integer variables. For example, if A has the value 3 and B has the value 4, then the statement CALL `Switch(A,  B)` causes A to have the value 4 and B the value 3.

3. Write a subroutine that accepts a measurement in centimeters and returns the corresponding measurement in yards, feet, and inches (1 cm = 0.3937 in).

4. Write a subroutine that accepts a weight in grams and returns the corresponding weight in pounds and ounces (1 g = 0.35274 oz).

5. Write a subroutine that accepts a time in military format and returns the corresponding time in the usual representation in hours, minutes, and A.M./P.M. For example, a time of 100 should be returned as 1 hour, 0 minutes, and AM; a time of 1545 should be returned as 3 hours, 45 minutes, and PM.

6. Write a subroutine that accepts a time in the usual representation in hours, minutes, and one of the strings AM or PM, and returns the corresponding military time. (See Exercise 5.)

7.2 APPLICATION: DESIGNING A COIN DISPENSER

Problem:

An automated cash register accepts two inputs: the amount of a purchase and the amount given as payment. It then computes the number of dollars, quarters, dimes, nickels, and pennies to be given in change. The cashier returns the dollars to the customer, but the coins are returned by an automatic coin dispenser. A subprogram to compute the number of dollars to be returned by the cashier and the number of coins of each denomination to be returned by the coin dispenser must be developed and tested.

Solution

Specification. The subprogram to be developed will accept the purchase amount and the amount paid by the customer and must return the number of dollars and the number of coins of each denomination to be returned to the customer. Thus a specification for this subprogram is

Accepts: The amount of the purchase
            The amount of the payment

Returns: The number of dollars in change
            The number of quarters in change
            The number of dimes in change
            The number of nickels in change
            The number of pennies in change

Since the subprogram must return more than one item, we will design it as a sub-routine rather than as a function.

Design. To determine what sequence of operations is needed to make change, consider a specific example. Suppose the amount of a purchase is $8.49 and the customer pays with a $10 bill. We clearly must begin by subtracting the purchase amount from the payment to get the total amount of change ($1.51). This is a real value, but our return values are integers, and so at some point we must convert this real value to an integer value. Because real values are not stored exactly (e.g., 1.51 might be stored as 1.50999...), it is best to convert the real amount of change (1.51) into an integer value (151) at the outset, ensuring that no significant digits are lost. An initial algorithm for the subroutine follows:

1. Compute the change to be returned in cents.

2. If the change is positive then
   Compute the number of dollars and the number of coins of each denomination to be returned.

   Else do the following:

   a. Display an appropriate message.
   b. Set the number of dollars and the number of coins of each denomination to zero.

Only the first part of step 2 needs to be refined to give a final version of the algorithm. We will use the following variables in our description:

VARIABLES FOR COIN-DISPENSER PROBLEM

Purchase	Amount of purchase
Payment	Amount of payment
Change	Change to be returned (in cents)
Dollars	Number of dollars to be returned
Quarters	Number of quarters to be returned
Dimes	Number of dimes to be returned
Nickels	Number of nickels to be returned
Pennies	Number of pennies to be returned

Once *Change* has been computed as the change in cents, the number of dollars of change can be computed using integer division, dividing the value of *Change* by 100:

$$Dollars = Change \: / \: 100$$

The remaining change is the remainder that results from this division:

$$Change = \text{remainder when } Change \text{ is divided by } 100$$

The number of quarters remaining in *Change* can then be computed in a similar manner by dividing *Change* by 25:

$$Quarters = Change / 25$$

The remainder of this division is then the amount of change remaining to be dispensed as dimes, nickels, and pennies.

$$Change = \text{remainder when } Change \text{ is divided by } 25$$

Similar calculations are used to determine the number of dimes, nickels, and pennies.

A complete algorithm for this problem follows.

ALGORITHM FOR COIN-DISPENSER PROBLEM

This algorithm computes the number of dollars, quarters, dimes, nickels, and pennies needed to make change for a given purchase amount and a given amount paid.

Receive: *Purchase* and *Payment*
Return: *Dollars, Quarters, Dimes, Nickels, Pennies*
Output: Error message if *Payment* < *Purchase*

1. Calculate *Change* = *Payment* − *Purchase* in cents.
2. If *Change* ≥ 0 do the following:

    a. Calculate *Dollars* = *Change* / 100.
    b. Calculate *Change* = remainder when *Change* is divided by 100.
    c. Calculate *Quarters* = *Change* / 25.
    d. Calculate *Change* = remainder when *Change* is divided by 25.
    e. Calculate *Dimes* = *Change* / 10.
    f. Calculate *Change* = remainder when *Change* is divided by 10.
    g. Calculate *Nickels* = *Change* / 5.
    h. Calculate *Pennies* = remainder when *Change* is divided by 5.

Else do the following:

    a. Display an appropriate message.
    b. Return 0 for each of *Dollars, Quarters, Dimes, Nickels,* and *Pennies.*

Coding, Execution, and Testing. The subroutine `Dispense` in Figure 7.4 implements this algorithm.

Figure 7.4 Computing change.

```
!Dispense-------------------------------------------------------------
! Subroutine to compute the dollars, quarters, dimes, nickels, and
! pennies in change given the amount of a purchase and the amount paid
! by the customer.  Local variable used:
!   Change : the amount to be returned in change (in cents)
!
! Accepts: Amount of Purchase and Payment made by customer
! Returns: Dollars, Quarters, Dimes, Nickels, Pennies, the number of
!          dollars, quarters, dimes, nickels, and pennies to be
!          returned in change.
!-------------------------------------------------------------------

SUBROUTINE Dispense(Purchase, Payment, &
                    Dollars, Quarters, Dimes, Nickels, Pennies)

  REAL, INTENT(IN) :: Purchase, Payment
  INTEGER, INTENT(OUT) :: Dollars, Quarters, Dimes, Nickels, Pennies
  INTEGER :: Change

  ! Calculate amount of change in cents
  Change = NINT(100 * (Payment - Purchase))

  IF (Change > 0) THEN
     ! Compute number of dollars
     Dollars = Change / 100
     Change = MOD(Change, 100)

     ! Compute number of quarters
     Quarters = Change / 25
     Change = MOD(Change, 25)

     ! Compute number of dimes
     Dimes = Change / 10
     Change = MOD(Change, 10)

     ! Compute number of nickels and pennies
     Nickels = Change / 5
     Pennies = MOD(Change, 5)
```

Figure 7.4 *(cont.)*

```
    ELSE
        ! Insufficient payment
        PRINT *, "*** Payment too small by", -Change, "cents ***"
        Dollars = 0
        Quarters = 0
        Dimes = 0
        Nickels = 0
        Pennies = 0

    END IF

END SUBROUTINE Dispense
```

        To test this function, we might write a **driver program** that simply reads two amounts, calls the subroutine Dispense to calculate the change that must be given, and then displays the amounts returned by Dispense. Figure 7.5 shows such a driver program and a sample run with several test values.

    Figure 7.5 Making change—driver program.

```
PROGRAM Change_Dispenser
!--------------------------------------------------------------------
! This is a driver program to test subroutine Dispense.  Variables used:
!    ItemCost     : cost of item
!    AmountPaid   : amount paid by customer
!    NumDollars   : number of dollars,
!    NumQuarters  :    quarters,
!    NumDimes     :    dimes,
!    NumNickels   :    nickels,
!    NumPennies   :    pennies   to be returned in change
!    Response     : user response to More data? query
!
! Input : ItemCost and AmountPaid
! Output: Change in dollars, quarters, dimes, nickels, and pennies
!--------------------------------------------------------------------

    IMPLICIT NONE
    REAL :: ItemCost, AmountPaid
    INTEGER :: NumDollars, NumQuarters, NumDimes, NumNickels, NumPennies
    CHARACTER(1) :: Response
```

Figure 7.5 *(cont.)*

```
PRINT *, "This program tests a change-dispensing subroutine."
PRINT *

! Do the following until user indicates no more data
DO
   WRITE (*, '(1X, A)', ADVANCE = "NO") &
          "Enter cost of item and amount paid by customer: "
   READ *, ItemCost, AmountPaid
   CALL Dispense(ItemCost, AmountPaid, &
          NumDollars, NumQuarters, NumDimes, NumNickels, NumPennies)
   PRINT '(1X, A / 6(1X, I3, 1X, A /))', &
             "The change from this purchase is", &
             NumDollars, "Dollars", NumQuarters, "Quarters", &
             NumDimes, "Dimes", NumNickels, "Nickels", &
             NumPennies, "Pennies"
   WRITE (*, '(/ 1X, A)', ADVANCE = "NO") "More data (Y or N)? "
   READ *, Response
   IF (Response /= "Y") EXIT
END DO

CONTAINS

   !----------------------------------------------------------
   !     Insert subroutine Dispense from Figure 7.4 here
   !----------------------------------------------------------


END PROGRAM Change_Dispenser
```

Sample run:

```
This program tests a change-dispensing subroutine.

Enter cost of item and amount paid by customer: 1.01, 2.00
The change from this purchase is
  0 Dollars
  3 Quarters
  2 Dimes
  0 Nickels
  4 Pennies
```

Figure 7.5 *(cont.)*

```
More data (Y or N)? Y
Enter cost of item and amount paid by customer: 1.59, 3.00
The change from this purchase is
  1 Dollars
  1 Quarters
  1 Dimes
  1 Nickels
  1 Pennies


More data (Y or N)? Y
Enter cost of item and amount paid by customer: 1.20, 1.00
*** Payment too small by 20 cents ***
The change from this purchase is
  0 Dollars
  0 Quarters
  0 Dimes
  0 Nickels
  0 Pennies


More data (Y or N)? Y
Enter cost of item and amount paid by customer: .99, 1.00
The change from this purchase is
  0 Dollars
  0 Quarters
  0 Dimes
  0 Nickels
  1 Pennies


More data (Y or N)? N
```

7.3 RANDOM NUMBERS AND SIMULATION

The term **simulation** refers to modeling a dynamic process and using this model to study the behavior of the process. The behavior of some **deterministic** processes can be modeled with an equation or a set of equations. For example, an equation of the form $A(t) = A_0(0.5)^{t/h}$ was used in Section 1.3 to model the radioactive decay of polonium, and a linear system is used in Section 9.7 to model an electrical network. In many problems, the process being studied involves **randomness**, for example, Brownian motion, the arrival of airplanes at an airport, and the number of defective parts a machine manufactures. Computer programs that simulate such processes use random number generators to introduce randomness into the values produced during execution.

Random Number Generators

A **random number generator** is a subprogram that produces a number selected "at random" from some fixed range in such a way that a sequence of these numbers tends to be uniformly distributed over the given range. Although it is not possible to develop an algorithm that produces truly random numbers, there are some methods that produce sequences of **pseudorandom numbers** that are adequate for most purposes. Most of these algorithms have two properties:

1. Some initial value called a **seed** is required to begin the process of generating random numbers. Different seeds will produce different sequences of random numbers.

2. Each random number produced is used in the computation of the next random number.

Fortran 90 provides the subroutine RANDOM_SEED to initialize the random number generator RANDOM_NUMBER, which is a subroutine that produces random real numbers uniformly distributed over the range 0 to 1. The numbers produced by such a generator can be used to generate random real numbers in other ranges or to generate random integers. For example, if RandomNumber is a random number in the range 0 to 1, the value of the expression

```
A + (B - A) * RandomNumber
```

will be a random real number in the range A to B, and the value of the expression

```
M + INT(K * RandomNumber)
```

will be a random integer in the range M through M + K - 1.

Example: Dice Tossing

To illustrate, suppose we wish to model the random process of tossing a pair of dice. Using the preceding expression for generating random integers, we might use the statements

```
Die_1 = 1 + INT(6*R1)
Die_2 = 1 + INT(6*R2)
Pair = Die_1 + Die_2
```

to simulate one roll of two dice, where R1 and R2 are random real numbers in the range 0 to 1. The value of Pair is the total number of dots showing, and the relative frequency of each value from 2 through 12 for Pair should correspond to the probability of that number occurring on one throw of a pair of dice. These probabilities (rounded to three decimal places) are given in the following table:

Outcome	Probability
2	0.028
3	0.056
4	0.083
5	0.111
6	0.139
7	0.167
8	0.139
9	0.111
10	0.083
11	0.056
12	0.028

The program in Figure 7.6 reads an integer indicating the number of times that two dice are to be tossed and then repeatedly asks the user to enter a possible outcome of a roll of the dice and displays the relative frequency of this outcome. For each outcome, a DO loop is used to produce the required number of dice rolls.

Figure 7.6 Dice-roll simulation.

```
PROGRAM Dice_Roll
!-------------------------------------------------------------------
! This program uses a random number generator to simulate rolling a
! pair of dice several times, counting the number of times a specified
! number of spots occurs.  Identifiers used are:
!  Spots     : number of spots to be counted
!  Count     : number of times Spots occurred
!  NumRolls  : number of rolls of dice
!  R1, R2    : two random real numbers in the range 0 to 1
!  Die_1,
!  Die_2     : number of spots on die #1, #2, respectively
!  Pair      : sum of Die_1 and Die_2 = total # of spots on the dice
!  Roll      : counts dice rolls
!  Response  : user response
!
! Input:  NumRolls, Spots, Response
! Output: User prompts, and the relative frequency of the number of
!         spots
!-------------------------------------------------------------------
```

Figure 7.6 *(cont.)*

```
IMPLICIT NONE
INTEGER :: Spots, Count, NumRolls, Die_1, Die_2, Pair, Roll
REAL :: R1, R2
CHARACTER(1) :: Response

WRITE (*, '(1X, A)', ADVANCE = "NO") &
      "Enter number of times to roll the dice: "
READ *, NumRolls

! Seed the random number generator
CALL RANDOM_SEED

! Begin the simulation
DO
   WRITE (*, '(1X, A)', ADVANCE = "NO") &
         "Enter number of spots to count: "
   READ *, Spots
   Count = 0
   DO Roll = 1, NumRolls
      CALL RANDOM_NUMBER(R1)
      CALL RANDOM_NUMBER(R2)
      Die_1 = 1 + INT(6*R1)
      Die_2 = 1 + INT(6*R2)
      Pair = Die_1 + Die_2
      IF (Pair == Spots) Count = Count + 1
   END DO

   PRINT '(1X, "Relative frequency of", I3, " was", F6.3)', &
         Spots,  REAL(Count) / REAL(NumRolls)

   WRITE (*, '(/ 1X, A)', ADVANCE = "NO") "More rolls (Y or N) ? "
   READ *, Response
   IF (Response /= "Y") EXIT
 END DO

END PROGRAM Dice_Roll
```

Sample run:

```
Enter number of times to roll the dice: 1000
Enter number of spots to count: 6
Relative frequency of  6 was 0.128
```

Figure 7.6 *(cont.)*

```
More rolls (Y or N)? Y
Enter number of spots to count: 7
Relative frequency of  7 was 0.148

More rolls (Y or N)? Y
Enter number of spots to count: 11
Relative frequency of 11 was 0.056

More rolls (Y or N)? N
```

Normal Distributions

Most random number generators produce random numbers having a **uniform distribution**, but they can also be used to generate random numbers having other distributions. **Normal distributions** are especially important because they model many physical processes. For example, the heights and weights of people, the lifetime of light bulbs, the tensile strength of steel produced by a machine, and, in general, the variations in parts produced in almost any manufacturing process have normal distributions. Normal distributions have the familiar bell-shaped curve,

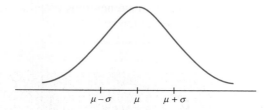

where μ is the mean of the distribution, σ is the standard deviation, and approximately two-thirds of the area under the curve lies between $\mu - \sigma$ and $\mu + \sigma$.

A normal distribution having $\mu = 0$ and $\sigma = 1$ is called a **standard normal distribution**. Random numbers having approximately this distribution can be generated quite easily from a uniform distribution with the following algorithm.

ALGORITHM FOR THE STANDARD NORMAL DISTRIBUTION

This algorithm generates random numbers having an approximate standard normal distribution from a uniform distribution over [0, 1].

1. Set *Sum* equal to 0.

2. Do the following 12 times:

   a. Generate a random number X from a uniform distribution.
   b. Add X to *Sum*.

3. Calculate $Z = Sum - 6$.

The numbers Z generated by this algorithm have an approximate standard normal distribution. To generate random numbers Y having a normal distribution with mean μ and standard deviation σ, we simply add the following step to the algorithm:

4. Calculate $Y = \mu + \sigma * Z$.

Implementing this algorithm as a program is left as an exercise.

7.4 APPLICATION: SHIELDING A NUCLEAR REACTOR

Problem:

When the enriched uranium fuel of a nuclear reactor is burned, high-energy neutrons are produced. Some of these are retained in the reactor core, but most of them escape. Since this radiation is dangerous, the reactor must be shielded. The problem is to simulate neutrons entering the shield and to determine what percentage of them get through it.

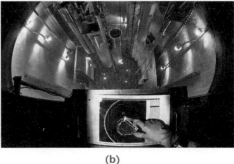

(a)   (b)

Nuclear power plant at Three Mile Island. (Photos courtesy of (a) Phil Degginger/Tony Stone Images, (b) Alexander Tsiaras/Stock Boston)

Solution

Specification. To model the shielding in such a way that we can simulate the paths of neutrons that enter it, we will make the simplifying assumption that neutrons entering the shield follow random paths by moving forward, backward, left, or right with equal likelihood, in jumps of one unit. We will also assume that losses of energy occur only when there is a change of direction, and that after a certain number of such direction changes, the neutron's energy is dissipated and it dies within the shield, provided that it has not already passed back inside the reactor core or outside through the shield.

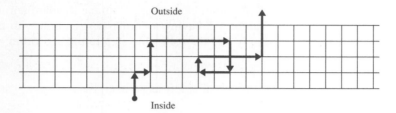

Outside

Inside

Making these simplifying assumptions, we can specify the problem as follows:

Input:	Thickness of the shield Limit on the number of direction changes Number of neutrons
Output:	Percentage of neutrons that reach the outside

Design.   To simulate the paths the neutrons take, we will generate random integers with values 1, 2, 3, or 4, corresponding to movement forward, backward, to the left, or to the right, respectively. If the net movement in the forward direction equals the thickness of the shield, the neutron escapes. If it becomes 0, the neutron returns back inside the reactor. If the number of direction changes reaches a specified limit, the neutron dies within the shield. We repeat this some given number of times and calculate what percentage of neutrons escape.

The following algorithm describes this simulation more precisely. It uses the following variables:

▼

VARIABLES FOR SHIELDING PROBLEM

Thickness	Thickness of shield
DirectionChangeLimit	Limit on number of direction changes (before energy is dissipated)
NewDirection	A random integer 1, 2, 3, or 4 representing direction
OldDirection	Previous direction of neutron
NumDirectionChanges	Number of changes of direction
Forward	Net units traveled in the forward direction
NumNeutrons	Number of neutrons simulated
NumEscaped	Number of neutrons escaping through the shield

ALGORITHM FOR SHIELDING PROBLEM

This algorithm simulates neutrons entering a shield and determines how many reach the outside. The neutrons are assumed to move forward, backward, left, and right with equal likelihood and to die within the shield if a certain number of direction changes occur. A random number generator is assumed.

Input: Thickness of the shield, limit on the number of direction changes, and number of particles

Output: Percentage of particles that reach the outside

1. Read *Thickness*, *DirectionChangeLimit*, and *NumNeutrons*.

2. Initialize *NumEscaped* to 0.

3. Do the following for *I* = 1 to *NumNeutrons*:

   a. Initialize *Forward* to 0, *OldDirection* to 0, and *NumDirectionChanges* to 0.

   b. Repeat the following until particle reaches the outside of the shield (*Forward* ≥ *Thickness*), returns inside the reactor (*Forward* ≤ 0), or dies within the shield (*NumDirectionChanges* ≥ *DirectionChangeLimit*):

      i. Generate a random integer 1, 2, 3, or 4 for the direction *NewDirection*.

      ii. If *NewDirection* ≠ *OldDirection*, increment *NumDirectionChanges* by 1 and set *OldDirection* equal to *NewDirection*.

      iii. If *NewDirection* = 1, increment *Forward* by 1. Else if *NewDirection* = 2, decrement *Forward* by 1.

   c. If *Forward* ≥ *Thickness*, increment *NumEscaped* by 1.

4. Display 100 * *NumEscaped* / *NumNeutrons*.

Coding. The program in Figure 7.7 implements this algorithm. It uses the intrinsic subroutine RANDOM_NUMBER to generate random real numbers in the range 0 to 1, which are then transformed into random integers 1, 2, 3, or 4, corresponding to the four directions forward, backward, left, and right, respectively.

Figure 7.7 Simulate shielding of nuclear reactor.

```
PROGRAM Shielding_a_Nuclear_Reactor
!-----------------------------------------------------------------------
! This program uses a random number generator to simulate neutrons
! entering a shield and to determine what percentage reaches the
! outside.  The neutrons are assumed to move forward, backward, left,
! and right with equal likelihood and to die within the shield if a
! certain number of changes of direction have occurred.  Identifiers
! used are:
!     Thickness            : thickness of shield
!     DirectionChangeLimit : limit on # of direction changes before
!                            energy dissipated
```

Figure 7.7 *(cont.)*

```
!      RandomReal              : a random real number in the range 0 to 1
!      NewDirection            : a random integer 1, 2, 3, or 4
!                                representing direction
!      OldDirection            : previous direction of neutron
!      NumDirectionChanges     : number of changes of direction
!      Forward                 : net units forward traveled
!      NumNeutrons             : number of neutrons simulated
!      NumEscaped              : number of neutrons reaching outside of
!                                shield
!      I                       : loop control variable
!
! Input:   Thickness, DirectionChangeLimit, and NumNeutrons
! Output:  Percentage of neutrons that reach the outside
!-------------------------------------------------------------------------

  IMPLICIT NONE
  REAL :: RandomReal
  INTEGER :: Thickness, DirectionChangeLimit, NewDirection, &
             OldDirection, NumDirectionChanges, Forward, &
             NumNeutrons, NumEscaped, I

  PRINT *, "Enter thickness of shield, limit on # of direction"
  PRINT *, "changes, and the number of neutrons to simulate:"
  READ *, Thickness, DirectionChangeLimit, NumNeutrons

  NumEscaped = 0

  ! Begin the simulation

  CALL RANDOM_SEED
  DO I = 1, NumNeutrons
     Forward = 0
     OldDirection = 0
     NumDirectionChanges = 0

     ! Repeat the following until neutron reaches outside of
     ! shield, returns inside reactor, or dies within shield

     DO
        CALL RANDOM_NUMBER(RandomReal)
        NewDirection = 1 + INT(4 * RandomReal)
        IF (NewDirection /= OldDirection) THEN
           NumDirectionChanges = NumDirectionChanges + 1
           OldDirection = NewDirection
        END IF
```

Figure 7.7 *(cont.)*

```
      IF (NewDirection == 1) THEN
         Forward = Forward + 1
      ELSE IF (NewDirection == 2) THEN
         Forward = Forward - 1
      END IF
      IF ((Forward >= Thickness) .OR. (Forward <= 0) .OR.  &
          (NumDirectionChanges >= DirectionChangeLimit)) EXIT
   END DO

   IF (Forward >= Thickness)  NumEscaped = NumEscaped + 1

 END DO

 PRINT '(1X, F5.2, "% of the neutrons escaped")', &
       100 * REAL(NumEscaped) / REAL(NumNeutrons)

END PROGRAM Shielding_a_Nuclear_Reactor
```

Execution and Testing. The following are four sample runs of the program. The first two are test runs. In the first test case, the neutron will move only once, since each first move is interpreted as a change of direction and the limit on the number of direction changes is 1. Since each of the four possible moves is equally likely, we would expect 25 percent of the neutrons to escape, and the result produced by the program is consistent with this value. In the second test case, the shielding is 100 units thick and the limit on the number of direction changes is small. Thus we expect almost none of the neutrons to escape through the shield.

Sample run #1:

```
Enter thickness of shield, limit on # of direction
changes, and the number of neutrons to simulate:
1, 1, 1000
25.80% of the neutrons escaped
```

Sample run #2:

```
Enter thickness of shield, limit on # of direction
changes, and the number of neutrons to simulate:
100 5 1000
 0.00% of the neutrons escaped
```

Sample run #3:

```
Enter thickness of shield, limit on # of direction
changes, and the number of neutrons to simulate:
4, 5, 100
 3.00% of the neutrons escaped
```

Sample run #4:

```
Enter thickness of shield, limit on # of direction
changes, and the number of neutrons to simulate:
8, 10, 500
 0.20% of the neutrons escaped
```

7.5 APPLICATION: CHECKING ACADEMIC STANDING

Top-Down Design

At several places in this text we have indicated that large and complex problems can best be solved using **top-down design.** In this approach, a **divide-and-conquer** strategy is used to divide the original problem into simpler subproblems. Each of these subproblems can then be solved independently, perhaps using this same divide-and-conquer strategy to divide them into still simpler subproblems. This refinement process continues until the subproblems are simple enough that algorithms can be easily developed to solve them. Subprograms are then written to implement these algorithms, and these subprograms are combined with a main program into a complete program that solves the original problem. Because this software engineering technique is so important and because we have now considered subprograms in some detail, we will now illustrate this technique by solving a relatively complex problem.

PROBLEM:

Problem

Suppose that the engineering department at a certain university wants a program to determine the academic standing of its students. The academic standing of each student is to be checked at the end of each of the first three years of the student's academic career and is based on two criteria: the number of hours that the student has successfully completed and his or her cumulative grade point average (GPA). To be in good standing, the student must have completed at least 25 hours with a minimum GPA of 1.7 by the end of the first year. At the end of the second year, 50 hours must have been completed with a cumulative GPA of 1.85 or higher, and at the end of the third year, 85 hours must have been completed with a minimum cumulative GPA of 1.95.

Solution

The program should display the student's ID number, class level, cumulative hours, GPA for the current year, and cumulative GPA, as well as an indication of his or her academic standing. At the end of this report, the program should also display the total number of students processed, the number who are in good standing, and the average current GPA for all students. The information to be supplied to the program is the student's ID number, class level, hours accumulated, cumulative GPA, and hours and grades for courses taken during the current year. Thus, we have the following input and output specifications for this problem:

Input: Student's ID number
    Class level (1, 2, or 3)
    Cumulative hours
    Cumulative GPA
    Hours and grade for each course completed in the current year

Output: Student's ID number
    Class level
    Current GPA
    Updated cumulative hours and cumulative GPA
    Indication of academic standing
    Number of students processed
    Number of students in good standing
    Average of all current GPAs

Using top-down design to develop this program, we begin by identifying three main tasks needed to solve it, describing them in fairly general terms:

1. *Inform.* Since the program will be used by personnel who are generally not regular users of a computer system, some instructions must be displayed each time the program is used.

2. *Process.* The second task is to accept the given information for each student, calculate the relevant statistics, and determine eligibility.

3. *WrapUp.* The final task is to generate and display the desired summary statistics after all the student information has been processed.

It is helpful to display these tasks and their relationship to one another in a **structure diagram** like the following:

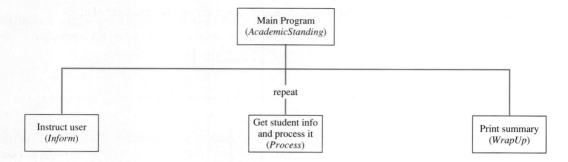

Typically, one or more of these first-level tasks are still quite complex and so must be divided into subtasks. In this example, the tasks *Inform* and *WrapUp* are straightforward, but the task *Process*, which is central to the entire program, is more complicated and requires further analysis. We can identify three main subtasks in *Process*:

1. *CalculateStats*. Read information about a student and calculate relevant statistics.
2. *CheckEligibility*. Determine a student's eligibility based on the statistics calculated in *CalculateStats*.
3. *Report*. Report information about a student, including eligibility status.

The following refinement of the earlier structure diagram summarizes this analysis:

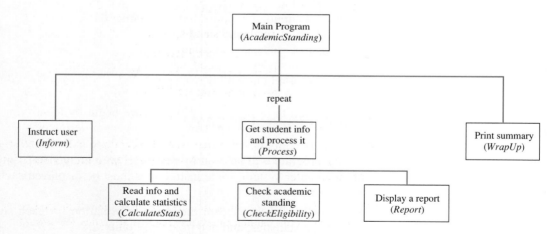

A student's eligibility is based on two criteria: an hours condition and a GPA condition. This means that two subtasks of *CheckEligibility* can be identified:

1. *HoursCheck*. Check if a student's cumulative hours satisfy the hours condition.
2. *GPACheck*. Check if a student's cumulative GPA satisfies the GPA condition.

The final refinement of the structure diagram for the program thus is

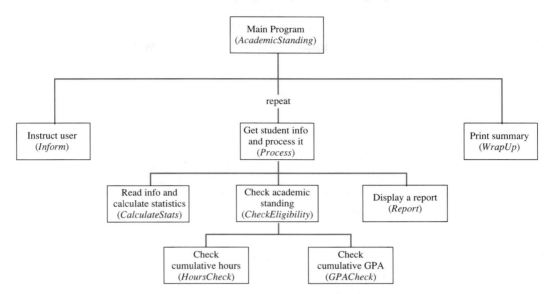

The next step is to develop algorithms for each of these tasks and subtasks. We begin with an algorithm for the main program.

VARIABLES FOR MAIN PROGRAM

NumStudents	Total number of students
Num_in_Good_Standing	Number in good standing
Response	User response to more-data query
Sum_of_GPAs	Sum of all current GPAs

ALGORITHM FOR MAIN PROGRAM

Determine academic eligibility of individual students according to two criteria—cumulative hours and cumulative GPA—and display several summary statistics for all students processed.

Input: For each of several students, the student's number, class level, cumulative hours, cumulative GPA, hours and grades for current courses; also, user responses to "More data?" query

Output: For each student, the student's number, class level, current GPA, updated cumulative hours and cumulative GPA, and an indication of eligibility; also, a summary report showing the number of students processed, number who are eligible, and average of all current GPAs

1. Call subalgorithm *Inform*.
2. Initialize *NumStudents*, *Num_in_Good_Standing*, and *Sum_of_GPAs* to 0.
3. Repeat the following until user indicates no more data:
   a. Call subalgorithm *Process*.
   b. Ask user if there is more data.
4. Call *WrapUp*.

The three tasks we have identified can be implemented as three subroutines, In-form, Process, and WrapUp. Since the procedure Inform simply displays instructions to the user, it requires no information from other program units and thus has no formal arguments. The subroutine WrapUp, which prints the summary, requires the total number of students (NumStudents), the total number who are in good standing (Num_in_Good_Standing), and the sum of all the current GPAs (Sum_of_GPAs). These values must be calculated by the subroutine Process and shared with WrapUp. Thus, the main program has the form

```fortran
PROGRAM Academic_Standing

    IMPLICIT NONE
    INTEGER :: NumStudents = 0, Num_in_Good_Standing = 0
    REAL :: Sum_of_GPAs = 0.0
    CHARACTER(1) :: Response

    CALL Inform

    ! Repeat the following until no more data
    DO
        CALL Process(NumStudents, Num_in_Good_Standing, Sum_of_GPAs)
        WRITE (*, '(// 1X, A)', ADVANCE = "NO") "More (Y or N)? "
        READ *, Response
        IF (Response /= "Y") EXIT
    END DO

    CALL WrapUp(NumStudents, Num_in_Good_Standing, Sum_of_GPAs)

CONTAINS

    ! Subprograms must be inserted here

END PROGRAM Academic_Standing
```

Next we must develop the three subroutines Inform, Process, and WrapUp. Since Process is central to the entire program, we will consider it first:

VARIABLES FOR Process

NumStudents, *Num_in_Good_Standing*, and *Sum_of_GPAs* as in main algorithm

StudentNumber:	Student's number
Class:	Student's class
CumulativeHours:	Student's cumulative hours
CumulativeGPA:	Student's cumulative GPA
CurrentGPA:	Student's current GPA
InGoodStanding:	Indicates whether student is in good standing

ALGORITHM FOR Process

Read student information, determine eligibility, and maintain counts of the number of students processed and the number eligible, and a sum of current GPAs.

Accepts: *NumStudents*, *Num_in_Good_Standing*, and *Sum_of_GPAs*
Returns: Updated values of *NumStudents*, *Num_in_Good_Standing*, and *Sum_of_GPAs*

1. Call subalgorithm *CalculateStats* to get values for *StudentNumber*, *Class*, *CumulativeHours*, *CumulativeGPA*, and *CurrentGPA*.

2. Call subalgorithm *CheckEligibility* to get value for *InGoodStanding*.

3. Call subalgorithm *Report* to display information about student.

The three second-level subtasks of Process can be implemented as subroutines CalculateStats, CheckEligibility, and Report. An algorithm for CalculateStats is as follows:

VARIABLES FOR CalculateStats

NumStudents, *Sum_of_GPAs* as in main algorithm

StudentNumber, *Class*, *CumulativeHours*, *CumulativeGPA*, *CurrentGPA* as in
   Process

Hours, *Grade*:	Student's hours and grade for a current course
NewHours:	Total hours earned in current year
NewHonorPoints:	Honor points earned in current year
OldHonorPoints:	Honor points earned in past years

ALGORITHM FOR `CalculateStats`

Read information about a student and calculate current GPA, updated cumulative hours, cumulative GPA, count of students processed, and sum of cumulative GPAs for all students.

Accepts: *NumStudents* and *Sum_of_GPAs*
Input: *StudentNumber*, *Class*, *CumulativeHours*, *CumulativeGPA*,
                Hours and *Grade* for each current course
Returns: *StudentNumber*, *Class*, *CumulativeHours*, *CumulativeGPA*,
                CurrentGPA, updated values of *NumStudents* and *Sum_of_GPAs*

1. Read *StudentNumber*, *Class*, *CumulativeHours*, and *CumulativeGPA* for student.
2. Calculate the number of honor points the student already has earned:

$$OldHonorPoints = CumulativeHours * CumulativeGPA$$

3. Initialize *NewHours* and *NewHonorPoints* to 0.
4. Repeat the following:

    a. Read *Hours* of credit and numeric *Grade* for a course taken by student.
    b. If the end-of-data flag has been read, terminate the repetition.
       Otherwise continue with the following:
    c. Add *Hours* to *NewHours*.
    d. Add *Hours* * *Grade* to *NewHonorPoints*.

5. Calculate student's current GPA (*CurrentGPA*): 0 if student took no new courses; else

$$CurrentGPA = \frac{NewHonorPoints}{NewHours}$$

6. Update cumulative hours for student by adding *NewHours* to *CumulativeHours*.
7. Calculate student's cumulative GPA:

$$CumulativeGPA = \frac{OldHonorPoints + NewHonorPoints}{CumulativeHours}$$

8. Increment *NumStudents* by 1 and add *CurrentGPA* to *Sum_of_GPAs*.

Implementing the algorithm for `CalculateStats` as a subroutine is straightforward. Note that `StudentNumber`, `Class`, `CumulativeHours`, `CumulativeGPA`, `CurrentGPA`, `NumStudents`, and `Sum_of_GPAs` will be arguments of `CalculateStats` since they must be shared with other program units.

Once the subroutine `CalculateStats` has been written, it can be incorporated into the total program and tested before the other subprograms are developed, as shown in Figure 7.8. We simply insert output statements in the undeveloped subprograms to signal when they are called. In this program, the execution parts of subroutines `Inform`, `WrapUp`, and `CheckEligibility` contain **program stubs** to signal their execution, and `Report` and `WrapUp` produce temporary outputs to enable us to verify the correctness of `CalculateStats`. The subroutine `CalculateStats` is in its final form, as is the main program.

Figure 7.8 Academic standing—version 1.

```
PROGRAM Academic_Standing
!-----------------------------------------------------------------------
! Program to determine academic standing of engineering students
! according to two criteria:  cumulative hours and cumulative GPA.
! It also counts the total # of students checked and the # found to
! be in good standing, and calculates the average current GPA for all
! students.  Variables used are:
!   NumStudents              : total number of students
!   Num_in_Good_Standing     : number in good standing
!   Response                 : user response to more-data inquiry
!   Sum_of_GPAs              : sum of all current GPAs
!
! Input:  Response; also several items of student information in
!         subroutine CalculateStats
! Output: Student report by subroutine Report and summary statistics
!         by subroutine WrapUp
!-----------------------------------------------------------------------

  IMPLICIT NONE
  INTEGER :: NumStudents = 0, Num_in_Good_Standing = 0
  REAL :: Sum_of_GPAs = 0.0
  CHARACTER(1) :: Response

  CALL Inform

  ! Repeat the following until no more data
  DO
     CALL Process(NumStudents, Num_in_Good_Standing, Sum_of_GPAs)
     WRITE (*, '(// 1X, A)', ADVANCE = "NO") "More (Y or N)? "
     READ *, Response
     IF (Response /= "Y") EXIT
  END DO

  CALL WrapUp(NumStudents, Num_in_Good_Standing, Sum_of_GPAs)

CONTAINS
```

Figure 7.8 *(cont.)*

```
!-Inform-----------------------------------------------------------

SUBROUTINE Inform

  PRINT *, "*********** Inform called ***********"

END SUBROUTINE Inform


!--Process---------------------------------------------------------
! Accepts student information, determines academic standing, and
! maintains counts of # processed and # in good standing, and a sum
! of current GPAs.  Variables used are:
!    NumStudents          : total number of students
!    Num_in_Good_Standing : number in good standing
!    Sum_of_GPAs          : sum of all current GPAs
!    StudentNumber        : student's number
!    Class                : student's class
!    CumulativeHours      : student's cumulative hours
!    CumulativeGPA        : student's cumulative GPA
!    CurrentGPA           : student's current GPA
!    InGoodStanding       : indicates whether student is in good
!                           standing
!
! Accepts:  NumStudents, Num_in_Good_Standing, and Sum_of_GPAs
! Returns:  Updated values of NumStudents, Num_in_Good_Standing, and
!           Sum_of_GPAs
!------------------------------------------------------------------

SUBROUTINE Process(NumStudents, Num_in_Good_Standing, Sum_of_GPAs)

  INTEGER, INTENT(INOUT) :: NumStudents, Num_in_Good_Standing
  REAL, INTENT(INOUT) :: Sum_of_GPAs
  REAL :: CumulativeHours, CumulativeGPA, CurrentGPA
  INTEGER :: StudentNumber, Class
  LOGICAL :: InGoodStanding

  CALL CalculateStats(StudentNumber, Class, NumStudents, &
                      CumulativeHours, CumulativeGPA, CurrentGPA,  &
                      Sum_of_GPAs)
  CALL CheckEligibility
  CALL Report(StudentNumber, Class, CumulativeHours, CurrentGPA, &
              CumulativeGPA)

END SUBROUTINE Process
```

Figure 7.8 *(cont.)*

```fortran
!-WrapUp-------------------------------------------------------------

SUBROUTINE WrapUp(NumStudents, Num_in_Good_Standing, Sum_of_GPAs)

  INTEGER, INTENT(IN) ::  NumStudents, Num_in_Good_Standing
  REAL, INTENT(IN) :: Sum_of_GPAs

  PRINT *, "*********** WrapUp called ***********"
  PRINT *, "Number of Students =", NumStudents
  PRINT *, "Sum of GPAs =", Sum_of_GPAs

END SUBROUTINE WrapUp

!-CalculateStats----------------------------------------------------
! Subroutine to read a student's number, class, cumulative hours,
! and cumulative GPA; then read Hours and Grade for courses taken
! during the current year; calculate current GPA and update
! cumulative hours, cumulative GPA, and count (NumStudents) of
! students processed.  Hours = 0 and Grade = 0 are used to signal the
! end of data for a student.  Other local variables used are:
!   NewHours       : total hours earned during current year
!   NewHonorPoints : honor points earned in current year
!   OldHonorPoints : honor points earned in past years
!
! Accepts:  NumStudents and Sum_of_GPAs
! Input:    StudentNumber, Class, CumulativeHours, CumulativeGPA;
!           also Hours and Grade for each of several courses
! Returns:  StudentNumber, Class, CumulativeHours, CumulativeGPA,
!           CurrentGPA and updated values of NumStudents and
!           Sum_of_GPAs
!-------------------------------------------------------------------

SUBROUTINE CalculateStats(StudentNumber, Class, NumStudents,  &
                          CumulativeHours, CumulativeGPA, &
                          CurrentGPA, Sum_of_GPAs)

  INTEGER, INTENT(INOUT) ::  NumStudents
  INTEGER, INTENT(OUT) :: StudentNumber, Class
  REAL, INTENT(INOUT) :: Sum_of_GPAs
  REAL, INTENT(OUT) :: CumulativeHours, CumulativeGPA, CurrentGPA
  REAL :: Hours, Grade, NewHours, NewHonorPoints, OldHonorPoints
```

Figure 7.8 *(cont.)*

```fortran
      WRITE (*, '(1X, A)', ADVANCE = "NO") &
            "Enter student number, class, cum. hours, cum. GPA: "
      READ *, StudentNumber, Class, CumulativeHours, CumulativeGPA
      OldHonorPoints = CumulativeHours * CumulativeGPA
      NewHours = 0.0
      NewHonorPoints = 0.0

      DO
         WRITE (*, '(1X, A)', ADVANCE = "NO") "Hours and grade? "
         READ *, Hours, Grade
         IF (Hours <= 0.0) EXIT
         ! Terminate repetition if end-of-data signaled
         ! Otherwise continue with the following

         NewHours = NewHours + Hours
         NewHonorPoints = NewHonorPoints + Hours * Grade
      END DO

      IF (NewHours == 0.0) THEN
         CurrentGPA = 0.0
      ELSE
         CurrentGPA = NewHonorPoints / NewHours
      END IF
      CumulativeHours = CumulativeHours + NewHours
      CumulativeGPA = (OldHonorPoints + NewHonorPoints) / CumulativeHours
      NumStudents = NumStudents + 1
      Sum_of_GPAs = Sum_of_GPAs + CurrentGPA

END SUBROUTINE CalculateStats

!-CheckEligibility----------------------------------------------------

SUBROUTINE CheckEligibility

   PRINT *, "*********** CheckEligibility called ***********"

END SUBROUTINE CheckEligibility

!-Report-------------------------------------------------------------

SUBROUTINE Report(StudentNumber, Class, CumulativeHours, &
                  CurrentGPA, CumulativeGPA)
```

Figure 7.8 *(cont.)*

```
    INTEGER, INTENT(IN) :: StudentNumber, Class
    REAL, INTENT(IN) :: CumulativeHours, CurrentGPA, CumulativeGPA

    PRINT *, "*********** Report called ***********"

    !----- Temporary printout -----
    PRINT *, "StudentNumber:", StudentNumber
    PRINT *, "Class:          ", Class
    PRINT *, "Cum. Hours:  ", CumulativeHours
    PRINT *, "Curr. GPA:   ", CurrentGPA
    PRINT *, "Cum. GPA:    ", CumulativeGPA

  END SUBROUTINE Report

END PROGRAM Academic_Standing
```

Sample run:

```
*********** Inform called ***********
Enter student number, class, cum. hours, cum. GPA: 1234, 1, 0, 0
Hours and grade? 5, 3.0
Hours and grade? 4, 3.0
Hours and grade? 3.5, 3.0
Hours and grade? 4, 3.0
Hours and grade? 3, 3.0
Hours and grade? 2, 3.0
Hours and grade? 0, 0
*********** CheckEligibility called ***********
*********** Report called ***********
StudentNumber: 1234
Class:         1
Cum. Hours:    21.5000000
Curr. GPA:      3.0000000
Cum. GPA:       3.0000000

More (Y or N)? Y
Enter student number, class, cum. hours, cum. GPA: 55555, 5, 10, 0
Hours and grade? 3, 3.0
Hours and grade? 0, 0
*********** CheckEligibility called ***********
```

Figure 7.8 *(cont.)*

```
*********** Report called ***********
StudentNumber: 55555
Class:         5
Cum. Hours:    13.0000000
Curr. GPA:      3.0000000
Cum. GPA:       0.6923077

More (Y or N)? N
*********** WrapUp called ***********
Number of Students = 2
Sum of GPAs =    6.0000000
```

The sample run in the preceding figure is part of the testing that must be done to ensure that the procedure `CalculateStats` is correct. Such **unit testing** should be performed on each subprogram as it is developed and added to the program. When a subprogram has been thoroughly tested, we can proceed to develop and test other subprograms. This process continues until all of the algorithms in the design plan have been coded, tested, and added to the program.

In this example, once we are convinced of the correctness of `Calculate-Stats`, we may turn to developing the other subprograms. An algorithm for `CheckEligibility` is as follows:

▼▼▼───

VARIABLES FOR `CheckEligibility`

InGoodStanding and *Num_in_Good_Standing* as in main algorithm

Class, *CumulativeHours*, *CumulativeGPA*, *CurrentGPA* as in *Process*

SUBALGORITHM `CheckEligibility`

Check if student's cumulative hours and cumulative GPA satisfy the hours and GPA conditions for good academic standing.

Accepts: A student's *Class*, *CumulativeHours*, *CumulativeGPA*, *Num_in_Good_Standing*

Returns: Student's eligibility status (*InGoodStanding*)
           Updated value of *Num_in_Good_Standing*

Output: Message indicating an illegal class code

If *Class* is not one of 1, 2, or 3 then
    Display an illegal-class-code message and set *InGoodStanding* to false
Else do the following:

1. Call subalgorithm *HoursCheck* to determine whether student satisfies the hours condition for good standing.

2. Call subalgorithm *GPACheck* to determine whether student satisfies the GPA condition for good standing.

3. If student is in good standing, increment *Num_in_Good_Standing* by 1.

The subtasks *HoursCheck* and *GPACheck* can be conveniently implemented as logical-valued functions `HoursCheck` and `GPACheck`, which return the value `.TRUE.` or `.FALSE.`, depending on whether the student satisfies the corresponding criteria to be in good standing. Algorithms for these functions are as follows:

VARIABLES FOR `HoursCheck`

Class and *CumulativeHours* as in *Process*

ALGORITHM FOR `HoursCheck`

Check if student satisfies the hours condition for good standing.

Accepts: A student's *Class* and *CumulativeHours*
Returns: True if student meets the hours criterion, and false otherwise

If *Class* = 1 then
  Set *HoursCheck* to true if *CumulativeHours* ≥ hours required for freshman good standing and to false otherwise.
Else if *Class* = 2 then
  Set *HoursCheck* to true if *CumulativeHours* ≥ hours required for sophomore good standing and to false otherwise.
Else
  Set *HoursCheck* to true if *CumulativeHours* ≥ hours required for junior good standing and to false otherwise.

VARIABLES FOR `GPACheck`

Class and *CumulativeGPA* as in *Process*

ALGORITHM FOR `GPACheck`

Check if student satisfies the GPA condition for good standing.

Accepts: A student's *Class* and *CumulativeGPA*
Returns: True if student meets the GPA criterion, and false otherwise

> If *Class* = 1 then
>> Set *GPACheck* to true if *CumulativeGPA* ≥ GPA required for freshman good standing and to false otherwise.
>
> Else if *Class* = 2 then
>> Set *GPACheck* to true if *CumulativeGPA* ≥ GPA required for sophomore good standing and to false otherwise.
>
> Else
>> Set *GPACheck* to true if *CumulativeGPA* ≥ GPA required for junior good standing and to false otherwise.

Replacing the temporary version of `CheckEligibility` in the preceding program and adding the functions `HoursCheck` and `GPACheck` produce the refined program in Figure 7.9. Note that we have also modified the temporary version of `Report` and the reference to it in order to display the value of `InGoodStanding` and the temporary version of `WrapUp` to display `Num_in_Good_Standing`, the number of students in good standing.

Figure 7.9 Academic standing—version 2.

```
PROGRAM Academic_Standing
          ⋮
CONTAINS

   !-Inform--------------------------------------------------------------
          ⋮
   SUBROUTINE Process(NumStudents, Num_in_Good_Standing, Sum_of_GPAs)
          ⋮
     CALL CalculateStats(StudentNumber, Class, NumStudents, &
                          CumulativeHours, CumulativeGPA, CurrentGPA, &
                          Sum_of_GPAs)
     CALL CheckEligibility(Class, CumulativeHours, CumulativeGPA, &
                           InGoodStanding, Num_in_Good_Standing)
     CALL Report(StudentNumber, Class, CumulativeHours, CurrentGPA, &
                 CumulativeGPA, InGoodStanding)
          ⋮
   !-WrapUp--------------------------------------------------------------
          ⋮
     PRINT *, "Number in good standing =", Num_in_Good_Standing
          ⋮
   !-CalculateStats-----------------------------------------------------
          ⋮
```

Figure *7.9* (cont.)

```fortran
!-CheckEligibility------------------------------------------------------
! Subroutine to check academic standing.  Two criteria are used:
! cumulative hours and cumulative GPA.  Functions HoursCheck and
! GPACheck are used to check these.  Class, CumulativeHours, and
! CumulativeGPA are the class, cumulative hours, and cumulative GPA
! for the student being checked.  InGoodStanding is true or false
! according to whether or not the student is found to be in good
! standing, and Num_in_Good_Standing is the count of students who
! are in good standing.
!
! Accepts:  Class, CumulativeHours, CumulativeGPA, and
!           Num_in_Good_Standing
! Returns:  InGoodStanding and updated value of Num_in_Good_Standing
! Output:   Message indicating an illegal class code
!-----------------------------------------------------------------------

SUBROUTINE CheckEligibility(Class, CumulativeHours, CumulativeGPA, &
                            InGoodStanding, Num_in_Good_Standing)

   INTEGER, INTENT(IN) :: Class
   INTEGER, INTENT(INOUT) :: Num_in_Good_Standing
   REAL, INTENT(IN) :: CumulativeHours, CumulativeGPA
   LOGICAL, INTENT(OUT) :: InGoodStanding

   IF ((Class < 1) .OR. (Class > 3)) THEN
      PRINT *, "*** Illegal class code ***"
      InGoodStanding = .FALSE.
   ELSE
      InGoodStanding = HoursCheck(Class, CumulativeHours) .AND. &
                       GPACheck(Class, CumulativeGPA)
   END IF

   IF (InGoodStanding) Num_in_Good_Standing = Num_in_Good_Standing + 1

END SUBROUTINE CheckEligibility

!-Report----------------------------------------------------------------

SUBROUTINE Report(StudentNumber, Class, CumulativeHours, &
                  CurrentGPA, CumulativeGPA, InGoodStanding)
            ⋮
```

Figure 7.9 *(cont.)*

```
    LOGICAL, INTENT(IN) :: InGoodStanding
              ⋮
    PRINT *, "Good standing: ", InGoodStanding


END SUBROUTINE Report


!-HoursCheck------------------------------------------------------------
! Check cumulative hours (CumulativeHours) of student in Class.  Local
! constants Freshman_Hours, Sophomore_Hours, and Junior_Hours give
! the minimum number of hours required of freshmen, sophomores, and
! juniors, respectively.
! Accepts: Class and CumulativeHours
! Returns: True or false according to whether student has accumulated
!          enough hours
!----------------------------------------------------------------------


FUNCTION HoursCheck(Class, CumulativeHours)

    LOGICAL :: HoursCheck
    INTEGER, INTENT(IN) :: Class
    REAL, INTENT(IN) ::  CumulativeHours
    REAL, PARAMETER :: Freshman_Hours = 25.0, Sophomore_Hours = 50.0, &
                       Junior_Hours = 85.0

    IF (Class == 1) THEN
       HoursCheck = (CumulativeHours >= Freshman_Hours)
    ELSE IF (Class == 2) THEN
       HoursCheck = (CumulativeHours >= Sophomore_Hours)
    ELSE
       HoursCheck = (CumulativeHours >= Junior_Hours)
    END IF

END FUNCTION HoursCheck


!-GPACheck--------------------------------------------------------------
! Check cumulative GPA of student in Class. Local constants
! Freshman_GPA, Sophomore_GPA, and Junior_GPA give the minimum
! GPA required of freshmen, sophomores, and juniors, respectively.
!
! Accepts: Class and CumulativeGPA
! Returns: True or false according to whether student's GPA is high
!          enough
!----------------------------------------------------------------------
```

Figure 7.9 *(cont.)*

```
FUNCTION GPACheck(Class, CumulativeGPA)

   LOGICAL :: GPACheck
   INTEGER, INTENT(IN) :: Class
   REAL, INTENT(IN) :: CumulativeGPA
   REAL, PARAMETER :: Freshman_GPA = 1.7, Sophomore_GPA = 1.85, &
                      Junior_GPA = 1.95

   IF (Class == 1) THEN
      GPACheck = (CumulativeGPA >= Freshman_GPA)
   ELSE IF (Class == 2) THEN
      GPACheck = (CumulativeGPA >= Sophomore_GPA)
   ELSE
      GPACheck = (CumulativeGPA >= Junior_GPA)
   END IF

END FUNCTION GPACheck

END PROGRAM Academic_Standing
```

Sample run:

```
*********** Inform called ***********
Enter student number, class, cum. hours, cum. GPA: 1234, 1, 0, 0
Hours and grade? 5, 3.0
Hours and grade? 4, 3.0
Hours and grade? 3.5, 3.0
Hours and grade? 4, 3.0
Hours and grade? 3, 3.0
Hours and grade? 2, 3.0
Hours and grade? 0, 0
*********** Report called ***********
StudentNumber: 1234
Class:          1
Cum. Hours:    21.5000000
Curr. GPA:      3.0000000
Cum. GPA:       3.0000000
Good standing: F

More (Y or N)? Y
Enter student number, class, cum. hours, cum. GPA: 55555, 5, 10, 0
Hours and grade? 3, 3.0
Hours and grade? 0, 0
*** Illegal class code ***
```

Figure 7.9 *(cont.)*

```
*********** Report called ***********
StudentNumber:  55555
Class:  5
Cum. Hours:    13.0000000
Curr. GPA:      3.0000000
Cum. GPA:       0.6923077
Good standing: F


More (Y or N)? N
*********** WrapUp called ***********
Number of Students = 2
Number in good standing = 0
Sum of GPAs =    6.0000000
```

Testing the newly added subprograms indicates that they are correct. Thus we can proceed to develop algorithms for the remaining subtasks, Report, Inform, and WrapUp :

VARIABLES FOR Report

StudentNumber, Class, CumulativeHours, CumulativeGPA, InGoodStanding as in *Process*

ALGORITHM FOR Report

Display statistics and eligibility status for a given student.

Accepts: Student's *StudentNumber, Class, CumulativeHours, CurrentGPA, CumulativeGPA,* and *InGoodStanding*

Output: *StudentNumber, Class, CumulativeHours, CurrentGPA, CumulativeGPA,* and a message indicating whether student is in good standing

A series of output statements to display the required information in an acceptable format.

VARIABLES FOR Inform

None

ALGORITHM FOR Inform

Display instructions to the user.

Output: User instructions

A series of output statements that inform the user of the purpose of the program and provide instructions for entering the data.

VARIABLES FOR WrapUp

NumStudents, *Num_in_Good_Standing*, *Sum_of_GPAs* as in main algorithm

ALGORITHM FOR WrapUp

Display summary statistics.

Accepts: *NumStudents*, *Num_in_Good_Standing*, and *Sum_of_GPAs*
Output: Number of students processed, average current GPA for all
            students, and the number found to be eligible

1. Display *NumStudents*.
2. If *NumStudents* is not zero
    a. Calculate and display the average current GPA for all students.
    b. Display *Num_in_Good_Standing*.

We write and test each of these subprograms and add them to the program, producing the final version of the program shown in Figure 7.10. Each of the subprograms was tested as it was developed and added to the program. Although each was tested individually, it must also be verified that these subprograms were integrated into the program correctly, that is, that they interact with one another correctly, passing the required information to and from one another. This is called **integration testing**.

When all of the subprograms have been developed and integrated into the program, the complete program should be tested to determine that the overall system functions correctly. This is known as **system testing.**

Figure 7.10 Academic standing—version 3.

```
PROGRAM Academic_Standing
        ⋮
CONTAINS

    !-Inform----------------------------------------------------------
    ! Subroutine to display instructions to the user.
    ! Output:  Several lines of instructions
    !-----------------------------------------------------------------
```

Figure 7.10 *(cont.)*

```
SUBROUTINE Inform
  PRINT *, "You will first be asked to enter the student's number,"
  PRINT *, "class, cumulative hours, and cumulative GPA.  Enter these"
  PRINT *, "with at least one space or comma separating them."
  PRINT *
  PRINT *, "You will then be asked to enter the number of hours and"
  PRINT *, "the numeric grade earned for each of the courses the"
  PRINT *, "student took during the current year.  Separate the"
  PRINT *, "number of hours from the grade by at least one space"
  PRINT *, "or by a comma.  Enter 0 for hours and 0 for grades when"
  PRINT *, "you are finished entering the information for each &
           &student."
  PRINT *
  PRINT *
  PRINT *


END SUBROUTINE Inform
            ⋮
SUBROUTINE Process(NumStudents, Num_in_Good_Standing, Sum_of_GPAs)
            ⋮
  CALL CalculateStats(StudentNumber, Class, NumStudents, &
                      CumulativeHours, CumulativeGPA, CurrentGPA, &
                      Sum_of_GPAs)
  CALL CheckEligibility(Class, CumulativeHours, CumulativeGPA, &
                        InGoodStanding, Num_in_Good_Standing)
  CALL Report(StudentNumber, Class, CumulativeHours, CurrentGPA, &
              CumulativeGPA, InGoodStanding)
            ⋮
!-WrapUp---------------------------------------------------------------
! Subroutine to print some summary statistics.
! Accepts:  Number of students (NumStudents), number in good standing
!           (Num_in_Good_Standing), and sum of all GPAs (Sum_of_GPAs)
! Output:   Report containing values of NumStudents,
!           Num_in_Good_Standing, and average GPA
!---------------------------------------------------------------------

SUBROUTINE WrapUp(NumStudents, Num_in_Good_Standing, Sum_of_GPAs)

  INTEGER, INTENT(IN) :: NumStudents, Num_in_Good_Standing
  REAL, INTENT(IN) :: Sum_of_GPAs
```

Figure 7.10 *(cont.)*

```fortran
   PRINT *
   PRINT *
   PRINT *, "*********************************************************"
   PRINT *, "*                   SUMMARY STATISTICS                  *"
   PRINT *, "*********************************************************"
   PRINT *
   PRINT '(1X, A, T34,  I5)', "Number of students processsed: ", &
         NumStudents
   IF (NumStudents /= 0) THEN
      PRINT '(1X, A, T34, F5.2)', "Average current GPA of students:", &
            Sum_of_GPAs / REAL(NumStudents)
      PRINT '(1X, A, T34, I5)', "Number in good standing:", &
            Num_in_Good_Standing
   END IF

END SUBROUTINE WrapUp
            ⋮
!-CalculateStats-----------------------------------------------------
            ⋮
!-CheckEligibility--------------------------------------------------
            ⋮
!-Report------------------------------------------------------------
! Subroutine to display the statistics for a given student.
!
! Accepts:  Student's number, class, cumulative hours, current GPA,
!           cumulative GPA, and indicator whether student is in good
!           standing
! Output:   StudentNumber, Class, CumulativeHours, CurrentGPA, and a
!           message indicating  whether student is in good standing
!-------------------------------------------------------------------

SUBROUTINE Report(StudentNumber, Class, CumulativeHours, CurrentGPA, &
          CumulativeGPA, InGoodStanding)

  INTEGER, INTENT(IN) :: StudentNumber, Class
  REAL, INTENT(IN) :: CumulativeHours, CurrentGPA, CumulativeGPA
  LOGICAL, INTENT(IN) :: InGoodStanding
```

Figure 7.10 *(cont.)*

```
    PRINT *
    PRINT '(1X, "***** report for student", I6, " *****")', &
          StudentNumber
    PRINT '(1X, A, I6)', "Class:              ", Class
    PRINT 10, "Cumulative Hours:", CumulativeHours
    PRINT 10, "Current GPA:     ", CurrentGPA
    PRINT 10, "Cumulative GPA:  ", CumulativeGPA
    10 FORMAT(1X, A, F6.2)


    IF (InGoodStanding) THEN
       PRINT 20, "In good standing"
    ELSE
       PRINT 20, "*** Not in good standing ***"
    END IF
    20 FORMAT(1X, A / 1X, 35("*"))


  END SUBROUTINE Report
              ⋮
  !-HoursCheck--------------------------------------------------------
              ⋮
  !-GPACheck----------------------------------------------------------
              ⋮
END PROGRAM Academic_Standing
```

Sample run:

```
You will first be asked to enter the student's number,
class, cumulative hours, and cumulative GPA.  Enter these
with at least one space or comma separating them.

You will then be asked to enter the number of hours and
the numeric grade earned for each of the courses the
student took during the current year.  Separate the
number of hours from the grade by at least one space
or by a comma.  Enter 0 for hours and 0 for grades when
you are finished entering the information for each student.

Enter student number, class, cum. hours, cum. GPA: 1234, 1, 0, 0
Hours and grade? 5, 3.0
Hours and grade? 4, 3.0
Hours and grade? 3.5, 3.0
```

Figure 7.10 *(cont.)*

```
Hours and grade? 4, 3.0
Hours and grade? 3, 3.0
Hours and grade? 2, 3.0
Hours and grade? 0, 0

***** Report for Student  1234 *****
Class:               1
Cumulative Hours: 21.50
Current GPA:      3.00
Cumulative GPA:    3.00
*** Not in good standing ***
***********************************

More (Y or N)? Y
Enter student number, class, cum. hours, cum. GPA: 3333, 2, 30, 3.3
Hours and grade? 5, 3.3
Hours and grade? 5, 4.0
Hours and grade? 5, 2.7
Hours and grade? 5, 3.0
Hours and grade? 3, 3.7
Hours and grade? 0, 0

***** Report for Student  3333 *****
Class:               2
Cumulative Hours: 53.00
Current GPA:      3.31
Cumulative GPA:    3.30
In good standing
***********************************

More (Y or N)? Y
Enter student number, class, cum. hours, cum. GPA: 4444, 3, 60, 2.0
Hours and grade? 5, 1.0
Hours and grade? 5, 1.3
Hours and grade? 4, 0.7
Hours and grade? 3, 0.7
Hours and grade? 5, 1.0
Hours and grade? 0, 0
```

Figure 7.10 *(cont.)*

```
***** Report for Student   4444 *****
Class:                 3
Cumulative Hours: 82.00
Current GPA:        0.97
Cumulative GPA:     1.72
*** Not in good standing ***
*********************************


More (Y or N)? N


*********************************************************
*                 SUMMARY STATISTICS                    *
*********************************************************


Number of students processsed:      3
Average current GPA of students: 2.43
Number in good standing:             1
```

7.6   SUBPROGRAMS AS ARGUMENTS

In our examples of subprograms thus far, the actual arguments have been constants, variables, or expressions, but Fortran also permits functions and subroutines as arguments for other subprograms. In this case, the function or subroutine must be a *module* subprogram, an *external* subprogram, or an *instrinsic* subprogram. Also, no INTENT attribute is used for a formal argument that is a subprogram.

Module Subprograms as Arguments

To illustrate the use of a module function as an argument, consider a subroutine Integrate that approximates the definite integral

$$\int_a^b f(x)\, dx$$

using the trapezoidal method of Section 6.3. We wish to use this subprogram in another program to calculate the integral of the function Integrand(x), defined by Integrand(x) = e^{x^2}, for $0 \le x \le 1$. The program in Figure 7.11 imports this function from the module Integrand_Function and passes it along with the interval endpoints A and B to the subroutine Integrate, which displays the approximate value of the integral

$$\int_A^B e^{x^2}\, dx$$

Figure 7.11 Trapezoidal approximation of an integral—version 2.

```fortran
PROGRAM Definite_Integral_2
!-------------------------------------------------------------------------
! Program to approximate the integral of a function over the interval
! [A,B] using the trapezoidal method.  This approximation is calculated
! by the subroutine Integrate; the integrand, the interval of
! integration, and the # of subintervals are passed as arguments to
! Integrate.  The function Integrand is imported from the module
! Integrand_Function.  Identifiers used are:
!   A, B       : endpoints of interval of integration
!   Integrate : subroutine to approximate integral of F on [A, B]
!   Integrand : the integrand
!   Number_of_Subintervals : # of subintervals into which [A, B] is cut
!
! Input:  A, B, and Number_of_Subintervals
! Output: Approximation to integral of F on [A, B]
!-------------------------------------------------------------------------

  USE Integrand_Function        ! module containing Integrand

  IMPLICIT NONE
  REAL :: A, B
  INTEGER :: Number_of_Subintervals

  WRITE (*, '(1X, A)', ADVANCE = "NO") &
        "Enter the interval endpoints and the # of subintervals: "
  READ *, A, B, Number_of_Subintervals

  CALL Integrate(Integrand, A, B, Number_of_Subintervals)

CONTAINS

  ! Integrate ----------------------------------------------------
  ! Subroutine to calculate the trapezoidal approximation of the
  ! integral of the function F over the interval [A,B] using N
  ! subintervals.  Local variables used are:
  !     I       : counter
  !     DeltaX  : the length of the subintervals
  !     X       : a point of subdivision
  !     Y       : the value of the function at X
  !     Sum     : the approximating sum
  !
  !Accepts: Function F, endpoints A and B, and number N of subintervals
  !Output:  Approximate value of integral of F over [A, B]
  !--------------------------------------------------------------
```

no type declare (handwritten annotation near `CALL Integrate`)

Figure 7.11 *(cont.)*

```
SUBROUTINE Integrate(F, A, B, N)


  REAL, INTENT(IN) :: A, B
  INTEGER, INTENT(IN) :: N
  REAL :: F, DeltaX, X, Y, Sum
  INTEGER ::   I


  ! Calculate subinterval length
  ! and initialize the approximating sum and X


  DeltaX = (B - A) / REAL(N)
  X = A
  Sum = 0.0


  ! Now calculate the approximating sum
  DO I = 1, N - 1
     X = X + DeltaX
     Y = F(X)
     Sum = Sum + Y
  END DO
  Sum = DeltaX * ((F(A) + F(B)) / 2.0 + Sum)
  PRINT 10, Number_of_Subintervals, Sum
  10 FORMAT (1X, "Trapezoidal approximate value using", I4, &
                 " subintervals is", F10.5)


END SUBROUTINE Integrate

END PROGRAM Definite_Integral_2
```

Sample run:

```
Enter the interval endpoints and the # of subintervals: 0, 1, 100
Trapezoidal approximate value using 100 subintervals is   1.46270
```

Here `Integrand_Function` is a module like that shown in Figure 7.12 which contains the function `Integrand`.

Figure 7.12 A module function.

```
MODULE Integrand_Function
!-------------------------------------------------------------------------
!  Module containing a function Integrand
!-------------------------------------------------------------------------

CONTAINS
  FUNCTION Integrand(X)

    REAL :: Integrand
    REAL, INTENT(IN) :: X

    Integrand = EXP(X**2)

  END FUNCTION Integrand

END MODULE Integrand_Function
```

External Subprograms as Arguments

If an external function is to be passed as an argument to some other subprogram, it must be declared to have the EXTERNAL attribute. This can be done by using an EXTERNAL specifier in its type declaration,

> *type*, EXTERNAL :: *function-name*

or by using a separate **EXTERNAL statement** of the form

> EXTERNAL *list of external subprogram names*

like <u>Use</u> "module name"

Only the second form can be used for subroutines, because they are not declared (since they have no type associated with them).

For example, the program in Figure 7.11 can be easily modified to use an external function, as shown in Figure 7.13. We indicate that Integrand is an external function by including the EXTERNAL specifier in its type declaration in the main program.

Figure 7.13 Trapezoidal approximation of an integral—version 3.

```
PROGRAM Definite_Integral_3
!-------------------------------------------------------------------------
! Program to approximate the integral of a function over the interval
! [A,B] using the trapezoidal method.  This approximation is calculated
! by the subroutine Integrate; the integrand, the interval of
! integration, and the # of subintervals are passed as arguments to
! Integrate.  Identifiers used are:
!    A, B        : endpoints of interval of integration
!    Integrate : subroutine to approximate integral of F on [A, B]
!    Integrand : the integrand
!    Number_of_Subintervals : # of subintervals into which [A, B] is cut
!
! Input:  A, B, and Number_of_Subintervals
! Output: Approximation to integral of F on [A, B]
!-------------------------------------------------------------------------

  IMPLICIT NONE
  REAL :: A, B
  REAL, EXTERNAL :: Integrand
  INTEGER :: Number_of_Subintervals

  WRITE (*, '(1X, A)', ADVANCE = "NO") &
        "Enter the interval endpoints and the # of subintervals: "
  READ *, A, B, Number_of_Subintervals

  CALL Integrate(Integrand, A, B, Number_of_Subintervals)

CONTAINS

  !-------------------------------------------------------------------
  !          Insert subroutine Integrate (see Figure 7.11) here
  !-------------------------------------------------------------------

END PROGRAM Definite_Integral_3


! Integrand -------------------------------------------------------------
!                              The integrand
!-----------------------------------------------------------------------

FUNCTION Integrand(X)
```

Figure 7.13 *(cont.)*

```
  REAL :: Integrand
  REAL, INTENT(IN) :: X
  Integrand = EXP(X**2)

END FUNCTION Integrand
```

Intrinsic Subprograms as Arguments

To approximate the integral of the sine function from 0 to 0.5, we can simply change the definition of `Integrand` to

```
Integrand = SIN(X)
```

and reexecute the program in Figure 7.11 or 7.13. An alternative is to remove the `USE` statement in Figure 7.11, or delete the function subprogram `Integrand` in Figure 7.13, and pass the intrinsic function `SIN` as an argument to `Integrate`. In this case we must indicate that it is an intrinsic function by using an **INTRINSIC statement** of the form

```
INTRINSIC list of intrinsic subprogram names
```

as in the program in Figure 7.14, or by using an `INTRINSIC` specifier in a type declaration:

```
type, INTRINSIC :: function-name
```

Figure 7.14 Trapezoidal approximation of an integral—version 4.

```
PROGRAM Definite_Integral_4
!-----------------------------------------------------------------------
! Program to approximate the integral of a function over the interval
! [A,B] using the trapezoidal method.  This approximation is calculated
! by the subroutine Integrate; the integrand, the interval of
! integration, and the # of subintervals are passed as arguments to
! Integrate.   Identifiers used are:
!    A, B       : endpoints of interval of integration
!    Integrate : subroutine to approximate integral of F on [A, B]
!    Number_of_Subintervals : # of subintervals into which [A, B] is cut
!
! Input:  A, B, and Number_of_Subintervals
! Output: Approximation to integral of F on [A, B]
!-----------------------------------------------------------------------
```

Figure 7.14 *(cont.)*

```
IMPLICIT NONE
REAL :: A, B
INTRINSIC SIN
INTEGER :: Number_of_Subintervals

WRITE (*, '(1X, A)', ADVANCE = "NO") &
      "Enter the interval endpoints and the # of subintervals: "
READ *, A, B, Number_of_Subintervals

CALL Integrate(SIN, A, B, Number_of_Subintervals)

CONTAINS

  !------------------------------------------------------------------
  !          Insert subroutine Integrate (see Figure 7.11) here
  !------------------------------------------------------------------

END PROGRAM Definite_Integral_4
```

Sample run:

```
Enter the interval endpoints and the # of subintervals: 0, 0.5, 50
Trapezoidal approximate value using  50 subintervals is   0.12242
```

In our discussion of Fortran's intrinsic functions, in most cases we have used the *generic* names of these functions. These generic names simplify references to the functions, because the same function may be used with more than one type of argument. Some intrinsic functions may, however, also be referenced by *specific* names, as indicated in Appendix D. These specific names—but not the generic names—of the Fortran intrinsic functions may be used as arguments in a subprogram reference. Appendix D indicates which intrinsic functions do not have specific names and which functions have specific names but may not be used as arguments.

Interface Blocks

When an external subprogram is used in a program, the actual arguments must be associated correctly with the corresponding formal arguments and for a function, the value returned by the function must be used appropriately. As we noted in Section 6.6, in some cases the compiler does not have enough information about the arguments to ensure that the subprogram is being used correctly.

To illustrate the problem, suppose that in the program in Figure 7.13, the function subprogram Integrand was changed to

```
! Integrand -----------------------------------------------------
!                          The integrand
!-----------------------------------------------------------------

FUNCTION Integrand(X, Y)

  REAL :: Integrand
  REAL, INTENT(IN) :: X, Y

  Integrand = X ** 2 + 3 * X * Y + Y ** 2

END FUNCTION Integrand
```

Most compilers would not detect any errors even though this function with two arguments is passed to the formal argument F of the subroutine Integrate, which assumes that F is a function with only one argument.

The problem is that the only information specified for the function Integrand is that it is a real-valued function; the number of arguments and their types are not specified. Consequently, the compiler cannot detect the incorrect usage of Integrand. What is needed is a complete declaration of this function, comprised of

1. The number of arguments
2. The type of each argument
3. The type of the value returned by the function

These complete declarations can be given using interface blocks. Figure 7.15 illustrates the use of an interface block to ensure that the function Integrand is a real-valued function that has one real argument.

Figure 7.15 Trapezoidal approximation of an integral—version 5.

```
PROGRAM Definite_Integral_5
!-----------------------------------------------------------------------
! Program to approximate the integral of a function over the interval
! [A,B] using the trapezoidal method.  This approximation is calculated
! by the subroutine Integrate; the integrand, the interval of
! integration, and the # of subintervals are passed as arguments to
! Integrate.  Identifiers used are:
!   A, B       : endpoints of interval of integration
!   Integrate : subroutine to approximate integral of F on [A, B]
!   Integrand : the integrand
!   Number_of_Subintervals : # of subintervals into which [A, B] is cut
!
! Input:  A, B, and Number_of_Subintervals
! Output: Approximation to integral of F on [A, B]
!-----------------------------------------------------------------------
```

Figure 7.15 *(cont.)*

```
IMPLICIT NONE
REAL :: A, B

INTERFACE
  FUNCTION Integrand(X)
    REAL :: Integrand
    REAL, INTENT(IN) :: X
  END FUNCTION Integrand
END INTERFACE

INTEGER :: Number_of_Subintervals

WRITE (*, '(1X, A)', ADVANCE = "NO") &
      "Enter the interval endpoints and the # of subintervals: "
READ *, A, B, Number_of_Subintervals

CALL Integrate(Integrand, A, B, Number_of_Subintervals)

CONTAINS

  !-------------------------------------------------------------------
  !          Insert subroutine Integrate (see Figure 7.11) here
  !-------------------------------------------------------------------

END PROGRAM Definite_Integral_5

! Integrand --------------------------------------------------------
!                          The integrand
!-------------------------------------------------------------------

FUNCTION Integrand(X)

  REAL :: Integrand
  REAL, INTENT(IN) :: X

  Integrand = EXP(X**2)

END FUNCTION Integrand
```

As Figure 7.15 illustrates, the EXTERNAL attribute is not specified for the function Integrand. In general, interface blocks and EXTERNAL specifiers cannot both be used to declare subprograms, nor can interface blocks be used for module subprograms or intrinsic subprograms.

Quick Quiz 7.6

1. (True or false) An internal subprogram may not be passed as an argument to another subprogram.

2. (True or false) An intrinsic subprogram may not be passed as an argument to another subprogram.

3. An external subprogram passed as an argument to another subprogram must have the _____ attribute.

4. What three items comprise a complete declaration of a function?

5. Write an interface block for the following function:

```
FUNCTION F(X, Y, N)

  REAL :: F
  REAL, INTENT(IN) :: X, Y
  INTEGER, INTENT(IN) :: N

  F = X**N + Y**N

END FUNCTION F
```

7.7 OPTIONAL AND KEYWORD ARGUMENTS OF SUBPROGRAMS

In all of our examples of subprograms thus far, the number and types of the actual arguments in a subprogram reference have matched the number and type of the formal arguments in the subprogram heading. In Fortran 90, however, it is possible to design a subprogram in which there may be fewer actual arguments in a reference to a subprogram than there are formal arguments. This is accomplished by specifying that some of the arguments are optional. Keyword arguments make it possible to list the actual arguments in a subprogram reference in an order different from the corresponding formal arguments. We will illustrate the use of optional and keyword arguments with an example.

Optional Arguments

Consider the problem of constructing a function that will evaluate any real-valued polynomial function of degree 4 or less for a given real value X. The general form of such a polynomial is

$$A + BX + CX^2 + DX^3 + EX^4$$

where the coefficients $A, B, C, D,$ and E are real constants.

One solution to the problem is to define a function that has six arguments, the X value and the five real coefficients A, B, C, D, and E:

```
FUNCTION Polynomial(X, A, B, C, D, E)

    REAL :: Polynomial
    REAL, INTENT(IN) :: X, A, B, C, D, E

    Polynomial = A + B*X + C*X**2 + D*X**3 + E*X**4

END FUNCTION Polynomial
```

The function reference

```
Polynomial(2.5, 1.5, 2.0, 3.0, -1.0, 7.2)
```

could then be used to evaluate the polynomial $1.5 + 2X + 3X^2 - X^3 + 7.2X^4$ at $X = 2.5$, and the function reference

```
Polynomial(2.5, 1.0, 2.0, 0.0, 0.0, 0.0)
```

could be used to evaluate the linear polyonomial $1 + 2X$ at $X = 2.5$.

Note that in this last function reference it is necessary to supply zero coefficients for any term that does not appear in the polynomial. An alternative is to specify that the arguments specifying the coefficients B, C, D, and E are optional by using the OPTIONAL specifier in their declarations:

```
FUNCTION Polynomial(X, A, B, C, D, E)

    REAL :: Polynomial
    REAL, INTENT(IN) :: X, A
    REAL, INTENT(IN), OPTIONAL :: B, C, D, E
```

Subprograms that contain optional arguments must be module subprograms, internal subprograms, or external subprograms for which an interface block is given in the program unit that references them. Figure 7.16 shows the complete function Polynomial and a simple program that references this function to evaluate several different polynomials.

The function Polynomial can be referenced as described earlier:

```
Polynomial(2.5, 1.5, 2.0, 3.0, -1.0, 7.2)
```

However, it can also be referenced with fewer actual arguments; for example,

```
Polynomial(2.5, 1.0, 2.0)
```

can be used to evaluate the linear polyonomial $1 + 2X$ at $X = 2.5$; the actual arguments 2.5, 1.0, and 2.0 will be passed to the formal arguments X, A, and B, respectively, and no values are passed to the remaining arguments C, D, and E. When there are fewer actual arguments than formal arguments, as in this last example, the arguments are associated in order, beginning with the first item in the argument lists; arguments for which no values are supplied will be at the end of the formal argument list.

Keyword Arguments

The associations of actual arguments with formal arguments can also be given explicitly by using **keyword arguments** of the form

```
formal-argument = actual-argument
```

in the function reference. For example, we could use the function reference

```
Polynomial(X = 2.5, A = 2.0, E = 1.0)
```

to evaluate the fourth-degree polynomial $2 + X^4$ at $X = 2.5$. Note that the use of keyword arguments makes it possible to omit a value for any of the formal arguments, not just those at the end of the argument list. Keyword arguments also make it possible to list the actual arguments in any order; for example,

```
Polynomial(E = 1.0, A = 2.0, X = 2.5)
```

Both keyword arguments and ordinary actual arguments may be used in a subprogram reference, provided the keyword arguments are at the end of the list. In this case, the ordinary arguments are associated with the arguments at the beginning of the formal argument list in the usual manner. For example, in the function reference

```
Polynomial(2.5, 2.0, E = 1.0)
```

2.5 will be passed to X, 2.0 to A, and 1.0 to E; no values will be passed to B, C, and D.

The main program in Figure 7.16 demonstrates these various function references. The function subprogram Polynomial uses the predefined function **PRESENT** to determine which arguments have been supplied values by the reference. A reference to this function has the form

```
PRESENT(formal-argument)
```

and returns true if a value was supplied for *formal-argument* and false otherwise.

Figure 7.16 Optional and keyword arguments.

```
PROGRAM Optional_Keyword_Argument_Demo
!-------------------------------------------------------------------------
! Program to demonstrate the use of optional arguments and keyword
! arguments.
!
! Input:  None
! Output: Values of function Polynomial for various arguments
!-------------------------------------------------------------------------

  IMPLICIT NONE

  PRINT *, "Ordinary function references:"
  PRINT *, "============================="
  PRINT *, "Polynomial(2.5, 1.5, 2.0, 3.0, -1.0, 7.2) =", &
           Polynomial(2.5, 1.5, 2.0, 3.0, -1.0, 7.2)
  PRINT *, "Polynomial(2.5, 1.0, 2.0, 0.0, 0.0, 0.0) =", &
           Polynomial(2.5, 1.0, 2.0, 0.0, 0.0, 0.0)

  PRINT *
  PRINT *, "References with missing arguments:"
  PRINT *, "================================="
  PRINT *, "Polynomial(2.5, 1.0, 2.0) =", &
           Polynomial(2.5, 1.0, 2.0)
  PRINT *, "Polynomial(2.5, 1.0) =", &
           Polynomial(2.5, 1.0)

  PRINT *
  PRINT *, "References with keyword arguments:"
  PRINT *, "=================================="
  PRINT *, "Polynomial(X = 2.5, A = 2.0, E = 1.0) =", &
           Polynomial(X = 2.5, A = 2.0, E = 1.0)
  PRINT *, "Polynomial(E = 1.0, A = 2.0, X = 2.5) =", &
           Polynomial(E = 1.0, A = 2.0, X = 2.5)
  PRINT *, "Polynomial(2.5, 2.0, E = 1.0) =", &
           Polynomial(2.5, 2.0, E = 1.0)

CONTAINS

  !--Polynomial-----------------------------------------------------------
  ! Function to evaluate any polynomial of degree <= 4:
  !                     2    3    4
  !         A + BX + CX  + DX  + EX
  !
  ! Accepts:  X value, and coefficients A, B, C, D, E;  B, C, D, and E
  !             are optional.
  ! Returns:  Value of Polynomial at X
  !-----------------------------------------------------------------------
```

Figure 7.16 *(cont.)*

```
FUNCTION Polynomial(X, A, B, C, D, E)

  REAL :: Polynomial
  REAL, INTENT(IN) :: X, A
  REAL, INTENT(IN), OPTIONAL :: B, C, D, E

  Polynomial = A
  IF (PRESENT(B)) Polynomial = Polynomial + B*X
  IF (PRESENT(C)) Polynomial = Polynomial + C*X**2
  IF (PRESENT(D)) Polynomial = Polynomial + D*X**3
  IF (PRESENT(E)) Polynomial = Polynomial + E*X**4


END FUNCTION Polynomial

END PROGRAM Optional_Keyword_Argument_Demo
```

Sample run:

```
Ordinary function references:
==============================
Polynomial(2.5, 1.5, 2.0, 3.0, -1.0, 7.2) =   2.9087500E+02
Polynomial(2.5, 1.0, 2.0, 0.0, 0.0, 0.0) =   6.0000000

References with missing arguments:
===================================
Polynomial(2.5, 1.0, 2.0) =   6.0000000
Polynomial(2.5, 1.0) =   1.0000000

References with keyword arguments:
===================================
Polynomial(X = 2.5, A = 2.0, E = 1.0) =  41.0625000
Polynomial(E = 1.0, A = 2.0, X = 2.5) =  41.0625000
Polynomial(2.5, 2.0, E = 1.0) =  41.0625000
```

7.8 APPLICATION: RECURSION AND ARTIFICIAL INTELLIGENCE

In Section 6.7 we described recursion and how recursive functions are written in Fortran. In this section we give some examples of recursive subroutines.

Recall that there are two parts to a recursive definition of a function: an *anchor* (or *base case*) and an *inductive* (or *recursive*) *step*. Recursive subroutines also have two parts:

1. An anchor or base case, in which the action of the subroutine is specified for one or more values of the argument(s)

2. An inductive or recursive step, in which the subroutine's action for the current value of the argument(s) is defined in terms of previously defined actions and/or argument values

Example: Reversing an Integer

To illustrate a recursive subroutine, consider the problem of printing the digits of a nonnegative integer in reverse order. Although this problem can easily be solved without recursion (as the exercises ask you to do), it can also be solved by a recursive subroutine.

The recursive approach to solving this problem is motivated by considering how the problem would be solved by hand. To write the digits of the number 16285 in reverse order, we first look at the last digit 5 and write it. Next we look to the left and consider the number formed by the remaining digits and process it *in exactly the same way* (inductive step). We continue in this way until we reach the left end of the number (anchor step). Viewed in this way, the processing is recursive and leads naturally to the following recursive subroutine for solving this problem:

```
!--PrintReverse--------------------------------------------
! Subroutine to display recursively the digits of Number
! in reverse order.  Local variable used:
!    LeftDigits : leftmost digits of Number
!
! Accepts: An integer Number >= 0
! Output:  Reversal of Number
!----------------------------------------------------------

RECURSIVE SUBROUTINE PrintReverse(Number)

  INTEGER, INTENT(IN) :: Number
  INTEGER :: LeftDigits

  WRITE(*, '(I1)', ADVANCE = "NO") MOD(Number, 10)
  LeftDigits = Number / 10
  IF (LeftDigits == 0) THEN           ! anchor
     PRINT *
  ELSE                                ! inductive step
     CALL PrintReverse(LeftDigits)
  END IF

END SUBROUTINE PrintReverse
```

To show how this subroutine carries out its processing, we will trace the execution of the reference `Call PrintReverse(16285)`. The statement

```
WRITE(*, '(I1)', ADVANCE = "NO") MOD(Number, 10)
```

displays the rightmost digit, and the number that remains when this last digit is removed is calculated by the statement

```
LeftDigits = Number / 10
```

Since the value of `LeftDigits` is not 0, the inductive step generates a new subroutine call with argument `LeftDigits` = 1628, as pictured in the following diagram:

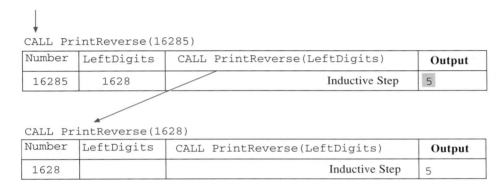

The new subroutine reference, with argument 1628, displays the rightmost digit 8 and calculates `LeftDigits` = 162, and the inductive step generates another subroutine reference with argument 162:

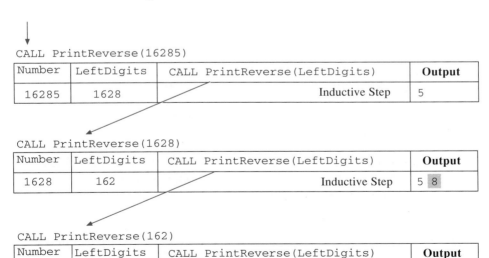

This reference displays the rightmost digit 2 and generates another subroutine reference with argument `LeftDigits = 16`. This reference displays the digit 6 and generates another reference with argument `LeftDigits = 1`, which displays the digit 1 and computes `LeftDigits = 0`:

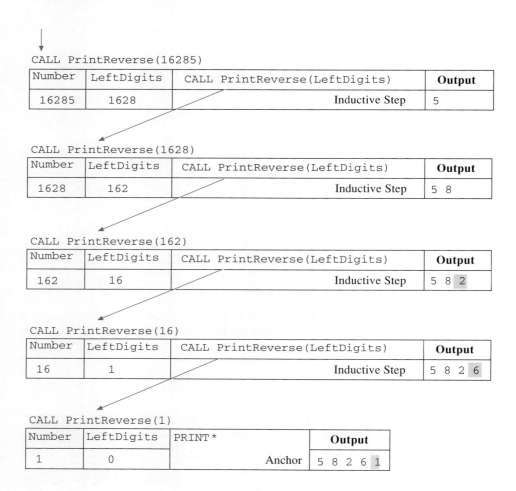

```
CALL PrintReverse(16285)
```

Number	LeftDigits	CALL PrintReverse(LeftDigits)	Output
16285	1628	Inductive Step	5

```
CALL PrintReverse(1628)
```

Number	LeftDigits	CALL PrintReverse(LeftDigits)	Output
1628	162	Inductive Step	5 8

```
CALL PrintReverse(162)
```

Number	LeftDigits	CALL PrintReverse(LeftDigits)	Output
162	16	Inductive Step	5 8 2

```
CALL PrintReverse(16)
```

Number	LeftDigits	CALL PrintReverse(LeftDigits)	Output
16	1	Inductive Step	5 8 2 6

```
CALL PrintReverse(1)
```

Number	LeftDigits	PRINT *	Output
1	0	Anchor	5 8 2 6 1

Since the anchor case has now been reached, this last subroutine reference executes the `PRINT *` statement, which terminates output on the current line. Execution of the preceding reference to subroutine `PrintReverse` is resumed. Since the subroutine reference in the inductive step was at the end of the subroutine, no additional processing is done, and control simply returns to the preceding reference. The earlier references to `PrintReverse` terminate in the same way. The following diagram summarizes this execution trace of `PrintReverse(16285)`:

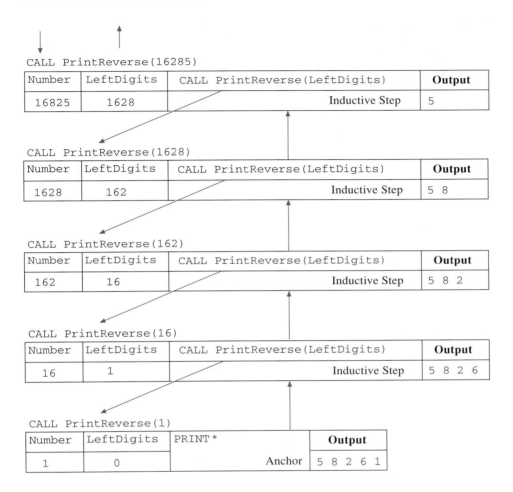

Many problems can be solved with equal ease using either a recursive or a non-recursive algorithm. For example, the factorial and power functions were implemented in Section 6.7 as recursive functions, and the subroutine `PrintReverse` is a recursive subroutine, but these subprograms can be written nonrecursively just as easily. Nonrecursive subprograms may execute more rapidly and utilize memory more efficiently than the corresponding recursive subprograms do. Thus, if an algorithm can be described either recursively or nonrecursively with little difference in effort, it is usually better to use the nonrecursive formulation.

For some problems, recursion is the most natural and straightforward technique. This is especially true for many problems in the area of artificial intelligence, which we describe next. For these problems, nonrecursive algorithms may not be obvious, may be more difficult to develop, and may be less readable than recursive ones. For such problems, the simplicity of the recursive algorithms compensates for any inefficiency. Unless the programs are to be executed many times, the extra effort required to develop nonrecursive solutions is not warranted.

Artificial Intelligence

Artificial intelligence (AI) is concerned with designing computer systems that exhibit characteristics associated with human intelligence; for example, learning, deductive reasoning, problem solving, language understanding, and recognizing visual images. Areas currently studied in AI include

- Expert systems: Designing systems that use a knowledge base of information obtained from a human expert in some area and logical rules to answer questions, analyze problems, and provide advice, much as a human expert would. Successful expert systems include MYCIN for medical consultations, DENDRAL for chemical inference, PROSPECTOR for dealing with geological data, and XCON to configure computer systems.
- Pattern recognition: Recognizing speech, handwriting, patterns of amino acids in DNA strands, and so on.
- Computer vision: Designing machines that can accept input in visual form and can recognize and classify the images they receive.
- Robotics: Attempting to build machines that have sensing capabilities (vision, force, touch), can manipulate objects (grasp them, pick them up, put them down), and solve various object- and space-oriented problems (moving without bumping into things, fitting parts together).
- Search techniques: Searching large data sets in problems such as airline scheduling and routing in which the number of possible search paths is so large that it is not feasible to examine them all.
- Game playing: Devising programs that solve puzzles and play board games such as Tic Tac Toe, chess, and checkers.

Recursion is an important technique in many of these areas of AI. In fact, it is the basic control structure in the programming language LISP, which is one of the major programming languages in AI. We will consider one problem from the area of game playing that can easily be solved using recursion, but for which a nonrecursive solution is quite difficult.

PROBLEM:

Problem

The **Towers of Hanoi** problem is to solve the puzzle shown in the following figure, in which one must move the disks from the left peg to the right peg according to the following rules:[1]

[1] Legend has it that the priests in the Temple of Bramah were given a puzzle consisting of a golden platform with three golden needles on which 64 golden disks were placed. Time was to end when they had successfully finished moving the disks to another needle, following the given rules. (*Query:* If the priests moved one disk per second and began their work in year 0, when would time end?)

1. When a disk is moved, it must be placed on one of the three pegs.
2. Only one disk may be moved at a time, and it must be the top disk on one of the pegs.
3. A larger disk may never be placed on top of a smaller one.

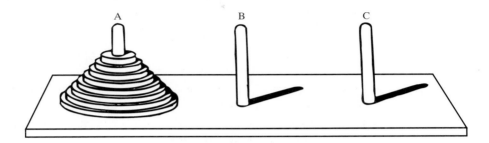

Solution

The Towers of Hanoi puzzle is easy to solve for a small number of disks, but it becomes more difficult as the number of disks grows to seven, eight, and beyond. The puzzle can be solved easily, however, for any number of disks using recursion:

ALGORITHM FOR TOWERS OF HANOI PROBLEM

Recursive algorithm to solve the Towers of Hanoi puzzle

Input: Number N of disks to be moved
Output: A sequence of moves that solves the puzzle

1. Enter N.
2. If there is one disk,
       Anchor step:
       Move it from Peg A to Peg C, solving the puzzle.
   Else do the following:
       Inductive step:
       a. Move the topmost $N - 1$ disks from Peg A to Peg B, using C as an auxiliary peg.
       b. Move the large disk remaining on Peg A to Peg C.
       c. Move the $N - 1$ disks from Peg B to Peg C, using Peg A as an auxiliary peg.

This scheme is implemented by the recursive subroutine `Move` in the program of Figure 7.17, which solves the Towers of Hanoi puzzle.

Figure 7.17 Towers of Hanoi.

```fortran
PROGRAM Towers_of_Hanoi
!-------------------------------------------------------------------------
! Program to solve the Towers of Hanoi puzzle recursively, using
! subroutine Move.  Identifiers used are:
!   Peg_1, Peg_2, Peg_3 : labels for the pegs
!   Number_of_Disks     : number of disks
!   Move                : subroutine to move the disks
!
!   Input:    Number_of_Disks
!   Output:   User prompts and a sequence of moves that solves
!             the puzzle
!-------------------------------------------------------------------------

  CHARACTER(*), PARAMETER :: Peg1 = "A",  Peg2 = "B", Peg3 = "C"
  INTEGER :: Number_of_Disks

  WRITE (*, '(1X, A)', ADVANCE = "NO") "Enter number of disks: "
  READ *, Number_of_Disks
  PRINT *
  CALL Move(Number_of_Disks, Peg1, Peg2, Peg3)

CONTAINS

  !--Move------------------------------------------------------------
  ! Recursive subroutine to move N disks from StartPeg to EndPeg using
  ! AuxPeg as an auxiliary peg.  Variables used are:
  !   N         : number of disks
  !   StartPeg  : peg containing the disks
  !   EndPeg    : peg to which disks are to be moved
  !   AuxPeg    : extra peg used to store disks being moved
  !
  ! Accepts: N, StartPeg, AuxPeg, EndPeg
  ! Output : A sequence of moves that solves the puzzle
  !------------------------------------------------------------------

  RECURSIVE SUBROUTINE Move(N, StartPeg, AuxPeg, EndPeg)

    INTEGER, INTENT(IN) :: N
    CHARACTER(*), INTENT(IN) :: StartPeg, AuxPeg, EndPeg
```

Figure 7.17 *(cont.)*

```
    IF (N == 1) THEN   ! Anchor
        PRINT *, "Move disk from ", StartPeg, " to ", EndPeg

    ELSE                  ! Inductive step
        ! Move n - 1 disks from StartPeg to AuxPeg
        ! using EndPeg as an auxiliary peg
        CALL Move(N - 1, StartPeg, EndPeg, AuxPeg)

        ! Move disk from StartPeg to EndPeg
        CALL Move(1, StartPeg, " ", EndPeg)

        ! Move n - 1 pegs from AuxPeg to EndPeg
        ! using StartPeg as an auxiliary peg
        CALL Move(N - 1, AuxPeg, StartPeg, EndPeg)
    END IF

  END SUBROUTINE Move

END PROGRAM Towers_of_Hanoi
```

Sample run:

```
Enter number of disks: 4

Move disk from A to B
Move disk from A to C
Move disk from B to C
Move disk from A to B
Move disk from C to A
Move disk from C to B
Move disk from A to B
Move disk from A to C
Move disk from B to C
Move disk from B to A
Move disk from C to A
Move disk from B to C
Move disk from A to B
Move disk from A to C
Move disk from B to C
```

Exercises 7.8

Exercises 1–4 assume the following recursive subroutine S:

```
RECURSIVE SUBROUTINE S(Num)

   INTEGER, INTENT(IN) :: Num
   IF (1 <= Num .AND. Num <= 8) THEN
      CALL S(Num - 1)
      WRITE (*, '(I1)', ADVANCE = "NO") Num
   ELSE
      PRINT *
   END IF

END SUBROUTINE S
```

1. What output is produced by each of the following subroutine calls?

    (a) CALL S(3)   (b) CALL S(7)   (c) CALL S(10)

2. If Num – 1 is replaced by Num + 1 in the procedure, what output will be produced by the subroutine calls in Exercise 1?

3. If the WRITE statement and the recursive call to S are interchanged, what output will be produced by the calls in Exercise 1?

4. If a copy of the WRITE statement is inserted before the recursive call to S, what output will be produced by the calls in Exercise 1?

Exercises 5–7 assume the following recursive subroutine Q:

```
RECURSIVE SUBROUTINE Q(Num1, Num2)

   INTEGER, INTENT(IN) :: Num1, Num2

   IF (Num2 <= 0) THEN
      PRINT *
   ELSE
      CALL Q(Num1 - 1, Num2 - 1);
      WRITE (*, '(I1)', ADVANCE = "NO") Num1
      CALL Q(Num1 + 1, Num2 - 1)
   END IF
END SUBROUTINE Q
```

5. What output is produced by CALL Q(14, 4)? (*Hint*: First try CALL Q(14, 2), then try CALL Q(14, 3).)

6. How many lines of output are produced by CALL Q(14, 10)?

7. If the WRITE statement is moved before the first recursive call to Q, what output will be produced by CALL Q(14, 4)?

8. Write a nonrecursive version of the recursive subroutine PrintReverse in the text.

9. Write a recursive subroutine that displays a nonnegative integer with commas in the correct locations. For example, it should display 20131 as 20,131.

10. Trace the execution of Move(4, "A", "B", "C") far enough to produce the first five moves. Does your answer agree with the program output in Figure 7.17? Do the same for Move(5, "A", "B", "C").

CHAPTER REVIEW

Summary

Like most programming languages, Fortran provides two kinds of subprograms, functions and subroutines. The focus of this chapter is on subroutines. The chapter begins by describing and illustrating with several examples how subroutines are written and how the CALL statement is used to reference them. Simulation, an important tool in solving problems that involve randomness, is discussed in Sections 7.3 and 7.4. Top-down design using a divide-and-conquer strategy is illustrated in Section 7.5 by developing a large program for a fairly complex software engineering project. The chapter closes with a discussion of using subprograms as arguments of other subprograms, optional and keyword arguments, and an application of recursive subroutines in artificial intelligence.

FORTRAN SUMMARY

Subroutine Subprogram

subroutine heading
specification part   (same as for a program)
execution part   (same as for a program)
END SUBROUTINE statement

Subroutine Heading

SUBROUTINE subroutine-name(formal-argument-list)

where subroutine-name may be any legal Fortran identifier, and formal-argument-list is a list of identifiers.

For a recursive subroutine, the heading must be modified as follows:

RECURSIVE SUBROUTINE subroutine-name(formal-argument-list)

Example:

```
SUBROUTINE PrintDegrees(Degrees, Minutes, Seconds)
RECURSIVE SUBROUTINE Move(N, StartPeg, AuxPeg, EndPeg)
```

Purpose:
Names the subroutine and lists its arguments.

CALL Statement

```
CALL subroutine-name(actual-argument-list)
```

where *subroutine-name* is the subroutine being called, and *actual-argument-list* contains the variables, constants, or expressions that are the actual arguments.

Example:

```
CALL PrintDegrees(NumDegrees, NumMinutes, NumSeconds)
```

Purpose:
Calls the named subroutine. Execution of the current program unit is suspended, and execution of the subroutine begins. When execution of the subroutine is completed, execution of the original program unit resumes with the statement following the CALL statement.

Declarations of EXTERNAL Subprograms

```
EXTERNAL name₁, name₂, . . .
```

```
type, EXTERNAL :: name₁, name₂, . . .
```

where $name_1$, $name_2$, . . . are the names of external subprograms. Only the first form can be used for subroutines.

Example:

```
EXTERNAL Integrand
```

```
REAL, EXTERNAL :: Integrand
```

Purpose:
Specifies that $name_1$, $name_2$, . . . may be used as arguments to other subprograms. This statement must appear in the specification part of the program unit in which $name_1$, $name_2$, . . . are being used as actual arguments.

Declarations of INTRINSIC Subprograms

```
INTRINSIC name₁, name₂, . . .

type, INTRINSIC :: name₁, name₂, . . .
```

where $name_1$, $name_2$, . . . are the specific (not generic) names of intrinsic subprograms. Only the first form can be used for intrinsic subroutines.

Example:

```
INTRINSIC RANDOM_NUMBER

REAL, INTRINSIC :: SIN, EXP
```

Purpose:
Specifies that intrinsic functions $name_1$, $name_2$, . . . may be used as arguments to other subprograms. This statement must appear in the specification part of the program unit in which $name_1$, $name_2$, . . . are being used as actual arguments.

Interface Block

```
INTERFACE
    interface-body
END INTERFACE
```

where *interface-body* consists of

1. The subprogram heading (except that different names may be used for the formal arguments)
2. Declarations of the arguments and the result type in the case of a function
3. An END FUNCTION or END SUBROUTINE statement

Example:

```
INTERFACE
   FUNCTION Integrand(X)
      REAL :: Integrand
      REAL, INTENT(IN) :: X
   END FUNCTION Integrand
END INTERFACE
```

Purpose:
Provides a complete declaration of a subprogram.

Optional Arguments

```
type, OPTIONAL :: name₁, name₂, . . .
```

or

```
OPTIONAL name₁, name₂, . . .
```

where $name_1$, $name_2$, . . . are formal arguments. The second form must be used for an optional argument that is a subroutine.

Example:

```
REAL, OPTIONAL :: B, C, D, E
```

Purpose:
Specifies that $name_1$, $name_2$, . . . are optional arguments.

Keyword Arguments

```
formal-argument = actual-argument
```

Example:

```
Polynomial(X = 2.5, A = 2.0, E = 1.0)
```

Purpose:
Used in a function reference to associate the specified actual argument and formal argument.

PROGRAMMING POINTERS

Program Style and Design

1. *Subprograms should be documented in the same manner as the main program.* The documentation should include a brief description of the processing carried out by the subprograms, the values passed to them, the values returned by them, and what the arguments and local variables represent.

2. *Subprograms are separate program units, and the subprogram format should reflect this fact.* In this text, we
   - Insert a blank comment line before and after each subprogram to set it off from other program units
   - Follow the stylistic standards described in earlier chapters when writing subprograms

3. *In the formal argument list of a subroutine, it is usually considered good practice to list arguments whose values are passed to the subroutine (IN arguments) before arguments whose values are returned by the subroutine (OUT and IN-OUT arguments).*

4. *Programs for solving complex problems should be designed in a top-down fashion.* The problem should be divided into simpler subproblems, perhaps several times, so that subprograms can be written to solve each of them.

Potential Problems

1. *Unless some arguments of a subprogram have been declared to be optional, when that subprogram is referenced, the number of actual arguments must be the same as the number of formal arguments, and the type of each actual argument must agree with the type of the corresponding formal argument.* For example, consider the declarations

```
SUBROUTINE Sub(Num_1, Num_2)
INTEGER, INTENT(IN) :: Num_1, Num_2
       :
```

If K, L, and M are integer variables, the subroutine references

```
CALL Sub(K, L, M)
```

and

```
CALL SUB(K, 3.5)
```

are incorrect. In the first case, the number of actual arguments does not agree with the number of formal arguments, and in the second case, the real value 3.5 cannot be associated with the integer argument Num_2.

2. *Information is shared among different subprograms only via the arguments and the function name for function subprograms.* Thus, if the value of a variable in one subprogram is needed by another subprogram, it must be passed as an argument, as this variable is not otherwise accessible to the other subprogram. One consequence is that *local variables*—those not used as arguments —as well as statement labels in one subprogram may be used in another subprogram without conflict.

3. *When control returns from a subprogram, local variables in that subprogram do not retain their values unless they are initialized in their declarations or are declared to have the SAVE attribute.*

4. *Failure to declare the INTENT of formal arguments can lead to subtle errors.* For example, if a subroutine is defined by

```
SUBROUTINE Subber(NumItems, Sum)

   INTEGER :: NumItems, Sum, I

   Sum = 0
   DO I = 1, NumItems
      Sum = Sum + I
   END DO
   NumItems = 0

END SUBROUTINE Subber
```

then when the subroutine is called by a statement such as

```
CALL Subber(Count, Total)
```

where `Count` and `Total` are integer variables, the value of `Total` will change
to the value of `Sum`. However, the value of `Count` will also be changed (to 0)
since it is associated with the formal argument `NumItems`, whose value is
changed in the subprogram—this was probably not intended. For some compilers, the value of a constant might be changed in this manner! For example, if the
named constant `Limit` is declared by

```
INTEGER, PARAMETER :: Limit = 100
```

the subroutine call

```
CALL Subber(Limit, Total)
```

might change the value of the `Limit` to 0. Changing the declarations of the formal arguments `NumItems` and `Sum` and the local variable `I` to

```
INTEGER, INTENT(IN) :: NumItems
INTEGER, INTENT(OUT) :: Sum
INTEGER :: I
```

would prevent both problems from occurring.

5. *Local variables that are initialized in a subprogram retain their values from one
   subprogram reference to the next.* For example, consider the following subroutine subprogram to read, count, and find the mean of a set of lengths:

```
SUBROUTINE Get_Length_Info(Count, Mean)

   INTEGER, INTENT(OUT) :: Count
   REAL, INTENT(OUT) :: Mean
   REAL :: Length, Sum = 0.0
```

```
      Count = 0
      DO
         WRITE (*, '(1X, A)', ADVANCE = "NO") &
               "Enter length in meters (negative to stop): "
         READ *, Length
         IF (Length < 0) EXIT    ! End of data
         ! Otherwise process the length
         Count = Count + 1
         Sum = Sum + Length
      END DO

      IF (Count > 0) Mean = Sum / REAL(Count)

   END SUBROUTINE Get_Length_Info
```

Suppose this subroutine is called several times from a program to calculate the means of two data sets:

```
      CALL Get_Length_Info(Count_1, Mean_1)
         ⋮
      CALL Get_Length_Info(Count_2, Mean_2)
```

The mean of the first data set will be calculated correctly, but the mean of the second set will not be correct since Sum will not be reset to 0 but will instead retain its values from the first call to Get_Length_Info. The problem can be avoided by setting Sum to 0 in the executable part of the subroutine rather than in its declaration:

```
      SUBROUTINE Get_Length_Info(Count, Mean)

         INTEGER, INTENT(OUT) :: Count
         REAL, INTENT(OUT) :: Mean
         REAL :: Length, Sum

         Count = 0
         Sum = 0.0
            ⋮
```

6. *Programmer-defined subprograms used as actual arguments in a subprogram reference must be module subprograms or external subprograms that are declared to have the EXTERNAL attribute in the program unit that contains that reference.*

7. *Specific names, but not generic names, of intrinsic functions may be used as actual arguments in a subprogram reference, provided that they are declared to have the INTRINSIC attribute in the program unit that contains that reference.*

PROGRAMMING PROBLEMS

Section 7.1

1. Write a program that reads the number of a month and calls the subprogram of Exercise 1 of Section 7.1 to display the name of the month.

2. Write a program that reads several pairs of integers and for each pair calls the subprogram `Switch` in Exercise 2 of Section 7.1 to interchange their values, and then displays their values.

3. Write a program that reads several measurements in centimeters and for each measurement calls the subprogram of Exercise 3 of Section 7.1 to find the corresponding measurement in yards, feet, and inches and then displays this converted measurement.

4. Write a program that reads several weights in grams and for each measurement calls the subprogram of Exercise 4 of Section 7.1 to find the corresponding weight in pounds and ounces and then displays this converted weight.

5. Write a program that reads several times in military format and for each time calls the subprogram of Exercise 5 of Section 7.1 to find the corresponding hours–minutes–A.M./P.M. representation and then displays this representation.

6. Write a program that reads several times in hours–minutes–A.M./P.M. format and for each time calls the subprogram of Exercise 6 of Section 7.1 to find the corresponding military representation and then displays this representation.

7. Write a subroutine `Print_Stick_Number` to produce "stick numbers" like those on a calculator display for the digits 0, 1, 2, and 3, respectively:

   Write a program to test your subroutines.

8. Extend the subroutine from Problem 7 to display any digit. Write a program to read an integer and call the subroutine to display each digit of the integer.

9. Write a program that reads the diameters and heights of several right circular cylinders and displays the circumference, total surface area (including the ends), and the volume of each. The circumference, surface area, and volume should be calculated and returned by a subroutine.

10. Consider a simply supported beam to which a single concentrated load is applied:

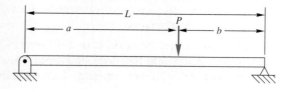

For $a \geq b$, the maximum deflection is given by

$$MaxDeflection = \frac{-Pb(L^2 - b^2)^{3/2}}{9\sqrt{3}\ EIL}$$

the deflection at the load by

$$Deflection\_at\_Load = \frac{-Pa^2b^2}{3EIL}$$

and the deflection at the center of the beam by

$$Deflection\_at\_Center = \frac{-Pb(3L^2 - 4b^2)}{48EI}$$

where P is the load, E is the modulus of elasticity, and I is the moment of iner-tia. For $a \leq b$, simply replace b with a and a with b in the preceding equations.
Write a program that produces a table of values for *MaxDeflection*, *Deflection_at_Load*, and *Deflection_at_Center* as the load position is moved along the beam in 6-inch increments. It should use a subroutine to calculate these values. Run your program with the following values: $L = 360$ inches, $P = 24,000$ pounds, $E = 30 \times 10^6$ psi, and $I = 795.5$ in^4.

11. The *greatest common divisor* GCD(A, B) of two integers A and B, not both of which are zero, can be calculated by the Euclidean Algorithm described in Ex-ercise 11 of Section 6.1. The *least common multiple* of A and B, LCM(A, B), is the smallest nonnegative integer that is a multiple of both A and B and can be calculated using

$$LCM(A, B) = \frac{|A * B|}{GCD(A, B)}$$

Write a program that reads two integers, calls a subroutine that calculates and returns their greatest common divisor and least common multiple, and displays these two values.

12. Write a program that reads a positive integer and then calls a subprogram that displays its prime factorization, that is, a subprogram that expresses a positive in-teger as a product of primes or indicates that it is a prime (see Exercise 12 of Sec-tion 6.1 for the definition of a prime number).

13. One simple method of calculating depreciation is the *straight-line* method de-scribed in Section 4.2. Write a subprogram that calculates and displays annual depreciation using this method for a given amount and a given number of years. Test your subprogram with a program that reads the current year, the amount to be depreciated, and the number of years, and then calls the subprogram to cal-culate and display the annual depreciation.

14. Another method of depreciation described in Section 4.2 is the *sum-of-the-years'-digits* method. Write a subroutine that receives the amount to be depreciated us-ing this method and the number of years and then displays a depreciation table

that shows each year number and the amount to be depreciated for that year, beginning with the current year and continuing for the specified number of years. Test your subprogram with a program that reads the current year, an amount to be depreciated, and the number of years over which it is to be depreciated, and then calls this subprogram to generate a depreciation table.

A possible addition to your program: To find how much is saved in taxes, assume a fixed tax rate over these years, and assume that the amounts saved in taxes by claiming the depreciation as a deduction are invested and earn interest at some fixed annual rate.

15. Another method of calculating depreciation is the *double-declining-balance* method described in Programming Problem 9 of Chapter 4. Write a subroutine that receives the amount to be depreciated using this method, the number of years, and the year in which to switch to the straight-line method (Problem 13); it then displays a depreciation table that shows each year number and the amount to be depreciated for that year, beginning with the current year and continuing for the specified number of years. Test your subprogram with a program that reads the current year, an amount to be depreciated, the number of years over which it is to be depreciated, and the year in which to switch to the straight-line method, and then calls this subprogram to generate a depreciation table.

A possible addition to your program: Calculate the tax savings as described in the previous problem.

16. Proceed as in Exercise 15, but print one table giving the amount to be depreciated each year, assuming that we switch in year 1 (use the straight-line method for all years), and another table giving the amount to be depreciated each year, assuming that we switch in year 2, and so on.

17. Write a subroutine that calculates the amount of city income tax and the amount of federal income tax to be withheld from an employee's pay for one pay period. Assume that the city income tax withheld is computed by taking 1.15 percent of gross pay on the first $15,000 earned per year and that the federal income tax withheld is computed by taking the gross pay less $15 for each dependent claimed and multiplying it by 20 percent.

Use this subroutine in a program that for each of several employees reads his or her employee number, number of dependents, hourly pay rate, city income tax withheld to date, federal income tax withheld to date, and hours worked for this pay period and that calculates and prints the employee number, gross pay and net pay for this pay period, the amount of city income tax and the amount of federal income tax withheld for this pay period, and the total amounts withheld through this pay period.

Section 7.4

18. The tensile strength of a certain metal component has an approximate normal distribution with a mean of 10,000 pounds per square inch and a standard deviation of 100 pounds per square inch. Specifications require that all components have

a tensile strength greater than 9800; all others must be scrapped. Write a program that uses the algorithm described in Section 7.3 to generate 1000 normally distributed random numbers representing the tensile strength of these components, and determine how many must be rejected.

19. Modify the shield program in Figure 7.7 to allow the particle to travel in any direction rather than simply left, right, forward, or backward. Choose a direction (angle) at random, and let the particle travel a fixed (or perhaps random) distance in that direction.

20. Write a program to simulate the random path of a particle in a box. A direction (angle) is chosen at random, and the particle travels a fixed (or random) distance in that direction. This procedure is repeated until the particle either passes out through the top of the box or collides with one of the sides or the bottom and stops. Calculate the average number of times the particle escapes from the box and the average number of jumps needed for it to get out.

   Some modifications are as follows: Use a two-dimensional box if a three-dimensional one seems too challenging. Let the particle bounce off the sides or the bottom of the box at the same angle with which it hits rather than stop when it collides with these boundaries.

21. The classic *drunkard's walk problem:* Over an eight-block line, the home of an intoxicated chap is at block 8, and a pub is at block 1. Our poor friend starts at block n, $1 \leq n \leq 8$, and wanders at random, one block at a time, either toward or away from home. At any intersection, he moves toward the pub with a certain probability, say 2/3, and toward home with a certain probability, say 1/3. Having gotten either home or to the pub, he remains there. Write a program to simulate 500 trips in which he starts at block 2, another 500 in which he starts at block 3, and so forth up to block 7. For each starting point, calculate and print the percentage of the time he ends up at home and the average number of blocks he walked on each trip.

22. The famous *Buffon Needle problem* is as follows: A board is ruled with equidistant parallel lines, and a needle whose length is equal to the distance between these lines is dropped at random on the board. What is the probability that it crosses one of these lines? The answer to this problem is $2/\pi$. Write a program to simulate this experiment and obtain an estimate for π.

23. Consider a quarter-circle inscribed in a square whose sides have length 1:

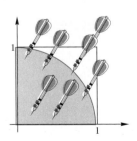

Imagine throwing q darts at this square and counting the total number p that hit within the quarter-circle. For a large number of throws, we would expect

$$\frac{p}{q} \approx \frac{\text{area of quarter-circle}}{\text{area of square}} = \frac{\pi}{4}$$

Write a program to approximate π using this method. To simulate throwing the darts, generate two random numbers X and Y and consider point (X, Y) as being where the dart hits.

24. A method of approximating π by throwing darts at a quarter-circle inscribed in a square is described in Problem 23. This method can be generalized to find the area under the graph of any function and is known as a *Monte Carlo* method of approximating integrals. To illustrate it, consider a rectangle that has base $[a, b]$ and height m, where $m \geq f(x)$ for all x in $[a, b]$:

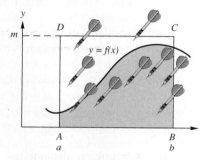

Imagine throwing q darts at rectangle $ABCD$ and counting the total number p that hit the shaded region. For a large number of throws, we would expect

$$\frac{p}{q} \approx \frac{\text{area of shaded region}}{\text{area of rectangle } ABCD}$$

Write a program to calculate areas using this Monte Carlo method. To simulate throwing the darts, generate two random numbers, X from $[a, b]$ and Y from $[0, m]$, and consider the point (X, Y) as being where the dart hits. Use your program to compute the current passing through a capacitor as described in Exercise 8 of Section 6.4.

25. Use Monte Carlo integration (see Problem 24) to find the fraction of fission neutrons with energies above a certain threshold as described in Exercise 10 of Section 6.4.

26. Use Monte Carlo integration (see Problem 24) to find the absorbed energy for the spring described in Exercise 12 of Section 6.4.

Section 7.5

27. Write a menu-driven program that allows the user to select one of the following methods of depreciation:

1. Straight-line (see Problem 13)
2. Sum-of-the-years'-digits (see Problem 14)
3. Double-declining-balance (see Problem 15)

Design the program to be modular, using subprograms to implement the various options.

28. (Project) Many everyday situations involve *queues* (waiting lines): at supermarket checkout lanes, at ticket counters, at bank windows, and so on. Consider the following example: An airport has one runway. Each airplane takes three minutes to land and two minutes to take off. On the average, in one hour, eight planes land and eight take off. Assume that the planes arrive randomly. (Delays make the assumption of randomness quite reasonable.) There are two types of queues: airplanes waiting to land and airplanes waiting to take off. Because it is more expensive to keep a plane airborne than to have one waiting on the ground, we assume that an airplane waiting to land has priority over one waiting to take off.

Write a computer simulation of this airport's operation. To simulate landing arrivals, generate a random number corresponding to a one-minute interval; if it is less than 8/60, then a "landing arrival" occurs and joins the queue of planes waiting to land. Generate another random number to determine whether a "takeoff" arrival occurs; if so, it joins the takeoff queue. Next, check to determine whether the runway is free. If so, first check the landing queue, and if planes are waiting, allow the first airplane in the landing queue to land; otherwise, consider the queue of planes waiting to take off. Have the program calculate the average queue lengths and the average time an airplane spends in a queue. For this problem, you might simulate a 24-hour day. You might also investigate the effect of varying arrival and departure rates to simulate prime and slack times of the day, or what happens if the amount of time it takes to land or take off is increased or decreased.

Section 7.6

29. Design a subprogram whose arguments are a function f and the endpoints of an interval known to contain a zero of the function and that uses the bisection method described in Programming Problem 19 of Chapter 6 to find an approximation to this zero. Use this subprogram in a program to find a zero of the function $f(x) = x - \cos x$ in the interval $[0, \pi/2]$.

30. Proceed as in Exercise 29, but use Newton's method (see Section 6.3) instead of the bisection method. Both the function and its derivative should be passed as arguments to the root-finding subprogram.

Section 7.8

31. Write a program to test the subroutine `PrintReverse` in Section 7.8 and add output statements to the subroutine to trace its actions as it executes. For example, the trace displayed for `PrintReverse(9254)` might have a form like

```
PrintReverse(9254):  Output 4, then call PrintReverse(925)
   PrintReverse(925):  Output 5, then call PrintReverse(92)
      PrintReverse(92):  Output 2, then call PrintReverse(9)
         PrintReverse(9):  Output 9
         PrintReverse(9) returns
      PrintReverse(92) returns
   PrintReverse(925) returns
PrintReverse(9254) returns
```

where the indentation level reflects the depth of the recursion. (See the hint in Programming Problem 51 of Chapter 6.)

32. Write a program that reads several nonnegative integers and calls the recursive subroutine of Exercise 9 of Section 7.8 to display each integer with commas in the correct locations.

33. Write a recursive subroutine to find the prime factorization of a positive integer (see Problem 12).

FEATURES NEW TO FORTRAN 90

Fortran 90 has added a number of new features that facilitate modular programming, including the following:

- A number of new intrinsic functions and subroutines have been added, including RANDOM_SEED and RANDOM_NUMBER.

- Function and subroutines may be recursive. The program in Figure 6.12 illustrates the use of recursive functions, and Section 7.8 illustrates the use of recursive subroutines.

- Program units may contain internal subprograms. A CONTAINS statement in a program unit signals that internal subprogram definitions follow.

- A formal argument of a subprogram may be declared to be an IN argument, an OUT argument, or an INOUT argument by using an INTENT clause in the type statement that specifies the type of that argument. IN arguments may not be modified within the subprogram; OUT arguments are intended to return values to the corresponding actual arguments, which must therefore be variables; IN-OUT arguments are intended both to receive and to return values.

- Explicit interfaces with a subprogram may be provided by means of an interface block of the form

```
INTERFACE
    interface-body
END INTERFACE
```

where *interface-body* is a copy of the heading and specification part of the subprogram followed by an END statement.

- Any formal argument of a subprogram may be declared to be optional by including an OPTIONAL attribute in the type statement that specifies the type of that argument.

- An interface block of the form

```
INTERFACE OPERATOR ASSIGN (=)
    interface-block for subroutine₁
    interface-block for subroutine₂
        ⋮
END INTERFACE
```

may be used to extend the assignment operator (=) to other data types. (See Chapter 10.)

- An interface block of the form

```
INTERFACE generic-name
    interface-block for subprogram₁
    interface-block for subprogram₂
        ⋮
END INTERFACE
```

may be used to define a subprogram name *generic-name* that may be used to reference any of *subprogram₁*, *subprogram₂*, ... (See Chapter 10.)

- A new kind of program unit, a *module*, is provided for packaging definitions and declarations of parameters, variables, types, and subprograms so that they can be used by other program units.

8

One-Dimensional Arrays

With silver bells, and cockle shells
And pretty maids all in a row.

MOTHER GOOSE

I've got a little list, I've got a little list.

GILBERT AND SULLIVAN, *The Mikado*

There is nothing more difficult to take in hand, more perilous to
conduct, or more uncertain in its success, than to take the lead in
the introduction of a new order of things.

NICCOLO MACHIAVELLI, *The Prince*

*I*n Chapter 2 we introduced the predefined Fortran data types, three for processing numeric data—integer, real, and complex—one for processing character data, and one for processing logical data. These data types are called **simple** types because a data value of one of these types consists of a single item. In many situations, however, it is necessary to process a collection of values, for example, a list of test scores, a collection of measurements resulting from some experiment, or a matrix. Processing such collections using only simple data types can be extremely cumbersome, and for this reason, most high-level languages include special features for structuring such data. Fortran 90 provides arrays and derived types. In this chapter we consider one-dimensional arrays; in Chapter 9, multidimensional arrays; and in Chapter 10, derived types.

8.1   EXAMPLE: PROCESSING A LIST OF FAILURE TIMES

In many of our examples, we processed a collection of data values by reading the data values one at a time and processing each value individually, for example, reading a failure time and assigning it to a variable, counting it, and adding it to a running sum. When the value was no longer needed, a new value was read for the same variable, counted, and added to the running sum. This process was repeated again and again. For many problems, however, the collection of data items must be processed several times. The following example illustrates.

PROBLEM:

Problem

Consider again the mean-time-to-failure problem from Section 4.4. Recall that in this problem a number of components in a circuit were tested and the time at which each component failed was recorded. As a measure of the reliability of a component, the mean of these failure times was calculated. This computation required processing the list of failure times only once. Suppose now we wish to analyze these failure times using a program to

1. Find the mean time to failure
2. Print a list of failure times greater than the mean
3. Sort the failure times so that they are in ascending order

Clearly, this will require processing the list several times. The following are two possible solutions.

Solution 1: Use One Variable for Each Failure Time

Suppose, for example, there are 50 failure times to be read from a data file. We might use 50 different variables, `FailureTime_1`, `FailureTime_2`, ..., `FailureTime_50`, to create 50 different memory locations to store the failure times:

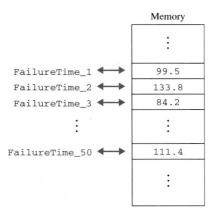

Although this approach might be practical if we have only a few data values to process, it is obviously cumbersome for large data sets, as the following program skeleton vividly demonstrates:

```
PROGRAM FailureTimes
   INTEGER :: OpenStatus, InputStatus
   REAL :: FailureTime_1, FailureTime_2, FailureTime_3, &
           FailureTime_4, FailureTime_5, FailureTime_6, &
                           ⋮
           FailureTime_48, FailureTime_49, FailureTime_50, &
           Mean_Time_to_Failure

   ! Read the failure times
   OPEN (UNIT = 10, FILE = "FAILTIME.DAT", STATUS = "OLD", &
         IOSTAT = OpenStatus)
   IF (OpenStatus > 0) STOP "*** Cannot open the file ***"

   READ (10, *, IOSTAT = InputStatus) &
         FailureTime_1, FailureTime_2, FailureTime_3, &
         FailureTime_4, FailureTime_5, FailureTime_6, &
                         ⋮
         FailureTime_48, FailureTime_49, FailureTime_50
   IF (InputStatus > 0) STOP "*** Input error ***"
   IF (InputStatus < 0) STOP "*** Not enough data ***"

   ! Calculate the mean time to failure

   Mean_Time_to_Failure = &
     (FailureTime_1 + FailureTime_2 + FailureTime_3 + &
      FailureTime_4 + FailureTime_5 + FailureTime_6 + &
                         ⋮
```

```
                    FailureTime_46 + FailureTime_47 + FailureTime_48 + &
                    FailureTime_49 + FailureTime_50) / 50.0
            PRINT *, "Mean time to failure = ", Mean_Time_to_Failure

            ! Display failure times above the mean

            IF (FailureTime_1 > Mean_Time_to_Failure) &
                PRINT *, FailureTime_1
            IF (FailureTime_2 > Mean_Time_to_Failure) &
                PRINT *, FailureTime_2
            IF (FailureTime_3 > Mean_Time_to_Failure) &
                PRINT *, FailureTime_3
                            ⋮
            IF (FailureTime_50 > Mean_Time_to_Failure) &
                PRINT *, FailureTime_50

            ! After about 200 lines of code, sort them?
            ! There must be a better way!

        END PROGRAM FailureTimes
```

Solution 2: Reread the Data

If we do not use 50 different memory locations to store all of the failure times, then we must read the values several times, rewinding the file each time we need to reread the values.

```
        PROGRAM FailureTimes

            INTEGER :: OpenStatus, InputStatus, Number_of_Times, I
            REAL :: FailureTime, Sum, Mean_Time_to_Failure

            ! Read and count the failure times

            OPEN (UNIT = 10, FILE = "FAILTIME.DAT", &
                    STATUS = "OLD", IOSTAT = OpenStatus)
            IF (OpenStatus > 0) STOP "*** Cannot open the file ***"

            Number_of_Times = 0
            DO
                READ (10, *, IOSTAT = InputStatus) FailureTime
                IF (InputStatus > 0) STOP "*** Input error ***"
                IF (InputStatus < 0) EXIT  ! end of file
                Number_of_Times = Number_of_Times + 1
            END DO
```

```
! Calculate the mean time to failure

REWIND (UNIT = 10)
Sum = 0.0
DO I = 1, Number_of_Times
   READ (10, *) FailureTime
   Sum = Sum + FailureTime
END DO
Mean_Time_to_Failure = Sum / REAL(Number_of_Times)
PRINT *, "Mean time to failure =", Mean_Time_to_Failure

! Display failure times above the mean

REWIND (UNIT = 10)
DO I = 1, Number_of_Times
   READ (10, *) FailureTime
   IF (FailureTime > Mean_Time_to_Failure) &
      PRINT *, FailureTime
END DO

! Sort them???   Hm-m-m-m

END PROGRAM FailureTimes
```

Although this program is more manageable than that in Solution 1, it is not a good solution to the problem because files are usually stored in secondary memory, from which data retrieval is slow.

Arrays

To solve this problem efficiently, we need a **data structure** to store and organize the entire collection of failure times. We prefer that the structure be stored in main memory so that storage and retrieval are fast (unlike Solution 2). However, instructions to access the values stored in the structure should be relatively simple and straightforward (unlike Solution 1). Also, many kinds of list processing, such as sorting, cannot be done efficiently if the data values can be accessed only **sequentially**, that is, a value can be accessed only by searching from the beginning of the list (as in Solution 2). What is needed instead is a **direct access** structure that allows a data value to be stored or retrieved directly by specifying its location in the structure, so that it takes no longer to access the value in location 50 than to access the value in location 5. One such data structure is an **array**, in which a fixed number of data values, all of the same type, are organized in a sequence and direct access to each value is possible by specifying its position in this sequence.

```
REAL, DIMENSION(50) :: FailureTime
```

instructs the compiler to establish an array with the name `FailureTime` consisting of 50 memory locations in which values of type `REAL` can be stored:

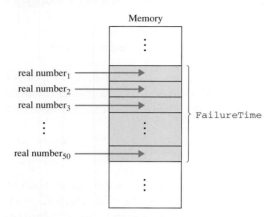

In the program we can then refer to this entire array of real numbers by using the **array variable** `FailureTime`, but we can also access each individual **element** of the array by using a **subscripted variable** formed by appending a **subscript** (or **index**) enclosed in parentheses to the array variable. This subscript specifies the position of an array element. Thus, `FailureTime(1)` refers to the first element of the array `FailureTime`, `FailureTime(2)` to the second element, and so on. The preceding specification statement thus not only reserves a block of memory locations in which to store the elements of the array `FailureTime`, but it also associates the subscripted variables `FailureTime(1)`, `FailureTime(2)`, `FailureTime(3)`,..., `FailureTime(50)` with these locations:

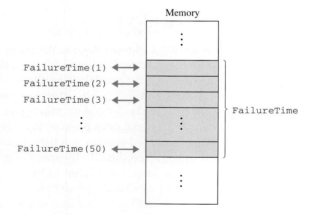

Each subscripted variable `FailureTime(1)`, `FailureTime(2)`, ..., `FailureTime(50)` names an individual memory location and hence can be used in much the same way as a simple variable. For example, the assignment statement

```
FailureTime(4) = 177.8
```

stores the value 177.8 in the fourth location of the array `FailureTime`, and the output statement

```
PRINT *, FailureTime(10)
```

displays the value stored in the tenth location of the array `FailureTime`.

An important feature of the notation used for arrays is that the subscript attached to the array name may be an integer variable or expression. For example, the statement

```
READ *, FailureTime(N)
```

reads a value and stores it in the Nth location of the array `FailureTime`.

Using an array reference in which the subscript is a variable or an expression within a loop that changes the value of the subscript on each pass through the loop is a convenient way to process each item in the array. Thus, the DO loop

```
DO I = 1, 50
   READ (10, *) FailureTime(I)
END DO
```

is equivalent to the following sequence of 50 READ statements,

```
READ (10, *) FailureTime(1)
READ (10, *) FailureTime(2)
READ (10, *) FailureTime(3)
            ⋮
READ (10, *) FailureTime(50)
```

and thus reads 50 values and stores them in the array `FailureTime`. Since each execution of a READ statement requires a new line of input data, the 50 failure times must be on 50 separate lines, one value per line.

An alternative method of reading or displaying an array is to use an input or output statement containing the array name. The effect is the same as listing all of the array elements in the input/output statement. For example, the input statement

```
READ (10, *) FailureTime
```

is equivalent to

```
READ (10, *) FailureTime(1), FailureTime(2), ..., FailureTime(50)
```

Because the READ statement is executed only once, the values for `FailureTime` need not be read from separate lines. All of the values may be on one line, or thirty values may be on the first line with twenty on the next, or ten values may be on each of five lines, and so on. The program in Figure 8.1 uses this method to read failure times and store them in the array `FailureTime`. The mean of these failure times is then calculated using

```
Sum = 0.0
DO I = 1, NumTimes
    Sum = Sum + FailureTime(I)
END DO
Mean_Time_to_Failure = Sum / REAL(NumTimes)
```

where `NumTimes` is a named constant declared by

```
INTEGER, PARAMETER :: NumTimes = 50
```

Another DO loop containing array references with a variable subscript is then used to display a list of failure times greater than this mean:

```
DO I = 1, NumTimes
    IF (FailureTime(I) > Mean_Time_to_Failure) &
        PRINT '(1X, F9.1)', FailureTime(I)
END DO
```

Figure 8.1 Processing a list of failure times.

```
PROGRAM Processing_Failure_Times_1
!-----------------------------------------------------------------------
! Program to read a list of failure times, calculate the mean time to
! failure, and then print a list of failure times that are greater
! than the mean.  Identifiers used are:
!     OpenStatus          : status variable for OPEN
!     InputStatus         : status variable for READ
!     FailureTime         : one-dimensional array of failure times
!     NumTimes            : size of the array (constant)
!     I                   : subscript
!     Sum                 : sum of failure times
!     Mean_Time_to_Failure : mean of the failure times
!
! Input (file):  A list of NumTimes failure times
! Output:        Information to user about the data file,
!                Mean_Time_to_Failure, and a list of failure times
!                greater than Mean_Time_to_Failure
!-----------------------------------------------------------------------
```

Figure 8.1 *(cont.)*

```
IMPLICIT NONE
INTEGER, PARAMETER :: NumTimes = 50
REAL, DIMENSION(NumTimes) :: FailureTime
INTEGER :: OpenStatus, InputStatus, I
REAL :: Sum, Mean_Time_to_Failure

PRINT *, "Program reads", NumTimes, "failure times from fil8-1.dat."
OPEN (UNIT = 10, FILE = "fil8-1.dat", STATUS = "OLD", IOSTAT = OpenStatus)
IF (OpenStatus > 0) STOP "*** Cannot open the file ***"

! Read the failure times and store them in array FailureTime

READ (10, *, IOSTAT = InputStatus) FailureTime
IF (InputStatus > 0) STOP "*** Input error ***"
IF (InputStatus < 0) STOP "*** Not enough data ***"

! Calculate the mean time to failure

Sum = 0.0
DO I = 1, NumTimes
   Sum = Sum + FailureTime(I)
END DO
Mean_Time_to_Failure = Sum / REAL(NumTimes)
PRINT '(/ 1X, "Mean time to failure =", F6.1)', Mean_Time_to_Failure

! Print list of failure times greater than the mean

PRINT *
PRINT *,  "List of failure times greater than the mean:"
DO I = 1, NumTimes
   IF (FailureTime(I) > Mean_Time_to_Failure) &
      PRINT '(1X, F9.1)', FailureTime(I)
END DO

END PROGRAM Processing_Failure_Times_1
```

Listing of `fil8-1.dat` used in sample run:

```
99.5, 133.8, 84.2, 217.5, 188.8, 103.1, 93.9, 165.0, 68.3, 111.4
88.8, 88.2, 90.1, 70.2, 150.5, 122.9, 138.8, 99.9, 111.6, 155.7
133.4, 122.2, 93.4, 101.5, 109.9, 103.3, 177.7, 188.1, 99.8, 144.4
87.5, 79.3, 190.2, 190.3, 170.1, 160.9, 121.1, 95.6, 140.5, 177.2
150.1, 140.3, 139.2, 113.8, 155.9, 144.4, 88.3, 83.5, 101.1, 112.8
```

Figure 8.1 *(cont.)*

Sample run:

```
Program reads 50 failure times from fil8-1.dat

Mean time to failure = 126.0

List of failure times greater than the mean:
    133.8
    217.5
    188.8
    165.0
    150.5
    138.8
    155.7
    133.4
    177.7
    188.1
    144.4
    190.2
    190.3
    170.1
    160.9
    140.5
    177.2
    150.1
    140.3
    139.2
    155.9
    144.4
```

The program in Figure 8.1 uses a list-directed input statement to read values for an array. A formatted READ statement can also be used to input an array. The number of values to be read from each line of input is then determined by the corresponding format specifier. For example, the statement

```
READ (10, '(5F6.1)') FailureTime
```

reads the values for FailureTime(1),..., FailureTime(5) from the first line of data, the values for FailureTime(6),..., FailureTime(10) from the second line, and so on.

An array can be displayed in a similar manner. For example, the statement

```
PRINT '(1X, 5F10.1)', FailureTime
```

is equivalent to

```
PRINT '(1X, 5F10.1)', FailureTime(1), FailureTime(2), ..., &
      FailureTime(50)
```

and displays the elements of the array FailureTime on ten lines, five values per line, right-justified in fields of width 10 with one digit to the right of the decimal point.

Putting an **implied DO loop** in an input or output statement provides a third method of array input/output. Implied DO loops have the form

```
(list-of-variables, control-var = init-value, limit, step)
```

where the control variable *control-var*, initial value *init-value*, *limit*, and *step* size are the same as for a DO loop. The effect of an implied DO loop is exactly that of a DO loop—it is as if the left parenthesis were a DO, with indexing information immediately before the matching right parenthesis and the *list-of-variables* constituting the body of the DO loop. For example, the statement

```
READ (10, *) (FailureTime(I), I = 1, NumTimes)
```

which is equivalent to

```
READ (10, *) Failure(1), Failure(2), ...,  Failure(NumTimes)
```

could be used in the program in Figure 8.1 to read the failure times and store them in the array FailureTime. Since the READ statement is encountered only once, the input values need not be read from separate lines but may be on any number of lines. Implied DO loops can also be used to display the elements of an array. For example, the statement

```
PRINT *, (FailureTime(I), I = 1, NumTimes)
```

would have the same effect as

```
PRINT *, FailureTime(1),..., FailureTime(NumTimes)
```

Arrays such as FailureTime involve only a single subscript and are called **one-dimensional arrays.** Fortran programs, however, may process arrays of more than one dimension, in which case each element of the array is designated by attaching the appropriate number of subscripts to the array name. In this chapter we consider only one-dimensional arrays; in the next chapter we discuss multidimensional arrays.

8.2 COMPILE-TIME ARRAYS AND RUN-TIME ARRAYS

As we noted in the preceding section, memory for the array `FailureTime` was allocated at compile time. This means that the size of such *compile-time arrays* is fixed before execution begins. If the data set stored in the array is very small, a considerable waste of memory may result; if the data set is too large, it cannot be stored in the array and processed correctly. To deal with this problem, Fortran 90 provides *run-time* (or *allocatable*) *arrays* for which memory is allocated during execution, making it possible to allocate an array of appropriate size. In this section we will show how such arrays are declared and processed.

Compile-Time Arrays

The general form of a declaration of a compile-time array is as follows:

Declaration of Compile-Time Array

Form:

> *type*, DIMENSION(*l:u*) :: *list-of-array-names*

or

> *type* :: *list-of-array-specifiers*

where
    list-of-array-names is a list of array names;
    list-of-array-specifiers is a list of array specifiers of the form

> *array-name(l:u)*

and the pair *l:u* is a pair of integer constants.

Purpose:
Declares that each of the identifiers in the *list* is an array for which memory is allocated at compile time and for which the range of values of the subscript will be from the lower limit *l* through the upper limit *u*. If the minimum value of the subscript for an array is 1, then only the maximum subscript need be specified.

Up to now, the subscripts in our examples of arrays have been positive valued, ranging from 1 through some upper limit. Although this is the most common subscript range, Fortran does allow a subscript to be any integer value, positive, negative, or zero, provided that it does not fall outside the range specified in the array declaration. For example, the array declarations

```
INTEGER, PARAMETER :: LowerLimit_1 = -1, UpperLimit_1 = 3, &
                      LowerLimit_2 = 0, UpperLimit_2 = 5

INTEGER, DIMENSION(LowerLimit_1 : UpperLimit_1) :: Gamma
REAL, DIMENSION(LowerLimit_2 : UpperLimit_2) :: Delta
```

establish two one-dimensional arrays. The integer array Gamma may have subscript values ranging from -1 through 3; thus, the following subscripted variables may be used: Gamma(-1), Gamma(0), Gamma(1), Gamma(2), Gamma(3). The real array Delta has subscript values ranging from 0 through 5 so that any of the subscripted variables Delta(0), Delta(1),..., Delta(5) may be used. The integer array FailureTime with subscript ranging from 1 through 50 was declared in the program in Figure 8.1 by

```
REAL, DIMENSION(50) :: FailureTime
```

It could also have been declared by any of the following:

```
REAL, DIMENSION(1:50) :: FailureTime
```

```
REAL :: FailureTime(1:50)
```

```
REAL :: FailureTime(50)
```

Allocatable Arrays

A declaration of a compile-time array of the form

```
INTEGER, PARAMETER :: NumElements = 10
REAL, DIMENSION(NumElements) :: Array
```

causes the compiler to allocate a block of memory large enough to hold 10 real values. The size of this block cannot be altered, except by changing the value of the named constant NumElements and then recompiling the program. As we noted earlier, such fixed-size arrays suffer from two problems:

- If the size of the array exceeds the number of values to be stored in it, then memory is wasted by the unused elements.
- If the size of the array is smaller than the number of values to be stored in it, there is the problem of array overflow.

Both of these problems would be solved if memory could be allocated to an array as the program executes. However, Fortran does *not* allow us to write

```
INTEGER :: N                      ! Declare a variable

PRINT *, "How many elements?"     ! At run time, let the user
READ *, N                         !    input the size of the array

REAL, DIMENSION(N) :: Array       !    and then allocate
                                  !    storage for the array
                                  ! ***NOT ALLOWED***
```

which would tailor the size of the array to the number of values being entered.

Fortran 90 does, however, provide **allocatable** or **run-time arrays** for which memory is allocated during execution (i.e., *run-time allocation*) instead of when it is compiled (i.e., *compile-time allocation*). The declaration of an allocatable array must specify that it has the **ALLOCATABLE** attribute:

Declaration of Allocatable Array

Forms:

```
type, DIMENSION(:), ALLOCATABLE :: list
```

or

```
type, DIMENSION(:) :: list
ALLOCATABLE :: list
```

where
   list is a list of array names.

Purpose:
Declares that each of the identifiers in the *list* is an array whose size will be specified during execution.

For example,

```
REAL, DIMENSION(:), ALLOCATABLE :: A, B
```

declares A and B to be one-dimensional allocatable arrays.

The actual bounds of an allocatable array are specified in an ALLOCATE statement:

ALLOCATE *Statement*

Form:

        ALLOCATE(*list*)

or

        ALLOCATE(*list*, STAT = *status-variable*)

where
        list is a list of array specifications of the form

            array-name(*l:u*)

        where the pair *l:u* is a pair of integer expressions;
status-variable is an integer variable.

Purpose:
Allocates space for each array listed. The range of subscripts for each array will be from the specified lower limit *l* through the upper limit *u*. If the minimum value of the subscript for an array is 1, then only the maximum subscript need be specified. In the second form, the integer variable *status-variable* will be set to zero if allocation is successful, but will be assigned some system-dependent error value if there is insufficient memory or if the array has already been allocated.

For example, consider the statements

```
WRITE (*, '(1X, A)', ADVANCE = "NO") &
      "Enter size of arrays A and B:"
READ *, N
ALLOCATE(A(N), B(0:N+1), STAT = AllocateStatus)
IF (AllocateStatus /= 0) STOP "*** Not enough memory ***"
```

where N and AllocateStatus are integer variables. If memory is available, enough will be allocated for arrays A and B so that A can store N real values in A(1), A(2), ..., A(N) and B can store N + 2 real values in B(0), B(1), ..., B(N+1). Once this memory has been allocated, these arrays may be used in the same way as other (compile-time) arrays.

When execution of a program begins, the program has a "pool" of available memory locations called the **free store**. The effect of the ALLOCATE statement is to request the operating system to

1. Remove a block of memory from the free store
2. Allocate that block to the executing program

Since the size of the free store is limited, each execution of ALLOCATE causes the pool of available memory to shrink.

Memory that is no longer needed should be returned to the free store so that it can be reallocated. This is accomplished by using the **DEALLOCATE** statement:

DEALLOCATE *Statement*

Forms:

    DEALLOCATE(*list*)

or

    DEALLOCATE(*list*, STAT = *status-variable*)

where
    list is a list of names of currently allocated arrays;
    status-variable is an integer variable.

Purpose:
Releases the memory allocated to the arrays listed. In the second form, the integer variable *status-variable* will be set to zero if deallocation is successful, but it will be assigned some system-dependent error value if it is not successful, for example, if no memory was previously allocated to an array.

Just as ALLOCATE is a request by the executing program to obtain memory from the free store, DEALLOCATE is a request to return memory to the free store. The ALLOCATE and DEALLOCATE statements are thus complementary.

Example: Processing a List of Failure Times—Revisited

In the preceding section we considered the problem of processing a list of failure times of components in a circuit, calculating their mean, and displaying a list of failure times greater than the mean. We assumed that there were 50 failure times, and we used a compile-time array of size 50 to store them.

Suppose, however, that the program in Figure 8.1 to do this processing is to be used with data sets of various sizes. For a compile-time array like FailureTime, the compiler must be informed of how many elements the array will have so that the correct size memory block can be allocated to it. For example, to process 100 failure times, we would change the definition of the named constant NumTimes,

```
INTEGER, PARAMETER :: NumTimes = 100
```

and recompile the program. Note the advantage of *using a named constant to specify the size of an array rather than a specific number.* If we used 50 in the declaration of the array `FailureTime` and in each of the DO loops for processing its elements, we would have to search through the entire program to locate all these occurrences of 50 and change them to 100. Instead, we need only change one statement in the program.

A more attractive solution is to make `FailureTime` an allocatable array. The number of failure times can then be entered during execution of the program, and an array of exactly the right size can be allocated at that time. The program in Figure 8.2 shows how the program in Figure 8.1 can be modified to use an allocatable array.

Figure 8.2 Processing a list of failure times.

```
PROGRAM Processing_Failure_Times_2
!------------------------------------------------------------------
! Program to read a list of failure times, calculate the mean time to
! failure, and then print a list of failure times that are greater
! than the mean.  An allocatable array is used to store the failure
! times.  Identifiers used are:
!     FileName            : name of data file
!     OpenStatus          : status variable for OPEN
!     InputStatus         : status variable for READ
!     AllocateStatus      : status variable for ALLOCATE
!     FailureTime         : one-dimensional array of failure times
!     NumTimes            : size of the array
!     I                   : subscript
!     Sum                 : sum of failure times
!     Mean_Time_to_Failure : mean of the failure times
!
! Input (keyboard): FileName
! Input (file):  NumTimes and a list of NumTimes failure times
! Output: Mean_Time_to_Failure and a list of failure times greater
!         than Mean_Time_to_Failure
! Note:  First value in data file must be the number of failure times.
!------------------------------------------------------------------

   IMPLICIT NONE
   CHARACTER(20) :: FileName
   REAL, DIMENSION(:), ALLOCATABLE :: FailureTime
   INTEGER :: OpenStatus, InputStatus, AllocateStatus, NumTimes, I
   REAL :: Sum, Mean_Time_to_Failure
```

Figure 8.2 *(cont.)*

```fortran
! Get the name of the data file and open it for input

WRITE (*, '(1X, A)', ADVANCE = "NO") "Enter name of data file: "
READ *, FileName
OPEN (UNIT = 10, FILE = FileName, STATUS = "OLD", IOSTAT = OpenStatus)
IF (OpenStatus > 0) STOP "*** Cannot open the file ***"

! Get the number of failure times and allocate an array
! with that many elements to store the failure times

READ (10, *, IOSTAT = InputStatus) NumTimes
IF (InputStatus > 0) STOP "*** Input error ***"
IF (InputStatus < 0) STOP "*** Not enough data ***"
ALLOCATE(FailureTime(NumTimes), STAT = AllocateStatus)
IF (AllocateStatus /= 0) STOP "*** Not enough memory ***"

! Read the failure times and store them in array FailureTime

READ (10, *, IOSTAT = InputStatus) FailureTime
IF (InputStatus > 0) STOP "*** Input error ***"
IF (InputStatus < 0) STOP "*** Not enough data ***"

! Calculate the mean time to failure

Sum = 0.0
DO I = 1, NumTimes
    Sum = Sum + FailureTime(I)
END DO
Mean_Time_to_Failure = Sum / REAL(NumTimes)
PRINT '(/ 1X, "For the", I4, " failure times read, " / 1X, &
      &"the mean time to failure =", F6.1)', NumTimes, Mean_Time_to_Failure

! Print list of failure times greater than the mean

PRINT *
PRINT *,  "List of failure times greater than the mean:"
DO I = 1, NumTimes
   IF (FailureTime(I) > Mean_Time_to_Failure) &
      PRINT '(1X, F9.1)', FailureTime(I)
END DO

! Deallocate the array of failure times
DEALLOCATE(FailureTime)

END PROGRAM Processing_Failure_Times_2
```

Note the use of the STAT = clause in the ALLOCATE statement to check whether the allocation is successful. If there is not enough memory to allocate to the array FailureTime, execution of the program will be terminated:

```
Cannot ALLOCATE ALLOCATABLE array - out of memory
Program terminated by fatal error
Abort
```

An error will also result if an attempt is made to allocate memory for an array to which memory has already been allocated or to deallocate memory for an array to which no memory has been allocated. The **ALLOCATED function** can be used to guard against this:

```
IF (ALLOCATED(FailureTime)) DEALLOCATE(FailureTime)
```

Quick Quiz 8.2

1. An array is a(n) _____ access structure.

2. Each individual element of an array is accessed by using a(n) _____ variable.

3. In the array reference X(I), I is called a(n) _____.

4. Arrays that involve only a single subscript are called _____ arrays.

5. (True or false) INTEGER, DIMENSION :: CODE(10) is a legal array declaration.

6. (True or false) The array declaration REAL, DIMENSION(5) :: X is equivalent to the array declaration REAL, DIMENSION(1:5) :: X.

7. (True or false) Given the declaration REAL, DIMENSION(10) :: X, the statement READ *, X is equivalent to the statement READ *, (X(I), I = 1, 10).

8. (True or false) Given the declaration REAL, DIMENSION(10) :: X, the statement PRINT *, X is equivalent to the DO loop

```
DO I = 1, 10
   PRINT *, X(I)
END DO
```

9. (True or false) For the statement READ *, X, the values to be stored in X must be entered one per line.

Which of the statements in Questions 10–13 are in correct form?

10. READ *, (X(I), I = 1, 5)

11. READ (X(I), I = 1, 5)

12. READ (*, *) X(I), I = 1, 5

13. X(I) (READ, I = 1, 5)

For Questions 14–17, assume the following declarations have been made:

```
INTEGER, DIMENSION(5) :: Number
REAL, DIMENSION(5) ::  X_Value
INTEGER :: I
```

What values will be assigned to the array elements by the given statements?

14. ```
DO I = 1, 5
    IF (MOD(I,2) == 0) THEN
        Number(I) = 2 * I
    ELSE
        Number(I) = 2 * I + 1
    END IF
END DO
```

15. ```
Number(1) = 2
DO I = 2, 5
    Number(I) = 2 * Number(I - 1)
END DO
```

16. ```
DO I = 1, 5
    X_Value(I) = REAL(I) / 2.0
END DO
```

17. ```
I = 0
DO
    I = I + 1
    Number(I) = MIN(I, 3)
    IF (I >= 5) EXIT
END DO
```

Exercises 8.2

For Exercises 1–4, write declarations for the given arrays.

1. An array whose subscript values are integers from 0 through 10 and in which each element is a real value.

2. An array whose subscript values are integers from −5 through 5 and in which each element is an integer.

3. An array whose subscript values are integers from 1 through 20 and in which each element is a character string of length 10.

4. An array whose subscript values are integers from 1 through 100 and in which each element is either .TRUE. or .FALSE..

For Exercises 5–8, write declarations and statements to construct the given array.

5. An array whose subscript values are integers from 0 through 5 and in which each element is the same as the subscript value.

6. An array whose subscript values are integers from -5 through 5 and in which the elements are the subscripts in reverse order.

7. An array whose subscript values are the integers from 1 through 20 and in which an array element is true if the corresponding subscript is even and is false otherwise.

8. An array whose subscript values are the integers from 0 through 359 and whose elements are the values of the sine function at the angles $0°, 1°, \ldots, 359°$.

In Exercises 9–17 assume that the following declarations have been made:

```
INTEGER, DIMENSION(10) :: Number
INTEGER :: I
REAL, DIMENSION(-4:5) :: Point
```

and that the following data is entered:

```
1, 2, 3, 4, 5, 6, 7, 8, 9, 0
```

Tell what value (if any) is assigned to each array element or explain why an error occurs:

9.
```
DO I = 1, 10
    Number(I) = I / 2
END DO
```

10.
```
DO I = 1, 6
    Number(I) = I * I
END DO
DO I = 7, 10
    Number(I) = Number(I - 5)
END DO
```

11.
```
I = 1
DO
    IF (I == 10) EXIT
    IF (MOD(I,3) == 0) THEN
        Number(I) = 0
    ELSE
        Number(I) = I
    END IF
    I = I + 1
END DO
```

12. ```
Number(1) = 1
I = 2
DO
    Number(I) = Number(I - 1)
    I = I + 1
    IF (I >= 10) EXIT
END DO
```

13. ```
DO  I  =  1,  10
    READ  *,  Number(I)
END  DO
```

14. `READ  *,  Number`

15. `READ  *,  (Number(I),  I  =  1,  10)`

16. `READ  *,  (Point(I),  I  =  -4,  5)`

17. ```
READ *, Number
DO I = 1, 5
    IF (Number(I) < 5) THEN
        Point(I - 5) = -1.1 * I
        Point(I) = 1.1 * I
    ELSE
        Point(I - 5) = 0
        Point(I) = 0
    END IF
END DO
```

Exercises 18–23 assume the following declarations have been made:

```
INTEGER, DIMENSION(5) :: Number
CHARACTER(2), DIMENSION(5) :: Code
```

For each exercise, assume that the data is entered as indicated (beginning in position 1). Tell what values will be assigned to each array element.

18. `READ  *,  Number`

   Data-line: 12, 34, 56, 78, 90

19. `READ  *,  Number`

   Data-line-1:   12, 34
   Data-line-2:   56, 78
   Data-line-3:   90

20. `READ  '(2I2)',  Number`

   Data-line-1:   12345678
   Data-line-2:   23456789
   Data-line-3:   34567890
```

21. ```
DO I = 1, 5
    READ *, Number(I)
END DO
```

    Data-line-1:  12 23 34
    Data-line-2:  23 34 45
    Data-line-3:  34 45 56
    Data-line-4:  45 56 67
    Data-line-5:  56 67 78

22. `READ '(A2)', Code`

    Data-line-1:  ABCD
    Data-line-2:  BCDE
    Data-line-3:  CDEF
    Data-line-4:  DEFG
    Data-line-5:  EFGH

23. `READ '(2I3)', (Number(I), I = 1, 5)`

    Data-line-1: 123
    Data-line-2: 345678
    Data-line-3: 567890123
    Data-line-4: 789

For Exercises 24–29, assume that the following declarations have been made:

```
INTEGER, DIMENSION(10) :: Number
REAL, DIMENSION(-4:5) :: Point
CHARACTER(1), DIMENSION(10) :: Symbol
INTEGER :: I
```

Assume also that the following format statements are given,

```
100 FORMAT(10(1X, I1))
110 FORMAT(10(1X, F1.0))
120 FORMAT(5(A1, 1X))
130 FORMAT(5A1)
200 FORMAT(1X, 5I2)
210 FORMAT(1X, 5F4.0)
220 FORMAT(1X, 5A2)
```

and that the following data is entered:

```
A1B2C3D4E5F6G7H8I9J0
```

Tell what output will be produced, or explain why an error occurs.
```

```
24. READ 100, Number
    DO I = 1, 10
        PRINT 200, Number(I)
    END DO
25. READ 100, (Number(I), I = 1, 10)
    PRINT 200, (Number(I), I = 1, 10)
26. READ 110, (Point(I), I = -4, 5)
    DO I = -4, 5
        PRINT 210, Point(I)
    END DO
27. READ 110, Point
    PRINT 210, (Point(I-4), I = 0, 9)
28. READ 120, Symbol
    PRINT 220, Symbol
29. READ 130, (Symbol(I), I = 1, 5)
    PRINT 220, (Symbol(I), I = 1, 5)
```

8.3   APPLICATION: AVERAGE CORN YIELDS

Problem

Several different hybrids of corn are being tested in a large number of 10-acre test plots. A collection of data pairs consisting of hybrid codes and yields in bushels from these test plots has been recorded in a data file. The average yield for each of the hybrids is to be calculated.

Solution

Specification. The input and output specifications of this problem are clear:

Input: Pairs of hybrid codes and yields
Output: For each hybrid, the average yield or a message indicating that no test results were reported for that particular hybrid

Design. In solving this problem, we will use the following variables:

VARIABLES FOR THE CORN-YIELD PROBLEM

NumHybrids   Number of hybrids of corn being tested
Hybrid   A code (1, 2, . . . , *NumHybrids*) for a hybrid

Count	A one-dimensional array; *Count*(*Hybrid*) is the number of plots planted with a particular *Hybrid*
TotalYield	A one-dimensional array; *TotalYield*(*Hybrid*) is the total yield for a particular *Hybrid*

An appropriate algorithm is the following:

ALGORITHM FOR THE CORN-YIELD PROBLEM

Algorithm to find the average yields for each of several hybrids of corn.

Input: Hybrid codes and yields
Output: For each hybrid, the average yield or a message indicating
             there were no results to report for that particular hybrid

1. Open for input the file containing the corn-yield data; if not successful, terminate execution.

2. Read the number of hybrids (*NumHybrids*) from the first line of the file. If an input error occurs, terminate execution.

3. Allocate memory for arrays *Count* and *TotalYield*; if not enough memory is available, terminate execution.

4. Initialize the arrays *Count* and *TotalYield* to 0.

5. Do the following:
   a. Read a *Hybrid* code and a *Yield*.
   b. If an input error occurs, terminate execution.
      If the end of the file has been reached, terminate repetition.
      Otherwise continue with the following.
   c. Add 1 to *Count*(*Hybrid*).
   d. Add *Yield* to *TotalYield*(*Hybrid*).

6. Do the following for *Hybrid* ranging from 1 through *NumHybrids*:
   If *Count*(*Hybrid*) > 0 then
       Display *TotalYield*(*Hybrid*) / *Count*(*Hybrid*).
   Else
       Display a message that no test results were reported for this hybrid.

7. Deallocate the memory allocated to arrays *Count* and *TotalYield*.

Coding and Execution. The program in Figure 8.3 implements this algorithm. Note that arrays Count and TotalYield are allocatable arrays.

Figure 8.3 Average corn yields.

```
PROGRAM Average_Corn_Yields
!----------------------------------------------------------------------
! Program to find the average yield for each of several hybrids of
! corn, using data consisting of a hybrid code and yield obtained from
! tests of these hybrids on several test plots.  Identifiers used are:
!    FileName        : name of data file containing the corn-yield data
!    OpenStatus      : status variable for OPEN
!    InputStatus     : status variable for READ
!    AllocateStatus  : status variable for ALLOCATE
!    NumHybrids      : number of hybrids being tested
!    Count           : Count(I) = number of tests of hybrid I
!    TotalYield      : TotalYield(I) = sum of yields for hybrid I
!    Hybrid          : current hybrid code
!    Yield           : current yield being processed
!    I               : subscript
!
! Input:  Pairs of hybrid codes and yields (stored in Hybrid and Yield)
! Output: For each hybrid, the average yield or a message that no test
!         results were reported for that particular hybrid
!----------------------------------------------------------------------

  IMPLICIT NONE
  CHARACTER(10) :: FileName
  INTEGER, DIMENSION(:), ALLOCATABLE :: Count
  INTEGER :: OpenStatus, InputStatus, AllocateStatus, &
             NumHybrids, Hybrid, I
  REAL, DIMENSION(:), ALLOCATABLE :: TotalYield
  REAL :: Yield

  ! Get the name of the file containing the corn-yield data
  ! and open it for input

  PRINT *, "This program reads pairs of hybrid codes and yields"
  PRINT *, "from a data file.  The first line of the file contains"
  PRINT *, "the number of hybrids.  Each subsequent line contains"
  PRINT *, "a hybrid code and a yield."
  WRITE (*, '(/ 1X, A)', ADVANCE = "NO") &
        "Enter the name of the data file to be used: "
  READ *, FileName
  OPEN (UNIT = 10, FILE = FileName, STATUS = "OLD", IOSTAT = OpenStatus)
  IF (OpenStatus > 0) STOP "*** Cannot open the file ***"
```

Figure 8.3 *(cont.)*

```fortran
! Read number of hybrids from the first line of the file,
! allocate memory for arrays Count and TotalYield
READ (10, *, IOSTAT = InputStatus) NumHybrids
IF (InputStatus > 0) STOP "*** Input error ***"
IF (InputStatus < 0) STOP "*** No test results in the file ***"

ALLOCATE(Count(NumHybrids), TotalYield(NumHybrids), STATUS = AllocateStatus)
IF (AllocateStatus /= 0) STOP "*** Not enough memory ***"

! Zero out the arrays Count and TotalYield.
! Note:  As described in Section 8.4, this could be done more
!           simply by:    Count = 0    and    TotalYield = 0.0

DO I = 1, NumHybrids
   Count(I) = 0
   TotalYield(I) = 0.0
END DO

! While there is more data, read a hybrid code and yield,
! increment the appropriate counter, and add the yield to the
! appropriate sum

DO
   READ (10, *, IOSTAT = InputStatus) Hybrid, Yield
   IF (InputStatus > 0) STOP "*** Input error ***"
   IF (InputStatus < 0) EXIT ! End of data--terminate repetition

   ! Otherwise process the corn-yield data
   IF (Hybrid < NumHybrids) THEN
      Count(Hybrid) = Count(Hybrid) + 1
      TotalYield(Hybrid) = TotalYield(Hybrid) + Yield
   ELSE
      PRINT *, "*** Illegal hybrid code:", Hybrid
   END IF
END DO

! Calculate and print average yields

PRINT '(//1X, "For hybrid")'
DO Hybrid = 1, NumHybrids
   IF (Count(Hybrid) > 0) THEN
      PRINT '(1X, I10, ":  Average yield is", F6.2)', &
            Hybrid, TotalYield(Hybrid) / REAL(Count(Hybrid))
   ELSE
      PRINT '(1X, I10, ":  There were no test results reported")', &
         Hybrid
   END IF
END DO
```

Figure 8.3 *(cont.)*

```
DEALLOCATE(Count, TotalYield)

END PROGRAM Average_Corn_Yields
```

Listing of data file `fi18-3.dat` used in sample run:

```
4
1 34.0
1 32.7
2 30.1
5 29.8
3 29.8
2 32.8
1 32.0
3 28.1
1 29.4
2 28.9
3 27.4
```

Sample run:

```
This program reads pairs of hybrid codes and yields
from a data file.  The first line of the file contains
the number of hybrids.  Each subsequent line contains
a hybrid code and a yield.

Enter the name of the data file to be used: fil8-3.dat
*** Illegal hybrid code: 5

For hybrid
        1:  Average yield is 32.02
        2:  Average yield is 30.60
        3:  Average yield is 28.43
        4:  There were no test results reported
```

8.4   ARRAY PROCESSING

In the preceding sections, we considered array declarations, input/output of arrays, and some simple processing of lists using arrays. In this section we describe how other kinds of array processing are carried out in Fortran.

Array Constants

An **array constant** may be constructed as a *list of values* enclosed between (/ and /),

```
(/ value₁, value₂, ..., valueₖ /)
```

where each `valueᵢ` is a constant expression. For example,

```
(/ 2, 4, 6, 8, 10, 12, 14, 16, 18, 20 /)
```

is a one-dimensional array constant of size 10 consisting of the first 10 positive even integers. A value in an array constant may also be an **implied-DO constructor** of the form

```
(value-list, implied-do-control)
```

For example,

```
(/ (2*I, I = 1, 10) /)
```

constructs the preceding array constant of size 10. Array constants may also be formed using a combination of these two methods; for example,

```
(/ 2, 4, (I, I = 6, 18, 2), 20 /)
```

constructs the same array constant.

Constants of any of these forms can be assigned to arrays of the same size and type. (Mixed-mode assignments are carried out as described in Section 2.4.) For example, if A is declared by

```
INTEGER, DIMENSION(10) :: A
```

it can be assigned the sequence 2, 4, 6, . . . , 20 by any of the following statements:

```
A = (/ 2, 4, 6, 8, 10, 12, 14, 16, 18, 20 /)
A = (/ (2*I, I = 1, 10) /)
A = (/ 2, 4, (I, I = 6, 18, 2), 20 /)
```

Each of these has the same effect as the elementwise assignment

```
DO I = 1, 10
   A(I) = 2*I
END DO
```

Array Expressions

Operators and functions normally applied to simple expressions may also be applied to arrays having the same number of elements and to arrays and simple expressions. In this case, operations applied to an array are carried out elementwise. To illustrate, consider the following declarations:

```
INTEGER, DIMENSION(4) :: A, B
INTEGER, DIMENSION(0:3) :: C
INTEGER, DIMENSION(6:9) :: D
LOGICAL, DIMENSION(4) :: P
```

If A and B are assigned values

```
A = (/ 1, 2, 3, 4 /)
B = (/ 5, 6, 7, 8 /)
```

then the assignment statement

```
A = A + B
```

assigns to A the sequence 6, 8, 10, 12. If C is assigned a value

```
C = (/ -1, 3, -5, 7 /)
```

the statement

```
D = 2 * ABS(C) + 1
```

assigns to D the sequence 3, 7, 11, 15. Logical operations are also allowed. For example, the statement

```
P = (C > 0) .AND. (MOD(B, 3) == 0)
```

assigns to P the sequence of truth values .FALSE., .TRUE., .FALSE., .FALSE..

Array Assignment

As we know, a value can be assigned to a simple variable by an assignment statement of the form *variable = expression*. As we have seen, assignment statements may also be used for array variables:

```
array-variable = expression
```

The value of the expression assigned to an array variable must be either

1. An array of the same size as the array variable, or

2. A simple value

In the second case, the value is *broadcast to all the array elements*, with the result that each is assigned this value. For example, the assignment statement

```
A = 0
```

assigns 0 to each of the elements of A.

Array Sections and Subarrays

Sometimes it is necessary to construct arrays by selecting elements from another array, called a **parent array**. These new arrays, called **array sections** or **subarrays**, are constructed by using expressions of the form

```
array-name(subscript-triplet)
```

or

```
array-name(vector-subscript)
```

A **subscript triplet** has the form

```
lower : upper : stride
```

and specifies the elements in positions *lower*, *lower* + *stride*, *lower* + 2*stride, . . . , going as far as possible without going beyond *upper* if *stride* > 0, or below *upper* if *stride* < 0. If *lower* is omitted, the lower bound in the array declaration is used; if *upper* is omitted, the upper bound in the array declaration is used; if *stride* is omitted, it is taken to be 1. For example, if A, B, and I are arrays declared by

```
INTEGER, DIMENSION(10) :: A
INTEGER, DIMENSION(5) :: B, I
INTEGER :: J
```

and A is assigned a value by

```
A = (/ 11, 22, 33, 44, 55, 66, 77, 88, 99, 110 /)
```

then

```
A(2:10:2)
```

is the section of array A consisting of the elements 22, 44, 66, 88, and 110.

A **vector subscript** is a sequence of subscripts of the parent array. For example, if A is the array considered earlier,

```
A = (/ 11, 22, 33, 44, 55, 66, 77, 88, 99, 110 /)
```

and I is the subscript vector

```
I = (/ 6, 5, 3, 9, 1 /)
```

then

```
B = A(I)
```

assigns to B the section of array A consisting of the elements 66, 55, 33, 99, and 11 that are in positions 6, 5, 3, 9, and 1 of A. The statement

```
B = A((/ 5, 3, 3, 4, 3 /))
```

assigns B the sequence of elements 55, 33, 33, 44, and 33.

Subarrays may also appear on the left-hand side of an assignment statement. For example, suppose that A is the one-dimensional array considered earlier:

```
INTEGER, DIMENSION(10) :: A

A = (/ 11, 22, 33, 44, 55, 66, 77, 88, 99, 110 /)
```

The statement

```
A(1:10:2) = (/ (I**2, I = 1, 5) /)
```

changes the elements in the odd positions of A to 1, 4, 9, 16, 25.

Subarrays may also appear in input or output statements to read or display part of an array. For example, the statement

```
READ *, FailureTime(1:NumTimes)
```

is an alternative to using an implied DO loop as described in Section 8.1 to read values into the first NumTimes locations of the array FailureTime:

```
READ (10, *) (FailureTime(I), I = 1, NumTimes)
```

Similarly,

```
PRINT *, FailureTime(1:NumTimes)
```

has the same effect as using an implied DO loop to display the first NumTimes elements of FailureTime:

```
PRINT *, (FailureTime(I), I = 1, NumTimes)
```

The WHERE Construct

A WHERE construct may be used to assign values to arrays depending on the value of a logical array expression. This construct has the form

---

WHERE *Construct*

Forms:

WHERE (*logical-array-expr*) *array-var₁* = *array-expr₁*

or

WHERE (*logical-array-expr*)
   array-var₁ = *array-expr₁*
            ⋮
   array-varₘ = *array-exprₘ*
ELSEWHERE
   array-varₘ₊₁ = *array-exprₘ₊₁*
            ⋮
   array-varₙ = *array-exprₙ*
END WHERE

where
   logical-array-expr is a logical-valued array expression;
   and each *array-varᵢ* has the same size as the value of *logical-array-expr*; in the second form, the ELSEWHERE part is optional.

Purpose:
Evaluates *logical-array-expr* element by element. Whenever the expression is true (false), assigns the value of the corresponding element of each *array-exprᵢ* (in the ELSEWHERE part) to the corresponding element of *array-varᵢ*. All other elements are left unchanged in the first form.

For example, if arrays A and B are declared by

```
INTEGER, DIMENSION(5) :: A = (/ 0, 2, 5, 0, 10 /)
REAL, DIMENSION(5) :: B
```

the WHERE construct

```
WHERE (A > 0)
   B = 1.0 / REAL(A)
ELSEWHERE
   B = -1.0
END WHERE
```

assigns to B the sequence $-1.0, 0.5, 0.2, -1.0, 0.1$.

Arrays as Arguments

Intrinsic Array-Processing Subprograms. Fortran 90 provides several intrinsic functions whose arguments are arrays. Some of the more useful ones for one-dimensional arrays are

`ALLOCATED(A)`	Returns true if memory has been allocated to the allocatable array A and false otherwise
`DOT_PRODUCT(A, B)`	Returns the dot product of (numeric or logical) arrays A and B (see Section 8.6)
`MAXVAL(A)`	Returns the maximum value in array A
`MAXLOC(A)`	Returns a one-dimensional array containing one element whose value is the position of the first occurrence of the maximum value in A
`MINVAL(A)`	Returns the minimum value in array A
`MINLOC(A)`	Returns a one-dimensional array containing one element whose value is the position of the first occurrence of the minimum value in A
`PRODUCT(A)`	Returns the product of the elements in A
`SIZE(A)`	Returns the number of elements in A
`SUM(A)`	Returns the sum of the elements in A

Other forms of these functions and other intrinsic array-processing subprograms are described in Chapter 9 and in Appendix D.

Programmer-Defined Array-Processing Subprograms. For programmer-defined subprograms, *the actual array argument must be declared in the calling program unit, and the corresponding formal array argument must be declared in the subprogram.* When the subprogram is referenced, the first element of the actual array argument is associated with the first element of the corresponding formal array argument. Successive actual array elements are then associated with the corresponding formal array elements.

The program in Figure 8.4 illustrates the use of array arguments. It reads a list of numbers and then calls a function to calculate the mean of the numbers. Note that function Mean uses the intrinsic function Sum to calculate the sum of the elements of array X.

Figure 8.4 Calculating the mean of a list—version 1.

```fortran
PROGRAM Mean_of_a_List_1
!-----------------------------------------------------------------------
! Program to read a list of numbers Item(1), Item(2), ... ,
! Item(NumItems) and to calculate their mean using the function
! subprogram Mean.  Identifiers used are:
!   Item      : one-dimensional array of numbers
!   NumItems : number of items (named constant)
!   Mean      : function that finds the mean of a set of numbers
!
! Input:  NumItems and a list of NumItems real numbers
! Output: The mean of the numbers
!-----------------------------------------------------------------------

  IMPLICIT NONE
  INTEGER, PARAMETER :: NumItems = 10
  REAL, DIMENSION(NumItems) :: Item

  PRINT *, "Enter the", NumItems, "real numbers:"
  READ *, Item
  PRINT '(1X, "Mean of the ", I3, " numbers is ", F6.2)', &
        NumItems, Mean(Item)

CONTAINS

  !-Mean------------------------------------------------------------
  ! Function to find the mean of the elements of array X.  Local
  ! identifier used is
  !   NumElements : number of elements in array X (named constant)
  !
  ! Accepts:  Array X
  ! Returns:  The mean of the numbers stored in X
  !-----------------------------------------------------------------

  FUNCTION Mean(X)

    INTEGER, PARAMETER :: NumElements = 10
    REAL, DIMENSION(NumElements), INTENT(IN) :: X
    REAL :: Mean

    Mean = SUM(X) / REAL(NumElements)

  END FUNCTION Mean

END PROGRAM Mean_of_a_List_1
```

Figure 8.4 *(cont.)*

Sample run:

```
Enter the 10 real numbers:
55, 88.5, 90, 71.5, 100, 66.5, 70.3, 81.2, 93.7, 41
Mean of the  10 numbers is  75.77
```

An actual array argument and the corresponding formal array argument must have the same size, but they need not have the same subscript range. For example, if the array X in the subprogram Mean was declared by

```
REAL, DIMENSION(0:9) :: X
```

then the first element Item(1) of the actual array Item would be associated with the first element X(0) of the formal array X, the second element Item(2) of the actual array Item with the second element X(1) of the formal array X, and so on.

As we noted earlier, when an array is used as a formal argument, it must be declared in the subprogram, and the corresponding actual array argument must be declared in the calling program unit. To make it possible to design subprograms that can be used to process arrays of various sizes, Fortran allows both the array and its size or range of subscripts to be passed to the subprogram. For example, the program in Figure 8.4 that uses the function subprogram Mean to calculate the mean of a list of numbers can be rewritten as shown in Figure 8.5. Note that the formal argument NumElements is used to specify the dimension of the formal array X in this subprogram. The actual dimension NumItems = 10 and the actual array Item are passed to the subprogram from the main program when the function is referenced.

Figure 8.5 Calculating the mean of a list—version 2.

```
PROGRAM Mean_of_a_List_2
!---------------------------------------------------------------
! Program to read a list of numbers Item(1), Item(2), ... ,
! Item(NumItems) and to calculate their mean using the function
! subprogram Mean.  Identifiers used are:
!    Item     : one-dimensional array of numbers
!    NumItems : number of items (named constant)
!    Mean     : function that finds the mean of a set of numbers
!
! Input:  NumItems and a list of NumItems real numbers
! Output: The mean of the numbers
!---------------------------------------------------------------
```

Figure 8.5 *(cont.)*

```
IMPLICIT NONE
INTEGER, PARAMETER :: NumItems = 10
REAL, DIMENSION(NumItems) :: Item

PRINT *, "Enter the", NumItems, " real numbers:"
READ *, Item
PRINT '(1X, "Mean of the ", I3, " Numbers is ", F6.2)', &
      NumItems, Mean(Item, NumItems)

CONTAINS

  !-Mean-----------------------------------------------------------
  ! Function to find the mean of the NumElements elements of the array
  ! X.  The size (NumElements) of X is passed as an argument.
  !
  ! Accepts:  Array X and NumElements
  ! Returns:  The mean of the numbers stored in X
  !-----------------------------------------------------------------

  FUNCTION Mean(X, NumElements)

    INTEGER, INTENT(IN) :: NumElements
    REAL, DIMENSION(NumElements), INTENT(IN) :: X
    REAL :: Mean

    Mean = SUM(X) / REAL(NumElements)

  END FUNCTION Mean

END PROGRAM Mean_of_a_List_2
```

The actual array element `Item` in the program in Figure 8.5 is a compile-time array, but it could also be an allocatable array:

```
INTEGER :: NumItems, AllocateStatus
REAL, DIMENSION(:), ALLOCATABLE :: Item
REAL :: Mean

WRITE (*, '(1X, A)', ADVANCE = "NO") &
      "How many numbers are in the data set? "
READ *, NumItems
ALLOCATE(Item(NumItems), STAT = AllocateStatus)
IF (AllocateStatus /= 0) STOP "*** Not enough memory ***"
```

```
PRINT *, "Enter the", NumItems, " real numbers:"
READ *, Item
PRINT '(1X, "Mean of the ", I3, " Numbers is ", F6.2)', &
       NumItems, Mean(Item, NumItems)
```

However, *a formal array argument may not be an allocatable array.*

Assumed-Shape Arrays. An alternative to passing the size of a formal array argument to a subprogram is to use an **assumed-shape array** as the formal argument. In this case, the size of the formal array will assume the size of the corresponding actual array.

For an assumed-shape array, the `DIMENSION` specifier in its declaration has the form

$$\text{DIMENSION(:)} \quad \text{or} \quad \text{DIMENSION}(lower\text{-}bound \;:)$$

where in the second form, `lower-bound` specifies the lower bound on the subscripts for the formal array; in the first form, 1 will be used for the lower bound. For an external subprogram, an interface block must be used in the program unit that calls the subprogram. For example, function subprogram `Mean` in the program in Figure 8.6 declares the formal array `X` to be an assumed-shape array using

```
REAL, DIMENSION(:), INTENT(IN) :: X
```

and the main program uses the interface block

```
INTERFACE
   FUNCTION Mean(X)
      REAL :: Mean
      REAL, DIMENSION(:), INTENT(IN) :: X
   END FUNCTION Mean
END INTERFACE
```

for the function `Mean`. The size of `X` will be the size of the corresponding actual argument `Item`. The predefined function `SIZE` is used to determine what this size is.

Figure 8.6 Calculating the mean of a list—version 3.

```
PROGRAM Mean_of_a_List_3
!-----------------------------------------------------------------
! Program to read a list of numbers Item(1), Item(2), ...,
! Item(NumItems) and calculate their mean using the external
! function subprogram Mean.  Variables used are:
!   NumItems       : number of items
!   AllocateStatus : status variable for ALLOCATE
!   Item           : one-dimensional array of items
!   Mean           : external function to find the mean
!
! Input:  NumItems and a list of NumItems real numbers
! Output: The mean of the numbers
!-----------------------------------------------------------------
```

Figure 8.6 *(cont.)*

```
  IMPLICIT NONE
  REAL, DIMENSION (:), ALLOCATABLE :: Item
  INTEGER :: NumItems, AllocateStatus

  INTERFACE
    FUNCTION Mean(X)
      REAL :: Mean
      REAL, DIMENSION(:), INTENT(IN) :: X
    END FUNCTION Mean
  END INTERFACE

  WRITE (*, '(1X, A)', ADVANCE = "NO") &
        "How many numbers are in the data set? "
  READ *, NumItems
  ALLOCATE(Item(NumItems), STAT = AllocateStatus)
  IF (AllocateStatus /= 0) STOP "*** Not enough memory ***"

  PRINT *, "Enter the", NumItems, " real numbers:"
  READ *, Item

  PRINT '(1X, "Mean of the ", I3, " Numbers is ", F6.2)', &
          NumItems, Mean(Item)
  DEALLOCATE(Item)

END PROGRAM Mean_of_a_List_3


! Mean-------------------------------------------------------------
! External function to find the mean of the elements of the
! array X.  Local variables used are:
!   Sum : sum of the numbers
!   I   : subscript
!
! Accepts:  Assumed-shape array X
! Returns:  The mean of the numbers stored in X
!-----------------------------------------------------------------

FUNCTION Mean(X)

  IMPLICIT NONE
  REAL :: Mean
  REAL, DIMENSION(:), INTENT(IN) :: X

  Mean = SUM(X) / REAL(SIZE(X))

END FUNCTION Mean
```

Automatic Arrays. A subprogram that uses assumed-shape arrays may also need local array variables, called **automatic arrays**, whose sizes vary from one subprogram reference to the next. The SIZE function can be used to dimension such local arrays. For example, the following subroutine for interchanging two real arrays of the same size uses the automatic array Temp:

```
!-Swap--------------------------------------------------------
! Subroutine to swap two assumed-shape arrays A and B.
! Local array used is:
!    Temp : An automatic array used to interchange A and B
!
! Accepts:  A and B
! Returns:  A and B with elements interchanged
!------------------------------------------------------------

SUBROUTINE Swap(A, B)

  REAL, DIMENSION(:), INTENT(INOUT) :: A, B
  REAL, DIMENSION(SIZE(A)) :: Temp

  Temp = A
  A = B
  B = Temp

END SUBROUTINE Swap
```

Array-Valued Functions. The value returned by some of the intrinsic functions such as MaxLoc and MinLoc is an array, and programmer-defined functions may also return arrays. The function Reverse in Figure 8.7 illustrates this. It accepts an array and returns the reversal of that array. A simple driver program is used to test this function.

Figure 8.7 Reversing a list.

```
PROGRAM Reversing_a_List
!------------------------------------------------------------------
! Driver program to test the function subprogram Reverse.  It reads
! a list of numbers Item(1), Item(2), ..., Item(NumItems), calls
! Reverse to contruct the list in reverse order, and displays the
! reversed list.  Identifiers used are:
!   NumItems  : number of items (constant)
!   Item      : one-dimensional array of items
!   Reverse   : function to reverse an array
!
! Input:  NumItems and a list of NumItems integers
! Output: The reversal of the list
!------------------------------------------------------------------
```

Figure 8.7 *(cont.)*

```
IMPLICIT NONE
INTEGER, PARAMETER :: NumItems = 10
INTEGER, DIMENSION (NumItems) :: Item

WRITE (*, '(1X, A, I3, A)', ADVANCE = "NO") &
      "Enter", NumItems, " integers: "
READ *, Item

PRINT *, "The reversal of this list is"
PRINT *, Reverse(Item)

CONTAINS

  ! Reverse-------------------------------------------------
  ! Internal function to find the reversal of an array X. Local
  ! variables used are:
  !   NumElements : number of elements in X
  !   I           : subscript
  !
  ! Accepts:  Assumed-shape array X
  ! Returns:  The reversal of X
  !-------------------------------------------------------

  FUNCTION Reverse(X)

    INTEGER, DIMENSION(:), INTENT(IN) :: X
    INTEGER, DIMENSION(SIZE(X)) :: Reverse
    INTEGER :: NumElements, I

    NumElements = SIZE(X)
    DO I = 1, NumElements
       Reverse(I) = X(NumElements - I + 1)
    END DO

  END FUNCTION Reverse

END PROGRAM Reversing_a_List
```

Sample run:

```
Enter 10 integers: 1 2 3 4 5 6 7 8 9 10
The reversal of this list is
10 9 8 7 6 5 4 3 2 1
```

For an external function that returns an array, a program unit that references the function must contain an interface block for that function. For example, if the function subprogram Reverse in Figure 8.7 were an external function, we would include the following interface block in the specification part of the main program:

```
INTERFACE
   FUNCTION Reverse(X)
      INTEGER, DIMENSION(:), INTENT(IN) :: X
      INTEGER, DIMENSION(SIZE(X)) :: Reverse
   END FUNCTION Reverse
END INTERFACE
```

Quick Quiz 8.4

1. (True or false)   If A and B are arrays declared by REAL, DIMENSION(5) :: A, B, the statement A = B can be used to copy the values stored in B into A.

Questions 2–9 assume the following declarations have been made:

```
INTEGER, DIMENSION(6) :: A = (/ 11, 22, 33, 44, 55, 66 /), &
                         B = (/ (I**2, I = 1, 6) /), &
                         C = (/ 1, 6, 2, 4, 3, 5 /), &
                         D, E, F, G
```

2. List the elements of B, or explain why the declaration is not legal.

3. List the elements of A(2:4), or explain why this expression is not legal.

4. List the elements of A(1:5:2), or explain why this expression is not legal.

5. List the elements of A(C), or explain why this expression is not legal.

6. For D = 3*B + A, list the elements of D, or explain why this statement is not legal.

7. For E = 3, list the elements of E, or explain why this statement is not legal.

8. For F = A(1:4), list the elements of F, or explain why this statement is not legal.

9. For

```
WHERE (A < 50)
   G = A + B
ELSEWHERE
   G = A - B
END WHERE
```

list the elements of G, or explain why this WHERE construct is not legal.

10. (True or false)

```fortran
SUBROUTINE Print(Array, NumElements)

   INTEGER, DIMENSION(NumElements), INTENT(IN) :: Array
   INTEGER :: I

   DO I = 1, NumElements
      PRINT *, Array(I)
   END DO

END SUBROUTINE Print
```

   is a legal Fortran subroutine.

11. What output will the following program produce?

```fortran
PROGRAM Demo

   CHARACTER(3), DIMENSION(3) :: &
      Animal = (/ "ape", "bat", "cat" /)

   CALL Change(Animal, 2)
   PRINT '(1X, A, 3A4)', "Animal = ", Animal

CONTAINS

   SUBROUTINE Change(Array, Index)

      CHARACTER(3), DIMENSION(3), INTENT(INOUT) :: Array
      INTEGER, INTENT(IN) :: Index
      CHARACTER(3) :: Dirty = "rat"

      Array(Index) = Dirty

   END SUBROUTINE Change

END PROGRAM Demo
```

Exercises 8.4

Exercises 1–13 assume the following declarations have been made:

```fortran
REAL, DIMENSION(10) :: &
      A = (/ 0.0, 1.1, 2.2, 3.3, 4.4, 5.5, 6.6, 7.7, 8.8, 9.9 /), &
      B = (/ (32.0 / 2.0**I, I = 0, 9) /),  C
INTEGER, DIMENSION(0:9) :: D = (/ (I + 5, I = 0, 5), 1, 2, 3, 4/)
```

```
INTEGER :: M = 3, N = 9
REAL, DIMENSION(0:9) :: E
REAL, DIMENSION(-3:6) :: F
REAL, DIMENSION(100:109) :: G
```

1. List the elements of B, or explain why the declaration is not legal.

2. List the elements of D, or explain why the declaration is not legal.

3. List the elements of A(3:7), or explain why this expression is not legal.

4. List the elements of A(1:9:2), or explain why this expression is not legal.

5. List the elements of D(M:N:M), or explain why this expression is not legal.

6. List the elements of B(N:M), or explain why this expression is not legal.

7. List the elements of A(D), or explain why this expression is not legal.

8. List the elements of D(A), or explain why this expression is not legal.

9. For C = A + 2*B, list the elements of C, or explain why this statement is not legal.

10. For F = A + 2*B, list the elements of F, or explain why this statement is not legal.

11. For E = REAL(D) + 5, list the elements of E, or explain why this statement is not legal.

12. For G = B(1:10), list the elements of G, or explain why this statement is not legal.

13. For

```
WHERE (B > A)
    G = B - A
ELSEWHERE
    G = A - B
END WHERE
```

list the elements of G, or explain why this WHERE construct is not legal.

14. Write a function subprogram that accepts a positive integer and returns an array containing the first N powers of 2: $2^1, 2^2, \ldots, 2^N$.

15. Proceed as in Exercise 14 but write a subroutine subprogram.

16. Write a function subprogram that accepts two one-dimensional arrays A and B and returns another array in which each element is the maximum of the corresponding elements of A and B. Use assumed-shape arrays for the formal array arguments.

17. Proceed as in Exercise 16 but write a subroutine subprogram.

18. Write a function subprogram that accepts a one-dimensional array A and returns another array containing the elements of A but with all negative elements replaced by 0. Use an assumed-shape array for the formal array argument.

19. Proceed as in Exercise 18 but write a subroutine subprogram.

Direct access to the elements in an array is accomplished by means of **address translation.** The address of the first byte (or word) in the memory block reserved for an array is called the **base address** of the array, and the address of any other element is calculated in terms of this base address. For example, if the base address for the array Code is B and each array item can be stored in one byte, then the address of Code(1) is B, the address of Code(2) is $B + 1$, the address of Code(3) is $B + 2$, and in general, the address of Code(I) is $B + I - 1$:

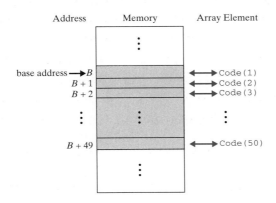

If W bytes are required for each element, then Code(1) is stored in W consecutive bytes, beginning at the byte with address B; Code(2) in a block beginning at address $B + W$; and in general, Code(I) in a block of size W beginning at address $B + (I - 1)*W$. Each time an array element is accessed using a subscripted variable, this address translation must be performed by the system software and/or hardware to determine the location of that element in memory.

In Exercises 20–27, assume that character and logical values require one byte of storage, that integers require four bytes, and that real values require eight bytes. Indicate with a diagram like that for Code, where each element of an array A as declared would be stored if the base address of A is B. Also, give the general address-translation formula for A(I).

20. INTEGER, DIMENSION(5) :: A

21. REAL, DIMENSION(5) :: A

22. LOGICAL, DIMENSION(5) :: A

23. CHARACTER(8), DIMENSION(5) :: A

24. INTEGER, DIMENSION(-5:5) :: A

25. REAL, DIMENSION(5:15) :: A

26. LOGICAL, DIMENSION(0:9) :: A

27. CHARACTER(1), DIMENSION(0:9) :: A

8.5   APPLICATION: QUALITY CONTROL

Problem

A quality-control engineer monitors a machine by recording the number of defective parts the machine produces each hour. This information is to be summarized in a *frequency distribution* that shows the number of one-hour periods in which there were no defective parts, one defective part, two defective parts, . . . , five or more defective parts.

Solution

Specification. The input/output specifications for this problem are clear:

Input: Integers representing counts of defective parts
Output: A frequency distribution

Design. To solve this problem, we will use the following variables:

VARIABLES FOR QUALITY-CONTROL PROBLEM

NumDefects: Number of defective parts counted in a one-hour period
FileName: The name of a data file that contains these counts
Count: An array: *Count*(*I*) is the number of one-hour periods during which *I* defective parts were produced, *I* = 0, 1, . . . , 5

Testing Motorola pagers. (Photo courtesy of Hewlett-Packard)

An appropriate algorithm is the following:

ALGORITHM FOR QUALITY-CONTROL PROBLEM

Algorithm to read several values for *NumDefects*, the number of defective parts produced by a machine in a given one-hour period, and to determine *Count*(I) = the number of periods in which there were I defective parts.

Input: Name of data file, and values stored in this file
Output: Values stored in array *Count*

1. Get the name of the data file and open it for input; if failure, stop execution.
2. Initialize array *Count* to all zeros.
3. Do the following:
   a. Attempt to read a value for *NumDefects*.
   b. If an input error occurs, stop execution. If the end of the file has been reached, terminate repetition. Otherwise continue with the following.
   c. If *NumDefects* > 5, set *NumDefects* to 5.
   d. Increase *Count*(*NumDefects*) by 1.
4. Display the values stored in array *Count*.

Coding, Testing, and Execution. The program in Figure 8.8 implements this algorithm. Also shown is a listing of a data file of test values and the frequency distribution produced by the program.

Figure 8.8 Generating a frequency distribution.

```
PROGRAM Frequency_Distribution_1
!------------------------------------------------------------------
! Program to generate a frequency distribution of the number of 1-hour
! periods in which there were 0, 1, 2, ... defective parts produced by
! a machine.  The data is read from a file.  Identifiers used are:
!     MaxDefective : constant representing maximum # of defective
!                    parts
!     Count        : Count(I) = # of 1-hour periods with I defective
!                    parts
!     FileName     : name of the data file
!     OpenStatus   : status variable for OPEN
!     InputStatus  : status variable for READ
!     NumDefects   : number of defective parts read from file
!     I            : subscript
!
```

Figure 8.8 *(cont.)*

```
! Input (keyboard): FileName
! Input (file):     Number of defects per hour
! Output:           Frequency distribution -- elements of array Count
!-------------------------------------------------------------------

  IMPLICIT NONE
  INTEGER, PARAMETER :: MaxDefective = 5
  INTEGER, DIMENSION(0:MaxDefective) :: Count = 0
  INTEGER :: OpenStatus, InputStatus, NumDefects, I
  CHARACTER(20) :: FileName

  ! Get file name, open the file as unit 15

  WRITE (*, '(1X, A)', ADVANCE = "NO") "Enter name of data file: "
  READ *, FileName
  OPEN (UNIT = 15, FILE = FileName, STATUS = "OLD", IOSTAT = OpenStatus)
  IF (OpenStatus > 0) STOP "*** Cannot open the file ***"

  ! While there is more data, read # of defective parts and
  ! increment appropriate counter

  DO
     READ (15, *, IOSTAT = InputStatus) NumDefects
     IF (InputStatus > 0) STOP "*** Input error ***"
     IF (InputStatus < 0) EXIT  ! end of file

     ! Otherwise continue with the following
     NumDefects = MIN(NumDefects, MaxDefective)
     Count(NumDefects) = Count(NumDefects) + 1
  END DO

  ! Print the frequency distribution

  PRINT *
  PRINT *, "# of defectives   # of hours"
  PRINT *, "===============   ========="
  DO I = 0, MaxDefective
     PRINT '(1X, I8, I15)', I, Count(I)
  END DO

  CLOSE (15)

END PROGRAM Frequency_Distribution_1
```

Figure 8.8 *(cont.)*

Listing of `fil8-8.dat` used in sample run:

```
0
1
0
2
2
0
1
6
3
0
3
1
2
0
1
2
0
```

Sample run:

```
Enter name of data file: fil8-8.dat

# of defectives    # of hours
===============    ==========
        0               6
        1               4
        2               4
        3               2
        4               0
        5               1
```

A Graphical Solution

A **bar graph** or **histogram** is often used to display frequency distributions graphically. Each of the categories is represented by a bar whose length corresponds to the number of items in that category. Thus the frequency distribution produced by the sample run in Figure 8.8 could be represented by the following bar graph:

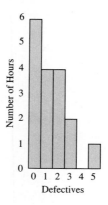

The program in Figure 8.9 is a modification of the preceding program that displays a similar bar graph.

Figure 8.9 Generating a bar graph.

```
PROGRAM Frequency_Distribution_2
!------------------------------------------------------------------
! Program to generate a bar graph of the number of 1-hour periods in
! which there were 0, 1, 2, ... defective parts produced by a machine.
! The data is read from a file.  Identifiers used are:
!     MaxDefective : constant representing maximum # of defective
!                    parts
!     Count        : Count(I) = # of 1-hour periods with I defective
!                    parts
!     FileName     : name of the data file
!     OpenStatus   : status variable for OPEN
!     InputStatus  : status variable for READ
!     NumDefects   : number of defective parts read from file
!     DrawBarGraph : subroutine to plot a bar graph
!
! Input (keyboard): FileName
! Input (file):     Number of defects per hour
! Output:           Bar graph displaying elements of array Count
!------------------------------------------------------------------

  IMPLICIT NONE
  INTEGER, PARAMETER :: MaxDefective = 5
  INTEGER, DIMENSION(0:MaxDefective) :: Count = 0
  INTEGER :: OpenStatus, InputStatus, NumDefects, I
  CHARACTER(20) :: FileName
```

Figure 8.9 *(cont.)*

```
! Get file name, open the file as unit 15

WRITE (*, '(1X, A)', ADVANCE = "NO") "Enter name of data file: "
READ *, FileName
OPEN (UNIT = 15, FILE = FileName, STATUS = "OLD", IOSTAT = OpenStatus)
IF (OpenStatus > 0) STOP "*** Cannot open the file ***"

! While there is more data, read # of defective parts and
! increment appropriate counter

DO
   READ (15, *, IOSTAT = InputStatus) NumDefects
   IF (InputStatus > 0) STOP "*** Input error ***"
   IF (InputStatus < 0) EXIT  ! end of file

   ! Otherwise continue with the following
   NumDefects = MIN(NumDefects, MaxDefective)
   Count(NumDefects) = Count(NumDefects) + 1
END DO

CALL DrawBarGraph(Count, MaxDefective, "Defectives", &
                  "Number of Hours")

CLOSE (15)

CONTAINS

   !-DrawBarGraph---------------------------------------------------------
   ! Subroutine to plot a bar graph representation of a frequency
   ! distribution.  Identifiers used are:
   !    Frequency               : array of frequencies
   !    NumFrequencies          : number of frequencies
   !    MaxFrequency            : largest frequency
   !    Vertical_Axis_Label     : label for vertical axis
   !    Horizontal_Axis_Label   : label for horizontal axis
   !    Number_of_Bars          : size of the array Bar (named constant)
   !    Bar                     : character array used to print one bar
   !                                of bar graph
   !    I, J                    : subscripts
   !
   ! Accepts:  Array Frequency, integer NumFrequencies, and character
   !           strings Vertical_Axis_Label and Horizontal_Axis_Label
   ! Output:   A bar graph of the elements of Frequency
   !----------------------------------------------------------------------
```

Figure 8.9 *(cont.)*

```
SUBROUTINE DrawBarGraph(Frequency, NumFrequencies, &
          Vertical_Axis_Label, Horizontal_Axis_Label)

   INTEGER, INTENT(IN) :: NumFrequencies
   INTEGER, DIMENSION (0:NumFrequencies), INTENT(IN) :: Frequency
   CHARACTER(*) :: Vertical_Axis_Label, Horizontal_Axis_Label
   INTEGER ::  I, J, MaxFrequency
   INTEGER, PARAMETER :: Number_of_Bars = 20
   CHARACTER(3), DIMENSION(Number_of_Bars) :: Bar

   PRINT '(//1X, A)', Vertical_Axis_Label
   MaxFrequency = MAXVAL(Frequency)

   DO I = 0, MaxFrequency
      Bar = " "
      DO J = 1, Frequency(I)
         Bar(J) = "***"
      END DO
      PRINT '(1X, I10, 21A)', I, ":", Bar
   END DO

   PRINT '(11X, 80A)', (".", I = 0, 3 * MaxFrequency)
   PRINT '(9X, 20I3)', (I, I = 0, MaxFrequency)
   PRINT '(11X, A)', Horizontal_Axis_Label

  END SUBROUTINE DrawBarGraph

END PROGRAM Frequency_Distribution_2
```

Sample run:

```
Enter name of data file: fil8-9.dat


Defectives
          0:******************
          1:************
          2:************
          3:******
          4:
          5:***
          6:
           .................
           0  1  2  3  4  5  6
           Number of Hours
```

8.6   EXAMPLE: VECTOR PROCESSING

Vectors are quantities that have two attributes: magnitude and direction. They are used in science and engineering to model forces, velocities, accelerations, and many other physical quantities.

A vector in the plane or in three-dimensional space can be represented by a directed line segment whose length represents the magnitude of the vector and whose orientation specifies its direction. Two vectors are equal if they have the same magnitude and direction. Thus all the vectors in the following diagram are equal:

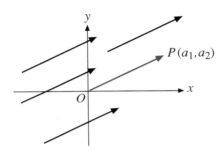

A vector like $\overrightarrow{OP}$, whose initial point is the origin, is called a *position vector*. This position vector (and all vectors equal to it) can be represented algebraically by the coordinates (a_1, a_2) of the terminal point P. The x- and y-coordinates a_1 and a_2 are called the *components* of the vector.

Similarly, vectors in three-dimensional space can be represented algebraically by ordered triples (a_1, a_2, a_3). In general, *n-dimensional vectors* can be represented algebraically by ordered n-tuples $(a_1, a_2, \ldots, a_n)$. This algebraic representation is convenient for computation because the components of a vector can be stored in an array and the basic vector operations can be easily implemented using this array representation.

To illustrate, the *norm* of a vector **a** is its magnitude and is usually denoted by |**a**|. For a vector in two and three dimensions, the norm is the length of the line segment that represents the vector and can be computed using the formula for the distance between two points. For example, in the preceding diagram, if **a** is the vector $\overrightarrow{OP}$, the norm of **a** is given by

$$|\mathbf{a}| = \sqrt{(a_1 - 0)^2 + (a_2 - 0)^2} = \sqrt{a_1^2 + a_2^2}$$

In general, the norm of an *n*-dimensional vector $\mathbf{a} = (a_1, a_2, \ldots, a_n)$ is given by

$$|\mathbf{a}| = \sqrt{a_1^2 + a_2^2 + \cdots + a_n^2}$$

Writing a function subprogram to compute the norm of a vector using this formula is straightforward. Note that A * A computes the squares of the elements of A, and the Sum function adds them:

```
!-Norm---------------------------------------------------------
! Function to calculate the norm of a vector.  Variables used:
!     A : array that stores the vector
!     N : number of components in the vector (its dimension)
!
! Accepts: A and N
! Returns: Norm of the N-dimensional vector stored in A
!--------------------------------------------------------------

FUNCTION Norm(A, N)

   REAL :: Norm
   REAL, INTENT(IN), DIMENSION(N) :: A
   INTEGER, INTENT(IN) :: N


   Norm = SQRT(SUM(A*A))

END FUNCTION Norm
```

The *sum* and *difference* of two vectors can be computed algebraically by simply adding and subtracting corresponding components. For example, if $\mathbf{a} = (3, 5)$ and $\mathbf{b} = (-2, 7)$, then

$$\mathbf{a} + \mathbf{b} = (1, 12)$$

$$\mathbf{a} - \mathbf{b} = (5, -2)$$

In general, if $\mathbf{a} = (a_1, a_2, \ldots, a_n)$ and $\mathbf{b} = (b_1, b_2, \ldots, b_n)$, then

$$\mathbf{a} + \mathbf{b} = (a_1 + b_1, a_2 + b_2, \ldots, a_n + b_n)$$

$$\mathbf{a} - \mathbf{b} = (a_1 - b_1, a_2 - b_2, \ldots, a_n - b_n)$$

Since the basic arithmetic Fortran operations are performed elementwise on arrays, + and – can be used to compute the sum and difference of vectors stored in arrays.

Like addition and subtraction, *multiplication of a vector by a scalar* (i.e., number) is performed componentwise:

$$c\mathbf{a} = (ca_1, ca_2, \ldots, ca_n)$$

For example, for the vector $\mathbf{a}$ given earlier,

$$2\mathbf{a} = (6, 10)$$

Since multiplication of an array by a scalar is carried out elementwise, implementing this vector operation in Fortran is trivial.

The *dot* (or *scalar*) *product* $\mathbf{a} \cdot \mathbf{b}$ of two vectors is the scalar obtained by adding the products of corresponding components:

$$\mathbf{a} \cdot \mathbf{b} = \sum_{i=1}^{n} a_i b_i = a_1 b_1 + a_2 b_2 + \cdots + a_n b_n$$

For example, for the vectors **a** and **b** given earlier,

$$\mathbf{a} \cdot \mathbf{b} = 29$$

In Fortran, if A and B are two one-dimensional arrays, the function reference DOT_PRODUCT(A, B) returns the dot product of A and B and can thus be used to compute dot products of vectors stored in arrays.

Other vector operations are described in the exercises. Function subprograms to implement them are straightforward.

Exercises 8.6

1. The *cross* (or *vector*) *product* $\mathbf{a} \times \mathbf{b}$ of two vectors is a vector. This product is defined only for three-dimensional vectors: if $\mathbf{a} = (a_1, a_2, a_3)$ and $\mathbf{b} = (b_1, b_2, b_3)$, then

$$\mathbf{a} \times \mathbf{b} = (a_2 b_3 - a_3 b_2, a_3 b_1 - a_1 b_3, a_1 b_2 - a_2 b_1)$$

Write a function subprogram that accepts a value for n and two n-dimensional vectors and that returns the cross product of the vectors if $n = 3$ or displays an error message otherwise. Write a program to test your subprogram.

2. Write a function subprogram that finds a unit vector having the same direction as a given vector.

3. A formula that can be used to find the angle between two vectors is

$$\cos \theta = \frac{\mathbf{a} \cdot \mathbf{b}}{|\mathbf{a}| \, |\mathbf{b}|}$$

Write a function subprogram to compute the angle between two vectors.

8.7 SORTING

A common programming problem is **sorting**, that is, arranging the items in a list so that they are in either ascending or descending order. There are many sorting methods, most of which assume that the items to be sorted are stored in an array. In this section we describe one of the simplest methods, **simple selection sort**, and one of the most efficient methods, **quicksort**. Other sorting schemes are described in the programming problems at the end of this chapter.

Simple Selection Sort

The basic idea of a selection sort of a list is to make a number of passes through the list or a part of the list, and on each pass to select one item to be correctly positioned. For example, on each pass through a sublist, the smallest item in the sublist might be found and moved to its proper position.

As an illustration, suppose that the following list is to be sorted into ascending order:

$$67, 33, 21, 84, 49, 50, 75$$

We locate the smallest item and find it in position 3:

$$67, 33, \boxed{21}, 84, 49, 50, 75$$

We interchange this item with the first item and thus properly position the smallest item at the beginning of the list:

$$\boxed{21}, 33, \boxed{67}, 84, 49, 50, 75$$

We now consider the sublist consisting of the items from position 2 on,

$$21, \boxed{33}, 67, 84, 49, 50, 75$$

to find the smallest item and exchange it with the second item (itself in this case) and thus properly position the next-to-smallest item in position 2:

$$21, \boxed{33}, 67, 84, 49, 50, 75$$

We continue in this manner, locating the smallest item in the sublist of items from position 3 on and interchanging it with the third item, then properly positioning the smallest item in the sublist of items from position 4 on, and so on until we eventually do this for the sublist consisting of the last two items:

$$21, 33, \boxed{49}, 84, \boxed{67}, 50, 75$$

$$21, 33, 49, \boxed{50}, 67, \boxed{84}, 75$$

$$21, 33, 49, 50, \boxed{67}, 84, 75$$

$$21, 33, 49, 50, 67, \boxed{75}, \boxed{84}$$

Positioning the smallest item in this last sublist obviously also positions the last item correctly and thus completes the sort.

An algorithm for this simple selection sort is as follows.

SIMPLE SELECTION SORT ALGORITHM

Algorithm to sort the list of items $X(1)$, $X(2)$, . . . , $X(N)$ so they are in ascending order. To sort them into descending order, find the largest item rather than the smallest item on each pass.

Accepts: List $X(1)$, $X(2)$, . . . , $X(N)$
Returns: Modified list $X(1)$, $X(2)$, . . . , $X(N)$; elements are sorted
            into ascending order

For I ranging from 1 to $N - 1$, do the following:

1. On the Ith pass, first find the *SmallestItem* in the sublist $X(I)$, . . . , $X(N)$ and its position *LocationSmallest*.

   Now interchange this smallest item with the item at the beginning of this sublist.

2. Set $X(LocationSmallest)$ equal to $X(I)$.
3. Set $X(I)$ equal to *SmallestItem*.

The following subroutine uses this algorithm to sort a list of integers.

Figure 8.10 Selection sort.

```
!-SelectionSort-----------------------------------------------
! Subroutine to sort an array Item into ascending order using
! the simple selection sort algorithm.  For descending order,
! change MINVAL to MAXVAL and MINLOC to MAXLOC.   Local
! variables used are:
!   NumItems          : number of elements in array Item
!   SmallestItem      : smallest item in current sublist
!   MINLOC_array      : one-element array returned by MINLOC
!   LocationSmallest  : location of SmallestItem
!   I                 : subscript
!
! Accepts:  Array Item
! Returns:  Array Item (modified) with elements in ascending
!           order
!
```

Figure 8.10 *(cont.)*

```
! Note:   Item is an assumed-shape array, so a program unit that
!         calls this subroutine must:
!         1. contain this subroutine as an internal subprogram,
!         2. import this subroutine from a module, or
!         3. contain an interface block for this subroutine.
!-------------------------------------------------------------

SUBROUTINE SelectionSort(Item)

  INTEGER, DIMENSION(:), INTENT(INOUT) :: Item
  INTEGER :: NumItems, SmallestItem, I
  INTEGER, DIMENSION(1) :: MINLOC_array

  NumItems = SIZE(Item)
  DO I = 1, NumItems - 1

     ! Find smallest item in the sublist
     ! Item(I), ..., Item(NumItems)

     SmallestItem = MINVAL(Item(I:NumItems))
     MINLOC_array = MINLOC(Item(I:NumItems))
     LocationSmallest = (I - 1) + MINLOC_array(1)

     ! Interchange smallest item with Item(I) at
     ! beginning of sublist

     Item(LocationSmallest) = Item(I)
     Item(I) = SmallestItem

  END DO

END SUBROUTINE SelectionSort
```

In this subroutine we have used the intrinsic functions MINVAL and MINLOC to locate the smallest value in each sublist and its position in that sublist. The function reference in the assignment statement

```
MINLOC_array = MINLOC(Item(I:N))
```

returns a one-element array whose value is the position, counting from 1, of the smallest value in the array section Item(I:N). The location of this smallest value in the entire list is thus given by

```
LocationSmallest = (I - 1) + MINLOC_array(1)
```

and the element in the list at this location is interchanged with the element at location I.

Quicksort

The **quicksort** method of sorting is more efficient than simple selection sort. It is, in fact, one of the fastest methods of sorting and is most often implemented by a recursive algorithm. The basic idea of quicksort is to choose some element called a **pivot** and then to perform a sequence of exchanges so that all elements that are less than this pivot are to its left and all elements that are greater than the pivot are to its right. This correctly positions the pivot and divides the (sub)list into two smaller sublists, each of which may then be sorted independently in the *same* way. This **divide-and-conquer** strategy leads naturally to a recursive sorting algorithm.

To illustrate this splitting of a list into two sublists, consider the following list of integers:

$$50, 30, 20, 80, 90, 70, 95, 85, 10, 15, 75, 25$$

If we select the first number as the pivot, we must rearrange the list so that 30, 20, 10, 15, and 25 are placed before 50, and 80, 90, 70, 95, 85, and 75 are placed after it. To carry out this rearrangement, we search from the right end of the list for an element less than 50 and from the left end for an item greater than 50.

$$50 , 30, 20, \boxed{80}, 90, 70, 95, 85, 10, 15, 75, \; 25$$

This locates the two numbers 25 and 80, which we now interchange to obtain

$$50, 30, 20, \boxed{25}, 90, 70, 95, 85, 10, 15, 75, \; 80$$

We then resume the search from the right for a number less than 50 and from the left for a number greater than 50:

$$50, 30, 20, 25, \boxed{90}, 70, 95, 85, 10, \; 15 , 75, 80$$

This locates the numbers 15 and 90, which are then interchanged:

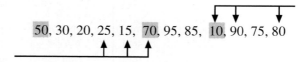

A continuation of the searches locates 10 and 70:

$$50, 30, 20, 25, 15, \boxed{70}, 95, 85, \boxed{10}, 90, 75, 80$$

Interchanging these gives

$$50, 30, 20, 25, 15, \boxed{10}, 95, 85, \boxed{70}, 90, 75, 80$$

When we resume our search from the right for a number less than 50, we locate the value 10, which was found on the previous left-to-right search. This signals the end of the two searches, and we interchange 50 and 10, giving

$$10, 30, 20, 25, 15, \boxed{50}, 95, 85, 70, 90, 75, 80$$

The two underlined sublists now have the required properties: All elements in the first sublist are less than 50, and all those in the right sublist are greater than 50. Consequently, 50 has been properly positioned.

Both the left sublist

$$10, 30, 20, 25, 15$$

and the right sublist

$$95, 85, 70, 90, 75, 80$$

can now be sorted independently. Each must be split by choosing and correctly positioning one pivot element (the first) in each of them. For this, a subroutine is needed to split a list of items in the array positions given by two parameters Low and High, denoting the beginning and end positions of the sublist, respectively. A recursive subroutine to sort a list is then easy to write. The anchor case occurs when the list being examined is empty or contains a single element; in this case the list is in order, and nothing needs to be done. The inductive case occurs when the list contains multiple elements, in which case the list can be sorted by:

1. Splitting the list into two sublists;
2. Recursively sorting the left sublist and
3. Recursively sorting the right sublist.

Figure 8.11 Quicksort.

```
!---------------------------------------------------------------
! Note: In the following subroutines, Item is an assumed-shape
!       array so a program unit that calls these subroutines must:
!          1. contain this subroutine as an internal subprogram,
!          2. import this subroutine from a module, or
!          3. contain an interface block for this subroutine.
!---------------------------------------------------------------


!-Quicksort-----------------------------------------------------
! Subroutine to sort a list using the quicksort method.  Call
! it with First = the lower bound on the subscripts of the
! array and Last = the upper bound.  Local variable used:
!    Mid : position of the split point
!
! Accepts:  Array Item
! Returns:  Array Item (modified) with elements in ascending
!           order
!---------------------------------------------------------------

RECURSIVE SUBROUTINE Quicksort(Item, First, Last)

   INTEGER, DIMENSION(:), INTENT(INOUT) :: Item
   INTEGER, INTENT(IN) :: First, Last
   INTEGER :: Mid

   IF (First < Last) THEN                    !If list size >= 2
      CALL Split(Item, First, Last, Mid) !  split it
      CALL Quicksort(Item, First, Mid-1) !  sort left half
      CALL Quicksort(Item, Mid+1, Last)  !  sort right half
   END IF

END SUBROUTINE Quicksort

!-Split---------------------------------------------------------
! Subroutine to split a list into two sublists, using the
! first element as pivot, and return the position of the
! element about which the List was divided.   Local variables
! used are:
!   Left  : position of first element
!   Right : position of last element
!   Pivot : pivot element
!   Swap  : used to swap two elements
!
```

Figure 8.11 *(cont.)*

```
! Accepts:   Array Item and positions Low and High of the first
!            and last elements
! Returns:   Array Item (modified) with elements in ascending
!            order
!
! Note:   Item is an assumed-shape array so a program unit that
!         calls this subroutine must:
!            1. contain this subroutine as an internal subprogram,
!            2. import this subroutine from a module, or
!            3. contain an interface block for this subroutine.
!-------------------------------------------------------------

SUBROUTINE Split(Item, Low, High, Mid)

  INTEGER, DIMENSION(:), INTENT(INOUT) :: Item
  INTEGER, INTENT(IN) :: Low, High
  INTEGER, INTENT(OUT) :: Mid
  INTEGER :: Left, Right, Swap

  Left = Low
  Right = High
  Pivot = Item(Low)

  ! Repeat the following while Left and Right haven't met
  DO
     IF (Left >= Right) EXIT

     ! Scan right to left to find element < Pivot
     DO
        IF (Left >= Right .OR. Item(Right) < Pivot) EXIT
        Right = Right - 1
     END DO

     ! Scan left to right to find element > Pivot
     DO
        IF (Item(Left) > Pivot) EXIT
        Left = Left + 1
     END DO

     ! If Left and Right haven't met, exchange the items
     IF (Left < Right) THEN
        Swap = Item(Left)
        Item(Left) = Item(Right)
        Item(Right) = Swap
     END IF
  END DO
```

Figure 8.11 *(cont.)*

```
! Switch element in split position with pivot
Item(Low) = Item(Right)
Item(Right) = Pivot
Mid = Right

END SUBROUTINE Split
```

8.8 APPLICATION: ANALYZING CONSTRUCTION COSTS

Problem

A company is planning to build a new manufacturing facility. One of the factors in selecting the site is the cost of labor in the various cities under consideration. To help analyze this data, the labor costs for these cities must be sorted so that they can be displayed in order and so that the median labor cost can be found.

Solution

Specification

Input:	A list of labor costs
Output:	Sorted list of labor costs
	Median labor cost

Design. The following variables will be used:

VARIABLES USED IN CONSTRUCTION-COST PROBLEM

Cost	Array that stores the labor costs
N	Number of labor costs

The **median** of a set of numbers $X_1, \ldots, X_n$ is the middle value when these numbers have been arranged in ascending order. One-half of the numbers are greater than or equal to this median value and one-half are smaller. After the list of numbers has been sorted, the median value is in position $(n + 1)/2$ if n is odd and is the average of the numbers in positions $n/2$ and $n/2 + 1$ if n is even. The following algorithm reads and stores the labor costs, sorts these costs, and then finds the median cost using this approach.

ALGORITHM FOR CONSTRUCTION-COST PROBLEM

Algorithm to sort a list of labor costs $Cost(1)$, $Cost(2)$, . . . , $Cost(N)$ so they are in ascending order and then find the median cost.

Input: A list of labor costs
Output: Sorted list of labor costs and the median cost

1. Read the labor costs and store them in array *Cost*.
2. Sort the array *Cost*.
3. Display the sorted list of costs.
4. Calculate and display the median cost as follows:
     If N is odd
          Display $Cost((N + 1) / 2)$.
     Else
          Display $\dfrac{Cost\,(N/2) + Cost\,(N/2 + 1)}{2}$.

Coding, Execution, and Testing. The program in Figure 8.12 implements the preceding algorithm. It calls the (internal) subroutine `ReadCosts` to read the list of costs, calls the subroutine `SelectionSort` (imported from module `Sort_Routines`) to sort them using the selection sort algorithm, and then calls the (internal) subroutine `Output` to display the sorted list and the median cost. Also shown is one of the test runs with a small set of test data.

Figure 8.12 Sorting labor costs and finding median cost.

```
PROGRAM Sort_and_Find_Median_Cost
!-------------------------------------------------------------------
! This program reads and counts a list of labor costs, uses a module
! subroutine to sort them in ascending order, and finds the median cost.
! Variables used are:
!   Cost             : list of labor costs (in millions)
!   MaxNumCosts      : maximum number of costs
!   AllocateStatus   : status variable for ALLOCATE
!   NumCosts         : number of costs
!
! Input:  Elements of Cost -- using internal subroutine ReadCosts
! Output: Sorted elements of Cost -- using internal subroutine Output
!-------------------------------------------------------------------
```

Figure 8.12 *(cont.)*

```fortran
  USE Sort_Routines, ONLY : SelectionSort

  IMPLICIT NONE
  INTEGER, DIMENSION(:), ALLOCATABLE :: Cost
  INTEGER :: MaxNumCosts, AllocateStatus, NumCosts

  ! Allocate the array Cost
  WRITE (*, '(1X, A)', ADVANCE = "NO") &
        "Enter the maximum number of costs to be processed: "
  READ *, MaxNumCosts
  ALLOCATE(Cost(MaxNumCosts), STAT = AllocateStatus)
  IF (AllocateStatus /= 0) STOP "*** Not enough memory ***"

  CALL ReadCosts(Cost, NumCosts)
  CALL SelectionSort(Cost(1:NumCosts))
  CALL Output(Cost(1:NumCosts))

  DEALLOCATE(Cost)

CONTAINS

  !-ReadCosts-------------------------------------------------------
  ! Subroutine to read a list of up to MaxNumCosts costs, store them in
  ! array Cost, and return this list and a count NumCosts of the number
  ! of values read.  Local variables used are:
  !   MaxNumCosts : maximum number of costs
  !   InputData   : data value read (an actual cost or end-of-data
  !                 signal)
  !
  ! Input:    Elements of Cost
  ! Returns:  NumCosts and the array Cost
  !-----------------------------------------------------------------

  SUBROUTINE ReadCosts(Cost, NumCosts)

    INTEGER, DIMENSION(:), INTENT(OUT) :: Cost
    INTEGER, INTENT(OUT) :: NumCosts
    INTEGER :: MaxNumCosts, InputData

    MaxNumCosts = SIZE(Cost)
```

Figure 8.12 *(cont.)*

```
   PRINT *, "Enter labor costs in millions (0 or negative to stop)."
   NumCosts = 0
   DO
      ! Check if there is still room in the array Costs.  If not,
      ! terminate input and process the costs that have been entered
      IF (NumCosts == MaxNumCosts) THEN
         PRINT *, "No more costs can be entered.  Processing the first"
         PRINT *, MaxNumCosts, " costs."
         RETURN
      END IF

      ! Otherwise read and store more costs
      READ *, InputData
      IF (InputData <= 0) EXIT  ! End of data -- terminate repetition

      ! Otherwise, count and store the data value
      ! in the next location of array Cost
      NumCosts = NumCosts + 1
      Cost(NumCosts) = InputData
   END DO

END SUBROUTINE ReadCosts


!-Output-----------------------------------------------------------
! Subroutine to display the sorted list of costs and the median cost.
! Local variables used are:
!    I          : subscript
!    NumCosts   : number of costs
!
! Accepts:  Array Cost and integer NumCosts
! Output:   First NumCosts elements of Cost and the median cost
!------------------------------------------------------------------

SUBROUTINE Output(Cost)

  INTEGER, DIMENSION(:), INTENT(IN) :: Cost
  INTEGER :: NumCosts, I

  NumCosts = SIZE(Cost)

  PRINT '(2(/, 1X, A))', "Sorted List", "====== ===="
  DO I = 1, NumCosts
     PRINT '(1X, I6)', Cost(I)
  END DO
```

Figure 8.12 *(cont.)*

```
    IF (MOD(NumCosts, 2) /= 0) THEN
        PRINT 10, REAL(Cost((NumCosts + 1)/2))
    ELSE
        PRINT 10, REAL(Cost(NumCosts/2) + Cost(NumCosts/2 + 1)) / 2.0
    END IF
    10 FORMAT(/1X, "Median =", F7.1, " million dollars")


  END SUBROUTINE Output

END PROGRAM Sort_and_Find_Median_Cost
```

Sample run:

```
Enter the maximum number of costs to be processed: 50
Enter labor costs in millions (0 or negative to stop).
870
778
655
640
956
538
1050
529
689
0


Sorted List
====== ====
    529
    538
    640
    655
    689
    778
    870
    956
   1050


Median =  689.0 million dollars
```

Exercises 8.8

For each of the arrays X in Exercises 1–4, show X after each of the first four passes of simple selection sort.

1.

i	1	2	3	4	5	6	7	8
$X(i)$	30	50	80	10	60	20	70	40

2.

i	1	2	3	4	5	6	7	8
$X(i)$	20	40	70	60	80	50	30	10

3.

i	1	2	3	4	5	6	7	8
$X(i)$	80	70	60	50	40	30	20	10

4.

i	1	2	3	4	5	6	7	8
$X(i)$	10	20	30	40	50	60	70	80

5. One variation of simple selection sort for a list $X(1), \ldots, X(n)$ is to locate both the smallest and the largest elements while scanning the list and to position them at the beginning and the end of the list, respectively. On the next scan, this process is repeated for the sublist $X(2), \ldots, X(n-1)$, and so on. Write an algorithm to implement this double-ended selection sort.

For each of the arrays X in Exercises 6–9, show X after each pass of the double-ended selection sort described in Exercise 5.

6. The list in Exercise 1.

7. The list in Exercise 2.

8. The list in Exercise 3.

9. The list in Exercise 4.

10. For the following array Item, show the contents of Item after the statement

```
CALL Split(Item, 1, 10, Mid)
```

is executed, and give the value of Mid:

I	1	2	3	4	5	6	7	8	9	10
Item(I)	45	20	50	30	80	10	60	70	40	90

11. The subroutine Quicksort always sorts the left sublist before the right. Its performance will improve if the shorter of the two sublists is sorted first. Modify Quicksort to sort the shorter sublist first.

12. The subroutine `Split` always selects the first element of the sublist as the pivot. Another common practice is to use the "median-of-three" rule, in which the pivot is the median of the three numbers `Item(Low)`, `Item(Middle)`, and `Item(High)` where `Middle = (Low + High) / 2`. (The median of three numbers *a*, *b*, and *c*, arranged in ascending order, is the middle number *b*.) Modify `Split` to use this median-of-three rule.

8.9   SEARCHING

Another important problem is **searching** a collection of data for a specified item and retrieving some information associated with that item. For example, one searches a telephone directory for a specific name in order to retrieve the phone number listed with that name. We consider two kinds of searches, linear search and binary search.

Linear Search

A **linear search** begins with the first item in a list and searches sequentially until either the desired item is found or the end of the list is reached. The following algorithm describes this method of searching:

LINEAR SEARCH ALGORITHM

Algorithm to linear search a list $X(1), X(2), \ldots, X(N)$ for *ItemSought*.
The logical variable *Found* is set to true and *Location* is set to the position of *ItemSought* if the search is successful; otherwise, *Found* is set to false.

Accepts: List $X(1), X(2), \ldots, X(N)$ and *ItemSought*.
Returns: If *ItemSought* is found in the list:
      Found = true and *Location* = position of *ItemSought*.
    If *ItemSought* is not found in the list:
      Found = false (and *Location* = $N + 1$).

1. Initialize *Location* to 1 and *Found* to false.
2. While *Location* $\leq N$ and not *Found*, do the following:
    If *ItemSought* = $X(Location)$, then
      Set *Found* to true.
    Else
      Increment *Location* by 1.

The following subroutine uses this algorithm to search a list of character strings.

Figure 8.13 Linear search.

```
!-LinearSearch------------------------------------------------
! Subroutine to search the list Item for ItemSought using
! linear search.  If ItemSought is found in the list, Found
! is returned as true and the Location of the item is
! returned; otherwise Found is false.
!
! Accepts:   Array Item and ItemSought
! Returns:   If ItemSought is found in the list Item:
!                 Found = true and
!                 Location = position of ItemSought
!            Otherwise:
!                 Found = false
!                 (and Location = last position examined)
!
! Note:   Item is an assumed-shape array, so a program unit
!         that calls this subroutine must
!         1. contain this subroutine as an internal subprogram,
!         2. import this subroutine from a module, or
!         3. contain an interface block for this subroutine.
!------------------------------------------------------------

SUBROUTINE LinearSearch(Item, ItemSought, Found, Location)

  CHARACTER(*), DIMENSION(:), INTENT(IN) :: Item
  CHARACTER(*), INTENT(IN) :: ItemSought
  LOGICAL, INTENT(OUT) :: Found
  INTEGER, INTENT(OUT) :: Location
  INTEGER :: NumItems


  NumItems = SIZE(Item)
  Location = 1
  Found = .FALSE.


  ! While Location less than or equal to NumItems and not Found do

  DO
     IF ((Location > NumItems) .OR. Found) RETURN
     ! If end of list reached or item found, terminate the search
```

Figure 8.13 *(cont.)*

```
      ! Otherwise check the next list element
      IF (ItemSought == Item(Location)) THEN
         Found = .TRUE.
      ELSE
         Location = Location + 1
      END IF
   END DO

END SUBROUTINE LinearSearch
```

Binary Search

If a list has been sorted, binary search can be used to search for an item more efficiently than linear search. Linear search may require n comparisons to locate a particular item, but binary search will require at most $\log_2 n$ comparisons. For example, for a list of 1024 ($= 2^{10}$) items, binary search will locate an item using at most 10 comparisons, whereas linear search may require 1024 comparisons.

In the binary search method, we first examine the middle element in the list, and if this is the desired element, the search is successful. Otherwise we determine whether the item being sought is in the first half or in the second half of the list and then repeat this process, using the middle element of that list.

To illustrate, suppose the list to be searched is

$$
\begin{array}{c}
1279 \\
1331 \\
1373 \\
1555 \\
1824 \\
1898 \\
1995 \\
2002 \\
2335 \\
2665 \\
3103
\end{array}
$$

and we are looking for 1995. We first examine the middle number 1898 in the sixth position. Because 1995 is greater than 1898, we can disregard the first half of the list and concentrate on the second half.

$$
\begin{array}{c}
1995 \\
2002 \\
2335 \\
2665 \\
3103
\end{array}
$$

The middle number in this sublist is 2335, and the desired item 1995 is less than 2335, so we discard the second half of this sublist and concentrate on the first half.

<u>1995</u>
2002

Because there is no middle number in this sublist, we examine the number immediately preceding the middle position; that is, the number 1995.

In general, the algorithm for binary search is as follows:

BINARY SEARCH ALGORITHM

Algorithm to binary search a list $X(1)$, $X(2)$, . . . , $X(N)$ that has been ordered so the elements are in ascending order. The logical variable *Found* is set to true and *Location* is set to the position of the *ItemSought* being sought if the search is successful; otherwise, *Found* is set to false.

Accepts: List $X(1)$, $X(2)$, . . . , $X(N)$ and *ItemSought*.
Returns: If *ItemSought* is found in the list:
            Found = true and *Location* = position of *ItemSought*.
          If *ItemSought* is not found in the list:
            Found = false.

1. Initialize *First* to 1 and *Last* to *N*. These values represent the positions of the first and last items of the list or sublist being searched.

2. Initialize the logical variable *Found* to false.

3. While *First* ≤ *Last* and not *Found*, do the following:
    a. Find the middle position in the sublist by setting *Middle* equal to the integer quotient $(First + Last) / 2$.
    b. Compare *ItemSought* with $X(Middle)$. There are three possibilities:
        i. *ItemSought* < $X(Middle)$:   *ItemSought* is in the first half of the sublist; set *Last* equal to *Middle* − 1.
       ii. *ItemSought* > $X(Middle)$:   *ItemSought* is in the second half of the sublist; set *First* equal to *Middle* + 1.
      iii. *ItemSought* = $X(Middle)$:   *ItemSought* has been found; set *Location* equal to *Middle* and *Found* to true.

The following subroutine uses this algorithm to search a list of character strings.

Figure 8.14 Binary search.

```
!-BinarySearch------------------------------------------------
! Subroutine to search the list Item for ItemSought using
! binary search.  If ItemSought is found in the list, Found
! is returned as true and the Location of the item is
! returned; otherwise Found is false.  In this version of
! binary search, ItemSought and the elements of Item are
! character strings.  Local variables used are:
!   First   :  first item in (sub)list being searched
!   Last    :  last    "    "    "       "       "
!   Middle  :  middle  "    "    "       "       "
!
! Accepts:  Array Item and ItemSought in the list Item
! Returns:  If ItemSought is found:
!                 Found = true and
!                 Location = position of ItemSought
!             Otherwise:
!                 Found = false (and Location = last
!                 position examined)
!
! Note:  Item is an assumed-shape array, so a program unit
!        that calls this subroutine must
!        1. contain this subroutine as an internal subprogram,
!        2. import this subroutine from a module, or
!        3. contain an interface block for this subroutine.
!-------------------------------------------------------------

SUBROUTINE BinarySearch(Item, ItemSought, Found, Location)

  CHARACTER(*), DIMENSION(:), INTENT(IN) :: Item
  CHARACTER(*), INTENT(IN) :: ItemSought
  LOGICAL, INTENT(OUT) :: Found
  INTEGER, INTENT(OUT) :: Location
  INTEGER :: First, Last, Middle

  First = 1
  Last = SIZE(Item)
  Found = .FALSE.

! While First less than or equal to Last and not Found do the following:

  DO
     IF ((First > Last) .OR. Found) RETURN
     ! If empty list to be searched or item found, return
```

Figure 8.14 *(cont.)*

```
   ! Otherwise continue with the following
   Middle = (First + Last) / 2
   IF (ItemSought < Item(Middle)) THEN
      Last = Middle - 1
   ELSE IF (ItemSought > Item(Middle)) THEN
      First = Middle + 1
   ELSE
      Found = .TRUE.
      Location = Middle
   END IF
END DO

END SUBROUTINE BinarySearch
```

8.10   APPLICATION: SEARCHING A CHEMISTRY DATABASE

Problem

Each line of a data file contains the chemical formula and name of an inorganic compound and its specific heat (the ratio of the amount of heat required to raise the temperature of a body 1° C to that required to raise an equal mass of water 1° C). The file has been sorted so that the chemical formulas are in alphabetical order. A table-lookup program is to be developed that will allow the user to enter a formula and that will then search the list of formulas and display the name and specific heat corresponding to that formula.

Solution

Specification. From the statement of the problem, we see that part of the input for this problem is a list of chemical formulas, names, and specific heats stored in a file and arranged so that the formulas are in alphabetical order. After these have been read and stored, the user will input various formulas from the keyboard. The output will be the corresponding names and specific heats or a message indicating that none could be found. We thus have the following input/output specifications:

Input: A list of chemical formulas, names, and specific heats (data file)
            User-entered chemical formulas (keyboard)

Output: Names and specific heats for formulas entered, or a message indicating that the formula could not be found

Experimenting in a chemistry lab. (Photo courtesy of Uniphoto Picture Agency)

Design. We will use the following variables for this problem:

VARIABLES FOR TABLE-LOOKUP PROBLEM

Formula	Array that stores the chemical formulas
Name	Array that stores the names
SpecificHeat	Array that stores the specific heats
InputFormula	A formula entered by the user
Location	Location of *InputFormula* in the array *Formula*

The following algorithm uses binary search to search the array *Formula* for the formulas the user enters:

ALGORITHM FOR TABLE-LOOKUP PROBLEM

Algorithm to read a list of chemical formulas, names, and specific heats, store these in arrays, and then search this list for specific formulas and retrieve the corresponding names and specific heats.

Input: A list of chemical formulas, names, and specific heats
Output: Names and specific heats for specific formulas or a
            message indicating that a formula could not be found

1. Read the formulas, names, and specific heats and store them in arrays *Formula*, *Name*, and *SpecificHeat*, respectively.

2. Repeat the following:
   a. Enter *InputFormula* ("QUIT" to stop).
   b. If *InputFormula* = "QUIT" terminate repetition.
      Otherwise continue with the following:
   c. Use binary search to find the *Location* of *InputFormula* in the array *Formula* or to determine that it is not present.
   d. If *InputFormula* is found,
         Display *Name*(*Location*) and *SpecificHeat*(*Location*).
      Else
         Display a "Not Found" message.

Coding, Execution, and Testing. The program in Figure 8.15 implements the preceding algorithm. It calls the (internal) subroutine `ReadData` to read and store the chemical formulas, names, and specific heats and then calls the (internal) subroutine `LookUp` to read formulas entered by the user and calls the (module) subroutine `Search` to search the array `Formula` for each formula. The program was tested with various data files, and a sample run with a small file is included.

Figure 8.15 Searching a list of chemical formulas.

```
PROGRAM Chemical_Formulas
!-----------------------------------------------------------------
! Program to read a file containing the chemical formula, name, and
! specific heat for various inorganic compounds and store these in
! parallel arrays.  The first line contains the number of items in
! these lists.  Also, the file is sorted so that the formulas are in
! alphabetical order.  The user enters a formula; the list of formulas
! is searched using the binary search algorithm; and if the formula is
! found, its name and specific heat are displayed.   Identifiers used
! are:
!   Length          : length of character strings (constant)
!   Formula         : array of formulas
!   Name            : array of names
!   SpecificHeat    : array of specific heats
!   MaxRecords      : maximum number of records in the file
!   NumRecords      : actual number of records in the file
!   AllocateStatus  : status variable for ALLOCATE
!
```

Figure 8.15 *(cont.)*

```
! Input:  Arrays Formula, Name, and SpecificHeat (by ReadData)
! Output: Names and specific heats for certain formulas (by LookUp)
!-------------------------------------------------------------------

  USE Search_Routines, ONLY : BinarySearch

  IMPLICIT NONE
  INTEGER, PARAMETER :: Length = 10
  CHARACTER(Length), DIMENSION(:), ALLOCATABLE :: &
                    Formula, Name*(2*Length)
  REAL, DIMENSION(:), ALLOCATABLE :: SpecificHeat
  INTEGER :: MaxRecords, NumRecords, AllocateStatus

  ! Get the number of records to be stored and allocate
  ! the arrays Formula, Name, and SpecificHeat of this size
  WRITE (*, '(1X, A)', ADVANCE = "NO") &
        "Enter the maximum number of records in the file: "
  READ *, MaxRecords

  ALLOCATE(Formula(MaxRecords), Name(MaxRecords), &
          (SpecificHeat(MaxRecords), IOSTAT = AllocateStatus)
  IF (AllocateStatus /= 0) STOP "*** Not enough memory ***"

  CALL ReadData(Formula, Name, SpecificHeat, MaxRecords, NumRecords)
  CALL LookUp(Formula, Name, SpecificHeat, NumRecords)

CONTAINS

  !-ReadData----------------------------------------------------
  ! Subroutine to read a list of up to MaxRecords chemical formulas,
  ! names, and specific heats; store them in parallel arrays Formula,
  ! Name, and SpecificHeat; and count (NumRecords) how many sets of
  ! readings are stored.   Local variables used are:
  !   FileName    : name of data file
  !   OpenStatus  : status variable for OPEN
  !   InputStatus : status variable for READ
  !
  ! Accepts:          Arrays Formula, Name, SpecificHeat,
  !                   integers MaxRecords and NumRecords
  ! Input (keyboard): FileName
  ! Input (file):     Elements of Formula, Name, SpecificHeat
  ! Returns:          Arrays Formula, Name, SpecificHeat and NumRecords
  !-------------------------------------------------------------------
```

Figure 8.15 *(cont.)*

```fortran
SUBROUTINE ReadData(Formula, Name, SpecificHeat, MaxRecords, &
                    NumRecords)

  CHARACTER(*), DIMENSION(:), INTENT(INOUT) :: Formula, Name
  REAL, DIMENSION(:), INTENT(INOUT) :: SpecificHeat
  INTEGER, INTENT(IN) :: MaxRecords
  INTEGER, INTENT(OUT) :: NumRecords
  INTEGER :: OpenStatus, InputStatus
  CHARACTER(20) :: FileName

  ! Open the file, then read, count, and store the records

  WRITE (*, '(1X, A)', ADVANCE = "NO") "Enter name of file: "
  READ *, FileName
  OPEN (UNIT = 15, FILE = FileName, STATUS = "OLD", IOSTAT = OpenStatus)
  IF (OpenStatus > 0) STOP "*** Cannot open the file ***"

  NumRecords = 0
  DO
     ! Check if there is still room in the arrays.  If not,
     ! terminate input and process the records that have been read.
     IF (NumRecords == MaxRecords) THEN
        PRINT *, "No more data can be read.  Processing the first"
        PRINT *, MaxRecords, " formulas."
        RETURN
     END IF


     ! Otherwise read and store more records
     NumRecords = NumRecords + 1
     READ (UNIT = 15, FMT = '(2A, F6.0)', IOSTAT = InputStatus) &
       Formula(NumRecords), Name(NumRecords), SpecificHeat(NumRecords)
     IF (InputStatus > 0) STOP "*** Input error ***"


     ! If end of data, adjust count, close the file and terminate repetition
     IF (InputStatus < 0) THEN
        NumRecords = NumRecords - 1
        CLOSE (15)
        EXIT
     END IF

  END DO

END SUBROUTINE ReadData
```

Figure 8.15 *(cont.)*

```
!-LookUp-------------------------------------------------------------
! Subroutine that allows user to enter formulas.  The first NumRecords
! chemical formulas in array Formula are then searched for this
! formula.  If found, the corresponding elements of the parallel
! arrays Name and SpecificHeat are displayed.  User enters QUIT to
! stop searching.  Local identifiers used are:
!     InputFormula :  formula entered by the user
!     Found        :  signals if InputFormula found in array Formula
!     Location     :  location of InputFormula in Formula if found
!     Length       :  constant used to specify length of InputFormula
!
! Accepts:          Arrays Formula, Name, SpecificHeat, and
!                   integer NumRecords
! Input (keyboard): Several values of InputFormula or a "QUIT" signal
! Output:           For each formula that is found, its name and
!                   specific heat; otherwise a "not found" message
!-------------------------------------------------------------------

SUBROUTINE LookUp(Formula, Name, SpecificHeat, NumRecords)

  CHARACTER(*), DIMENSION(:), INTENT(IN) :: Formula, Name
  REAL, DIMENSION(:), INTENT(IN) ::   SpecificHeat
  INTEGER, INTENT(IN) :: NumRecords
  INTEGER :: Location
  INTEGER, PARAMETER :: Length = 10
  CHARACTER(Length) :: InputFormula
  LOGICAL :: Found


  PRINT *

  ! While there are formulas to search for, do the following:

  DO
     WRITE (*, '(1X, A)', ADVANCE = "NO") &
          "Enter formula to search for, (QUIT to stop): "
     READ *, InputFormula
     IF (InputFormula == "QUIT") EXIT
     ! If done searching for formulas, terminate repetition

     ! Otherwise, search Formula array for InputFormula
     ! and display information found

     CALL BinarySearch(Formula(1:NumRecords), InputFormula, &
                   Found, Location)
```

Figure 8.15 *(cont.)*

```
        IF (Found) THEN
            PRINT '(1X, A, 1X, A, F7.4)', Name(Location), &
                  "has specific heat",  SpecificHeat(Location)
        ELSE
            PRINT *, "         *** not found ***"
        END IF
    END DO

  END SUBROUTINE LookUp

END PROGRAM Chemical_Formulas
```

Listing of `fi18-15.dat` used in sample run:

```
AGCL        Silver Chloride        0.0804
ALCL3       Aluminum Chloride      0.188
AUI         Gold Iodide            0.0404
BACO3       Barium Carbonate       0.0999
CACL2       Calcium Chloride       0.164
CACO3       Calcium Carbonate      0.203
FE2O3       Ferric Oxide           0.182
H2O2        Hydrogen Peroxide      0.471
KCL         Potassium Chloride     0.162
LIF         Lithium Flouride       0.373
NABR        Sodium Bromide         0.118
NACL        Sodium Chloride        0.204
PBBR2       Lead Bromide           0.0502
SIC         Silicon Carbide        0.143
SNCL2       Stannous Chloride      0.162
ZNSO4       Zinc Sulfate           0.174
```

Sample run:

```
Enter the maximum number of records in the file: 25
Enter name of file: fi18-15.dat

Enter formula to search for, (QUIT to stop): AGCL
Silver Chloride     has specific heat 0.0804

Enter formula to search for, (QUIT to stop): NACL
Sodium Chloride     has specific heat 0.2040

Enter formula to search for, (QUIT to stop): FECO3
     *** not found ***
```

Figure 8.15 *(cont.)*

```
Enter formula to search for, (QUIT to stop): FE2O3
Ferric Oxide        has specific heat 0.1820

Enter formula to search for, (QUIT to stop): ZNSO4
Zinc Sulfate        has specific heat 0.1740

Enter formula to search for, (QUIT to stop): QUIT
```

CHAPTER REVIEW

Summary

In this chapter we described arrays and subscripted variables. We began by describing how arrays are declared and how subscripts can be used to provide direct access to the elements in an array. We described four methods of input/output of array elements: (1) using a DO loop; (2) using the array name; (3) using an implied DO loop; and in Section 8.4, (4) using an array section. In addition to array sections (or subarrays), we also described array constants and expressions, array assignment, the WHERE construct, and how arrays can be used as arguments of subprograms. The important problem of sorting was considered in Section 8.7. Two sorting methods were described and illustrated with examples: simple selection sort and quicksort. In Section 8.9 we considered another important list-processing problem—searching. We described two search methods: linear search, which may be used with any list; and binary search, which may be used with sorted lists. Applications of arrays included averages of group data (corn yields), frequency distributions and bar graphs (quality control), vector processing, finding the median of a list of numbers (construction costs), and binary and linear search (searching a chemistry database).

FORTRAN SUMMARY

Declaration of Compile-Time Arrays

```
type, DIMENSION(l:u) :: list-of-array-names
```

or

```
type :: list-of-array-specifiers
```

where each array specifier has the form

```
array-name(l:u)
```

Here l is the minimum value of a subscript and u is the maximum value. If the minimum subscript value is 1, only the maximum subscript need be specified.

Examples:

```
REAL, DIMENSION(50) :: FailTime

INTEGER, DIMENSION(0:20) :: Count

INTEGER, PARAMETER :: Limit = 50
REAL, DIMENSION(Limit) :: FailTime
```

or, using the alternative form:

```
REAL :: FailTime(50)

INTEGER :: Count(0:20)

INTEGER, PARAMETER :: Limit = 50
REAL :: FailTime(Limit)
```

Purpose:
Declares that each identifier *array-name* in the list of array declarations is an array for which memory will be allocated at compile time and for which the range of values of the subscript will be from the lower limit *l* through the upper limit *u*.

Declaration of Allocatable Arrays

```
type, DIMENSION(:), ALLOCATABLE :: list-of-array-names
```

or

```
type, DIMENSION(:) :: list-of-array-names
ALLOCATABLE :: list-of-array-names
```

Example:

```
REAL, DIMENSION(:), ALLOCATABLE :: A, B
```

Purpose:
Declares that each of the identifiers in the list is an array whose size will be specified during execution.

ALLOCATE Statement

```
ALLOCATE(list, STAT = status-variable)
```

where *list* is a list of array specifications of the form

```
array-name(l:u)
```

Here *l* is the minimum value of a subscript and *u* is the maximum value. If the minimum subscript is 1, only the maximum subscript need be specified.
The variable *status-variable* is an integer variable.

Examples:

```
WRITE (*, '(1X, A)', ADVANCE = "NO") &
      "Enter size of arrays A and B: "
READ *, N
ALLOCATE(A(N), B(0:N+1), STAT = AllocateStatus)
IF (AllocateStatus /= 0) STOP "*** Not enough memory ***"
```

Purpose:
Allocates space for each array listed. If the (optional) STAT = clause is present, the integer variable *status-variable* will be set to zero if allocation is successful, but will be assigned some system-dependent error value if there is insufficient memory or if the array has already been allocated.

DEALLOCATE Statement

```
DEALLOCATE(list)
```

or

```
DEALLOCATE(list, STAT = status-variable)
```

where *list* is a list of currently allocated arrays and *status-variable* is an integer variable.

Example:

```
DEALLOCATE(A, B)
```

Purpose:
Releases the memory allocated to the arrays listed. In the second form, the integer variable *status-variable* will be set to zero if deallocation is successful, but it will be assigned some system-dependent error value if it is not successful, for example, if no memory was previously allocated to an array.

Array Constants

```
(/ value₁, value₂, ..., valueₖ /)
```

where each *value*$_i$ is a constant expression or an *implied* DO *constructor* of the form

```
(value-list, implied-do-control)
```

Examples:

```
(/ 2, 4, 6, 8, 10, 12, 14, 16, 18, 20 /)

(/ 2*I, (I = 1, 10) /)

(/ 2, 4, (I, I = 6, 18, 2), 20 /)
```

Purpose:

To construct an array whose size and elements are given by the constant. Array constants may be assigned to array variables.

Array Sections and Subarrays

```
array-name(subscript-triplet)
```

or

```
array-name(vector-subscript)
```

A subscript triplet has the form

```
lower : upper : stride
```

and specifies the elements in positions *lower*, *lower* + *stride*, *lower* + 2 * *stride*, ... going as far as possible without going beyond *upper* if *stride* > 0, or below *upper* if *stride* < 0. If *lower* is omitted, the lower bound in the array declaration is used; if *upper* is omitted, the upper bound in the array declaration is used; if *stride* is omitted, it is taken to be 1.

A vector subscript is a sequence of subscripts of the array; in this case, the array section consists of the elements in those positions.

Examples:

```
A(2:10:2)
B(:20:)
C(::)

A((/ 6, 5, 3, 9, 1 /))
```

Purpose:

Forms an array consisting of the selected elements of the specified parent array.

Array Assignment

```
array = expression
```

where *array* is an array variable or an array section and the value of *expression* must be either

1. An array of the same size as the array variable, or
2. A simple value

In the second case, the value is *broadcast to all the array elements*, with the result that each is assigned this value.

Examples:

```
INTEGER, DIMENSION(5) :: A, B, C

A = (/ 11, 22, 33, 44, 55 /)
B = 0
C = A + B
C(1:2) = (/ 111, 222 /)
```

Purpose:
To assign a value to an array or to a section of an array.

The WHERE Construct

```
WHERE (logical-array-expr) array-var₁ = array-expr₁
```

or

```
WHERE (logical-array-expr)
   array-var₁ = array-expr₁
      ⋮
   array-varₘ = array-exprₘ
ELSEWHERE
   array-varₘ₊₁ = array-exprₘ₊₁
      ⋮
   array-varₙ = array-exprₙ
END WHERE
```

where *logical-array-expr* is a logical-valued array expression, and each *array-varᵢ* has the same size as the value of *logical-array-expr*. In the second form, the ELSEWHERE part is optional.

Example:

```
WHERE (A > 0)
    B = SQRT(A)
ELSEWHERE
    B = 0.0
END WHERE
```

Purpose:

Constructs arrays by checking *logical-array-expr* element by element, and whenever it is true (in the ELSEWHERE part), assigning the value of the corresponding element of each *array-expr$_i$* (false) to the corresponding element of *array-var$_i$*. In the first form, all other elements are left unchanged.

Intrinsic Array-Processing Functions

ALLOCATED(A)	Returns true if memory has been allocated to the allocatable array A and false otherwise
DOT_PRODUCT(A, B)	Returns the dot product of A and B (see Section 8.6)
MAXVAL(A)	Returns the maximum value in array A
MAXLOC(A)	Returns a one-dimensional array containing one element whose value is the position of the first occurrence of the maximum value in A
MINVAL(A)	Returns the minimum value in array A
MINLOC(A)	Returns a one-dimensional array containing one element whose value is the position of the first occurrence of the minimum value in A
PRODUCT(A)	Returns the product of the elements in A
SIZE(A)	Returns the number of elements in A
SUM(A)	Returns the sum of the elements in A

PROGRAMMING POINTERS

Program Style and Design

1. *One-dimensional arrays can be used to store lists of values.* If the data values must be processed more than once in a program, it is appropriate to store them in an array. Otherwise, it is usually better to use simple variables.

2. *Use named constants to dimension compile-time arrays.* If it is necessary to change the size of an array, only the named constant needs to be changed.

3. *Use allocatable arrays in programs that must process arrays whose sizes vary from one execution of the program to the next.* Unlike programs that use com-

pile-time arrays, no changes in declarations are required to process arrays of different sizes.

4. *Specify reasonable sizes for arrays.* The size of an array is determined by the number of data values to be stored. Specifying too large an array wastes memory.

5. *Use broadcasting rather than a loop to construct an array whose elements are all the same.* For example, using the assignment statement

```
A = 0
```

to zero out the array A is simpler than using the DO loop

```
DO I = 1, SIZE(A)
   A(I) = 0
END DO
```

6. *The basic arithmetic operations and intrinsic functions can be applied to arrays and are performed elementwise.* For example, two arrays A and B of the same size can be added to give array C by a simple assignment statement

```
C = A + B
```

7. *Assumed-shape arrays can be used to design general subprograms for processing arrays.* For example, the subroutines for sorting and searching arrays—see Sections 8.7 and 8.9—can be used with arrays of any size.

Potential Problems

1. *Declarations of array variables must include dimension information.* If, for example, Alpha has been declared by

```
REAL :: Alpha
```

with no DIMENSION specified, the compiler may interpret a reference to an element of Alpha, as in

```
X = Alpha(1)
```

as a reference to a function named Alpha, which is an error.

2. *Subscripts must be integer valued and must stay within the range specified in the array declarations.* Related to this requirement are two kinds of errors that can easily occur when using arrays. The first error results from forgetting to declare a subscript to be of integer type. For example, consider the program segment

```
INTEGER, DIMENSION(10) :: Alpha

DO Element = 1, 10
   Alpha(Element) = Element**2
END DO
      ⋮
```

Because the type of `Element` has not been declared and `IMPLICIT NONE` has not been used, the Fortran naming convention implies that it is of real type. Consequently, an error results when the array `Alpha` is referenced by the statement

```
Alpha(Element) = Element**2
```

because the subscript is not of integer type.

Another error results when a subscript gets "out of bounds," that is, it has a value less than the lower bound or greater than the upper bound specified in the array declaration. The result of an out-of-range subscript is compiler-dependent. If a compiler does range checking, an error will result, and execution is usually terminated. For some compilers, however, no such range checking is done, and the memory location that is accessed is determined simply by counting forward or backward from the base address of the array. This is illustrated by the program in Figure 8.16. Here A, B, and C are arrays declared by

```
INTEGER, DIMENSION(4) :: A, B, C
```

and the illegal array references `B(-2)` and `B(7)` caused by the statements

```
I = -2
B(I) = -999
B(I+9) = 999
```

access the memory locations associated with `A(2)` and `C(3)`:

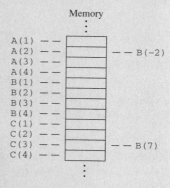

Thus modifying `B(-2)` and `B(7)` changes `A(2)` and `C(3)`, respectively. This change to arrays A and C caused by seeming modifications of array B is obviously undesirable. An array reference that is very much out of range may even cause a program instruction to be modified! Consequently, *it is important to ensure that subscripts do not get out of range.*

Figure 8.16 Why array subscripts must stay in bound.

```
PROGRAM Out_of_Bounds_Subscripts
!-----------------------------------------------------------------------
! Program to demonstrate what may result when subscripts get out of
! bounds.  Variables used are:
!     A, B, C : one-dimensional arrays of integers
!
! Output:  Arrays A, B, and C before and after subscripts get out of
!          range
!-----------------------------------------------------------------------

  INTEGER, DIMENSION(4) :: &
      A = (/ 1, 2, 3, 4 /), &
      B = (/ 5, 6, 7, 8 /), &
      C = (/ 9, 10, 11, 12 /)
  INTEGER :: I

  ! Display the original arrays

  PRINT 100, "A =", A
  PRINT 100, "B =", B
  PRINT 100, "C =", C
  100 FORMAT(1X, A, 4I5)

  ! Reference array B with a subscript that is out of bounds

  I = -2
  B(I) = -999
  B(I+9) = 999

  ! Print each of the arrays again

  PRINT *
  PRINT 100, "A =", A
  PRINT 100, "B =", B
  PRINT 100, "C =", C

END PROGRAM Out_of_Bounds_Subscripts
```

Figure 8.16 *(cont.)*

Sample run:

```
A =    1    2    3    4
B =    5    6    7    8
C =    9   10   11   12
A =    1 -999   3    4

B =    5    6    7    8
C =    9   10  999   12
```

3. *In an assignment of one array to another, the arrays must be the same size.* **For example, consider arrays** A, B, **and** C **declared by**

```
INTEGER, DIMENSION(6)  :: A = (/ 11, 22, 33, 44, 55, 66 /)
INTEGER, DIMENSION(10) :: B
INTEGER, DIMENSION(0:5) :: C
```

Array A cannot be assigned to array B since these arrays have different sizes. However, array A can be assigned to array C; even though they have different subscript ranges, they do have the same size.

4. *Subprograms that use assumed-shape arrays and array-valued functions must be internal subprograms or module subprograms, or there must be an interface block in each program unit that references them.*

5. *Allocatable arrays may not be formal arguments.*

PROGRAMMING PROBLEMS

Sections 8.2 and 8.3

1. The Cawker City Candy Company maintains two warehouses, one in Chicago and one in Detroit, each of which stocks at most 25 different items. Write a program that first reads the product numbers of the items stored in the Chicago warehouse and stores them in an array and then repeats this for the items stored in the Detroit warehouse, storing these product numbers in another array. The program should then find and display the *intersection* of these two lists of numbers, that is, the collection of product numbers common to both lists. Do not assume that the lists have the same number of elements.

2. Repeat Problem 1, but find and display the *union* of the two lists, that is, the collection of product numbers that are elements of at least one of the lists.

3. A hardware store sells lawn sprinklers. Past experience has indicated that the selling season is only six months long, lasting from April 1 through September 30. The sales division has forecast the following sales for next year:

Month	Demand
April	40
May	20
June	30
July	40
August	30
September	20

All sprinklers are purchased from an outside source at a cost of $8.00 per sprinkler. However, the supplier sells them only in lots of 10, 20, 30, 40, or 50; monthly orders for fewer than 10 sprinklers or more than 50 are not accepted. Discounts based on the size of the lot ordered are as follows:

Lot Size	Discount (percent)
10	5
20	5
30	10
40	20
50	25

For each order placed, the store is charged a fixed cost of $15.00 to cover shipping costs, insurance, packaging, and so on, regardless of the number ordered (except that there is no charge for a month when none is ordered). Assume that orders are placed on the first of the month and are received immediately. The store also incurs a carrying charge of $1.80 for each sprinkler remaining in stock at the end of any one month.

Write a program to calculate the total seasonal cost, the price that must be charged per sprinkler in order for the hardware store to break even, and the price that must be charged to realize a profit of 30 percent. Run your program with each of the following six ordering policies, and determine which is the best:

Policy Number	Number Ordered/Month					
	April	May	June	July	August	September
1	40	20	30	40	30	20
2	50	50	50	30	0	0
3	40	50	0	40	50	0
4	50	50	40	40	0	0
5	50	10	50	20	50	0
6	50	50	0	50	30	0

4. Suppose that a row of mailboxes are numbered 1 through 150 and that begin-ning with mailbox 2, we open the doors of all the even-numbered mailboxes. Next, beginning with mailbox 3, we go to every third mailbox, opening its door if it is closed and closing it if it is open. We repeat this procedure with every fourth mailbox, then every fifth mailbox, and so on. Write a program to deter-mine which mailboxes will be closed when this procedure is completed.

5. A *prime number* is an integer greater than 1 whose only positive divisors are 1 and the integer itself. One method for finding all the prime numbers in the range 2 through n is known as the *Sieve of Eratosthenes*. Consider the list of numbers from 2 through n. Here 2 is the first prime number, but the multiples of 2 (4, 6, 8, . . .) are not, and so they are "crossed out" in the list. The first number after 2 that was not crossed out is 3, the next prime. We then cross out all higher mul-tiples of 3 (6, 9, 12, . . . from the list. The next number not crossed out is 5, the next prime; we cross out all higher multiples of 5 (10, 15, 20, . . .). We repeat this procedure until we reach the first number in the list that has not been crossed out and whose square is greater than n. Then all the numbers that remain in the list are the primes from 2 through n. Write a program that uses this sieve method to find all the prime numbers from 2 through n. Run it for $n = 50$ and for $n = 500$.

6. Write a program to investigate the *birthday problem:* If there are n persons in a room, what is the probability that two or more of them have the same birthday? You might consider values of n, say from 10 through 40, and for each value of n, generate n random birthdays, and then scan the list to see whether two of them are the same. To obtain some approximate probabilities, you might do this 100 times for each value of n.

Sections 8.4 and 8.5

7. Write a program to test the subprogram in Exercise 14 or 15 of Section 8.4.

8. Write a program to test the subprogram in Exercise 16 or 17 of Section 8.4.

9. Write a program to test the subprogram in Exercise 18 of Section 8.4.

10. Write a program that calls subprograms to read and count a list of numbers and to calculate their mean, variance, and standard deviation. Print how many num-bers there are and their mean, variance, and standard deviation with appropriate labels. If $\bar{x}$ denotes the mean of the numbers $x_1, . . . , x_n$, the *variance* is the av-erage of the squares of the deviations of the numbers from the mean:

$$\text{variance} = \frac{1}{n} \sum_{i=1}^{n} (x_i - \bar{x})^2$$

and the *standard deviation* is the square root of the variance.

11. Letter grades are sometimes assigned to numeric scores by using the grading scheme commonly called *grading on the curve*. In this scheme, a letter grade is assigned to a numeric score, according to the following table:

x = Numeric Score	Letter Grade
$x < m - \dfrac{3}{2}\sigma$	F
$m - \dfrac{3}{2}\sigma \le x < m - \dfrac{1}{2}\sigma$	D
$m - \dfrac{1}{2}\sigma \le x < m + \dfrac{1}{2}\sigma$	C
$m + \dfrac{1}{2}\sigma \le x < m + \dfrac{3}{2}\sigma$	B
$m + \dfrac{3}{2}\sigma \le x$	A

where m is the mean score and σ is the standard deviation. Extend the program of Problem 10 to read a list of real numbers representing numeric scores, calculate their mean and standard deviation, and then find and display the letter grade corresponding to each numeric score.

12. Write a subprogram to evaluate a polynomial $a_0 + a_1x + a_2x^2 + \cdots + a_nx^n$ for any degree n, coefficients $a_0, a_1, \ldots, a_n$, and values of x that are supplied to it as arguments. Then write a program that reads a value of n, the coefficients, and various values of x and then uses this subprogram to evaluate the polynomial at these values.

13. A more efficient way of evaluating polynomials is *Horner's method* (also known as *nested multiplication*), in which a polynomial $a_0 + a_1x + a_2x^2 + \cdots + a_nx^n$ is rewritten as

$$a_0 + (a_1 + (a_2 + \cdots + (a_{n-1} + a_nx)x) \cdots x)x$$

For example:

$$7 + 6x + 5x^2 + 4x^3 + 3x^4 = 7 + (6 + (5 + (4 + 3x)x)x)x$$

Proceed as in Problem 12, but use Horner's method to evaluate the polynomial.

14. Write a program to read the files STUDENT.DAT and STUPDATE.DAT (see Appendix B) and produce an updated grade report. This grade report should show
    (a) the current date
    (b) the student's name and student number
    (c) a list of the names, grades, and credits for each of the current courses under the headings COURSE, GRADE, and CREDITS
    (d) current GPA (multiply the credits by the numeric grade—A = 4.0, A− = 3.7, B+ = 3.3, B = 3.0, . . . , D− = 0.7, F = 0.0—for each course to find honor points earned for that course; sum these to find the total new honor points, then divide the total new honor points by the total new credits to give the current GPA, rounded to two decimal places)

(e)   total credits earned (old credits from STUDENT.DAT plus total new credits)

(f)   new cumulative GPA (first, calculate old honor points = old credits times old cumulative GPA, then new cumulative GPA = sum of old honor points and new honor points divided by updated total credits)

15. Write a subroutine to add two large integers of any length, say up to 300 digits. A suggested approach is as follows: treat each number as a list, each of whose elements is a block of digits of that number. For example, the integer 179,534,672,198 might be stored with $N(1) = 198$, $N(2) = 672$, $N(3) = 534$, $N(4) = 179$. Then add the two integers (lists) element by element, carrying from one element to the next when necessary. Test your subroutine with a program that reads two large integers and calls the subroutine to find their sum.

16. Proceed as in Problem 15, but write a subroutine to multiply two large integers, say of length up to 300 digits.

17. A data structure that is sometimes implemented using an array is a *stack*. A stack is a list in which elements may be inserted or deleted at only one end of the list, called the *top* of the stack. Because the last element added to a stack will be the first one removed, a stack is called a *Last-In–First-Out (LIFO)* structure. A stack can be implemented as an array Stack, with Stack(1) representing the bottom of the stack and Stack(Top) the top, where Top is the position of the top element of the stack. Write subprograms Push and Pop to implement insertion and deletion operations for a stack. Use these subprograms in a program that reads a command I (Insert) or D (Delete); for I, an integer is then read and inserted into ("pushed onto") the stack; for D, an integer is deleted ("popped") from the stack and displayed.

18. Another data structure that can be implemented using an array is a *queue*. A queue is a list in which elements may be inserted at one end, called the *rear*, and removed at the other end, called the *front*. Because the first element added is the first to be removed, a queue is called a *First-In–First-Out (FIFO)* structure. Write subprograms to implement insertion and deletion operations for a queue. Use these subprograms in a program like that in Problem 17 to insert integers into or delete integers from a queue. (*Note:* The most efficient representation of a queue as an array is obtained by thinking of the array as being circular, with the first array element immediately following the last array element.)

19. (Project)   A problem from the area of *artificial intelligence:* The game of *Nim* is played by two players. There are three piles of objects, and each player is allowed to take any number (at least one) of objects from any pile on his or her turn. The player taking the last object wins. Write a program in which the computer "learns" to play Nim. One way to "teach" the computer is to have the program assign a value to each possible move based on experience gained from playing games. The value of each possible move is stored in some array, and each value is set to 0. The program then keeps track of each move the computer makes as it plays the game. At the end of each game that the computer wins,

the value of each move the computer made is increased by 1. At the end of any game that the computer loses, the value of each move the computer made is decreased by 1. The computer plays by selecting, from all legal moves, the one that has the largest value. When there are several possible moves having this same largest value, some strategy must be chosen. (One possibility is to have it select a move randomly.)

20. (Project)   The spread of a contagious disease and the propagation of a rumor have a great deal in common. Write a program to simulate the spread of a disease or a rumor. You might proceed as follows: establish a population of N individuals, and assign to each individual four parameters (perhaps different numbers to various individuals):

    (a) a "resistance" parameter: the probability that the individual will be infected by the disease (rumor) upon transmission from a carrier

    (b) a "recovery" (or "forgetting") parameter: the probability that the infected individual will recover from the disease (forget the rumor) before transmitting it to others in the population

    (c) an "activity" parameter: the probability that the individual will contact another person

    (d) a "transmission" parameter: the probability that the individual will in fact transmit the disease (rumor) to another person he or she contacts

    A person who comes in contact with an infected person either becomes infected or does not; a random number can be compared with the individual's resistance parameter to determine the result.

    Once a person is infected, that is, becomes a carrier, another random number can be compared with his or her recovery (forgetting) parameter to determine whether or not he or she will recover from the disease (forget the rumor) before contacting other persons.

    The activity parameter of a person who does not recover from the disease (forget the rumor) before contacting other persons determines how many persons he or she will contact. The transmission parameter determines the actual number of persons to whom the disease (rumor) will be transmitted. The specific individuals can then be selected at random from the population and the disease (rumor) transmitted to them.

    Select one individual to initiate the process. You might keep track of the number of persons infected in each stage; the "degrees of exposure (credibility)," that is, the number of persons exposed once, twice, and so on; the effect of using certain percentages to indicate the decreased chances of reinfection; and so on.

Section 8.6

21. Write a program to test the function subprogram for calculating cross products in Exercise 1 of Section 8.6.

22. Write a program to test the function subprogram for unit vectors in Exercise 2 of Section 8.6.

23. Write a program to test the function subprogram for finding the angle between two vectors in Exercise 3 of Section 8.6.

Sections 8.7 and 8.8

24. Write a program that reads a list of numbers, calls the double-ended selection sort subroutine in Exercise 5 of Section 8.8 to sort the list, and then displays the sorted list.

25. Write a program that reads a list of numbers, calls the modified subroutine Quicksort in Exercise 10 of Section 8.8 to sort the list, and then displays the sorted list.

26. Proceed as in Problem 25, but use the modified subroutine Split described in Exercise 11 of Section 8.8.

27. Write a program that reads two lists of integers that have been sorted so that they are in ascending order and then calls a subroutine to *merge* these lists into a third list in which the integers are also in ascending order. Run the program for at least the following lists:

    (a) $List_1$: 1, 3, 5, 7, 9
              $List_2$: 2, 4, 6, 8, 10
    (b) $List_1$: 1, 4, 5, 6, 9, 10
              $List_2$: 2, 3, 7, 8
    (c) $List_1$: 1, 2, 3, 4, 5, 6, 7
              $List_2$: 8, 9, 10
    (d) $List_1$: 10
              $List_2$: 1, 2, 3, 4, 5, 6, 7, 8, 9

28. *Insertion sort* is an efficient sorting method for small data sets. It begins with the first item $X(1)$, then inserts $X(2)$ into this one-item list in the correct position to form a sorted two-element list, then inserts $X(3)$ into this two-element list in the correct position, and so on. For example, to sort the list 7, 1, 5, 2, 3, 4, 6, 0, the steps are as follows (the element being inserted is highlighted):

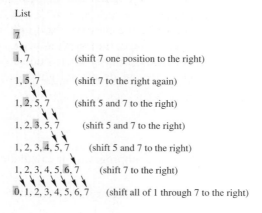

Write a subroutine to sort a list of items using this insertion-sort method and then write a main program that reads a set of values and calls this subroutine to sort them.

29. Insertion sort (see Problem 28) performs best for small lists and for partially sorted lists. *Shell sort* (named after Donald Shell) uses insertion sort to sort small sublists to produce larger, partially ordered sublists. Specifically, one begins with a "gap" of a certain size g and then uses insertion sort to sort sublists of elements that are g positions apart: first, $X(1), X(1 + g), X(1 + 2g), \ldots$; then the sublist $X(2), X(2 + g), X(2 + 2g), \ldots$; then $X(3), X(3 + g), X(3 + 2g), \ldots$, and so on. Next the size of the gap g is reduced, and the process is repeated. This continues until the gap g is 1, and the final insertion sort results in the sorted list.

Write a subroutine to sort a list of items using this Shell sort method, beginning with a gap g of the form $(3^k - 1)/2$ for some integer k, and dividing it by 3 at each stage. Then write a main program that reads a set of values and calls this subroutine to sort them.

30. The investment firm of Pikum and Loozum has been recording the trading price of a particular stock over a 15-day period. Write a program that reads these prices and sorts them into increasing order, using the insertion-sort scheme described in Problem 28. The program should display the trading range, that is, the lowest and highest prices recorded, and also the median price.

31. One way to improve quicksort is to use some faster sorting method for small sublists. For example, the insertion-sort method described in Problem 28 is usually faster than quicksort for lists with 20 items or less. Modify quicksort to use insertion sort if a sublist has fewer than `LowerBound` items for some constant `LowerBound`, and otherwise, use quicksort. Then redo Problem 30 using this modified quicksort method.

Sections 8.9 and 8.10

32. In general, it is not necessary to perform a linear search on an entire list to determine that it does not contain a given item if the list has been previously sorted. Write a modified linear search algorithm for such an ordered list. Then implement this algorithm as a subroutine and write a program that reads a list of real values, stores them in an array `List`, and then calls the subroutine to search the list for a given real number entered during execution.

33. The following data was collected by a company and represents discrete values of a function for which an explicit formula is not known:

x	f(x)
1.123400	167.5600
2.246800	137.6441
3.370200	110.2523
4.493600	85.38444
5.617000	63.04068
6.740400	43.22099
7.863800	25.92535
8.987200	11.15376
10.11060	−1.093781
11.23400	−10.81726
12.35740	−18.01665
13.48080	−22.69202
14.60420	−24.84334
15.72760	−24.47060
16.85100	−21.57379
17.97440	−16.15295
19.09780	−8.208008
20.22120	2.260895
21.34460	15.25394
22.46800	30.77100
23.59140	48.81213
24.71480	69.37738
25.83820	92.46655
26.96160	118.0799
28.08500	146.2172

One can, however, use *linear interpolation* to approximate the $f(x)$-value for any given x-value between the smallest and the largest x-values. First, find the two x-values x_i and x_{i+1} in the list that bracket the given x-value, using a modified linear search procedure similar to that in Problem 32, and then interpolate to find the corresponding $f(x)$-value:

$$f(x) = f(x_i) + \frac{f(x_{i+1}) - f(x_i)}{x_{i+1} - x_i} (x - x_i)$$

(If the x-value is out of range, print a message.) Test your program with the following x-values: −7.8, 1.1234, 13.65, 22.5, 23.5914, 25, 25.085, and 33.8.

34. The Cawker City Candy Company records the number of cases of candy produced each day over a four-week period. Write a program that reads these production numbers and stores them in an array. The program should then accept from the user a week number and a day number and display the production level for that day. Assume that each week consists of five workdays.

35. The Cawker City Candy Company manufactures different kinds of candy, each identified by a product number. Write a program that reads two arrays, `Number` and `Price`, in which `Number(1)` and `Price(1)` are the product number and the unit price for the first item, `Number(2)` and `Price(2)` are the product number and the unit price for the second item, and so on. The program should then allow the user to select one of the following options:

1. Retrieve and display the price of a product whose number is entered by the user.
2. Print a table displaying the product number and the price of each item.

Make the program modular by using subprograms to perform the various tasks.

FEATURES NEW TO FORTRAN 90

- Array assignment
- Array constants of the form

$$(/ \; value_1, \; value_2, \; ..., \; value_k \; /)$$

or

$$(value\text{-}list, \; implied\text{-}do\text{-}control)$$

- Elementwise application of operators and functions to arrays
- Array sections of the form

$$array\text{-}name(lower \; : \; upper \; : \; stride)$$

or

$$array\text{-}name(vector\text{-}subscript)$$

- The `WHERE` construct to assign values to arrays depending on the value of a logical array expression
- Assumed-shape arrays as formal array arguments in subprograms
- Array inquiry functions `SIZE`, `LBOUND`, and `UBOUND`
- Functions may return arrays.
- Several new predefined functions for processing arrays, including `DOT_PRODUCT`, `MAXVAL`, `MAXLOC`, `MINVAL`, `MINLOC`, `PRODUCT`, and `SUM`
- Allocatable arrays and the `ALLOCATE` and `DEALLOCATE` statements

9

Multidimensional Arrays

Everyone knows how laborious the usual Method is of attaining to Arts and Sciences; whereas by his Contrivance, the most ignorant Person at a reasonable Charge, and with a little bodily Labour, may write Books in Philosophy, Poetry, Politicks, Law, Mathematicks, and Theology, without the least Assistance from Genius or Study. He then led me to the Frame, about the sides whereof all his Pupils stood in Ranks. It was Twenty Foot square ... linked by slender Wires. These Bits ... were covered on every Square with Paper pasted upon them; and on These Papers were written all the Words of their Language. ...

The Professor then desired me to observe, for he was going to set his Engine at work. The Pupils at this Command took each of them hold of an Iron Handle, whereof there were Forty fixed round the Edges of the Frame; and giving them a sudden Turn, the whole Disposition of the Words was entirely changed. ...

JONATHAN SWIFT, *Gulliver's Travels*

*I*n the preceding chapter, we considered one-dimensional arrays and used them to process lists of data. We also observed that Fortran provides arrays of more than one dimension and that two-dimensional arrays are useful when the data being processed can be arranged in rows and columns. Similarly, a three-dimensional array is appropriate when the data can be arranged in rows, columns, and ranks. When there are several characteristics associated with the data, still higher dimensions may be appropriate, with each dimension corresponding to one of these characteristics. In this chapter we consider how such multidimensional arrays are processed in Fortran programs.

9.1   INTRODUCTION TO MULTIDIMENSIONAL ARRAYS AND MULTIPLY SUBSCRIPTED VARIABLES

There are many problems in which the data being processed can be naturally organized as a table. For example, suppose that water temperatures are recorded four times each day at each of three locations near the discharge outlet of a nuclear power plant's cooling system. These temperature readings can be arranged in a table having four rows and three columns:

615

		Location	
Time	1	2	3
1	65.5	68.7	62.0
2	68.8	68.9	64.5
3	70.4	69.4	66.3
4	68.5	69.1	65.8

In this table, the three temperature readings at time 1 are in the first row, the three temperatures at time 2 are in the second row, and so on.

These 12 data items can be conveniently stored in a two-dimensional array. The array declaration

```
REAL, DIMENSION(4, 3) :: Temperature
```

or

```
REAL, DIMENSION(1:4, 1:3) :: Temperature
```

reserves 12 memory locations for these data items. The doubly subscripted variable

```
Temperature(2,3)
```

then refers to the entry in the second row and third column of the table, that is, to the temperature 64.5 recorded at time 2 at location 3. In general

```
Temperature(I,J)
```

refers to the entry in the Ith row and Jth column, that is, to the temperature recorded at time I at location J.

To illustrate the use of an array with more than two dimensions, suppose that the temperature readings are made for one week, and so seven temperature tables are collected:

A three-dimensional array `TemperatureArray` declared by

    REAL, DIMENSION(4, 3, 7) :: TemperatureArray

or

    REAL, DIMENSION(1:4, 1:3, 1:7) :: TemperatureArray

can be used to store these 84 temperature readings. The value of the triply subscripted variable

    TemperatureArray(1,3,2)

is the temperature recorded at time 1 at location 3 on day 2, that is, the value 64.3 in the first row and third column of the second table. In general,

    TemperatureArray(Time,Location,Day)

is the temperature recorded at time `Time` at location `Location` on day `Day`.

The general form of a **compile-time array declaration** is

Declaration of Compile-Time Array

Forms:

        type, DIMENSION($l_1:u_1$, $l_2:u_2$, . . . , $l_k:u_k$) :: &
            list-of-array-names

or

        type :: list-of-array-specifiers

where
   list-of-array-names is a list of array names, separated by commas
     if there is more than one array;
   list-of-array-specifiers is a list of array specifiers of the form

        array-name($l_1:u_1$, $l_2:u_2$, . . . , $l_k:u_k$)

the number k of dimensions, called the **rank** of the array, is at most seven; and each pair $l_i:u_i$ must be a pair of integer constants specifying the range of values for the ith subscript to be from l_i through u_i; l_i may be omitted if its value is 1.

Purpose:
Declares that each of the identifiers in the *list* is a *k*-dimensional array for which memory is allocated at compile time and for which the range of values of the subscript will be from the specified lower limit l_i through the upper limit u_i. If the minimum value of the subscript for an array is 1, then only the maximum subscript need be specified.

For example, the declarations

```
REAL, DIMENSION(1:2, -1:3) :: Gamma
REAL, DIMENSION(0:2, 0:3, 1:2) :: Beta
INTEGER, DIMENSION(5:12) :: Kappa
```

or

```
REAL :: Gamma(1:2, -1:3), Beta(0:2, 0:3, 1:2)
INTEGER :: Kappa(5:12)
```

establish three arrays. The array `Gamma` is a two-dimensional 2×5 real array, with the first subscript either 1 or 2 and the second subscript ranging from -1 through 3. Thus, the doubly subscripted variables `Gamma(1,-1)`, `Gamma(1,0)`, `Gamma(1,1)`, `Gamma(1,2)`, `Gamma(1,3)`, `Gamma(2,-1)`, `Gamma(2,0)`, `Gamma(2,1)`, `Gamma(2,2)`, and `Gamma(2,3)` may be used. The first subscript in the three-dimensional $3 \times 4 \times 2$ real array `Beta` is equal to 0, 1, or 2; the second subscript ranges from 0 through 3; and the third subscript is equal to 1 or 2. The one-dimensional integer array `Kappa` has subscripts ranging from 5 through 12.

The general form of an **allocatable** (or **run-time**) **array declaration** is

Declaration of Allocatable Array

Forms:

```
type, DIMENSION(:, :, ..., :), ALLOCATABLE :: list
```

or

```
type, DIMENSION(:, :, ..., :) :: list
ALLOCATABLE :: list
```

where
    list is a list of array names;
    the rank *k* of the array (the number of dimensions) is at most seven.

Purpose:
Declares that each of the identifiers in the *list* is a k-dimensional array, where k is the number of colons (:) in the DIMENSION specifier. The number of subscripts in each dimension, called the **extent** of the array, will be specified during execution.

For example,

```
REAL, DIMENSION(:, :, :), ALLOCATABLE :: Beta
REAL, DIMENSION(:, :), ALLOCATABLE :: Gamma
```

declare that Beta is a three-dimensional allocatable array and that Gamma is a two-dimensional allocatable array.

Memory is allocated and the actual ranges of subscripts are specified for an allocatable array by an ALLOCATE statement:

ALLOCATE *Statement*

Forms:

ALLOCATE(*list*)

or

ALLOCATE(*list*, STAT = *status-variable*)

where
list is a list of array specifications of the form

$$array\text{-}name(l_1:u_1, \ l_2:u_2, \ . \ . \ . \ , \ l_k:u_k)$$

where each pair $l_i:u_i$ is a pair of integer expressions; *status-variable* is an integer variable.

Purpose:
Allocates space for each k-dimensional array listed. The range of subscripts in the ith dimension of each array will be from the specified lower limit l_i through the upper limit u_i. If the minimum value of any subscript is 1, then only the maximum subscript need be specified. In the second form, the integer variable *status-variable* will be set to zero if allocation is successful, but it will be assigned some system-dependent error value if there is insufficient memory or if the array has already been allocated.

For example, consider the statement

```
ALLOCATE(Beta(0:2, 0:3, 1:2), Gamma(1:N, -1:3), &
         STAT = AllocateStatus)
```

where `Beta` and `Gamma` are the allocatable arrays declared earlier, and `N` and `AllocateStatus` are integer variables. If memory is available, enough will be allocated for `Beta` and `Gamma`. The first subscript of the three-dimensional $3 \times 4 \times 2$ real array `Beta` will be 0, 1, or 2, the second subscript ranges from 0 through 3, and the third subscript is equal to 1 or 2. For the two-dimensional array `Gamma`, the first subscript will be one of 1, 2, . . . , N and the second subscript can range from -1 through 3.

The `DEALLOCATE` statement used to release memory allocated to multidimensional allocatable arrays has the same form as that for one-dimensional arrays in Chapter 8.

9.2 INPUT/OUTPUT OF MULTIDIMENSIONAL ARRAYS

In the preceding section, we gave several examples of multidimensional arrays and showed how such arrays are declared in a Fortran program. We also noted that each element of an array can be accessed directly by using a multiply subscripted variable consisting of the array name followed by the subscripts that specify the location of that element in the array. In this section we consider the input and output of multidimensional arrays.

Elementwise Processing

As we observed in the preceding chapter, the most natural order for processing the elements of a one-dimensional array is the usual sequential order, from first item to last. For multidimensional arrays, however, there are several orders in which the subscripts may be varied when processing the array elements.

Two-dimensional arrays are often used when the data can be organized as a table consisting of rows and columns. This suggests two natural orders for processing the elements of a two-dimensional array: **rowwise** and **columnwise.** Rowwise processing means that the array elements in the first row are processed first, then those in the second row are processed next, and so on, as shown in Figure 9.1(a) for the 3×4 array A, which has three rows and four columns. In columnwise processing, the elements in the first column are processed first, then those in the second column are processed next, and so on, as illustrated in Figure 9.1(b). In most cases, a programmer can select one of these orderings by controlling the way the subscripts vary. *If this is not done, the Fortran convention is that two-dimensional arrays will be processed columnwise.*

In the list of array elements shown in Figure 9.1(a), we observe that in rowwise processing of a two-dimensional array, the second subscript varies first and the first

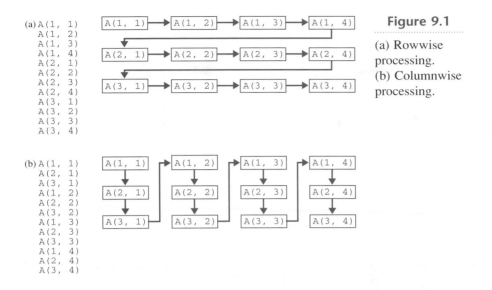

Figure 9.1

(a) Rowwise processing.
(b) Columnwise processing.

subscript varies second; that is, the second subscript must vary over its entire range before the first subscript changes. It is just the opposite for columnwise processing, as we see from Figure 9.1(b): the first subscript varies first and the second subscript second; that is, the first subscript must vary over its entire range before the second subscript changes.

For arrays of three or more dimensions, the elements can be processed in many ways. One of the common orders is the analogue of columnwise processing for the two-dimensional case; that is, the first subscript varies first, followed by the second subscript, then by the third, and so on. This order of processing an array is called **array-element order** and is illustrated in Figure 9.2 for the 2 × 4 × 3 array B.

In Section 8.1 we considered four methods of input/output of array elements:

1. Using a DO loop
2. Using the array name
3. Using an implied DO loop
4. Using an array section

Each of these four techniques can also be used for the input and output of multidimensional arrays, and in this section, we consider each of the first three methods in turn, paying particular attention to the order in which the elements are processed. Array sections are considered in the next section.

Input/Output Using DO Loops

When DO loops are used to read or display a multidimensional array, the input/output statement is placed within a set of nested DO loops, each of which controls

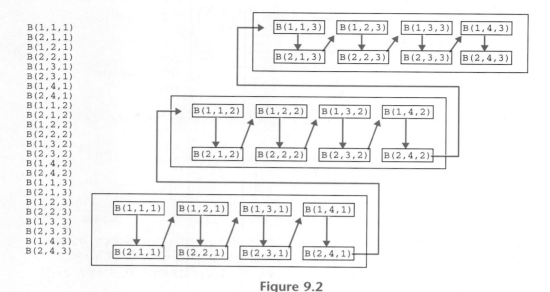

```
B(1,1,1)
B(2,1,1)
B(1,2,1)
B(2,2,1)
B(1,3,1)
B(2,3,1)
B(1,4,1)
B(2,4,1)
B(1,1,2)
B(2,1,2)
B(1,2,2)
B(2,2,2)
B(1,3,2)
B(2,3,2)
B(1,4,2)
B(2,4,2)
B(1,1,3)
B(2,1,3)
B(1,2,3)
B(2,2,3)
B(1,3,3)
B(2,3,3)
B(1,4,3)
B(2,4,3)
```

Figure 9.2

Processing a three-dimensional array.

one of the array's subscripts. For example, consider the problem of reading values into the 3×4 real array `Table` declared by

```
INTEGER, DIMENSION(3,4)  ::  Table
```

so that it has the value

$$\begin{bmatrix} 77 & 56 & 32 & 25 \\ 99 & 10 & 100 & 46 \\ 48 & 89 & 77 & 33 \end{bmatrix}$$

Suppose we use the following statements:

```
DO Row = 1, 3
   DO Col = 1, 4
      READ *, Table(Row, Col)
   END DO
END DO
```

Here the outer DO loop sets the value of the control variable Row to 1, and the inner DO loop is then executed using 1 as the value for Row. The effect is the same as executing

```
DO Col = 1, 4
   READ *, Table(1, Col)
END DO
```

which is equivalent to the following four READ statements:

```
READ *, Table(1,1)
READ *, Table(1,2)
READ *, Table(1,3)
READ *, Table(1,4)
```

The first pass through the outer DO loop thus reads values for the first row of Table, so that the first four values entered must be

```
77
56
32
25
```

Note that they must be entered on separate lines, one per line, because the READ statement is executed four times and each execution requires a new line of input.

Now the outer DO loop sets the value of Row to 2, and the inner DO loop is executed again,

```
DO Col = 1, 4
   READ *, Table(2, Col)
END DO
```

which is equivalent to the four READ statements

```
READ *, Table(2,1)
READ *, Table(2,2)
READ *, Table(2,3)
READ *, Table(2,4)
```

so that the next four values entered must be

```
99
10
100
46
```

again on separate lines. The outer DO loop then causes the inner DO loop to be executed again, with Row set equal to 3,

```
DO Col = 1, 4
   READ *, Table(3, Col)
END DO
```

which is equivalent to

```
READ *, Table(3,1)
READ *, Table(3,2)
READ *, Table(3,3)
READ *, Table(3,4)
```

so that the four values for the third row of `Table` must be entered on separate lines:

```
48
89
77
33
```

Columnwise input is also possible; we need only reverse the order of the two DO loops:

```
DO Col = 1, 4
   DO 10 Row = 1, 3
      READ *, Table(Row, Col)
   END DO
END DO
```

These statements are equivalent to the following sequence of 12 READ statements:

```
READ *, Table(1,1)
READ *, Table(2,1)
READ *, Table(3,1)
READ *, Table(1,2)
READ *, Table(2,2)
READ *, Table(3,2)
READ *, Table(1,3)
READ *, Table(2,3)
READ *, Table(3,3)
READ *, Table(1,4)
READ *, Table(2,4)
READ *, Table(3,4)
```

Because the READ statement is executed 12 times, the data values must be entered on 12 separate lines, 1 per line:

```
77
99
48
56
10
89
32
```

```
100
77
25
46
33
```

Since the data values must appear on separate lines, one value per line, this method is cumbersome for large arrays. A similar problem also occurs with output, since each execution of a PRINT or WRITE statement within nested DO loops such as

```
DO Row = 1, 3
   DO Col = 1, 4
       PRINT *, Table(Row, Col)
   END DO
END DO
```

causes output to begin on a new line. Thus, the elements of the array are displayed on separate lines, one value per line, rather than in a tabular format.

Input/Output Using the Array Name

In this method of reading or displaying an array, the array name without subscripts appears in the input/output statement. As we observed for one-dimensional arrays, this is equivalent to listing a *complete* set of array elements in the input/output list. The total number of elements specified in the array declaration must be read or displayed, and it is therefore not possible to read or display only part of an array using this method.

Another disadvantage of this method is the order in which multidimensional arrays are read or displayed. Because the order in which the subscripts vary is not specified by the programmer, array element order is used. For example, the statement

```
READ *, Table
```

causes values to be read columnwise into the array Table. Thus, for the input data

```
77, 99, 48, 56, 10, 89
32, 100, 77, 25, 46, 33
```

the value assigned to Table is

$$
\begin{bmatrix}
77 & 56 & 32 & 25 \\
99 & 10 & 100 & 46 \\
48 & 89 & 77 & 33
\end{bmatrix}
$$

The output statement

```
PRINT '(1X, 4I5/)', Table
```

displays the elements in columnwise order and so produces the following output:

```
|    77    99    48    56
|   ------------------------
|   ------------------------
|        10    89    32   100
|   ------------------------
|   ------------------------
|        77    25    46    33
|   ------------------------
|   ------------------------
```

Input/Output Using Implied DO Loops

An implied DO loop, introduced in Section 8.1, has the form

```
(i/o-list, control-variable  = initial-value, limit)
```

or

```
(i/o-list, control-variable  = initial-value, limit, step-size)
```

Since the input/output list may contain other implied DO loops, it is possible to use implied DO loops to read or display multidimensional arrays. For example, the statement

rowwise

```
READ *, ((Table(Row, Col), Col = 1, 4), Row = 1, 3)
```

is equivalent to the statement

```
READ *, (Table(Row,1), Table(Row,2), &
         Table(Row,3), Table(Row,4), Row = 1, 3)
```

which has the same effect as

```
READ *, Table(1,1), Table(1,2), Table(1,3), Table(1,4), &
        Table(2,1), Table(2,2), Table(2,3), Table(2,4), &
        Table(3,1), Table(3,2), Table(3,3), Table(3,4)
```

and thus reads the elements of the array Table in rowwise order.

Columnwise input is possible by interchanging the indexing information in the nested implied DO loop:

```
READ *, ((Table(Row, Col), Row = 1, 3), Col = 1, 4)
```

Similarly, the statement

```
READ *, (((B(I,J,K), I = 1, 2), J = 1, 4), K = 1, 3)
```

reads values into the three-dimensional array B in the order indicated in Figure 9.2.

Note the use of parentheses and commas in these statements. They should be used exactly as indicated. Each implied DO loop must be enclosed in parentheses, and a comma must separate the list from the indexing information in the implied DO loop.

Because the READ statement is executed only once, all the data values for Table to be read can be entered on the same line, or with four values on each of three lines, or with seven values on one line, four on the next, and one on another line, and so on. For this reason, using such nested implied DO loops provides the most flexibility for input of multidimensional arrays and is the method we will use in most of our examples.

The most flexible method for outputting a multidimensional array is to use a combination of DO loops and implied DO loops. For example, to produce tabular output of the array Table, we can use

```
DO Row = 1, 3
    PRINT '(1X, 4I5)', (Table(Row, Col), Col = 1, 4)
END DO
```

which is equivalent to the statements

```
PRINT '(1X, 4I5)', (Table(1, Col), Col = 1, 4)
PRINT '(1X, 4I5)', (Table(2, Col), Col = 1, 4)
PRINT '(1X, 4I5)', (Table(3, Col), Col = 1, 4)
```

Since each PRINT statement causes output to begin on a new line, each row of Table will appear on a separate line. This would also be true if the format specifier were changed to allow it to be used with tables with more columns:

```
'(1X, 15I5)'
```

The output of Table would still be a table with three rows and four columns:

```
    77    56    32    25
    99    10   100    46
    48    89    77    33
```

Example: Temperature Table

The program in Figure 9.3 illustrates the input and output of two-dimensional arrays. It reads the number of times NumTimes at which temperatures are recorded and the number of locations NumLocations at which these readings are made; allocates memory for an allocatable array Temperature having NumTimes rows and NumLocations columns; reads NumTimes × NumLocations values into this array; and displays these temperatures in tabular format. Note the use of nested implied DO loops to input the temperatures into the array and an implied DO loop within a DO loop to display them.

Figure 9.3 I/O of two-dimensional arrays.

```
PROGRAM Table_of_Temperatures
!-----------------------------------------------------------------------
! Program illustrating i/o of a two-dimensional array. Variables
! used are:
!   Temperature     : two-dimensional array of temperatures
!   NumTimes        : number of times temperatures are recorded
!   NumLocs         : number of locations at which temperatures
!                       are recorded
!   AllocateStatus  : status variable for ALLOCATE
!   Time            : row subscript for the table
!   Location        : column subscript for the table
!
! Input:  NumTimes, NumLocs, and elements of Temperature
! Output: The array Temperature in table format
!-----------------------------------------------------------------------

  IMPLICIT NONE
  REAL, DIMENSION(:, :), ALLOCATABLE :: Temperature
  INTEGER :: NumTimes, NumLocs, AllocateStatus, Time, Location

  PRINT *, "Enter number of times temperatures are recorded"
  PRINT *, "and number of locations where recorded:"
  READ *, NumTimes, NumLocs

  ALLOCATE (Temperature(NumTimes, NumLocs), STAT = AllocateStatus)
  IF (AllocateStatus /= 0) STOP "*** Not enough memory ***"

  PRINT *, "Enter the temperatures at the first location,"
  PRINT *, "then those at the second location, and so on:"

  READ *, ((Temperature(Time, Location), &
           Location = 1, NumLocs), Time = 1, NumTimes)

  PRINT *
  PRINT '(1X, T13, "Location" / 1X, "Time", 10I6)', &
        (Location, Location = 1, NumLocs)
```

Figure 9.3 *(cont.)*

```
DO Time = 1, NumTimes
    PRINT '(/1X, I3, 2X, 10F6.1/)', &
          Time, (Temperature(Time, Location), Location = 1, NumLocs)
END DO

DEALLOCATE (Temperature)

END PROGRAM Table_of_Temperatures
```

Sample run:

```
Enter number of times temperatures are recorded
and number of locations where recorded:
4, 3
Enter the temperatures at the first location,
then those at the second location, and so on:
65.5, 68.7, 62.0
68.8, 68.9, 64.5
70.4, 69.4, 66.3
68.5, 69.1, 65.8


              Location
Time      1    2    3

 1      65.5 68.7 62.0

 2      68.8 68.9 64.5

 3      70.4 69.4 66.3

 4      68.5 69.1 65.8
```

The following examples exhibit some of the additional flexibility that implied DO loops provide. In these examples, the integer variable `Total` has the value 152; `Number` is the one-dimensional integer array containing the four numbers 16, 37, 76, and 23; and `Rate` is a 3 × 4 real array

$$\begin{bmatrix} 16.1 & 7.3 & 18.4 & 6.5 \\ 0.0 & 1.0 & 1.0 & 3.5 \\ 18.2 & 16.9 & 0.0 & 0.0 \end{bmatrix}$$

Input/output statement:

```
READ *, N, (Number(I), I = 1, N), M, &
        ((Rate(I,J), J = 1, N), I = 1, M)
```

Possible lines of input data:

```
4
16, 37, 76, 23
3
16.1,  7.3, 18.4, 6.5
0.0,   1.0,  1.0, 3.5
18.2, 16.9,  0.0, 0.0
```

Input/output statement:

```
PRINT 5, ("Row", I, (Rate(I,J), J = 1, 4), I = 1, 3)
5 FORMAT(1X, A, I2, "--", 4F6.1/)
```

Output produced:

```
Row 1--  16.1   7.3  18.4     6.5
---------------------------------
---------------------------------
Row 2--   0.0   1.0   1.0     3.5
---------------------------------
---------------------------------
Row 3--  18.2  16.9   0.0     0.0
---------------------------------
```

Input/output statement:

```
PRINT 6, (J, (Rate(I,J), I = 1,3), Number(J), J = 1,4), &
        "Total", Total
6 FORMAT (4(1X, I4, 5X, 3F6.1, I10/), 1X, A, T35, I3)
```

Output produced:

```
    1     16.1   0.0  18.2        16
-------------------------------------
    2      7.3   1.0  16.9        37
-------------------------------------
    3     18.4   1.0   0.0        76
-------------------------------------
    4      6.5   3.5   0.0        23
-------------------------------------
Total                            152
-------------------------------------
```

Quick Quiz 9.2

1. (True or false)   The array declaration `REAL, DIMENSION(5,10) :: X` is equivalent to the declaration `REAL, DIMENSION(1:5, 5:10) :: X`.

2. (True or false)   The declaration `INTEGER Alpha(1:10, 1:10)` is equivalent to the declaration `INTEGER, DIMENSION(10,10) :: Alpha`.

3. The following is an example of _____ processing (rowwise or columnwise):

```
DO J = 1, 10
   DO I = 1, 10
      READ *, Alpha(I,J)
   END DO
END DO
```

4. Unless specified otherwise, two-dimensional arrays in Fortran are input or output in a _____ (rowwise or columnwise) manner.

For Questions 5–9, assume that `Beta` is an integer array declared by

```
INTEGER, DIMENSION(2,2) :: Beta
```

and that the following values are entered: 1, 2, 3, 4. Tell what value (if any) will be assigned to `Beta(1,2)` by the given statements.

5. `READ *, Beta`

6. `READ *, ((Beta(I,J), J = 1, 2), I = 1, 2)`

7. `READ *, ((Beta(J,I), J = 1, 2), I = 1, 2)`

8.
```
DO I = 1, 2
   DO J = 1, 2
      READ *, Beta(I,J)
   END DO
END DO
```

9. Which of the input statements or loops in Questions 6–8 is equivalent to the READ statement in Question 5?

10. Given the declaration `INTEGER, DIMENSION(2,2,2) :: T` and that the values entered in response to the statement

```
READ *, (((T(I,J,K), I = 1,2), J = 1,2), K = 1,2)
```

are 1, 2, 3, 4, 5, 6, 7, 8, what value will be assigned to `T(1,2,1)`?

11. (True or false) The array `T` in Question 10 has six elements.

12. The rank of the array `Beta` in Question 5 is _____ , and the rank of the array `T` in Question 10 is _____ .

13. (True or false) Input using implied DO loops is the most flexible method of array input.

14. How many lines of output will be produced if the READ statement in Question 8 is replaced by `PRINT *, Beta(I,J)`?

Which of the statements in Questions 15–20 will reserve 200 storage locations?

15. `REAL, DIMENSION(100,100) :: List`

16. `INTEGER, DIMENSION(10,20) :: Array`

17. `REAL, DIMENSION(4:50) :: List`

18. `REAL :: XRay(-50:49, 0:1)`

19. `REAL, DIMENSION(2,2,2,5,5), :: Dim5`

20. `REAL :: Number(100:299)`

Exercises 9.2

1. Write a declaration for a two-dimensional array whose rows are numbered from 1 through 5, whose columns are numbered from 1 through 10, and in which each element is a real value.

2. Write a declaration for a two-dimensional array whose rows are numbered from 0 through 4, whose columns are numbered from 1900 through 1910, and in which each element is a character string of length 5.

3. Write statements to set each element in the array of Exercise 1 to the sum of the row number and the column number in which that element appears.

4. Write statements to set each element in the array of Exercise 2 to a string of blanks.

For Exercises 5–16, assume that the following declarations have been made:

```
INTEGER, DIMENSION(3,3) :: Array
INTEGER, DIMENSION(6) :: Number
INTEGER :: I, J
```

and assume that the following data is entered for those statements that involve input:

```
1, 2, 3, 4, 5, 6, 7, 8, 9
```

Tell what value (if any) is assigned to each array element, or explain why an error results:

5. ```
DO I = 1, 3
    DO J = 1, 3
        Array(I,J) = I + J
    END DO
END DO
```

6. ```
DO I = 1, 3
    DO J = 3, 1, -1
        IF (I == J) THEN
            Array(I,J) = 0
        ELSE
            Array(I,J) = 1
        END IF
    END DO
END DO
```

7. ```
DO I = 1, 3
    DO J = 1, 3
        IF (I < J) THEN
            Array(I,J) = -1
        ELSE IF (I == J) THEN
            Array(I,J) = 0
        ELSE
            Array(I,J) = 1
        END IF
    END DO
END DO
```

8. ```
DO I = 1, 3
    DO J = 1, I
        Array(I,J) = 0
    END DO
    DO J = I + 1, 3
        Array(I,J) = 2
    END DO
END DO
```

9. ```
DO I = 1, 3
    DO J = 1, 3
        READ *, Array(I,J)
    END DO
END DO
```

10. ```
READ *, Array
```

11. ```
READ *, ((Array(I,J), J = 1, 3), I = 1, 3)
```

12. ```
READ *, ((Array(J,I), I = 1, 3), J = 1, 3)
```

13. ```
READ *, ((Array(I,J), I = 1, 3), J = 1, 3)
```

14. ```
DO I = 1, 3
    READ *, (Array(I,J), J = 1, 3)
END DO
```

15.
```
READ *, Number
    DO I = 1, 3
        DO J = 1, 3
            Array(I,J) = Number(I) + Number(J)
        END DO
    END DO
```

16.
```
READ *, Number, (Array(1,J), J = 1, 3)
    DO I = 1, 2
        DO J = 1, 3
            Array(Number(I + 1), Number(J)) = Number(I + J)
        END DO
    END DO
```

For Exercises 17–20, assume that the following declaration has been made:

```
REAL, DIMENSION(5,5) :: Table
```

and assume that the following lines of data are entered:

data-line-1:	123456789876543
data-line-2:	564738291928374
data-line-3:	135798642123456
data-line-4:	123454321567896
data-line-5:	498376251427485

Tell what values (if any) will be assigned to the array Table, or explain why an error results:

17.
```
READ '(5F3.2)', Table
```

18.
```
READ '(5F3.0)', ((Table(I,J), J = 1, 5), I = 1, 5)
```

19.
```
READ '(5F3.0)', ((Table(J,I), J = 1, 5), I = 1, 5)
```

20.
```
DO I = 1, 5
    READ '(5F2.1)', (Table(I,J), J = 1, 5)
END DO
```

9.3 PROCESSING MULTIDIMENSIONAL ARRAYS

In the preceding sections, we described how multidimensional arrays are declared and various ways they can be input and output. In this section we show how the other kinds of array processing described for one-dimensional arrays in Section 8.4 can be extended to multidimensional arrays.

Array Constants

One-dimensional array constants like those described in Section 8.4 can be used to assign values to multidimensional arrays, but first they must be *reshaped* to match the dimensions of the array. The intrinsic function **RESHAPE** can be used to reshape any array. A reference to this function has the form

```
RESHAPE(source-array, shape, pad, order)
```

It returns an array with values obtained from the specified *source-array*, with the specified *shape*, followed by elements of the array *pad* (used repeatedly if necessary). *order* is a one-dimensional array that specifies the order in which the subscripts are to be varied when filling in the resulting array. The arguments *pad* and *order* are optional and may also be given in the form PAD = *pad* and ORDER = *order*, respectively.

To illustrate, suppose that A is a two-dimensional array declared by

```
INTEGER, DIMENSION(2,3) :: A
```

The statement

```
A = RESHAPE((/ 11, 22, 33, 44, 55, 66 /), (/ 2, 3 /))
```

or

```
A = RESHAPE((/ (11*N, N = 1, 6) /), (/ 2, 3 /))
```

assigns to A the 2 × 3 array

$$\begin{bmatrix} 11 & 33 & 55 \\ 22 & 44 & 66 \end{bmatrix}$$

Note that the array is filled columnwise. The fourth argument of the RESHAPE function can be given to specify that the subscripts are to be varied in a different order. For example, the statement

```
A = RESHAPE((/ 11, 22, 33, 44, 55, 66 /), (/2, 3/), &
            ORDER = (/2, 1/))
```

assigns to A the array

$$\begin{bmatrix} 11 & 22 & 33 \\ 44 & 55 & 66 \end{bmatrix}$$

The order (/2, 1/) specifies that the second subscript is to be varied before the first, which causes the array to be filled rowwise. If there are not enough values in the source array to fill the reshaped array, the values specified in argument *pad* will be used. For example, the statement

```
A = RESHAPE((/ 11, 22, 33, 44/), (/2, 3/), &
            PAD = (/0, 0/), ORDER = (/2, 1/))
```

or equivalently,

```
A = RESHAPE((/ 11, 22, 33, 44/), (/2, 3/), &
            (/0, 0/), (/2, 1/))
```

assigns to A the array

$$\begin{bmatrix} 11 & 22 & 33 \\ 44 & 0 & 0 \end{bmatrix}$$

Since *pad* will be used repeatedly if necessary, it could also have been given simply as `(/ 0 /)`.

The instrinsic function **SHAPE** can be used to determine the *shape* of an array, which consists of the number of dimensions for the array and the *extent* (the number of subscripts) in each dimension. A reference to SHAPE has the form

```
SHAPE(array)
```

and returns a one-dimensional array, each of whose elements is the extent in the corresponding dimension of *array*. For example, for the above array A, SHAPE(A) will return (2, 3).

Array Expressions

As described for one-dimensional arrays in Section 8.4, operators and functions normally applied to simple expressions may also be applied to multidimensional arrays having the same shape and to arrays and simple expressions, and they are carried out elementwise. To illustrate, consider the following declarations:

```
INTEGER, DIMENSION(2,2) :: A, B
```

and suppose that A is the 2×2 array

$$A = \begin{bmatrix} -8 & 12 \\ 0 & -1 \end{bmatrix}$$

The statement

```
B = 2*A + 1
```

assigns to B the array

$$B = \begin{bmatrix} -15 & 25 \\ 1 & -1 \end{bmatrix}$$

and the statement

```
B = ABS(A)
```

assigns to B the array

$$B = \begin{bmatrix} 8 & 12 \\ 0 & 1 \end{bmatrix}$$

Array Sections and Subarrays

Array sections or subarrays, which are arrays consisting of selected elements from a parent array, may also be constructed from multidimensional arrays. Such array sections are defined by specifications of the form

```
array-name(section-subscript-list)
```

where each item in the *section-subscript-list* is a subscript, or a subscript triplet, or a vector subscript. (See Section 8.4 for a description of subscript triplets and vector subscripts.) For example, if A is an array declared by

```
INTEGER, DIMENSION(2,3) :: A
```

with value

$$A = \begin{bmatrix} 11 & 22 & 33 \\ 44 & 55 & 66 \end{bmatrix}$$

the array section `A(1:2:1, 2:3:1)`, or simply `A(:, 2:3)`, is the 2 × 2 subarray consisting of the last two columns of A:

$$\begin{bmatrix} 22 & 33 \\ 55 & 66 \end{bmatrix}$$

The value of the array section `A(2, 1:3:1)`, or simply, `A(2, :)`, is the one-dimensional array consisting of the last row of A:

```
[ 44 55 66 ]
```

The value of the array section `A((/ 2, 1 /), 2:3)`, in which the first item in the section subscript list is the subscript vector `(/2, 1/)` and the second item is the subscript triplet `2:3` with stride 1, is the 2 × 2 array

$$\begin{bmatrix} 55 & 66 \\ 22 & 33 \end{bmatrix}$$

Array Assignment

Assignment of one array to another is permitted,

array-variable = expression

provided that the value of *expression* is either

1. An array of the same shape as the array variable, or
2. A simple value

In the second case, the value is broadcast to all the array elements, with the result that each is assigned this value. For example, if A and B are declared by

```
INTEGER, DIMENSION(2,3) :: A
INTEGER, DIMENSION(3,2) :: B
```

the assignment statement

```
A = 0
```

assigns to A a 2 × 3 array containing all zeros:

$$A = \begin{bmatrix} 0 & 0 & 0 \\ 0 & 0 & 0 \end{bmatrix}$$

The statement

array   shape

```
B = RESHAPE(A, (/3, 2/))
```

then assigns to B a 3 × 2 array containing all zeros:

$$B = \begin{bmatrix} 0 & 0 \\ 0 & 0 \\ 0 & 0 \end{bmatrix}$$

Subarrays may also appear on the left-hand side of an assignment statement. For example, for the preceding 2 × 3 array A containing all zeros, the statement

```
A(:, 2:3) = RESHAPE((/ (I**2, I = 1, 4) /), (/2, 3/))
```

changes the value of A to

$$A = \begin{bmatrix} 0 & 1 & 9 \\ 0 & 4 & 16 \end{bmatrix}$$

The WHERE construct may also be used with multidimensional arrays. For example, if arrays Alpha and Beta are declared by

```
REAL, DIMENSION(2,3) :: Alpha, Beta
```

and Alpha has the value

$$Alpha = \begin{bmatrix} 1.0 & 2.0 & 0.0 \\ 0.0 & 10.0 & 5.0 \end{bmatrix}$$

the WHERE construct

```
WHERE (Alpha /= 0)
   Beta = 1.0 / REAL(Alpha)
ELSEWHERE
   B = 0.0
END WHERE
```

assigns Beta the value

$$Beta = \begin{bmatrix} 1.0 & 0.5 & 0.0 \\ 0.0 & 0.1 & 0.2 \end{bmatrix}$$

Multidimensional Arrays as Arguments

Intrinsic Array-Processing Subprograms. In Section 8.4 we described a number of intrinsic functions that can be used to process one-dimensional arrays. Several of these can also be used for multidimensional arrays. The following is a list of the most useful functions; others have been described earlier in this section, and more are described in Section 9.6 and in Appendix D.

ALLOCATED(A)	Returns true if memory has been allocated to the allocatable array A and false otherwise
MATMUL(A, B)	Returns the matrix product of A and B, provided this product is defined (see Section 9.6)
MAXVAL(A, D)	Returns an array of one less dimension than A containing the maximum values in array A along dimension D. If D is omitted, the maximum value in the entire array is returned.
MAXLOC(A)	Returns a one-dimensional array containing the position of the first occurrence of the maximum value in A
MINVAL(A, D)	Returns an array of one less dimension than A containing the minimum values in array A along dimension D. If D is omitted, the minimum value in the entire array is returned.
MINLOC(A)	Returns a one-dimensional array containing the position of the first occurrence of the minimum value in A

PRODUCT(A, D)	Returns an array of one less dimension than A containing the products of the elements of A along dimension D. If D is omitted, the elementwise product of the elements in the entire array is returned.
RESHAPE(A, S, P, O)	Returns an array with values obtained from A, with the specified shape S, followed by elements of array P (used repeatedly if necessary); and one-dimensional array O specifies the order in which the subscripts are to be varied when filling in the resulting array. P and O are optional arguments.
SHAPE(A)	Returns a one-dimensional array, each of whose elements is the extent in the corresponding dimension of A
SUM(A, D)	Returns an array of one less dimension than A containing the sums of the elements of A along dimension D. If D is omitted, the sum of the elements in the entire array is returned.

SPREAD(A, D, N)   Returns an array of dimension one more than the dimension of A obtained by broadcasting N copies of A along dimension D. For example, SPREAD((/ 11, 22, 33 /), 1, 2) returns the array

$$\begin{bmatrix} 11 & 22 & 33 \\ 11 & 22 & 33 \end{bmatrix}$$

and SPREAD((/ 11, 22, 33 /), 2, 2) returns the array

$$\begin{bmatrix} 11 & 11 \\ 22 & 22 \\ 33 & 33 \end{bmatrix}$$

TRANSPOSE(A)   Returns the transpose of A (see Section 9.6)

Programmer-Defined Array-Processing Subprograms. The fundamental rule governing the use of arrays as arguments of subprograms is

An actual array argument and the corresponding formal array argument must have the same type and shape.

This means that the elements of the two arrays must have the same type, the arrays must have the same rank (number of dimensions), and each dimension must have the same extent (same number of subscripts but not necessarily the same range).

As described and illustrated in Section 8.4 for one-dimensional arrays, the type of an array that is a formal argument must be specified within the subprogram, but there are three ways that its shape can be specified. We will describe and illustrate each with an example.

The shape of the formal array can be given explicitly in the subprogram. This is illustrated by the program in Figure 9.4. It reads a square array of numbers and then calls an internal subroutine to find and display the largest value in each row. Note that the subroutine `FindRowMaxima` uses the intrinsic function `MAXVAL` to find these maximum row entries.

 Figure 9.4 Finding row maxima—version 1.

```
PROGRAM Finding_Row_Maxima_1
!-------------------------------------------------------------------
! Program to read an array of numbers and to find the maximum value in
! each row using the subroutine FindRowMaxima.  Identifiers used are:
!    IntArray       : two-dimensional array of numbers
!    NumRows        : number of rows in IntArray (constant)
!    NumColumns     : number of columns in IntArray (constant)
!    FindRowMaxima  : subroutine to find the row maxima
!    I, J           : subscripts
!
! Input:  NumRows, NumColumns, and IntArray
! Output: The maximum value in each row (using FindRowMaxima)
!-------------------------------------------------------------------

  IMPLICIT NONE
  INTEGER, PARAMETER :: NumRows = 4, NumColumns = 5
  INTEGER, DIMENSION(NumRows, NumColumns) :: IntArray
  INTEGER :: I, J

  PRINT *, "Enter the", NumRows, "X", NumColumns, "array of integers &
          &in a rowwise manner:"
  READ *, ((IntArray(I,J), J = 1, NumColumns), I = 1, NumRows)

  CALL FindRowMaxima(IntArray)

CONTAINS
```

Figure 9.4 *(cont.)*

```
!-FindRowMaxima--------------------------------------------------------
! Subroutine to find and display the maximum value in each row of an
! array Table of integers.  Local identifiers used are:
!   Rows    : number of rows in array Table (named constant)
!   Cols    : number of columns in array Table (named constant)
!   RowMax  : one-dimensional array of row maxima
!   I       : subscript
!
! Accepts: Array Table
! Output:  The maximum value in each row of Table
!----------------------------------------------------------------------

SUBROUTINE FindRowMaxima(Table)

   INTEGER, PARAMETER :: Rows = 4, Cols = 5
   INTEGER, DIMENSION(Rows, Cols), INTENT(IN) :: Table
   INTEGER, DIMENSION(Rows) :: RowMax
   INTEGER :: I

   RowMax = MAXVAL(Table, 2)  ! Find max values along dimension 2
   DO I = 1, Rows
      PRINT *, "Maximum entry in row", I, "is", RowMax(I)
   END DO

 END SUBROUTINE FindRowMaxima

END PROGRAM Finding_Row_Maxima_1
```

Sample run:

```
Enter the 4 X 5 array of integers in a rowwise manner:
1 2 3 4 5
6 6 6 6 6
4 3 2 1 0
2 9 4 8 6
Maximum entry in row 1 is 5
Maximum entry in row 2 is 6
Maximum entry in row 3 is 4
Maximum entry in row 4 is 9
```

Although an actual array argument and the corresponding formal array argument must have the same extent in each dimension, they need not have the same subscript range. For example, the array Table in the subprogram FindRowMaxima could have been declared by

```
INTEGER, DIMENSION(0:Rows-1, 0:Cols-1) :: Table
```

The first row (column) of `IntArray` would be associated with row (column) 0 of `Table`, the second row (column) of `IntArray` with row (column) 1 of `Table`, and so on.

A second way to specify the shape of a formal array is to pass the extent (or subscript range) of each dimension—but not the rank—as an argument and use these to declare the array. This makes it possible to design subprograms that can be used to process arrays of a certain rank but of various extents. For example, the program in Figure 9.5 is a modification of that in Figure 9.4 in which the formal arguments `Rows` and `Cols` are used to specify the extents of the formal array `Table` in the subroutine `FindRowMaxima`. The actual extents `NumRows` and `NumColumns` and the actual array `IntArray`, which is an allocatable array, are passed to the subprogram from the main program when the function is referenced.

Figure 9.5 Finding fow maxima—version 2.

```
PROGRAM Finding_Row_Maxima_2
!-----------------------------------------------------------------------
! Program to read an array of numbers and to find the maximum value in
! each row using the subroutine FindRowMaxima.  Identifiers used are:
!    IntArray        : two-dimensional allocatable array of numbers
!    NumRows         : number of rows in IntArray
!    NumColumns      : number of columns in IntArray
!    AllocateStatus : status variable for ALLOCATE
!    FindRowMaxima  : subroutine to find the row maxima
!    I, J            : subscripts
!
! Input:  NumRows, NumColumns, and IntArray
! Output: The maximum value in each row (using FindRowMaxima)
!-----------------------------------------------------------------------

  IMPLICIT NONE
  INTEGER, DIMENSION(:, :), ALLOCATABLE :: IntArray
  INTEGER :: NumRows, NumColumns, AllocateStatus
  INTEGER :: I, J

  WRITE (*, '(1X, A)', ADVANCE = "NO") &
       "How many rows and how many columns are in the array? "
  READ *, NumRows, NumColumns

  ALLOCATE(IntArray(NumRows, NumColumns), STAT = AllocateStatus)
  IF (AllocateStatus /= 0) STOP "*** Not enough memory ***"
```

Figure 9.5 *(cont.)*

```
   PRINT *, "Enter the", NumRows, "X", NumColumns, "array of integers &
           & in a rowwise manner:"
   READ *, ((IntArray(I,J), J = 1, NumColumns), I = 1, NumRows)

   CALL FindRowMaxima(IntArray, NumRows, NumColumns)

CONTAINS

   !-FindRowMaxima------------------------------------------------------
   ! Subroutine to find and display the maximum value in each row of a
   ! Rows X Cols array Table of integers.  Local variables used are:
   !    I      : subscript
   !    RowMax : one-dimensional array of row maxima
   !
   ! Accepts: Array Table, Rows, Cols
   ! Output:  The maximum value in each row of Table
   !--------------------------------------------------------------------

   SUBROUTINE FindRowMaxima(Table, Rows, Cols)

      INTEGER, INTENT(IN):: Rows, Cols
      INTEGER, DIMENSION(Rows, Cols), INTENT(IN) :: Table
      INTEGER, DIMENSION(Rows) :: RowMax
      INTEGER :: I

      RowMax = MAXVAL(Table, 2)   ! Find max values along dimension 2
      DO I = 1, Rows
         PRINT *, "Maximum entry in row", I, "is", RowMax(I)
      END DO

   END SUBROUTINE FindRowMaxima

END PROGRAM Finding_Row_Maxima_2
```

Sample run:

```
How many rows and how many columns are in the array? 4, 5
Enter the 4 X 5 array of integers in a rowwise manner:
1 2 3 4 5
6 6 6 6 6
4 3 2 1 0
2 9 4 8 6
Maximum entry in row 1 is 5
Maximum entry in row 2 is 6
Maximum entry in row 3 is 4
Maximum entry in row 4 is 9
```

A third way to specify the shape of a formal array is to use an assumed-shape array, which will assume the extents of the corresponding actual array. The program in Figure 9.6 illustrates. The subroutine `FindRowMaxima` declares the formal array `Table` to be an assumed-shape array using

```
INTEGER, DIMENSION(:, :), INTENT(IN) :: Table
```

The extents of `Table` will be the extents of the corresponding actual argument `Item`. Note the use of the predefined function `SIZE` to determine the number of rows in `Table`. Also note that no interface block is required in the main program, because `FindRowMaxima` is an internal subroutine.

Figure 9.6 Finding row maxima—version 3.

```fortran
PROGRAM Finding_Row_Maxima_3
!----------------------------------------------------------------------
! Program to read an array of numbers and to find the maximum value in
! each row using the subroutine FindRowMaxima.  Identifiers used are:
!   IntArray        : two-dimensional allocatable array of numbers
!   NumRows         : number of rows in IntArray
!   NumColumns      : number of columns in IntArray
!   AllocateStatus  : status variable for ALLOCATE
!   FindRowMaxima   : subroutine to find the row maxima
!   I, J            : subscripts
!
! Input:  NumRows, NumColumns, and IntArray
! Output: The maximum value in each row (using FindRowMaxima)
!----------------------------------------------------------------------

  IMPLICIT NONE
  INTEGER, DIMENSION(:, :), ALLOCATABLE :: IntArray
  INTEGER :: NumRows, NumColumns, AllocateStatus
  INTEGER :: I, J

  WRITE (*, '(1X, A)', ADVANCE = "NO") &
        "How many rows and how many columns are in the array? "
  READ *, NumRows, NumColumns

  ALLOCATE(IntArray(NumRows, NumColumns), STAT = AllocateStatus)
  IF (AllocateStatus /= 0) STOP "*** Not enough memory ***"

  PRINT *, "Enter the", NumRows, "X", NumColumns, "array of integers &
           & in a rowwise manner:"
  READ *, ((IntArray(I,J), J = 1, NumColumns), I = 1, NumRows)
```

Figure 9.6 *(cont.)*

```
CALL FindRowMaxima(IntArray)

CONTAINS

  !-FindRowMaxima-----------------------------------------------------
  ! Subroutine to find and display the maximum value in each row of an
  ! array Table of integers, which is an assumed-shape array. Local
  ! variables used are:
  !   I      : subscript
  !   RowMax : one-dimensional array of row maxima
  !
  ! Accepts: Array Table
  ! Output:  The maximum value in each row of Table
  !-------------------------------------------------------------------

  SUBROUTINE FindRowMaxima(Table)

    INTEGER, DIMENSION(:, :), INTENT(IN) :: Table
    INTEGER, DIMENSION(SIZE(Table, 1)) :: RowMax
    INTEGER:: I

    RowMax = MAXVAL(Table, 2)   ! Find max values along dimension 2
    DO I = 1, SIZE(RowMax)
       PRINT *, "Maximum entry in row", I, "is", RowMax(I)
    END DO

  END SUBROUTINE FindRowMaxima

END PROGRAM Finding_Row_Maxima_3
```

Automatic arrays may be multidimensional, and a function may return a multidimensional array. These properties of arrays were described in detail for one-dimensional arrays in Chapter 8 and are used in the same manner for multidimensional arrays.

Quick Quiz 9.3

1. (True or false) If A and B are arrays declared by

```
   REAL, DIMENSION(3, 0:4) ::  A
   REAL, DIMENSION(2:4, 5) ::  B
```

the statement A = B can be used to copy the values stored in B into A.

Questions 2–11 assume the following declarations have been made:

```
INTEGER, DIMENSION(2,3) ::  &
  A = RESHAPE( (/ 10, 20, 30, 40, 50, 60 /), (/2, 3/) )
INTEGER :: I
INTEGER, DIMENSION(3,2) ::  &
  B = RESHAPE( (/ (I**2, I = 1, 6) /), (/3, 2/) )
INTEGER, DIMENSION(3) :: C = (/ 1, 3, 2 /)
INTEGER, DIMENSION(0:1, 2:4) :: D, E, F, G, H
```

Give answers in a table format (where appropriate), or explain why the expression or statement is not legal.

2. A

3. B

4. A(2, 2:3)

5. B(1:3:2, :)

6. B(C, :)

7. D = 2*A

8. E = 3*A + B

9. F = A*A

10. G = 3

11. H, whose value is given by

```
WHERE (A < 40)
  H = A + 1
ELSEWHERE
  H = A - 1
END WHERE
```

For Questions 12–14, assume the following declaration has been made:

```
INTEGER, DIMENSION(3,3) :: Table = 0
```

What values will be assigned to the array Table by the given statements?

12.
```
DO I = 1, 3
   Table(I,I) = 1
END DO
```

13.
```
DO I = 1, 3
   DO J = I, 3
      Table(I,J) = 1
   END DO
END DO
```

14.
```
DO I = 1, 3
   DO J = 1, 3
      Table(I,J) = I * J
   END DO
END DO
```

Exercises 9.3

Exercises 1–15 assume the following declarations have been made:

```
REAL, DIMENSION(2,5) :: A = &
        RESHAPE( (/0.0, 1.1, 2.2, 3.3, 4.4, &
                   5.5, 6.6, 7.7, 8.8, 9.9 /), (/2, 5/) ), &
        B
INTEGER :: I, M = 1, N = 3
REAL, DIMENSION(3,4) :: &
        C = RESHAPE( (/ (128.0/2.0**I, I = 0, 11) /), (/3, 4/) ), &
        D
INTEGER, DIMENSION(4) :: E = (/ 4, 2, 1, 3 /)
REAL, DIMENSION(0:1, 5:9) :: F, G, L
REAL, DIMENSION(-1:0, 0:5) :: H
REAL, DIMENSION(0:2, 100:104) :: K
```

Give answers in a table format (where appropriate), or explain why the expression or statement is not legal.

1. A
2. C
3. C(2:3, 3:4)
4. A(1, 1:5:2)
5. C(M:N, M:N)
6. C(M:2, M:N:N-1)
7. C(E(2:3), E)
8. E(A)
9. D = 3.14
10. B = 2.0 * A + 1.0
11. F = A + 2*B
12. G = A/2 + 1.0
13. H = RESHAPE(A, (/2, 6/), REAL(E))
14. K = RESHAPE(A, (/3, 5/), REAL(E), E(2:3))
15. L, whose value is given by

```
WHERE (A > 1)
   L = 10.0 * A
ELSEWHERE
   L = A - 1.0
END WHERE
```

9.4 APPLICATION: POLLUTION TABLES

Problem

In a certain city, the air pollution is measured at two-hour intervals, beginning at midnight. These measurements are recorded for a one-week period and stored in a file, the first line of which contains the pollution levels for day 1, the second line for day 2, and so on. For example, the pollution file for a certain week contains the following data:

```
30 30 31 32 35 40 43 44 47 45 40 38
33 32 30 34 40 48 46 49 53 49 45 40
38 35 34 37 44 50 51 54 60 58 51 49
49 48 47 53 60 70 73 75 80 75 73 60
55 54 53 65 70 80 90 93 95 94 88 62
73 70 65 66 71 78 74 78 83 75 66 58
50 47 43 35 30 33 37 43 45 52 39 31
```

A program must be written to produce a weekly report that displays the pollution levels in a table of the form

```
                            TIME
DAY:   1   2   3   4   5   6   7   8   9  10  11  12
      ---------------------------------------------
  1 :  30  30  31  32  35  40  43  44  47  45  40  38
  2 :  33  32  30  34  40  48  46  49  53  49  45  40
  3 :  38  35  34  37  44  50  51  54  60  58  51  49
  4 :  49  48  47  53  60  70  73  75  80  75  73  60
  5 :  55  54  53  65  70  80  90  93  95  94  88  62
  6 :  73  70  65  66  71  78  74  78  83  75  66  58
  7 :  50  47  43  35  30  33  37  43  45  52  39  31
```

and that also displays the average pollution level for each day and the average pollution level for each sampling time.

Solution

Specification

Input: Air pollution levels (from a file)

Output: A table of pollution levels
            Average pollution level for each day
            Average pollution level for each sampling time

Design. The following variables will be used:

VARIABLES FOR POLLUTION REPORT PROBLEM

Pollution_Table	A two-dimensional array containing pollution levels
Sum	Used to add the rows/columns of *Pollution_Table*
NumTimes	Number of sampling times
NumDays	Number of days
Day, Time	Subscripts

Monitoring air pollution. (Photo courtesy of Bruce Roberts/Photo Researchers, Inc.)

The required algorithm is as follows:

ALGORITHM FOR POLLUTION REPORT PROBLEM

Algorithm to read a two-dimensional array *Pollution_Table* from a file containing pollution levels measured at selected times for several days. The first line of the file contains the size of the array *Pollution_Table*. These measurements are displayed in tabular form. The average pollution level for each day and the average pollution level for each sampling time are then calculated.

Input: Pollution levels

Output: A table of pollution levels, the average pollution level for each day (row averages), and the average pollution level for each sampling time (column averages)

1. Open the pollution file for input and read the number of days and the number of times per day when pollution levels were read.

2. Read the contents of the pollution file into the array *Pollution_Table* so that each row contains the pollution measurements for a given day and each column contains the pollution measurements for a given time.

3. Print the array *Pollution_Table* with appropriate headings.

4. Calculate the average pollution level for each day, that is, the average of each of the rows, as follows:

    For *Day* ranging from 1 through *NumDays*, do the following:

        a. Calculate the *Sum* of the pollution levels in row *Day*.

        b. Display *Sum/NumTimes*.

5. Calculate the average pollution level for each sampling time, that is, the average of each of the columns, as follows:

    For *Time* ranging from 1 through *NumTimes*, do the following:

        a. Calculate the *Sum* of the pollution levels in column *Time*.

        b. Display *Sum/NumDays*.

Coding, Execution and Testing. The program in Figure 9.7 implements this algorithm. Also included is a sample run with the data file described previously. The program was tested with several small data files to check its correctness, but sample runs with these files are not shown here.[1]

---

[1] To save space, we will generally not include listings of test data and the output they produce for the remaining programs in this text.

Figure 9.7 Pollution report.

```fortran
PROGRAM Pollution_Report
!-----------------------------------------------------------------------
! This program reads the elements of the two-dimensional array
! Pollution_Table from a file and produces a report showing a table
! of pollution levels, the average pollution level for each day,
! and the average pollution level for each sampling time.  The
! first line of the file contains the number of days and the number
! of times when readings were made.  Variables used are:
!    FileName        : name of pollution file
!    OpenStatus      : status variable for OPEN
!    InputStatus     : status variable for READ
!    AllocateStatus  : status variable for ALLOCATE
!    NumDays         : the number of rows (days)
!    NumTimes        : the number of columns (times)
!    Pollution_Table : a NumDays X NumTimes allocatable array of
!                        pollution levels
!    Day, Time       : row, column subscripts
!
! Input (keyboard): The name of the pollution file
! Input (file):     NumDays, NumTimes, and the pollution levels
! Output (screen):  The array Pollution_Table in table format, the
!                     average pollution level for each day, and the
!                     average pollution level for each sampling time
!-----------------------------------------------------------------------

  IMPLICIT NONE
  INTEGER, DIMENSION(:, :), ALLOCATABLE :: Pollution_Table
  INTEGER :: OpenStatus, InputStatus, AllocateStatus, &
             NumDays, NumTimes, Day, Time
  CHARACTER(20) :: FileName

  ! Open the file and read the number of days and number of times
  ! per day when pollution levels were read. Then allocate the
  ! array Pollution_Table

  WRITE (*, '(1X, A)', ADVANCE = "NO") &
        "Enter the name of the pollution file: "
  READ *, FileName
  OPEN (UNIT = 15, FILE = FileName, STATUS = "OLD", IOSTAT = OpenStatus)
  IF (OpenStatus > 0) STOP "*** Cannot open the file ***"
```

Figure 9.7 *(cont.)*

```
READ (15, *, IOSTAT = InputStatus) NumDays, NumTimes
IF (InputStatus > 0) STOP "*** Input error ***"
IF (InputStatus < 0) STOP "*** No pollution readings in the file ***"

ALLOCATE(Pollution_Table(NumDays, NumTimes), STAT = AllocateStatus)
IF (AllocateStatus /= 0) STOP "*** Not enough memory ***"

! Read the pollution levels, store them in Pollution_Table, and display
! them in a table of the required form

DO Day = 1, NumDays
   READ (15, *, IOSTAT = InputStatus) &
        (Pollution_Table(Day, Time), Time = 1, NumTimes)
   IF (InputStatus > 0) STOP "*** Input error ***"
   IF (InputStatus < 0) STOP "*** End of file reached ***"
END DO

PRINT '(T30, "Time" / 1X, "Day:", 12I4 / 1X, 53("-"))', &
  (Time, Time = 1, NumTimes)

DO Day = 1, NumDays
   PRINT '(1X, I2, " :", 15I4)', &
      Day, (Pollution_Table(Day,Time), Time = 1, NumTimes)
END DO

! Calculate average pollution level for each day (row averages)

PRINT *
DO Day = 1, NumDays
   PRINT 10,  "for day", Day, &
      REAL(SUM(Pollution_Table(Day,:))) / REAL(NumTimes)
   10 FORMAT(1X, "Average pollution level ", A7, I3, ":", F6.1)
END DO

! Calculate average pollution level for each time (column averages)

PRINT *
DO Time = 1, NumTimes
   PRINT 10, "at time", Time, &
      REAL(SUM(Pollution_Table(:,Time))) / REAL(NumDays)
END DO

CLOSE (15)

END PROGRAM Pollution_Report
```

Figure 9.7 *(cont.)*

Sample run:

```
Enter the name of the pollution file: fil9-7.dat

                           Time
Day:   1    2    3    4    5    6    7    8    9   10   11   12
------------------------------------------------------------
  1 :  30   30   31   32   35   40   43   44   47   45   40   38
  2 :  33   32   30   34   40   48   46   49   53   49   45   40
  3 :  38   35   34   37   44   50   51   54   60   58   51   49
  4 :  49   48   47   53   60   70   73   75   80   75   73   60
  5 :  55   54   53   65   70   80   90   93   95   94   88   62
  6 :  73   70   65   66   71   78   74   78   83   75   66   58
  7 :  50   47   43   35   30   33   37   43   45   52   39   31

Average pollution level for day   1:   37.9
Average pollution level for day   2:   41.6
Average pollution level for day   3:   46.8
Average pollution level for day   4:   63.6
Average pollution level for day   5:   74.9
Average pollution level for day   6:   71.4
Average pollution level for day   7:   40.4

Average pollution level at time   1:   46.9
Average pollution level at time   2:   45.1
Average pollution level at time   3:   43.3
Average pollution level at time   4:   46.0
Average pollution level at time   5:   50.0
Average pollution level at time   6:   57.0
Average pollution level at time   7:   59.1
Average pollution level at time   8:   62.3
Average pollution level at time   9:   66.1
Average pollution level at time  10:   64.0
Average pollution level at time  11:   57.4
Average pollution level at time  12:   48.3
```

9.5 APPLICATION: OCEANOGRAPHIC DATA ANALYSIS

Problem

A petroleum exploration company has collected some depth readings for a square section of the ocean. The diagonal of this square is parallel to the equator. The company has divided the square into a grid with each intersection point (node) of the grid separated by five miles. The entire square is 50 miles on each side. Two separate crews did exploratory drilling in this area, one in the northern half (above the diagonal) and the other in the southern half. A program is to be written to find the approximate average ocean depth for each crew and the overall average for the entire square. The following depth data (in feet) was collected by the crews.

301.3	304.5	312.6	312.0	325.6	302.0	299.8	297.6	304.6	314.7	326.8
287.6	294.5	302.4	315.6	320.9	315.7	300.2	312.7	308.7	324.5	322.8
320.8	342.5	342.5	323.5	333.7	341.6	350.5	367.7	354.2	342.8	330.9
312.6	312.0	325.6	301.3	304.5	302.0	314.7	326.8	299.8	297.6	304.6
302.4	308.7	324.5	315.6	287.6	294.5	320.9	315.7	300.2	312.7	322.8
320.8	333.7	341.6	350.5	367.7	354.2	342.8	342.5	342.5	323.5	330.9
312.0	325.6	326.8	302.0	299.8	297.6	304.6	314.7	301.3	304.5	312.6
294.5	302.4	315.6	320.9	315.7	300.2	312.7	308.7	324.5	287.6	322.8
320.8	342.5	323.5	333.7	341.6	350.5	367.7	342.5	354.2	342.8	330.9
312.0	304.6	314.7	326.8	301.3	304.5	312.6	325.6	302.0	299.8	297.6
312.7	308.7	324.5	322.8	287.6	294.5	302.4	315.6	320.9	315.7	300.2

NORTH

Solution

Specification. From the description of the problem, we have the following input/output specifications:

Input: A collection of depth readings
Output: The average of the readings in the northern half of the grid
                The average of the readings in the southern half of the grid
                The average of all the readings

Famed sea explorer Jacques Cousteau (Photo courtesy of Teresa Zabala/Uniphoto
Picture Agency)

Design. We will use the following variables for this problem:

VARIABLES FOR OCEANOGRAPHIC DATA ANALYSIS

Depth	A two-dimensional array of depth readings
N	The size of the grid ($N \times N$)
Readings_per_Half	Number of readings in each half of the grid
NorthSum	Sum of the northern readings
SouthSum	Sum of the southern readings
DiagonalSum	Sum of the readings on the diagonal
OverallSum	Sum of all readings
NorthAverage	Average of the northern readings
SouthAverage	Average of the southern readings
OverallAverage	Average of all readings
I	Subscript

An algorithm for solving this problem is as follows:

ALGORITHM FOR OCEANOGRAPHIC DATA ANALYSIS

Algorithm to find the average ocean depth in each half (separated by the diagonal) of a square section of the ocean and the overall average. The depth readings are stored in the $N \times N$ two-dimensional array *Depth*.

Input: The size N and the depth readings
Output: The average of elements above the diagonal, the average of elements below the diagonal, and the average of all the elements

1. Get the name of the data file and open the file for reading.
2. Read N and the depth readings from the file, storing in the array *Depth*.
3. Calculate

$$NorthSum = \text{the sum of the entries above the diagonal}$$

$$SouthSum = \text{the sum of the entries below the diagonal}$$

$$DiagonalSum = \text{the sum of the diagonal entries}$$

4. Calculate *OverallSum* = *NorthSum* + *SouthSum* + *DiagonalSum*.
5. Calculate *Readings_per_Half* = $(N^2 - N)/2$.
6. Calculate the north, south, and overall average depths by

$$NorthAverage = \frac{NorthSum}{Readings\_per\_Half}$$

$$SouthAverage = \frac{SouthSum}{Readings\_per\_Half}$$

$$OverallAverage = \frac{OverallSum}{N^2}$$

7. Display *NorthAverage*, *SouthAverage*, and *OverallAverage*.

Coding, Execution, and Testing. The program in Figure 9.8 implements this algorithm. In addition to calculating and displaying the three required averages, it also displays the grid of depth readings so that the input data is echoed and can be used to check the results. Note the use of the intrinsic function SUM and array sections to find NorthSum and SouthSum. Also included is a sample run using the given data file.

Figure 9.8 Oceanographic data analysis.

```
PROGRAM Oceanograpic_Data_Analysis
!-----------------------------------------------------------------
! Program to find the average ocean depth in each half (separated by
! the diagonal) of a square section of the ocean.  Variables used are:
!    Depth              : a two-dimensional allocatable array of
!                              depth readings
!    FileName           : name of the file containing depth readings
!    OpenStatus         : status variable for OPEN
!    InputStatus        : status variable for READ
!    AllocateStatus     : status variable for ALLOCATE
!    N                  : the number of rows (or columns)
!    I                  : subscript
!    NorthSum           : the sum of the northern depths
!    SouthSum           : the sum of the southern depths
!    DiagonalSum        : the sum of the depths on the diagonal
!    OverallSum         : the overall sum
!    NorthAverage       : the average of the northern depths
!    SouthAverage       : the average of the southern depths
!    OverallAverage     : the overall average
!    Readings_per_Half : number of elements in each half
!
! Note: It is assumed that the elements on the diagonal are included
!       in the overall average but not in either half. Also, the
!       first line of the data file must contain the value of N.
!
! Input (keyboard): The file name
! Input (file):     The elements of array Depth
! Output (screen):  The array Depth in table format, NorthAverage,
!                   SouthAverage, and OverallAverage
!-----------------------------------------------------------------

  CHARACTER(20) :: FileName
  INTEGER :: OpenStatus, InputStatus, AllocateStatus, &
             N, I, J, Readings_per_Half
  REAL, DIMENSION(:, :), ALLOCATABLE :: Depth
  REAL :: NorthSum = 0.0, NorthAverage, SouthSum = 0.0, SouthAverage, &
          OverallSum = 0.0, OverallAverage

  ! Get the name of the input file, open it for input
  WRITE (*, '(1X, A)', ADVANCE = "NO") "Enter name of data file: "
  READ *, FileName
  OPEN (UNIT = 10, FILE = FileName, STATUS = "OLD", IOSTAT = OpenStatus)
  IF (OpenStatus > 0) STOP "*** Cannot open the file ***"
```

Figure 9.8 *(cont.)*

```
! Read N, allocate the N x N array Depth, and
! read values for its entries from the file
READ (10, *, IOSTAT = InputStatus) N
IF (InputStatus > 0) STOP "*** Input error ***"
IF (InputStatus < 0) STOP "*** No depth readings in the file ***"

ALLOCATE(Depth(N,N))
IF (AllocateStatus /= 0) STOP "*** Not enough memory ***"

DO I = 1, N
   READ (10,*, IOSTAT = InputStatus) (Depth(I,J), J = 1, N)
   IF (InputStatus > 0) STOP "*** Input error ***"
   IF (InputStatus < 0) STOP "*** End of file reached ***"
END DO

DiagonalSum = Depth(1,1)
DO I = 2,N
   ! Add entries in Ith column above diagonal to North
   NorthSum = NorthSum + SUM(Depth(1:I-1, I))

   ! Add entries in Ith row below diagonal to SouthSum
   SouthSum = SouthSum + SUM(Depth(I, 1:I-1))

   ! Add diagonal entry to DiagonalSum
   DiagonalSum = DiagonalSum + Depth(I,I)
END DO

OverallSum = NorthSum + SouthSum + DiagonalSum

! Calculate the north, south, and overall average depths
Readings_per_Half = (N**2 - N) / 2
NorthAverage = NorthSum / REAL(Readings_per_Half)
SouthAverage = SouthSum / REAL(Readings_per_Half)
OverallAverage = OverallSum / REAL(N**2)

! Display the Depth array and the average depths
PRINT '(/ 1X, T29, "Ocean Depths")'
DO I = 1, N
   PRINT '(/1X, 13F6.1)', (Depth(I,J), J = 1, N)
END DO

PRINT *
PRINT 10, "Northern half average depth", NorthAverage
PRINT 10, "Southern half average depth", SouthAverage
PRINT 10, "Overall average depth", OverallAverage
10 FORMAT(/ 1X, A, T30, F6.2, " feet")

END PROGRAM Oceanograpic_Data_Analysis
```

Figure 9.8 *(cont.)*

Sample run:

```
Enter name of data file: fil9-8.dat

                      Ocean Depths

 301.3 304.5 312.6 312.0 325.6 302.0 299.8 297.6 304.6 314.7 326.8

 287.6 294.5 302.4 315.6 320.9 315.7 300.2 312.7 308.7 324.5 322.8

 320.8 342.5 342.5 323.5 333.7 341.6 350.5 367.7 354.2 342.8 330.9

 312.6 312.0 325.6 301.3 304.5 302.0 314.7 326.8 299.8 297.6 304.6

 302.4 308.7 324.5 315.6 287.6 294.5 320.9 315.7 300.2 312.7 322.8

 320.8 333.7 341.6 350.5 367.7 354.2 342.8 342.5 342.5 323.5 330.9

 312.0 325.6 326.8 302.0 299.8 297.6 304.6 314.7 301.3 304.5 312.6

 294.5 302.4 315.6 320.9 315.7 300.2 312.7 308.7 324.5 287.6 322.8

 320.8 342.5 323.5 333.7 341.6 350.5 367.7 342.5 354.2 342.8 330.9

 312.0 304.6 314.7 326.8 301.3 304.5 312.6 325.6 302.0 299.8 297.6

 312.7 308.7 324.5 322.8 287.6 294.5 302.4 315.6 320.9 315.7 300.2

Northern half average depth 318.31 feet

Southern half average depth 318.63 feet

Overall average depth       318.02 feet
```

9.6   MATRIX PROCESSING

A two-dimensional array with numeric entries having *m* rows and *n* columns is called an **_m_ × _n_ matrix**. Matrices arise naturally in many problems in engineering and applied mathematics. In this section we descibe some of the basic matrix operations that are useful in these applications.

Matrix Operations

Several matrix operations such as addition and subtraction are defined element-wise; that is, two matrices of the same shape are added or subtracted by adding or subtracting corresponding elements. For example, if

$$A = \begin{bmatrix} 1 & 0 & 2 \\ -1 & 3 & 5 \end{bmatrix}$$

and

$$B = \begin{bmatrix} 4 & 2 & 1 \\ 7 & 0 & 3 \end{bmatrix}$$

then

$$A + B = \begin{bmatrix} 5 & 2 & 3 \\ 6 & 3 & 8 \end{bmatrix}$$

$$A - B = \begin{bmatrix} -3 & -2 & 1 \\ -8 & 3 & 2 \end{bmatrix}$$

Similarly, a matrix is multipled by a scalar (number) elementwise; for example,

$$2A = \begin{bmatrix} 2 & 0 & 4 \\ -2 & 6 & 10 \end{bmatrix}$$

Since arithmetic operations in Fortran are applied elementwise to arrays, they can be used to carry out these matrix operations. For example, if A and B are two arrays of the same shape, then A + B is the sum and A - B is the difference of the matrices stored in A and B; 2*A is the matrix obtained by multiplying each element by 2.

One important matrix operation that is not defined elementwise is matrix multiplication. Suppose that A is an $m \times n$ matrix and B is an $n \times p$ matrix. The **product** **AB** is the $m \times p$ matrix for which

the entry in row i and column j

= the sum of the products of the entries in row i of A with the entries in column j of B

$= A_{i1}B_{1j} + A_{i2}B_{2j} + \cdots + A_{in}B_{nj}$

$= \displaystyle\sum_{k=1}^{n} A_{ik}B_{kj}$

Note that the number of columns (n) in A is equal to the number of rows in B, which must be the case for the product of A with B to be defined.

For example, suppose that A is the 2×3 matrix

$$A = \begin{bmatrix} 1 & 0 & 2 \\ 3 & 0 & 4 \end{bmatrix}$$

and B is the 3×4 matrix

$$B = \begin{bmatrix} 4 & 2 & 5 & 3 \\ 6 & 4 & 1 & 8 \\ 9 & 0 & 0 & 2 \end{bmatrix}$$

Because the number of columns (3) in A equals the number of rows in B, the product matrix AB is defined. The entry in the first row and the first column is

$$1 \times 4 + 0 \times 6 + 2 \times 9 = 22$$

Similarly, the entry in the first row and the second column is

$$1 \times 2 + 0 \times 4 + 2 \times 0 = 2$$

The complete product matrix AB is the 2×4 matrix given by

$$AB = \begin{bmatrix} 22 & 2 & 5 & 7 \\ 48 & 6 & 15 & 17 \end{bmatrix}$$

The Fortran multiplication operator * cannot be used to compute the product of matrices. An expression of the form A * B will compute the *elementwise* product of A and B, provided both matrices have the same shape, and will be undefined otherwise. However, Fortran 90 does provide a predefined function MATMUL that returns the product of two matrices.

One other important intrinsic function provided for processing matrices is TRANSPOSE, which returns the transpose of a matrix. The **transpose** of an $m \times n$ matrix A is the $n \times m$ matrix whose rows are the columns of A.

Example: Production Costs

Suppose that a company produces three different items. They are processed through four different departments, A, B, C, and D. The following table gives the number of hours that each department spends on each item:

Item	A	B	C	D
1	20	10	15	13
2	18	11	11	10
3	28	0	16	17

The cost per hour of operation in each of the departments is as follows:

Department	A	B	C	D
Cost per hour	$140	$295	$225	$95

We wish to determine the total cost of each item.

This problem can be solved using matrices. If we let *Hours* be the 3 × 4 array

$$Hours = \begin{bmatrix} 20 & 10 & 15 & 13 \\ 18 & 11 & 11 & 10 \\ 28 & 0 & 16 & 17 \end{bmatrix}$$

and *HourlyCost* be the 4 × 1 array

$$HourlyCost = \begin{bmatrix} 140 \\ 295 \\ 225 \\ 95 \end{bmatrix}$$

then the product *Hours · HourlyCost* will be a 3 × 1 array whose elements are the total costs of producing each of the three items. The program in Figure 9.9 uses the intrinsic function MATMUL to compute this product.

Figure 9.9 Production costs.

```
PROGRAM Production_Costs
!-----------------------------------------------------------------
! This program reads the two-dimensional array Hours whose elements
! are the number of hours required by various departments to produce
! various items.  It also reads an array containing the cost per hour
! of operation in each department.  It uses the intrinsic function
! MATMUL to compute an array whose elements are the total costs of
! producing each of the items.  Variables used are:
!    NumItems        : the number of rows (items)
!    NumDepartments : the number of columns (departments)
!    AllocateStatus : status variable for ALLOCATE
!    Hours           : a NumItems X NumDepartments allocatable array:
!                      Hours(I,J) is the number required for item I
!                      by department J
!    HourlyCost      : a NumDepartments X 1 allocatable array in which the
!                      Ith entry is the hourly cost of operation by
!                      department I
!    TotalCost       : Hours * HourlyCost.  Its Ith element is the
!                      total cost of producing item I
!    Item, Dept      : row, column subscripts
!
! Input:  NumItems, NumDepartments, Hours, and HourlyCost
! Output: TotalCost
!-----------------------------------------------------------------
```

Figure 9.9 *(cont.)*

```
IMPLICIT NONE
INTEGER, DIMENSION(:, :), ALLOCATABLE :: Hours, HourlyCost, TotalCost
INTEGER :: NumItems, NumDepartments, AllocateStatus, Item, Dept

! Read values for NumItems and NumDepartments and allocate arrays
! Hours, HourlyCost, and TotalCost

PRINT *, "Enter the number of items produced and the number of &
        &departments:"
READ *, NumItems, NumDepartments

ALLOCATE(Hours(NumItems, NumDepartments), &
        HourlyCost(NumDepartments, 1), &
        TotalCost(NumItems, 1), STAT = AllocateStatus
IF (AllocateStatus /= 0) STOP "*** Not enough memory ***"

! Read the arrays Hours and HourlyCost

PRINT *, "Enter the hours table in rowwise order:"
READ *, ((Hours(Item, Dept), Dept = 1, NumDepartments), &
                        Item = 1, NumItems)
PRINT *, "Enter the ", NumDepartments, " hourly costs:"
READ *, (HourlyCost(Item, 1), Item = 1, NumDepartments)

! Calculate and display the array TotalCost

PRINT *
TotalCost = MATMUL(Hours, HourlyCost)
DO Item = 1, NumItems
   PRINT '(1X, "Cost of item", I2, " is $", I6)', Item, &
        TotalCost(Item,1)
END DO

END PROGRAM Production_Costs
```

Sample run:

```
Enter the number of items produced and the number of departments:
3, 4
```

Figure 9.9 *(cont.)*

```
Enter the hours table in rowwise order:
20, 10, 15, 13
18, 11, 11, 10
28, 0,  16, 17
Enter the 4 hourly costs:
140, 295, 225, 95

Cost of item 1 is $ 10360
Cost of item 1 is $  9190
Cost of item 1 is $  9135
```

9.7 APPLICATION: ELECTRICAL NETWORKS

Problem

Consider the following electrical network containing six resistors and a battery:

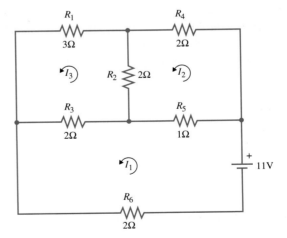

We wish to find the currents I_1, I_2, and I_3 in the three loops (where current is considered positive when the flow is in the direction indicated by the arrows).

Solution

Specification. The input information for this problem is the circuit pictured in the diagram; in particular, the six resistances $R_1, R_2, \ldots, R_6$ will be needed to solve the problem. The output consists of the currents $I_1, I_2,$ and I_3 in the three loops.

Design. The current through resistor R_1 is I_3, the current through resistor R_2 is $I_2 - I_3$, and so on. Ohm's law states that the voltage drop across a resistor is $R * I$, where R is the resistance in ohms and I is the current in amperes. One of Kirchhoff's laws states that the algebraic sum of the voltage drops around any loop is equal to the applied voltage. This law gives rise to the following system of linear equations for the loop currents $I_1, I_2,$ and I_3:

$$2I_1 + 1(I_1 - I_2) + 2(I_1 - I_3) = 11$$

$$2I_2 + 2(I_2 - I_3) + 1(I_2 - I_1) = 0$$

$$3I_3 + 2(I_3 - I_1) + 2(I_3 - I_2) = 0$$

Collecting terms gives the simplified linear system

$$5I_1 - 1I_2 - 2I_3 = 11$$

$$-1I_1 + 5I_2 - 2I_3 = 0$$

$$-2I_1 - 2I_2 + 7I_3 = 0$$

To find the loop currents, we must solve this **linear system**; that is, we must find the values for $I_1, I_2,$ and I_3 that satisfy these equations simultaneously.

Linear systems arise in many areas of mathematics, science, and engineering, such as solving differential equations, electrical circuit problems, statical systems, and dynamical systems. Several methods for solving them have been developed, including the method called **Gaussian elimination.** To use this method to solve the preceding system, we first eliminate I_1 from the second equation by adding 1/5 times the first equation to the second equation. Similarly, we eliminate I_1 from the third equation by adding 2/5 times the first equation to the third equation. This yields the linear system

$$5I_1 - 1I_2 - 2I_3 = 11$$

$$4.8I_2 - 2.4I_3 = 2.2$$

$$-2.4I_2 + 6.2I_3 = 4.4$$

which is equivalent to the original system in that the two systems have the same solution. We then eliminate I_2 from the third equation by adding 2.4/4.8 = 1/2 times the second equation to the third, yielding the new equivalent linear system

$$5I_1 - 1I_2 - 2I_3 = 11$$

$$4.8I_2 - 2.4I_3 = 2.2$$

$$5I_3 = 5.5$$

Once the original system has been reduced to such a *triangular* form, it is easy to find the solution. It is clear from the last equation that the value of I_3 is

$$I_3 = \frac{5.5}{5} = 1.100$$

Substituting this value for I_3 in the second equation and solving for I_2 gives

$$I_2 = \frac{2.2 + 2.4(1.1)}{4.8} = 1.008$$

and substituting these values for I_2 and I_3 in the first equation gives

$$I_1 = \frac{11 + 1.008 + 2(1.100)}{5} = 2.842$$

Refining the Method. The computations required to solve a linear system can be carried out more conveniently if the coefficients and constants of the linear system are stored in a matrix. For the preceding linear system, this gives the following 3×4 matrix:

$$LinSys = \begin{bmatrix} 5 & -1 & -2 & 11 \\ -1 & 5 & -2 & 0 \\ -2 & -2 & 7 & 0 \end{bmatrix}$$

The first step in the reduction process was to eliminate I_1 from the second and third equations by adding multiples of the first equation to these equations. This corresponds to adding multiples of the first row of the matrix *LinSys* to the second and third rows so that all entries in the first column except *LinSys*(1, 1) are zero. Thus, we add $-LinSys(2, 1)/LinSys(1, 1) = 1/5$ times the first row of *LinSys* to the second row, and $-LinSys(3, 1)/LinSys(1, 1) = 2/5$ times the first row of *LinSys* to the third row, to obtain the new matrix:

$$LinSys = \begin{bmatrix} 5 & -1 & -2 & 11 \\ 0 & 4.8 & -2.4 & 2.2 \\ 0 & -2.4 & 6.2 & 4.4 \end{bmatrix}$$

The variable I_2 was then eliminated from the third equation. The corresponding operation on the rows of the preceding matrix is to add $-LinSys(3, 2)/LinSys(2, 2) = 1/2$ times the second row to the third row. The resulting matrix, which corresponds to the final triangular system, thus is

$$LinSys = \begin{bmatrix} 5 & -1 & -2 & 11 \\ 0 & 4.8 & -2.4 & 2.2 \\ 0 & 0 & 5 & 5.5 \end{bmatrix}$$

From this example, we see that the basic row operation performed at the *i*th step of the reduction process is

$$\text{For } j = i + 1, i + 2, \ldots, n$$

$$\text{Replace row}_j \text{ by row}_j - \frac{LinSys(j, i)}{LinSys(i, i)} \times \text{row}_i$$

Clearly, for this to be possible, the element $LinSys(i, i)$, called a **pivot element,** must be nonzero. If it is not, we must interchange the ith row with a later row to produce a nonzero pivot. In fact, to minimize the effect of roundoff error in the computations, it is best to rearrange the rows to obtain a pivot element that is largest in absolute value.

The following algorithm, which summarizes the Gaussian elimination method for solving a linear system, uses this pivoting strategy. Note that if it is not possible to find a nonzero pivot element at some stage, the linear system is said to be a **singular** system and does not have a unique solution.

GAUSSIAN ELIMINATION ALGORITHM

Algorithm to solve a linear system of N equations with N unknowns using Gaussian elimination. *LinSys* is the $N \times (N + 1)$ matrix that stores the coefficients and constants of the linear system.

Input: Coefficients and constants of the linear system
Output: Solution of the linear system or a message indicating that
            the system is singular

1. Enter the coefficients and constants of the linear system and store them in the matrix *LinSys.*

2. For I ranging from 1 to N, do the following:
   a. Find the entry $LinSys(K, I)$, $K = I, I + 1, \ldots, N$ that has the largest absolute value to use as a pivot.
   b. If the pivot is zero, display a message that the system is singular, and terminate the algorithm. Otherwise proceed.
   c. Interchange row I and row K.
   d. For J ranging from $I + 1$ to N, do the following:

   $$\text{Add } \frac{-LinSys(J, I)}{LinSys(I, I)} \text{ times the } I\text{th row of } LinSys \text{ to the } J\text{th row of}$$

   $LinSys$ to eliminate $X(I)$ from the Jth equation.

3. Set $X(N)$ equal to $\dfrac{LinSys(N, N + 1)}{LinSys(N, N)}$.

4. For J ranging from $N - 1$ to 1 in steps of -1, do the following:

   Substitute the values of $X(J + 1), \ldots, X(N)$ in the Jth equation and solve for $X(J)$.

Coding and Execution. The program in Figure 9.10 implements this algorithm for Gaussian elimination. Because real numbers cannot be stored exactly, the statement implementing step 2b checks if ABS(LinSys(I,I)) is less than some small positive number Epsilon rather than if LinSys(I,I) is exactly 0.

Figure 9.10 Gaussian elimination.

```fortran
PROGRAM Linear_Systems
!-------------------------------------------------------------------------
! Program to solve a linear system using Gaussian elimination.
! Variables used are:
!   N                 : number of equations and unknowns
!   AllocateStatus  : status variable for ALLOCATE
!   LinSys           : matrix for the linear system
!   X                 : solution
!   I, J              : subscripts
!   Singular          : indicates if system is (nearly) singular
!
! Input:   The number of equations, the coefficients, and the
!          constants of the linear system
! Output:  The solution of the linear system or a message indicating
!          that the system is (nearly) singular
!-------------------------------------------------------------------------

  IMPLICIT NONE
  REAL, DIMENSION(:, :), ALLOCATABLE :: LinSys
  REAL, DIMENSION(:), ALLOCATABLE :: X
  INTEGER :: N, AllocateStatus, I, J
  LOGICAL :: Singular

  ! Read N and allocate N x (N + 1) matrix LinSys
  ! and one-dimensional array X of size N

  WRITE (*, '(1X, A)', ADVANCE = "NO")  "Enter number of equations: "
  READ *, N
  ALLOCATE(LinSys(N, N+1), X(N), STAT = AllocateStatus)
  IF (AllocateStatus /= 0) STOP "*** Not enough memory ***"

  ! Read coefficients and constants

  DO I = 1, N
     PRINT *, "Enter coefficients and constant of equation", I, ":"
     READ *, (LinSys(I,J), J = 1, N + 1)
  END DO
```

Figure 9.10 *(cont.)*

```fortran
! Use subroutine Gaussian_Elimination to find the solution,
! and then display the solution

CALL Gaussian_Elimination(LinSys, N, X, Singular)
IF (.NOT. Singular) THEN
   PRINT *, "Solution is:"
   DO I = 1, N
      PRINT '(1X, "X(", I2, ") =", F8.3)', I, X(I)
   END DO
ELSE
   PRINT *, "Matrix is (nearly) singular"
END IF

DEALLOCATE(LinSys, X)

CONTAINS

!-Gaussian_Elimination--------------------------------------------
! Subroutine to find solution of a linear system of N equations in N
! unknowns using Gaussian elimination, provided a unique solution
! exists.  The coefficients and constants of the linear system are
! stored in the matrix LinSys.  If the system is singular, Singular
! is returned as true, and the solution X is undefined.  Local
! variables used are:
!   I, J        : subscripts
!   Multiplier  : multiplier used to eliminate an unknown
!   AbsPivot    : absolute value of pivot element
!   PivotRow    : row containing pivot element
!   Epsilon     : a small positive real value ("almost zero")
!   Temp        : used to interchange rows of matrix
!
! Accepts: Two-dimensional array LinSys and integer N
! Returns: One-dimensional array X and logical value Singular
!----------------------------------------------------------------

SUBROUTINE Gaussian_Elimination(LinSys, N, X, Singular)

  INTEGER, INTENT(IN) :: N
  REAL, DIMENSION(N, N+1), INTENT(IN) :: LinSys
  REAL, DIMENSION(N), INTENT(OUT) :: X
  LOGICAL, INTENT(OUT) :: Singular
  REAL, DIMENSION(N+1) :: Temp
  REAL :: AbsPivot, Multiplier
  REAL, PARAMETER :: Epsilon = 1E-7
  INTEGER :: PivotRow
```

Figure 9.10 *(cont.)*

```fortran
      Singular = .FALSE.
      DO I = 1, N

         ! Locate pivot element

         AbsPivot = ABS(LinSys(I, I))
         PivotRow = I
         DO J = I + 1, N
            IF (ABS(LinSys(J,I)) > AbsPivot) THEN
               AbsPivot = ABS(LinSys(J,I))
               PivotRow = J
            END IF
         END DO

         ! Check if matrix is (nearly) singular

         IF (AbsPivot < Epsilon) THEN
            Singular = .TRUE.
            RETURN
         END IF

         ! It isn't, so interchange rows PivotRow and I if necessary

         IF (PivotRow /= I) THEN
            Temp(I:N+1) = LinSys(I, I:N+1)
            LinSys(I, I:N+1) = LinSys(PivotRow, I:N+1)
            LinSys(PivotRow, I:N+1) = Temp(I:N+1)
         END IF

         ! Eliminate Ith unknown from equations I + 1, ..., N

         DO J = I + 1, N
            Multiplier = -LinSys(J,I) / LinSys(I,I)
            LinSys(J, I:N+1) = LinSys(J, I:N+1)   &
                            + Multiplier * LinSys(I, I:N+1)
         END DO

      END DO

      ! Find the solutions by back substitution

      X(N) = LinSys(N, N + 1) / LinSys(N,N)
      DO J = N - 1, 1, -1
         X(J) = (LinSys(J, N + 1) -    &
                SUM(LinSys(J, J+1:N) * X(J+1:N))) / LinSys(J,J)
      END DO

      END SUBROUTINE Gaussian_Elimination

END PROGRAM Linear_Systems
```

Figure 9.10 *(cont.)*

Sample runs:

```
Enter number of equations: 3
Enter coefficients and constant of equation 1:
 5 -1 -2 11
Enter coefficients and constant of equation 2:
-1  5 -2  0
Enter coefficients and constant of equation 3:
-2 -2  7  0
Solution is:
X( 1) =   2.842
X( 2) =   1.008
X( 3) =   1.100


Enter number of equations: 3
Enter coefficients and constant of equation 1:
1 1 1  1
Enter coefficients and constant of equation 2:
2 3 4  2
Enter coefficients and constant of equation 3:
3 4 5  3
Matrix is (nearly) singular
```

Exercises 9.7

1. Write the system of linear equations for the loop currents I_1, I_2, and I_3 in the following simple resistor and battery circuit. Then use Gaussian elimination to find these currents.

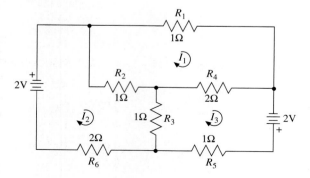

2. Consider the following electrical network:

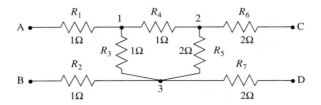

If the voltages at the endpoints are $V_A = V_B = V_C = V_D = 1V$, then applying Kirchoff's law of currents at the nodes 1, 2, and 3 yields (after some simplification) the following system of linear equations for the voltages V_1, V_2, and V_3 at these nodes:

$$\frac{5}{2} V_1 - \frac{1}{2} V_2 - V_3 = 1$$

$$-\frac{1}{2} V_1 + \frac{3}{2} V_2 - \frac{1}{2} V_3 = \frac{1}{2}$$

$$-V_1 - \frac{1}{2} V_2 + 3V_3 = \frac{3}{2}$$

Use Gaussian elimination to find these voltages.

3. Consider the following material-balance problem: A solution that is 80 percent oil, 15 percent usable byproducts, and 5 percent impurities enters a refinery. One output is 92 percent oil and 6 percent usable byproducts. The other output is 60 percent oil and flows at the rate of 1000 liters per hour (L/h).

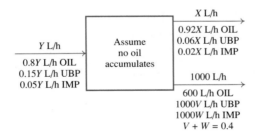

We thus have the following system of material-balance equations:

Total:	$Y = X + 1000$
Oil:	$0.8Y = 0.92X + 600$
Usable byproducts:	$0.15Y = 0.06X + 1000V$
Impurities:	$0.05Y = 0.02X + 1000W$
Also:	$V + W = 0.4$

Use Gaussian elimination to solve this linear system. Check that your solution also satisfies the last equation.

4. Consider the following statical system:

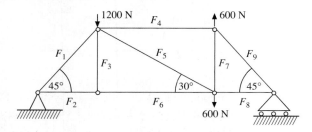

Since the sum of all forces acting horizontally or vertically at each pin is zero, the following system of linear equations can be used to obtain the tensions F_1, $F_2, \ldots, F_9$:

$$
\begin{bmatrix}
\sqrt{2}/2 & 0 & 0 & -1 & -\sqrt{3}/2 & 0 & 0 & 0 & 0 \\
\sqrt{2}/2 & 0 & 1 & 0 & 1/2 & 0 & 0 & 0 & 0 \\
0 & 1 & 0 & 0 & 0 & -1 & 0 & 0 & 0 \\
0 & 0 & -1 & 0 & 0 & 0 & 0 & 0 & 0 \\
0 & 0 & 0 & 0 & 0 & 0 & 1 & 0 & \sqrt{2}/2 \\
0 & 0 & 0 & 1 & 0 & 0 & 0 & 0 & -\sqrt{2}/2 \\
0 & 0 & 0 & 0 & 3/2 & 1 & 0 & -1 & 0 \\
0 & 0 & 0 & 0 & -1/2 & 0 & -1 & 0 & 0 \\
0 & 0 & 0 & 0 & 0 & 0 & 0 & 1 & \sqrt{2}/2
\end{bmatrix}
\begin{bmatrix}
F_1 \\ F_2 \\ F_3 \\ F_4 \\ F_5 \\ F_6 \\ F_7 \\ F_8 \\ F_9
\end{bmatrix}
=
\begin{bmatrix}
0 \\ -1200 \\ 0 \\ 0 \\ 600 \\ 0 \\ 0 \\ -600 \\ 0
\end{bmatrix}
$$

Use Gaussian elimination to find these tensions.

5. The population of a country (or of a region) is divided into age groups. If n is the number of age groups and $P_i(t)$ is the number of individuals in age group i at time t, the dynamic model describing the populations of the different age groups is given by

$$ P_1(t + 1) = b_1 P_1(t) + b_2 P_2(t) + \cdots + b_n P_n(t) + c_1 $$

$$ P_{i+1}(t + 1) = a_i P_i(t) + c_i, \quad \text{for } i = 1, \ldots, n - 1 $$

Here, each a_i is the percentage of persons in age group i who move into age group $i + 1$ at the next time period; each b_i is the birthrate for age group i; and each c_i is the number of persons belonging to age group i that move into the region.

If this dynamic system reaches equilibrium at a certain time period t so that for each age group i, $P_i(t) = P_i(t + 1) = P_i(t + 2) = \cdots = $ some constant value p_i, then the preceding system of difference equations can be rewritten as the following system of steady-state equations:

$$p_1 = b_1 p_1 + b_2 p_2 + \cdots + b_n p_n + c_1$$

$$p_2 = a_1 p_1 + c_2$$

$$p_3 = a_2 p_2 + c_3$$

$$\vdots$$

$$p_n = a_{n-1} p_{n-1} + c_n$$

Use Gaussian elimination to solve this linear system for $n = 4$, $a_1 = 0.8$, $a_2 = 0.7$, $a_3 = 0.6$, $b_1 = 0$, $b_2 = 0.05$, $b_3 = 0.15$, $b_4 = 0.1$, and each $c_i = 100$.

6. In Section 4.6 we described the method of least squares for finding the equation of a line that best fits a set of data points. This method can also be used to find best-fitting curves of higher degree. For example, to find the equation of the parabola

$$y = A + Bx + Cx^2$$

that best fits a set of n data points, the values of A, B, and C must be determined for which the sum of the squares of the deviations of the observed y-values from the predicted y-values (using the equation) is as small as possible. These values are found by solving the linear system

$$nA + (\Sigma x)B + (\Sigma x^2)C = \Sigma y$$

$$(\Sigma x)A + (\Sigma x^2)B + (\Sigma x^3)C = \Sigma xy$$

$$(\Sigma x^2)A + (\Sigma x^3)B + (\Sigma x^4)C = \Sigma x^2 y$$

Find the equation of the least-squares parabola for the following set of data points:

x	y
0.05	0.957
0.12	0.851
0.15	0.832
0.30	0.720
0.45	0.583
0.70	0.378
0.84	0.295
1.05	0.156

7. Linear systems similar to those in Exercise 6 must be solved to find least-squares curves of higher degrees. For example, for a least-squares cubic

$$y = A + Bx + Cx^2 + Dx^3$$

the coefficients A, B, C, and D can be found by solving the following system of equations:

$$nA + (\Sigma x)B + (\Sigma x^2)C + (\Sigma x^3)D = \Sigma y$$

$$(\Sigma x)A + (\Sigma x^2)B + (\Sigma x^3)C + (\Sigma x^4)D = \Sigma xy$$

$$(\Sigma x^2)A + (\Sigma x^3)B + (\Sigma x^4)C + (\Sigma x^5)D = \Sigma x^2 y$$

$$(\Sigma x^3)A + (\Sigma x^4)B + (\Sigma x^5)C + (\Sigma x^6)D = \Sigma x^3 y$$

Find the equation of the least-squares cubic for the set of data points in Exercise 6.

CHAPTER REVIEW

Summary

In this chapter we described multidimensional arrays and multiply subscripted variables. We began by describing how such arrays are declared and how multiple subscripts are used to access the elements of the array. Sections 9.2 and 9.3 describe several techniques for processing multidimensional arrays and described various orders in which array elements can be processed, such as rowwise and columnwise. The three methods of array input/output described in Chapter 8 for one-dimensional arrays—using DO loops, using the array name, and using implied DO loops—are described for multidimensional arrays, as are array constants and expressions, array sections and subarrays, array assigment, the WHERE construct, and using multidimensional arrays as arguments of subprograms. Several applications of two-dimensional arrays are given, including their use in processing data tables (pollution tables and oceanographic data analysis) and matrices and in solving linear systems (electrical networks).

FORTRAN SUMMARY

Declaration of Compile-Time Arrays

```
type, DIMENSION(1:u) :: list-of-array-names
```

or

```
type :: list-of-array-specifiers
```

where each array specifier has the form

```
array-name(l₁:u₁, l₂:u₂, . . . , lₖ:uₖ)
```

the number k of dimensions (called the *rank*) is at most 7; and each pair $l_i : u_i$ must be a pair of integer constants specifying the range of values for the ith subscript to be from l_i through u_i.

Examples:

```
REAL, DIMENSION(4, 3) :: Temperature
REAL, DIMENSION(1:4, 1:3, 1:7) :: TemperatureArray
```

or

```
REAL :: Temperature(4, 3)
REAL :: TemperatureArray(1:4, 1:3, 1:7)
```

Purpose:

Declares that each identifier *array-name* in the list of array declarations is an array for which memory will be allocated at compile time and for which the range of values of the first subscript will be from the lower limit l_1 through the upper limit u_1, the range of values of the second subscript will be from the lower limit l_2 through the upper limit u_2, and so on.

Declaration of Allocatable (Run-Time) Arrays

```
type, DIMENSION(:, :, ..., :), ALLOCATABLE :: list-of-array-names
```

or

```
type, DIMENSION((:, :, ..., :) :: list-of-array-names
ALLOCATABLE :: list-of-array-names
```

Examples:

```
REAL, DIMENSION(:, :), ALLOCATABLE :: A, B
REAL, DIMENSION(:, :, :), ALLOCATABLE :: Three_Dim_Array
```

Purpose:

Declares that each of the identifiers in the list is an array whose shape will be specified during execution.

ALLOCATE Statement

```
ALLOCATE (list)
```

or

```
ALLOCATE (list, STAT = status-variable)
```

where *list* is a list of array specifications of the form

```
array-name(l₁:u₁, l₂:u₂, . . . , lₖ:uₖ)
```

Here each l_i is the minimum value of the ith subscript and u_i is the maximum value. If a minimum subscript is 1, only the maximum subscript need be specified. The variable $status\text{-}variable$ is an integer variable.

Examples:

```
PRINT *, "Enter the number of rows and the number of columns &
        &in arrays A and B: "
READ *, M, N
ALLOCATE (A(M, N), B(0:M, 10:2*M))
```

Purpose:
Allocates space for each array listed. In the second form, the integer variable $status\text{-}variable$ will be set to zero if allocation is successful, but it will be assigned some system-dependent error value if there is insufficient memory or if the array has already been allocated.

DEALLOCATE Statement

See the Fortran summary of Chapter 8.

Array Constants

See the Fortran summary of Chapter 8.

Array Sections and Subarrays

```
array-name(range₁, range₂, ..., rangeₖ)
```

where each $range_i$ is a subscript, a subscript triplet, a vector subscript, or a colon (:) denoting the entire subscript range. (See the Fortran summary of Chapter 8 for a description of subscript triplets and vector subscripts.)

Examples:

```
Temperature(1, :)
TemperatureArray((/ 4, 3, 2, 1 /), :, 1:7:2)
```

Purpose:
Forms an array consisting of the selected elements of the specified parent array.

Array Assignment

array = expression

where *array* is an array variable or an array section and the value of *expression* must be either

1. An array of the same shape as the array variable, or
2. A simple value

In the second case, the value is *broadcast to all the array elements*, with the result that each is assigned this value.

Examples:

```
INTEGER, DIMENSION(2, 3) :: A, B, C

A = RESHAPE( (/ 11, 22, 33, 44, 55,66 /), (/2, 3/) )
B = 0
C = A + B
C(1:2, 1) = (/ 111, 222 /)
```

Purpose:
To assign a value to an array or to a section of an array.

The WHERE Construct

See the Fortran summary of Chapter 8.

Intrinsic Array-Processing Functions

ALLOCATED(A)	Returns true if memory has been allocated to the allocatable array A and false otherwise
MATMUL(A, B)	Returns the matrix product of A and B, provided this product is defined (see Section 9.6)
MAXVAL(A, D)	Returns an array of one less dimension than A containing the maximum values in array A along dimension D. If D is omitted, the maximum value in the entire array is returned.
MAXLOC(A)	Returns a one-dimensional array containing the position of the first occurrence of the maximum value in A
MINVAL(A, D)	Returns an array of one less dimension than A containing the minimum values in array A along

	dimension D. If D is omitted, the minimum value in the entire array is returned.
MINLOC(A)	Returns a one-dimensional array containing the position of the first occurrence of the minimum value in A
PRODUCT(A, D)	Returns an array of one less dimension than A containing the products of the elements of A along dimension D. If D is omitted, the element-wise product of the elements in the entire array is returned.
RESHAPE(A, S, P, Q)	Returns an array with values obtained from A, with the specified shape S, followed by elements of array P (used repeatedly if necessary); and one-dimensional array Q specifies the order in which the subscripts are to be varied when filling in the resulting array. P and Q are optional arguments and may also be given in the forms PAD = P and ORDER = Q, respectively.
SHAPE(A)	Returns a one-dimensional array each of whose elements is the extent in the corresponding dimension of A
SUM(A, D)	Returns an array of one less dimension than A containing the sums of the elements of A along dimension D. If D is omitted, the sum of the elements in the entire array is returned.
SPREAD(A, D, N)	Returns an array of dimension one more than the dimension of A obtained by broadcasting N copies of A along dimension D.
TRANSPOSE(A)	Returns the transpose of A (see Section 9.6)

PROGRAMMING POINTERS

Program Style and Design

1. *Two-dimensional arays are especially useful for storing tables of values.* If the data values can be viewed as arranged in rows and columns and they must be processed more than once in a program, it is convenient to store them in a two-dimensional array.

2. *Use named constants to dimension compile-time arrays.* If it is necessary to change any extent or subscript range of an array, only the named constant needs to be changed.

3. *Use allocatable arrays in programs that must process arrays whose extents or subscript ranges vary from one execution of the program to the next.* Unlike pro-

grams that use compile-time arrays, no changes in declarations are required to process arrays of different extents or subscript ranges.

4. *Specify reasonable extents for arrays.* The extents of an array are determined by the number of data values to be stored. Making the extents too large wastes memory.

5. *Use broadcasting rather than a loop to construct an array whose elements are all the same.* For example, using the assignment statement

```
A = 0
```

to zero out a two-dimensional array A is simpler than using nested DO loops:

```
DO I = 1, SIZE(A, 1)
   DO J = 1, SIZE(A, 2)
      A(I,J) = 0
   END DO
END DO
```

6. *The basic arithmetic operations and instrinsic functions can be applied to arrays having the same shape and are performed elementwise.* For example, A + B gives the sum of two matrices A and B, provided they have the same shape.

7. *Assumed-shape arrays can be used to design general subprograms for processing arrays.*

Potential Problems

The difficulties encountered in using multidimensional arrays are similar to those for one-dimensional arrays considered in the preceding chapter. The first two potential problems listed here are simply restatements of some of the programming pointers in Chapter 8, and the reader should refer to those pointers for an expanded discussion.

1. *Declarations of array variables must include dimension information.*

2. *Subscripts must be integer valued and must stay within the range specified in the array declarations.*

3. *Unless some other order is specified, two-dimensional arrays are processed columnwise.* In general, the Fortran convention for processing multidimensional arrays is to vary each subscript over its entire range before varying the subscript that follows it. Any other processing order must be established by the programmer.

To illustrate, suppose that the two-dimensional array Table is declared by

```
INTEGER, DIMENSION(3,4) :: Table
```

and the following data is to be read into the array:

```
11, 22, 27, 35, 39, 40, 48, 51, 57, 66, 67, 92
```

If these values are to be read and assigned in a rowwise manner, so that the value of Table is

$$\begin{bmatrix} 11 & 22 & 27 & 35 \\ 39 & 40 & 48 & 51 \\ 57 & 66 & 67 & 92 \end{bmatrix}$$

the following READ statement is appropriate:

```
READ *, ((Table(I,J), J = 1, 4), I = 1, 3)
```

If the values are to be read and assigned in a columnwise manner, so that the value of Table is

$$\begin{bmatrix} 11 & 35 & 48 & 66 \\ 22 & 39 & 51 & 67 \\ 27 & 40 & 57 & 92 \end{bmatrix}$$

the statements should be

```
READ *, ((Table(I,J), I = 1, 3), J = 1, 4)
```

or

```
READ *, Table
```

4. *In an assignment of one array to another, the arrays must have the same shape.*
   For example, consider arrays A, B, and C declared by

```
INTEGER, DIMENSION(2, 3) :: &
   A = RESHAPE( (/ 11, 22, 33, 44, 55, 66 /), (/ 2, 3/) )
INTEGER, DIMENSION(10) :: B
INTEGER, DIMENSION(3, 2) :: C
INTEGER, DIMENSION(0:1, 5::7) :: D
```

Array A cannot be assigned to array B nor to array C since the shapes of these arrays are different than A. However, array A can be assigned to array D; even though they have different subscript ranges, they do have the same shape.

5. *Subprograms that use assumed-shape arrays and array-valued functions must be internal subprograms or module subprograms, or there must be an interface block in each program unit that references them.*

6. *Allocatable arrays may not be formal arguments.*

PROGRAMMING PROBLEMS

Section 9.3

1. A car manufacturer has collected data on the noise level (measured in decibels) produced by six different models of cars at seven different speeds. This data is summarized in the following table:

Car	Speed (mph)						
	20	30	40	50	60	70	80
1	88	90	94	102	111	122	134
2	75	77	80	86	94	103	113
3	80	83	85	94	100	111	121
4	68	71	76	85	96	110	125
5	77	84	91	98	105	112	119
6	81	85	90	96	102	109	120

Write a program that will display this table in a nice format and that will calculate and display the average noise level for each car model, the average noise level at each speed, and the overall average noise level.

2. A number of students from three different engineering sections, 1, 2, and 3, performed the same experiment to determine the tensile strength of sheets made from two different alloys. Each of these strength measurements is a real number in the range 0 through 10. Write a program to read several lines of data, each consisting of a section number and the tensile strength of the two types of sheets recorded by a student in that section, and calculate
   (a) for each section, the average of the tensile strengths for each type of alloy,
   (b) the number of persons in a given section who recorded strength measures of 5 or higher,
   (c) the average of the tensile strengths recorded for alloy 2 by students who recorded a tensile strength lower than 3 for alloy 1.

3. A certain company manufactures four electronic devices using five different components that cost $10.95, $6.30, $14.75, $11.25, and $5.00, respectively. The number of components used in each device is given in the following table:

Device Number	Component Number				
	1	2	3	4	5
1	10	4	5	6	7
2	7	0	12	1	3
3	4	9	5	0	8
4	3	2	1	5	6

Write a program to

(a)   calculate the total cost of each device,

(b)   calculate the total cost of producing each device if the estimated labor cost for each device is 10 percent of the cost in part (a).

4. An electronics firm manufactures four types of radios. The number of capacitors, resistors, and transistors (denoted by C, R, and T, respectively) in each of these is given in the following table:

Radio Type	C	R	T
1	2	6	3
2	6	11	5
3	13	29	10
4	8	14	7

Each capacitor costs $0.35, a resistor costs $0.25, and a transistor costs $1.40. Write a program to find the total cost of the components for each of the types of radios.

5. Write a program to calculate and print the first 10 rows of *Pascal's triangle*. The first part of the triangle has the form

```
        1
      1   1
    1   2   1
  1   3   3   1
1   4   6   4   1
```

in which each row begins and ends with ones and each other entry in a row is the sum of the two entries just above it. If displaying the triangle in this form seems too challenging, you might display it in the form

```
1
1  1
1  2  1
1  3  3  1
1  4  6  4  1
```

6. A *magic square* is an $n \times n$ array in which all of the integers $1, 2, 3, \ldots, n^2$ appear exactly once, and all the column sums, row sums, and diagonal sums are equal. For example, the following is a 5×5 magic square in which all rows, columns, and diagonals sum to 65:

17	24	1	8	15
23	5	7	14	16
4	6	13	20	22
10	12	19	21	3
11	18	25	2	9

The following is a procedure for constructing an $n \times n$ magic square for any odd integer n. Place 1 in the middle of the top row. Then after placing integer k, move up one row and one column to the right to place the next integer $k + 1$, unless one of the following occurs:

(a)   If a move takes you above the top row in the jth column, move to the bottom of the jth column and place the integer there.

(b)   If a move takes you outside to the right of the square in the ith row, place the integer in the ith row at the left side.

(c)   If a move takes you to an already filled square or if you move out of the square at the upper right-hand corner, place $k + 1$ immediately below k.

Write a program to construct a magic square for any odd value of n.

7. Suppose that each of the four edges of a thin square metal plate is maintained at a constant temperature and that we wish to determine the steady-state temperature at each interior point of the plate. To do this, we divide the plate into squares (the corners of which are called *nodes*) and find the temperature at each interior node by averaging the four neighboring temperatures; that is, if T_{ij} denotes the old temperature at the node in row i and column j, then

$$\frac{T_{i-1,j} + T_{i,j-1} + T_{i,j+1} + T_{i+1,j}}{4}$$

will be the new temperature.

To model the plate, we can use a two-dimensional array, with each array element representing the temperature at one of the nodes. Write a program that first reads the four constant temperatures (possibly different) along the edges of the plate, and some estimate of the temperature at the interior points, and then uses these values to initialize the elements of the array. Then determine the steady-state temperature at each interior node by repeatedly averaging the temperatures at its four neighbors, as just described. Repeat this procedure until the new temperature at each interior node differs from the old temperature by no more than some specified small amount. Then print the array and the number of iterations used to produce the final result. (It may also be of interest to print the array at each stage of the iteration.)

8. Write a program similar to that in Problem 7 to find steady-state temperatures in a fireplace, a diagram of which follows. The north, west, and east wall temperatures are held constant, and the south wall (a fire wall) is insulated. The steady-state temperatures at each interior node are to be calculated using the averaging

process described in Problem 7, but those for the nodes along the south wall are to be calculated using the formula

$$\frac{2T_{i-1,j} + T_{i,j-1} + T_{i,j+1}}{4}$$

Your program should read the constant north, west, and east temperatures and a constant fire wall temperature (e.g., 10, 50, 40, 1500), the number of rows and columns in the grid (e.g., 4, 7), the numbers of the fire wall's first and last rows and the first and last columns (e.g., 3, 4, and 3, 6), a small value to be used as a termination criterion (e.g., .0001), and an initial guess for the interior temperatures (e.g., 500).

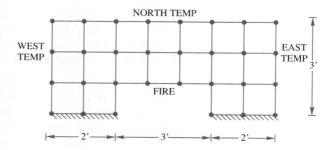

9. The game of *Life*, invented by the mathematician John H. Conway, is intended to model life in a society of organisms. Consider a rectangular array of cells, each of which may contain an organism. If the array is assumed to extend indefinitely in both directions, each cell will have eight neighbors, the eight cells surrounding it. Births and deaths occur according to the following rules:
   (a) An organism is born in an empty cell that has exactly three neighbors.
   (b) An organism dies from isolation if it has fewer than two neighbors.
   (c) An organism dies from overcrowding if it has more than three neighbors.
   The following display shows the first five generations of a particular configuration of organisms:

Write a program to play the game of Life and investigate the patterns produced by various initial configurations. Some configurations die off rather quickly; others repeat after a certain number of generations; others change shape and size and may move across the array; and still others may produce "gliders" that detach themselves from the society and sail off into space.

Section 9.6

10. Proceed as in Problem 3, but use the intrinsic function MATMUL to compute the required matrix products.

11. Proceed as in Problem 4, but use the intrinsic function MATMUL to find the total cost of the components for each of the types of radios.

12. The vector-matrix equation

$$\begin{bmatrix} N \\ E \\ D \end{bmatrix} = \begin{bmatrix} \cos\alpha & -\sin\alpha & 0 \\ \sin\alpha & \cos\alpha & 0 \\ 0 & 0 & 1 \end{bmatrix} \begin{bmatrix} \cos\beta & 0 & \sin\beta \\ 0 & 1 & 0 \\ -\sin\beta & 0 & \cos\beta \end{bmatrix} \begin{bmatrix} 1 & 0 & 0 \\ 0 & \cos\gamma & -\sin\gamma \\ 0 & \sin\gamma & \cos\gamma \end{bmatrix} \begin{bmatrix} I \\ J \\ K \end{bmatrix}$$

is used to transform local coordinates (I, J, K) for a space vehicle to inertial co-ordinates (N, E, D). Write a program that reads values for α, β, and γ and a set of local coordinates (I, J, K) and then uses the predefined intrinsic function MATMUL to determine the corresponding inertial coordinates.

13. A *Markov chain* is a system that moves through a discrete set of states in such a way that when the system is in state i, there is probability P_{ij} that it will next move to state j. These probabilities are given by a *transition matrix P*, whose (i, j) entry is P_{ij}. It is easy to show that the (i, j) entry of P^n gives the probability of starting in state i and ending in state j after n steps.

    One model of gas diffusion is known as the *Ehrenfest urn model*. In this model, there are two urns A and B containing a given number of balls (molecules). At each instant, a ball is chosen at random and is transferred to the other urn. This is a Markov chain if we take as a state the number of balls in urn A and let P_{ij} be the probability that a ball is transferred from A to B if there are i balls in urn A. For example, for four balls, the transition matrix P is given by

$$\begin{bmatrix} 0 & 1 & 0 & 0 & 0 \\ 1/4 & 0 & 3/4 & 0 & 0 \\ 0 & 1/2 & 0 & 1/2 & 0 \\ 0 & 0 & 3/4 & 0 & 1/4 \\ 0 & 0 & 0 & 1 & 0 \end{bmatrix}$$

Write a program that reads a transition matrix P for such a Markov chain and calculates and displays the value of n and P^n for several values of n.

14. A *directed graph*, or *digraph*, consists of a set of *vertices* and a set of *directed arcs* joining certain of these vertices. For example, the following diagram pictures a directed graph having five vertices numbered 1, 2, 3, 4, and 5 and seven directed arcs joining vertices 1 to 2, 1 to 4, 1 to 5, 3 to 1, 3 to itself, 4 to 3, and 5 to 1:

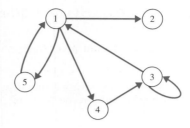

A directed graph having n vertices can be represented by its *adjacency matrix*, which is an $n \times n$ matrix, with the entry in the ith row and jth column a 1 if vertex i is joined to vertex j, and 0 otherwise. The adjacency matrix for this graph is

$$
\begin{bmatrix}
0 & 1 & 0 & 1 & 1 \\
0 & 0 & 0 & 0 & 0 \\
1 & 0 & 1 & 0 & 0 \\
0 & 0 & 1 & 0 & 0 \\
1 & 0 & 0 & 0 & 0
\end{bmatrix}
$$

If A is the adjacency matrix for a directed graph, the entry in the ith row and jth column of A^k gives the number of ways that vertex j can be reached from the vertex i by following k edges. Write a program to read the number of vertices in a directed graph and a collection of ordered pairs of vertices representing directed arcs, to construct the adjacency matrix, and then to find the number of ways that each vertex can be reached from every other vertex by following k edges for some value of k.

Section 9.7

15. The *inverse* of an $n \times n$ matrix A is a matrix A^{-1} for which both the products $A * A^{-1}$ and $A^{-1} * A$ are equal to the *identity matrix*, which is a square matrix with 1s on the diagonal from the upper left to the lower right and 0s elsewhere. The inverse of a matrix A can be calculated by solving the linear systems $Ax = b$ for each of the following constant vectors b:

$$
\begin{bmatrix} 1 \\ 0 \\ 0 \\ \vdots \\ 0 \end{bmatrix}
\begin{bmatrix} 0 \\ 1 \\ 0 \\ \vdots \\ 0 \end{bmatrix}
\begin{bmatrix} 0 \\ 0 \\ 1 \\ \vdots \\ 0 \end{bmatrix}
\cdots
\begin{bmatrix} 0 \\ 0 \\ 0 \\ \vdots \\ 1 \end{bmatrix}
$$

These solutions give the first, second, third, ..., nth columns of A^{-1}. Write a program that uses Gaussian elimination to solve these linear systems and thus calculate the inverse of a matrix.

16. A general three-term equation for fitting a curve is

$$y = A + Bf(x) + Cg(x)$$

where f and g can be any functions of x. The least-squares curve of this type can be found by solving the linear system

$$nA + (\Sigma f(x))B + (\Sigma g(x))C = \Sigma y$$

$$(\Sigma f(x))A + (\Sigma f(x)^2)B + (\Sigma f(x)g(x))C = \Sigma f(x)y$$

$$(\Sigma g(x))A + (\Sigma f(x)g(x))B + (\Sigma g(x)^2)C = \Sigma g(x)y$$

for A, B, and C. Write a subprogram whose arguments are the functions f and g and a set of data points and that finds the coefficients A, B, and C for this least-squares curve.

FEATURES NEW TO FORTRAN 90

The Fortran 90 features described at the end of the preceding chapter for one-dimensional arrays apply to multidimensional arrays as well. They include

- Array assignment
- An intrinsic function RESHAPE to reshape arrays
- Elementwise application of operators and functions to arrays
- Array sections of the form

  ```
  array-name(section-subscript-list)
  ```

  where each item in the *section-subscript-list* is a subscript, or a subscript triplet, or a vector subscript
- The WHERE construct to assign values to arrays depending on the value of a logical array expression
- Assumed-shape arrays as formal array arguments in subprograms
- Array inquiry functions SIZE, LBOUND, and UBOUND
- Functions may return arrays.
- Several new predefined functions for processing arrays, including MAXVAL, MAXLOC, MINVAL, MINLOC, PRODUCT, SUM, SPREAD, MATMUL, and TRANSPOSE
- Allocatable arrays and the ALLOCATE and DEALLOCATE statements

10

Derived Data Types

*F*ortran provides six *intrinsic* data types: INTEGER, REAL, COMPLEX, CHARAC-
TER, and LOGICAL, which are simple types, and the array, which is a structured data type. In Fortran 90, it is also possible to define new data types. These programmer-
defined types are called **derived types,** and an item of such a type is called a
structure. In this chapter we describe how derived types and structures are defined
and used.

10.1 INTRODUCTION TO DERIVED TYPES AND STRUCTURES

Arrays are used to store elements of the same type. In many situations, however, we need to process items that are related in some way but that are not all of the
same type. For example, a date consists of a month name (of character type), a day
(of integer type), and a year (of integer type); a record of computer usage might contain, among other items, a user's name and password (character strings), identification number (integer), resource limit (integer), and resources used to date (real). In
Fortran 90, a derived data type can be used to declare a structure, which can be used
to store such related data items of possibly different types. The positions in the structure in which these data items are stored are called the **components** of the structure.
Thus, a structure for storing computer usage information might contain a last-name
component, a first-name component, a password component, an identification number component, and a resources-used component.

Definition of a Derived Type

A simple form of a derived type definition is

Definition of a Derived Type

Form:

```
TYPE type-name
   declaration₁
   declaration₂
      ⋮
   declarationₖ
END TYPE type-name
```

where

> *type-name* is a valid Fortran identifier that names the derived type, and each *declarationᵢ* declares one or more components in a structure of this type.

Purpose:

Defines a derived type whose components are named and declared in *declaration₁, declaration₂, ...* These definitions are placed in the specification part of a program unit.

For example, the type definition

```
TYPE Computer_Usage_Info
   CHARACTER(15) :: LastName, FirstName
   INTEGER :: IdNumber
   CHARACTER(6) :: Password
   INTEGER :: ResourceLimit
   REAL :: ResourcesUsed
END TYPE Computer_Usage_Info
```

defines the derived type `Computer_Usage_Info`. A structure of this type will have six components: `LastName` and `FirstName`, which are of character type with values of length 15; `IdNumber` of integer type; `Password` of character type with values of length 6; `ResourceLimit` of integer type; and `ResourcesUsed` of real type. A typical value of type `Computer_Usage_Info` might be pictured as follows:

LastName	FirstName	IdNumber	Password	ResourceLimit	ResourcesUsed
Babbage	Charles	10101	ADA	750	380.81

The components of a structure need not be of different types. For example, the type definition

```
TYPE Point
   REAL :: X, Y
END TYPE Point
```

defines the derived type `Point`, and a structure of type `Point` will have two components named X and Y, each of which is of real type:

X	Y
2.5	3.2

Type identifiers like `Computer_Usage_Info` and `Point` can then be used to declare the types of structures in declarations of the form

> ### Declarations of Structures
>
> **Form:**
>
> ```
> TYPE(type-name) :: list-of-identifiers
> ```
>
> **Purpose:**
> Declares the identifiers in the given list to be names of structures whose components are named and declared in the definition of derived type *type-name*.

For example,

```
TYPE(Point) :: P, Q
```

declares structure variables P and Q of type `Point`;

```
TYPE(Computer_Usage_Info) :: User
```

declares a structure variable `User` of type `Computer_Usage_Info`; and

```
TYPE(Computer_Usage_Info), DIMENSION(50) :: UserList
```

or

```
TYPE(Computer_Usage_Info) :: UserList(50)
```

declares a one-dimensional array `UserList`, each of whose elements is a structure of type `Computer_Usage_Info`.

Derived Type Constructors

Values of a derived type are sequences of values for the components of that derived type. Their form is

```
type-name(list of component values)
```

For example,

```
Point(2.5, 3.2)
```

is a value of type `Point` and can be assigned to variable `P` of type `Point`,

```
P = Point(2.5, 3.2)
```

or associated with a named constant `Center` of type `Point`,

```
TYPE(Point), PARAMETER :: Center = Point(2.5, 3.2)
```

Similarly,

```
Computer_Usage_Info("Babbage", "Charles", &
                    10101, "ADA", 750, 380.81)
```

is a value of type `Computer_Usage_Info` and can be assigned to the variable `User` or to a component of the array `UserList`:

```
User = Computer_Usage_Info("Babbage", "Charles",  &
                           10101, "ADA", 750, 380.81)
UserList(1) = User
```

The components in such **derived type constructors** may also be variables or expressions. For example, if `A` is a real variable with value 1.1, the assignment statement

```
P = Point(A, 2*A)
```

assigns the structure having real components 1.1 and 2.2 to the variable `P`.

Accessing Components

Individual components of a structure are accessed using **qualified variables** formed by joining the structure name to the component name with the **component selector** character (%):

```
structure-name%component-name
```

For example, P%X is the first component of the structure P of type Point, and P%Y is the second component; UserList(1)%LastName, UserList(1)%First-Name, UserList(1)%IdNumber, UserList(1)%Password, UserList(1)%ResourceLimit, and UserList(1)%ResourcesUsed refer to the six components of the structure UserList(1).

Each component of a structure has a specified type and may be used in the same way as any item of that type. For example, since User%LastName is of character type, it may be assigned a value in an assignment statement

```
User%LastName = "Babbage"
```

or by an input statement:

```
READ *, User%LastName
```

Its value can be displayed by using an output statement

```
PRINT *, User%LastName
```

and its value can be modified by a substring reference:

```
User%LastName(1:1) = "C"
```

Nested Structures

The components of a structure may be of any type; in particular, they may be other structures. For example, the declarations

```
TYPE Point
   REAL :: X, Y
END TYPE Point

TYPE Circle
   TYPE(Point) :: Center
   REAL :: Radius
END TYPE Circle

TYPE(Circle) :: C
```

declare C to be a structure whose values are of type `Circle`. Such a structure has two components: the first component `Center` is of type `Point` and is itself a structure having two real components named X and Y; the second component `Radius` is of type `REAL`.

The components within such a **nested structure** may be accessed by simply affixing a second component identifier to the name of the larger structure. Thus, if C is assigned a value by

```
C = Circle(Point(2.5, 3.2), 10.0)
```

representing a circle of radius 10.0, centered at (2.5, 3.2), the value of `C%Center%X` is 2.5, the value of `C%Center%Y` is 3.2, and the value of `C%Radius` is 10.0.

10.2 PROCESSING STRUCTURES

In the previous section, we saw that structures can be used to store several related data items that may be of different types and that each item or component in a structure can be accessed with a qualified variable of the form

```
structure-name%component-name
```

In this section we discuss input/output of structures, assignment of values to structures, and use of structures as arguments of subprograms.

Input/Output of Structures

Unlike arrays, an entire structure may not be input simply by including a structure variable in the input list of a `READ` statement; nor may an entire structure be displayed simply by including a structure expression in the output list of a `PRINT` or `WRITE` statement. Instead, input or output of a structure must be done componentwise, that is, by reading or displaying the value of each component in the structure individually.

To illustrate, consider a structure variable `User` of type `Computer_Usage_Info` described in the preceding section. To input a value for `User`, we must read values for each component of `User` separately:

```
READ *, User%LastName, User%FirstName, User%IdNumber, &
        User%Password, User%ResourceLimit, User%ResourcesUsed
```

Similarly, to display the value of `User`, we must display each component individually, as in

```
PRINT '(1X, "Name:            ", 2A)', &
      User%FirstName, User%LastName
PRINT '(1X, "Id Number:       ", I5)', User%IdNumber
PRINT '(1X, "Resource Limit: ", I5)', User%ResourceLimit
PRINT '(1X, "Used to date:   ", F6.1)', User%ResourcesUsed
```

The following example illustrates input and output of structures. It reads and displays values for only some of the components of the structures.

Example: Retrieving Computer Usage Records

To illustrate processing of structures, suppose that a data file contains information about computer users like that we have been considering: the user's last name, first name, id-number, and login password, amount of resources allocated to the user, and the amount of computer resources used to date:

```
Babbage        Charles        10101ADA    75038081
Newton         Isaac          10102APPLE  65059884
Leibniz        Gottfried      10103CALC   25019374
Fahrenheit     Freda          10104FRZ32  25017793
Celsius        Christine      10105FRZ0   85019191
Tower          Lean           10106PISA   35022395
VanderVan      Henry          10107VAN    75016859
Freeloader     Freddie        10108RED    450 7661
   ⋮             ⋮              ⋮           ⋮
Yale           Harvard        20125IVY    15012770
```

Each line of the file consists of a user's last name, first name, five-digit id number, password with up to six characters, resource limit (in dollars) with at most four digits, and resources used to date, which appears with no decimal point but is to be processed as a number with three digits before the decimal point and two following it. A program is to be written to search this file for a specified user; if the user is found, the program will display the user's id number, name, and percentage of resources remaining.

Since each line of information in this file consists of a user's last name, first name, id number, password, resource limit, and resources used to date, it is natural to organize this information in structures of type Computer_Usage_Info as in the program in Figure 10.1. This program repeatedly reads an id number from the keyboard and then reads id numbers from the file until a match is found, an input error occurs, or the end of the file is reached. If the id number is found, the program then reads values for the remaining components of the structure User and displays the required information.

Figure 10.1 Retrieving computer-usage records.

```
PROGRAM Computer_Usage_Records
!-----------------------------------------------------------------------
! Program to read id numbers from the keyboard, search a file of
! computer-usage records to determine if this is the number of a
! computer user, and if so, retrieve and display information about
! that user.  Identifiers used are:
!   Computer_Usage_Info : name of a derived type
!   FileName            : name of computer-usage file
!   OpenStatus          : status variable for OPEN
!   InputStatus         : status variable for READ
!   User                : structure of type Computer_Usage_Info
!   InputNumber         : an id number entered from the keyboard
!   UserNumber          : an id number in the computer-usage file
!   Found               : indicates if InputNumber matches some
!                           user's id number in the file
!
! Input (keyboard): InputNumber
! Input (file)    : UserNumber and computer usage record assigned
!                   to User
! Output (screen) : User's id number, name, and percentage of computer
!                   resources remaining or a message that the id number
!                   was not found in the file
!-----------------------------------------------------------------------

  IMPLICIT NONE

  TYPE Computer_Usage_Info
     CHARACTER(15):: LastName, FirstName
     INTEGER :: IdNumber
     CHARACTER(6) :: Password
     INTEGER :: ResourceLimit
     REAL :: ResourcesUsed
  END TYPE Computer_Usage_Info

  CHARACTER(20) :: FileName
  TYPE(Computer_Usage_Info) :: User
  INTEGER :: InputNumber, UserNumber, EndOfFile
  LOGICAL :: Found
```

Figure 10.1 *(cont.)*

```fortran
! Get name of file and open it for input
WRITE (*, '(1X, A)', ADVANCE = "NO") "Enter name of computer-usage file: "
READ *, FileName
OPEN (UNIT = 10, FILE = FileName, STATUS = "OLD", IOSTAT = OpenStatus)
IF (OpenStatus > 0) STOP "*** Cannot open file ***"


! Read id numbers and search file for matches
DO
   PRINT *
   WRITE (*, '(1X, A)', ADVANCE = "NO") "Enter id number (0 to stop): "
   READ *, InputNumber
   IF (InputNumber == 0) EXIT
   ! If no more id numbers to process, terminate repetition

   ! Otherwise search file for id number
   DO
      READ (10, '(T31, I5)', IOSTAT = InputStatus) UserNumber
      IF (InputStatus > 0) STOP "*** Input error ***"
      IF (InputStatus < 0) EXIT
      ! If end of file reached, stop searching

      ! Else check if ids match
      Found = (InputNumber == UserNumber)
      IF (Found) EXIT
   END DO

   ! Id found -- back up in the file, read the user info,
   ! and display the required information

   IF (Found) THEN
      BACKSPACE 10
      READ (10, '(2A15, 10X, I4, F5.2)') &
         User%LastName, User%FirstName, &
         User%ResourceLimit, User%ResourcesUsed
      PRINT &
         '(1X, I5, 1X, 2A / 1X, "has used", F5.1, "% of resources")',&
         UserNumber, User%FirstName, User%LastName, &
         100.0 * (User%ResourceLimit - User%ResourcesUsed) &
         / User%ResourceLimit
   ELSE
      PRINT *, InputNumber, " not found"
   END IF
```

Figure 10.1 *(cont.)*

```
     ! Rewind file and get new id number
     REWIND 10
   END DO

END PROGRAM Computer_Usage_Records
```

Sample run:

```
Enter name of computer-usage file: USERS.DAT

Enter id number (0 to stop): 10101
10101 Charles        Babbage
has used 49.2% of resources

Enter id number (0 to stop): 10108
10108 Freddie        Freeloader
has used 83.0% of resources

Enter id number (0 to stop): 20125
20125 Harvard        Yale
has used 14.9% of resources

Enter id number (0 to stop): 10199
10199  not found

Enter id number (0 to stop): 0
```

Structure Assignment

Sometimes it is necessary to copy the components of one structure into another structure. This can be done with a series of assignment statements that copy the individual components of the first structure to the components of the second structure. For example, if User_1 and User_2 are structure variables of type Computer_Usage_Info and we wish to copy the components of User_1 into User_2, we could use

```
User_2%LastName = User_1%LastName
User_2%FirstName = User_1%FirstName
User_2%IdNumber = User_1%IdNumber
User_2%Password = User_1%Password
User_2%ResourceLimit = User_1%ResourceLimit
User_2%ResourcesUsed = User_1%ResourcesUsed
```

If the structures have the same type, this can be done more conveniently with a single assignment statement of the form

```
structure-variable = structure-expression
```

For example, the six assignment statements above could be replaced by the single assignment statement

```
User_2 = User_1
```

Remember, however, that *the structure variable and the structure expression must have the same type.*

Structures as Arguments

Structures may be used as arguments of subprograms provided the corresponding actual and formal structure arguments have the same type. The value returned by a function may also be a structure.

The following example illustrates the use of structures as arguments. Two structures P1 and P2 of type Point are passed to the function Distance, which calculates and returns the distance between P1 and P2. The structures P1 and P2 are then passed to the subroutine FindLine, which finds the equation of the line through P1 and P2.

Example: Equations of Lines

The distance between point P_1 with coordinates (x_1, y_1) and point P_2 with coordinates (x_2, y_2) is given by

$$\sqrt{(x_2 - x_1)^2 + (y_2 - y_1)^2}$$

The **slope-intercept** form of the equation of the line through points P_1 and P_2 is

$$y = mx + b$$

where m is the **slope** of the line and is calculated by

$$m = \frac{y_2 - y_1}{x_2 - x_1}$$

(provided that $x_1 \neq x_2$); and b is the **y-intercept** of the line; that is, $(0, b)$ is the point where the line crosses the y-axis. Using the slope m, we can calculate b as

$$b = y_1 - mx_1$$

If $x_1 = x_2$, there is no y-intercept and the slope is not defined; the line through P_1 and P_2 is the vertical line having the equation

$$x = x_1$$

The program in Figure 10.2 uses the function `Distance` to calculate the distance between two points and then calls the subroutine `FindLine` to find the equation of the line passing through the two points. Points are represented as structures having two components X and Y of `real` type, which represent the *x*- and *y*-coordinates, respectively.

```
TYPE Point
   REAL :: X, Y
END TYPE Point
```

Figure 10.2 Equations of lines.

```
PROGRAM Points_and_Lines
!------------------------------------------------------------------------
! Program to read two points P1 and P2 represented as structures,
! calculate the distance between P1 and P2, and find the slope-
! intercept equation of the line determined by P1 and P2. Identifiers
! used are:
!    Point    : derived type representing points in two dimensions
!    P1, P2   : two points being processed
!    Distance : function to calculate distance between points
!    FindLine : subroutine to find the equation of a line
!    Response : user response
!
! Input:   Coordinates of points
! Output:  User prompts, labels, distance between two points, and
!          slope-intercept of equation of line through the points
!------------------------------------------------------------------------

  IMPLICIT NONE
  TYPE Point
    REAL :: X, Y
  END TYPE Point

  TYPE(Point) :: P1, P2
  CHARACTER(1) :: Response

  DO
     WRITE (*, '(1X, A)', ADVANCE = "NO") &
         "Enter coordinates of points P1 and P2: "
     READ *, P1%X, P1%Y, P2%X, P2%Y
     PRINT '(1X, 2(A, "(", F5.2, ",", F5.2, ")"), " is ", F5.2)', &
         "Distance between ", P1%X, P1%Y, " and ", P2%X, P2%Y, &
         Distance(P1, P2)
     CALL FindLine(P1, P2)
```

Figure 10.2 *(cont.)*

```
      WRITE (*, '(/ 1X, A)', ADVANCE = "NO") "More points (Y or N)? "
      READ *, Response
      IF (Response /= "Y") EXIT
   END DO

CONTAINS

   !--Distance-----------------------------------------------------------
   ! Function to calculate the distance between points P1 and P2
   !
   ! Accepts:   Structures P1 and P2 of type Point
   ! Returns:   Distance between P1 and P2
   !--------------------------------------------------------------------

   FUNCTION Distance(P1, P2)

      TYPE(Point), INTENT(IN) :: P1, P2
      REAL :: Distance

      Distance = SQRT((P2%x - P1%x)**2 + (P2%y - P1%y)**2)

   END FUNCTION Distance

   !--FindLine-----------------------------------------------------------
   ! Subroutine to find the slope-intercept equation  y = mx + b of the
   ! line passing though points P1 and P2.  Local variables used are:
   !   M : slope of line
   !   B : y-intercept of line
   !
   ! Accepts: Structures P1 and P2 of type Point
   ! Output:  Equation of line determined by P1 and P2
   !--------------------------------------------------------------------

   SUBROUTINE FindLine(P1, P2)

      TYPE(Point), INTENT(IN) :: P1, P2
      REAL :: M,  B

      IF (P1%X == P2%X) THEN
         PRINT '(1X, A, F5.2)', "Line is vertical line  x = ", P1%X
      ELSE
         M = (P2%Y - P1%Y) / (P2%X - P1%X)
         B = P1%Y - M * P1%X
         PRINT '(1X, 2(A, F5.2))', "Equation of line is y = ", &
                                   M, "x + ", B
      END IF
   END SUBROUTINE FindLine

END PROGRAM Points_and_Lines
```

Figure 10.2 *(cont.)*

Sample run:

```
Enter coordinates of points P1 and P2: 0,0  1,1
Distance between ( 0.00, 0.00) and ( 1.00, 1.00) is 1.41
Equation of line is y =  1.00x +  0.00

More points (Y or N)? Y
Enter coordinates of points P1 and P2: 1,1  1,5
Distance between ( 1.00, 1.00) and ( 1.00, 5.00) is 4.00
Line is vertical line  x =  1.00

More points (Y or N)? Y
Enter coordinates of points P1 and P2: 3.1, 4.2   -5.3, 7.2
Distance between ( 3.10, 4.20) and (-5.30, 7.20) is 8.92
Equation of line is y =  -.36x +  5.31

More points (Y or N)? N
```

10.3 APPLICATION: SEARCHING A CHEMISTRY DATABASE—REVISITED

Problem

In Section 8.10, we considered the problem of looking up a chemical formula in a file and retrieving the name and specific heat of the inorganic compound corresponding to that formula. Each line of the file contains the formula, name, and specific heat of a compound. The file has been sorted so that the formulas are in alphabetical order.

Solution

The input for this problem is a list of chemical formulas, names, and specific heats stored in a file. In the solution in Section 8.10, we read these values and stored them in three separate arrays, Formula, Name, and SpecificHeat. A better solution is to define a derived type ChemicalData to represent the information stored in the file,

```
INTEGER, PARAMETER :: Length = 10
TYPE ChemicalData
   CHARACTER(Length) :: Formula
   CHARACTER(2*Length) :: Name
   REAL :: SpecificHeat
END TYPE ChemicalData
```

and use an array whose elements are structures of this type to store this information:

```
TYPE(ChemicalData), DIMENSION(:), ALLOCATABLE :: Compound
```

The program in Figure 10.3 reads the chemical formulas, names, and specific heats from the file and stores them in Compound, an array of structures. After these have been read and stored, the user inputs various formulas from the keyboard. For each formula, the array Compound is searched to locate a structure whose Formula component contains this formula. If such a structure is found, its Name and SpecificHeat components are displayed. Note that the subroutine Binary-Search from Chapter 8 has been modified so that it searches an array of structures to locate a structure that contains the input value in a specified component. Such a component is called a **key component**.

Figure 10.3 Searching a list of chemical formulas—version 2

```
PROGRAM Chemical_Formulas_2
!-----------------------------------------------------------------------
! Program to read a file containing the chemical formula, name, and
! specific heat for various inorganic compounds and store these in
! an array of structures.  The first line of the file contains the
! number of compounds.  Also, the file is sorted so that the formulas
! are in alphabetical order.  The user enters a formula; the array is
! searched using binary search to locate a structure containing this
! formula as one of its components.  If such a structure is found,
! the name and specific heat components are displayed.   Identifiers
! used are:
!   Length         : length of character strings (constant)
!   ChemicalData   : derived type
!   Compound       : array of structures of type ChemicalData
!   MaxRecords     : maximum number of records in the file
!   NumRecords     : number of records in the file
!   AllocateStatus : status variable for ALLOCATE
!
! Input:  Formulas, names, and specific heats (from ReadData)
!            -- stored in array Compound
! Output: Names and specific heats for certain formulas (by LookUp)
!-----------------------------------------------------------------------
```

Figure 10.3 *(cont.)*

```fortran
IMPLICIT NONE
INTEGER, PARAMETER :: Length = 10
TYPE ChemicalData
   CHARACTER(Length) :: Formula
   CHARACTER(2*Length) :: Name
   REAL :: SpecificHeat
END TYPE ChemicalData

TYPE(ChemicalData), DIMENSION(:), ALLOCATABLE :: Compound
INTEGER :: MaxRecords, NumRecords, AllocateStatus

! Get the number of records to be stored, and
! allocate the array Compound of this size
WRITE (*, '(1X, A)', ADVANCE = "NO") &
      "Enter the maximum number of records in the file: "
READ *, MaxRecords
ALLOCATE(Compound(MaxRecords), IOSTAT = AllocateStatus)
IF (AllocateStatus /= 0) STOP "*** Not enough memory ***"

CALL ReadData(Compound, MaxRecords, NumRecords)
CALL LookUp(Compound, NumRecords)

CONTAINS

!-ReadData-------------------------------------------------------
! Subroutine to read a list of up to MaxRecords chemical formulas,
! names, and specific heats, store them in an array of structures
! (Compound), and count (NumRecords) how many sets of readings are
! stored.  Local variables used are:
!   FileName    : name of data file
!   OpenStatus  : status variable for OPEN
!   InputStatus : status variable for READ
!
! Accepts:          Array Compound and integer MaxRecords
! Input (keyboard): FileName
! Input (file):     Formulas, names, and specific heats
! Returns:          Array Compound
!-------------------------------------------------------------------

SUBROUTINE ReadData(Compound, MaxRecords, NumRecords)

   TYPE(ChemicalData), DIMENSION(:), INTENT(INOUT) :: Compound
   INTEGER, INTENT(IN) :: MaxRecords
   INTEGER, INTENT(OUT) :: NumRecords
   INTEGER :: OpenStatus, InputStatus
   CHARACTER(20) :: FileName
```

Figure 10.3 *(cont.)*

```
! Open the file, then read, count, and store the records

WRITE (*, '(1X, A)', ADVANCE = "NO") "Enter name of file: "
READ *, FileName
OPEN (UNIT = 15, FILE = FileName, STATUS = "OLD", IOSTAT = OpenStatus)
IF (OpenStatus > 0) STOP "*** Cannot open the file ***"

NumRecords  = 0
DO
    ! Check if there is still room in the array.  If not,
    ! terminate input and process the records that have been read.
    IF (NumRecords == MaxRecords) THEN
       PRINT *, "No more data can be read.  Processing the first"
       PRINT *, MaxRecords, " formulas."
       RETURN
    END IF

    ! Otherwise read and store more records
    NumRecords = NumRecords + 1
    READ (UNIT = 15, FMT = '(2A, F6.0)', IOSTAT = InputStatus) &
       Compound(NumRecords)%Formula, Compound(NumRecords)%Name, &
       Compound(NumRecords)%SpecificHeat
    IF (InputStatus > 0) STOP "*** Input error ***"

    ! If end of data, adjust count, close the file and terminate repetition
    IF (InputStatus < 0) THEN
       NumRecords = NumRecords - 1
       CLOSE (15)
       EXIT
    END IF

  END DO

END SUBROUTINE ReadData


!-LookUp--------------------------------------------------------------
! Subroutine that allows user to enter formulas.  The first NumRecords
! structures in array Compound are then searched to locate a structure
! whose Formula component matches this formula, and if found, the
! Name and SpecificHeat components are displayed.  User enters QUIT to
! stop searching.  Local identifiers used are:
!     InputFormula :  formula entered by the user
!     Found        :  signals if InputFormula found in array Compound
!     Location     :  location of InputFormula in Compound if found
!     Length       :  constant used to specify length of InputFormula
!
```

Figure 10.3 *(cont.)*

```
! Accepts:            Array Compound
! Input (keyboard):   Several values of InputFormula or a "QUIT" signal
! Output:             For each formula that is found, its name and
!                     specific heat; otherwise a "NOT Found" message
!-------------------------------------------------------------------

SUBROUTINE LookUp(Compound, NumRecords)

   TYPE(ChemicalData), DIMENSION(:), INTENT(IN) :: Compound
   INTEGER, INTENT(IN) :: NumRecords
   INTEGER :: Location
   INTEGER, PARAMETER :: Length = 10
   CHARACTER(Length) :: InputFormula
   LOGICAL :: Found

   ! While there are formulas to search for, do the following:

   DO
      WRITE (*, '(/ 1X, A)', ADVANCE = "NO") &
            "Enter formula to search for, (QUIT to stop): "
      READ *, InputFormula
      IF (InputFormula == "QUIT") EXIT
      ! If done searching for formulas, terminate repetition

      ! Otherwise, search Formula array for InputFormula
      ! and display information found

      CALL BinarySearch(Compound(1:NumRecords), InputFormula, &
                        Found, Location)
      IF (Found) THEN
         PRINT '(1X, A, 1X, A, F7.4)', Compound(Location)%Name, &
            "has specific heat", Compound(Location)%SpecificHeat
      ELSE
         PRINT *, "        *** not found ***"
      END IF
   END DO

END SUBROUTINE LookUp

!-BinarySearch-----------------------------------------------------
! Subroutine to search the first NumRecords of array Compound to
! locate a structure whose Formula component matches InputFormula
! using binary search.  If InputFormula is found, Found is returned as
! true and the Location of the structure is returned; otherwise Found
! is false. Local variables used are:
!   First  :  first item in (sub)list being searched
!   Last   :  last    "    "       "         "     "
!   Middle :  middle  "    "       "         "     "
!
```

Figure 10.3 *(cont.)*

```
! Accepts:   Array Compound and InputFormula
! Returns:   If InputFormula is found:
!                 Found = true and Location = its position in array
!                 Compound
!            Otherwise:
!                 Found = false (and Location = last position examined)
!------------------------------------------------------------------

SUBROUTINE BinarySearch(Compound, InputFormula, Found, Location)

   TYPE(ChemicalData), DIMENSION(:), INTENT(IN) :: Compound
   CHARACTER(*), INTENT(IN) :: InputFormula
   LOGICAL, INTENT(OUT) :: Found
   INTEGER, INTENT(OUT) :: Location
   INTEGER :: First, Last, Middle

   First = 1
   Last = SIZE(Compound)
   Found = .FALSE.

   ! While First less than or equal to Last and not Found do
   DO
      IF ((First > Last) .OR. Found) RETURN
      ! If empty list to be searched or item found, return

      ! Otherwise continue with the following

      Middle = (First + Last) / 2
      IF (InputFormula < Compound(Middle)%Formula) THEN
         Last = Middle - 1
      ELSE IF (InputFormula > Compound(Middle)%Formula) THEN
         First = Middle + 1
      ELSE
         Found = .TRUE.
         Location = Middle
      END IF
   END DO

 END SUBROUTINE BinarySearch

END PROGRAM Chemical_Formulas_2
```

Figure 10.3 *(cont.)*

Listing of `fil10-3.dat` **used in sample run:**

```
AGCL      Silver Chloride     0.0804
ALCL3     Aluminum Chloride   0.188
AUI       Gold Iodide         0.0404
BACO3     Barium Carbonate    0.0999
CACL2     Calcium Chloride    0.164
CACO3     Calcium Carbonate   0.203
FE2O3     Ferric Oxide        0.182
H2O2      Hydrogen Peroxide   0.471
KCL       Potassium Chloride  0.162
LIF       Lithium Flouride    0.373
NABR      Sodium Bromide      0.118
NACL      Sodium Chloride     0.204
PBBR2     Lead Bromide        0.0502
SIC       Silicon Carbide     0.143
SNCL2     Stannous Chloride   0.162
ZNSO4     Zinc Sulfate        0.174
```

Sample run:

```
Enter the maximum number of records in the file: 25
Enter name of file: fil10-3.dat

Enter formula to search for, (QUIT to stop): AGCL
Silver Chloride      has specific heat 0.0804

Enter formula to search for, (QUIT to stop): NACL
Sodium Chloride      has specific heat 0.2040

Enter formula to search for, (QUIT to stop): FECO3
     *** not found ***

Enter formula to search for, (QUIT to stop):FE2O3
     *** not found ***

Enter formula to search for, (QUIT to stop): FE2O3
Ferric Oxide         has specific heat 0.1820

Enter formula to search for, (QUIT to stop): ZNSO4
Zinc Sulfate         has specific heat 0.1740

Enter formula to search for, (QUIT to stop): QUIT
```

Quick Quiz 10.3

1. Programmer-defined types in Fortran are called _____ types, and an item of such a type is called a(n) _____.

2. (True or false) All components of a structure must have the same type.

3. Each component of a structure can be accessed using _____.

4. A structure contained inside another structure is called a(n) _____.

5. (True or false) One structure may be assigned to another provided they are of the same type.

6. Define a derived type for processing dates consisting of a month name, day of the month (number), and the year.

7. For a structure variable `Day` whose type is defined in Question 6, write a single assignment statement that assigns a value to `Day` that represents the date July 4, 1776.

8. Write statements to input a value for a structure variable `Day` whose type is defined in Question 6.

9. Define a derived type for processing inventory information including the name of an item (up to 20 characters), its stock number, and date received, which is a structure containing the month name, day, and year (see Question 6).

10. For a structure variable `Item` whose type is defined in Question 9, write a single assignment statement that assigns a value to `Item` that represents a camera with stock number 12384 that was received on December 10, 1995.

11. Write statements to input a value for a structure variable `Item` whose type is defined in Question 9.

Exercises 10.3

Exercises 1–11 assume the following declarations have been made:

```
TYPE PersonalComputer
   CHARACTER(10) :: Manufacturer
   INTEGER :: DiskSpace, RAM, ClockSpeed
   LOGICAL :: CDROM
END TYPE PersonalComputer

TYPE InventoryRecord
   INTEGER :: StockNumber
   TYPE(PersonalComputer) :: PC
   REAL, DIMENSION(6) :: ListPrice
END TYPE InventoryRecord
```

```
TYPE(PersonalComputer) :: MyPC
TYPE(PersonalComputer), DIMENSION(10) :: PCArray
TYPE(InventoryRecord) :: Item
```

Write statements to do what each exercise requests.

1. Assign the character string "IBM" to the appropriate component of `MyPC`.
2. Read a clock speed (in megahertz) and store it in the appropriate field of `MyPC`.
3. Display the disk space of `MyPC`.
4. Read an amount of RAM for `PCArray(5)`.
5. Display the manufacturer, disk space, amount of RAM, clock speed of `PCArray(3)`, and whether or not it contains a CD ROM.
6. Read values for the disk space, amount of RAM, and clock speed of each structure in the array `PCArray`.
7. Assign 11782 to the stock number in `Item`.
8. Read values for the disk space, amount of RAM, and clock speed for the personal computer stored in `Item`.
9. Display a message indicating whether the manufacturer of the personal computer stored in `Item` is Apple.
10. Assign a price of $1999.99 to the third list price in `Item`.
11. Display all of the prices in `Item`.

Suppose that the following type definition is added to those for Exercises 1–11:

```
TYPE OrderRecord
   INTEGER :: Quantity
   TYPE(InventoryRecord) :: Item
END TYPE OrderRecord
```

and suppose that `Order` is of type `OrderRecord`. For each of Exercises 12–15, write statements to do what is asked.

12. Read the stock number of the `Item` in `Order`.
13. Display all of the personal computer information in `Order` (in the field `Item`).
14. Assign a price of $3895.00 to the third list price of an item in `Order`.
15. Display all of the list prices in `Order` (in the component `Item`).

For Exercises 16–21, assume that `Shipment` is an array that records shipments of 20 different items, each of type `InventoryRecord`, where `InventoryRecord` is the record type defined in Exercises 1–11. Write statements to do what is asked.

16. Display the stock number of the fifth item shipped.
17. Read a list of stock numbers for all 20 items.

18. Display an appropriate message indicating whether the personal computers in the first shipment were manufactured by IBM.

19. Read the stock number, disk space, and amount of RAM for the tenth shipment.

20. Assign $1775.95 to the third list price in the second shipment.

21. Display a table of list prices in all of the shipments.

For Exercises 22–30, develop an appropriate record structure for the given information, and then write type declarations for the records.

22. Temperature (degrees and scale)

23. Time measured in hours, minutes, and seconds

24. Length measured in yards, feet, and inches

25. Angles measured in degrees, minutes, and seconds

26. Cards in a deck of playing cards

27. Description of an automobile (make, model, style, color, and so on)

28. Listings in a telephone directory

29. Teams in a baseball league (name, won–lost record, and so on)

30. Position of a checker on a board

For Exercises 31–33, write appropriate record declarations to describe the information in the files (see Appendix B).

31. STUDENT.DAT

32. INVENTOR.DAT

33. USERS.DAT

10.4 CREATING NEW DATA TYPES

A **data type** consists of a collection of values together with basic operations and relations that are defined on these values. For example, the type INTEGER in Fortran is a subset of the mathematical set of integers, $\{\ldots, -3, -2, -1, 0, 1, 2, 3, \ldots\}$ together with the basic arithmetic operations $+$, $-$, $*$, $/$, and $**$, and the relations $<$, $>$, $==$, $/=$, $<=$, and $>=$. Similarly, the type REAL is a subset of the set of real numbers together with the usual arithmetic operations and relations. The type LOGICAL has only two values, .TRUE. and .FALSE., and the basic operations are .NOT., .AND., .OR., .EQV., and .NEQV.. Values of type CHARACTER are strings of characters, and basic operations include concatenation and substring extraction (as described in Section 11.5).

We have seen how derived types are useful in organizing the data of certain problems, but the only intrinsic operation provided for derived types is the assignment operation (=). All other processing must be carried out using the individual components. In some cases, however, it would be convenient to define operations and relations on objects of these types. In this section, we show how this can be done by extending arithmetic operations, relational operators as well, and the assignment operation to new data types and by defining new operations.

Example: A `Rectangle` Data Type

To illustrate how new data types are implemented, we will construct a data type `Rectangle` for modeling rectangles whose sides are parallel to the *x*- and *y*-axes and have one vertex at the origin. Values of type `Rectangle` will be structures containing two components representing the two sides of a rectangle:

```
TYPE Rectangle
   REAL :: Side1, Side2
END TYPE Rectangle
```

The basic operations and relations we will consider are the following:

+	R1 + R2 is the smallest rectangle containing R1 and R2
.int.	R1 .int. R2 is the intersection of R1 and R2
*	c * R with c a scalar (number) is the rectangle obtained by scaling the sides of R by |c|
==	R1 == R2 is true if R1 and R2 have the same width and the same length

Other operations can be defined and implemented in much the same way.

The type definitions and the definitions of the basic operations are usually placed in a module so that this data type can be used in any program simply by importing it from that module. A module for the data type `Rectangle` might thus have the form

```
MODULE Rectangle_Type
!-------------------------------------------------------------
! Module to define the derived data type Rectangle for
! processing rectangles with sides parallel to the x- and y-
! axes and with one vertex at the origin.  Basic operations
! are:
!    +     : R1 + R2 is the smallest rectangle containing
!            R1 and R2
!   .int. : R1 .int. R2 is the intersection of  R1 and R2
!    *     : c * R where c is a scalar (number) is the
!            rectangle obtained by scaling the sides of R
!            by |c|
!    ==    : R1 == R2 is true if R1 and R2 have the same width
!            and the same length
!-------------------------------------------------------------
```

```
    TYPE Rectangle
       REAL :: Side1, Side2
    END TYPE Rectangle

    ! Basic operations and relations
            ⋮
 END MODULE Rectangle_Type
```

Extending Intrinsic Operations and Relations

Intrinsic operations such as + and * and intrinsic relations such as == can be extended to new data types by using interface blocks of the form

```
INTERFACE OPERATOR(Δ)
   MODULE PROCEDURE function-name
END INTERFACE
```

where Δ is the symbol for the operation or relation being extended and *function-name* is the name of a function that implements this operation. This function has one argument if the operator is a unary operator and two arguments if it is a binary operator. For a binary operator Δ, an expression of the form

$$operand_1 \ \Delta \ operand_2$$

is evaluated by using the function reference

$$function\text{-}name(operand_1, \ operand_2)$$

Similarly, if Δ is a unary operator, an expression of the form

$$\Delta operand$$

will be evaluated by using the function reference

$$function\text{-}name(operand)$$

For example, to extend the operator + to type Rectangle, we add the interface block

```
    INTERFACE OPERATOR(+)
       MODULE PROCEDURE Plus
    END INTERFACE
```

to the module Rectangle_Type and a module function Plus that carries out this operation:

```
!-Plus-----------------------------------------------------
! Function to implement the + operation on type Rectangle.
! Accepts:  Rectangles R1 and R2
! Returns:  R1 + R2
!-----------------------------------------------------------

FUNCTION Plus(R1, R2)

  TYPE(Rectangle) :: Plus
  TYPE(Rectangle), INTENT(IN) :: R1, R2

  Plus%Side1 = MAX(R1%Side1, R2%Side1)
  Plus%Side2 = MAX(R1%Side2, R2%Side2)

END FUNCTION Plus
```

The operands for a binary operator being extended need not be of the same type. For example, for a scalar multiple of a rectangle, c * R, the first operand is of type REAL and the second is of type Rectangle. To extend * in this manner, we would add the interface block

```
INTERFACE OPERATOR(*)
   MODULE PROCEDURE ScalarMultiple
END INTERFACE
```

to the module Rectangle_Type and a module function ScalarMultiple that carries out this operation:

```
!-ScalarMultiple-------------------------------------------
! Function to implement the * operation on type Rectangle.
! Accepts:  Real number c and Rectangle R
! Returns:  c * R
!-----------------------------------------------------------

FUNCTION ScalarMultiple(c, R)

  TYPE(Rectangle) :: ScalarMultiple
  REAL, INTENT(IN) :: c
  TYPE(Rectangle), INTENT(IN) :: R

  ScalarMultiple%Side1 = ABS(c) * R%Side1
  ScalarMultiple%Side2 = ABS(c) * R%Side2

END FUNCTION ScalarMultiple
```

Intrinsic relational operators can also be extended to new data types. For example, to extend == to type `Rectangle`, we would use the interface block

```
INTERFACE OPERATOR(==)
   MODULE PROCEDURE Equal
END INTERFACE
```

and a module function `Equal`:

```
!-Equal-------------------------------------------------------
! Function to implement the == relation on type Rectangle.
! Accepts:  Rectangles R1 and R2
! Returns:  Truth or falsity of logical expression R1 == R2
!-------------------------------------------------------------

FUNCTION Equal(R1, R2)

   LOGICAL :: Equal
   TYPE(Rectangle), INTENT(IN) :: R1, R2

   Equal = (R1%Side1 == R2%Side1) .AND. (R1%Side2 == R2%Side2)

END FUNCTION Equal
```

Public and Private Specifications

By default, all items in a module are accessible outside the module and thus are said to be *public*. But in some cases we may wish to deny access to certain items, that is, to make them *private*. For example, subprograms like `Plus`, `ScalarMultiple`, and `Equal` used to implement operations on a derived data type normally would not be accessible outside the module since it is not necessary to know anything about these functions to use the operations.

A **PRIVATE statement** of the form

```
PRIVATE :: list
```

can be used in the specification part of a module to declare that certain items in the module are to be private. For example, we would put the statement

```
PRIVATE :: Plus, ScalarMultiple, Equal
```

in the specification part of the module `Rectangle_Type` to declare that the functions `Plus`, `ScalarMultiple`, and `Equal` used to implement +, *, and ==, respectively, are not accessible outside the module.

An alternate way to control access to the items in a module is to set the default access to private using the statement

```
PRIVATE
```

and then list the items to be publicly accessible in a **PUBLIC statement** of the form

```
PUBLIC :: list
```

For example, we could set the default access for the module `Rectangle_Type` to private and make the type `Rectangle` and the operators +, *, and == accessible outside the module by using the statements

```
PRIVATE
PUBLIC :: Rectangle, OPERATOR(+), OPERATOR(*), OPERATOR(==)
```

For many new data types, access to the components used to store values of that type is not permitted. Programs and other modules are allowed to interface with the new type only by means of public operations. In this case, the components of the type can be declared to be private; for example,

```
TYPE Rectangle
   PRIVATE
   REAL :: Side1, Side2
END TYPE Rectangle
```

In addition to their use as statements, `PUBLIC` and `PRIVATE` can be used as attributes in declarations of items. For example, if `Alpha` and `Beta` are local real variables that are to be used only within a module, they might be declared as

```
REAL, PRIVATE :: Alpha, Beta
```

Defining New Operations

New operations can be defined for a data type. In this case, the symbol for the operation must have the form

```
.operator.
```

For example, to define the `.int.` operation for type `Rectangle`, we would add the interface block

```
INTERFACE OPERATOR(.int.)
   MODULE PROCEDURE Intersect
END INTERFACE
```

to module `Rectangle_Type` and function `Intersect` to implement this operation:

```
!-Intersect-----------------------------------------------
! Function to implement the .int. operation on type Rectangle.
! Accepts:  Rectangles R1 and R2
! Returns:  The intersection of R1 and R2
!----------------------------------------------------------

FUNCTION Intersect(R1, R2)

   TYPE(Rectangle) :: Intersect
   TYPE(Rectangle), INTENT(IN) :: R1, R2

   Intersect%Side1 = MIN(R1%Side1, R2%Side1)
   Intersect%Side2 = MIN(R1%Side2, R2%Side2)

END FUNCTION Intersect
```

Alternatively, we could use * for both the intersection operation and scalar multiplication. In this case, we would replace the two interface blocks with

```
INTERFACE OPERATOR(*)
   MODULE PROCEDURE ScalarMultiple
   MODULE PROCEDURE Intersect
END INTERFACE
```

If the expression 2.0 * R is encountered, where R is of type Rectangle, the compiler will use the function ScalarMultiple to evaluate this expression. For an expression R1 * R2, where R1 and R2 are of type Rectangle, it will use the function Intersect. An expression 2.0 * X, where X is of type REAL, will be evaluated using ordinary multiplication of real numbers.

An operator like * that can be applied to various types of operators is said to be **overloaded**. When the compiler encounters an expression containing an overloaded operator, it uses the types of the operands to determine which function to use to evaluate the expression. Consequently, *the formal arguments of any function that implements an operator must not have the same types as the formal arguments of another function that implements the same operator.*

Extending the Assignment Operation

Assignment is defined for arrays and structures, and since new data types are constructed using derived types and arrays, the assignment operation is also defined for them. For example, if R1 and R2 are of type Rectangle, we can assign a value to R1 using

```
R1 = Rectangle(2.5, 4.8)
```

This statement assigns the value 2.5 to the component `Side1` of `R1` and the value 4.8 to the component `Side2`. Similarly, the assignment statement

```
R2 = 2.0 * R1
```

assigns the values 5.0 and 9.6 to `R2%Side1` and `R2%Side2`, respectively.

This elementwise assignment is usually adequate, but in some cases, a different kind of assignment may be necessary or convenient. For example, to assign a value to `R1` so that it represents a square of side 2.5, we could use

```
R1 = Rectangle(2.5, 2.5)
```

but it would be more convenient to write

```
R1 = 2.5
```

(This is analogous to mixed-mode assignment of an integer value to a real variable.)

To extend the assignment operator to a new data type, an interface block of the form

```
INTERFACE ASSIGNMENT(=)
   MODULE PROCEDURE subroutine-name
END INTERFACE
```

is used. Here *subroutine-name* is the name of a subroutine having two arguments. The first is an `INOUT` argument, and the second is an `IN` argument. The effect of a call to this subroutine is to carry out the assignment

$$argument_1 = argument_2$$

For example, to extend = to allow assignment of a real value to a variable of type `Rectangle`, we could add the interface block

```
INTERFACE ASSIGNMENT(=)
   MODULE PROCEDURE Assign
END INTERFACE
```

to module `Rectangle_Type`. We would also add a subroutine `Assign` to implement this assignment:

```
!-Assign-----------------------------------------------------
! Subroutine to extend = to type Rectangle to allow statements
! of the form   Rectangle-variable = real-expression
! Accepts:  Rectangle R and real value RealValue
! Returns:  R with both its components set to RealValue
!------------------------------------------------------------
```

```
SUBROUTINE Assign(R, RealValue)

  TYPE(Rectangle), INTENT(INOUT) :: R
  REAL, INTENT(IN) :: RealValue

  R%Side1 = RealValue
  R%Side2 = RealValue

END SUBROUTINE Assign
```

Figure 10.4 shows the complete module `Rectangle_Type`, and Figure 10.5 shows a small driver program used to test the module.

Figure 10.4 The data type `Rectangle`.

```
MODULE Rectangle_Type
!-------------------------------------------------------------------
! Module to define the derived data type Rectangle for processing
! rectangles with sides parallel to the x- and y-axes and with
! one vertex at the origin.  Basic operations are:
!    +     : R1 + R2 is the smallest rectangle containing
!            R1 and R2
!   .int. : R1 .int. R2 is the intersection of R1 and R2
!    *     : c * R, where c is a scalar (number), is the
!            rectangle obtained by scaling the sides of R
!            by |c|
!   ==     : R1 == R2 is true if R1 and R2 have the same width
!            and the same length
!-------------------------------------------------------------------

  TYPE Rectangle
    REAL :: Side1, Side2
  END TYPE Rectangle

  ! Basic operations and relations

  INTERFACE OPERATOR(+)
    MODULE PROCEDURE Plus
  END INTERFACE

  INTERFACE OPERATOR(*)
    MODULE PROCEDURE ScalarMultiple
  END INTERFACE
```

Figure 10.4 *(cont.)*

```
  INTERFACE OPERATOR(==)
    MODULE PROCEDURE Equal
  END INTERFACE

  INTERFACE OPERATOR(.int.)
    MODULE PROCEDURE Intersect
  END INTERFACE

  INTERFACE ASSIGNMENT(=)
    MODULE PROCEDURE Assign
  END INTERFACE

CONTAINS

  !-Plus-------------------------------------------------------
  ! Function to implement the + operation on type Rectangle.
  ! Accepts:  Rectangles R1 and R2
  ! Returns:  R1 + R2
  !-----------------------------------------------------------

  FUNCTION Plus(R1, R2)

    TYPE(Rectangle) :: Plus
    TYPE(Rectangle), INTENT(IN) :: R1, R2

    Plus%Side1 = MAX(R1%Side1, R2%Side1)
    Plus%Side2 = MAX(R1%Side2, R2%Side2)

  END FUNCTION Plus

  !-ScalarMultiple---------------------------------------------
  ! Function to implement the * operation on type Rectangle.
  ! Accepts:  Real number c and Rectangle R
  ! Returns:  c * R
  !-----------------------------------------------------------

  FUNCTION ScalarMultiple(c, R)

    TYPE(Rectangle) :: ScalarMultiple
    REAL, INTENT(IN) :: c
    TYPE(Rectangle), INTENT(IN) :: R

    ScalarMultiple%Side1 = ABS(c) * R%Side1
    ScalarMultiple%Side2 = ABS(c) * R%Side2

  END FUNCTION ScalarMultiple
```

Figure 10.4 *(cont.)*

```
!-Equal-----------------------------------------------------------
! Function to implement the == relation on type Rectangle.
! Accepts:  Rectangles R1 and R2
! Returns:  Truth or falsity of logical expression R1 == R2
!----------------------------------------------------------------

FUNCTION Equal(R1, R2)

  LOGICAL :: Equal
  TYPE(Rectangle), INTENT(IN) :: R1, R2

  Equal = (R1%Side1 == R2%Side1) .AND. (R1%Side2 == R2%Side2)

END FUNCTION Equal

!-Intersect------------------------------------------------------
! Function to implement the .int. operation on type Rectangle.
! Accepts:  Rectangles R1 and R2
! Returns:  The intersection of R1 and R2
!----------------------------------------------------------------

FUNCTION Intersect(R1, R2)

  TYPE(Rectangle) :: Intersect
  TYPE(Rectangle), INTENT(IN) :: R1, R2

  Intersect%Side1 = MIN(R1%Side1, R2%Side1)
  Intersect%Side2 = MIN(R1%Side2, R2%Side2)

END FUNCTION Intersect

!-Assign---------------------------------------------------------
! Subroutine to extend = to type Rectangle to allow statements
! of the form Rectangle-variable = real-expression.
! Accepts:  Rectangle R and real value RealValue
! Returns:  R with both its components set to RealValue
!----------------------------------------------------------------

SUBROUTINE Assign(R, RealValue)

  TYPE(Rectangle), INTENT(INOUT) :: R
  REAL, INTENT(IN) :: RealValue
```

Figure 10.4 *(cont.)*

```
    R%Side1 = RealValue
    R%Side2 = RealValue

  END SUBROUTINE Assign

END MODULE Rectangle_Type
```

Figure 10.5 Testing data type `Rectangle`.

```
PROGRAM RectangleTester
!-----------------------------------------------------------------------
! Driver program to test the data type Rectangle defined in module
! Rectangle_Type.  Variables used are:
!   A, B, C : three rectangles
!    RealVal : a real value
! Input  : Sides of rectangles, a real value
! Output : Sides of rectangles
!-----------------------------------------------------------------------

  USE Rectangle_Type

  TYPE(Rectangle) :: A, B, C
  REAL :: RealVal

  PRINT *, "Enter the lengths of the sides of a rectangle:"
  READ *, A%Side1, A%Side2
  PRINT *, "Enter the lengths of the sides of another rectangle:"
  READ *, B%Side1, B%Side2

  PRINT *, "Testing the +, *, and == operations:"
  C = A + B
  PRINT *, "Sum of the rectangles: ",  C%Side1, C%Side2

  C = 2.0*A
  PRINT *, "2*(first rectangle): ",  C%Side1, C%Side2

  PRINT *, "Rectangles equal (T or F)? ", A == B

  PRINT *
  PRINT *, "Testing the .int. operation:"
  C = A .int. B
  PRINT *, "Intersection: ",  C%Side1, C%Side2
```

Figure 10.5 *(cont.)*

```
   PRINT *
   PRINT *, "Testing the extended assignment operation:"
   PRINT *, "Enter the length of a side of a square"
   READ *, RealVal
   C = RealVal
   PRINT *, "Square: ",  C%Side1, C%Side2

END PROGRAM RectangleTester
```

Sample run:<

```
Enter the lengths of the sides of a rectangle:
2.0, 5.0
Enter the lengths of the sides of another rectangle:
1.0, 6.0
Testing the +, *, and == operations:
Sum of the rectangles:    2.0000000    6.0000000
2*(first rectangle):    4.0000000   10.0000000
Rectangles equal (T or F)?   F

Testing the .int. operation:
Intersection:    1.0000000    5.0000000

Testing the extended assignment operation:
Enter the length of a side of a square
4
Square:    4.0000000    4.0000000
```

Defining Generic Subprograms

We have seen that several of the intrinsic operators in Fortran have been overloaded so that they can be applied to various types of operands. Several of the intrinsic subprograms in Fortran have also been overloaded so they can be applied to various types of arguments; for example, the ABS function can be used to find the absolute value of an integer value, of a real value, of a complex value, or of each element of a numeric array. Such subprograms are said to be **generic** subprograms.

It is also possible to extend or to define generic subprograms for new data types. The names of such subprograms are declared in interface blocks of the form

```
INTERFACE generic-name
   specific-interface-body₁
   specific-interface-body₂
      ⋮
   specific-interface-bodyₙ
END INTERFACE
```

where each *specific-interface-body$_i$* has the form described in Chapter 7 for external subprograms or one of the forms given in previous interface blocks for module procedures. They must all be functions or they must all be subroutines.

For example, suppose that module `Rectangle_Type` contains a function `RectArea`, which returns the area of a rectangle, and that another module `Circle_Type` contains a function `CircleArea`, which returns the area of a circle. To define a generic function called `Area` that could be used to find the area of either a rectangle or a circle, the following interface block might be used:

```
INTERFACE Area
   MODULE PROCEDURE RectArea
   MODULE PROCEDURE CircleArea
END INTERFACE Area
```

A reference `Area(R1)` where R1 is of type `Rectangle` will generate the reference `RectArea(R1)`, and a reference `Area(C1)` where C1 is of type `Circle` will generate the reference `CircleArea(C1)`.

CHAPTER REVIEW

Summary

In this chapter, we described derived types and structures and how they are used to process nonhomogenous data sets. We began by describing how derived types are defined, how derived type constructors are used, and how the component selector % is used to access the components of a structure. The last section of the chapter described how derived types can be used to construct new data types. Intrinsic operations can be extended to these new data types, and new operations can be defined. Several applications of structures are given, including processing computer-usage records, representing points in two dimensions, and processing the information in a chemical database.

FORTRAN SUMMARY

Declaration of Derived Types

```
TYPE type-name
   declaration₁
   declaration₂
      ⋮
   declarationₖ
END TYPE type-name
```

where *type-name* names the derived type and each *declaration$_i$* declares one or more components in a structure of this type.

Examples:

```
TYPE Computer_Usage_Info
   CHARACTER(15):: LastName, FirstName
   INTEGER :: IdNumber
   CHARACTER(6) :: Password
   INTEGER :: ResourceLimit
   REAL :: ResourcesUsed
END TYPE Computer_Usage_Info

TYPE Point
   REAL :: X, Y
END TYPE Point
```

Purpose:

Defines a derived type whose components are named and declared in $declaration_1$, $declaration_2$, ... These definitions are placed in the specification part of a program unit.

Declaration of Structures

```
TYPE(type-name) :: list-of-identifiers
```

Examples:

```
TYPE(Computer_Usage_Info) :: User1, User2
TYPE(Point) :: P, Q
```

Purpose:

Declares identifiers to be names of structures whose components are named and declared in the definition of derived type `type-name`.

Derived Type Constructors

```
type-name(list of component values)
```

Examples:

```
Point(2.5, 3.2)
Computer_Usage_Info("Babbage", "Charles", &
                    10101, "ADA", 750, 380.81)
```

Purpose:

Constructs a value of the specified derived type `type-name`.

Accessing Components

```
structure-name%component-name
```

Examples:

```
User%LastName
P%X
```

Purpose:
Constructs a *qualified variable* whose value is the value stored in the specified component of the structure.

Structure Assignment

```
structure-variable = structure-expression
```

where `structure-variable` and `structure-expression` must have the same type.

Examples:

```
User_2 = User_1
P = Point(2.5, 3.2)
```

Purpose:
Copies the components of one structure into another.

Interface Blocks for Extending and Defining Operators

```
INTERFACE OPERATOR(op)
  MODULE PROCEDURE function-name
END INTERFACE
```

where `op` is the symbol for the intrinsic operation being extended or has the form `.operation.` for a new operation, and `function-name` is the name of a function that implements this operation.

Examples:

```
INTERFACE OPERATOR(+)
  MODULE PROCEDURE Plus
END INTERFACE
```

```
INTERFACE OPERATOR(.int.)
   MODULE PROCEDURE Intersect
END INTERFACE
```

Purpose:

Extends or defines operator *op* for objects whose types are the types of the argument(s) of *function-name*. An expression of the form *x op y* is evaluated by *function-name(x, y)*.

Interface Block for Extending Assignment Operator

```
INTERFACE ASSIGNMENT(=)
   MODULE PROCEDURE subroutine-name
END INTERFACE
```

where *subroutine-name* is the name of a subroutine that implements the assignment.

Example:

```
INTERFACE ASSIGNMENT(=)
   MODULE PROCEDURE Assign
END INTERFACE
```

Purpose:

Extends the assignment operator to objects whose types are the types of the argument(s) of *subroutine-name*. A call to this subroutine carries out the assignment $argument_1 = argument_2$.

Interface Block for Defining Generic Subprograms

```
INTERFACE generic-name
   specific-interface-body₁
   specific-interface-body₂
        ⋮
   specific-interface-bodyₙ
END INTERFACE
```

where each *specific-interface-body$_i$* has the form described in Chapter 7 for external subprograms or the form

```
MODULE PROCEDURE subprogram-name
```

for module procedures. They must all be functions or they must all be subroutines.

Example:

```
INTERFACE Area
   MODULE PROCEDURE RectArea
   MODULE PROCEDURE CircleArea
END INTERFACE Area
```

Purpose:
Allows the subprogram *generic-name* to be referenced with arguments whose types are the types of arguments of any of the specific subprograms.

Public and Private Specifications

```
PUBLIC :: list
PRIVATE :: list
```

where each item in *list* is an identifier or has the form OPERATOR(Δ).

Example:

```
PUBLIC :: Rectangle, OPERATOR(+), OPERATOR(*), OPERATOR(==)
PRIVATE :: Plus, ScalarMultiple, Equal
```

Purpose:
These statements may be used in a module to specify the type of access (public or private) allowed for items in the module. PRIVATE and PUBLIC may also be used as attributes in declarations.

PROGRAMMING POINTERS

Program Style and Design

1. *A derived type is an appropriate data type to use for nonhomogeneous data collections, that is, those in which the items of information to be processed are of different types.* For example, in this chapter we considered computer-usage information consisting of a user's last name and first name (CHARACTER), id number (INTEGER), password (CHARACTER), resource limit (INTEGER), and resources used to date (REAL). Using a structure to store these data items makes it possible to treat them as a single object that can be passed to subprograms for processing. This would not be possible if individual simple variables were used to store these items.

2. *In a definition of a derived type, it is good style to indent and align the component declarations:*

```
TYPE type-name
   declaration₁
   declaration₂
      ⋮
   declarationₖ
END TYPE type-name
```

Potential Problems

1. *A component of a structure is accessed with a qualified variable of the form* `structure-name%component-name`. Using a component name without qualifying it with the name of the structure to which it belongs (by attaching the structure name to it) will in fact process a different item that has the same name as the component. For example, for the structure variable P declared by

```
TYPE Point
   REAL :: X, Y
END TYPE Point

TYPE(Point) :: P
```

the statement

```
PRINT *, X
```

will display the value of a variable or constant named X and not the first component of a structure of type `Point`.

2. *The scope of each component identifier is the structure in which it appears.* This means that
   - *The same identifier may not be used to name two different components within the same structure.*
   - *An identifier that names a component within a structure may be used for some other purpose outside that structure.*

3. *Structures cannot be read or written as units; instead, individual components must be read or written.* For example, if `InfoRec` is a structure of type `InformationRecord` defined by

```
TYPE AddressRecord
   CHARACTER(20) :: StreetAddress
   CHARACTER(12) :: City, State
   INTEGER :: ZipCode
END TYPE AddressRecord

TYPE InformationRecord
   CHARACTER(20) :: Name
```

```
        TYPE(AddressRecord)  ::  Address
        INTEGER :: Age
        CHARACTER(1) :: MaritalStatus
      END TYPE InformationRecord
```

its components can be displayed as follows:

```
      PRINT *, InfoRec%Name
      PRINT *, InfoRec%Address%StreetAddress
      PRINT *, InfoRec%Address%City, ",", InfoRec%Address%State, &
               InfoRec%Address%ZipCode
      PRINT *, "Age: ", InfoRec%Age
      PRINT *, "Marital Status: ", InfoRec%MaritalStatus
```

4. *In an assignment of one structure to another, the structures must have the same type.*

5. *Structures may be used as arguments in subprograms, but each actual argument must have the same type as the corresponding formal argument. The value of a function may be a structure.*

PROGRAMMING PROBLEMS

1. Extend the program in Figure 10.2 to find
   (a) The midpoint of the line segment joining two points.
   (b) The equation of the perpendicular bisector of this line segment.

2. The **point-slope** equation of a line having slope m and passing through point P with coordinates (x_1, y_1) is

$$y - y_1 = m(x - x_1)$$

   (a) Define a derived type for a line, given its slope and a point on the line.
   (b) Write a program that reads the slope of a line and the coordinates of a point on the line and then
      (i) Finds the point-slope equation of the line.
      (ii) Finds the slope-intercept equation of the line.
   (c) Write a program that reads the point and slope information for two lines and determines whether they intersect or are parallel. If they intersect, find the point of intersection and also determine whether they are perpendicular.

3. Write a program that accepts a time of day in military format and finds the corresponding standard representation in hours, minutes, and A.M/P.M., or accepts the time in the usual format and finds the corresponding military representation. For example, the input 0100 should produce 1:00 A.M. as output, and the input 3:45 P.M. should give 1545. Use a structure to store the time in the two formats.

4. Define a derived type for cards in a standard deck of 52 cards consisting of 4 suits (hearts, diamonds, spades, clubs) and 13 cards per suit. Then write a program to deal two 10-card hands from such a deck. (See Section 7.3 regarding random number generation.) Be sure that the same card is not dealt more than once.

5. Define derived types to store information about four geometric figures: circle, square, rectangle, and triangle. For a circle, the structure should store its radius and its center; for a square, the length of a side; for a rectangle, the lengths of two adjacent sides; and for a triangle, the lengths of the three sides. Then write a program that reads one of the letters C (circle), S (square), R (rectangle), T (triangle), and the appropriate numeric quantity or quantities for a figure of that type, and then calculates its area. For example, the input R 7.2 3.5 represents a rectangle with length 7.2 and width 3.5; and T 3 4 6.1 represents a triangle having sides of lengths 3, 4, and 6.1. (The area of a triangle can be found by using **Hero's formula:**

$$\text{area} = \sqrt{s(s-a)(s-b)(s-c)}$$

where a, b, and c are the lengths of the sides and s is one-half of the perimeter.)

6. Write a program to read the records in the file INVENTOR.DAT (see Appendix B) and store them in an array of structures, read a stock number entered by the user, and then search this array for the item having that stock number. If a match is found, the item name and number currently in stock should be displayed; otherwise, a message indicating that it was not found should be displayed.

7. Write a program to read the records in the file STUDENT.DAT (see Appendix B) and store them in an array of structures, sort them so that cumulative GPAs are in descending order, and then display the student numbers, names, majors, and GPAs of the records in this sorted array.

Section 10.4

8. Construct a data type Temperature for modeling temperatures. Use a structure with two components to store temperatures; one component stores degrees and other component stores the scale (F for Fahrenheit, C for Celsius, and possibly others). Develop and test a module that implements the following basic operations:
   - (a) Input   A subprogram that reads a value for a Temperature variable
   - (b) Output   A subprogram that displays the value of a Temperature expression
   - (c) ==   Determines if two temperatures are equal
   - (d) <   Determines if one temperature is less than another
   - (e) +

9. Construct a data type Time for processing time measured in both standard format (hours, minutes, A.M. or P.M.) and in military format. Develop and test a module that implements the following basic operations:
   - (a) Input   A subprogram that reads a value for a Time variable

   (b) Output   A subprogram that displays the value of a `Time` expression

   (c) ==

   (d) <

   (e) +

   (f) −

10. Construct a data type `Angle` for processing angles measured in degrees, minutes, and seconds; use a structure with three components to store an angle measurement. Develop and test a module that implements the following basic operations:

   (a) Input   A subprogram that reads a value for an `Angle` variable

   (b) Output   A subprogram that displays the value of an `Angle` expression

   (c) ==

   (d) <

   (e) +

   (f) −

11. Construct a data type `Fraction` for processing fractions, storing each fraction in a structure that has a numerator component and a denominator component. Develop and test a module that implements the following basic operations:

   (a) Input   A subprogram that reads a value for a `Fraction` variable

   (b) Output   A subprogram that displays the value of a `Fraction` expression

   (c) `.red.`   A unary operator that reduces a fraction to lowest terms

   (d) + $a/b + c/d = (ad + bc)/bd$ reduced to lowest terms

   (e) − $a/b − c/d = (ad − bc)/bd$ reduced to lowest terms

   (f) * $a/b * c/d = ac/bd$ reduced to lowest terms

   (g) / $a/b / c/d = ad/bc$ reduced to lowest terms

   (h) ==

   (i) <

   (j) >

12. Construct a data type `LongInt` for processing large integers of any length (see Programming Problems 15 and 16 of Chapter 8). Develop and test a module that implements the following basic operations:

   (a) Input   A subprogram that reads a value for a `LongInt` variable

   (b) Output   A subprogram that displays the value of a `LongInt` expression

   (c) +

   (d) −

   (e) ==

   (f) <

   (g) >

   (h) *

13. Construct a data type `Polynomial` for processing polynomials (see Programming Problems 12 and 13 of Chapter 8). Store polynomials in a structure in which one component stores the degree of the polynomial and another component is an array that stores its coefficients. Develop and test a module that implements the following basic operations:

   (a) Input   A subprogram that reads a value for a `Polynomial` variable

(b) Output   A subprogram that displays the value of a `Polynomial` expression

(c) +

(d) –

(e) ==

(f) `.deg.`   A unary operator that gives the degree of the polynomial

(g) `.eval.`   A binary operator whose operands are a polynomial and a real value and which produces the value of the polynomial at that real value

(h) *

FEATURES NEW TO FORTRAN 90

All of the features described in this chapter are new to Fortran 90:

- Derived types and structures
- Derived type constructors
- Component selector and qualified variables
- Modules
- Extension of intrinsic operations and relations to new data types
- Definitions of new operations on new data types
- Extension of assignment to new data types
- Generic subprograms
- Public and private specifications

11

Other Data Types

Ten decimals are sufficient to give the circumference of the earth to the fraction of an inch.

S. NEWCOMB

All such expressions as $\sqrt{-1}$, $\sqrt{-2}$, ... are neither nothing, nor greater than nothing, nor less than nothing, which necessarily constitutes them imaginary or impossible.

L. EULER

An average English word is four letters and a half. By hard, honest labor I've dug all the large words out of my vocabulary and shaved it down till the average is three and a half. ...

MARK TWAIN

*O*n most machines, 32 bits are used to store integers, which provides values in the range $-2,147,483,648$ through $2,147,483,647$; 32 bits are also commonly used for real values, also called *single-precision* values, which provides approximately seven digits of precision and a range of values from approximately -10^{38} to 10^{38}. In some computations, however, these ranges or this precision may be inadequate. To allow integers with larger (or smaller) ranges and to allow reals with larger (or smaller) ranges and more (or less) precision, Fortran 90 provides *parameterized* data types, which are described in this chapter.

A new numeric data type introduced in this chapter is the complex type. A **complex number** is a number of the form

$$a + bi$$

where *a* and *b* are real numbers and

$$i^2 = -1$$

The first real number, *a*, is called the **real part** of the complex number, and the second real number, *b*, is called the **imaginary part**.[1] In Fortran a complex number is represented as a pair of real numbers.

The character data type is also considered in this chapter. In earlier chapters we described character constants, character variables and their declarations, assignment of values to character variables, input and output of character data, and comparison of character values in a logical expression. In this chapter we consider some of the more advanced character-processing capabilities of Fortran.

11.1   PARAMETERIZED DATA TYPES

In Section 2.11, we considered the internal representation of data and noted that because of the finite length of memory words, most real numbers cannot be stored exactly. Even such "nice" decimal fractions as 0.1 do not have terminating binary representations and thus cannot be represented exactly in the computer's memory. In this connection, we observed in Section 3.2 that because of this approximate representation, logical expressions formed by comparing two real quantities with == often are evaluated as false, even though the quantities are algebraically equal. In particular, we observed in Figure 3.3 that even though

```
X * (1.0 / X)
```

is algebraically equal to 1 for all nonzero values of X, the logical expression

```
X * (1.0 / X) == 1.0
```

is false for most real values of X. We also observed that many other familiar algebraic equalities fail to hold for real data values.

As another example of the effect of approximate representation, consider again the following program, used in Section 2.11 to illustrate the effect of roundoff error:

```
PROGRAM Demo_1

   IMPLICIT NONE
   REAL :: A, B, C

   READ *, A, B
   C = ((A + B) ** 2 - 2.0 * A * B - B ** 2) / A ** 2
   PRINT *, C

END PROGRAM Demo_1
```

The following table shows the output produced by one computer system for various values of A and B:

---

[1] It is customary in electrical engineering to use *j* instead of *i* to denote the complex number $\sqrt{-1}$. This helps to avoid confusion with *I* or *i* used to denote current.

A	B	C
0.5	888.0	1.0000000
0.1	888.0	-6.2499995
0.05	888.0	-24.9999981
0.03	888.0	69.4444427
0.02	888.0	$1.5625000E+02$

Except for the first value, the values of C are completely inaccurate. They should all be 1.0, since the expression

$$\frac{(A + B)^2 - 2AB - B^2}{A^2}$$

used to compute C simplifies to

$$\frac{A^2}{A^2}$$

and thus is identically 1 (provided $A \neq 0$).

For computations in which more (or less) precision is needed than is available using the default real data type, Fortran provides parameterized real types. When the preceding program was executed with A, B, and C declared to have twice as much precision, the value displayed for C differed from 1 by less than 0.0000003 for the given values for A and B.

Parameterized Type Declarations

A parameterized type declaration has the form

Parameterized Type Declaration

Forms:

```
type-specifier(KIND = kind-number), attributes :: list
```

or

```
type-specifier(kind-number), attributes :: list
```

where
    `type-specifier` is usually one of the following:

```
INTEGER
REAL
```

```
COMPLEX
LOGICAL
```

kind-number, called a **kind type parameter**, is a positive integer constant or a constant integer expression whose value is positive;
attributes is a list of attributes and may be omitted (along with the comma preceding them); and
list is a list of identifiers, separated by commas.

Purpose:
Declares that the identifiers in *list* have the specified type and kind.

The kind numbers for the various types are machine and compiler dependent. There must be at least two kinds of real types, one for single-precision values and another for **double-precision** values, which provides approximately twice as many significant digits as single precision. The kind numbers for these two types typically are 1 and 2:

Type	Kind Number	Description
REAL	1	Single-precision values with approximately 7 significant digits; usually stored in 32 bits (normally the default real type)
REAL	2	Double-precision values with approximately 14 significant digits; usually stored in 64 bits

For example,

```
REAL(KIND = 2) :: Z
REAL(KIND = 2), DIMENSION(5, 5) :: Beta
```

declare the variable Z and the 5×5 array Beta to be real variables of kind 2 (commonly, double precision).

The number of kinds of integer types varies from one Fortran compiler to another, but most compilers provide at least three, and some provide four kinds:

Type	Kind Number	Description
INTEGER	1	8-bit integers: -2^7 through $2^7 - 1$
INTEGER	2	16-bit integers: -2^{15} through $2^{15} - 1$
INTEGER	3	32-bit integers: -2^{31} through $2^{31} - 1$
INTEGER	4	64-bit integers: -2^{63} through $2^{63} - 1$

Parameterized LOGICAL types are provided primarily for consistency with the other data types. They are seldom used, and there is no requirement that a compiler support more than one kind. Parameterized COMPLEX and CHARACTER types are also provided and are described in Sections 11.3 and 11.5, respectively.

Intrinsic Functions for Use with Parameterized Types

Because the number of integer and real kinds and their meaning differ from one compiler to another, Fortran provides several intrinsic functions for use with parameterized types. Two of the most useful functions are SELECTED_REAL_KIND and SELECTED_INT_KIND because they facilitate writing programs that are portable from one machine to another. A reference to SELECTED_REAL_KIND has the form

```
SELECTED_REAL_KIND(p, r)
```

where p and r are integers, with r optional. It returns a kind type parameter that will provide at least p decimal digits of precision and a range of at least -10^r to 10^r, provided such a kind is available. It returns -1 if there is no kind with the requested range, -2 if there is no kind with the requested precision, and -3 if no kind with either the requested range or precision is available. For example, the statement

```
REAL(KIND = SELECTED_REAL_KIND(20, 50)) :: X
```

declares that X is to be a real variable whose values are to have at least 20 decimal digits of precision and may be in the range -10^{50} to 10^{50}. If no such kind is available, the specified kind number is negative and the declaration causes a compilation error. The statements

```
INTEGER, PARAMETER :: Prec10 = SELECTED_REAL_KIND(10)
REAL(KIND = Prec10) :: A, B
```

declare that A and B are real variables whose values are to have at least 10 decimal digits of precision. This declaration cannot fail, because, as we have noted, a real kind that provides approximately 14 digits of precision must be supported.

The intrinsic function PRECISION can be used to determine the precision of a real or complex value (which may be an array). A reference to this function has the form

```
PRECISION(expression)
```

and returns the number of digits of precision for the expression. Thus, for the variable A just declared, PRECISION(A) would return the value 10. A reference to the function RANGE,

```
RANGE(expression)
```

returns the decimal exponent range of the expression, that is, the exponent r for which -10^r to 10^r is the range of values of the expression.

A reference to `SELECTED_INT_KIND` has the form

```
SELECTED_INT_KIND(r)
```

where r is an integer. It returns a kind type parameter that will provide a range of at least -10^r to 10^r if such a kind is available; otherwise, it returns -1. For example, the statements

```
INTEGER, PARAMETER :: Range20 = SELECTED_INT_KIND(20)
INTEGER(KIND = Range20) :: M, N
```

declare that M and N are integer variables whose values may have up to 20 digits. If no such integer kind is available, a compiler error will result.

The intrinsic function `KIND` can be used to find kind numbers. A reference to it has the form

```
KIND(expression)
```

and returns the kind number of the expression. For example, the value returned by

```
KIND(1.23)
```

would typically be 1.

Several of the intrinsic functions considered earlier may also have an optional kind argument. These include `AINT`, `ANINT`, `INT`, `NINT`, and `REAL`. For example, the statement

```
M = INT(A, KIND = KIND(M))
```

or simply

```
M = INT(A, KIND(M))
```

can be used to convert the value of the real variable A to an integer whose kind number is `Range20` and assigns this value to M. For the variable M declared above, these statements could also be written

```
M = INT(A, KIND = Range20)
```

or

```
M = INT(A, Range20)
```

Other intrinsic functions that may be used with parameterized types are described in the following sections and in Appendix D.

Specifying Kinds of Constants

To specify the kind of a constant, an underscore (_) followed by a kind number is appended to the constant (except for characters as noted in Section 11.5). For example,

```
123456789_3
```

is an integer constant whose kind number is 3, and

```
12345678901234567890_Range20
```

is an integer constant whose kind number is `Range20`, where `Range20` is the named constant defined earlier by

```
INTEGER, PARAMETER :: Range20 = SELECTED_INT_KIND(20)
```

Similarly,

```
1.23456789123_2
```

is a real constant whose kind number is 2, and

```
0.1234554321_Prec10
```

is a real constant whose kind number is `Prec10`, where the named constant `Prec10` was defined earlier by

```
INTEGER, PARAMETER :: Prec10 = SELECTED_REAL_KIND(10)
```

When a value is assigned to a parameterized real variable in a program, it is important that the kind of the value being assigned is the same as the kind of the variable. For example, consider the following program:

```
PROGRAM Demo_2

   IMPLICIT NONE
   REAL :: X
   INTEGER, PARAMETER :: DP = SELECTED_REAL_KIND(14)
   REAL(KIND = DP) :: A, B
```

```
X = 0.1
B = 0.1_DP
A = X
PRINT *, A
A = B
PRINT *, A

END PROGRAM Demo_2
```

On some systems, the values displayed for A by the first two PRINT statements resemble the following:

```
0.1000000014901161
0.1000000000000000
```

The value 0.1_DP of the real variable B of kind DP is stored with more precision than the value 0.1 of the single-precision variable X. This accounts for the discrepancy between the two values displayed for A.

It is also important to ensure that all variables, arrays, and functions that are to have values of a particular kind are declared to be of that kind. For example, if R is a real variable of kind DP and Area is an ordinary (single-precision) real variable, the computation in the statement

```
Area = 3.1415926535898_DP * R ** 2
```

will be carried out in extended precision, but the resulting value will then be assigned to the single-precision variable Area, thus losing approximately half of the significant digits.

As these examples illustrate, although mixed-kind expressions are permitted, accuracy may be lost because of the presence of lower-precision constants or variables. For example, if the assignment statement

```
A = (B + 3.7) ** 2
```

were used in the program Demo_2, the value for A would be limited to single-precision accuracy because of the single-precision constant 3.7. To ensure that the expression has the same kind as A, the assignment statement

```
A = (B + 3.7_DP) ** 2
```

should be used.

11.2 APPLICATION: ILL-CONDITIONED LINEAR SYSTEMS

Problem

In Section 9.7, we considered the problem of solving systems of linear equations. Such systems arise in the analysis of electrical networks, in analyzing statical systems, in finding least-squares approximations, in solving differential equations, and in many other problems in science and engineering.

Some linear systems, called *ill-conditioned systems*, are very difficult to solve accurately. One characteristic of such systems is that they are very sensitive to perturbations of the coefficients and constant terms. Small changes in one or more of these coefficients or constants may produce large changes in the solution. For example, consider the linear system

$$(\text{I}) \qquad 2x + 6y \qquad\quad = 8$$
$$2x + 6.0000003y = 8.0000003$$

for which the solution is

$$x = 1$$
$$y = 1$$

If this linear system is changed to

$$(\text{II}) \qquad 2x + 6y \qquad\quad = 8$$
$$2x + 6.0000003y = 7.9999994$$

the solution becomes

$$x = 10$$
$$y = -2$$

The change in the solution is on the order of 10^7 times the change in the constant term in the second equation.

Solution

When these linear systems were solved using the program in Figure 9.10 for solving linear systems with Gaussian elimination, the results were

$$x = 4.000$$
$$y = 0.000$$

for system (I) and

$$x = 7.000$$

$$y = -1.000$$

for system (II).

The program in Figure 11.1 uses double-precision variables and constants in the computations involved in Gaussian elimination. Note that in the sample runs, the correct solutions to these linear systems are obtained.

Figure 11.1 Gaussian elimination.

```
PROGRAM Linear_Systems
!-----------------------------------------------------------------------
! Program to solve a linear system using Gaussian elimination.
! Identifiers used are:
!   DP               : kind number for double precision
!   N                : number of equations and unknowns
!   AllocateStatus   : status variable for ALLOCATE
!   LinSys           : matrix for the linear system
!   X                : solution
!   I, J             : subscripts
!   Singular         : indicates if system is (nearly) singular
!
! Input:    The number of equations, the coefficients, and the
!           constants of the linear system
! Output:   The solution of the linear system or a message indicating
!           that the system is (nearly) singular
!-----------------------------------------------------------------------

  IMPLICIT NONE
  INTEGER, PARAMETER :: DP = SELECTED_REAL_KIND(14)
  REAL(KIND = DP), DIMENSION(:, :), ALLOCATABLE :: LinSys
  REAL(KIND = DP), DIMENSION(:), ALLOCATABLE :: X
  INTEGER :: N, AllocateStatus, I, J
  LOGICAL :: Singular

  ! Read N and allocate N x (N + 1) matrix LinSys
  ! and one-dimensional array X of size N

  WRITE (*, '(1X, A)', ADVANCE = "NO")  "Enter number of equations: "
  READ *, N
  ALLOCATE(LinSys(N, N+1), X(N), STAT = AllocateStatus)
  IF (AllocateStatus /= 0) STOP "*** Not enough memory ***"
```

Figure 11.1 *(cont.)*

```
! Read coefficients and constants

DO I = 1, N
   PRINT *, "Enter coefficients and constant of equation", I, ":"
   READ *, (LinSys(I,J), J = 1, N + 1)
END DO

! Use subroutine Gaussian_Elimination to find the solution,
! and then display the solution

CALL Gaussian_Elimination(LinSys, N, X, Singular)
IF (.NOT. Singular) THEN
   PRINT *, "Solution is:"
   DO I = 1, N
      PRINT '(1X, "X(", I2, ") =", F8.3)', I, X(I)
   END DO
ELSE
   PRINT *, "Matrix is (nearly) singular"
END IF

DEALLOCATE(LinSys, X)

CONTAINS

!-Gaussian_Elimination-------------------------------------------
! Subroutine to find solution of a linear system of N equations in N
! unknowns using Gaussian elimination, provided a unique solution
! exists.  The coefficients and constants of the linear system are
! stored in the double-precision matrix LinSys and the solution in
! the double-precision array X.  If the system is singular, Singular
! is returned as true, and the solution X is undefined.  Local
! variables used are:
!   I, J       : subscripts
!   Multiplier : multiplier used to eliminate an unknown
!   AbsPivot   : absolute value of pivot element
!   PivotRow   : row containing pivot element
!   Epsilon    : a small positive real value ("almost zero")
!   Temp       : used to interchange rows of matrix
!
! Accepts: Two-dimensional array LinSys and integer N
! Returns: One-dimensional array X and logical value Singular
!----------------------------------------------------------------

   SUBROUTINE Gaussian_Elimination(LinSys, N, X, Singular)
```

Figure 11.1 *(cont.)*

```fortran
INTEGER, INTENT(IN) :: N
REAL(KIND = DP), DIMENSION (N, N+1), INTENT(IN) :: LinSys
REAL(KIND = DP), DIMENSION(N), INTENT(OUT) :: X
LOGICAL, INTENT(OUT) :: Singular
REAL(KIND = DP), DIMENSION(N+1) :: Temp
REAL(KIND = DP) :: AbsPivot, Multiplier
REAL(KIND = DP), PARAMETER :: Epsilon = 1E-15_DP
INTEGER :: PivotRow

Singular = .FALSE.
DO I = 1, N

   ! Locate pivot element

   AbsPivot = ABS(LinSys(I, I))
   PivotRow = I
   DO J = I + 1, N
      IF (ABS(LinSys(J,I)) > AbsPivot) THEN
         AbsPivot = ABS(LinSys(J,I))
         PivotRow = J
      END IF
   END DO

   ! Check if matrix is (nearly) singular

   IF (AbsPivot < Epsilon) THEN
      Singular = .TRUE.
      RETURN
   END IF

   ! It isn't, so interchange rows PivotRow and I if necessary

   IF (PivotRow /= I) THEN
      Temp(I:N+1) = LinSys(I, I:N+1)
      LinSys(I, I:N+1) = LinSys(PivotRow, I:N+1)
      LinSys(PivotRow, I:N+1) = Temp(I:N+1)
   END IF

   ! Eliminate Ith unknown from equations I + 1, ..., N

   DO J = I + 1, N
      Multiplier = -LinSys(J,I) / LinSys(I,I)
      LinSys(J, I:N+1) = LinSys(J, I:N+1)  &
                      + Multiplier * LinSys(I, I:N+1)
   END DO

END DO
```

Figure 11.1 *(cont.)*

```
    ! Find the solutions by back substitution

    X(N) = LinSys(N, N + 1) / LinSys(N,N)
    DO J = N - 1, 1, -1
       X(J) = (LinSys(J, N + 1) -    &
               SUM(LinSys(J, J+1:N) * X(J+1:N))) / LinSys(J,J)
    END DO

  END SUBROUTINE Gaussian_Elimination

END PROGRAM Linear_Systems
```

Sample runs:

```
Enter number of equations: 2
Enter coefficients and constant of equation 1:
2  6  8
Enter coefficients and constant of equation 2:
2  6.0000003  8.0000003
Solution is:
X( 1) =    1.000
X( 2) =    1.000


Enter number of equations: 2
Enter coefficients and constant of equation 1:
2  6  8
Enter coefficients and constant of equation 2:
2  6.0000003  7.9999994
Solution is:
X( 1) =   10.000
X( 2) =   -2.000
```

It should be noted that although extended precision reduces the effects of limited precision, it is not a panacea. Simply declaring everything in the program to have higher precision does not avoid all of the problems caused by single precision, because even extended-precision representations of most real numbers still are only approximate.

11.3 THE COMPLEX DATA TYPE

Although the complex number system has many important applications, it is perhaps not as familiar as the real number system. Thus, in this section, we review the basic properties of and operations on complex numbers and describe how they are represented and used in Fortran programs.

Representation of Complex Numbers

Since complex numbers have two parts, a real part and an imaginary part, they can be plotted in a coordinatized plane by taking the horizontal axis to be the real axis and the vertical axis to be the imaginary axis, so that the complex number $a + bi$ is represented as the point $P(a, b)$:

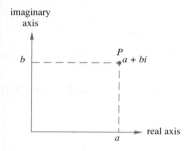

An alternative geometric representation is to associate the complex number $z = a + bi$ with the vector $\overrightarrow{OP}$ from the origin to the point $P(a, b)$:

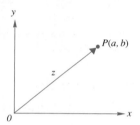

In Fortran, a complex constant is represented as a pair of real constants

```
(a, b)
```

where a and b represent the real part and the imaginary part of the complex number, respectively. For example,

```
(1.0, 1.0)
(-6.0, 7.2)
(-5.432, -1.4142)
```

are complex constants equivalent to

$$1.0 + 1.0i$$

$$-6.0 + 7.2i$$

$$-5.432 - 1.4142i$$

respectively.

The COMPLEX Type Statement

The names of variables, arrays, or functions that are complex may be any legal Fortran names, but their types must be declared using the **COMPLEX type statement.** For example, the statements

```
COMPLEX :: A, B
COMPLEX, DIMENSION(10,10) :: Rho
```

declare A, B, and the 10×10 array Rho to be complex variables. The statements

```
INTEGER, PARAMETER :: DP = SELECTED_REAL_KIND(14)
COMPLEX(KIND = DP) :: Gamma
```

or

```
INTEGER, PARAMETER :: DP = SELECTED_REAL_KIND(14)
COMPLEX(DP) :: Gamma
```

declare Gamma to be a variable whose type is complex of kind DP. For a complex value, this means that both the real part and the imaginary part are real values of kind DP (that is, both are double-precision values).

Operations on Complex Numbers

The **sum** of two complex numbers $z = a + bi$ and $w = c + di$ is

$$z + w = (a + c) + (b + d)i$$

If vector representation is used for complex numbers, this corresponds to the usual sum of vectors; that is, the vector representing $z + w$ is the sum of the vectors representing z and w:

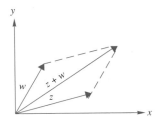

Similarly, the **difference** of z and w defined by

$$z - w = (a - c) + (b - d)i$$

corresponds to vector subtraction:

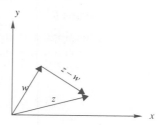

The **product** of two complex numbers $z = a + bi$ and $w = c + di$ is

$$z \cdot w = (ac - bd) + (ad + bc)i$$

This complex number is represented by a vector whose magnitude is the product of the magnitudes of the vectors representing z and w and whose angle of inclination is the sum $\theta_1 + \theta_2$ of the angles of inclination of the vectors:

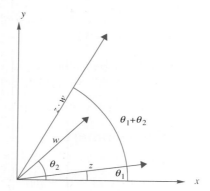

To see why this geometric representation of the product of two complex numbers is correct, it is helpful to consider the **polar representation** of complex numbers. To describe this representation, consider a vector $\overrightarrow{OP}$ from the origin to point P, and suppose that r is the length of $\overrightarrow{OP}$ and that θ is the angle from the positive x-axis to $\overrightarrow{OP}$, so that the polar coordinates of point P are (r, θ):

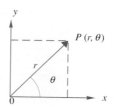

It is clear from this diagram that the relation between the rectangular coordinates (a, b) of point P and its polar coordinates (r, θ) is

$$a = r \cos \theta$$

$$b = r \sin \theta$$

It follows that the complex number represented by $\overrightarrow{OP}$ can be written in polar form as

$$r \cos \theta + ir \sin \theta = r(\cos \theta + i \sin \theta)$$

A basic property of complex numbers is that

$$e^{i\theta} = \cos \theta + i \sin \theta$$

and thus an alternative form of the polar representation of a complex number is

$$re^{i\theta}$$

Now consider two complex numbers:

$$z = r_1 e^{i\theta_1}$$

$$w = r_2 e^{i\theta_2}$$

The familiar properties of exponents then give

$$z \cdot w = (r_1 e^{i\theta_1})(r_2 e^{i\theta_2}) = r_1 r_2 e^{i(\theta_1 + \theta_2)}$$

which agrees with the geometric representation of the product of two complex numbers described earlier.

The **quotient** of two complex numbers z and w is

$$\frac{z}{w} = \frac{ac + bd}{c^2 + d^2} + \frac{bc - ad}{c^2 + d^2} i \quad \text{(provided } c^2 + d^2 \neq 0)$$

In the same manner as for multiplication, we can use polar representation and properties of exponents to show that this quotient corresponds to a vector whose magnitude is the quotient of the magnitudes of the vectors representing z and w and whose angle of inclination is the difference $\theta_1 - \theta_2$ of the vectors' angles of inclination.

These basic arithmetic operations for complex numbers are denoted in Fortran by the usual operators +, -, *, /, and **. Mixed-mode expressions and assignments involving integer, real, and complex values are allowed. For example, suppose that C and Z are complex variables, with the value of C given by

```
C = (6.2, 2.4)
```

Then the assignment statement

```
Z = 4.0 * C / 2
```

assigns the complex value (12.4, 4.8) to Z. If this same expression is assigned to the real variable X,

```
X = 4.0 * C / 2
```

only the real part of the expression's value is assigned to X; thus, X has the value 12.4. Similarly, if N is an integer variable, the statement

```
N = 4.0 * C / 2
```

assigns the integer part of this value to N, so that N has the value 12.

The only relational operators that may be used with complex values are == and /=. Two complex values are **equal** if, and only if, their real parts are equal and their imaginary parts are equal.

Complex Functions

Some of the mathematical functions commonly used with complex numbers are the absolute value, conjugate, and complex exponential functions. For the complex number $z = a + bi$, these functions are defined as follows:

Absolute value:	$\|z\| = \sqrt{a^2 + b^2}$
Conjugate:	$\bar{z} = a - bi$
Complex exponential:	$e^z = e^a(\cos b + i \sin b)$

If vector representation is used for complex numbers, $|z|$ is the magnitude of the vector representing z; $\bar{z}$ is represented by the vector obtained by reflecting the vector representing z in the x-axis; and the complex exponential e^z is associated with the polar representation of z.

These three functions are implemented in Fortran by the library functions ABS, CONJG, and EXP, respectively. Several of the other library functions listed in Table 6.1, such as SIN, COS, and LOG, may also be used with complex arguments. Three library functions that are useful in converting from real type to complex type, and vice versa, are

AIMAG(z)	Gives the imaginary part of the complex argument z as a real value whose kind is the same as the kind of z
CMPLX(x, y, KIND = k) or CMPLX(x, KIND = k)	Converts the two integer, real, or double-precision arguments x and y into a complex number. The first argument x becomes the real part of the complex number, and the second argument y becomes the imaginary part. The second form is equivalent to CMPLX(x, 0, KIND = k). The KIND = specifier is optional.
REAL(z, KIND = k)	Gives the real part of the complex argument z. The KIND = specifier is optional.

Complex I/O

Complex values may be read using a list-directed READ statement, with the complex numbers entered as pairs of real numbers enclosed in parentheses. They may also be read using a formatted READ statement. In this case, a pair of F, E, EN, ES, or G descriptors is used for each complex value to be read, and parentheses are not used to enclose the parts of the complex number when it is entered. Complex values displayed using a list-directed output statement appear as a pair of real values separated by a comma and enclosed within parentheses. For formatted output of complex values, a pair of F, E, EN, ES, or G descriptors is used for each complex value.

The following program illustrates the input and output of complex numbers and complex arithmetic:

```
PROGRAM Demo_3

   IMPLICIT NONE
   COMPLEX :: X, Y, W, Z, A

   READ *, X, Y
   READ '(2F2.0)', W
   PRINT *, X, Y
   PRINT *, W
   PRINT 10, X, Y, W
10 FORMAT(1X, F5.2, " +", F8.2, "I")
   Z = (X + Y) / (1.0,2.2)
   A = X * Y
   PRINT 10, Z, A

END PROGRAM Demo_3
```

If the following data is entered,

```
(3,4), (0.75,-2.23)
 5 7
```

the output produced will be

```
(  3.0000000,   4.0000000) (  0.7500000,  -2.2300000)
(  5.0000000,   7.0000000)
  3.00 +     4.00I
  0.75 +    -2.23I
  5.00 +     7.00I
  1.31 +    -1.11I
 11.17 +    -3.69I
```

Example: Solving Equations

Quadratic Equations. In Section 3.2, we considered the problem of solving quadratic equations

$$Ax^2 + Bx + C = 0$$

and noted that if the discriminant $B^2 - 4AC$ is negative, there are no real roots. In this case, the quadratic equation has two complex solutions, which can be found by using the quadratic formula. For example, the discriminant for the equation

$$x^2 + 2x + 5 = 0$$

is

$$2^2 - 4 \cdot 1 \cdot 5 = -16$$

and so the roots are complex. The quadratic formula gives the roots

$$\frac{-2 \pm \sqrt{-16}}{2} = \frac{-2 \pm 4i}{2} = -1 \pm 2i$$

The program in Figure 11.2 reads the complex coefficients A, B, and C of a quadratic equation, uses the quadratic formula to calculate the roots, and displays them as complex numbers.

Figure 11.2 Quadratic equations—complex roots.

```
PROGRAM Complex_Quadratic_Equations
!-----------------------------------------------------------------
! Program to solve a quadratic equation having complex coefficients
! using the quadratic formula.  Variables used are:
!    A, B, C           : the coefficients of the quadratic equation
!    Discriminant      : square root of B ** 2 - 4 * A * C
!    Root_1, Root_2    : the two roots of the equation
!    Response          : user response to "more data" query
!
! Input:   The coefficients A, B, and C
! Output: The two roots of the equation
!-----------------------------------------------------------------

  IMPLICIT NONE
  CHARACTER(1) :: Response
  COMPLEX :: A, B, C, Discriminant, Root_1, Root_2
```

Figure 11.2 *(cont.)*

```
  DO
     ! Get the coefficients
     PRINT *, "Enter the coefficients of the quadratic equation as"
     PRINT *, "complex numbers of the form (a, b):"
     READ *, A, B, C

     ! Calculate the discriminant
     Discriminant = SQRT(B**2 - 4.0*A*C)

     ! Find the roots
     Root_1 = (-B + Discriminant) / (2.0 * A)
     Root_2 = (-B - Discriminant) / (2.0 * A)
     PRINT *, "The roots are:"
     PRINT '(5X, F7.3, " +", F7.3, "I")', Root_1, Root_2

     WRITE (*, '(/ 1X, A)', ADVANCE = "NO") "More data (Y or N)? "
     READ *, Response
     IF (Response == "N") EXIT
  END DO

END PROGRAM Complex_Quadratic_Equations
```

Sample run:

```
Enter the coefficients of the quadratic equation as
complex numbers of the form (a, b):
(1,0), (-5,0), (6,0)
The roots are:
     3.000 +   0.000I
     2.000 +   0.000I

More data (Y or N)? Y
Enter the coefficients of the quadratic equation as
complex numbers of the form (a, b):
(1,0), (2,0), (5,0)
The roots are:
    -1.000 +   2.000I
    -1.000 + -2.000I

More data (Y or N)? Y
Enter the coefficients of the quadratic equation as
complex numbers of the form (a, b):
(1,0), (0,0), (1,0)
The roots are:
     0.000 +   1.000I
     0.000 + -1.000I

More data (Y or N)? N
```

Polynomial Equations. For higher-degree polynomials, there is no general formula analogous to the quadratic formula for finding roots. For such polynomials, we can use Newton's method, as described in Section 6.3, to approximate a real root if there is one. However, as the preceding example with quadratic equations demonstrates, a polynomial equation may have no real roots. In this case, Newton's method can still be used to find a complex root. Modifying the program in Figure 6.4 to use Newton's method to find complex roots of polynomials is left as an exercise (see Programming Problem 7).

Linear Systems. In Section 9.7, we considered the problem of determining the loop currents in a direct-current (d-c) circuit and found these currents by solving a system of linear equations. Whereas the current, voltage, and resistance of a d-c circuit can be represented by real numbers, these same quantities are represented by complex numbers for alternating-current (a-c) circuits. Consequently, the equations in a linear system for finding loop currents in an a-c circuit have coefficients that are complex numbers. Such a system can be solved using the Gaussian elimination method if the real operations are replaced by complex operations.

11.4   APPLICATION: A-C CIRCUITS

Problem

An a-c circuit contains a capacitor, an inductor, and a resistor in series:

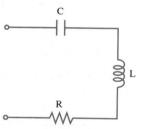

A program must be written to calculate the current in this circuit for several frequencies and voltages.

Solution

Specification. The input to the problem will be the resistance, the inductance, the capacitance, the frequency of the a-c source, and the voltage. The output will be the current in the circuit. Thus, a specification for the problem is as follows:

Input: Resistance (ohms)
Inductance (henrys)
Capacitance (farads)
Frequency (radians/second)
Voltage (volts)

Output: Current (amperes)

Design. The impedance Z_R for a resistor is simply the resistance R, but for inductors and capacitors, it is a function of the frequency. The impedance Z_L of an inductor is the complex value given by

$$Z_L = \omega L i$$

where ω is the frequency (in radians per second) of the a-c source and L is the self-inductance (in henrys). For a capacitor, the impedance is

$$Z_C = \frac{-i}{\omega C}$$

where C is the capacitance (in farads). The total impedance Z is then given by

$$Z = Z_R + Z_L + Z_C$$

and the current I by

$$I = \frac{V}{Z}$$

An algorithm for this problem is straightforward:

ALGORITHM FOR A-C CIRCUIT PROBLEM

Algorithm to compute the current in an a-c circuit containing a capacitor, an inductor, and a resistor in series.

Input: Resistance (R), inductance (L), capacitance (C), frequency (*Omega*)
Output: Current (I)

1. Enter R, L, C.

2. Enter *Omega*.

3. Enter the voltage V as a complex number.

4. Compute the impedance Z.

5. Compute the current I.

6. Display I.

Coding, Execution and Testing.   The program in Figure 11.3 implements this
algorithm. A sample run is also shown.

Figure 11.3   A-C circuit.

```
PROGRAM AC_Circuit
!------------------------------------------------------------------
! Program to compute the current in an a-c circuit containing a
! capacitor, an inductor, and a resistor in series.   Variables
! used are:
!     R      : resistance (ohms)
!     L      : inductance (henrys)
!     C      : capacitance (farads)
!     Omega : frequency (radians/second)
!     V      : voltage (volts)
!     Z      : total impedance
!     I      : current (amperes)
!
! Input:  R, L, C, Omega, and V
! Output: I
!------------------------------------------------------------------

  IMPLICIT NONE
  REAL :: R, L, C, Omega
  COMPLEX :: V, Z, I

  WRITE (*, '(1X, A)', ADVANCE = "NO") &
        "Enter resistance (ohms), inductance (henrys), ", &
        "and capacitance (farads): "
  READ *, R, L, C
  WRITE (*, '(1X, A)', ADVANCE = "NO") "Enter frequency (radians/second): "
  READ *, Omega
  WRITE (*, '(1X, A)', ADVANCE = "NO") &
        "Enter voltage as a complex number in the form (x, y): "
  READ *, V

  ! Calculate resistance using complex arithmetic
  Z = R +  Omega * L * (0.0, 1.0)  - (0.0, 1.0) / (Omega * C)

  ! Calculate and display current using complex arithmetic
  I = V / Z
  PRINT *
  PRINT 10, I, ABS(I)
  10 FORMAT(1X, "Current = ", F10.4, " + ",  &
            F10.4, "I" / 1X, "with magnitude = ", F10.4)

END PROGRAM AC_Circuit
```

Figure 11.3 *(cont.)*

Sample run:

```
Enter resistance (ohms), inductance (henrys),
and capacitance (farads): 5000, .03, .02
Enter frequency (radians/second): 377
Enter voltage as a complex number in the form (x, y): (60000, 134)


Current =     12.0000 +      0.0000I
with magnitude =    12.0000
```

Quick Quiz 11.4

1. (True or false) Parameterized real data types make it possible to store the exact representation of a real number.

2. The declaration

   ```
   INTEGER(KIND = _____) :: Number
   ```

   declares that Number is an integer variable whose value may contain up to 15 digits.

3. (True or false) Every Fortran 90 compiler must provide at least two kinds of reals.

4. The declaration

   ```
   REAL(KIND = _____) :: X
   ```

   declares that X is an real variable whose values have at least 12 digits of precision and for which the range is from -10^{40} to 10^{40}.

5. (True or false) In the complex number $a + bi$, a and b are called the real parts and i the imaginary part.

6. (True or false) If Z is a complex variable, then the statement Z = (2.0, 3.0) is a valid assignment statement.

7. (True or false) If Z is a complex variable and X and Y are real variables, then the statement Z = (X, Y) is a valid assignment statement.

8. If Z is a complex variable, the statement Z = (2, 3) * (1, 4) assigns the value _____ to Z.

9. (True or false) The formatted output of a complex value is accomplished using a Cw.d format descriptor.

10. (True or false) Real values may be assigned to complex variables.

11. (True or false) If Z is a complex variable, Z > (0, 0) is a valid logical expression.

For Questions 12–16, calculate the given expression given that $z = 8 + 3i$ and $w = 7 + 2i$.

12. $z + w$

13. $z - w$

14. $z \cdot w$

15. z/w

16. $|z|$

Questions 17–21 assume the following declarations and assignments have been executed:

```
REAL :: R1, R2, R3
COMPLEX :: C1, C2, C3

R1 = 1.5
R2 = 2.1
C1 = (1.0, 3.0)
C2 = (2.0, 1.0)
```

What values will be assigned to the given variable in each of the assignment statements?

17. C3 = C1 * C2

18. C3 = CONJG(C2)

19. C3 = CMPLX(R1, R2)

20. R3 = C2

21. C3 = R1

For Questions 22 and 23, tell how the data must be entered for the given READ statement so that the value assigned to C1 is the complex constant $1.5 + 2.5i$.

22. READ *, C1

23. READ '(2F4.1)', C1

Exercises 11.4

For Exercises 1–12, calculate each expression, given that $z = 1 + 2i$ and $w = 3 - 4i$.

1. $z + w$
2. $z - w$
3. $z \cdot w$
4. $\dfrac{z}{w}$

5. z^2 6. $\bar{z}$ 7. $\overline{w}$ 8. $\dfrac{z + \bar{z}}{2}$

9. $\dfrac{z - \bar{z}}{2i}$ 10. $z \cdot \bar{z}$ 11. $\dfrac{1}{z}$ 12. $\dfrac{z + w}{z - w}$

13-24. Repeat Exercises 1–12 for $z = 6 - 5i$ and $w = 5 + 12i$.

25-36. Repeat Exercises 1–12 for $z = 1 + i$ and $w = 1 - i$.

For Exercises 37–49, assume the declarations

```
INTEGER :: N1, N2
REAL :: R1, R2
INTEGER, PARAMETER :: DP = SELECTED_REAL_KIND(14)
REAL(KIND = DP) :: D1, D2
COMPLEX :: C1, C2
```

and the assignment statements

```
N1 = 2
R1 = 0.5
D1 = 0.1_DP
C1 = (6.0, 8.0)
```

have been executed. Find the value assigned to the specified variable by the given assignment statement, or indicate why there is an error.

37. `D2 = 1.23456_DP * D1`

38. `C2 = C1 ** N1`

39. `R2 = C1`

40. `R2 = REAL(C1)`

41. `R2 = AIMAG(C1)`

42. `C2 = C1 * (0,1)`

43. `C2 = 1 / C1`

44. `R2 = ABS(C1)`

45. `C2 = CONJG(C1)`

46. `C2 = CMPLX(N1, R1)`

47. `C2 = REAL(C1) + AIMAG(C1)`

48. `C2 = EXP((0,0))`

49. `C2 = EXP((0,1))`

50. Write declarations for integer variables `Num_1` and `Num_2` whose values will be between $-1{,}000{,}000$ and $1{,}000{,}000$.

51. Write declarations for a real variable `Alpha` whose values will have at least 12 digits of precision.

52. Write declarations for real variables X and Y whose values will have at least 9 digits of precision and will be between $-1,000,000$ and $1,000,000$.

53. For Alpha as in Exercise 51, write a statement to assign Alpha the first 10 digits of π ($\pi = 3.141592653589793238...$).

54. Write declarations for a complex variable Beta whose values will have real and imaginary parts with at least 9 digits of precision and will be between $-1,000,000$ and $1,000,000$.

11.5 THE CHARACTER DATA TYPE

Recall that a character constant is a string of characters from the Fortran character set enclosed in quotation marks (double quotes) or in apostrophes (single quotes) and that the number of characters enclosed is the length of the constant. The **empty string** has length 0 and is denoted by two consecutive quotation marks or two consecutive apostrophes.

As we have seen, character variables are declared using a type statement of the form

```
CHARACTER(LEN = n) :: list
```

or simply

```
CHARACTER(n) :: list
```

where *list* is a list of variables being typed as character and *n* is the length of their values.

For example, the statement

```
CHARACTER(10) :: Street, City, State
```

declares Street, City, and State to be of character type with string values of length 10. The length specification may be overridden for any variable in the list by appending a length descriptor of the form *m to its name; thus

```
CHARACTER(10) :: Street*20, City, State
```

declares City and State to have values of length 10 and Street to have values of length 20. In Chapter 6, we also noted that when a formal argument of character type is being declared in a function or subroutine subprogram, a declaration of the form

```
CHARACTER(*) :: list-of-identifiers
```

which contains the **assumed length specifier** *, may be used. In this case, the formal argument will have the same length as the corresponding actual argument.

The CHARACTER type may also be parameterized.[2] In this case the declaration has one of the following forms:

```
CHARACTER(LEN = n, KIND = kind-number) :: list
CHARACTER(n, KIND = kind-number) :: list
CHARACTER(n, kind-number) :: list
CHARACTER(KIND = kind-number, LEN = n) :: list
CHARACTER(KIND = kind-number) :: list
```

The kind numbers may specify the coding scheme (e.g., ASCII, EBCDIC) and/or the character set (e.g., English, Japanese, Russian). Which (if any) are provided and how they are used is machine dependent, and we will consider only the default type in this text.

Character Operations

Concatenation. There is one binary operation that can be used to combine two character values. This operation is **concatenation** and is denoted by `//`. Thus

```
"centi" // "meters"
```

produces the string

```
"centimeters"
```

and if `SquareUnit` is a variable declared by

```
CHARACTER(7) :: SquareUnit
```

and is assigned a value by

```
SquareUnit = "square "
```

then

```
SquareUnit // "centi" // "meters"
```

yields the string

```
"square centimeters"
```

---

[2] For parameterized character constants, the kind number *precedes* the character string. For example, for a character type with kind number `Greek = 5`, `Greek_"αβγ"` would be a character constant of this type.

Substring.   Another operation commonly performed on character strings is accessing a sequence of consecutive characters in a string. Such a sequence is called a **substring** of the given string. For example, the substring consisting of the fourth through seventh characters of the character constant

```
"centimeters"
```

is the string

```
"time"
```

In Fortran, a substring can be extracted from the value of a character variable or character constant by specifying the variable or constant followed by the positions of the first and last characters of the substring, separated by a colon (:) and enclosed in parentheses. For example, if character variable Units has the value

```
"centimeters"
```

then

```
Units (4:7)
```

has the value

```
"time"
```

The initial and final positions of the substring may be specified by integer constants, variables, or expressions. If the initial position is not specified, it is assumed to be 1; if the final position is not specified, it is assumed to be the last position in the value of the character variable. To illustrate, consider the following statements:

```
CHARACTER(15) :: Course, Name*20

Course = "Engineering"
```

Then

```
Course(:6)
```

has the value

```
"Engine"
```

and the value of

```
Course(8:)
```

is

```
"ringⱠⱠⱠⱠ"
```

where ᵬ denotes a blank. If N has the value 3, then

```
Course(N : N+2)
```

has the value

```
"gin"
```

Care must be taken to ensure that the first position specified for a substring is positive and that the last position is greater than or equal to the first position but not greater than the length of the given string.

Substring references may be used to form character expressions in the same way that character variables are used. For example, they may be concatenated with other character values, as in

```
Course(:3) // Course(8:8) // " 141"
```

the value of which is the string

```
"Engr 141"
```

An assignment statement or an input statement may also be used to modify part of a string by using a substring reference. Only the character positions specified in the substring name are assigned values; the other positions are not changed. To illustrate, consider the statements

```
CHARACTER(8) :: Course

Course = "CPSC 141"
```

The assignment statement

```
Course(1:4) = "Engr"
```

or

```
Course(:4) = "Engr"
```

changes the value of Course to

```
"Engr 141"
```

Positions to which new values are being assigned may not be referenced, however, in the character expression on the right side of such assignment statements. Thus

```
Course(2:4) = Course(5:7)
```

is valid, but

```
Course(2:4) = Course(3:5)
```

is not, because the substring being modified overlaps the substring being referenced.

Character Input/Output

Output. Character values can be displayed using either list-directed or formatted output. List-directed output of a character value consists of the string of characters in that value, displayed in a field whose width is equal to the length of that value. For example, if Str_1 and Str_2 are declared by

```
CHARACTER(8) :: Str_1, Str_2
```

and are assigned values by

```
Str_1 = "square"
Str_2 = "centimeters"
```

the statement

```
PRINT *, "***", Str_1, "***", Str_2, "***"
```

produces the output

```
***square  ***centimet***
-------------------------
```

Note the two trailing blanks in the value of Str_1 that result from the padding that occurs when a string of length 6 is assigned to a character variable of length 8. Note also that the last three characters in the string "centimeters" are not displayed because they were truncated in the assignment of the value to Str_2.

Character expressions may also appear in the output list of a PRINT or WRITE statement. For example,

```
PRINT *, Str_1(:2) // ". " // Str_2(:1) // Str_2(6:6) // "."
```

produces as output

```
sq. cm.
```

An A descriptor is used for formatted output of character values. To illustrate, consider the following program segment:

```
CHARACTER(15) :: Item, Color*5

Item= "mm camera"
Color = "black"
PRINT '(1X, A, A4)', Color, "red"
PRINT '(1X, A1)', Color
PRINT '(1X, A)', "movie-" // Item(4:9)
PRINT '(1X, I2, A)', 35, Item
```

These statements produce the following output:

```
 black red
 b
 movie-camera
 35mm camera
```

Input. Character values can be read using either list-directed or formatted input. For list-directed input, character values need not be enclosed in quotation marks or apostrophes unless one of the following is true:

1. They contain blanks, commas, or slashes.
2. They extend over more than one line.
3. The leading non-blank character is a quotation mark or an apostrophe.
4. A repetition indicator is used.

In this case the input value is terminated by the first blank, comma, or end of line that is encountered.

For formatted input, when a value is read for a character variable, *all* characters in the field associated with the corresponding A descriptor are read. For example, if the line of data

```
Scientific Fortran
```

is read by the statements

```
CHARACTER(8) :: Str_1, Str_2

READ '(2A)', Str_1, Str_2
```

the value

    Scientif

is assigned to Str_1 and

    ic Fortr

to Str_2.

A substring reference may also appear in an input list. For example, if Course has the value

    "CPSC 141"

and the input for the statement

    READ '(A)', Course (2:6)

is

    LAS 3
    -----

the value of Course is changed to

    'CLAS 341'

11.6 APPLICATION: FINITE-STATE MACHINES

In our discussion of system software in Chapter 1, we described compilers, which are programs whose function is to translate a source program written in some high-level language such as Fortran into an object program written in machine code. This object program is then executed by the computer.

The basic phases of the compiler are summarized in the following diagram:

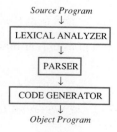

The input to a compiler is a stream of characters that comprise the source program. Before the translation can actually be carried out, this stream of characters must be broken up into meaningful groups, such as identifiers, key words, constants, and operators. For example, for the assignment statement

```
Alpha = Beta*200 + 5
```

or as a "stream" of characters

```
Alphab=bBeta*200b+b5
```

(where ƀ is a blank), the lexical analyzer must identify the following units:

Alpha	⟷	identifier
=	⟷	assignment operator
Beta	⟷	identifier
*	⟷	arithmetic operator
200	⟷	integer constant
+	⟷	arithmetic operator
5	⟷	integer constant

These units are called **tokens,** and the part of the compiler that recognizes these tokens is called the **lexical analyzer.**

It is the task of the **parser** to group these tokens together to form the basic **syntactic structures** of the language as determined by the syntax rules. For example, it must recognize that the three consecutive tokens

identifier   arithmetic-operator   integer-constant
↓   ↓   ↓
Beta   *   200

can be grouped together to form a valid arithmetic expression; that

arithmetic-expression   arithmetic-operator   integer-constant
↓   ↓
+   5

constitutes a valid arithmetic expression; and then that

identifier   assignment-operator   arithmetic-expression
↓   ↓
Alpha   =

forms a valid assignment statement. The complete **parse tree** constructed during compilation of the preceding statement is

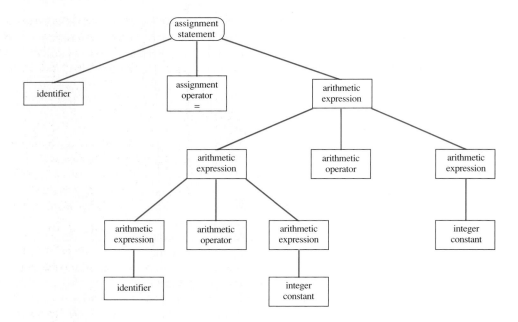

Later phases of the compiling process generate the machine code for this assignment statement.

A tool that is useful in designing lexical analyzers and in modeling many other processes made up of a finite sequence of events is the **finite-state machine** (also called a **finite automaton**), which has a finite number of states with transitions from one state to another that depend on the current state of the machine and the current input character. If the machine is in one of certain states called *accepting states* after an input string is processed, then that string is said to be *recognized* or *accepted* by the machine. For example, a finite-state machine to recognize bit strings that contain 01 is

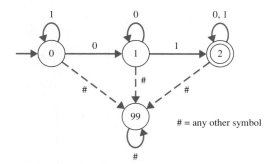

Here, the arrow pointing to state 0 indicates that this is the initial state, and the double circle for state 2 indicates that it is an accepting state. The machine begins processing input symbols in the initial state and makes transitions from one state to another or remains in the current state as specified by the labels on the arrows.

To illustrate, consider the input string 0011. The finite-state machine begins in state 0, and because the first input symbol is 0, it transfers to state 1. Since the next input symbol is a 0, the machine remains in state 1. However, the third symbol is a 1, which causes a transition to state 2. The final symbol is a 1 and causes no state change. The end of the input string has now been reached, and because the finite-state machine is in an accepting state, it has accepted the string 0011. It is easy to see that any bit string containing 01 will be processed in a similar manner and lead to the accepting state and that only such strings will cause the machine to terminate in state 2. For example, the string 11000 is not accepted because the machine will be in state 1 after processing this string, and state 1 is not an accepting state. Neither is the bit string 100201 accepted, since the "illegal" symbol 2 causes a transition from state 1 to state 99, which is not an accepting state.

State 99 is a "reject" or "dead" state: once it is entered, it is never exited. The transitions to this state are shown as dashed lines since the existence of such a state is usually assumed and transitions are not drawn in the diagram; for any state and any input symbol for which no transition is specified, it is assumed that the transition is to such a reject state. Thus, the finite-state machine is usually drawn as

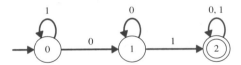

As another example, consider the following finite-state machine:

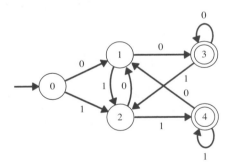

After some analysis and experimentation, it should become clear that to terminate processing in one of the accepting states 3 or 4, the last two input symbols must both be 0s or both be 1s. This finite-state machine thus recognizes bit strings ending in 00 or 11.

To show how a finite-state machine can be used to advantage in the design of lexical analyzers, we consider the problem of recognizing (nonparameterized) Fortran integer constants. A finite-state machine that does this is

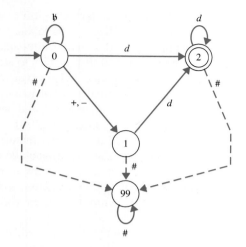

where d denotes one of the digits $0, 1, \ldots, 9$; ƀ denotes a blank; and state 2 is the only accepting state. The machine begins in state 0. If the first input symbol is a blank, it stays in state 0, "gobbling up" leading blanks; if it is a $+$ or $-$, it goes to state 1; if it is a digit, it goes to state 2. Otherwise, the input character is not valid, and thus the string does not represent a valid integer.

Writing program statements corresponding to such a finite-state machine is then straightforward. The program in Figure 11.4 illustrates this. It reads a string of characters and determines whether it represents a valid Fortran integer. The part of the program highlighted in color implements the preceding finite-state machine.

Figure 11.4 Lexical analysis.

```
PROGRAM Lexical_Analysis
!--------------------------------------------------------------------
! This program implements a simple lexical analyzer for Fortran integer
! constants. A finite-state machine that recognizes integer constants was
! used in designing the program.  Identifiers used are:
!   DeadState           : dead state
!   CurrentState        : current state
!   I                   : index
!   InputString         : input string to be checked
!   Symbol              : a character in InputString
!   End_of_String_Mark  : character used to indicate the end of the string
!   Response            : user response to "more data" query
!
! Input:  InputString, Response
! Output: User prompt, message indicating if string is a valid integer
!--------------------------------------------------------------------
```

Figure 11.4 *(cont.)*

```fortran
INTEGER, PARAMETER :: DeadState = 99
INTEGER :: CurrentState, I
CHARACTER(1) :: Symbol, End_of_String_Mark = ";", Response, InputString*80



! Repeat the following until no more strings to check
DO
   PRINT *, "Enter the string to be checked (end with ", &
            End_of_String_Mark, ") "
   READ '(A)', InputString
   I = 1

   ! Begin in initial state
   CurrentState = 0

   DO
      IF (InputString(I:I) == End_of_String_Mark) EXIT
      ! If Ith symbol in InputString is the end-of-string mark,
      ! terminate repetition

      ! Otherwise continue processing InputString

      Symbol = InputString(I:I)

      SELECT CASE (CurrentState)
        CASE(0)
           IF (Symbol == " ") THEN                          ! blank
              CurrentState = 0
           ELSE IF (Symbol == "+" .OR. Symbol ==  "-") THEN ! sign
              CurrentState = 1
           ELSE IF (Symbol >= "0" .AND. Symbol <= "9") THEN ! digit
              CurrentState = 2
           ELSE                                             ! other char
              CurrentState = DeadState
           END IF
        CASE(1, 2)
           IF (Symbol >= "0" .AND. Symbol <= "9") THEN      ! digit
              CurrentState = 2
           ELSE                                             ! other char
              CurrentState = DeadState
           END IF
      END SELECT

      I = I + 1
   END DO
```

Figure 11.4 *(cont.)*

```
      IF (CurrentState == 2) THEN
         PRINT *, "Valid integer"
      ELSE
         PRINT *, "Not a valid integer"
      END IF

      WRITE (*, '(/ 1X, A)', ADVANCE = "NO") "More data (Y or N)? "
      READ *, Response
      IF (Response /= "Y") EXIT
   END DO

END PROGRAM Lexical_Analysis
```

Sample run:

```
Enter the string to be checked (end with ;)
1234;
Valid integer

More data (Y or N)? Y
Enter the string to be checked (end with ;)
+9999;
Valid integer

More data (Y or N)? Y
Enter the string to be checked (end with ;)
-1;
Valid integer

More data (Y or N)? Y
Enter the string to be checked (end with ;)
123+4;
Not a valid integer

More data (Y or N)? Y
Enter the string to be checked (end with ;)
ABCDEF;
Not a valid integer

More data (Y or N)? N
```

Exercises 11.6

1. ASCII is a coding scheme that uses seven bits to represent characters. An extra bit is commonly added for error detection. In an *even-parity* error-detecting scheme, this extra bit is set to 1 if the number of ones in the ASCII code is odd and to 0 otherwise. Design a finite-state machine to recognize bit strings containing an odd number of ones.

2. Design a finite-state machine to recognize bit strings containing 00 or 11.

3. Design a finite-state machine to recognize bit strings containing an even number of zeros and an even number of ones.

4. Design a finite-state machine to recognize bit strings in which the remainder is 1 when n is divided by 3, where n is the number of ones.

11.7 CHARACTER FUNCTIONS

In Section 11.5, we described the CHARACTER data type and some of the basic character operations. Fortran also provides several functions for processing characters strings. In this section we describe these functions and continue the description of character comparison begun in Section 3.1.

String-to-String Functions

The intrinsic string operations concatenation and substring extraction operate on strings to produce other strings. There also are several intrinsic functions that accept a string and produce another string. These string-to-string functions are

ADJUSTL(*str*)	Returns the string obtained from *str* by moving leading blanks to the right end
ADJUSTR(*str*)	Returns the string obtained from *str* by moving trailing blanks to the left end
REPEAT(*str*, *n*)	Returns the string formed by concatenating *n* copies of *str*
TRIM(*str*)	Returns the string formed by removing trailing blanks from *str*

For example, suppose that String is declared by

```
CHARACTER(10) :: String = " ABCDE"
```

The output produced by the statements

```
PRINT *, "***", String, "***"
PRINT *, "***", ADJUSTL(String), "***"
PRINT *, "***", ADJUSTR(String), "***"
PRINT *, "***", TRIM(String), "***"
PRINT *, "***", REPEAT(String, 3), "***"
```

is

```
*** ABCDE      ****
***ABCDE       ****
***       ABCDE****
*** ABCDE****
*** ABCDE      ABCDE      ABCDE      ****
```

Length Functions

Fortran provides two instrinsic functions for determining the length of a string:

LEN(str)   Length of string str, including leading and trailing blanks

LEN_TRIM(str) Length of string str, ignoring trailing blanks

For example, for the character variable String declared by

```
CHARACTER(10) :: String = " ABCDE"
```

the value returned by the function reference

```
LEN(String)
```

is 10, because the value of String is " ABCDE   " since the character string used to initialize String is padded with four blanks. The value returned by

```
LEN_TRIM(String)
```

is 6.

Search Functions

When processing strings, it is often convenient to locate a given pattern within a string. Three instrinsic functions that can be used to search strings are

INDEX(str_1, str_2) or INDEX(str_1, str_2, $back$)	The first form and the second form with $back$ = .FALSE. return the position of the first occurrence of str_2 in str_1. The second form with $back$ = .TRUE. returns the last occurrence of str_2 in str_1. Both forms return 0 if str_2 does not appear in str_1.

SCAN(*str₁*, *str₂*)
or
SCAN(*str₁*, *str₂*, *back*)

The first form and the second form with *back* = .FALSE. return the position of the leftmost character of *str₁* that appears in *str₂*. The second form with *back* = .TRUE. returns the position of the rightmost character of *str₁* that appears in *str₂*. Both forms return 0 if no character of *str₁* appears in *str₂*.

VERIFY(*str₁*, *str₂*)
or
VERIFY(*str₁*, *str₂*, *back*)

The first form and the second form with *back* = .FALSE. return the position of the leftmost character of *str₁* that is not in *str₂*. The second form with *back* = .TRUE. returns the position of the rightmost character of *str₁* that is not in *str₂*. Both forms return 0 if all characters of *str₁* appear in *str₂*.

For example, suppose that Units is declared by

```
CHARACTER(25) :: Units = "centimeters and meters"
```

The output produced by the statements

```
PRINT *, INDEX(Units, "meters")
PRINT *, INDEX(Units, "meters", .FALSE.)
PRINT *, INDEX(Units, "meters", .TRUE.)
PRINT *, INDEX(Units, "cents")
PRINT *, SCAN("kilometer", Units)
PRINT *, SCAN("kilometer", Units, .FALSE.)
PRINT *, SCAN("kilometer", Units, .TRUE.)
PRINT *, SCAN("floor", Units)
PRINT *, VERIFY("kilometer", Units)
PRINT *, VERIFY("kilometer", Units, .FALSE.)
PRINT *, VERIFY("kilometer", Units, .TRUE.)
PRINT *, VERIFY("tennis", Units)
```

is

```
6
6
17
0
2
2
```

```
9
5
1
1
4
0
```

Example: Text Editing

The preparation of textual material such as research papers, books, and computer programs often involves the insertion, deletion, and replacement of parts of the text. The software of most computers systems includes an **editing** package that makes it easy to carry out these operations. As an example showing the text-processing capabilities of Fortran, we consider the editing problem of replacing a specified substring in a given line of text with another string. A solution to this problem is given in the program in Figure 11.5. The sample run shows that in addition to string replacements, the program can be used to make insertions and deletions. For example, changing the substring

```
a n
```

in the line of text

```
a nation conceived in liberty and and dedicated
```

to

```
a new n
```

yields the edited line

```
a new nation conceived in liberty and and dedicated
```

Entering the edit change

```
and //
```

changes the substring

```
andb
```

(where ƀ denotes a blank) in the line of text to an *empty* or *null* string containing no characters, and so the edited result is

```
a new nation conceived in liberty and dedicated
```

Figure 11.5 Text editor.

```fortran
PROGRAM Text_Editor
!----------------------------------------------------------------------
! Program to perform some basic text-editing functions on lines of
! text.  The basic operation is replacing a substring of the text
! with another string.  This replacement is accomplished by a command
! of the form
!                       oldstring/newstring/
! where oldstring specifies the substring in the text to be replaced
! with newstring; newstring may be an empty string, which then causes
! oldstring (if found) to be deleted.  The text lines are read from a
! file, and after editing, the edited lines are written to another
! file.   Identifiers used are:
!   InputFile  : name of the input file
!   OutputFile : name of the output file
!   OpenStatus : status variable for OPEN
!   IOStatus   : status variable for READ and WRITE
!   TextLine   : a character string representing a line of text
!   Length     : length of text line (constant)
!   Change     : a character string specifying the edit operation
!                 Value is of the form:
!                       "oldstring/newstring/"
!   Response   : user response (Y or N)
!
! Input (keyboard):  InputFile, OutputFile, Change, Response
! Output (screen):   User prompts, TextLine
! Input (file):      Lines of text
! Output (file):     Edited lines of text
!----------------------------------------------------------------------

  IMPLICIT NONE
  INTEGER, PARAMETER :: Length = 70
  CHARACTER(Length) TextLine, Change, InputFile*20, OutputFile*20, &
                    Response*1
  INTEGER :: OpenStatus, IOStatus

  ! Get names of input and output files and open the files
  WRITE (*, '(1X, A)', ADVANCE = "NO") "Enter the name of the input file: "
  READ *, InputFile
  WRITE (*, '(1X, A)', ADVANCE = "NO") "Enter the name of the output file: "
  READ *, OutputFile
```

Figure 11.5 *(cont.)*

```fortran
OPEN (UNIT = 15, FILE = InputFile, STATUS = "OLD", IOSTAT = OpenStatus)
IF (OpenStatus > 0) STOP "*** Cannot open input file ***"
OPEN (UNIT = 16, FILE = OutputFile, STATUS = "NEW", IOSTAT = OpenStatus)
IF (OpenStatus > 0) STOP "*** Cannot open output file ***"

! While there is more data, read a line of text and edit it
DO
    READ (15, "(A)", IOSTAT = IOStatus) TextLine
    IF (IOStatus > 0) STOP "*** Input error ***"

    IF (IOStatus < 0) EXIT
    ! If end of file reached, stop text editing

    ! Otherwise continue with the following
    PRINT *
    PRINT *, TextLine

    DO
        WRITE (*, '(1X, A)', ADVANCE = "NO") "Edit this line (Y OR N)? "
        READ *, Response
        IF (Response == "N") EXIT
        ! No editing needed -- terminate loop

        ! Otherwise get editing change, modify the
        ! line of text, and display the edited line
        PRINT *, "Enter edit change:"
        READ '(A)', Change
        CALL Edit(TextLine, Change)
        PRINT *, TextLine
    END DO

    ! Write the edited line to the output file
    WRITE (16, *, IOSTAT = IOStatus) TextLine
    IF (IOStatus > 0) STOP "*** Output error ***"

END DO

CLOSE(15)
CLOSE(16)

CONTAINS
```

Figure 11.5 *(cont.)*

```
!-Edit-----------------------------------------------------------
! Subroutine to edit a line of TextLine by replacing a substring of the
! text by another string as specified by the command Change, which has
! the form
!                   oldstring/newstring/
! newstring (which may be empty) replaces the first occurrence of
! oldstring in TextLine.  Local identifiers used are:
!   FirstSlash            : position of first slash (/) in Change
!   SecondSlash           : position of second slash (/) in Change
!   OldString             : old string -- to be replaced
!   OldLength             : actual length of OldString
!   NewString             : new replacement string
!   NewLength             : actual length of NewString
!   Index_of_OldString    : index of old string in TextLine
!
! Accepts:  TextLine, Change
! Returns:  TextLine (modified)
!----------------------------------------------------------------

SUBROUTINE Edit(TextLine, Change)

  CHARACTER(Length), INTENT(INOUT) :: TextLine
  CHARACTER(Length), INTENT(IN) :: Change
  INTEGER :: FirstSlash, SecondSlash, OldLength, NewLength, &
             Index_of_OldString
  CHARACTER(Length) :: OldString, NewString

  ! Attempt to locate slash delimiters in Change
  FirstSlash = INDEX(Change, "/")
  SecondSlash = INDEX(Change, "/", .TRUE.)
  IF (FirstSlash == 0 .OR. SecondSlash == FirstSlash) THEN
     PRINT *, "Missing slash"
     RETURN
  END IF

  ! Slashes were found, so continue with editing
  ! First extract OldString and NewString from Change, and locate
  ! OldString in TextLine
```

Figure 11.5 *(cont.)*

```
    OldLength = FirstSlash - 1
    OldString = Change( : OldLength)
    NewLength = SecondSlash - FirstSlash - 1
    NewString = Change(FirstSlash + 1: SecondSlash - 1)
    Index_of_OldString = INDEX(TextLine, TRIM(OldString))
    IF (Index_of_OldString > 0) THEN
        TextLine = TextLine( : Index_of_OldString - 1) // &
                TRIM(NewString) // TextLine(Index_of_OldString + OldLength : )
    END IF

  END SUBROUTINE Edit

END PROGRAM Text_Editor
```

Listing of `fil11-5.dat` used in sample run:

```
Fourscore and five years ago, our mothers
brought forth on continent
a nation conceived in liberty and and dedicated
to the preposition that all men
are created equal.
```

Sample run:

```
Enter the name of the input file: fil11-5.dat
Enter the name of the output file: fil11-5.out

Fourscore and five years ago, our mothers
Edit this line (Y OR N)? Y
Enter edit change:
five/seven/
Fourscore and seven years ago, our mothers
Edit this line (Y OR N)? Y
Enter edit change:
mo/fa/
Fourscore and seven years ago, our fathers
Edit this line (Y OR N)? N

brought forth on continent
Edit this line (Y OR N)? Y
Enter edit change:
on/on this/
brought forth on this continent
Edit this line (Y OR N)? N
```

Figure 11.5 *(cont.)*

```
a nation conceived in liberty and and dedicated
Edit this line (Y OR N)? Y
Enter edit change:
a n/a new n/
a new nation conceived in liberty and and dedicated
Edit this line (Y OR N)? Y
Enter edit change:
and //
a new nation conceived in liberty and dedicated
Edit this line (Y OR N)? N

to the preposition that all men
Edit this line (Y OR N)? Y
Enter edit change:
pre/pro/
to the proposition that all men
Edit this line (Y OR N)? N

are created equal.
Edit this line (Y OR N)? N
```

Listing of `fi11-5.out` produced by sample run:

```
Fourscore and seven years ago, our fathers
brought forth on this continent
a new nation conceived in liberty and dedicated
to the proposition that all men
are created equal
```

Character Comparison

In Section 3.1, we stated that character strings are compared using the encoding schemes (such as ASCII and EBCDIC) that represent character information in a computer. Each such encoding scheme assigns a unique integer to each character that the machine can process. These characters can then be arranged in an order in which one character precedes another if its numeric code is less than the numeric code of the other. This ordering of characters based on their numeric codes is called a **collating sequence** and varies from one computer to another. The Fortran standard, however, partially specifies this sequence. It requires that letters and digits be ordered in the usual way and that the letters and digits not overlap. The blank character must precede both letters and digits in the ordering.

When characters are compared in a logical expression, this collating sequence is used. Thus,

```
"C" < "D"
"Z" > "W"
```

are true logical expressions since C must precede D and Z must follow W in every collating sequence. However, the truth or falsity of the logical expressions

```
"1" < "A"
"*" > ")"
```

depends on the encoding scheme used in a particular computer. Both logical expressions are true for ASCII but false for EBCDIC.

Similarly, the logical expressions

```
"HCL" < "NACL"
"CO2" > "C"
```

are true, since strings are compared character by character using the collating sequence and, in the first case, H must precede N, and in the second case, O must follow a blank character. (Recall that strings of different lengths are compared as though the shorter string is blank-padded so that two strings of equal length are compared.) However, the truth or falsity of such logical expressions as

```
"3" < "B"
"PDQ+123" > "PDQ*123"
```

depends on the collating sequence used in a particular computer.

Comparison Functions

The variation in collating sequences may cause the same program to execute differently on different machines. This difficulty can be circumvented, however, by using the special functions LLT, LLE, LGT, and LGE. The LLT function has the form

```
LLT(string₁, string₂)
```

where $string_1$ and $string_2$ are character expressions. The value of this function is true if $string_1$ precedes $string_2$ using the collating sequence *determined by ASCII encoding* and is false otherwise. Thus

```
LLT("1", "A")
```

is true *regardless* of which collating sequence is in effect.

Similarly,

```
LLE(string₁, string₂)
```

is true if $string_1$ precedes or is equal to $string_2$ using the ASCII collating sequence;

```
LGT(string₁, string₂)
```

is true if $string_1$ follows $string_2$; and

```
LGE(string₁, string₂)
```

is true if $string_1$ follows or is equal to $string_2$ using the ASCII collating sequence.

Conversion Functions

Fortran provides four intrinsic functions for converting characters to their numeric codes and vice versa:

`ICHAR(char)`	The position of character `char` in the collating sequence
`IACHAR(char)`	The ASCII code of character `char`
`CHAR(int)`	The character whose position in the collating sequence is `int`
`ACHAR(int)`	The character whose ASCII code is `int`

For example,

```
IACHAR("A")
```

returns 65, the ASCII code of `"A"`, and

```
ACHAR(65)
```

returns `"A"`.

Quick Quiz 11.7

1. (True or false) The default length of a character variable is 6.
2. (True or false) Given the variable declaration CHARACTER(4) :: Course, the statement Course = "Mathematics" assigns COURSE the value "Math".
3. (True or false) If Str is a character variable of length 5, then the assignment Str = "ABC" assigns the value "ƂƂABC" to Str.
4. (True or false) Given the declaration CHARACTER(6) :: C1, C2, C3, the following statements

```
C1 = "shell"
C2 = "seashore"
C3 = C1(2:) // C2(6:6)
```

assign C3 the value "hello".

5. (True or false) The logical expression "human" > "helium" has the value .TRUE..

6. (True or false) The logical expression "human" > "hum" has the value .TRUE..

7. (True or false) Character constants must be enclosed in single or double quotation marks for both list-directed and formatted input.

For Questions 8–15, find the value returned by the function reference.

8. INDEX("Fortran 90", "or")

9. SCAN("not", "Fortran 90")

10. VERIFY("knot", "Fortran 90")

11. ADJUSTL("   12345")

12. TRIM(" 1 2 3 4 ")

13. REPEAT("12", 5)

14. LLT("A", "B")

15. CHAR(ICHAR("A"))

For Questions 16–19, assume the following statements have been executed:

```
CHARACTER(5) :: Beta, Animal, Robot, R2D2*8, Star
ROBOT = "Three"
STAR = "wars"
```

Find the value (if any) assigned to the character variable (indicate each blank with a ƀ).

16. Beta = "B"

17. Animal = "kangaroo"

18. R2D2 = Robot // "CPO"

19. Star(4:5) = Robot(:1) // "s"

Exercises 11.7

For Exercises 1–17, assume that the declarations

```
CHARACTER(10) :: Alpha, Beta*5, Gamma*1, &
                 Label_1*4,Label_2*3, Str_1*3, Str_2*4
```

have been made and that `Str_1 = "For"`, `Str_2 = "tran"`, `Label_1 = "foot"`, `Label_2 = "lbs"`. Find the value assigned to the given variable, or indicate why the statement is not valid.

1. `Gamma = 123`
2. `Gamma = "123"`
3. `Alpha = "one" // "two"`
4. `Alpha = "1" // "2"`
5. `Beta = "antidisestablishmentarianism"`
6. `Beta = "1,000,000,000"`
7. `Beta = "one" // 23`
8. `Alpha = Str_1 // Str_2 // -"90"`
9. `Beta = Str_1 // Str_2 // -"90"`
10. `Alpha = Label_1 // Label_2`
11. `Gamma = Label_1`
12. `Alpha = Label_1 // "-" // Label_2`
13. `Beta = Str_1 // Str_2(:1)`
14. `Alpha = Str_2(2:3) // "ndom"`
15. `Str_2(2:3) = "ur"`
16. `Str_2(:2) = Str_2(3:)`
17. `Str_1(:2) = Str_1(2:)`

For Exercises 18–22, assume that `First`, `Last`, and `Name` are character variables with lengths 5, 5, and 14, respectively. Find the value assigned to the specified variable.

18. `First = "Bill"`
19. `Last = "Smith"`
20. `Name = "Mr. " // First // Last`
21. `Name = "The Honorable " // First // Last`
22. `Name = Last // ", " // First(1:1)`

For Exercises 23–27, assume that `Name` is declared by

```
CHARACTER(7) :: Name = "Fortran"
```

Find the value assigned to `Name`, or indicate why an error occurs.

23. `Name(4:6) = "lor"`
24. `Name(4: ) = "est"`
25. `Name( :3) = "For"`

26. Name(5:) = Name(:3)

27. Name(3:) = Name(:5)

For Exercises 28–33, assume the following declarations have been made:

```
INTEGER :: N
REAL :: A
CHARACTER(40) :: Form, S1*10, S2*6
```

Show how the data should be entered so that the READ statement will assign N, A, S1, and S2 the values 1, 1.1, Model-XL11, and Camera, respectively.

28. READ *, N, A, S1, S2

29. READ '(I2, F4.1, 2A)', N, A, S1, S2

30. READ '(I1, A, F2, A)', N, S1, A, S2

31. Form = '(25X, I3, T1, F5.0, 1X, A, T18, A)'
    READ Form, N, A, S1, S2

32. Form = '(I5, F5.0, 2A15)'
    READ Form, N, A, S1, S2

33. READ 10, N, A, S1, S2
    10 FORMAT (T9, I1, TL1, F2.1, T1, 2A)

For each of Exercises 34–36, fill in the blank so the resulting statement(s) will produce the indicated output, or explain why it isn't possible or why an error occurs. Assume that X and Y are real variables with values 2.5341, 3.1619, respectively; Z is an integer variable with value 20; and Form is a character variable with length 40. Assume that printer controls are not in effect. *Note:* ƀ denotes a blank.

34. Xƀ=ƀ2.53ƀƀYƀ=ƀ0.316E+01   PRINT 20, "Xƀ=", X, "Yƀ=", Y
                                 20 FORMAT_____

35. (blank line)   Form = _____
    Z'sƀvalueƀisƀ20
    CubeƀofƀZƀ=ƀ***   PRINT Form, Z, "CubeƀofƀZƀ=ƀ", Z**3

36. ƀƀF   PRINT 20, "F", "ABCD", "ABCD", "2", 2
    ABCABCDƀƀ22   20 FORMAT_____

37. Write a statement to assign the first five characters of the value of the character variable String to the character variable SubString.

38. Assume that Name = "Smith, Bill" and that First and Last are character variables of length 5. Write a statement to extract the first and last names from Name and then combine them so that the value "Bill Smith" is assigned to the variable String. (String is a character variable of length 10.)

For each of Exercises 39–54, find the value returned by the function reference.

39. INDEX("She sells seashells", "he")

40. INDEX("She sells seashells", "he", .TRUE.)

41. INDEX("She sells seashells", "shore")

42. SCAN("coral reef", "She sells seashells")

43. SCAN("coral reef", "She sells seashells", .TRUE.)

44. SCAN("driftwood", "She sells seashells")

45. VERIFY("coral reef", "She sells seashells")

46. VERIFY("coral reef", "She sells seashells", .TRUE.)

47. VERIFY("shell", "She sells seashells")

48. ADJUSTL(REPEAT(" ABC ", 3))

49. ADJUSTR(REPEAT(" ABC ", 3))

50. TRIM(REPEAT(" ABC ", 3))

51. LEN(REPEAT(" ABC ", 3))

52. LEN_TRIM(REPEAT(" ABC ", 3))

53. IACHAR("X")

54. ACHAR(120)

55. Write a function that accepts a character and returns its uppercase equivalent if that character is a lowercase letter, and returns the character itself otherwise.

56. Write a function that accepts a character and returns its lowercase equivalent if that character is an uppercase letter, and returns the character itself otherwise.

11.8 APPLICATION: DATA SECURITY

Problem

It is often necesary to code information in order to keep it secure, for example, computer passwords, electronic mail, data transmitted when funds are transmitted electronically, and information stored in databases. The string of characters comprising the information is transformed into another string that is an encrypted form of the information, which may be safely stored or transmitted. At a later time it can be decrypted by reversing the encrypting process to recover the original information. The problem considered here is how to encrypt and decrypt information. We will describe several solutions to this problem.

Solution

Caesar Cipher. Data encryption has been used to send secret military and political messages from the days of Julius Caesar to the present. The **Caesar cipher** scheme consists of replacing each character by the character that appears k positions later in the character set for some integer k. In the original Caesar cipher, k was 3, so that each occurrence of A in the message was replaced by D, each B by E, each C by F, and so on, with "wraparound" at the end of the character set. For example, we would encrypt the string "IDESOFMARCH" as follows:

Original string: I D E S O F M A R C H
                  ↓ ↓ ↓ ↓ ↓ ↓ ↓ ↓ ↓ ↓ ↓
Encrypted string: L G H V R I P D U F K

The program in Figure 11.6 uses the character functions of the preceding section to implement the Caesar cipher encryption scheme. Its basic approach is to examine each character in the character string, and if it is a *printable* character (i.e., its ASCII value is in the range 32 through 126), it is shifted Key positions. This shifting is accomplished by converting each character to its numeric representation (ASCII) using the function IACHAR and then adding the offset Key to the numeric code of the character. For example, suppose that Key is 3 and the character being examined is 'A'. The ASCII code of 'A' is 65, and adding 3 gives 68, which is the ASCII code of 'D', the coded value of 'A'.

The shifting is complicated by the wraparound required for values near the end of the character set. For example, suppose that Key is 10 and the character being examined is 'z', whose ASCII code is 122. If we simply add 10 to 122, we get 132, which is not the ASCII code of a printable character. Instead, the values must wrap around to the beginning of the printable characters,

ASCII Value: 32, 33, 34, ..., 115, 116, 117, 118, ..., 126
Key = 10   ↓   ↓   ↓   ↓   ↓   ↓   ↓   ↓
Shifted Value: 42, 43, 44, ..., 126, 32, 33, 34, ..., 41

so that the value that is 10 positions from 'z' is 39, the ASCII value of the single-quote character ('). This wraparound can be accomplished by processing a character as follows:

1. Scale the value from the range 32 through 126 into the range 0 through 94 by subtracting 32.

2. Add the offset.

3. Since the resulting value may be outside the range 0 through 94, wrap it around by using the MOD function to find the remainder when the value is divided by 95, the number of printable chars.

4. Scale the resulting value from the range 0 through 94 back into the range 32 through 126 by adding 32.

The statement

```
Code = MOD((IACHAR(Message(I:I)) - 32 + Key), 95) + 32
```

in the program carries out this translation. The ACHAR function is then used to convert this numerical value back to a character:

```
Message(I:I) = ACHAR(Code)
```

Figure 11.6 Caesar cipher encryption.

```
PROGRAM Caesar_Cipher
!-----------------------------------------------------------------------
! This program encrypts a character string using the Caesar cipher
! scheme.  Variables used are the following:
!   Message : message to be encrypted
!   Key     : integer to be added in encrypting the message
!   Code    : numeric code for a symbol in Message
!   I       : counter
!
! Input:  Message and Key
! Output: User prompts and Message (coded)
!-----------------------------------------------------------------------

  IMPLICIT NONE
  CHARACTER(80) :: Message
  INTEGER :: Key, Code, I

  WRITE (*, '(1X, A)', ADVANCE = "NO") "Enter message: "
  READ '(A)', Message
  WRITE (*, '(1X, A)', ADVANCE = "NO") "Enter key: "
  READ *, Key

  I = 0
  DO
     ! Get next character in message
     I = I + 1
     IF (I > LEN_TRIM(Message)) EXIT
     ! If end of string, stop
     ! Otherwise continue coding characters
     Code = MOD((ICHAR(Message(I:I)) - 32 + Key), 95) + 32
     Message(I:I) = CHAR(Code)
  END DO

  PRINT *, "Coded message: ", Message

END PROGRAM Caesar_Cipher
```

Figure 11.6 *(cont.)*

Sample runs:

```
Enter message: IDESOFMARCH
Enter key: 3
Coded message: LGHVRIPDUFK


Enter message: My password is SECRET
Enter key: 17
Coded message: ^+1"r%%)!$u1z%1dVTcVe


Enter message: LGHVRIPDUFK
Enter key: -3
Coded message: IDESOFMARCH
```

Note that, as the last sample run demonstrates, the offset `Key` may be negative, which permits this program to be used both to encrypt and to decrypt strings. The negative offset `Key` $= -3$ is used to decrypt the string encrypted earlier with an offset of 3:

$$\text{Cryptogram:}\quad \text{L G H V R I P D U F K}$$
$$\downarrow\downarrow\downarrow\downarrow\downarrow\downarrow\downarrow\downarrow\downarrow\downarrow\downarrow$$
$$\text{Message:}\quad \text{I D E S O F M A R C H}$$

Vignère Cipher. The Caesar cipher is obviously not a very secure scheme, since it is easy to "break the code" simply by trying all possible values for the key. An improved substitution operation is to use a *keyword* to specify several different displacements of letters rather than the single offset of the Caesar cipher. In this **Vignère cipher** scheme, a keyword is added character by character to the string, where each letter is represented by its position in the character set and wraparound occurs as with the Caesar cipher scheme. For example, if the positions of A, B, C, ..., Z are given by 0, 1, 2, ..., 25, respectively, and the keyword is DAGGER, the string "IDESOFMARCH" is encrypted as follows:

$$\text{Original string:}\quad \text{I D E S O F M A R C H}$$
$$\downarrow\downarrow\downarrow\downarrow\downarrow\downarrow\downarrow\downarrow\downarrow\downarrow\downarrow$$
$$\text{Repeated keyword:}\quad \text{D A G G E R D A G G E}$$
$$\downarrow\downarrow\downarrow\downarrow\downarrow\downarrow\downarrow\downarrow\downarrow\downarrow\downarrow$$
$$\text{Encrypted string:}\quad \text{L D K Y S W P A X I L}$$

The original string can be recovered by subtracting the characters in this keyword from those in the encrypted string.

Substitution Tables. A different encryption method is to use a **substitution table**; for example:

Original character:	A	B	C	D	E	F	G	H	I	J	K	L	M
Substitute character:	Q	W	E	R	T	Y	U	I	O	P	A	S	D
	N	O	P	Q	R	S	T	U	V	W	X	Y	Z
	F	G	H	J	K	L	Z	X	C	V	B	N	M

The string "IDESOFMARCH" would then be encrypted using this substitution table as follows:

Original string: I D E S O F M A R C H

↓ ↓ ↓ ↓ ↓ ↓ ↓ ↓ ↓ ↓ ↓

Encrypted string: O R T L G Y D Q K E I

To decrypt, one simply uses the substitution table in reverse.

Since there are 95! (approximately 10^{148}) possible substitution tables, this scheme is considerably more secure than the simple Caesar cipher scheme. Experienced cryptographers can easily break the code, however, by analyzing frequency counts of certain letters and combinations of letters.

Permutation Operations. Another basic operation in some encryption schemes is **permutation**, in which characters or blocks of characters are rearranged. For example, we might divide a string into blocks (substrings) of size 3 and permute the characters in each block as follows:

Original position: 1 2 3

Permuted position: 3 1 2

Thus, the string "IDESOFMARCH" would be encrypted (after the addition of a randomly selected character X so that the string length is a multiple of the block length) as

Original string: I D E S O F M A R C H X

Encrypted string: D E I O F S A R M H X C

To decrypt a string, one must know the key permutation and its inverse:

Original position: 1 2 3

Permuted position: 2 3 1

DES. Many modern encryption schemes combine several substitution and permutation operations. Perhaps the best known is the **Data Encryption Standard (DES)** developed in the early 1970s by researchers at the IBM Corporation. The scheme is described in *Federal Information Processing Standards Publication 46* (FIPS Pub 46).[3] It consists essentially of a permutation followed by a sequence of 16

---

[3] Copies of this publication can be obtained from the National Institute of Standards and Technology of the U.S. Department of Commerce.

substitutions and a final permutation. The substitution operations are similar to those in earlier examples. Some are obtained by the addition of keywords (16 different ones), and others use substitution tables.

DES was adopted in 1977 by the National Institute of Standards and Technology (formerly the National Bureau of Standards) as the standard encryption scheme for sensitive federal documents. It has been the subject of some controversy, however, because of questions about its security. In fact, two Israeli scientists, E. Biham and A. Shamir (one of the developers of the popular public-key encryption scheme described next) recently announced a mathematical technique that makes it possible to break the DES code under certain circumstances.

Public-Key Encryption. Each of the preceding encryption schemes requires that both the sender and the receiver know the encryption key or keys. This means that although an encrypted message may be transmitted through some public channel such as a telephone line that is not secure, the keys must be transmitted in some secure manner, for example, by a courier. This problem of maintaining secrecy of the key is compounded when it must be shared by several persons.

Recently developed encryption schemes eliminate this problem by using two keys, one for encryption and one for decryption. These schemes are called **public-key encryption schemes** because the encryption key is made public by the receiver to all those who will transmit messages to him or her; the decryption key, however, is known only to the receiver. The security of these schemes depends on it being nearly impossible to determine the decryption key if one knows only the encryption key.

In 1978, R. L. Rivest, A. Shamir, and L. Adelman proposed one method of implementing a public-key encryption scheme.[4] The public key is a pair (e, n) of integers, and a message string M is encrypted by first dividing M into blocks $M_1, M_2, \ldots, M_k$ and converting each block M_i of characters to an integer P_i in the range 0 through $n - 1$ (for example, by concatenating the ASCII codes of the characters). M is then encrypted by raising each block to the power e and reducing modulo n:

$$\text{Message:} \quad M = M_1 M_2 \cdots M_k \rightarrow P_1 P_2 \cdots P_k$$

$$\text{Cryptogram:} \quad C = C_1 C_2 \cdots C_k, \; C_i = P_i^e \text{ modulo } n$$

(Here x modulo n is the remainder when x is divided by n.) The cryptogram C is decrypted by raising each block C_i to the power d and reducing modulo n, where d is a secret decryption key.

To illustrate, suppose that characters are converted to numeric values using the codes 0, 1, 2, ..., 25 for the letters A, B, C, ..., Z, respectively, and that (17, 2773) is the public encryption key. To encrypt the string $M =$ "IDESOFMARCH" using the RSA (Rivest–Shamir–Adelman) algorithm, we divide M into two-character blocks

---

[4] R. L. Rivest, A. Shamir, and L. Adelman, "A Method for Obtaining Digital Signatures and Public-Key Cryptosystems," *Communications of the ACM*, February 1978, pp. 120–126.

$M_1, M_2, \ldots, M_6$ (after appending a randomly selected character X) and represent each block M_i as an integer P_i in the range 0 through $2773 - 1 = 2772$ by concatenating the numeric codes of the characters that comprise the block:

	M_1	M_2	M_3	M_4	M_5	M_6
	|	|	|	|	|	|
Original string:	ID	ES	OF	MA	RC	HX
	↓	↓	↓	↓	↓	↓
	0803	0418	1405	1200	1702	0723
	|	|	|	|	|	|
	P_1	P_2	P_3	P_4	P_5	P_6

Each of these blocks P_i is then encrypted by calculating $C_i = P_i^{17}$ modulo 2773:

Encrypted codes:	0779	1983	2641	1444	0052	0802
	|	|	|	|	|	|
	C_1	C_2	C_3	C_4	C_5	C_6

For this encryption key, the corresponding decrypting key is $d = 157$. Thus, we decrypt by calculating C_i^{157} modulo 2773 for each block C_i. For the preceding encrypted string, this gives

Decrypted codes:	0803	0418	1405	1200	1702	0723

which is the numeric form of the original string.

The number n is the product of two large "random" primes p and q,

$$n = p \cdot q$$

In the preceding example, we used the small primes 47 and 59 to simplify the computations, but Rivest, Shamir, and Adelman suggest that p and q have several hundred digits. The decrypting key d is then selected to be some large integer that is relatively prime to both $p - 1$ and $q - 1$; that is, one that has no factors in common with either number. In our example, $d = 157$ has this property. The number e is then selected to have the property that

$$e \cdot d \text{ modulo } ((p - 1) \cdot (q - 1)) \text{ is equal to } 1$$

To break this code, one must be able to determine the value of d from the values of n and e. Because of the manner in which d and e are selected, this is possible if n can be factored into a product of primes. Thus, the security of the RSA encryption scheme is based on the difficulty of determining the prime factors of a large integer. Even with the best factorization algorithms known today, this is a prohibitively time-consuming task. A study a few years ago gave the following table displaying some estimated times, assuming that each operation required one microsecond:

Number of Digits in Number Being Factored	Time
50	4 hours
75	104 days
100	74 years
200	4 billion years
300	5×10^{15} years
500	4×10^{25} years

Although research on factorization continues, no algorithms have been found that significantly reduce the times in the preceding table. Improved algorithms and the use of high-speed computers have made factorization possible in less time than the table shows, but not significantly less for large numbers. This public-key encryption scheme thus appears (so far) to be quite secure and is being endorsed by a growing number of major computer vendors. The adoption of a public-key encryption standard is being considered by the National Institute of Standards and Technology.

Exercises 11.8

1. A pure permutation encryption scheme is very insecure. Explain why, by describing how an encryption scheme that merely permutes the bits in an n-bit string can easily be cracked by studying how certain basic bit strings are encrypted. Show this for $n = 4$.

For Exercises 2–7, use the character codes $0, 1, \ldots, 25$ given in the text.

2. Encrypt the string "PUBLIC" using the Caesar cipher scheme with key = 3.

3. Encrypt the string "PUBLIC" using the Vignère cipher scheme with keyword "AND".

4. Encrypt the string "PUBLIC" using the substitution table given in the text.

5. Encrypt the string "PUBLIC" using the permutation given in the text:

   Original position: 1 2 3

   Permuted position: 3 1 2

6. Encrypt the string "PUBLIC" using the RSA scheme with encryption key (e, n) = (5, 2881).

7. One decrypting key for the RSA scheme in Exercise 6 is $d = 1109$. Use it to decrypt the codes obtained in Exercise 6.

11.9 APPLICATION: COMPUTER GRAPHICS

The number and quality of software packages and even hand-held calculators that can be used to generate high-resolution graphs of functions are increasing rapidly. For example, Figure 11.7(a) shows the graph of $y = x * \cos(x)$ for $-8 \le x \le 8$ as plotted on a Texas Instruments TI-85 calculator, and Figure 11.7(b) shows the same graph as produced by the powerful software package Mathematica™.

The window containing each of the plots shown in Figure 11.7 is simply a two-dimensional array of points (called *pixels*) on the screen, some of which (those corresponding to points on the graph of the function) are "on" (black) and the rest of which are "off" (white). Figure 11.8 shows an enlarged view of the portion of the graphics window near the origin in Figure 11.7; the grid structure of this part of the window is evident.

Example 1: Scatter Plots

The subroutine `ScatterPlot` in the module `GraphingRoutines` of Figure 11.10 uses this same approach to produce a **scatter plot** of a collection of data points. For example, Figure 11.9 shows a scatter plot of cutting times (in minutes) using an oxyacetylene torch versus metal thicknesses (in inches—see Exercise 3 of Section 4.6). A listing of a file containing these (thickness, time) pairs is given in Figure 11.10. Such plots are used in exploratory data analysis. For example, as in Figure 11.9, they might suggest that the data points are clustered about some line (or about some other curve). The least-squares method described in Section 4.6 could then be used to find the equation of the line that best fits these data points, and this equation could then be used to predict cutting times for other metal thicknesses.

The subroutine `ScatterPlot` in module `GraphingRoutines` in Figure 11.10 produces a scatter plot of data points stored in a file whose name is passed as an argument to `ScatterPlot`. It uses a `Vert_Limit` × `Horiz_Limit` character array `Window`, each element of which is a single character corresponding to a point in a graphics window. The first line of the data file contains values for `X_Min`

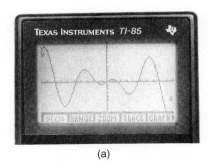

(a)

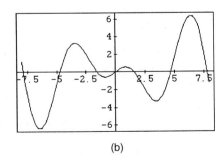

(b)

Figure 11.7

(a) Plot of $y = x * \cos(x)$ on a Texas Instruments TI-85 calculator. (Photo by Randal Nyhof, Nyhof School Pictures) (b) Plot of $y = x * \cos(x)$ produced by Mathematica.

Figure 11.8

Blow-up of
graphics
window.

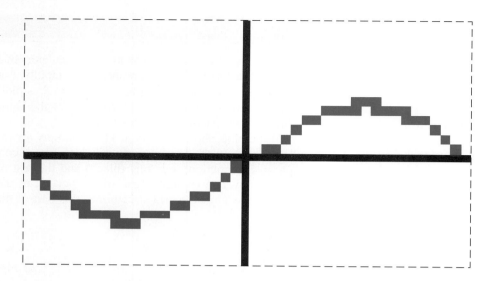

and X_Max, the minimum and maximum X values, and for Y_Min and Y_Max, the minimum and maximum Y values. The rows of the two-dimensional array `Window` correspond to X values ranging from X_Min to X_Max in increments of DeltaX = (X_Max - X_Min) / Horiz_Limit, and the rows correspond to Y values ranging from Y_Min to Y_Max in steps of DeltaY = (Y_Max - Y_Min) / Vert_Limit. For each X value, the Y value nearest the actual Y data value is determined, and the point `Window(X,Y)` is set to some plotting character such as `"*"` ("on"); all other elements of `Window` are blank ("off").

A Hewlett Packard Deskjet 600 plotter.

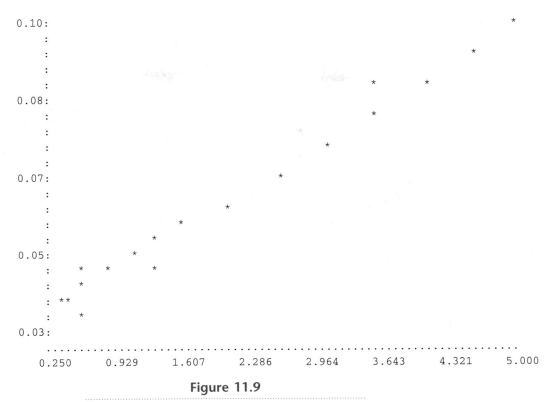

```
0.10:                                                                    *
    :
    :
    :
    :                                                              *
0.08:                                                        *        *
    :                                                  *
    :                                               *
    :
    :                                       *
    :
0.07:                                 *
    :
    :                            *
    :                      *
    :                  *
0.05:              *
    :     *    *     *
    :     *
    :  **
    :     *
0.03:
    .........................................................................
     0.250     0.929     1.607     2.286     2.964     3.643     4.321     5.000
```

Figure 11.9

Scatter plot produced by program in Figure 11.10.

Figure 11.10 Scatter plot.

```
MODULE GraphingRoutines
!-----------------------------------------------------------------------
! Module that contains the subroutines for producing various kinds
! of graphs:
!     ScatterPlot
!     DensityPlot
!     . . .
!-----------------------------------------------------------------------


CONTAINS
```

Figure 11.10 *(cont.)*

```
!-ScatterPlot------------------------------------------------------------
! Subroutine to produce a scatter plot of data points stored in a file,
! the first line of which contains values for X_Min, X_Max, Y_Min, and
! Y_Max, in this order. Local identifiers used are:
!    Horiz_Limit,
!    Vert_Limit      : limits on the size of the graphics window
!                       (constants)
!    Window          : two-dimensional character array -- the graphics
!                       window
!    PlotChar        : plotting character -- represents a point on the
!                       graph
!    X_Min, X_Max    : minimum and maximum X values
!    Y_Min, Y_Max    : minimum and maximum Y values
!    DeltaX, DeltaY  : X and Y increments
!    X, Y            : a point on the graph
!    X_Loc, Y_Loc    : location of a point in the window
!    Count           : counts units on Y-axis for labeling purposes
!    OpenStatus      : status variable for OPEN
!    InputStatus     : status variable for READ
!
! Accepts:          FileName
! Output (screen):  The graphics window
!------------------------------------------------------------------------

SUBROUTINE ScatterPlot(FileName)

  IMPLICIT NONE
  CHARACTER(*), INTENT(IN) :: FileName
  REAL :: X_Min, X_Max, Y_Min, Y_Max, DeltaX, DeltaY, X, Y
  INTEGER, PARAMETER :: Horiz_Limit = 70, Vert_Limit = 20
  INTEGER :: X_Loc, Y_Loc, OpenStatus, InputStatus, Count
  CHARACTER(1), DIMENSION(0:Horiz_Limit, 0:Vert_Limit) :: Window
  CHARACTER(1), PARAMETER :: PlotChar = "*"

  OPEN (UNIT = 20, FILE = FileName, STATUS = "OLD", IOSTAT = OpenStatus)
  IF (OpenStatus > 0) STOP "*** Cannot open input file ***"

  READ (20, *, IOSTAT = InputStatus)  X_Min, X_Max, Y_Min, Y_Max
  IF (IOStatus > 0) STOP "*** Input error ***"
  IF (IOStatus < 0) STOP "*** No data in file ***"

  DeltaX = (X_Max - X_Min) / REAL(Horiz_Limit)
  DeltaY = (Y_Max - Y_Min) / REAL(Vert_Limit)
```

Figure 11.10 *(cont.)*

```
Window = " "

! Read data pairs and turn on points in window corresponding to pairs

DO
    READ (20, *, IOSTAT = InputStatus) X, Y
    IF (IOStatus > 0) STOP "*** Input error ***"
    IF (IOStatus < 0) EXIT
    ! If end of file, terminate repetition

    ! Otherwise plot point
    X_Loc = NINT((X - X_Min)/ DeltaX)
    Y_Loc = NINT((Y - Y_Min)/ DeltaY)
    Window(X_Loc, Y_Loc) = PlotChar
END DO

! Draw the window together with labeled Y-axis

Y = Y_Max
Count = 5 * (Vert_Limit / 5)
DO Y_Loc = Vert_Limit, 0, -1
    IF (MOD(Count, 5) == 0) THEN
        PRINT '(1X, F8.2, ":", 200A)', &
            Y, (Window(X_Loc,Y_Loc), X_Loc = 0, Horiz_Limit)
    ELSE
        PRINT '(9X, ":", 200A)', &
            (Window(X_Loc,Y_Loc), X_Loc = 0, Horiz_Limit)
    END IF
    Count = Count - 1
    Y = Y - DeltaY
END DO

! Draw a labeled X-axis

PRINT '(9X, 200A)', (".", X_Loc = 0, Horiz_Limit)
PRINT '(3X, 50F10.3)', &
    (X_Min + X_Loc*DeltaX, X_Loc = 0, Horiz_Limit, 10)

END SUBROUTINE ScatterPlot

!    . . .

END MODULE GraphingRoutines
```

Figure 11.10 *(cont.)*

```
PROGRAM Scatter_Plot_of_Data
!-------------------------------------------------------------------------
! Program to produce a scatter plot of a data set stored in a file.
! The name of the file is passed to subroutine ScatterPlot imported
! from module GraphingRoutines.  Identifiers used are:
!    FileName : name of file containing data set to be plotted
!    Plot     : subroutine called to produce scatter plot
!
! Input:   FileName
! Output: User prompts and the scatter plot
!-------------------------------------------------------------------------

  USE GraphingRoutines, ONLY: ScatterPlot

  IMPLICIT NONE
  CHARACTER(20) :: FileName

  PRINT *, "This program produces a scatter plot of data points"
  PRINT *, "stored in a data file.  The first line of this file"
  PRINT *, "must contain the minimum and maximum x values and"
  PRINT *, "the minimum and maximum y values, in this order."
  PRINT *
  WRITE (*, '(/ 1X, A)', ADVANCE = "NO") "Enter the name of the data file: "
  READ *, FileName
  CALL ScatterPlot(FileName)

END PROGRAM Scatter_Plot_of_Data
```

Listing of file `fi11-10.dat` that produced Figure 11.9:

```
0.25, 5.0, 0.030, 0.102
0.25    0.036
0.5     0.039
0.375   0.037
3.5     0.078
2.0     0.058
1.0     0.046
5.0     0.102
0.75    0.042
1.25    0.050
4.5     0.093
1.5     0.053
3.0     0.073
```

Figure 11.10 *(cont.)*

```
2.5      0.065
4.0      0.085
0.5      0.044
1.25     0.044
3.5      0.084
0.5      0.030
```

Example 2: Plotting a Graph

If we order the points in Figure 11.9 and connect consecutive points with line segments, we obtain a polygonal path that passes through all the data points. If these points were on the graph of some function $y = f(x)$ and we ordered them by increasing x values, this polygonal path would approximate the graph of this function.

The program in Figure 11.11 uses this approach to graph the function $f(x) = x * \cos(x)$ considered at the beginning of this section. It generates two arrays XPlot and YPlot so that for each integer I, (XPlot(I), YPlot(I)) is a point in a 640 × 480 (pixels) graphic window that corresponds to a point on the graph. The subroutine PLOT_LINE@ provided in the graphics library of the Salford FTN90 compiler is then called to draw a polygonal path connecting these points. The output produced by the program is shown in Figure 11.12.

Figure 11.11 Graphing a function.

```
PROGRAM Plot_a_Graph
!-------------------------------------------------------------------
! Program to plot the graph of a function Y = F(X) on a given interval.
! The graphics routines of Salford FTN90 are used to draw the plot.
! Identifiers used are:
!   X, Y               : a point on the graph
!   X_Min, X_Max       : min. and max. X values
!   Y_Min, Y_Max       : min. and max. Y values
!   DeltaX, DeltaY     : X and Y increments
!   Horiz_Pixels       : number of pixels in horizontal direction
!   Vert_Pixels        : number of pixels in vertical direction
!   XPlot, YPlot       : (XPlot(I), YPlot(I)) is the position of a pixel that
!                        approximates a point on the graph
!
! Input:  Min. and Max. X and Y values
! Output: Graph of Y = F(X) over the interval [X_Min, X_Max]
!-------------------------------------------------------------------
```

Figure 11.11 *(cont.)*

```
   REAL :: X, Y, X_Min, X_Max, Y_Min, Y_Max, DeltaX, DeltaY
   INTEGER, PARAMETER :: Horiz_Pixels = 640, Vert_Pixels = 480
   INTEGER (KIND = 2) :: I, XPlot(640), YPlot(640)


   WRITE (*, '(1X, A)', ADVANCE = "NO") &
         "Enter min. & max. X values, then min. & max. Y values: "
   READ *, X_Min, X_Max, Y_Min, Y_Max
   DeltaX = (X_Max - X_Min) / REAL(Horiz_Pixels)
   DeltaY = (Y_Max - Y_Min) / REAL(Vert_Pixels)

   X = X_Min
   DO I = 1, Horiz_Pixels
      Y = F(X)
      XPlot(I) = NINT((X - X_Min)/ DeltaX)
      YPlot(I) = NINT((Y - Y_Min)/ DeltaY)
      X = X + DeltaX
   END DO

   ! The following graphics routines are from Salford FTN90

   ! Set up VGA graphics and clear the graphics screen and
   CALL VGA@
   CALL CLEAR_SCREEN_AREA@(0, 0, 639, 480, 11)

   ! Draw a polygonal line through the points (XPlot(I), YPlot(I))
   CALL POLYLINE@(XPlot, YPlot, 640, 16)

   ! Terminate the graphics session and return to text mode
   CALL GET_KEY@(K)
   CALL TEXT_MODE@

CONTAINS

   ! F(X) -----------------------------
   ! The function to be plotted
   !-----------------------------------

   FUNCTION F(X)

   REAL :: F, X

   F = X * COS(X)

   END FUNCTION F

END PROGRAM Plot_a_Graph
```

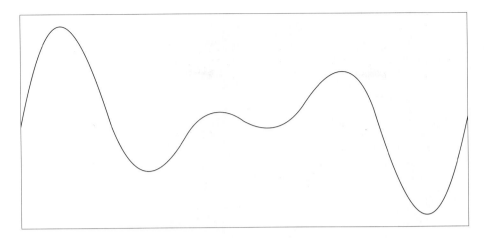

Figure 11.12

Graph of
$y = x * \cos x$
produced by
the program
in Figure
11.11.

Example 3: Density Plots and Level Curves

In the preceding example, we described how two-dimensional graphs of functions $y = f(x)$ of a single variable can be displayed. Graphs of functions $z = f(x, y)$ of two variables x and y are surfaces in three dimensions and are considerably more difficult to display on a two-dimensional screen. Some software packages are able to generate good two-dimensional representations of many three-dimensional surfaces. For example, Figure 11.13 shows a graph produced by Mathematica of the surface defined by the function

$$z = e^{-(x^2 + y^2)}$$

Note that in this representation, shading is used to represent the height of the function, with lighter shades for larger values and darker shades for smaller values. This shading, together with the curved grid lines and the enclosing box, produces a visu-

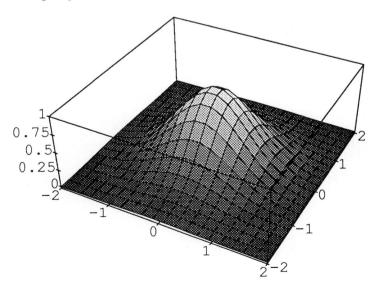

Figure 11.13

Mathematica
plot of $z = e^{-(x^2 + y^2)}$.

Figure 11.14

Density plot
of $z =$
$e^{-(x^2 + y^2)}$ in
Mathematica.

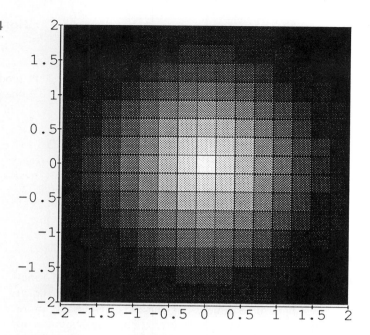

al illusion of a three-dimensional surface. Another representation of a surface that also uses shading but not perspective is a **density plot** obtained by projecting a representation like that in Figure 11.13 onto a plane. Figure 11.14 shows the density plot generated by Mathematica for this surface. The various densities of gray again indicate different heights of the function.

The program in Figure 11.15 produces a density plot for a function F. It uses a character array Window of 10 different characters, with Window(X,Y) representing the height of the function at point (X, Y). The order of the characters in the array Gray corresponds to increasing Z values, beginning with Z_Min, the minimum Z value. The sample run shows the output produced for the function $f(x, y) = e^{-(x^2 + y^2)}$ with Z_Min = 0 and Z_Max = 1, using the characters "0", "1", ..., "9".

Figure 11.15 Density plot.

```
MODULE Function_F
!-------------------------------------------------------------------
! Module that contains the function whose graph is to be plotted
!-------------------------------------------------------------------

CONTAINS

  FUNCTION F(X,Y)

    REAL :: F
    REAL, INTENT(IN) :: X, Y
```

Figure 11.15 *(cont.)*

```
    F = EXP(-(X**2 + Y**2))

  END FUNCTION F

END MODULE Function_F

MODULE GraphingRoutines
!-------------------------------------------------------------------------
! Module that contains the subroutines for producing various kinds
! of graphs:
!     ScatterPlot
!     DensityPlot
!     . . .
!-------------------------------------------------------------------------

CONTAINS

  !-ScatterPlot-----
  ! . . .

  !-DensityPlot------------------------------------------------------------
  ! Subroutine to generate a density plot of a function Z = F(X, Y) for
  ! X ranging from X_Min to X_Max and Y ranging from Y_Min to Y_Max; Z is
  ! allowed to range from Z_Min to Z_Max.  Local identifiers used are
  !    FileName     : name of file containing the output
  !    Horiz_Limit,
  !    Vert_Limit   : limits on the size of the graphics window (constants)
  !    Window       : two-dimensional character array -- the graphics window
  !    MaxGraySub   : constant: largest subscript in array Gray
  !    Gray         : array of symbols representing shades of gray
  !    DeltaX       : X-increment
  !    DeltaY       : Y-increment
  !    DeltaZ       : Z-increment
  !    X, Y, Z      : a point on the graph
  !    X_Loc,
  !    Y_Loc        : location of a point in the window
  !    Shade_for_Z  : shade of gray used to represent height Z
  !    OpenStatus   : status variable for OPEN
  !    OutputStatus : status variable for READ
  !
  ! Accepts:         F, X_Min, X_Max, Y_Min, Y_Max, Z_Min, Z_Max
  ! Input (keyboard): FileName
  ! Output (screen): User prompt
  ! Output (file):   The graphics window
  !------------------------------------------------------------------------
```

Figure 11.15 *(cont.)*

```
SUBROUTINE DensityPlot (X_Min, X_Max, Y_Min, Y_Max, Z_Min, Z_Max)

  USE Function_F

  IMPLICIT NONE
  REAL, INTENT(IN) ::  X_Min, X_Max, Y_Min, Y_Max, Z_Min, Z_Max
  REAL :: DeltaX, DeltaY, DeltaZ, X, Y, Z
  INTEGER, PARAMETER ::  Horiz_Limit = 75, Vert_Limit = 45, MaxGraySub = 9
  INTEGER :: X_Loc, Y_Loc, Shade_for_Z, OpenStatus, OutputStatus
  CHARACTER(1), DIMENSION(0:Horiz_Limit, 0:Vert_Limit) :: Window
  CHARACTER(1), DIMENSION(0:MaxGraySub) :: &
                  Gray = (/"0","1","2","3","4","5","6","7","8","9"/)
  CHARACTER(20) :: FileName

  WRITE (*, '(1X, A)', ADVANCE = "NO") &
        "Enter name of file to contain the density plot: "
  READ *, FileName
  OPEN (UNIT = 20, FILE = FileName, STATUS = "NEW", IOSTAT = OpenStatus)
  IF (OpenStatus > 0) STOP "*** Cannot open output file ***"

  DeltaX = (X_Max - X_Min) / REAL(Horiz_Limit)
  DeltaY = (Y_Max - Y_Min) / REAL(Vert_Limit)
  DeltaZ = (Z_Max - Z_Min) / REAL(MaxGraySub)

  ! "Shade" each element of Window with appropriate gray

  Y = Y_Min
  DO Y_Loc = 0, Vert_Limit
     X = X_Min
     DO X_Loc = 0, Horiz_Limit
        Z = F(X, Y)

        ! Find gray shade corresponding to Z value

        IF (Z > Z_Max) THEN
           Shade_for_Z = MaxGraySub
        ELSE
           Shade_for_Z = NINT((Z - Z_Min) / DeltaZ)
        END IF

        Window(X_Loc, Y_Loc) = Gray(Shade_for_Z)
        X = X + DeltaX
     END DO

     Y = Y + DeltaY
  END DO
```

Figure 11.15 *(cont.)*

```
    ! Draw the Window in the file

    DO Y_Loc = Vert_Limit, 0, -1
       WRITE(20, *, IOSTAT = OutputStatus) &
            (Window(X_Loc,Y_Loc), X_Loc = 0, Horiz_Limit)
       IF (IOStatus > 0) STOP "*** Input error ***"
    END DO

  END SUBROUTINE DensityPlot

PROGRAM Density_Plot_of_a_Function
!-----------------------------------------------------------------------
! Program to produce a density plot of a function Z = F(X, Y).  F is
! defined by a module function subprogram and is passed to
! subroutine DensityPlot imported from module GraphingRoutines.
! Identifiers used are:
!   F                 : function to be plotted
!   X_Min, X_Max : minimum and maximum X values
!   Y_Min, Y_Max : minimum and maximum Y values
!   Z_Min, Z_Max : minimum and maximum Z values
!
! Input:  X_Min, X_Max, Y_Min, Y_Max
! Output: User prompts and density plot of Z = F(X, Y)
!-----------------------------------------------------------------------

  USE GraphingRoutines, ONLY: DensityPlot

  IMPLICIT NONE

  REAL :: X_Min, X_Max, Y_Min, Y_Max, Z_Min, Z_Max

  WRITE (*, '(1X, A)', ADVANCE = "NO") &
       "Enter minimum and maximum x-values, then y-values: "
  READ *, X_Min, X_Max, Y_Min, Y_Max
  WRITE (*, '(1X, A)', ADVANCE = "NO") &
       "Enter minimum and maximum values of function: "
  READ *, Z_Min, Z_Max
  CALL DensityPlot(X_Min, X_Max, Y_Min, Y_Max, Z_Min, Z_Max)

END PROGRAM Density_Plot_of_a_Function
```

Figure 11.15 *(cont.)*

Sample run:

```
Enter minimum and maximum x-values, then y-values: -2, 2,  -2, 2
Enter minimum and maximum values of function: 0, 1
Enter name of file to contain the density plot: fil11-15.out
```

Listing of `fil11-15.OUT` (reduced)

```
00000000000000000000000000000000000000000000000000000000000000000000000
00000000000000000000000000000000000000000000000000000000000000000000000
00000000000000000000000000000000000000000000000000000000000000000000000
00000000000000000000000001111111111111111111110000000000000000000000000
00000000000000000000001111111111111111111111111110000000000000000000000
00000000000000000000011111111111111111111111111111111100000000000000000
00000000000000000011111111111111122222222222211111111111111000000000000
00000000000000011111111111112222222222222222222221111111111110000000000
00000000000000111111111111222222222233333333332222222221111111111000000
00000000000001111111111222222223333333333333332222222221111111110000000
0000000000011111111222222333333344444444444443333332222221111111100000000
00000000001111111122222333334444445555555544444433332222211111111000000
000000000111111112222233334444455555556665555555444443333222211111111000000
0000000011111111222233344445556666666666666655554443333222211111111100000
000000011111112222233344445556666777777777766665554443332222111111110000000
00000011111112222333445556667777788888777776665554443332222111111100000000
00000011111112222233344555666777888888888888877766655544433322221111111100000000
0000001111111222223334455566677788888999988887777665554433322221111111000000
0000001111111222233344555667778888999999998888777665554433322221111111000000
0000001111111222233344555667778888999999998888777665554433322221111111000000
0000001111111222233344555667778888999999998888777665554433322221111111000000
0000001111111222233344555667778888999988887777665554433322221111111000000
00000011111112222233344555666777888888888888877766655544433322221111111100000000
00000011111112222233344555666777777888877777666555444333222211111110000000
000000011111112222233344445556666666666666655554443333222211111111100000
000000001111111222223333444445555555566665555555544444333322222111111111000000
00000000011111111222223333334444444455555555544444433333222221111111100000000
0000000000111111112222223333333344444444444443333333222222111111111000000000
000000000001111111122222223333333333333333322222222221111111111000000000
0000000000001111111111112222222222222222222222221111111111110000000000
00000000000000111111111111122222222222222222221111111111111000000000000
000000000000000111111111111111111222111111111111111111000000000000000000
00000000000000000111111111111111111111111111111111111000000000000000000
000000000000000000001111111111111111111111111111110000000000000000000000
0000000000000000000000000011111111111111111111111000000000000000000000000
00000000000000000000000000000000000000000000000000000000000000000000000
00000000000000000000000000000000000000000000000000000000000000000000000
00000000000000000000000000000000000000000000000000000000000000000000000
00000000000000000000000000000000000000000000000000000000000000000000000
```

Characters other than "0", "1", ..., "9" can be used simply by changing the array constant used to initialize Gray in this program. For example, if "gray-scale characters" were available, a density plot similar to that in Figure 11.14 could be generated. Figure 11.16 shows the result obtained when ordinary characters such as "#", "@", and "+" are used to achieve various densities and the output is reduced still more than that in Figure 11.15.

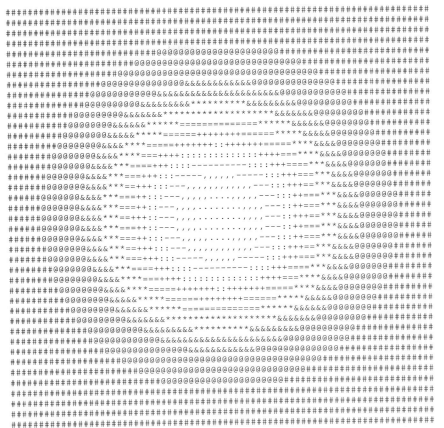

Figure 11.16

Density plot
of $e^{-(x^2 + y^2)}$.

Another common two-dimensional representation of a three-dimensional surface $z = f(x, y)$ is obtained by displaying its **level curves** or **contour maps.** A level curve consists of all points (x, y) where the function has a particular constant value. For example, if $f(x, y)$ represents the temperature at point (x, y), the level curve $f(x, y) = 30$ is an isothermal curve consisting of all points where the temperature is 30.

The level curves for $f(x, y) = e^{-(x^2 + y^2)}$ can be seen in the density plots produced by the program in Figure 11.15 as the circles that separate one level from another. Figure 11.17 shows the level curves that Mathematica produces for this function. The largest circle is the level curve $e^{-(x^2 + y^2)} = 0.1$, or equivalently $x^2 + y^2 = |\ln(0.1)|$; the smallest circle is the level curve $e^{-(x^2 + y^2)} = 0.9$, which can also be written $x^2 + y^2 = |\ln(0.9)|$; the other circles are level curves corresponding to $0.8, 0.7, \ldots,$ 0.2.

The ideas in this example can be modified to display an image that is represented in digitized form and then to enhance this image. This digitized representation might be a table of light intensities transmitted from a remote sensor such as a television camera in a satellite. This problem of visual image processing and enhancement is described in the programming projects.

Figure 11.17

Level curves
of $e^{-(x^2 + y^2)}$
in
Mathematica.

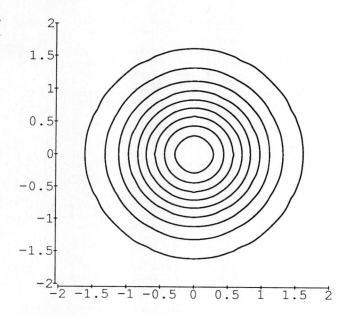

CHAPTER REVIEW

Summary

In this chapter we considered parameterized data types and the COMPLEX data type, and we extended the discussion of the CHARACTER data type begun in Chapter 2. We described parameterized real and integer constants, declarations of parameterized variables, and several intrinsic functions used with parameterized types. We illustrated how extended precision may be helpful in solving ill-conditioned linear systems. We described complex numbers, variables, and operations, input/output of complex values, and several complex library functions. We used the COMPLEX data type in a program for analyzing an a-c circuit. We reviewed character constants and variables and character input/output. We also described the concatenation and substring operations and an assortment of intrinsic functions for processing character data. Applications using these character-processing features included text processing, lexical analysis, cryptography, and computer graphics.

FORTRAN SUMMARY

Parameterized Type Statements

```
type-specifier(KIND = kind-number), attributes :: list
```

where "KIND =" is optional; *type-specifier* is one of INTEGER, REAL, COMPLEX, LOGICAL, CHARACTER; *kind-number* is a positive integer constant or a constant integer expression whose value is positive; and *list* is a list of identifiers, separated by commas.

Examples:

```
REAL(KIND = 2) :: Z
REAL(KIND = 2), DIMENSION(5,5) :: Beta
INTEGER, PARAMETER :: Prec10 = SELECTED_REAL_KIND(10)
REAL(KIND = Prec10) :: A, B
INTEGER, PARAMETER :: Range20 = SELECTED_INT_KIND(20)
INTEGER(KIND = Range20) :: M, N
```

Purpose:
Declare the type and kind of values that variables will have.

Parameterized Type Constants

```
numeric-constant_kind
kind_character-constant
```

Examples:

```
1.23_2
0.1234567890_Prec10
123456789012345_Range20
greek_"αβγδ"
```

Character Operations

Concatenation:

```
char-expression₁ // char-expression₂
```

Examples:
Given the declarations and assignment

```
CHARACTER(7) :: SquareUnits
SquareUnits = "square "
```

the expression

```
SquareUnits // "centi" // "meters"
```

produces the string

```
"square centimeters"
```

Substring:

```
char-variable(init-position : final-position)
```

Examples:
Given the declarations and assignment

```
CHARACTER(12) :: Units
Units = "centimeters"
```

the values of

```
Units(:4), Units(4:7), and Units(6:)
```

are

```
"cent", "time", and "meters"
```

respectively.

Functions

Function	Description
SELECTED_INT_KIND(r)	Kind number for an integer type with range -10^r to 10^r
SELECTED_REAL_KIND(p, r)	Kind number for a real type with precision p and range -10^r to 10^r; r is optional
KIND(x)	Kind number of x
PRECISION(x)	Precision of x
RANGE(x)	Decimal exponent range of x
INT(x, k)	Converts x to an integer value of kind k
REAL(x, k)	Converts x to a real value of kind k
AIMAG(z)	Imaginary part of z
REAL(z)	Real part of z
CMPLX(x, y)	Converts x, y into a complex number
CMPLX(x)	Converts x into a complex number
CONJG(z)	Conjugate of z
ADJUSTL(s)	String obtained by left-justifying s
ADJUSTR(s)	String obtained by right-justifying s
REPEAT(s, n)	String obtained by concatenating n copies of s
TRIM(s)	String obtained by trimming trailing blanks from s
LEN(s)	Length of string s, including leading and trailing blanks
LEN_TRIM(s)	Length of string s, not including trailing blanks
INDEX(s_1, s_2, b)	Position of first occurrence of string s_2 in string s_1 if b is omitted or is .FALSE.; the last occurrence if b is .TRUE.; returns 0 if s_2 is not found in s_1
SCAN(s_1, s_2, b)	Position of leftmost character of string s_1 that appears in string s_2 if b is omitted or is .FALSE.; the rightmost character if b is .TRUE.; returns 0 if none is found

Function	Description
VERIFY(s_1, s_2, b)	Position of leftmost character of string s_1 that does not appear in string s_2 if b is omitted or is .FALSE.; the rightmost character if b is .TRUE.; returns 0 if all are found
LLT(s_1, s_2)	Determines if string $s_1 <$ string s_2 (in ASCII)
LLE(s_1, s_2)	Determines if string $s_1 \leq s_2$ (in ASCII)
LGT(s_1, s_2)	Determines if string $s_1 >$ string s_2 (in ASCII)
LGE(s_1, s_2)	Determines if string $s_1 \geq$ string s_2 (in ASCII)
ICHAR(c)	Numeric code of c
IACHAR(c)	ASCII code of c
CHAR(i)	Character whose numeric code is i
ACHAR(i)	Character whose ASCII code is i

Like INT and REAL, several of the intrinsic functions may also have an optional kind argument. These include AINT, ANINT, and CMPLX.

PROGRAMMING POINTERS

Program Style and Design

1. *The default* REAL *data type provides approximately seven significant digits. Parameterized* REAL *types should be used for computations that require extended precision.*

2. *To increase program portability, intrinsic functions* SELECTED_INT_KIND *and* SELECTED_REAL_KIND *should be used for parameterized numeric types instead of specific kind numbers, since these numbers are compiler dependent.*

3. *The* COMPLEX *data type should be used for computations that require complex numbers and operations.*

4. *Formatted output of complex values requires two real descriptors.*

5. *For formatted input of complex data, complex values are not enclosed in parentheses.*

Potential Problems

1. *Precision may be lost in extended-precision expressions and assignments because of the presence of lower-precision constants and/or variables.*

To illustrate, consider the following declarations:

```
REAL :: X
INTEGER, PARAMETER :: DP = SELECTED_REAL_KIND(14)
REAL(KIND = DP) :: A, B
```

In the assignment statement

```
B = 0.1 * A ** 2
```

precision may be lost because of the single-precision constant 0.1. This statement should be written as

```
B = 0.1_DP * A ** 2
```

Similarly, in the assignment statement

```
X = (A + B) * (A - B)
```

the expression on the right side is evaluated in double precision, but the resulting value is then assigned to the single-precision variable X. Remember, however, that simply declaring everything to have extended precision does not solve all of the problems arising from limited precision. For example, the logical expression

```
A * (1.0_DP / A) == 1.0_DP
```

is still false for most values of A.

2. *A pair of real constants representing a complex data value is enclosed in parentheses for list-directed input but not for formatted input.*

3. *Formatted output of complex values requires two real descriptors.*

4. *Complex values may be compared only with the relational operators == and /=.*

The character data type was introduced in earlier chapters and was described in more detail in this chapter. Some of the following programming pointers are summaries of earlier programming pointers, and the reader should refer to those for an expanded discussion.

5. *The first position specified in a substring reference should be no greater than the last position; also, both positions should be positive and no greater than the length of the string.* For a substring consisting of the leftmost characters of a string, the position need not be specified. Thus, if String is declared by

```
CHARACTER(10) :: String
```

then the substring reference

```
String( :4)
```

is equivalent to

```
String(1:4)
```

Similarly, for a substring consisting of the rightmost characters, the last position need not be specified. Thus,

```
String(6: )
```

is equivalent to

```
String(6:10)
```

6. *In an assignment to a substring, the value being assigned may not be a character expression that references any of the same positions to which values are being assigned.* Thus, for the character variable declared by

```
CHARACTER(10) :: String
```

the following assignment statement is not allowed:

```
String(3:7) = String(6:10)
```

7. *The collating sequence used to compare characters depends on the encoding system used to store characters.* For example,

```
"123" < "A23"
```

is true if ASCII coding is used, but it is false for EBCDIC.

8. *Character constants must be enclosed in apostrophes or quotation marks for list-directed input if any of the following is true:*
   - *They contain blanks, commas, or slashes.*
   - *They extend over more than one line.*
   - *The leading non-blank character is a quotation mark or an apostrophe.*
   - *A repetition indicator is used.*

9. *In assignment statements and in list-directed input, if the value being assigned or read has a length greater than that specified for the character variable (or substring), the rightmost characters are truncated. If the value has a length less than that of the variable (or substring), blanks are added at the right.* An acronym sometimes used to remember this is
   - **APT:**   for **A**ssignment (and list-directed input), blank **P**adding and **T**runcation both occur on the right.

   See Potential Problem 12 in the Programming Pointers section of Chapter 2 for more details.

10. *For formatted input/output, characters are truncated or blanks are added according to whether the field width is too small or too large. For input, truncation occurs on the left and blank padding on the right; for output, truncation occurs on the right and blank padding on the left.*

    The acronyms similar to that in Potential Problem 9 are
    - **POT:**   **P**adding on the left with blanks occurs for formatted **O**utput, or **T**runcation of rightmost characters occurs.
    - **TIP:**   **T**runcation of leftmost characters occurs for formatted **I**nput, or **P**adding with blanks on the right occurs.

See Potential Problem 4 in the Programming Pointers section of Chapter 5 for more details.

PROGRAMMING PROBLEMS

Sections 11.1 and 11.2

1. For the sequence of numbers $a_0, a_1, a_2, \ldots$ defined by

$$a_0 = e^1 - 1$$

and

$$a_{n+1} = (n + 1)a_n - 1, \qquad \text{for } n = 0, 1, 2, \ldots$$

it can be shown that for each n,

$$a_n = n! \left[e^1 - \left(1 + 1 + \frac{1}{2!} + \cdots + \frac{1}{n!} \right) \right]$$

so that this sequence converges to 0. Write a program that prints a table of values of a_n for $n = 0, 1, 2, \ldots, 15$, calculated first in single precision and then in double precision.

2. Write a program to find a double-precision approximation to the zero of a function using Newton's method (see Section 6.3).

3. Write a program to find a double-precision approximation to an integral using the trapezoidal method or Simpson's rule (see Section 6.3 and Programming Problem 31 in Chapter 6).

4. Repeat Programming Problem 13 in Chapter 6 for calculating values of the hyperbolic sine function sinh by using a subprogram to calculate e^x, but perform all calculations in extended precision. In particular, use the series to calculate values for e^x using extended-precision arithmetic to achieve 10-decimal-place accuracy.

Sections 11.3 and 11.4

5. Write a program that reads three complex numbers P, Q, and R and then determines whether the triangle whose vertices are the points corresponding to P, Q, and R in the complex plane is a right triangle.

6. Write a subroutine that converts a complex number from its usual representation to its polar representation. Use the subroutine in a program that reads a complex number z and a positive integer n and finds the *nth roots of* z as given by

$$z^{1/n} = r^{1/n} \left[\cos\left(\frac{\theta + 2k\pi}{n} \right) + i \sin\left(\frac{\theta + 2k\pi}{n} \right) \right], \qquad \text{for } k = 0, 1, \ldots, n - 1$$

7. Modify the program in Figure 6.4 to use Newton's method to find complex roots of polynomials. Use Horner's method (i.e., nested multiplication) as described in Programming Problem 13 of Chapter 8 to evaluate the polynomials efficiently.

8. In a circuit containing a resistor and an inductor in series, the voltage is given by

$$V = (R + i\omega L)I$$

where V is the voltage (in volts), R is the resistance (in ohms), L is the inductance (in henrys), and ω is the angular velocity (in radians per second). Write a program that can be used to compute the voltage (complex) given the current (complex), or to find the current given the voltage. Use $R = 1.3\Omega$, $L = 0.55$ mH, and $\omega = 365.0$ rad/sec.

Sections 11.5 to 11.7

9. Write a program that reads a character string and prints it in reverse order, beginning with the last non-blank character.

10. Write a program to determine whether a specified string occurs in a given string, and if so, print an asterisk (*) under the first position of each occurrence.

11. Write a program to count the occurrences of a specified character in several lines of text.

12. Write a program to count the occurrences of a specified string in several lines of text.

13. Write a program that permits the input of a name consisting of a first name, a middle name or initial, and a last name, in that order, and then prints the last name followed by a comma and then the first and middle initials, each followed by a period. For example, the input John   Henry   Doe should produce Doe,   J. H..

14. Write a program to read STUDENT.DAT (see Appendix B) and display the name and cumulative GPA of all students with a given major.

15. A file contains grade records for students in a first-year engineering class. Each record consists of several lines of information. The first line contains the student's name in columns 1 through 30 and the letter T or F in column 31 to indicate whether a letter grade is to be assigned (T) or the course is to be graded on a pass/fail basis (F). The next 10 lines contain the test scores for this student, one integer score per line in columns 1 through 3. Write a program to read these records and, for each student, to display on a single line his or her name, term average (in the form xxx.x), and final grade. If the student has selected the pass/fail option, the final grade is "Pass" for a term average of 70.0 or above and "Fail" otherwise. If the student has selected the letter grade option, the final grade is "A" for a term average of 90.0 or above, "B" for a term average of 80.0 through 89.9, "C" for a term average of 70.0 through 79.9, "D" for a term average of 60.0 through 69.9, and "F" otherwise.

16. The following data file contains for each of several objects its shape (cube or sphere), its critical dimension (edge or radius), its density, and the material from which it is made:

```
sphere    2.0    .00264    aluminum
cube      3.0    .00857    brass
```

```
cub        1.5      .0113    lead
sphere     1.85     .0088    nickel
CUBE       13.7     .00035   cedar
SPHERE     2.85     .00075   oak
```

Write a program to read these records and produce a table displaying the following information for each object:

(a) Shape
(b) Critical dimension
(c) Material
(d) Volume
(e) Mass
(f) Whether the object will float when immersed in an oil bath
(g) Mass of oil displaced by the object

(An object will float if its density is less than or equal to the density of oil, .00088 kg/cm^3.) Your program should check that each object's shape is one of the strings `"cube"`, `"CUBE"`, `"sphere"`, or `"SPHERE"`.

17. Reverend Zeller developed a formula for computing the day of the week on which a given date fell or will fall. Suppose that we let a, b, c, and d be integers defined as follows:

> a = The month of the year, with March = 1, April = 2, and so on, with January and February being counted as months 11 and 12 of the preceding year
>
> b = The day of the month
>
> c = The year of the century
>
> d = The century

For example, July 31, 1929 gives $a = 5$, $b = 31$, $c = 29$, $d = 19$; January 3, 1988 gives $a = 11$, $b = 3$, $c = 87$, $d = 19$. Now calculate the following integer quantities:

> w = The integer quotient $(13a - 1)/5$
>
> x = The integer quotient $c/4$
>
> y = The integer quotient $d/4$
>
> $z = w + x + y + b + c - 2d$
>
> r = z reduced modulo 7; that is, r is the remainder of z divided by 7, $r = 0$ represents Sunday; $r = 1$ represents Monday, and so on

Write a program to accept a date as input and then calculate on what day of the week that date fell or will fall.

(a) Verify that December 12, 1960 fell on a Monday and that January 1, 1991 fell on a Tuesday.
(b) On what day of the week did January 25, 1963 fall?
(c) On what day of the week did June 2, 1964 fall?
(d) On what day of the week did July 4, 1776 fall?
(e) On what day of the week were you born?

18. Write a program that will convert ordinary Hindu-Arabic numerals into Roman numerals and vice versa. (I = 1, V = 5, X = 10, L = 50, C = 100, D = 500, and M = 1000. Roman numeration also uses a subtraction principle: IV = 5 − 1

= 4, IX = 10 − 1 = 9, XL = 50 − 10 = 40, XC = 100 − 10 = 90, CD = 500 − 100 = 400, CM = 1000 − 100 = 900, but no other cases of a smaller number preceding a larger are allowed.)

19. A string is said to be a *palindrome* if it does not change when the order of the characters in the string is reversed. For example,

       MADAM

       463364

       ABLE WAS I ERE I SAW ELBA

    are palindromes. Write a program to read a string and then determine whether it is a palindrome.

20. Write a simple *text-formatting* program that reads a file of text and produces another file in which blank lines are removed, multiple blanks are replaced with a single blank, and no lines are longer than some given length. Put as many words as possible on the same line. You will have to break some lines of the given file, but do not break any words or put punctuation marks at the beginning of a new line.

21. Extend the text-formatting program of Problem 20 to right-justify each line except the last in the new file by adding evenly distributed blanks in lines where necessary.

22. A (nonparameterized) real number in Fortran has one of the forms $m.n$, $+m.n$, or $-m.n$, where m and n are nonnegative integers and either (but not both) may be omitted; or it may be expressed in scientific form xEe, $xE+e$, or $xE-e$, where x is an integer or a real number not in scientific form and e is a nonnegative integer. Write a program that reads a string of characters and then checks to see if it represents a real constant having one of these forms.

23. Modify the input and output operations of the data type `Fraction` of Programming Problem 11 of Chapter 10 so that fractions are entered and displayed in the form a/b, or simply a if the denominator is 1.

24. Write a program for a lexical analyzer to recognize assignment statements of the form

       variable = constant

    where constant is an integer constant or a real constant.

25. Write a program for a lexical analyzer to recognize assignment statements of the form

       variable = string constant

26. Extend the program of Problem 25 to allow substrings and the concatenation operator.

27. Write a program for a lexical analyzer to process assignment statements of the form

```
logical-variable = logical-value
```

Have it recognize the following tokens: variable, logical constant, assignment operator, and logical operator (`.NOT.`, `.AND.`, `.OR.`, `.EQV.`, and `.NEQV.`).

Section 11.8

28. Write a program to encrypt and decrypt a message using the Vignère cipher scheme.

29. Write a program to encrypt and decrypt a message using a substitution table.

30. Write a program to encrypt and decrypt a message using a permutation scheme.

31. Write a program that implements the RSA scheme.

32. The *Morse code* is a standard encoding scheme that uses substitutions similar to those in the scheme described in this section. The substitutions used in this case are shown in the following table. Write a program to read a message and encode it using Morse code or to read a message in Morse code and decode it.

A	·—	M	——	Y	—·——
B	—···	N	—·	Z	——··
C	—·—·	O	———	1	·————
D	—··	P	·——·	2	··———
E	·	Q	——·—	3	···——
F	··—·	R	·—·	4	····—
G	——·	S	···	5	·····
H	····	T	—	6	—····
I	··	U	··—	7	——···
J	·———	V	···—	8	———··
K	—·—	W	·——	9	————·
L	·—··	X	—··—	0	—————

Section 11.9

33. Modify the program in Figure 11.10 to plot points on the graph of a function $y = f(x)$.

34. Modify the program in Figure 11.10 to plot points on the graph of parametric equations of the form

$$x = x(t), \quad y = y(t), \quad a \le t \le b$$

35. In Example 2, we noted that the ideas in that example can be modified to carry out *visual image processing* and *enhancement*. Make a file that represents light intensities of an image in digitized form, say, with intensities from 0 through 9.

Write a program that reads these intensities from the file and then reconstructs and displays them using a different character for each intensity. This image might then be enhanced to sharpen the contrast. For example, "gray" areas might be removed by replacing all intensities in the range 0 through some value by 0 (light) and intensities greater than this value by 9 (dark). Design your program to accept a threshold value that distinguishes light from dark and then enhances the image in the manner described.

36. An alternative method for enhancing an image (see Problem 35) is to accept three successive images of the same object and, if two or more of the intensities agree, to use that value; otherwise, use the average of the three values. Modify the program of Problem 35 to use this technique for enhancement.

FEATURES NEW TO FORTRAN 90

- Kind type parameters
- Intrinsic functions SELECTED_REAL_KIND, SELECTED_INT_KIND, PRE-CISION, and RANGE
- References to the REAL function with a kind type parameter:

      REAL(x, kind-type-parameter)˙

- References to the CMPLX function with a kind type parameter:

      CMPLX(x, y, kind-type-parameter)
      CMPLX(x, kind-type-parameter)˙

- Complex values with components of any precision
- Character strings enclosed either in apostrophes ('string') or in quotation marks ("string")
- Empty string consisting of two consecutive apostrophes or two consecutive quotation marks
- Attaching a substring specification to a string constant
- Character strings to be read by a list-directed input statement need not be enclosed in apostrophes or within quotation marks unless
    1. They contain blanks, commas, or slashes.
    2. They extend over more than one line.
    3. The leading non-blank character is a quotation mark or an apostrophe.
    4. A repetition indicator is used.
- Use of a DELIM = "APOSTROPHE" , "QUOTE", or "NONE" clause in an OPEN statement to specify the delimiter used for character strings written with list-directed or NAMELIST formatting
- Several new instrinsic string-processing functions: ACHAR, ADJUSTL, ADJUSTR, IACHAR, LEN_TRIM, REPEAT, SCAN, TRIM, and VERIFY

12

File Processing

The goal is information at your fingertips.

BILL GATES

*The next best thing to knowing something is knowing where
to find it.*

SAMUEL JOHNSON

*... It became increasingly apparent to me that, over the years,
Federal agencies have amassed vast amounts of information about
virtually every American citizen. This fact, coupled with
technological advances in data collection and dissemination, raised
the possibility that information about individuals conceivably could
be used for other than legitimate purposes and without the prior
knowledge or consent of the individuals involved.*

Former President GERALD R. FORD

*I*n Section 2.10 and in Chapter 5, we introduced file processing for those applications involving large data sets that can be processed more conveniently if stored on magnetic disk or some other form of external (secondary) memory. We considered simple forms of several Fortran statements that are used to process files. In this chapter, we review these statements, give their complete forms, and introduce some additional file concepts.

The files we have considered thus far are called **sequential files.** These are files in which the lines of data or **records** are written in sequence and must be read in that same order. This means that to read a particular record in a sequential file, all of the preceding records must first be read. In contrast, **direct access files** are files in which each record may be accessed directly, usually by referring to a record number. This means that a particular record may be accessed without reading (or writing) those records that precede it. All records in a direct access file must have the same fixed length, whereas records in a sequential file may be of varying lengths.

Another distinction between files is that they may be **formatted** or **unformatted.** All the files we have considered thus far have been formatted, which means that they consist of records in which information is represented in external character form. In contrast, unformatted files are those in which the information is represented in internal binary form. Thus, the precise form of the records in an unformatted file is machine dependent, as it depends on the way in which values are stored internally in a particular system. For this reason, unformatted files are discussed only briefly in this chapter. We focus our attention instead on formatted files.

12.1   THE OPEN, CLOSE, AND INQUIRE STATEMENTS

A file must be **connected** to a unit number before input from or output to that file can take place. Normally this is accomplished by using an OPEN statement, which was introduced in Sections 2.10 and 5.5. When such input/output is completed, the file should be disconnected from its unit number using the CLOSE statement, also introduced in Section 5.5. In some situations, it may also be convenient to inquire about certain properties of a file. The INQUIRE statement can be used for this purpose.

Opening Files

The OPEN **statement** has the general form

```
OPEN (open-list)
```

where *open-list* must include

1. A unit specifier indicating a unit number to be connected to the file being opened

In most cases, it also includes

2. A FILE = clause giving the name of the file being opened

3. A STATUS = clause specifying whether the file is new, old, or scratch or has an unknown status

4. An IOSTAT = clause indicating whether the file has been successfully opened

It may also include other specifiers selected from the following list:

5. An ACCESS = clause specifying the type of access as sequential or direct

6. An ACTION = clause specifying whether the file is to be opened for reading only, for writing only, or for both reading and writing

7. A BLANK = clause specifying whether blanks in a numeric field are to be interpreted as zeros or are to be ignored

8. A DELIM = clause specifying whether character strings to be written to the file are to be enclosed in apostrophes or quotation marks or with no enclosing delimiters

9. An ERR = clause specifying a statement to be executed if an error occurs while attempting to open the file

10. A FORM = clause specifying whether the file is formatted or unformatted

11. A PAD = clause specifying whether or not an input character value is to be padded with blanks

12. A POSITION = clause specifying whether the file is to be positioned at its initial point, to be positioned at the end of the file, or to have its position unchanged

13. A RECL = clause specifying the record length for a direct access file

Unit Specifier. The unit specifier has the form

    UNIT = *integer-expression*

or simply

    integer-expression

where the value of *integer-expression* is a nonnegative integer that is the unit number to be connected to this file. Reference to this file by subsequent READ or WRITE statements is by means of this unit number. If the second form of the unit specifier is used, it must be the first item in the open list.

FILE = Clause. The FILE = clause has the form

    FILE = *character-expression*

where the value of *character-expression* (ignoring trailing blanks) is the name of the file to be connected to the specified unit number.

STATUS = Clause. The STATUS = clause has the form

    STATUS = *character-expression*

where the value of *character-expression* (ignoring trailing blanks and case) is one of the following:

    OLD
    NEW
    SCRATCH
    UNKNOWN

If the value is OLD or NEW, the name of the file must have been given in the FILE = clause. OLD means that the file already exists in the system, and NEW means that the file does not yet exist and is being created by the program. The OPEN statement creates an empty file with the specified name and changes its status to OLD. If the status is SCRATCH, the file must not be named in a FILE = clause. The OPEN statement creates a work file that is used during execution of this program but that is deleted by a CLOSE statement or by normal termination of the program. A status of UNKNOWN means that none of the preceding applies. In this case, the status of the file depends on the particular system being used. If the STATUS = clause is omitted, the file is assumed to have an UNKNOWN status.

IOSTAT = Clause. The IOSTAT = clause is of the form

    IOSTAT = *status-variable*

where *status-variable* is an integer variable to which the value zero is assigned if the file is opened successfully and a positive value is assigned otherwise. A positive value usually represents the number of an appropriate error message in a list found in system manuals.

ACCESS = Clause. The ACCESS = clause is of the form

    ACCESS = *access-method*

where *access-method* is a character expression whose value (ignoring trailing blanks and case) is

    SEQUENTIAL   or   DIRECT

If this clause is omitted, the file is assumed to be sequential.

ACTION = Clause. The ACTION = clause is of the form

    ACTION = *i-o-action*

where *i-o-action* is a character expression whose value (ignoring trailing blanks and case) is one of the following:

    READ
    WRITE
    READWRITE

The file will be opened for reading only, for writing only, or for both reading and writing, respectively. If this clause is omitted, the action is compiler dependent, but normally the file will be opened for READWRITE.

BLANK = Clause. The BLANK = clause has the form

    BLANK = *blank-specifier*

where *blank-specifier* is a character expression whose value (ignoring trailing blanks and case) is either

    ZERO   or   NULL

The first specification causes blanks in the numeric fields of records in the file being opened to be interpreted as zeros for formatted input, whereas the NULL specifier causes such blanks to be ignored. In all cases, however, a numeric field consisting only of blanks is interpreted as zero. If this clause is omitted, NULL is used as the default value.

DELIM = Clause. The DELIM = clause has the form

    DELIM = delimiter

where *delimiter* is a character expression whose value (ignoring trailing blanks and case) is one of the following:

    APOSTROPHE
    QUOTE
    NONE

These specifiers cause character strings written to the file by list-directed output or by name-list formatting to be enclosed in apostrophes or quotation marks or with no enclosing delimiters, respectively. If this clause is omitted, no delimiters will be used.

ERR = Clause. The ERR = clause has the form

    ERR = n

where *n* is the label of the next statement to be executed if an error occurs in attempting to open the file.

FORM = Clause. The FORM = clause is of the form

    FORM = form-specifier

where *form-specifier* is a character expression whose value (ignoring trailing blanks) is either

    FORMATTED   or   UNFORMATTED

If this clause is omitted, the file being opened is assumed to be formatted if it is a sequential file or to be unformatted if it is a direct access file.

PAD = Clause. The PAD = clause has the form

    PAD = padding-indicator

where *padding-indicator* is a character expression whose value (ignoring trailing blanks and case) is either

    YES   or   NO

This clause specifies whether or not an input string is to be padded with blanks. If this clause is omitted, blank padding will occur.

POSITION = Clause. The POSITION = clause has the form

POSITION = *pos*

where *pos* is a character expression whose value (ignoring trailing blanks and case) is one of the following:

REWIND
APPEND
ASIS

These specifiers position the file at its initial point, position it at the end of the file, or leave its position unchanged, respectively. If this clause is omitted, there are three possibilities:

1. If the file is already open, the position of the file will be left unchanged.
2. If the file exists but has not been opened, the position is unspecified.
3. If the file does not exist, it will be created and positioned at its initial point.

RECL = Clause. The RECL = clause has the form

RECL = *record-length*

where *record-length* is an integer expression whose value must be positive. This clause is used only for direct access files and specifies the length of the records in the file. For a formatted file, the record length is the number of characters in each record of that file. For an unformatted file, it is a processor-dependent measure of the record length.

Illustration. As an illustration, suppose that a file has been previously created and saved under the name INFO1 and that data values are to be read from this file. A unit number such as 10 must first be connected to this file by an OPEN statement such as

```
OPEN (UNIT = 10, FILE = "INFO1", STATUS = "OLD", &
      ACTION = "READ", POSITION = "REWIND", IOSTAT = OpenStatus)
```

where OpenStatus is an integer variable. Alternatively, the name of the file can be read during execution:

```
CHARACTER(10) :: InputFile
WRITE (*, '(1X, A)', ADVANCE = "NO") &
      "Enter name of input file: "
READ *, InputFile
OPEN (UNIT = 10, FILE = InputFile, STATUS = "OLD", &
      ACTION = "READ", POSITION = "REWIND", IOSTAT = OpenStatus)
```

Because the other clauses are not used, the file is assumed to be sequential and formatted, and any character strings read from the file will be padded with blanks. If we wish to specify this explicitly, we can use

```
OPEN (UNIT = 10, FILE = InputFile, STATUS = "OLD", &
      ACTION = "READ", POSITION = "REWIND", &
      FORM = "FORMATTED", ACCESS = "SEQUENTIAL", &
      PAD = "YES", IOSTAT = OpenStatus)
```

The statement

```
OPEN (UNIT = 10, FILE = InputFile, STATUS = "OLD", &
      ACTION = "READ", POSITION = "REWIND", ERR = 50)
```

serves the same purpose, but if an error occurs during the opening of the file, the ERR = clause will cause execution to continue with the statement labeled 50.

If the program is to create a new output file named INFO2, we might attach the unit number 11 to it with the statement

```
OPEN (UNIT = 11, FILE = "INFO2", STATUS = "NEW", &
      ACTION = "WRITE", IOSTAT = OpenStatus)
```

Execution of this statement changes the status of this file to OLD, so that it will exist after execution of the program is completed. On the other hand, if a temporary work file is needed only during execution, we might use a statement such as

```
OPEN (UNIT = 12, STATUS = "SCRATCH", IOSTAT = OpenStatus)
```

This temporary file will then be deleted if it is closed by a CLOSE statement or when execution terminates.

Closing Files

The **CLOSE statement** is used to disconnect a file from its unit number. This statement is of the form

```
CLOSE (close-list)
```

where *close-list* must include

1. A unit specifier

It may also include items selected from the following:

2. An `IOSTAT` = clause
3. An `ERR` = clause
4. A `STATUS` = clause specifying whether the file is to be kept or deleted

The `IOSTAT` = and `ERR` = clauses are used to detect errors that may occur when attempting to close the file. They have the same form as the corresponding clauses in the `OPEN` statement. The `STATUS` = clause has the form

```
STATUS = character-expression
```

where the value of *character-expression* (ignoring trailing blanks) is

```
KEEP        or        DELETE
```

depending on whether the file is to continue to exist after the `CLOSE` statement is executed. `KEEP` may not be used for a `SCRATCH` file. If the `STATUS` = clause is omitted, scratch files are deleted, but all other types are kept. Thus, to close the file `INFO2` with the unit number 11 referred to earlier so that it is saved after execution, we could use any of the following statements:

```
CLOSE (11)
CLOSE (UNIT = 11)
CLOSE (UNIT = 11, STATUS = "KEEP")
```

A file that has been closed by a `CLOSE` statement may be reopened by an `OPEN` statement; the same unit number may be connected to it, or a different one may be used. All files that are not explicitly closed with a `CLOSE` statement are automatically closed when execution of the program is terminated (except when termination is caused by an error).

The INQUIRE Statement

The **INQUIRE statement** may be used to ascertain the properties of a file or of its connection to a unit number. The two most useful forms of this statement are

```
INQUIRE (UNIT = unit-number, inquiry-list)

INQUIRE (FILE = file-name, inquiry-list)
```

where `"UNIT ="` and `"FILE ="` are optional, and *inquiry-list* may include a number of clauses, each of which (except the `ERR` = clause) serves as a question concerning some property of the file. When the `INQUIRE` statement is executed, a value that answers the question is assigned to the variable in each clause. A list of the clauses and their meanings is given in Table 12.1.

Table 12.1 Clauses Allowed in an INQUIRE Statement

Clause	Variable Type	Values and Their Meanings
ACCESS = *variable*	Character	SEQUENTIAL if the file is opened for sequential access; DIRECT if it is opened for direct access; UNDEFINED if it is not connected to a unit number
ACTION = *variable*	Character	READ, WRITE, or READWRITE, according to the action specified in the OPEN statement for that file; UNDEFINED if it is not connected to a unit number
BLANK = *variable*	Character	ZERO if the blanks in numeric fields are to be interpreted as zeros; NULL if they are to be ignored; UNDEFINED if the file is not connected to a unit number or has not been opened for formatted I/O
DELIM = *variable*	Character	APOSTROPHE, QUOTE, or NONE, according to the delimiter specified in the OPEN statement for that file; UNDEFINED if the file is not connected to a unit number or has not been opened for formatted I/O
ERR = *statement-label*		Control transfers to the specified statement if an error occurs while executing the INQUIRE statement
EXIST = *variable*	Logical	.TRUE. if the file with the specified name or unit number exists; .FALSE. otherwise
FORM = *variable*	Character	FORMATTED if the file is open for formatted data transfer; UNFORMATTED if the file is open for unformatted data transfer; UNDEFINED if it is not connected to a unit number
FORMATTED = *variable*	Character	YES if the file is formatted; NO if the file is unformatted; UNKNOWN if the record type cannot be determined
IOSTAT = *variable*	Integer	Zero if no error condition exists; positive if an error exists
NAME = *variable*	Character	Either the name of the file or undefined if the file has no name
NAMED = *variable*	Logical	.TRUE. if the file has a name; .FALSE. otherwise
NEXTREC = *variable*	Integer	One plus the number of the last record read from or written to a direct access file; undefined if the file is not connected for direct access or the record number cannot be determined
NUMBER = *variable*	Integer	Either the file's unit number or -1 if there is no connection to a unit number

Table 12.1 *(cont.)*

Clause	Variable Type	Values and Their Meanings
OPENED = *variable*	Logical	.TRUE. if the specified file or unit number has been connected to a unit number or file, respectively; .FALSE. otherwise
PAD = *variable*	Character	YES or NO according to whether or not padding is specified in the OPEN statement for that file
POSITION = *variable*	Character	REWIND, APPEND, or ASIS, according to the file position specified in the OPEN statement for that file; UNDEFINED if the file is not connected to a unit number
READ = *variable*	Character	YES, NO, or UNKNOWN, according to whether READ is allowed, not allowed, or undetermined for the file
READWRITE = *variable*	Character	YES, NO, or UNKNOWN, according to whether READWRITE is allowed, not allowed, or undetermined for the file
RECL = *variable*	Integer	Record length for a direct access file; undefined if the file is not connected or is not connected for direct access
SEQUENTIAL = *variable*	Character	YES if the file can be connected for sequential access; NO if it cannot; UNKNOWN if the file's suitability for sequential access cannot be determined
UNFORMATTED = *variable*	Character	YES if the file is unformatted; NO if the file is formatted; UNKNOWN if the record type cannot be determined
WRITE = *variable*	Character	YES, NO, or UNKNOWN, according to whether WRITE is allowed, not allowed, or undetermined for the file

A third form of the INQUIRE statement is

```
INQUIRE (IOLENGTH = integer-variable) output-list
```

It assigns to *integer-variable* the length of an unformatted *output-list* in processor-dependent units. This form of the INQURE statement is useful for determining what value to use in a RECL = clause of an OPEN statement for unformatted direct access files.

12.2 FILE INPUT/OUTPUT AND POSITIONING

File input/output is accomplished using the general READ and WRITE statements introduced in Section 2.10 and in Chapter 5. The complete forms of these statements are considered in this section. Some file positioning is also carried out by these statements. Other positioning statements that may be used for sequential files are the REWIND, BACKSPACE, and ENDFILE statements.

File Input

Data can be read from a file using a **READ statement** of the general form

```
READ (control-list) input-list
```

The *input-list* is a list of variable names, substring names, array names, or implied DO loops, separated by commas. The *control-list* must include

1. A unit specifier indicating the unit number connected to the file

It may also include one or more of the following:

2. A format specifier describing the format of the information to be read
3. An ADVANCE = clause to enable or disable nonadvancing input/output
4. An END = clause specifying a statement to be executed when the end of a sequential file is reached
5. An EOR = clause specifying a statement to be executed when the end of a record is reached in nonadvancing input
6. An ERR = clause specifying a statement to be executed if an input error occurs
7. An IOSTAT = clause to check the status of the input operation, in particular, to detect an end-of-file condition or an input error
8. A NML = clause for NAMELIST input
9. A REC = clause indicating the number of the record to be read for a direct access file
10. A SIZE = clause to count characters during nonadvancing input

The forms of the unit specifier, the format specifier, the ADVANCE = clause, the END = clause, the IOSTAT = clause, and the NML = clause were described in detail in Chapter 5.

EOR = Clause. The EOR = clause has the form

```
EOR = n
```

where *n* is the label of a statement to be executed if during nonadvancing input, an attempt is made to read beyond the end of a record.

ERR = Clause. The ERR = clause has the form

```
ERR = n
```

where *n* is the label of a statement to be executed if an input error occurs. For example, suppose that `Number` and `Name` are declared by

```
INTEGER :: Number
CHARACTER(20) :: Name
```

For the `READ` statement,

```
READ (UNIT = 15, FMT = '(I5, A20)', ERR = 20) Number, Name
```

if the following data is read from the file with unit number 15,

```
123 John Henry Doe
```

an input error occurs because the character `J` in the fifth column is read as part of the value for the integer variable `Number`. The `ERR` = clause then causes execution to continue with the statement numbered 20, which might be a statement to print an error message such as

```
20 PRINT *, "Input data error"
```

`IOSTAT` = Clause. In Chapter 5 we noted that when a `READ` statement containing an `IOSTAT` = clause of the form

```
IOSTAT = integer-variable
```

is executed, the variable in this clause is assigned

1. A positive value (usually the number of an error message in a list found in system manuals) if an error occurs
2. A negative value if the end of data is encountered but no input error occurs
3. Zero if neither an input error nor the end of data occurs

We have used the `IOSTAT` = clause to detect input errors and to detect the end of data. It thus provides an alternative to the `ERR` = and `END` = clauses. For example, if `Error` is an integer variable, the preceding statements could also be written as

```
READ (UNIT = 15, FMT = '(I5, A20)', IOSTAT = Error) Number, Name
IF (Error > 0) PRINT *, 'Input data error'
```

`REC` = Clause. The `REC` = clause has the form

```
REC = integer-expression
```

where the value of the *integer-expression* is positive and indicates the number of the record to be read from a direct access file. The clause must be used if input is to be from a file connected for direct access. The control list may not contain both a REC = clause and an END = clause.

SIZE = Clause. The SIZE = clause has the form

SIZE = *integer-variable*

where the value of the *integer-variable* will be the number of characters read during nonadvancing input. This count of characters will not include any blanks used for padding.

Example 1: Direct Access Inventory File

All of the files used in the example programs in this text have thus far been sequential files. The program in Figure 12.1 uses a direct access file to retrieve information in a parts inventory file. The name of the file is read during execution and is then opened with the statement

```
OPEN (UNIT = 10, FILE = Filename, STATUS = "OLD", &
      ACCESS = "DIRECT", ACTION = "READ", &
      FORM = "FORMATTED", RECL = RecordLength, &
      IOSTAT = OpenStatus)
```

The user then enters a part number, which is used to access a record of the file:

```
READ (UNIT = 10, FMT = '(A)', REC = PartNumber, &
      IOSTAT = InputStatus) PartsRecord
```

The information in this record PartsRecord is then displayed to the user.

Figure 12.1 Direct access inventory file.

```
PROGRAM Direct_Access_File_Demo
!---------------------------------------------------------------------
! Program to read a part number during execution, access a record in
! a direct access parts inventory file, and display this record.
! Identifiers used are:
!    RecordLength  : length of records in the file (constant)
!    PartNumber    : a part number -- 0 to signal end of input
!    Filename      : name of the file
!    OpenStatus    : status variable for OPEN statement
!    InputStatus   : status variable for direct access READ
!    PartsRecord   : a record in the file
!
```

Figure 12.1 *(cont.)*

```
! Input (keyboard): FileName, PartNumber
! Input (file):     PartsRecord
! Output (screen):  User prompts
!                   PartsRecord, or an error message for an invalid
!                   part number
! NOTE:  In this version of Fortran, the end-of-record mark is
!        counted in the record length.
!-----------------------------------------------------------------------

  IMPLICIT NONE
  INTEGER, PARAMETER :: RecordLength = 31
  INTEGER :: OpenStatus, InputStatus, PartNumber
  CHARACTER(20) :: FileName, PartsRecord*(RecordLength)

  ! Get the name of the file and open it for direct access

  WRITE (*, '(1X, A)', ADVANCE = "NO") "Enter name of file: "
  READ *, FileName

  OPEN (UNIT = 10, FILE = FileName, STATUS = "OLD", &
        ACCESS = "DIRECT", ACTION = "READ", POSITION = "REWIND", &
        FORM = "FORMATTED", RECL = RecordLength, IOSTAT = OpenStatus)
  IF (OpenStatus > 0) STOP " *** Cannot open file ***"

  ! Repeat the following so long as there are more
  ! part numbers to process:

  DO
     WRITE (*, '(1X, A)', ADVANCE = "NO") &
           "Enter part number (0 to stop): "
     READ *, PartNumber

     IF (PartNumber == 0) EXIT
     ! If no more part numbers to process, terminate repetition

     ! Otherwise, try to find the inventory record for this part
     READ (UNIT = 10, FMT = '(A)', REC = PartNumber, &
           IOSTAT = InputStatus) PartsRecord
     IF (InputStatus == 0) THEN
        PRINT '(1X, "Part", I3, ": ", A)', PartNumber, PartsRecord
     ELSE
        PRINT '(1X, "Invalid part number: ", I3)', PartNumber
     END IF
  END DO
END DO
```

Figure 12.1 *(cont.)*

```
CLOSE(10)

END PROGRAM Direct_Access_File_Demo
```

Listing of test file used in sample run:

```
CHROME-BUMPER...$152.95.....15
SPARK-PLUG.......$1.25....125
DISTRIBUTOR-CAP..$39.95.....57
FAN-BELT..........$5.80.....32
DOOR-HANDLE......$18.85.....84
```

Sample run:

```
Enter name of file: fil12-1.dat
Enter part number (0 to stop): 4
Part  4: FAN-BELT.........$5.80.....32

Enter part number (0 to stop): 2
Part  2: SPARK-PLUG.......$1.25....125

Enter part number (0 to stop): 10
Invalid part number:   10
Enter part number (0 to stop): 0
```

File-positioning Statements

There are three Fortran statements that may be used to position a sequential file. Each of these statements has two possible forms:

REWIND *unit*	or	REWIND (*position-list*)
BACKSPACE *unit*	or	BACKSPACE (*position-list*)
ENDFILE *unit*	or	ENDFILE (*position-list*)

In the first form, *unit* is the unit number connected to the file. In the second form, *position-list* must contain

1. A unit specifier of the form *unit* or UNIT = *unit*

It may also contain

2. An ERR = clause specifying the number of a statement to be executed if an error occurs while positioning the file
3. An IOSTAT = clause specifying a status variable that is assigned 0 if the file is successfully positioned or a positive value if some error occurs

The **REWIND statement** positions the file at its initial point, that is, at the beginning of the file's first record. The **BACKSPACE statement** positions the file at the beginning of the preceding record. If the file is at its initial point, these statements have no effect.

The **ENDFILE statement** writes into the file a special record called an **end-of-file record**. When this record is encountered by a READ statement, an end-of-file condition occurs that can be detected by an IOSTAT = clause or an END = clause in the control list of the READ statement. After the execution of an ENDFILE statement, no more data can be transferred to or from this file until the file is repositioned at some record preceding the end-of-file record.

File Output

Data is written to a file using a **WRITE statement** of the general form

```
WRITE (control-list) output-list
```

The *output-list* is a list of expressions, array names, or implied DO loops separated by commas. The *control-list* must include

1. A unit specifier indicating the unit number connected to the file

It may also include one or more of the items that may appear in the control list of a READ statement. The most useful of these items are

2. A format specifier describing the form of the information being output
3. An ADVANCE = clause to enable or disable nonadvancing output
4. An ERR = clause specifying a statement to be executed if an output error occurs
5. An IOSTAT = clause to check the status of the output operation
6. A REC = clause indicating the number of the record to which the information is to be output for a direct access file
7. A SIZE = clause to count characters during nonadvancing output

The form of each of these items is the same as for a READ statement.

Output to a direct access file may not be list-directed. Also, the REC = clause may not appear when the output is list-directed (indicated by an asterisk for the format specifier).

Example 2: Merging Files

An important problem in file processing is merging two files that have been previously sorted so that the resulting file is also sorted. To illustrate, suppose that *File1* and *File2* have been sorted and contain the following integers:

File1:   2   4   5   7   9   15   16   20   *File2*:   1   6   8   10   12

To merge these files to produce *File3*, we read one element from each file, say *X* from *File1* and *Y* from *File2*:

File1: 2 4 5 7 9 15 16 20   *File2*: 1 6 8 10 12
      ↑   ↑
      X   *Y*

We write the smaller of these values, in this case *Y*, into *File3*

File3: 1

and then read another value for *Y* from *File2*:

File1: 2 4 5 7 9 15 16 20   *File2*: 1 6 8 10 12
      ↑   ↑
      X   *Y*

Now *X* is smaller than *Y*, and so it is written to *File3*, and a new value for *X* is read from *File1*:

File1: 2 4 5 7 9 15 16 20   *File2*: 1 6 8 10 12
         ↑   ↑
         X   *Y*

File3: 1 2

Again, *X* is less than *Y*, and so *X* is written to *File3* and a new *X*-value is read from *File1*:

File1: 2 4 5 7 9 15 16 20   *File2*: 1 6 8 10 12
            ↑   ↑
            X   *Y*

File3: 1 2 4

Continuing in this manner, we eventually reach the value 15 for *X* and the value 12 for *Y*:

File1: 2 4 5 7 9 15 16 20   *File2*: 1 6 8 10 12
                  ↑   ↑
                  X   *Y*

File3: 1 2 4 5 6 7 8 9 10

Because *Y* is smaller than *X*, we write *Y* to *File3*:

File3: 1 2 4 5 6 7 8 9 10 12

Because the end of *File2* has been reached, we simply copy the remaining values of *File1* to *File3* to obtain the final sorted file *File3*:

File3: 1 2 4 5 6 7 8 9 10 12 15 16 20

The general algorithm to merge two sorted files is as follows:

ALGORITHM TO MERGE FILES

Algorithm to merge sorted files *File1* and *File2* to produce the sorted file *File3*.

Input (files): Elements from *File1*, *File2*
Output (file): Elements to *File3*

1. Open *File1*, *File2*, and *File3*.

2. Read the first element X from *File1* and the first element Y from *File2*.

3. While the end of neither *File1* nor *File2* has been reached, do the following:
   If $X \leq Y$ then
      a. Write X to *File3*.
      b. Read a new X-value from *File1*.
   Else do the following:
      a. Write Y to *File3*.
      b. Read a new Y-value from *File2*.

4. If the end of *File1* has not been reached, copy the rest of *File1* into *File3*. If the end of *File2* has not been reached, copy the rest of *File2* into *File3*.

In this algorithm, we assumed that the file components are numbers, strings, and so on that can be compared. If the files contain records that are sorted on the basis of some key field in the records, then the key field of X is compared with the key field of Y in step 3. The program in Figure 12.2 implements this modified merge algorithm. It merges two files whose records consist of a student number, student name, and cumulative GPA. The files have been sorted so that the student numbers are in ascending order.

Figure 12.2 Merging files.

```
PROGRAM Merging_Files
!-------------------------------------------------------------------
! Program to read two files of records containing a student number, a
! student name, and a cumulative GPA, where the files have been sorted
! so that student numbers are in ascending order, and merge these two
! files to produce another that is also sorted.  Variables used are:
!    File           : array of 3 file names
!    OpenStatus     : array of 3 status variables for OPEN
!    InputStatus    : array of 2 status variables for READ
!    StudentName    : array of 2 student names
!    StudentNumber  : array of 2 student numbers
!    GPA            : array of 2 cumulative GPAs
!    I              : subscript
```

Figure 12.2 *(cont.)*

```
!
! Input (keyboard): File
! Output (screen):  User prompts and message that merging has been
!                   completed
! Input (files):    Student records from File(1) and File(2)
! Output (file):    Student records to File(3)
!-------------------------------------------------------------------

  IMPLICIT NONE
  CHARACTER(20), DIMENSION(3) :: File
  INTEGER, DIMENSION(3) :: OpenStatus
  CHARACTER(20), DIMENSION(2) :: StudentName
  INTEGER, DIMENSION(2) :: InputStatus, StudentNumber
  REAL,  DIMENSION(2) :: GPA
  INTEGER :: I

  ! Get the names of the files and open them

  PRINT *, "Enter the names of the files to be merged and the name"
  PRINT *, "of the file to be produced:"
  READ *, File
  DO I = 1, 2
     OPEN (UNIT = 10*I, FILE = File(I), STATUS = "OLD", &
           ACTION = "READ", POSITION = "REWIND", &
           ACCESS = "SEQUENTIAL", IOSTAT = OpenStatus(I))
  END DO

  OPEN (UNIT = 30, FILE = File(3), STATUS = "NEW", &
        ACTION = "WRITE", ACCESS = "SEQUENTIAL", IOSTAT = OpenStatus(3))

  DO I = 1, 3
     IF (OpenStatus(I) > 0) THEN
        PRINT *, "*** File #", I, "cannot be opened *** "
        STOP
     END IF
  END DO

  ! Read first record from each file
  DO I = 1, 2
     READ (UNIT = 10*I, FMT = 100, IOSTAT = InputStatus(I)) &
           StudentNumber(I), StudentName(I), GPA(I)
     IF (InputStatus(I) > 0) STOP "*** Input error ***"
  END DO
100 FORMAT(I5, 1X, A, F4.2)
```

Figure 12.2 *(cont.)*

```fortran
! While neither the end of File(1) or File(2) has been reached,
! do the following:
DO
    IF (InputStatus(1) < 0 .OR. InputStatus(2) < 0) EXIT
    ! If at the end of either file, terminate repetition

    ! Otherwise continue with the following
    IF (StudentNumber(1) < StudentNumber(2)) THEN
       I = 1
    ELSE
       I = 2
    END IF

    WRITE (UNIT = 30, FMT = 100) StudentNumber(I), StudentName(I), GPA(I)
    READ (UNIT = 10*I, FMT = 100, IOSTAT = InputStatus(I)) &
          StudentNumber(I), StudentName(I), GPA(I)
END DO

! If more records remain in either file, copy them to File_3

DO I = 1, 2
  DO
     IF (InputStatus(I) < 0) EXIT
     WRITE (UNIT = 30, FMT = 100) StudentNumber(I), StudentName(I), GPA(I)
     READ (UNIT = 10*I, FMT = 100, IOSTAT = InputStatus(I)) &
           StudentNumber(I), StudentName(I), GPA(I)
  END DO
END DO

PRINT *
PRINT *, "File merging is complete"

END PROGRAM Merging_Files
```

Sample run:

```
Enter the names of the files to be merged and the name
of the file to be produced:
fil12-2a.dat, fil12-2b.dat, fil12-2c.dat

File merging is complete
```

Figure 12.2 *(cont.)*

Data files used in sample run:

`fil12-2a.dat:`

```
12320 John Henry Doe        3.50
12346 Fred Samuel Doe       3.48
13331 Mary Jane Smith       3.85
13345 Peter Vander Van      2.99
14400 Alfred E. Newman      1.00
15555 Henry Smithsma        2.05
```

`fil12-2b.dat:`

```
12360 Alice M. Van Doe      2.15
12365 Jane E. Jones         1.89
13400 Jesse James           1.66
14001 Richard Van Van       4.00
```

`fil12-2c.dat` **produced by the sample run:**

```
12320 John Henry Doe        3.50
12346 Fred Samuel Doe       3.48
12360 Alice M. Van Doe      2.15
12365 Jane E. Jones         1.89
13331 Mary Jane Smith       3.85
13345 Peter Vander Van      2.99
13400 Jesse James           1.66
14001 Richard Van Van       4.00
14400 Alfred E. Newman      1.00
15555 Henry Smithsma        2.05
```

Example 3: External Sorting: Mergesort

The sorting algorithms we considered in Chapter 8 are *internal* sorting schemes; that is, the entire collection of items to be sorted must be stored in main memory. In many sorting problems, however, the data sets are too large to store in main memory and so must be stored in external memory. To sort such collections of data, an *external* sorting algorithm is required. One popular and efficient external sorting method is the **mergesort** technique, a variation of which, called **natural mergesort,** we examine here.

As the name *mergesort* suggests, the basic operation in this sorting scheme is merging data files. To see how the merge operation can be used in sorting a file, consider the following file F containing 15 integers:

F: 75 55 15 20 80 30 35 10 70 40 50 25 45 60 65

Notice that several segments of F contain elements that are already in order:

F: | 75 | 55 | 15 20 80 | 30 35 | 10 70 | 40 50 | 25 45 60 65 |

These segments, enclosed by vertical bars, are called *subfiles* or *runs* in F and subdivide F in a natural way.

We begin by reading these subfiles of F and alternately writing them to two other files, $F1$ and $F2$,

$F1$: | 75 | 15 20 80 | 10 70 | 25 45 60 65 |
$F2$: | 55 | 30 35 | 40 50 |

and then identifying the sorted subfiles in $F1$ and $F2$:

$F1$: | 75 | 15 20 80 | 10 70 | 25 45 60 65 |
$F2$: | 55 | 30 35 40 50 |

Note that although the subfiles of $F1$ are the same as those copied from F, two of the original subfiles written into $F2$ have combined to form a larger subfile. We now merge the first subfile of $F1$ with the first subfile of $F2$, storing the elements back in F:

F: | 55 75 |

Next, the second subfile of $F1$ is merged with the second subfile of $F2$ and written to F:

F: | 55 75 | 15 20 30 35 40 50 80 |

This merging of corresponding subfiles continues until the end of either or both of the files $F1$ and $F2$ is reached. If either file still contains subfiles, these are simply copied into F. Thus, in our example, because the end of $F2$ has been reached, the remaining subfiles of $F1$ are copied back into F:

F: | 55 75 | 15 20 30 35 40 50 80 | 10 70 | 25 45 60 65 |

Now file F is again split into files $F1$ and $F2$ by copying its subfiles alternately into $F1$ and $F2$:

$F1$: | 55 75 | 10 70 |
$F2$: | 15 20 30 35 40 50 80 | 25 45 60 65 |

Identifying the sorted subfiles in each of these files, we see that for this splitting, none of the original subfiles written into either $F1$ or $F2$ combine to form larger ones. Once again we merge corresponding subfiles of $F1$ and $F2$ back into F:

F: | 15 20 30 35 40 50 55 75 80 | 10 25 45 60 65 70 |

Now when we split F into $F1$ and $F2$, each of the files $F1$ and $F2$ contains a single sorted subfile, and each is, therefore, completely sorted:

$F1$: | 15 20 30 35 40 50 55 75 80 |
$F2$: | 10 25 45 60 65 70 |

Thus, when we merge *F1* and *F2* back into *F*, *F* will also contain only one sorted subfile and hence will be sorted:

F: | 10 15 20 25 30 35 40 45 50 55 60 65 70 75 80 |

This example shows that the mergesort method has two steps: (1) splitting file *F* into two other files, *F1* and *F2*, and (2) merging corresponding subfiles in these two files. These steps are repeated until each of the smaller files contains a single sorted subfile; when these are merged, the resulting file is completely sorted. Designing an algorithm to split the file and a program to implement the mergesort scheme is left as an exercise.

Unformatted Files

Information is stored in a formatted file using a standard coding scheme such as ASCII or EBCDIC. When such a file is listed, these codes are automatically converted to the corresponding characters by the terminal, printer, or other output device. In contrast, information is stored in an unformatted or binary file using the internal representation scheme for the particular computer being used. This representation usually cannot be correctly displayed in character form by the output device, nor can it be used easily with another computer system.

There are, however, some advantages in using unformatted files. When a Fortran program reads information from a formatted file, two separate processes are involved: (1) the transfer of the information from the file and (2) the conversion of this information to internal form. Similarly, the output of information to a formatted file involves two steps: (1) conversion to external form and (2) the actual transfer of this information to the file. Because such conversion is time-consuming, it may be desirable to eliminate it, especially when a file is to be read and processed only by the computer and not displayed to the user. Another advantage in using unformatted files is that data items are usually stored more compactly using their internal representation rather than their external representation in one of the standard coding schemes.

Unformatted file input/output is accomplished by using a READ or WRITE statement in which the format specification is omitted. For example, the statement

```
WRITE (UNIT = 10, ERR = 100) Number, Rate, Time
```

writes values of Number, Rate, and Time to the unformatted file having unit number 10.

The variables in the input list of a READ statement used to read information from an unformatted file should match in number and type the variables in the output lists of the WRITE statements that produced that file. Also, both formatted and unformatted input/output statements cannot be used with the same file.

Internal Files

An **internal file** is a sequence of memory locations containing information stored in character form and named by a character variable, a character array or array element, or a character substring. Such internal files are useful in converting information from character form to numeric form.

For example, suppose the character variable `Date` is assigned the value

```
Date = "July 4, 1776"
```

and we wish to extract the year `1776` from this character string and convert it to a numeric form suitable for computations. To do this, we first use a substring reference to extract the substring to be converted:

```
YearString = Date(9:12)
```

The value of the character variable `YearString` is the character string `"1776"`, and thus `YearString` can be viewed as an internal file. The information

```
1776
```

stored in this file can be read and assigned to a numeric variable `YearNumber` by using a `READ` statement in which the name `YearString` of this internal file is used as the unit specifier:

```
READ (UNIT = YearString, FMT = '(I4)') YearNumber
```

or simply

```
READ (YearString, '(I4)') YearNumber
```

The integer `1776` can also be read and assigned to `YearNumber` by using the character substring name `Date(9:12)` as the name of the internal file:

```
READ (UNIT = Date(9:12), FMT = '(I4)') YearNumber
```

or by considering `Date` as the name of the internal file and using the appropriate positioning descriptors in the format identifier:

```
READ (UNIT = Date, FMT = '(8X, I4)') YearNumber
```

In no case, however, is list-directed input allowed.

Conversely, a numeric constant can be converted to the corresponding character string and assigned to a character variable by considering that character variable to be an internal file and writing to it. For example, suppose the integer variable `N` has been assigned the value

```
N = 1776
```

and we wish to concatenate the corresponding character string `"1776"` to the character constant `"July 4,   "`. To do this, we first convert the value of N to character form and assign the resulting string to the character variable `Revolution` by the statement

```
WRITE (UNIT = Revolution, FMT = '(I4)') N
```

or simply

```
WRITE (Revolution, '(I4)') N
```

in which `Revolution` is viewed as an internal file. The value of `Revolution` can then be concatenated with `"July 4,  "` and assigned to the character variable `Date` by

```
Date = "July 4, " // Revolution
```

When a character array is viewed as an internal file, the number of records in that file is equal to the number of elements in the array, and the length of each record is equal to the declared length of the array elements. Each `READ` and `WRITE` statement using this array as an internal file begins transferring data with the first array element.

List-directed input/output is not allowed for internal files, nor may the auxiliary input/output statements

```
OPEN
CLOSE
INQUIRE
BACKSPACE
ENDFILE
REWIND
```

be used for such files.

12.3 APPLICATION: PHARMACY INVENTORY

Problem

Each day, the large pharmaceutical company Uppers and Downers receives and fills thousands of orders for the drugs and pharmaceutical supplies it manufactures. Since customers depend on these drugs for their health and well-being, it is critical that the company be able to process and fill these orders promptly. This means that an adequate inventory of the drugs and supplies must be maintained at all times. The computing services department has been requested to develop a program to manage this inventory.

Pharmaceutical supplies. (Photo courtesy of James Prince/Photo Researchers, Inc.)

Solution

Specification. The problem here is maintaining an inventory file. The program to be developed must accept as input an order number followed by a list of item numbers and order quantities for several items. For each of these items, the appropriate record in the inventory file must be read to determine whether there is sufficient stock to fill the order. If there is, the quantity ordered is subtracted from the number in stock, and a message is displayed indicating this fact. If the number remaining in stock is less than the reorder point for that item, an appropriate warning message must be displayed so that a production run can be scheduled. If there are not enough items to fill the order, a message indicating how much of the order can be filled at this time must be displayed.

In summary, the input/output specifications for this problem are

Input (user):	Order numbers
	Item numbers
	Order quantities
Input (file):	Records of information about items in inventory:
	Item number
	Name
	Lot size
	Price
	Reorder point

| | Number in stock |
| | Optimal inventory level |

Output (screen):   User prompts
                   Messages about the order being processed
                   and reordering information

Output (file):   Updated records for items in inventory

Design. Because an inventory file typically contains a large number of records, and because many transactions are processed using this file, sequential access is inefficient. Consequently, the inventory file will be organized as a direct access file, which allows one to access a specific record directly rather than to search sequentially through all the records preceding it. In order to access a specific record in a direct access file, it is necessary to know its record number. Thus, a correspondence must be established between the item number and the number of the record in the inventory file that contains the information relevant to this item. This is accomplished by constructing an array `Index`, consisting of a list of item numbers arranged in the same order as in the file. Thus, the position of a given item number in this array is the same as the number of the corresponding record in the file. When the program is executed, the elements of the array `Index` are read from a file that contains the item numbers. This file is unformatted because it is read only by the program and is not intended for display to the user.

There are two major tasks that the program must carry out. The first is the initialization task, which consists of opening the necessary files and constructing the array `Index`. The second task is the transaction processing, which consists of accepting the order information from the user, searching the index file to determine the appropriate record number, and carrying out the necessary processing using the order information and the information found in this record. The structure diagram in Figure 12.3 displays these tasks and subtasks and the relationship between them.

Most of these program components are quite simple. Instead of detailed algorithms, we will give informal descriptions of their purposes.

Main program	Calls the subprogram `Initialize` and then repeatedly calls the subprogram `ProcessTransaction` until the user indicates that there are no more transactions to process.
Initialize	Opens the inventory file and the index file by calling the subprogram `OpenFiles`. It then calls subprogram `ConstructIndex` to construct the array `Index` of item numbers.
ProcessTransaction	Accepts an order for a certain item and calls subprogram `Search` to search the array `Index` in order to find the position of this item in the inventory file. If the item is found, subprogram `ProcessOrder` then processes the order.

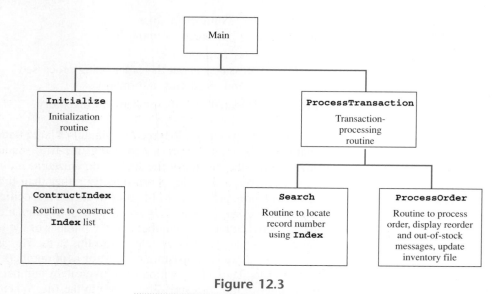

Figure 12.3

Structure diagram for inventory program.

ConstructIndex	Constructs the array Index of item numbers.
ProcessTransaction	Accepts an order for a certain item and calls subprogram Search to search the array Index in order to find the position of this item in the inventory file.
Search	Linear searches the array Index for a specified item number.
ProcessOrder	Processes a given order by determining if there is sufficient stock to fill the order, updates the record for that item, and checks if the in-stock level has fallen below the reorder point.

Coding, Execution, and Testing. The program in Figure 12.4 has the structure just described. The processing carried out by the subroutines Initialize, ProcessTransaction, ConstructIndex, Search, and ProcessOrder is straightforward, and their documentation explains clearly their input/output and accepts/returns specifications. Also shown is a small test file used in a sample run, a listing of the updated test file produced by this run, and a small program that can be used to create the unformatted index file fil12-4b.dat.

Figure 12.4 Inventory program.

```fortran
PROGRAM Inventory_Maintenance
!-Main------------------------------------------------------------------
! This program accepts an order from the keyboard, searches an inventory
! file to see if the item ordered is in stock, updates the file, and
! displays an out-of-stock message and reorder message when necessary.
! The search of the inventory file uses an index of item numbers.  This
! index is read into main memory from an unformatted file.  Identifiers
! used are:
!   ItemsLimit      : limit on number of items in inventory file
!   InputUnitNumber : unit number of input file
!   Index           : array of item numbers (Index(0) = # of items)
!   Response        : response from user (Y or N) about more orders
!                       to process
!
! Input:  Response
! Output: User prompts
!----------------------------------------------------------------------

  IMPLICIT NONE
  INTEGER, PARAMETER :: ItemsLimit = 1000
  INTEGER :: InputUnitNumber
  CHARACTER(1) Response
  INTEGER, DIMENSION(0:ItemsLimit) :: Index

  CALL Initialize (ItemsLimit, InputUnitNumber, Index)

  ! Repeat the following until there are no more transactions

  DO
     CALL ProcessTransaction(InputUnitNumber, Index, ItemsLimit)
     WRITE (*, '(/ 1X, A)', ADVANCE = "NO") &
           "More transactions (Y or N)? "
     READ *, Response
     IF (Response /= "Y") EXIT
  END DO

CONTAINS
```

Figure 12.4 *(cont.)*

```
!-Initialize--------------------------------------------------------------
! This subroutine opens the inventory file and the index file and
! constructs the array Index of ItemsLimit numbers. ItemsLimit,
! RecordLength, InputUnitNumber, Index as in Main.  Other local
! identifiers used are:
!    InventoryFile : name of inventory file
!    IndexFile     : name of index file
!    OpenStatus    : status variable for OPEN
!    RecordLength  : length of records in inventory file
!
! Accepts:   ItemsLimit
! Input:     InventoryFile, IndexFile
! Returns:   InputUnitNumber, Index
! Output:    User prompts
!-------------------------------------------------------------------------

SUBROUTINE Initialize(ItemsLimit, InputUnitNumber, Index)

  INTEGER, PARAMETER :: RecordLength = 80
  INTEGER, INTENT(IN) :: ItemsLimit
  INTEGER, INTENT(OUT) :: InputUnitNumber
  INTEGER, DIMENSION(0:ItemsLimit), INTENT(OUT) :: Index
  CHARACTER(20) :: InventoryFile, IndexFile
  INTEGER :: OpenStatus

  WRITE (*, '(1X, A)', ADVANCE = "NO") &
        "Enter name of inventory file: "
  READ *, InventoryFile
  InputUnitNumber = 10
  OPEN(FILE = InventoryFile, UNIT = 10, STATUS = "OLD", &
       FORM = "FORMATTED", POSITION = "REWIND", &
       ACTION = "READWRITE", ACCESS = "DIRECT", &
       RECL = RecordLength, IOSTAT = OpenStatus)
  IF (OpenStatus > 0) STOP "*** Cannot open inventory file ***"

  WRITE (*, '(1X, A)', ADVANCE = "NO") "Enter name of index file: "
  READ *, IndexFile

  OPEN (FILE = IndexFile, UNIT = 11, STATUS = "OLD", &
        FORM = "UNFORMATTED", POSITION = "REWIND", &
        ACTION = "READ",  ACCESS = "SEQUENTIAL", &
        IOSTAT = OpenStatus)
  IF (OpenStatus > 0) STOP "*** Cannot open index file ***"

  CALL ConstructIndex(11, ItemsLimit, Index)

END SUBROUTINE Initialize
```

Figure 12.4 *(cont.)*

```
!-ConstructIndex-------------------------------------------------------
! This subroutine constructs the array Index of item numbers from an
! (unformatted) file whose unit number is UnitNumber.  Index and
! ItemsLimit are as in Main.  Other local variables used are:
!    I             : count of records in inventory file (stored in
!                        Index(0) before return)
!    InputStatus : status variable for READ
!    ItemNumber  : item number
!
! Accepts:        UnitNumber, Index, ItemsLimit
! Input (file): Elements of the array Index
! Returns:        Index
!---------------------------------------------------------------------

SUBROUTINE ConstructIndex(UnitNumber, ItemsLimit, Index)

   INTEGER, INTENT(IN) :: UnitNumber, ItemsLimit
   INTEGER, DIMENSION(0:ItemsLimit), INTENT(INOUT) :: Index
   INTEGER :: I, InputStatus, ItemNumber

   I = 0

   ! While there is more data, do the following:
   DO
      READ (UNIT = UnitNumber, IOSTAT = InputStatus) ItemNumber
      IF (InputStatus > 0) STOP "*** Input error ***"
      IF (InputStatus < 0) EXIT   ! end of file

      ! Otherwise, store ItemNumber in array Index
      I = I + 1
      Index(I) = ItemNumber
   END DO

   ! Store the count in Index(0)
   Index(0) = I

END SUBROUTINE ConstructIndex

!-ProcessTransaction---------------------------------------------------
! This subroutine processes a transaction by accepting an order for
! a certain item from the keyboard, searching the array Index to find
! the number of the record in the inventory file with unit number
! InvFileUnitNumber describing this item, and then updating this
! record (displaying out-of-stock and/or reorder messages on the
! screen when necessary).  Index and ItemsLimit are as in Main and
! Initialize.  Other local variables used are:
```

Figure 12.4 *(cont.)*

```
!       OrderNumber    :   order number
!       ItemNumber     :   item number
!       Quantity       :   number of items ordered
!       RecordNumber   :   number of record containing information about
!                          ItemNumber (value 0 indicates item not found)

! Accepts:  InputUnitNumber, Index, ItemsLimit
! Input  :  OrderNumber, ItemNumber, Quantity
! Output :  User prompts
!-------------------------------------------------------------------

SUBROUTINE ProcessTransaction(InvFileUnitNumber, Index, ItemsLimit)

  INTEGER, INTENT(IN) ::  InvFileUnitNumber, ItemsLimit
  INTEGER, DIMENSION(0:ItemsLimit), INTENT(IN) :: Index
  INTEGER :: OrderNumber, ItemNumber, Quantity, RecordNumber

  WRITE (*, '(1X, A)', ADVANCE = "NO") "Enter order #: "
  READ *, OrderNumber

  DO
     PRINT *, "(Enter 0/ for item # to terminate order)"
     WRITE (*, '(1X, A)', ADVANCE = "NO") "Item #, Quantity: "
     READ *, ItemNumber, Quantity

     IF (ItemNumber == 0) EXIT
     ! If no more items, terminate repetition

     ! Otherwise process this item
     CALL Search(ItemNumber, Index, ItemsLimit, RecordNumber)
     IF (RecordNumber /=  0) &
        CALL ProcessOrder(RecordNumber, Quantity, OrderNumber, &
                          InvFileUnitNumber)
  END DO

END SUBROUTINE ProcessTransaction

!-Search-------------------------------------------------------------
! This subroutine searches the array Index of item numbers to locate
! the RecordNumber of the record in the inventory file containing
! information about the item ItemNumber.  ItemsLimit is as in Main.
! Other local variables used are:
!     I     : subscript
!     Found : indicates if item has been found
!
! Accepts:  Index, ItemNumber, ItemsLimit
! Returns:  RecordNumber (0 if ItemNumber not found in Index)
!-------------------------------------------------------------------
```

Figure 12.4 *(cont.)*

```fortran
SUBROUTINE Search(ItemNumber, Index, ItemsLimit, RecordNumber)

   INTEGER, INTENT(IN) :: ItemNumber, ItemsLimit
   INTEGER, DIMENSION(0:ItemsLimit), INTENT(IN) :: Index
   INTEGER, INTENT(OUT) :: RecordNumber
   LOGICAL :: Found
   INTEGER :: I


   I = 1
   Found = .FALSE.

   ! While Found is false and I is less than or equal to the
   ! number of items in the array Index, do the following:
   DO
      IF ((Found) .OR. (I > Index(0))) EXIT
      ! If ItemNumber Found or entire array Index
      ! has been searched, terminate repetition

      ! Otherwise continue the search
      IF (ItemNumber == Index(I)) THEN
         RecordNumber = I
         Found = .TRUE.
      ELSE
         I = I + 1
      END IF
   END DO

   IF (.NOT. Found) THEN
      PRINT *, "Bad item number"
      RecordNumber = 0
   END IF

END SUBROUTINE Search

!-ProcessOrder----------------------------------------------------
! This subroutine processes an order (order # OrderNumber) for
! Quantity items.  The RecordNumber-th record of the inventory file
! (unit number InputUnitNumber) is examined to determine whether the
! number in stock is sufficient to fill the order.  If not, an
! out-of-stock message will be displayed at the terminal.  In either
! case, this record will be updated. Also, if the new number in stock
! is below the reorder point, a reorder message will be displayed on
! the screen.  Local variables used are:
```

Figure 12.4 *(cont.)*

```
!      InventoryRecord : derived type for processing inventory records
!      IOStatus        : status variable for READ and WRITE
!      InvRecord       : an inventory record
!      StockRemaining  : stock remaining after filling order (negative
!                        if order can't be filled)
!
! Accepts:        RecordNumber, Quantity, OrderNumber, InputUnitNumber
! Input (file):   InvRecord
! Output(screen): Messages about the order being processed and
!                 reordering information
! Output(file):   InvRecord (updated)
!-------------------------------------------------------------------

SUBROUTINE ProcessOrder(RecordNumber, Quantity, OrderNumber, &
                        InputUnitNumber)

  IMPLICIT NONE
  INTEGER, INTENT(IN) :: RecordNumber, Quantity, OrderNumber, &
                         InputUnitNumber

  TYPE InventoryRecord
     INTEGER :: ItemNumber
     CHARACTER(25) :: ItemName
     INTEGER :: LotSize
     REAL :: Price
     INTEGER :: ReorderPoint, &
                NumberInStock, &
                OptimalInvLevel
  END TYPE InventoryRecord

  TYPE(InventoryRecord) :: InvRecord
  INTEGER ::  IOStatus, StockRemaining

  READ (UNIT = InputUnitNumber, FMT = 10, REC = RecordNumber, &
        IOSTAT = IOStatus) InvRecord%ItemNumber, InvRecord%ItemName, &
        InvRecord%LotSize, InvRecord%Price, InvRecord%ReorderPoint, &
        InvRecord%NumberInStock, InvRecord%OptimalInvLevel
  10 FORMAT(I4, A, I4, F6.2, 3I6)
  IF (IOStatus /= 0) STOP "*** Error reading inventory file ***"
```

Figure 12.4 *(cont.)*

```
    StockRemaining  = InvRecord%NumberInStock - Quantity
    IF (StockRemaining  < 0) THEN
    ! Not enough stock to fill order
       PRINT *, "Out of stock on item #", InvRecord%ItemNumber
       PRINT *, "Back order", -StockRemaining, " for order #", &
                OrderNumber
       PRINT *, "Only", InvRecord%NumberInStock, &
                " units can be shipped at this time"
       PRINT *, "The desired inventory level is", &
                InvRecord%OptimalInvLevel
       InvRecord%NumberInStock = 0

    ELSE
    ! Can fill the order
       InvRecord%NumberInStock = StockRemaining
       PRINT *, "Done"
    END IF

    ! Update inventory file
    WRITE (UNIT = InputUnitNumber, FMT = 10,  REC = RecordNumber,&
           IOSTAT = IOStatus) InvRecord%ItemNumber, InvRecord%ItemName, &
           InvRecord%LotSize, InvRecord%Price, InvRecord%ReorderPoint, &
           InvRecord%NumberInStock, InvRecord%OptimalInvLevel
    IF (IOStatus /= 0) STOP "*** Error writing to inventory file ***"

    IF ((0 <= StockRemaining ) .AND. &
        (StockRemaining <= InvRecord%ReorderPoint)) THEN
       PRINT *, "Only ", InvRecord%NumberInStock, " units of", &
                InvRecord%ItemNumber," remain in stock"
       PRINT *, "Reorder point is ", InvRecord%ReorderPoint
       PRINT *, "Desired inventory level is ", InvRecord%OptimalInvLevel
    END IF

  END SUBROUTINE ProcessOrder

END PROGRAM Inventory_Maintenance
```

Sample run:

```
Enter name of inventory file: fil12-4a.dat
Enter name of index file: fil12-4b.dat
Enter order #: 11111
(Enter 0/ for item # to terminate order)
Item #, Quantity: 1011, 1200
Done
```

Figure 12.4 *(cont.)*

```
(Enter 0/ for item # to terminate order)
Item #, Quantity: 1021, 700
Done
(Enter 0/ for item # to terminate order)
Item #, Quantity: 1040, 80
Done
(Enter 0/ for item # to terminate order)
Item #, Quantity: 0/
More transactions (Y or N)? Y
Enter order #: 11119
(Enter 0/ for item # to terminate order)
Item #, Quantity: 1021, 95
Done
Only  1962  units of 1021  remain in stock
Reorder point is  2000
Desired inventory level is  3000
(Enter 0/ for item # to terminate order)
Item #, Quantity: 1022, 945
Done
Only  2000  units of 1022  remain in stock
Reorder point is  2000
Desired inventory level is  3000
(Enter 0/ for item # to terminate order)
Item #, Quantity: 1040, 100
Done
(Enter 0/ for item # to terminate order)
Item #, Quantity: 0/
More transactions (Y or N)? N
```

Contents of direct access file `fil12-4a.dat` (record length = 80) used in sample run:

```
1011IBUPROFEN-600mg              500  2398 15000 21773 25000
1012CARBAMAZEPINE-200mg          500  7155  2500  2528  3500
1021LEVOTHYROXINE-0.2mg         1000  3900  2000  2757  3000
1022SULFAMEETHOXAZOLE DS         500  6775  2000  2945  3000
1023TERFENADINE-60mg             500 37953  2500  3302  3500
1031AMOXICILLIN-500mg            500  4773 10000 10175 15000
1033CIPROFLAXIN-500mg            100 30248  2000  2155  3000
1037HYDROCHLOROTHIAZIDE-50mg  5000  2565  1500  1770  2500
1040CYCLOBENZAPRINE-10mg         100  7925  2000  2188  2500
```

Figure 12.4 *(cont.)*

Contents of updated file produced by sample run:

```
1011IBUPROFEN-600mg              500   2398 15000 20573 25000
1012CARBAMAZEPINE-200mg          500   7155  2500  2528  3500
1021LEVOTHYROXINE-0.2mg         1000   3900  2000  1962  3000
1022SULFAMEETHOXAZOLE DS         500   6775  2000  2000  3000
1023TERFENADINE-60mg             500  37953  2500  3302  3500
1031AMOXICILLIN-500mg            500   4773 10000 10175 15000
1033CIPROFLAXIN-500mg            100  30248  2000  2155  3000
1037HYDROCHLOROTHIAZIDE-50mg    5000   2565  1500  1770  2500
1040CYCLOBENZAPRINE-10mg         100   7925  2000  2008  2500
```

Utility program to create unformatted index file:

```
PROGRAM Make_Unformatted_Index_File
! Program to create unformatted index file

  INTEGER :: ItemNumber
  CHARACTER(20) ::  IndexFile

  PRINT *, "Name of unformatted index file to be created?"
  READ *, IndexFile

  OPEN(UNIT = 10, FILE = IndexFile, FORM = "UNFORMATTED", &
       STATUS = "NEW", ACTION = "WRITE")
  DO
     PRINT *, "Item number (0 to stop):"
     READ *, ItemNumber
     IF (ItemNumber == 0) EXIT
     WRITE (UNIT = 10) ItemNumber
  END DO

END PROGRAM Make_Unformatted_Index_File
```

Quick Quiz 12.3

1. What are the major differences between sequential files and direct access files?
2. Write a statement that will associate an existing sequential file named TESTDATA with unit number 12 from which values will be read using formatted input, starting with the first record in the file; blanks in numeric fields will be ignored.

3. Write a statement that will associate unit number `10` with a formatted direct access file named `NEWDATA` to be created by the program by writing records of length 30.

4. Write a `READ` statement that will read an integer value for the variable `IdNumber` from the first 5 positions of the 100th record of the file in Question 3.

5. What is an unformatted file, and when is it appropriate to use such a file?

6. Describe how natural mergesort sorts the list 4, 1, 7, 3, 6, 2, 5.

Exercises 12.3

Following the example of the text, show the various splitting–merging stages of mergesort for the following lists of numbers:

1. 1, 5, 3, 8, 7, 2, 6, 4
2. 1, 8, 2, 7, 3, 6, 5, 4
3. 1, 2, 3, 4, 5, 6, 7, 8
4. 8, 7, 6, 5, 4, 3, 2, 1

CHAPTER REVIEW

Summary

This chapter took a detailed look at files. It described both sequential and direct access files as well as formatted and unformatted files. Section 12.1 completed the description of the OPEN and CLOSE statements begun in Chapter 5 and also described the INQUIRE statement. Section 12.2 described file input/output in detail, together with the file-positioning statements BACKSPACE, REWIND, and ENDFILE. It illustrated the use of direct access files with an information retrieval example using a direct access inventory file. The problems of merging and sorting files were also considered, and programs were given for their solutions. The application to a pharmacy inventory problem in the last section illustrates most of Fortran's file-processing capabilities.

FORTRAN SUMMARY

OPEN Statement

```
OPEN (open-list)
```

where *open-list* must include

1. A unit specifier indicating a unit number to be connected to the file being opened:

   UNIT = *integer-expression*

   or simply

   integer-expression

In most cases, it also includes

2. A clause of the form

   FILE = *character-expression*

   indicating the name of the file being opened

3. A

   STATUS = *character-expression*

   clause specifying whether the file is NEW, OLD, SCRATCH, or its status is UN-KNOWN (default)

4. An

   IOSTAT = *integer-variable*

   clause that assigns 0 to the integer variable if the file was opened successfully and a positive value otherwise

and may also include

5. An

   ACCESS = *character-expression*

   clause specifying the type of access as DIRECT or SEQUENTIAL (default)

6. An

   ACTION = *character-expression*

   clause specifying whether the file is opened for READ only, for WRITE only, or for READWRITE (The default value is compiler dependent, but is normally READWRITE.)

7. A clause of the form

   BLANK = *character-expression*

   specifying whether blanks in a numeric field are to be interpreted as ZERO or are to be ignored (NULL) in formatted I/O; NULL is the default value

8. A clause of the form

```
DELIMITER = character-expression
```

specifying whether list-directed or name-list formatted output of character strings should enclose the strings in APOSTROPHEs, QUOTEs, or with no delimiter (NONE), which is the default

9. An

```
ERR = statement-label
```

clause specifying a statement label to be executed if an error occurs while attempting to open the file

10. A

```
FORM = character-expression
```

clause specifying whether the file is FORMATTED or UNFORMATTED (The default value for a sequential file is FORMATTED and for a direct access file it is UNFORMATTED.)

11. A

```
PAD = character-expression
```

clause specifying whether (YES or NO) input strings are to be padded with blanks; default is NO

12. A

```
POSITION = character-expression
```

clause specifying if the file is to be positioned at its beginning (REWIND), to be positioned at its end (APPEND), or to have its position unchanged (ASIS); the default value is ASIS

13. A

```
RECL = record-length
```

clause specifying the record length for a direct access file

Examples:

```
OPEN (UNIT = 10, FILE = "INFO1", STATUS = "OLD", &
      ACTION = "READ", POSITION = "REWIND", IOSTAT = OpenStatus)
```

```
OPEN (UNIT = 11, FILE = InputFile, STATUS = "OLD", &
      ACTION = "READ", POSITION = "REWIND", &
      FORM = "FORMATTED", ACCESS = "SEQUENTIAL", &
      PAD = "YES", ERR = 50)
```

Purpose:
The OPEN statement connects a file with a specifed unit number and makes it available for input and/or output with the properties specified by the various clauses.

CLOSE Statement

```
CLOSE (close-list)
```

where *close-list* must include a unit specifier and may also include an IOSTAT = clause and an ERR = clause as described earlier, together with a STATUS = clause specifying whether the file is to be kept (KEEP) or deleted (DELETE).

Examples:

```
CLOSE(12)
CLOSE(UNIT = 12)
CLOSE (UNIT = 12, STATUS = "KEEP")
```

Purpose:
The CLOSE statement disconnects a file from its unit number.

INQUIRE Statement

```
INQUIRE (UNIT = unit-number, inquiry-list)

INQUIRE (FILE = file-name, inquiry-list)

INQUIRE (IOLENGTH = integer-variable) output-list
```

where "UNIT =" and "FILE =" are optional, and *inquiry-list* may include a number of different clauses, as described in Table 12.1:

```
ACCESS = variable
ACTION = variable
BLANK = variable
DELIM = variable
ERR = statement-label
EXIST = variable
FORM = variable
```

```
FORMATTED = variable
IOSTAT = variable
NAME = variable
NAMED = variable
NEXTREC = variable
NUMBER = variable
OPENED = variable
PAD = variable
POSITION = variable
READ = variable
READWRITE = variable
RECL = variable
SEQUENTIAL = variable
WRITE = variable
```

Examples:

```
LOGICAL :: FileExists
CHARACTER(10) :: ReadOrWrite, Str
INTEGER :: UnitNumber, RecordLength, A, B
REAL :: X, Y

INQUIRE(UNIT = 12, EXISTS = FileExists, &
        ACTION = ReadOrWrite)

INQUIRE(FILE = "FILX.Y.DAT", EXISTS = FileExists, &
        NUMBER = UnitNumber)

INQUIRE(UNIT = 12, IOLENGTH = RecordLength) &
        Str, A, B, X, Y
```

Purpose:

Each of the clauses (except the ERR = clause) in the inquiry list acts as a question concerning some property of the file; a value that answers the question is assigned to the variable in each clause. In the third form, the length of an unformatted output list in processor-dependent units is assigned to the variable.

READ Statement

```
READ format-specifier, input-list
```

or

```
READ (control-list) input-list
```

where *input-list* is a list of variables, substring names, array names, or implied
DO loops; and *control-list* must include

1. A unit specifier (as described earlier) indicating the unit number connected to the
   file

It may also include one or more of the following:

2. A format specifier describing the format of the information to be read:

   ```
   FMT = format-specifier
   ```

   or simply

   ```
   format-specifier
   ```

   where *format-specifier* is one of the following:
   a. * (an asterisk)
   b. A character constant or a character variable (or expression or array) whose
      value specifies the format for the output
   c. The label of a FORMAT statement

3. An

   ```
   ADVANCE = character-expression
   ```

   clause to enable (NO) or disable (YES) nonadvancing input

4. An

   ```
   END = statement-number
   ```

   clause specifying a statement to be executed when the end of the file is reached

5. An

   ```
   EOR = statement-number
   ```

   clause specifying a statement to be executed when the end of a record is reached
   in nonadvancing input

6. An

   ```
   ERR = statement-number
   ```

   clause specifying a statement to be executed if an input error occurs

7. An

   ```
   IOSTAT = integer-variable
   ```

clause that assigns a positive value to the integer variable if an input error occurs, a negative value if the end of data occurs, and zero if neither occurs

8. An

```
NML = group-name
```

clause for namelist input

9. A

```
REC = integer-expression
```

clause indicating the number of the record to be read for a direct access file

10. A

```
SIZE = integer-variable
```

clause that will assign to the integer variable the number of characters read during nonadvancing input (not counting blanks used for padding)

Example:

```
READ (*, *, IOSTAT = InputStatus) A, B, C

READ (UNIT = 10, FMT = '(A)', REC = PartNumber, &
      IOSTAT = InputStatus) PartsRecord
```

Purpose:
The READ statement reads values for the variables in the input list from the specified input device, using the format specified by the format specifier, and according to other specifications in the control list.

WRITE Statement

```
WRITE (control-list) output-list
```

where *output-list* has the same syntax as in the PRINT statement; and *control-list* must include a unit specifier (as described earlier) indicating the unit number connected to the file. It may also include one or more of the following (described earlier):

1. A format specifier describing the form of the information being output
2. An ADVANCE = clause to enable or disable nonadvancing output
3. An ERR = clause specifying a statement to be executed if an output error occurs

4. An `IOSTAT` = clause to check the status of the output operation

5. A `REC` = clause indicating the number of the record to which the information is to be output for a direct access file

6. A `SIZE` = clause to count characters during nonadvancing input

Each has the same form as for a `READ` statement.

Examples:

```
WRITE (*, *) "At time ", Time, " velocity is ", Velocity
WRITE (20, 10), Time, Velocity
10 FORMAT(1X, "At time ", F6.2, " velocity is ", F6.3)
WRITE (*, '(1X, A)', ADVANCE = "NO") "Enter coefficients: "
```

Purpose:
The `WRITE` statement writes the values of the expressions in the output list to the specified output file, using the format determined by the format specifier, and according to other specifications in the control list.

File-Positioning Statements

REWIND *unit*	or	REWIND (*position-list*)
BACKSPACE *unit*	or	BACKSPACE (*position-list*)
ENDFILE *unit*	or	ENDFILE (*position-list*)

where *unit* is the unit number connected to a file. In the second form, *position-list* must contain a unit specifier. It may also contain any of the following (defined earlier):

1. An `ERR` = clause specifying the number of a statement to be executed if an error occurs while positioning the file

2. An `IOSTAT` = clause specifying a status variable that is assigned 0 if the file is successfully positioned or a positive value if some error occurs

Example:

```
REWIND 12
BACKSPACE 12
ENDFILE 12
```

Purpose:
The `REWIND` statement positions the file at its beginning. The `BACKSPACE` statement positions the file at the beginning of the preceding record. The `ENDFILE` statement writes a special end-of-file record into the file.

PROGRAMMING POINTERS

Program Style and Design

1. *Unformatted files are useful when the time required to convert information between its text representation and its internal binary representation is prohibitive. Unformatted files can also usually be stored more compactly than text files.*

2. *Internal files are useful in converting information from character form to numeric form and vice versa.*

3. *Data values read from a file should be echoed to the screen as they are read, at least during program testing.*

Potential Problems

1. *Before a file can be used for input or output, it must be connected to a unit number, using the* OPEN *statement.*

2. *List-directed input/output is not allowed for internal files, nor may they be opened, closed, positioned, or used in* INQUIRE *statements.*

3. *List-directed input/output and formatted input/output are not allowed for unformatted files.*

4. *The result of opening a file without using an* ACTION = *clause or a* POSITION = *clause is machine dependent.* Consequently, a file-processing program that executes correctly on one computer may not execute correctly on another.

5. *The length of records in a direct access formatted file is machine dependent.* Thus, a program that uses direct access files may execute differently on one computer than on another.

PROGRAMMING PROBLEMS

1. Write a program to concatenate two files, that is, to append one file to the end of the other.

2. (a) Design an algorithm to perform the file splitting required by mergesort.
   (b) Write a program to read records from USERS.DAT (described in Appendix B) and sort them using mergesort so that the resources used to date are in increasing order.

3. Information about computer terminals in a computer network is maintained in a direct access file. The terminals are numbered 1 through 100, and information about the *n*th terminal is stored in the *n*th record of the file. This information consists of a terminal type (string), the building in which it is located (string), the transmission rate (integer), an access code (character), and the date of last ser-

vice (month, day, year). Write a program to read a terminal number, retrieve and display the information about that terminal, and modify the date of last service for that terminal.

4. (Project)   Some text formatters allow command lines to be placed in the file of unformatted text. These command lines might have forms such as the following:

.P *m n*	Insert *m* blank lines before each paragraph, and indent each paragraph *n* spaces.
.W *n*	Page width (line length) is *n*.
.L *n*	Page length (number of lines per page) is *n*.
.I *n*	Indent by *n* spaces all lines following this command line.
.U	Unindent all following lines, and reset to the previous left margin.

Write a program to read a file containing lines of text and some of these command lines throughout, and produce a new file in which these formatting commands have been implemented.

5. (Project)   Modify and extend the text editor program of Section 12.2 so that other editing operations can be performed. Include commands of the following forms in the menu of options:

F*n*	Find and display the *n*th line of the file.
P*n*	Print *n* consecutive lines, beginning with the current line.
M*n*	Move ahead *n* lines from the current line.
T	Move to the top line of the file.
C/*string*₁/*string*₂/	Change the current line by replacing *string₁* with *string₂*.
L *string*	Search the file starting from the current line to find a line containing *string*.
D*n*	Delete *n* consecutive lines, beginning with the current line.
I *line*	Insert the given *line* after the current line.

6. (Project)   A *pretty printer* is a special kind of text formatter that reads a file containing a source program and then prints it in a "pretty" format. For example, a pretty printer for Fortran might insert blank lines between subprograms, indent and align statements within other statements such as block IF statements and DO loops, and so on, to produce a format similar to that used in the sample programs in this text. Write a pretty-print program for Fortran programs to indent and align statements in a pleasing format.

7. (Project)   Write a menu-driven program that uses STUDENT.DAT and STUP-DATE.DAT (see Appendix B) and allows (some of) the following options. For each option, write a separate subprogram so that options and corresponding subprograms can be easily added or removed.

(1) Locate a student's permanent record when given his or her student number, and print it in a nicer format than that in which it is stored.

(2) Same as option 1, but locate the record when given the student's name.

(3) Print a list of all student names and numbers in a given class (1, 2, 3, 4, 5).

(4) Same as option 3 but for a given major.

(5) Same as option 3 but for a given range of cumulative GPAs.

(6) Find the average cumulative GPAs for (a) all females, (b) all males, (c) all students with a specified major, and (d) all students.

(7) Produce updated grade reports with the following format (where *xx* is the current year):

```
                    GRADE REPORT    SEMESTER 2    5/29/xx

                    DISPATCH UNIVERSITY

    10103           James L. Johnson

                         GRADE                   CREDITS
                         =====                   =======
    ENGL 176               C                        4
    EDUC 268               B                        4
    EDUC 330               B+                       3
    P E 281                C                        3
    ENGR 317               D                        4

    Cumulative Credits:        28
    Current GPA:               1.61
    Cumulative GPA:            2.64
```

Here, letter grades are assigned according to the following scheme: A = 4.0, A− = 3.7, B+ = 3.3, B = 3.0, B− = 2.7, C+ = 2.3, C = 2.0, C− = 1.7, D+ = 1.3, D = 1.0, D− = 0.7, and F = 0.0. (See Programming Problem 22 in Chapter 2 for details on the calculation of GPAs.)

(8) Same as option 7, but instead of producing grade reports, produce a new file containing the updated total credits and new cumulative GPAs.

(9) Produce an updated file when a student (a) drops or (b) adds a course.

(10) Produce an updated file when a student (a) transfers into or (b) withdraws from the university.

FEATURES NEW TO FORTRAN 90

The new file-processing features added in Fortran 90 consist mainly of new clauses that may be included in the OPEN, CLOSE, INQUIRE, READ, and WRITE statements.

- New clauses that may be used in an `OPEN` statement are the `POSITION` =, `ACTION` =, `DELIM` =, and `PAD` = clauses.

- New clauses that may be used in `READ` and `WRITE` statements are the `NML` =, `ADVANCE` =, `SIZE` =, and `EOR` = clauses.

- New clauses that may be used in the `INQUIRE` statement are the `POSITION` =, `ACTION` =, `READ` =, `WRITE` =, `READWRITE` =, `DELIM` =, `PAD` =, and `IOLENGTH` = clauses.

13

Pointers and Linked Structures

[Pointers] are like little jumps, leaping wildly from one part of a data structure to another. Their introduction into high-level languages has been a step backward from which we may never recover.

C. A. R. HOARE

To be sure of hitting the target, shoot first, and call whatever you hit the target.

ASHLEIGH BRILLIANT

I've got a little list, I've got a little list.

GILBERT and SULLIVAN, The Mikado

He's making a list, and checking it twice, gonna' find out who's naughty or nice ...

Santa Claus Is Coming to Town (CHRISTMAS CAROL)

... Is the sort of person who keeps a list of all of his lists.

V. OREHCK III (fictitious)

I think that I shall never see,
A poem lovely as a tree.

JOYCE KILMER

*I*n Chapters 8 and 9, we saw how the ALLOCATE and DEALLOCATE statements can be used to allocate and deallocate storage for arrays at run time. This made it possible to construct arrays that fit the amount of data to be stored. Such arrays avoid the wasted memory that is characteristic of arrays whose memory is allocated at compile time.

For data sets whose sizes are relatively constant, run-time allocation offers a convenient way to tailor the size of the array that stores the data set to the quantity of data. However, in programs that process data sets of very different sizes, any array-based structure—whether allocated at compile time or at run time—suffers from a significant drawback. Enlarging an array so that new values can be added requires that

- A new larger array is allocated.
- The elements of the old array are copied into the new array.
- The new elements are written into the new array.
- The old array is deallocated.

A similar sequence of steps is required to reduce the size of an array.

Processing arrays whose sizes vary can thus involve extensive copying of elements. The time to perform this copying coupled with the time to allocate the new array and deallocate the old array can make these operations very time-consuming.

Unlike **static data structures** such as arrays whose sizes are fixed once memory is allocated, **dynamic data structures** expand or contract as required during execution. A dynamic data structure is a collection of elements called *nodes* that are linked together. This linking is established by associating with each node a pointer that points to the next node in the structure. One of the simplest linked structures is a *linked list*, which might be pictured as follows:

Dynamic data structures are especially useful for storing and processing data sets whose sizes change during program execution, for example, the collection of jobs that have been entered into a computer system and are awaiting execution or the collection of passenger names and seat assignments on an airplane.

Construction of a dynamic data structure requires the ability to allocate memory locations as needed during program execution and to access these memory locations so that data can be stored in them or retrieved from them. For this a special kind of variable is needed to *point to* these locations. Such variables are called **pointer variables**, or simply **pointers**. In this chapter we will consider pointers in Fortran and how they can be used to build dynamic data structures.

13.1 INTRODUCTION TO LINKED LISTS

In Chapter 8, we described how arrays can be used to store and process lists. Although this array-based implementation of lists works well for static lists whose sizes remain quite constant, it is not an efficient way of processing dynamic lists that grow and shrink as elements are inserted and deleted. One reason is that the declared size of the array must be large enough to store the largest list, but this largest size may not be known. If the array is too small, it will not be possible to store the entire list; if the array is too large, considerable memory may be wasted. Even if the maximum size is known so that an array of this size can be declared, memory will still be wasted when the list is smaller. Another drawback of an array-based implementation of a list is that each time a new element is inserted into the list, array elements may have to be shifted to make room for it. For example, suppose we wish to insert the new value 56 after the element 48 in the list of integers

$$23, 25, 34, 48, 61, 79, 82, 89, 91, 99$$

to produce the new list

$$23, 25, 34, 48, 56, 61, 79, 82, 89, 91, 99$$

If the list elements are stored in an array, the array elements in positions 5 through 10 must first be shifted into positions 6 through 11 before the new element can be inserted at position 5:

| 23 | 25 | 34 | 48 | 61 | 79 | 82 | 89 | 91 | 99 | ? | ... | ? |

| 23 | 25 | 34 | 48 | 56 | 61 | 79 | 82 | 89 | 91 | 99 | ... | ? |

Removing a list element also requires shifting array elements. For example, to delete the second item in the list,

$$23, 25, 34, 48, 56, 61, 75, 79, 82, 89, 91, 99$$

we must shift the array elements in positions 3 through 12 into locations 2 through 11 to "close the gap" in the array:

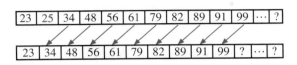

A linked list is an alternative structure for storing the elements of a list, and as we will see, it provides a better implementation of dynamic lists. A **linked list** consists of a collection of elements called **nodes,** each of which stores two items of information: (1) an element of the list and (2) a **link** or **pointer** that indicates the location of the node containing the successor of this list element. Access to the node storing the first list element must also be maintained. For example, a linked list storing the list of names Brown, Jones, and Smith might be pictured as follows:

In this diagram, arrows represent links, and List points to the first node in the list. The Data part of each node stores one of the names in the list, and the Next part stores the pointer to the next node. The "ground" symbol in the Next part of the last node represents a **null pointer** and indicates that this list element has no successor.

Inserting New Elements into a Linked List

One of the strengths of a linked list is that no list elements need be moved when a new element is inserted into the list or when an element is removed from the list. We demonstrate this first for insertion.

To insert a new data value into a linked list, we must first obtain a new node and store the new value in its data part. We assume that there is a storage pool of available nodes and some mechanism for obtaining nodes from it as needed. The second step is to connect this new node to the existing list, and for this, there are two cases to consider: (1) insertion at the beginning of the list and (2) insertion after some element in the list.

To illustrate the first case, suppose we wish to insert the name Adams at the beginning of the preceding linked list. We first obtain a new node and store the name Adams in its data part:

Get a node pointed to by `NewNodePtr`.
Store `"Adams"` in the `Data` part of this node.

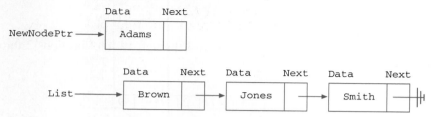

We then insert this node into the list by setting its link part to point to the first node in the list:

Set the `Next` part of the node pointed to by `NewNodePtr` equal to `List`.

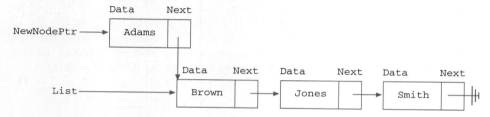

and then setting `List` to point to this new first node:

Set `List` equal to `NewNodePtr`.

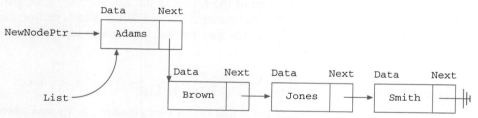

As an illustration of the second case, suppose that we wish to insert the name `Lewis` after the node containing `Jones` and that `PredPtr` is a pointer to this predecessor.

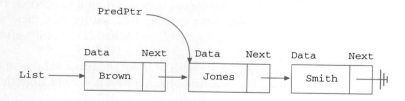

We begin as before by obtaining a new node in which to store the name Lewis:

Get a node pointed to by NewNodePtr.
Store "Lewis" in the Data part of this node.

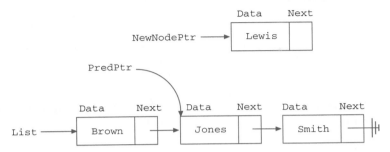

We insert this node into the list by first setting its link part equal to the pointer in the Next part of the node pointed to by PredPtr so that it points to its successor:

Set the Next part of the node pointed to by NewNodePtr equal to the Next part of the node pointed to by PredPtr.

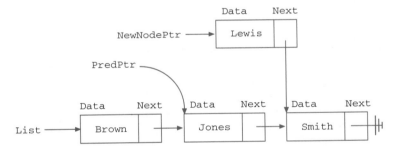

and then resetting the link part of the predecessor node to point to this new node:

Set the Next part of the node pointed to by PredPtr equal to NewNodePtr.

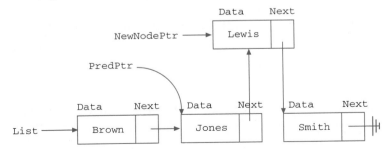

Deleting Items from a Linked List

Like insertion, there are two cases to consider for deletion: (1) deleting the first element in the list and (2) deleting an element that has a predecessor. To demonstrate the first case, suppose we have the list

and we wish to delete the name `Brown` from the preceding list. This case is easy and consists of simply resetting `List` to point to the second node in the list and then returning the first node to the storage pool of available nodes:

Set `TempPtr` equal to `List`.

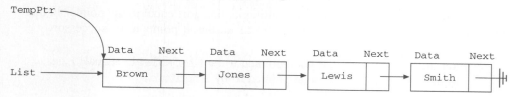

Set `List` equal to the `Next` part of the node pointed to by `TempPtr`.

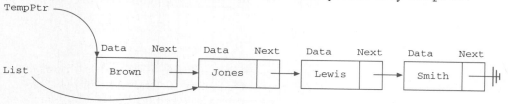

Return the node pointed to by `TempPtr` to the storage pool of available nodes.

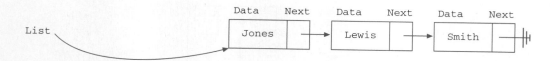

The second case is almost as easy as the first. For example, suppose that we wish to delete the node containing `Lewis` from the preceding list and that `PredPtr` points to the predecessor.

Set `TempPtr` equal to the `Next` part of the node pointed to by `PredPtr`.

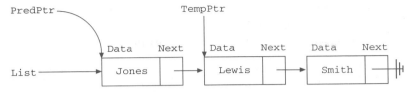

Set the `Next` part of the node pointed to by `PredPtr` equal to the `Next` part of the node pointed to by `TempPtr`.

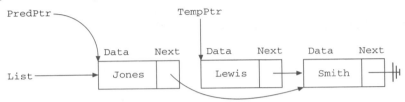

Return the node pointed to by `TempPtr` to the storage pool of available nodes.

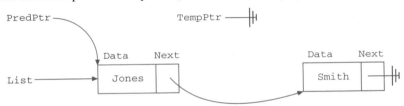

As the preceding examples demonstrate, it is possible to insert or delete items in a linked list without shifting list elements as required in the array-based implementation of a list. In the next section, we examine how a linked list can be implemented in Fortran.

Quick Quiz 13.1

1. Distinguish between static and dynamic data structures.
2. The elements of a linked list are called _____.
3. What two items of information are stored in the nodes of a linked list?
4. What advantages do linked lists have over lists stored in arrays?
5. A _____ pointer indicates that a list element has no successor.

Exercises 13.1

1. Write an algorithm to count the nodes in a linked list with first node pointed to by `List`.

2. Write an algorithm to determine the average of a linked list of real numbers with first node pointed to by `List`.

3. Write an algorithm to append a node at the end of a linked list with first node pointed to by `List`.

4. Write an algorithm to determine whether the data items in a linked list with first node pointed to by `List` are in ascending order.

5. Write an algorithm to search a linked list with first node pointed to by `List` for a given item, and if it is found, return a pointer to the predecessor of the node containing that item.

6. Write an algorithm to insert a new node into a linked list with first node pointed to by `List` after the nth node in this list for a given integer n.

7. Write an algorithm to delete the nth node in a linked list with first node pointed to by `List`, where n is a given integer.

8. Suppose the items stored in two linked lists are in ascending order. Write an algorithm to merge these two lists to yield a list with the items in ascending order.

9. Write an algorithm to reverse a linked list with first node pointed to by `List`. Do not copy the list elements; rather, reset links and pointers so that `List` points to the last node and all links between nodes are reversed.

13.2   POINTERS

We noted in the introduction to this chapter that construction of dynamic data structures requires the ability to allocate memory locations during program execution and that special kinds of variables called *pointer variables* (or simply *pointers*) are needed to access these locations. In this section we describe pointers in Fortran, and in the next section we will show how they can be used to implement linked lists.

Pointer Variables

A variable is declared to be a pointer variable by including the `POINTER` attribute in the attribute list of its declaration:

```
type, attribute-list, POINTER :: pointer-variable
```

This declares that `pointer-variable` can be used to access a memory location where a value having the specified type and attributes can be stored. For example, if the data values are strings, then a pointer to a memory location that can be used to store a string may be declared by

```
CHARACTER(8), POINTER :: StringPtr
```

This pointer variable `StringPtr` may be used only to access memory locations in which character strings of length 8 can be stored. Similarly,

```
TYPE Inventory_Info
   INTEGER :: Number
   REAL :: Price
END TYPE Inventory_Info

TYPE(Inventory_Info), POINTER :: InvPtr
```

declares that `InvPtr` is a pointer variable that can be used to access locations where structures of type `Inventory_Info` are stored.

The ALLOCATE Statement

The ALLOCATE statement was used in Chapters 8 and 9 to allocate memory for run-time arrays. It can also be used to acquire memory locations to associate with pointer variables during program execution. For example, the statement

```
ALLOCATE(StringPtr)
```

associates with `StringPtr` a memory location where a string such as `"Comput- er"` can be stored. We say that `StringPtr` "points" to this memory location, called a **target**, and we picture this with a diagram like the following:

Each execution of an ALLOCATE statement acquires a new memory location and associates it with the specified pointer. Thus, if `TempPtr` is also a pointer declared by

```
CHARACTER(8), POINTER :: TempPtr
```

the statement

```
ALLOCATE(TempPtr)
```

acquires a new memory location pointed to by `TempPtr`:

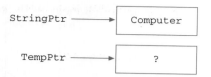

Pointer Association Status

Pointer variables may be in one of three states: undefined, associated, or disassociated. Like all variables, each pointer variable is initially **undefined**. When a pointer points to a target, its status changes to **associated**:

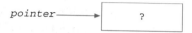

If this association is broken without associating the pointer variable with a new target, the pointer is said to be **null** or **disassociated**. A null pointer is commonly pictured using the ground symbol:

Fortran provides the intrinsic function ASSOCIATED to test whether a pointer variable is associated with a target. A reference of the form

ASSOCIATED(*pointer*)

returns .TRUE. if *pointer* is associated with a target and .FALSE. otherwise. The association status of *pointer* must not be undefined.

The NULLIFY statement can be used to change a pointer variable's status to null. This statement has the form

NULLIFY(*list-of-pointers*)

Any associations of memory locations with these pointer variables are broken, and these memory locations can no longer be accessed unless pointed to by some other pointer variables. If there are no such pointer variables, these memory locations are *marooned* and cannot be reused.

When execution of a program begins, the program has a "pool" of available memory locations, called the **free store**. The effect of an ALLOCATE statement is to

1. Remove a block of memory from the free store.
2. Allocate that block to the executing program.

Since the size of the free store is limited, each ALLOCATE statement causes the pool of available memory to shrink. If more memory is needed than is available, program execution is halted unless a STAT = clause is included in the ALLOCATE statement:

    ALLOCATE(*list*, STAT = *integer-variable*)

In this case, the integer variable will be assigned 0 if allocation is successful and a positive value otherwise.

Memory that is no longer needed can be returned to the free store by using a DEALLOCATE statement:

    DEALLOCATE(*list*, STAT = *integer-variable*)

The integer variable will be assigned 0 if deallocation is successful and a positive value otherwise; for example, if some of the pointer variables in the *list* are null. If the STAT = clause is omitted, unsuccessful deallocation will terminate program execution.

Memory returned to the free store can be reallocated by subsequent ALLOCATE statements. The ALLOCATE and DEALLOCATE operations are thus complementary.

Pointer Assignment

If $pointer_1$ and $pointer_2$ have the same type, an assignment statement of the form

    $pointer_1$ => $pointer_2$

causes $pointer_1$ to have the same association status as $pointer_2$, and if $pointer_2$ is associated, $pointer_1$ will point to the same target as $pointer_2$. The previous target (if any) pointed to by $pointer_1$ can no longer be accessed unless it is pointed to by some other pointer. The following diagrams illustrate:

Before assignment:

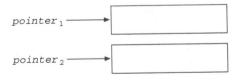

After assignment $pointer_1$ => $pointer_2$:

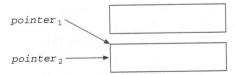

Before assignment:

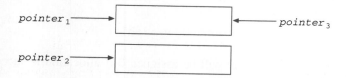

After assignment $pointer_1$ => $pointer_2$:

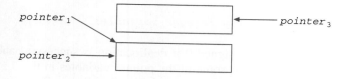

As an illustration, suppose that both `StringPtr` and `TempPtr` are pointer variables declared by

```
CHARACTER(8), POINTER :: StringPtr, TempPtr
```

and point to memory locations containing the strings `Computer` and `Software`, respectively:

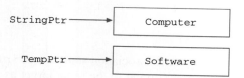

The assignment statement

```
TempPtr => StringPtr
```

causes `TempPtr` to point to the same memory location as `StringPtr`:

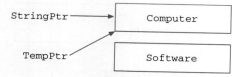

The string `Software` stored in the second location can no longer be accessed (unless it is pointed to by some other pointer).

A pointer assignment statement may also have the form

```
pointer-variable => target-variable
```

where *target-variable* has the same type as *pointer-variable* but has the TARGET attribute (and not the POINTER attribute). The declaration of such a variable has the form

> *type*, *attribute-list*, TARGET :: *target-variable*

This assignment statement causes *pointer-variable* to point to *target-variable*, that is, to the memory location allocated to *target-variable*.

To illustrate, consider the declarations:

```
CHARACTER(8), POINTER :: StringPtr
CHARACTER(8), TARGET :: Name = "John Doe"
```

The statement

```
StringPtr => Name
```

causes StringPtr to point to the memory location allocated to Name (at compile time):

A reference to the ASSOCIATED function of the form

> ASSOCIATED(*pointer*,*target*)

can be used to determine if *pointer* points to *target*. Thus after the preceding pointer assignment statement is executed,

```
ASSOCIATED(StringPtr, Name)
```

will return .TRUE.. A reference of the form

> ASSOCIATED(*pointer₁*,*pointer₂*)

can be used to determine if *pointer*$_1$ and *pointer*$_2$ point to the same target.

Pointers in Expressions

One important rule governs the use of pointers in expressions:

> When an associated pointer appears in an expression, it is automatically **dereferenced**; that is, the value stored in its target is used. If an associated pointer appears in an input list, an input value will be stored in its target.

To illustrate, consider the declarations

```
CHARACTER(8), POINTER :: StringPtr, NamePtr_1, NamePtr_2
CHARACTER(8), TARGET :: Name_1 = "Mary Doe", Name_2
CHARACTER(8) :: Product = "Computer"
```

and suppose that a memory location has been associated with StringPtr by

```
ALLOCATE(StringPtr)
```

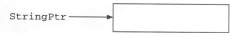

The statements

```
StringPtr = "Computer"
```

and

```
StringPtr = Product
```

are ordinary assignment statements and store the string "Computer" in the memory location pointed to by StringPtr:

The output statement

```
PRINT *, StringPtr
```

will display

```
Computer
```

as will

```
IF StringPtr(4:6) = "put" THEN
   PRINT *, StringPtr
END {IF}
```

A string that is input in response to the READ statement

```
READ '(A)', StringPtr
```

will be stored in the memory location pointed to by StringPtr.

Dereferencing also occurs for pointer variables that point to target variables. For example, suppose that `NamePtr1` and `NamePtr2` point to the variables `Name_1` and `Name_2`, respectively:

```
NamePtr_1 => Name_1
NamePtr_2 => Name_2
```

The output statement

```
PRINT *, NamePtr_1
```

would then display the value stored in `Name_1`:

```
Mary Doe
```

The assignment statement

```
NamePtr_2 = NamePtr_1
```

assigns the string `Mary Doe` stored in `Name_1` to `Name_2` and is therefore equivalent to the assignment statement

```
Name_2 = Name_1
```

As this example illustrates, there is a fundamental difference between the pointer assignment operator (=>) and the ordinary assignment operator (=). If both `TempPtr` and `StringPtr` are associated,

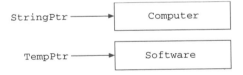

the statement

```
TempPtr = StringPtr
```

copies the contents of the memory location pointed to by `StringPtr` into the location pointed to by `TempPtr`:

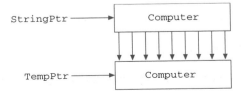

This result is quite different from that produced by the pointer assignment

```
TempPtr => StringPtr
```

which causes `TempPtr` to point to the same memory location pointed to by `StringPtr`:

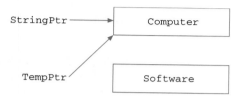

Pointers and Subprograms

Pointers (and targets) may be used as arguments of subprograms, provided they satisfy the following conditions:

1. If a formal argument is a pointer variable, the corresponding actual argument must also be a pointer variable of the same type.

2. A pointer formal argument cannot have an `INTENT` attribute.

3. If a formal argument is a pointer (or target) variable, the subprogram must have an explicit interface.

When the subprogram is invoked, the association status of each actual argument that is a pointer is passed to the corresponding formal argument.

The value returned by a function may also be a pointer. In this case, the value must be returned by using a `RESULT` clause (see Section 6.7) to return the value assigned within the function to a local pointer variable.

13.3   IMPLEMENTING LINKED LISTS

Pointer variables, which we introduced in the preceding section, are not very useful by themselves. Rather, their importance lies in the fact that they make it possible to implement dynamic data structures such as linked lists. As we have noted, dynamic structures are more suitable than static structures for modeling a data set whose size changes during processing. In this and the next section, we show how linked lists can be implemented using structures and pointers.

The nodes in a linked list are represented in Fortran as structures having two kinds of components, **data components** and **link components.** The data components have types that are appropriate for storing the necessary information, and the link components are pointers. For example, the type of the nodes in the linked list

may be defined by

```
TYPE List_Node
   INTEGER :: Data
   TYPE(List_Node), POINTER :: Next
END TYPE List_Node
```

Each node in this list is a structure of type `List_Node`, consisting of two components. The first component `Data` is of integer type and is used to store the data. The second component `Next` is a pointer and points to the next node in the list.

The nodes in a linked list of employee records,

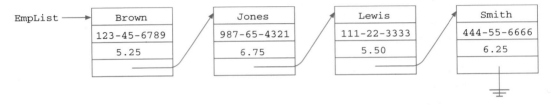

can be defined by

```
TYPE Employee_Record
   CHARACTER(10) :: Name
   CHARACTER(11) :: Social_Security_Number
   REAL :: HourlyRate
END TYPE Employee_Record

TYPE Emp_List_Node
   TYPE(Employee_Record) :: Data
   TYPE(Emp_List_Node), POINTER :: Next
END TYPE Emp_List_Node
```

Here the `Data` component is a structure of type `Employee_Record`.

In addition to the nodes of the list in which to store the data items, a pointer to the first node is needed. Thus we declare a pointer variable `NumList` by

```
TYPE(List_Node), POINTER :: NumList
```

for the linked list of integers, and

```
TYPE(Emp_List_Node), POINTER :: EmpList
```

for the linked list of employee records.

Constructing a Linked List

To illustrate the basic steps in the construction of a linked list, suppose that the integers 1996 and 1723 have already been stored in a linked list:

and suppose that we wish to add 1550 to this list. In the construction, we use two pointers, NumList to point to the first node in the list and TempPtr as a temporary pointer:

```
TYPE(List_Node), POINTER :: NumList, TempPtr
```

We first acquire a new node temporarily pointed to by TempPtr,

```
ALLOCATE(TempPtr)
```

and store 1550 in the data component of this structure:

```
TempPtr%Data = 1550
```

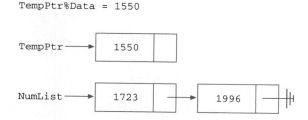

This node can then be joined to the list by setting its link component so that it points to the first node:

```
TempPtr%Next => NumList
```

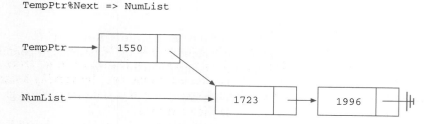

The pointer NumList is then updated to point to this new node:

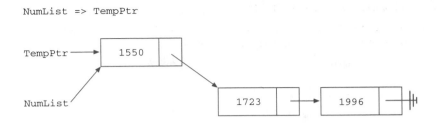

```
NumList => TempPtr
```

To construct the entire list, we could first initialize an empty list:

```
NULLIFY(NumList)
```

and then repeat the preceding four statements three times, replacing 1550 by 1996 in the second assignment statement, then by 1723, and finally again using the value 1550. In practice, however, such linked lists are usually constructed by reading the data values rather than by assigning them with assignment statements. In this example, the linked list could be constructed by using the following program segment, where Item and AllocateStatus are integer variables:

```
! Initially the list is empty
NULLIFY(NumList)

! Read the data values and construct the list
DO
    READ *, Item
    IF (Item == End_Data_Flag) EXIT
    ALLOCATE(TempPtr, STAT = AllocateStatus)
    IF (AllocateStatus /= 0) STOP "*** Not enough memory ***"
    TempPtr%Data = Item
    TempPtr%Next => NumList
    NumList => TempPtr
END DO
```

Traversing a Linked List

Once a linked list has been constructed, we may want to **traverse** it from beginning to end, displaying each element in it. To traverse a list stored in an array, we can easily move through the list from one element to the next by varying an array subscript in some repetition structure. To traverse a linked list, we move through the list by varying a pointer variable in a repetition structure.

To illustrate, suppose we wish to display the integers stored in the linked list:

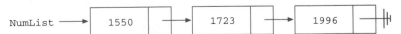

We begin by initializing a pointer variable `CurrPtr` to point to the first node

```
CurrPtr => NumList
```

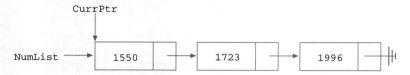

and display the integer stored in this node:

```
PRINT *, CurrPtr%Data
```

To move to the next node, we follow the link from the current node:

```
CurrPtr => CurrPtr%Next
```

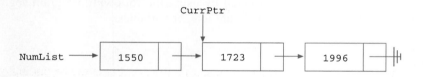

After displaying the integer in this node, we move to the next node:

```
CurrPtr => CurrPtr%Next
```

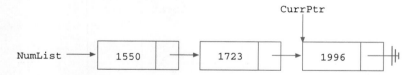

and display its data. Since we have now reached the last node, we need some way to signal this condition. But this is easy, for if we attempt to move to the next node, `CurrPtr` becomes null:

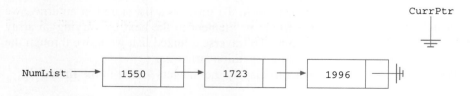

The function `ASSOCIATED` can be used to determine when this occurs:

```
CurrPtr => NumList
DO
    IF (.NOT. ASSOCIATED(CurrPtr)) EXIT   ! end of list
    PRINT *, CurrPtr%Data
    CurrPtr => CurrPtr%Next
END DO
```

Insertion and Deletion in Linked Lists

In general, linked lists are preferred over arrays for processing dynamic lists, whose sizes vary as items are added and deleted, because the number of nodes in a linked list is limited only by the available memory and because the insertion and deletion operations are easy to implement.

To insert an element into a linked list, we first obtain a new node temporarily accessed via a pointer TempPtr,

```
ALLOCATE(TempPtr, STAT = AllocateStatus)
```

and store the element in its data component:

```
TempPtr%Data = Element
```

There are now two cases to consider: (1) inserting the element at the beginning of the list, and (2) inserting it after some specified element in the list. The first case has already been illustrated. For the second case, suppose that the new node is to be inserted between the nodes pointed to by PredPtr and CurrPtr:

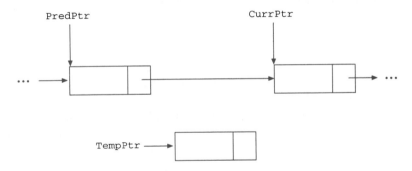

The node is inserted by setting the pointer in the link component of the new node to point to the node pointed to by CurrPtr,

```
TempPtr%Next => CurrPtr
```

and then resetting the pointer in the link component of the node pointed to by PredPtr to point to the new node:

```
PredPtr%Next => TempPtr
```

The following diagram illustrates:

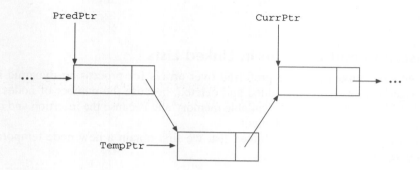

For deletion, there also are two cases to consider: (1) deleting the first element in the list, and (2) deleting an element that has a predecessor. The first case is easy and consists of the following steps:

1. Set `CurrPtr` to point to the first node in the list:

    ```
    CurrPtr => List
    ```

2. Set `List` to point to the second node in the list:

    ```
    List => CurrPtr%Next
    ```

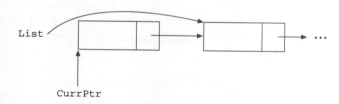

3. Release the node pointed to by `CurrPtr`:

    ```
    DEALLOCATE(CurrPtr)
    ```

For the second case, suppose that the predecessor of the node to be deleted is pointed to by `PredPtr`:

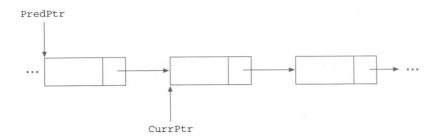

The node is deleted by setting the link component of the node pointed to by `Pred-Ptr` so that it points to the successor of the node to be deleted,

```
PredPtr%Next => CurrPtr%Next
```

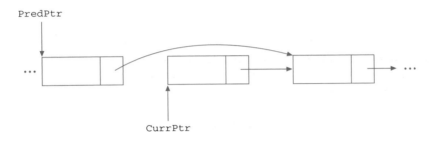

and then releasing the node pointed to by `CurrPtr`:

```
DEALLOCATE(CurrPtr)
```

13.4 APPLICATION: INTERNET ADDRESSES

TCP (Transmission Control Protocol) and **IP** (Internet Protocol) are communication protocols that specify rules computers use in exchanging messages in networks. TCP/IP addresses are used to uniquely identify computers in the Internet; for example,

titan.ksc.nasa.gov

is the address of a site at the NASA Kennedy Space Center. These addresses are made up of four fields that represent specific parts of the Internet:

host.subdomain.subdomain.rootdomain

which the computer will translate into a unique TCP/IP address. This address is a 32-bit value, but it is usually represented in a dotted-decimal notation by separating the 32 bits into four 8-bit fields, expressing each field as a decimal integer, and separating the fields with a period; for example,

128.159.4.20

is the TCP/IP address for the above site at the NASA Kennedy Space Center.

PROBLEM

Problem

A **gateway** is a device used to interconnect two different computer networks. Suppose that a gateway connects a university to the Internet and that the university's network administrator needs to monitor connections through this gateway. Each time a connection is made (for example, a student using the World Wide Web), the TCP/IP address of the student's computer is stored in a data file. The administrator wants to check periodically who has used the gateway and how many times they have used it.

Solution

Specification. The input and output for this problem are clear:

Input: The name of the data file containing the TCP/IP addresses
           TCP/IP addresses from the file

Output: A list of distinct TCP/IP addresses and the number of times they
           appear in the file

Design. The data file contains TCP/IP addresses, and these addresses must be read from the file and stored in a list. Since there are 2^{32} possible addresses and the number of distinct addresses is not known in advance, a static data structure such as an array cannot be used efficiently. The flexibility provided by a dynamic structure such as a linked list makes it a more appropriate storage structure. Each node will store an address and the number of times that address appeared in the data file.

The variables we will use are

IDENTIFIERS FOR TCP/IP-ADDRESS PROBLEM

FileName   The name of the data file containing the addresses

Address   A TCP/IP address

AddressList Linked list of addresses and counts

As each address is read from the file, we must determine if it is already in the list; if so, we increment its count by 1. If it is not in the list, we will simply insert the new address at the beginning of the list because the order in which the addresses occur is not important. After all the addresses in the file have been read, the list is traversed and the addresses and their counts displayed. The following algorithm summarizes this approach:

ALGORITHM FOR TCP/IP-ADDRESS PROBLEM

Algorithm to find the distinct TCP/IP addresses stored in a file and the number of times each address appears.

Input: *FileName*
            Addresses from the file
Output: A list of addresses and their counts

1. Get the name (*FileName*) of the data file containing the TCP/IP addresses, and open it for input. If the file cannot be opened, terminate execution.

2. Initialize *AddressList* as an empty linked list.

3. Repeat the following:
   a. Read an *Address* from the file.
   b. If an input error occurs, terminate execution.
      If there were no more addresses, terminate repetition.
      Otherwise continue with the following.
   c. Search *AddressList* to determine if *Address* already appears in the list.
   d. If *Address* is found
      Increment the count in the node containing the address by 1.
      Otherwise
      Insert a node containing *Address* and a count of 1 at the beginning of *AddressList*.

4. Traverse *AddressList*, displaying each TCP/IP address and its count.

Coding and Execution. The program in Figure 13.1 implements this algorithm. It uses the methods described in the preceding sections for inserting items into a linked list and for traversing a linked list.

Figure 13.1 Internet addresses.

```
PROGRAM Internet_Addresses
!--------------------------------------------------------------------------
! Program to read TCP/IP addresses from a file and produce a list of distinct
! addresses and a count of how many times each appeared in the file.  The
! addresses and counts are stored in a linked list.
! Variables used are:
!   FileName    : name of data file containing addresses
!   OpenStatus  : status variable for OPEN statement
!   InputStatus : status variable for READ statement
!   Address     : an address read from the file
!   AddressList : pointer to first node in the linked list of addresses
! Subroutines used to process linked list:
!   Add_To_List, Search, Output_Addresses
!
! Input (keyboard): FileName
! Input (file):     Addresses
! Output:           A list of distinct addresses and their counts
!--------------------------------------------------------------------------

  IMPLICIT NONE

  ! Define an address node type
  TYPE List_Node
     CHARACTER(15) :: TCP_IP_Address     ! Address data
     INTEGER :: Count                    ! Counter for this address
     TYPE(List_Node), POINTER :: Next    ! Pointer to next node
  END TYPE List_Node

  CHARACTER(15) :: Address, FileName*20
  INTEGER :: OpenStatus, InputStatus
  TYPE(List_Node), POINTER :: AddressList

  ! Get name of data file and open it for reading
  WRITE (*, '(1X, A)', ADVANCE = "NO") "Enter name of file of addresses: "
  READ *, FileName
  OPEN (UNIT = 10, FILE = FileName, STATUS = "OLD", IOSTAT = OpenStatus)
  IF (OpenStatus > 0) STOP "*** Cannot open address file ***"

  ! Create empty linked list
  NULLIFY(AddressList)
```

Figure 13.1 *(cont.)*

```
! Read addresses from the file and store them in the list,
! until end of file reached
DO
    READ(10, '(A)', IOSTAT = InputStatus) Address
    IF (InputStatus > 0) STOP "*** Input error ***"
    IF (InputStatus < 0) EXIT  ! end of file

    CALL Add_To_List(AddressList, Address)
ENDDO

CALL Output_Addresses(AddressList)

CONTAINS

   !-------------------------------------------------------------------------
   ! This subroutine determines if Address is already in the linked list
   ! AddressList (using Search).  If it is not, it is added at the beginning
   ! of the list; if it is, its count is incremented by 1.  Local variables:
   !   AllocateStatus : status variable for OPEN statement
   !   LocPtr         : pointer to a node containing Address or null if
   !                    not found
   !   In_the_List    : indicates if Address is already in AddressList
   ! Accepts:  AddressList and Address
   ! Returns:  Modified AddressList
   !-------------------------------------------------------------------------

   SUBROUTINE Add_To_List(AddressList, Address)

     TYPE(List_Node), POINTER :: AddressList
     CHARACTER(*), INTENT(IN) :: Address
     TYPE(List_Node), POINTER :: LocPtr
     INTEGER :: AllocateStatus
     LOGICAL :: In_the_List

     IF (.NOT. ASSOCIATED(AddressList)) THEN  ! List is empty

       ALLOCATE(AddressList, STAT = AllocateStatus)
       IF (AllocateStatus /= 0) STOP "*** Out of memory *** "

       AddressList%TCP_IP_Address = Address
       AddressList%Count = 1
       NULLIFY(AddressList%Next)
```

Figure 13.1 (*cont.*)

```
   ELSE  ! List not empty -- determine if Address is already in the list

      CALL Search(AddressList, Address, LocPtr, In_the_List)

      IF (In_the_List) THEN   ! Increment its count by 1
         LocPtr%Count = LocPtr%Count + 1

      ELSE                      ! Create a new node and insert it at the front
         ALLOCATE(LocPtr, STAT = AllocateStatus)
         IF (AllocateStatus /= 0) STOP "*** Out of memory *** "

         LocPtr%TCP_IP_Address = Address
         LocPtr%Count = 1
         LocPtr%Next => AddressList
         AddressList => LocPtr
      END IF
   END IF

END SUBROUTINE Add_To_List

!-------------------------------------------------------------------------
! This subroutine searches AddressList for a node containing Address.
! If it is found, LocPtr points to the node and In_the_List is set to
! true; otherwise LocPtr is NULL and In_the_List is false.
!
! Accepts: AddressList, Address
! Returns: LocPtr, In_the_List
!-------------------------------------------------------------------------

SUBROUTINE Search(AddressList, Address, LocPtr, In_the_List)

  TYPE(List_Node), POINTER :: AddressList, LocPtr
  CHARACTER(*), INTENT(IN) :: Address
  LOGICAL,INTENT(OUT) :: In_the_List

  LocPtr => AddressList
  In_the_List = .FALSE.

  ! Traverse the list until the address is found
  ! or the end of list is encountered
  DO
     IF( In_the_List .OR. .NOT. ASSOCIATED(LocPtr)) EXIT
     ! Address found or end of list -- terminate repetition
```

Figure 13.1 *(cont.)*

```
      IF(LocPtr%TCP_IP_Address == Address) THEN   ! Address found
         In_the_List = .TRUE.
      ELSE                                         ! Move to next node
         LocPtr => LocPtr%Next
      END IF
   END DO

END SUBROUTINE Search

!---------------------------------------------------------------------------
! This subroutine prints the contents of the linked list pointed to by
! AddressList.  For each node, it prints the address and count.  Local
! variable used:
!   Ptr : pointer that runs through the list
!
! Accepts: AddressList
! Output:  Addresses and counts stored in nodes of AddressList
!---------------------------------------------------------------------------

SUBROUTINE Output_Addresses(AddressList)

   TYPE(List_Node), POINTER :: AddressList, Ptr

   Ptr => AddressList

   PRINT *, "Summary of Internet address data"
   PRINT *
   PRINT *, "   Address         Count "
   PRINT *, "------------------------- "

   ! Print node information until end of list reached
   DO
      IF (.NOT. ASSOCIATED(Ptr)) EXIT  ! End of list reached

      ! Otherwise display contents of node pointed to by Ptr
      PRINT '(1X, A, 4X, I4)', Ptr%TCP_IP_Address, Ptr%Count

      ! Move to next node
      Ptr => Ptr%Next
   END DO

END SUBROUTINE Output_Addresses

END PROGRAM Internet_Addresses
```

Figure 13.1 *(cont.)*

Listing of `fil13-1.dat` used in sample run:

```
128.159.4.20
123.111.222.33
100.1.4.31
34.56.78.90
120.120.120.120
128.159.4.20
123.111.222.33
123.111.222.33
77.66.55.44
100.1.4.31
123.111.222.33
128.159.4.20
```

Sample run:

```
Enter name of file of addresses: fil13-1.dat
Summary of Internet address data

   Address           Count
---------------------------
77.66.55.44            1
120.120.120.120        1
34.56.78.90            1
100.1.4.31             2
123.111.222.33         4
128.159.4.20           3
```

Quick Quiz 13.4

1. Write a declaration for a variable P1 to be a pointer to a memory location in which an integer can be stored.

2. Write a declaration for a variable P2 to be a pointer to a memory location that can store structures having two components of type real, XCoord and YCoord.

3. Write statements that associate a memory location with P1 of Question 1 and store the value −1234 in this location.

4. Write statements that associate a memory location with P2 of Question 2 and store the values 3.15 and 12.9 in the XCoord and YCoord components associated with this location.

5. Name and describe three kinds of pointer association status.

6. Write a statement that displays the message "Not associated" if the variable P1 is not associated with a memory location.

7. The _____ statement can be used to change a pointer's status to null.

8. The _____ statement can be used to return the memory associated with a pointer to the free store.

9. (True or false)   For the variables P1 of Question 1 and P2 of Question 2, the statement P1 => P2 causes P1 and P2 to point to the same memory location.

10. Describe the output produced by the following program:

```
PROGRAM QUIZ10

    INTEGER, POINTER :: Foo, Goo

    ALLOCATE(Foo)
    Foo = 1
    PRINT *, Foo
    ALLOCATE(Goo)
    Goo = 3
    PRINT *, Foo, Goo
    Foo = Goo + 3
    PRINT *, Foo, Goo
    Foo = Goo
    Goo = 5
    PRINT *, Foo, Goo
    Foo => Goo
    Foo = 7
    PRINT *, Foo, Goo
    Goo => Foo
    Foo = 9
    PRINT *, Foo, Goo

END PROGRAM Quiz10
```

Exercises 13.4

1. Write type declarations needed for a linked list of structures from the file INVEN.DAT described in Appendix B.

2. Write type declarations needed for a linked list of structures from the file STUDENT.DAT described in Appendix B.

3. Write type declarations needed for a linked list of structures from the file USERS.DAT described in Appendix B.

For Exercises 4–10, assume that the following declarations have been made,

```
TYPE NumberNode
  INTEGER :: Data
  TYPE(NumberNode), POINTER :: Next
END TYPE NumberNode

TYPE(NumberNode), POINTER :: P1, P2
INTEGER, POINTER :: P3
```

and that the following three statements have already been executed:

```
ALLOCATE(P1)
ALLOCATE(P2)
ALLOCATE(P3)
```

Tell what will now be displayed by each of the following program segments or explain why an error occurs:

4. ```
P1%Data = 123
P2%Data = 456
P1%Next => P2
PRINT *, P1%Data
PRINT *, P1%Next%Data
```

5. ```
P1%Data = 12
P2%Data = 34
P1 => P2
PRINT *, P1%Data
PRINT *, P2%Data
```

6. ```
P1%Data = 12
P2%Data = 34
P1 = P2
PRINT *, P1%Data
PRINT *, P2%Data
```

7. ```
P1%Data = 123
P2%Data = 456
P1%Next => P2
PRINT *, P2%Data
PRINT *, P2%Next%Data
```

8. ```
P1%Data = 12
P2%Data = 34
P3%Data = 34
```
```

```
     P1%Next => P2
     P2%Next => P3
     PRINT *, P1%Data
     PRINT *, P1%Next%Data
     PRINT *, P2%Data
     PRINT *, P2%Next%Data
     PRINT *, P1%Next%Next%Data
     PRINT *, P3%Data
 9. P1%Data = 111
    P2%Data = 222
    P1%Next => P2
    P2%Next => P1
    PRINT *, P1%Data, P2%Data
    PRINT *, P1%Next%Data
    PRINT *, P1%Next%Next%Data
10. P1%Data = 12
    P2%Data = 34
    P1 => P2
    P2%Next => P1
    PRINT *, P1%Data
    PRINT *, P2%Data
    PRINT *, P1%Next%Data
    PRINT *, P2%Next%Data
```

For Exercises 11–20, use the following linked list and pointers P1, P2, P3, and P4:

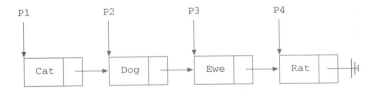

Draw a similar diagram for each of the following to show how this configuration changes when the given program segment is executed, or explain why an error occurs:

11. `P1 => P2%Next`

12. `P4 => P1`

13. `P4%Data = P1%Data`

14. `P4%Next%Data = P1%Data`

15. `P2%Next => P3%Next`

16. `P4%Next => P1`

17. `P1%Next => P3%Next`
    `P1 => P3`

18. `P1 => P3`
    `P1%Next => P3%Next`

19. `P4%Next => P3%Next`
    `P3%Next => P2%Next`
    `P2%Next => P1%Next`

20. `P4%Next => P3`
    `P4%Next%Next => P2`
    `P4%Next%Next%Next => P1`
    `NULLIFY(P1)`

21. Write a nonrecursive function to implement the algorithm in Exercise 1 of Section 13.1 for counting the nodes in a linked list.

22. Proceed as in Exercise 21 but write a recursive function.

23. Write a function to implement the algorithm in Exercise 2 of Section 13.1 for finding the average of a linked list of real numbers.

24. Write a subprogram to implement the algorithm in Exercise 3 of Section 13.1 for appending a node at the end of a linked list.

25. Write a logical-valued function to implement the algorithm in Exercise 4 of Section 13.1 for determining whether the data items in a linked list are arranged in ascending order.

26. Write a subprogram to implement the algorithm in Exercise 5 of Section 13.1 for searching a linked list.

27. Write a subprogram to implement the algorithm in Exercise 6 of Section 13.1 for inserting a new node into a linked list after the nth node in the list.

28. Write a subprogram to implement the algorithm in Exercise 7 of Section 13.1 for deleting the nth node in a linked list.

29. Write a subprogram to implement the algorithm in Exercise 8 of Section 13.1 for merging two linked lists that are in ascending order.

30. Write a subprogram to implement the algorithm in Exercise 9 of Section 13.1 for reversing a linked list.

31. Write a subprogram that erases a linked list, leaving it empty. It should traverse the linked list, removing each node and returning it to the free store.

13.5 MULTIPLY LINKED STRUCTURES: TREES

A **tree** consists of a finite set of elements called **nodes**, or **vertices,** and a finite set of **directed arcs** that connect pairs of nodes. If the tree is nonempty, then one of the nodes, called the **root**, has no incoming arcs, but every other node in the tree can be reached from the root by following a unique sequence of consecutive arcs.

Trees derive their names from the treelike diagrams that are used to picture them. For example,

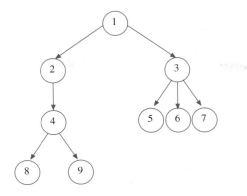

shows a tree having nine vertices in which vertex 1 is the root. As this diagram indicates, trees are usually drawn upside down, with the root at the top and the **leaves**—that is, vertices with no outgoing arcs—at the bottom. Nodes that are directly accessible from a given node (by using only one directed arc) are called the **children** of that node, and a node is said to be the **parent** of its children. For example, in the preceding tree, vertex 3 is the parent of vertices 5, 6, and 7, and these vertices are the children of vertex 3 and are called **siblings**.

Applications of trees are many and varied. For example, a **genealogical tree** such as the following is a convenient way to picture a person's descendants:

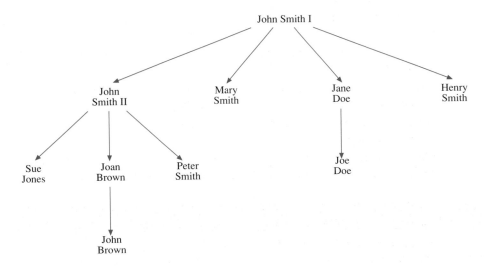

Game trees like the following, which shows the various configurations possible in the Towers of Hanoi problem with two disks (see Section 7.8), are used to analyze games and puzzles.

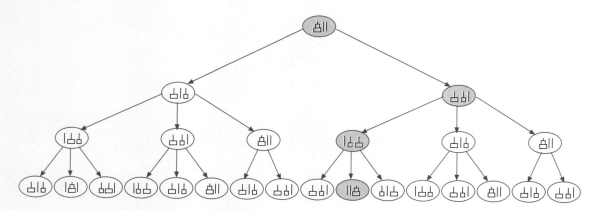

Parse trees constructed during the compilation of a program are used to check the program's syntax. For example, the following is a parse tree for the expression $2 * (3 + 4)$:

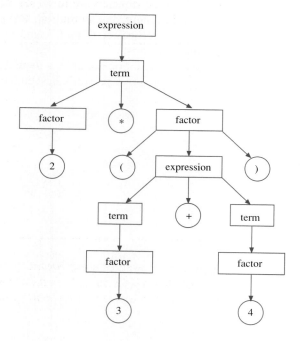

Binary Trees

Binary trees are trees in which each node has at most two children. Such trees are especially useful in modeling processes in which some experiment or test with two possible outcomes (for example, off or on, 0 or 1, false or true, down or up) is performed repeatedly. For example, the following binary tree might be used to represent the possible outcomes of flipping a coin three times:

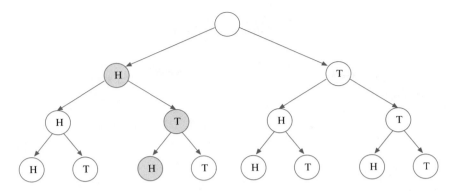

Each path from the root to one of the leaf nodes corresponds to a particular outcome, such as HTH (a head followed by a tail followed by another head), as highlighted in the diagram.

Similarly, a binary tree can be used in coding problems such as in encoding and decoding messages transmitted in Morse code, a scheme in which characters are represented as sequences of dots and dashes, as shown in the following table:

A	$\cdot-$	M	$--$	Y	$-\cdot--$
B	$-\cdot\cdot\cdot$	N	$-\cdot$	Z	$--\cdot\cdot$
C	$-\cdot-\cdot$	O	$---$	1	$\cdot----$
D	$-\cdot\cdot$	P	$\cdot--\cdot$	2	$\cdot\cdot---$
E	$\cdot$	Q	$--\cdot-$	3	$\cdot\cdot\cdot--$
F	$\cdot\cdot-\cdot$	R	$\cdot-\cdot$	4	$\cdot\cdot\cdot\cdot-$
G	$--\cdot$	S	$\cdot\cdot\cdot$	5	$\cdot\cdot\cdot\cdot\cdot$
H	$\cdot\cdot\cdot\cdot$	T	$-$	6	$-\cdot\cdot\cdot\cdot$
I	$\cdot\cdot$	U	$\cdot\cdot-$	7	$--\cdot\cdot\cdot$
J	$\cdot---$	V	$\cdot\cdot\cdot-$	8	$---\cdot\cdot$
K	$-\cdot-$	W	$\cdot--$	9	$----\cdot$
L	$\cdot-\cdot\cdot$	X	$-\cdot\cdot-$	0	$-----$

In this case, the nodes in a binary tree are used to represent the characters, and each arc from a node to its children is labeled with a dot or a dash, according to whether it leads to a left child or to a right child, respectively. Thus, part of the tree for Morse code is

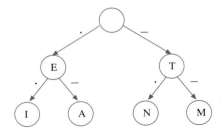

The sequence of dots and dashes labeling a path from the root to a particular node corresponds to the Morse code for that character; for example, ·· is the code for I, and −· is the code for N.

Here we confine our attention to binary trees. This is not a serious limitation, however, because any tree can be represented by a binary tree, using a technique described in the exercises.

Binary trees can be represented as multiply linked data structures in which each node has two link components, one being a pointer to the left child of that node and the other a pointer to the right child. Such nodes can be represented in Fortran using derived types of the form

```
TYPE BinTreeNode
   type :: Data
      TYPE(BinTreeNode), POINTER :: LChild, RChild
END TYPE BinTreeNode
```

The two link fields `LChild` and `RChild` are pointers to nodes representing the left child and right child, respectively,

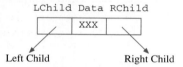

or are null if the node does not have a left or right child. A leaf node is thus characterized by having null values for both `LChild` and `RChild`:

The binary tree

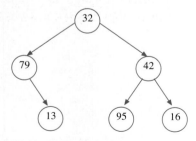

can thus be represented as the following linked tree of structures:

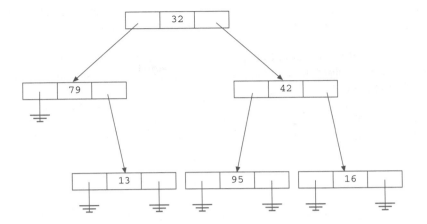

Binary Search Trees

One important class of binary trees are **binary search trees** (**BST**), in which the items in the left subtree (left child and all "descendants") of each node are less than the item in that node, which in turn is less than all items in the right subtree (right child and all descendants). They are so named because they can be searched efficiently using a technique much like the binary search method for arrays described in Section 8.9.

To illustrate, consider the binary search tree

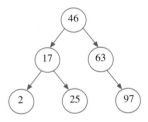

and suppose we wish to search this BST for 25. We begin at the root. Since 25 is less than the value 46 in this root, we know that the desired value is located to the left of the root; that is, it must be in the left subtree, whose root is 17:

Now we continue the search by comparing 25 with the value in the root of this subtree. Since 25 > 17, we know that the right subtree should be searched:

Examining the value in the root of this one-node subtree locates the value 25.

Similarly, to search for the value 55, after comparing 55 with the value in the root, we are led to search its right subtree:

Now. because $55 < 63$, if the desired value is in the tree, it will be in the left subtree. However, since this left subtree is empty, we conclude that the value 55 is not in the tree.

The following program segment for searching a binary search tree incorporates these techniques. It assumes that `Root` and `LocPtr` are declared by

```
TYPE(BinTreeNode), POINTER :: Root, LocPtr
```

where `BinTreeNode` is the derived type given earlier. The pointer `LocPtr` begins at the root of the BST and then is repeatedly replaced by its left or right link, according to whether the item for which we are searching is less than or greater than the value stored in this node. This process continues until either the desired item is found or `LocPtr` becomes null, indicating an empty subtree, in which case the item is not in the tree.

```
LocPtr = Root                                    ! begin at the root
Found = .FALSE.
DO
   IF (Found .OR. .NOT. ASSOCIATED(LocPtr))  EXIT
   IF ItemSought < LocPtr%Data THEN
      LocPtr = LocPtr%LChild                 ! search left subtree
   ELSE IF ItemSought > LocPtr%Data THEN
      LocPtr = LocPtr%RChild                 ! search right subtree
   ELSE
      Found = .TRUE.                         ! ItemSought found
END DO
```

A binary search tree can be constructed by repeatedly inserting elements into a BST that is initially empty using a method similar to the search technique just described. We move down to a left or right subtree of a node, beginning at the root, depending on whether the element is less than or greater than the value in that node. If the element is not already in the tree, we will eventually reach an empty subtree in which the item is to be inserted. Writing Fortran statements to implement this approach is left as an exercise.

Exercises 13.5

1. Complete the binary tree begun in this section for decoding messages in Morse code.
2. Write a subprogram for inserting an item into a binary search tree.

For Exercises 3–8, draw the binary search tree that results when the letters are inserted in the order given.

3. M, I, T, E, R
4. T, I, M, E, R
5. R, E, M, I, T
6. E, I, M, R, T
7. T, R, M, I, E
8. C, O, R, N, F, L, A, K, E, S

An *inorder traversal* of a binary search tree will visit the nodes in ascending order. A recursive algorithm for an inorder traversal is

> If the binary tree is empty then   ! anchor step
>   Do nothing.
> Else do the following: ! inductive step
>   L: Traverse the left subtree.
>   V: Visit the root.
>   R: Traverse the right subtree.

For each of Exercises 9–14, show the sequence of letters produced by an inorder traversal.

9. The BST in Exercise 3.
10. The BST in Exercise 4.
11. The BST in Exercise 5.
12. The BST in Exercise 6.
13. The BST in Exercise 7.
14. The BST in Exercise 8.
15. Write a recursive subroutine to implement the inorder traversal algorithm given above.
16. As noted in the text, every tree can be represented by a binary tree. This can be done by letting node x be a left child of node y in the binary tree if x is the leftmost child of y in the given tree, and by letting x be the right child of y if x and y are siblings (have the same parent) in the original tree. For example, the tree

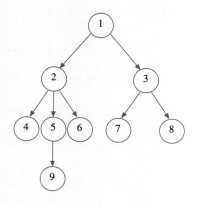

can be represented by the binary tree

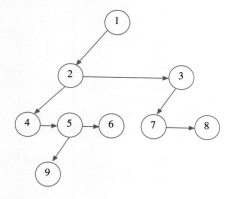

or, if it is drawn in the more customary manner,

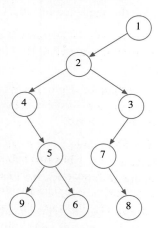

Represent each of the following by binary trees:

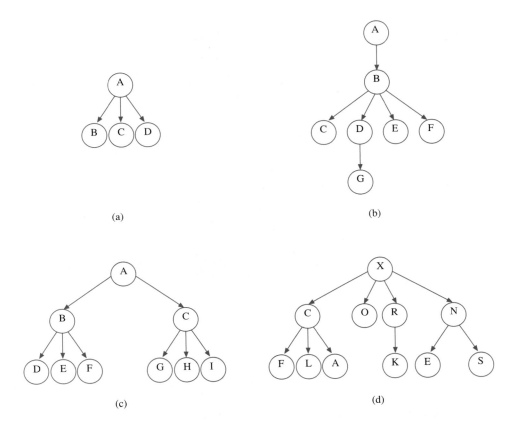

(a)

(b)

(c)

(d)

17. Write a recursive function to count the leaves in a binary tree. (*Hint*: How is the number of leaves in the entire tree related to the number of leaves in the left and right subtrees of the root?)

18. Write a recursive function to find the depth of a binary tree. The depth of an empty tree is 0, and for a nonempty tree it is one more than the larger of the depths of the left and right subtrees of the root.

19. To delete a node x from a BST, three cases must be considered: (1) x is a leaf; (2) x has only one subtree; and (3) x has two subtrees. Case 1 is handled easily. For case 2, simply replace x with the root of its subtree by linking the parent of x to this root. For case 3, x must be replaced with its inorder successor (or predecessor). The following diagram illustrates this case:

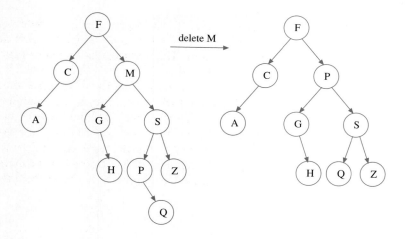

Write a subprogram to delete an item from a BST.

13.6 APPLICATION: DATA COMPRESSION

Problem:

Many data files used in computing are very large. A large amount of disk space is required to store these files, and it is very time-consuming to transfer such files. For example, files that contain digital representations of sound or images can take up many megabytes (or even gigabytes) of disk space. The problem considered in this section is how the information in such files can be compressed so that it takes up less disk space and requires less time to transfer through computer networks and communication channels.

In the preceding section, we indicated how a binary tree can be used in various encoding and decoding problems. In particular, we showed part of a binary tree for the Morse code, which represents each character by a sequence of dots and dashes. Unlike ASCII and EBCDIC coding schemes, in which the length of the code is the same for all characters, Morse code uses variable-length sequences. Other variable-length codes have been developed for data compression that can save as much as 20 percent to 50 percent of space over fixed-length codes.

Compression techniques are based on the fact that there is often a great deal of redundancy in data files. For example, digital representations of images have large homogenous areas; digital representations of sound have repeated patterns; and in text files, some characters appear more frequently than others. The basic idea in these compression schemes is to use shorter codes for those characters or patterns that occur more frequently and longer codes for those used less frequently. For example, 'E' in Morse code is a single dot, whereas 'Z' is represented as $--\cdot\cdot$. The objective is to minimize the expected length of the code for a character or pattern. This reduces the number of bits that must be stored or that must be transferred.

To state the problem more precisely, suppose that some character set $\{C_1, C_2, \ldots, C_n\}$ (or set of colors, gray scales, patterns, etc.) is given, and certain weights $w_1, w_2, \ldots, w_n$ are associated with these characters; w_i is the weight attached to character C_i and is a measure (e.g., probability or relative frequency) of how frequently this character occurs in messages to be encoded. If $l_1, l_2, \ldots, l_n$ are the lengths of the codes for characters $C_1, C_2, \ldots, C_n$, respectively, then the **expected length** of the code for any one of these characters is given by

$$\text{expected length} = w_1 l_1 + w_2 l_2 + \cdots + w_n l_n = \sum_{i=1}^{n} w_i l_i$$

As a simple example, consider the five characters A, B, C, D, and E, and suppose they occur with the following weights (probabilities):

character	A	B	C	D	E
weight	0.2	0.1	0.1	0.15	0.45

In Morse code with a dot replaced by 0 and a dash by 1, these characters are encoded as follows:

Character	Code
A	01
B	1000
C	1010
D	100
E	0

Thus, the expected length of the Morse code for a letter in this scheme is

$$0.2 \times 2 + 0.1 \times 4 + 0.1 \times 4 + 0.15 \times 3 + 0.45 \times 1 = 2.1$$

Another useful property of some coding schemes is that they are *immediately decodable*. This means that no sequence of bits that represents a character is a prefix of a longer sequence for some other character. Consequently, when a sequence of bits is received that is the code for a character, it can be decoded as that character immediately, without waiting to see whether subsequent bits change it into a longer code for some other character. Note that the preceding Morse code scheme is not immediately decodable because, for example, the code for E (0) is a prefix of the code for A (01), and the code for D (100) is a prefix of the code for B (1000). (For decoding, Morse code uses a third "bit," a pause, to separate letters.) A coding scheme for which the code lengths are the same as in the preceding scheme and that is immediately decodable is as follows:

Character	Code
A	01
B	0000
C	0001
D	001
E	1

Solutions Using Huffman Codes

The following algorithm, given by D. A. Huffman in 1952, can be used to construct coding schemes that are immediately decodable and for which each character has a minimal expected code length:

HUFFMAN'S ALGORITHM

Algorithm to construct a binary code for a given set of characters for which the expected length of the bit string for a character is minimal.

Accepts   A set of n characters $\{C_1, C_2, \ldots, C_n\}$ and a set of weights $\{w_1, w_2, \ldots, w_n\}$, where w_i is the weight of character C_i.

Returns: A collection of n bit strings representing codes for the characters.

1. Initialize a list of one-node binary trees containing the weights $w_1, w_2, \ldots, w_n$, one for each of the characters $C_1, C_2, \ldots, C_n$.

2. Do the following $n - 1$ times:
    a. Find two trees T' and T'' in this list with roots of minimal weights w' and w''.
    b. Replace these two trees with a binary tree whose root is $w' + w''$ and whose subtrees are T' and T'', and label the pointers to these subtrees 0 and 1, respectively:

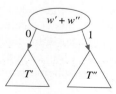

3. The code for character C_i is the bit string labeling a path in the final binary tree from the root to the leaf for C_i.

As an illustration of Huffman's algorithm, consider again the characters A, B, C, D, and E with the weights given earlier. We begin by constructing a list of one-node binary trees, one for each character:

The first two trees to be selected are those corresponding to letters B and C, since they have the smallest weights. These two trees are combined to produce a tree having weight $0.1 + 0.1 = 0.2$ and having these two trees as subtrees:

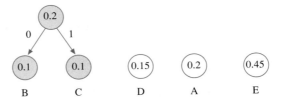

From this list of four binary trees, we again select two of minimal weights, the first and the second (or the second and the third), and replace them with another tree having weight $0.2 + 0.15 = 0.35$ and having these two trees as subtrees:

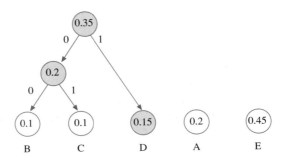

From this list of three binary trees, the first two have minimal weights and are combined to produce a binary tree having weight $0.35 + 0.2 = 0.55$ and having these trees as subtrees:

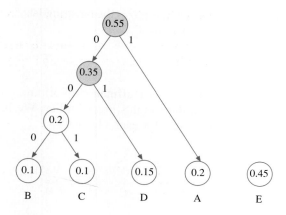

The resulting binary tree is then combined with the one-node tree representing E to produce the final Huffman tree:

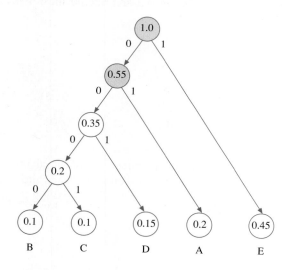

The Huffman codes obtained from this tree are as follows:

Character	Huffman Code
A	01
B	0000
C	0001
D	001
E	1

As we calculated earlier, the expected length of the code for each of these characters is 2.1.

A different assignment of codes to these characters for which the expected length is also 2.1 is possible because at the second stage we had two choices for trees of minimal weight:

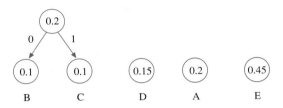

We selected the first and second trees from this list, but we could have used the second and third:

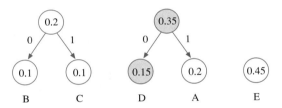

At the next stage, the resulting list of two binary trees would have been

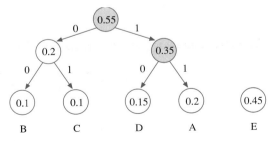

and the final Huffman tree would be

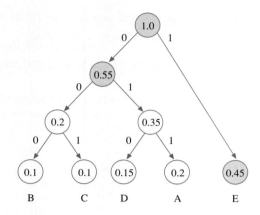

The assignment of codes corresponding to this tree is

Character	Huffman Code
A	011
B	000
C	001
D	010
E	1

The immediate decodability property of Huffman codes is clear. Each character is associated with a leaf node in the Huffman tree, and there is a unique path from the root of a tree to each leaf. Consequently, no sequence of bits comprising the code for some character can be a prefix of a longer sequence of bits for some other character.

Because Huffman codes are immediately decodable, a decoding algorithm is easy:

HUFFMAN DECODING ALGORITHM

Algorithm for decoding a bit string representing some string that was encoded using a Huffman code.

Accepts: A Huffman tree
Input: A bit string of codes of characters
Returns: The decoded string

1. Initialize pointer p to the root of the Huffman tree.

2. While the end of the message string has not been reached, do the following:
    a. Let x be the next bit in the string.

b. If $x = 0$ then
    Set p equal to its left child pointer.
  Else
    Set p equal to its right child pointer.
c. If p points to a leaf then
    i. Display the character associated with that leaf.
    ii. Reset p to the root of the Huffman tree.

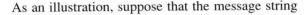

As an illustration, suppose that the message string

$$0\ 1\ 0\ 1\ 0\ 1\ 1\ 0\ 1\ 0$$

is received and that this message was encoded using the second Huffman tree constructed earlier. The pointer follows the path labeled 010 from the root of this tree to the letter D and is then reset to the root:

0 1 0	1 0 1 1 0 1 0
D	

The next bit, 1, leads immediately to the letter E:

0 1 0	1	0 1 1 0 1 0
D	*E*	

The pointer p next follows the path 011 to the letter A,

0 1 0	1	0 1 1	0 1 0
D	*E*	*A*	

and finally the path 010 to the letter D again:

0 1 0	1	0 1 1	0 1 0
D	*E*	*A*	*D*

The program in Figure 13.2 implements this decoding algorithm. The subroutine `BuildDecodingTree` initializes a tree consisting of a single node and then reads letters and their codes from a code file and constructs the decoding tree. For each letter in the file, it calls subroutine `AddToTree` to follow a path determined by the code of the character, creating nodes as necessary. When the end of the code string is reached, the character is inserted in the last (leaf) node created on this path. The subroutine `Decode` is then called to read a string of bits from `CompressedFile` and to decode it using the decoding tree. The subroutine `PrintTree` is included in this program simply to give an idea of what the tree looks like. It prints the tree "on its side" without the directed arcs and 0/1 labels. We leave it to the reader to draw these in and then rotate the tree 90 degrees so it has its usual orientation.

Figure 13.2 Huffman decoding.

```
PROGRAM Huffman_Decoding
!--------------------------------------------------------------------------
! Program to decode compressed text using a Huffman decoding tree.  Allowed
! characters and their codes (assumed to have been assigned using Huffman's
! algorithm) are read from a file.  Variable used:
!   Root : pointer to root of decoding tree
!
! Input(keyboard):   Name of file containing Huffman codes and the name
!                    of a compressed file
! Input(file):       Characters and their Huffman codes from CodeFile
!                    Compressed text from CompressedFile
! Output:            A graphical representation of the Huffman tree
!                    and the decoded text
!--------------------------------------------------------------------------

  IMPLICIT NONE
  TYPE BinTreeNode
    CHARACTER(1) :: Data
    TYPE(BinTreeNode), POINTER :: LChild, RChild
  END TYPE BinTreeNode

  TYPE(BinTreeNode), POINTER :: Root

  CALL BuildDecodingTree(Root)
  CALL PrintTree(Root, 8)
  PRINT *
  PRINT *
  CALL Decode(Root)

CONTAINS

  !-BuildDecodingTree----------------------------------------------------
  ! Subroutine that reads characters and their codes (assumed to be assigned
  ! using Huffman's algorithm) from CodeFile and constructs the Huffman
  ! decoding tree.  Local variables used are:
  !   CodeFile        : name of file containing characters and their codes
  !   OpenStatus      : status variable for OPEN
  !   InputStatus     : status variable for READ
  !   AllocateStatus  : status variable for ALLOCATE
  !   Ch              : character from code file
  !   Code            : Huffman code for Ch
  !
  ! Input (file): Characters and their Huffman codes
  ! Return:       Root
  !----------------------------------------------------------------------
```

Figure 13.2 *(cont.)*

```
SUBROUTINE BuildDecodingTree(Root)

  TYPE(BinTreeNode), POINTER :: Root
  CHARACTER(20) :: CodeFile, Ch*1, Code*10
  INTEGER :: OpenStatus, InputStatus, AllocateStatus

  ! Create an empty binary tree
  ALLOCATE(Root, STAT = AllocateStatus)
  IF (AllocateStatus /= 0) STOP "*** Not enough memory ***"

  Root%Data = "*"
  NULLIFY(Root%LChild)
  NULLIFY(Root%RChild)

  ! Get name of file containing Huffman codes and open it for input
  WRITE (*, '(1X, A)', ADVANCE = "NO") &
        "Enter name of file containing Huffman codes: "
  READ *, CodeFile
  OPEN (UNIT = 10, FILE = CodeFile, STATUS = "OLD", ACTION = "READ", &
        POSITION = "REWIND", IOSTAT = OpenStatus)
  IF (OpenStatus > 0) STOP "*** Cannot open code file ***"

  PRINT *
  ! Read characters and their codes from CodeFile
  DO
     READ(10, '(A, 1X, A)', IOSTAT = InputStatus) Ch, Code
     IF (InputStatus > 0) STOP "*** File input error ***"
     IF (InputStatus < 0) EXIT  ! End of file, terminate repetition

     ! Otherwise proceed
     CALL AddToTree (Ch, Code, Root)
  END DO

END SUBROUTINE BuildDecodingTree

!-AddToTree------------------------------------------------------------
! Subroutine that creates a node for character Ch and adds it to the
! Huffman decoding tree with root node pointed to by Root. Local variables
! used are:
!   AllocateStatus : status variable for ALLOCATE
!   I              : index
!   TempPtr        : pointer to new node(s)
!   P              : pointer to nodes in path labeled by Code
!
! Accepts:  Ch, Code, Root
! Returns:  Modified Huffman tree with specified Root
!----------------------------------------------------------------------
```

Figure 13.2 *(cont.)*

```fortran
SUBROUTINE AddToTree(Ch, Code, Root)

   TYPE(BinTreeNode), POINTER :: Root, TempPtr, P
   CHARACTER(1) :: Ch, Code*10
   INTEGER :: AllocateStatus, I

   ! Descend the Huffman tree using characters in Code
   I = 1
   P => Root

   DO
      IF (I > LEN_TRIM(Code)) EXIT
      ! If end of Code reached, terminate descent in tree

      ! Otherwise continue descent
      IF (Code(I:I) == "0") THEN                 ! Descend left
         IF (.NOT. ASSOCIATED(P%LChild)) THEN    ! Create node along path
            ALLOCATE(TempPtr, STAT = AllocateStatus)
            IF (AllocateStatus /= 0) STOP "*** Not enough memory ***"

            TempPtr%Data = "*"
            NULLIFY(TempPtr%LChild)
            NULLIFY(TempPtr%RChild)
            P%LChild => TempPtr
         END IF
         I = I + 1
         P => P%LChild
      ELSE IF (Code(I:I) == "1") THEN            ! Descend right
         IF (.NOT. ASSOCIATED(P%RChild)) THEN    ! Create node along path
            ALLOCATE(TempPtr, STAT = AllocateStatus)
            IF (AllocateStatus /= 0) STOP "*** Not enough memory ***"

            TempPtr%Data = "*"
            NULLIFY(TempPtr%LChild)
            NULLIFY(TempPtr%RChild)
            P%RChild => TempPtr
         END IF
         I = I + 1
         P => P%RChild
      END IF
      P%Data = Ch
   END DO

END SUBROUTINE AddToTree
```

Figure 13.2 *(cont.)*

```fortran
!-PrintTree-----------------------------------------------------------
! Subroutine that uses recursion to display a binary tree.  The tree is
! displayed "on its side" with each level indented by a specified value
! Indent, but with no arcs sketched in.  Local variable used is:
!   I : DO-loop counter
!
! Accepts:  Root and Indent
! Output :  Graphical representation of the binary tree
!---------------------------------------------------------------------

RECURSIVE SUBROUTINE PrintTree(Root, Indent)

  TYPE(BinTreeNode), POINTER :: Root
  INTEGER :: I, Indent

  IF (ASSOCIATED(Root)) THEN
     CALL PrintTree(Root%RChild, Indent + 7)
     DO I = 1, Indent
        WRITE (*, '(A)', ADVANCE = "NO") " "
     END DO
     PRINT *, Root%Data
     CALL PrintTree(Root%LChild, Indent + 7)
  END IF

END SUBROUTINE PrintTree

!-Decode--------------------------------------------------------------
! Subroutine that reads compressed text (a string of bits) from a file
! and decodes it using the Huffman decoding tree with specified Root.
! Local variables used are:
!   CompressedFile : name of file containing text to be decoded
!   Bit            : next bit
!   P              : pointer to trace path in decoding tree
!   OpenStatus     : status variable for OPEN
!   InputStatus    : status variable for READ
!
! Accepts:      Root
! Input (file): Individual bits from CompressedFile
! Output:       Decoded text
!---------------------------------------------------------------------

SUBROUTINE Decode (Root)
```

Figure 13.2 *(cont.)*

```fortran
      TYPE(BinTreeNode), POINTER :: Root, P
      CHARACTER(1) :: Bit, CompressedFile*20
      INTEGER :: OpenStatus, InputStatus

      ! Get name of compressed file and open it for input
      WRITE (*, '(1X, A)', ADVANCE = "NO") &
            "Enter name of file containing compressed text: "
      READ *, CompressedFile
      OPEN (UNIT = 20, FILE = CompressedFile, STATUS = "OLD", &
            ACTION = "READ", POSITION = "REWIND", IOSTAT = OpenStatus)
      If (OpenStatus > 0) STOP "*** Cannot open this file ***"

      PRINT *
      DO
         READ(20, '(A)', IOSTAT = InputStatus, ADVANCE = "NO") Bit

         IF (InputStatus < 0) EXIT
         ! End of file, terminate repetition
         IF (InputStatus > 0) Stop "***File input error***"

         ! Otherwise continue descent in Huffman tree to find character
         P => Root
         DO
            IF (.NOT. ASSOCIATED(P%LChild) .AND. &
                .NOT. ASSOCIATED(P%RChild)) EXIT
            ! If leaf node reached, terminate descent

            ! Otherwise, continue descent
            WRITE(*, '(A)', ADVANCE = "NO") Bit
            IF (Bit == "0") THEN
               P => P%LChild
            ELSE IF (Bit == "1") THEN
               P => P%RChild
            END IF
         END DO

         ! Print the decoded character
         PRINT *, "-- ", P%Data
      END DO

   END SUBROUTINE Decode

END PROGRAM Huffman_Decoding
```

Figure 13.2 *(cont.)*

Listing of **fil13-2a.dat**:

```
A 1101
B 001101
C 01100
D 0010
E 101
F 111100
G 001110
H 0100
I 1000
J 11111100
K 11111101
L 01111
M 01101
N 1100
O 1110
P 111101
Q 111111100
R 1001
S 0101
T 000
U 01110
V 001100
W 001111
X 111111101
Y 111110
Z 11111111
```

Listing of **fil13-2b.dat**:

```
0000100101100110100100110011101101000010111011001101011001110011011000110000111
```

Figure 13.2 *(cont.)*

Sample run:

```
Enter name of file containing Huffman codes: fil13-2a.dat
                                                              Z
                                                       *
                                                          *     X
                                                                Q
                                                  *
                                                       *  K
                                                          J
                                            *
                                      *
                                            *  Y
                                               P
                                               F
                                 *
                           *
                                 *  O
                                    A
                                    N
                     *
                           *  E
                                    R
                                 *  I
                                       L
                  *
                           *  U
                                       M
                                 *     C
                     *
                           *  S
                                 H
                                          W
                                    *     G
                                 *        B
                                    *     V
                        *
                           D
                     *     T
```

Figure 13.2 *(cont.)*

```
Enter name of file containing compressed text: fil13-2b.dat
000 -- T
0100 -- H
101 -- E
1001 -- R
101 -- E
0010 -- D
01100 -- C
1110 -- O
1101 -- A
000 -- T
0101 -- S
1101 -- A
1001 -- R
101 -- E
01100 -- C
1110 -- O
01101 -- M
1000 -- I
1100 -- N
001110 -- G
```

Exercises 13.6

1. Demonstrate that Morse code is not immediately decodable by showing that the bit string 100001100 can be decoded in more than one way.

Using the first Huffman code given in this section (A = 01, B = 0000, C = 0001, D = 001, E = 1), decode the bit strings in Exercises 2–5.

2. 000001001

3. 001101001

4. 000101001

5. 00001010011001

6. Construct the Huffman code for the Fortran key words and weights given in the following table:

Words	Weight
PROGRAM	.30
END	.30
DO	.05
IF	.20
THEN	.15

7. Repeat Exercise 6 for the following table of letters and weights:

Character	Weight
a	.20
b	.10
c	.08
d	.08
e	.40
f	.05
g	.05
h	.04

8. Using the Huffman code developed in Exercise 7, encode the string "feed a deaf aged hag".

9. Repeat Exercise 6 for the following table of Fortran key words and weights (frequencies):

Words	Weight
PROGRAM	22
SELECT	2
INTEGER	20
LOGICAL	2
ELSE	15
END	22
DO	5
GO TO	1
IF	20
CHARACTER	4
THEN	18
OPEN	3
CALL	4
REAL	15
CLOSE	3

10. Write a subroutine that reads a table of letters and their weights and constructs a Huffman code for these letters.

CHAPTER REVIEW

Summary

This chapter considered pointers and linked structures. It began by describing linked lists in general, what they are, why they are used, and how items can be inserted in and removed from a linked list efficiently. Section 13.2 described pointer variables, their three possible states (undefined, associated, disassociated), memory allocation and deallocation for them, pointer assignment, and automatic deferencing of pointers when they appear in expressions. Section 13.3 then showed how linked lists can be implemented in Fortran using pointers, and it gave algorithms for some of the basic linked list operations. The next section gave an application of linked lists to Internet addresses. The chapter closed with a discussion of binary trees and showed how they can be used to construct and use Huffman codes, which are useful in data compression.

FORTRAN SUMMARY

Pointer Declaration

```
type, attribute-list, POINTER :: pointer-variable
```

Examples:

```
CHARACTER(8), POINTER :: StringPtr, NamePtr

TYPE List_Node
   INTEGER :: Data
   TYPE(List_Node), POINTER :: Next
END TYPE List_Node

TYPE(List_Node), POINTER :: List, TempPtr
```

Purpose:

Declares that *pointer-variable* is a variable that can point to a memory location in which a value with the specified *type* can be stored.

Target Declaration

```
type, attribute-list, TARGET :: target-variable
```

Example:

```
CHARACTER(8), TARGET :: Name = "John Doe"
```

Purpose:
Declares that *target-variable* is a variable that can be pointed to by a pointer variable of the same type.

ALLOCATE Statement

```
ALLOCATE(list)
```

or

```
ALLOCATE(list, STAT = status-variable)
```

where *list* is a list of pointer variables (or array specficiations—see Chapter 8).

Examples:

```
ALLOCATE(StringPtr)
ALLOCATE(List, STAT = AllocateStatus)
```

Purpose:
Allocates memory locations for each variable in the list. In the second form, the integer variable *status-variable* will be set to zero if allocation is successful, but it will be assigned some system-dependent error value if there is insufficient memory or if memory has already been allocated to a variable.

DEALLOCATE Statement

```
DEALLOCATE(list)
```

or

```
DEALLOCATE(list, STAT = status-variable)
```

where *list* is a list of currently allocated pointer variables (or arrays) and *status-variable* is an integer variable.

Example:

```
DEALLOCATE(StringPtr)
```

Purpose:
Returns the memory allocated to the variables listed to the free store. In the second form, the integer variable *status-variable* will be set to zero if deallocation is successful, but it will be assigned some system-dependent error value if it is not successful, for example, if no memory was previously allocated to a variable.

NULLIFY Statement

```
NULLIFY(list-of-pointers)
```

Examples:

```
NULLIFY(StringPtr)
NULLIFY(TempPtr%Next)
```

Purpose:
Breaks the associations of memory locations with the pointer variables listed. These variables then become disassociated or null.

ASSOCIATED Function

```
ASSOCIATED(pointer)
```

Example:

```
IF (ASSOCIATED(TempPtr)) PRINT *, TempPtr%Data
```

Purpose:
Returns .TRUE. if *pointer* is associated with a target and .FALSE. otherwise.

Pointer Assignment

$$pointer_1 => pointer_2$$

or

$$pointer => target\text{-}variable$$

where *pointer*$_1$ and *pointer*$_2$ have the same type in the first form, and *pointer* and *target-variable* have the same type in the second form.

Examples:

```
TempPtr => List
NamePtr => Name
```

Purpose:
The first form causes $pointer_1$ to have the same association status as $pointer_2$, and if $pointer_2$ is associated, $pointer_1$ will point to the same target as $pointer_2$. The second form causes $pointer$ to point to $target\text{-}variable$, that is, to the memory location allocated to $target\text{-}variable$.

Automatic Dereferencing

When an associated pointer appears in an expression, it is automatically **dereferenced**; that is, the value stored in its target is used. If an associated pointer appears in an input list, an input value will be stored in its target.

Pointers and Subprograms

1. If a formal argument is a pointer variable, the corresponding actual argument must also be a pointer variable of the same type.
2. A pointer formal argument cannot have an intent attribute.
3. If a formal argument is a pointer (or target) variable, the subprogram must have an explicit interface.
4. A function that returns a pointer value must use a RESULT clause to return the value assigned within the function to a local pointer variable.

PROGRAMMING POINTERS

Program Style and Design

1. *Linked structures are appropriate for storing dynamic data sets, which grow and shrink during processing due to repeated insertions and deletions.*
2. *Memory locations allocated to pointer variables should be returned to the free store when they are no longer needed.*
3. *Binary search trees can be searched efficiently using a binary search technique.*

Potential Problems

The values assigned to variables considered in previous chapters have been specific data items such as integers, real numbers, complex numbers, character strings, logical values, arrays, and structures. Pointer variables, however, do not themselves have values but rather point to memory locations or variables where values are stored. Using pointer variables is quite different than using other kinds of variables, and consequently, pointers can cause special difficulties for both beginning and experienced programmers. Pointers are used to create dynamic data structures, such as linked lists, which are processed in a way quite different from that in which static data structures, such as arrays, are processed. The following are some of the main features to remember when using pointer variables and dynamic structures in Fortran programs:

1. *Each pointer variable is declared to have a specific type; a pointer points to a memory location in which only a value of that type can be stored.* For example, if P and Q are pointer variables declared by

```
INTEGER, POINTER :: P
CHARACTER(20), POINTER :: Q
```

then memory locations pointed to by P can store only integers, whereas those to which Q points can store only strings of length 20.

2. *Only limited operations can be performed on pointers.* In particular:
   - *A pointer P can be associated with a memory location in only the following ways:*
     (a) ALLOCATE(P) or ALLOCATE(P, STAT = *integer-variable*)
     (b) P => Q, *where Q is a pointer variable or a target variable with the same type as* P.
   - *A pointer P can be disassociated from a memory location by*

   DEALLOCATE(P) or DEALLOCATE(P, STAT = *integer-variable*)

   - *A function reference of the form* ASSOCIATED(P, Q) *can be used to determine if two pointers P and Q of the same type point to the same memory location.*
   - *A function reference of the form* ASSOCIATED(P, T) *can be used to determine if a pointer P points to a target T of the same type.*
   - *Pointers may be used as arguments in subprograms, but corresponding actual and formal arguments must have the same type, the formal argument cannot have an* INTENT *attribute, and the subprogram must have an explicit interface.*

3. *When a pointer P appears in an expression, it is automatically dereferenced.* For example, if P points to a memory location containing the integer 17, the statement PRINT *, P + 1 will display the value 18. Similarly, the value input for the statement READ *, P will be stored in the memory location pointed to by P.

4. *If P is a pointer that is undefined or null, then an attempt to use P in an expression is an error because P does not point to a memory location and thus cannot be dereferenced.*

5. *Don't confuse pointer assignment with ordinary assignment.* For example, suppose that P points to a memory location containing the integer 17 and Q points to a memory location containing the integer 900:

Then in the statement

```
P = Q
```

P and Q are dereferenced and the value 900 is copied into the memory location pointed to by P:

The statement

```
P => Q
```

however, causes P to point to the same memory location as Q:

6. *Null ≠ undefined.* A pointer becomes defined when it is associated with a memory location or is nullified using the NULLIFY statement. Nullifying a pointer is analogous to "blanking out" a character variable or "zeroing out" a numeric variable.

7. *Memory locations that were once associated with a pointer variable and that are no longer needed should be returned to the "storage pool" of available locations by using the* DEALLOCATE *statement.* Special care is required so that inaccessible memory locations are avoided. For example, as shown in Potential Problem 5, if P and Q are pointer variables of the same type, the assignment statement

```
P => Q
```

causes P to point to the same memory location as that pointed to by Q. Any memory location previously pointed to by P becomes inaccessible and cannot be disposed of properly unless it is pointed to by some other pointer. Temporary pointers should be used to maintain access, as the following statements demonstrate:

```
TempPtr => P
P => Q
DEALLOCATE(TempPtr)
```

8. *Pay attention to special cases in processing linked lists, and be careful not to lose access to nodes.* In particular, remember the following "programming proverbs":

- *Don't take a long walk off a short linked list.* It is an error to attempt to process elements beyond the end of the list. As an example, consider the following incorrect attempts to search a linked list with first node pointed to by List for some ItemSought:

Attempt 1:

```
CurrPtr => List
DO
    IF (CurrPtr%Data == ItemSought) EXIT
    CurrPtr => CurrPtr%Next
END DO
```

If the item is not present in any node of the linked list, CurrPtr will eventually reach the last node in the list. CurrPtr then becomes null, and an attempt is made to examine the Data field of a nonexistent node, resulting in a run-time error.

Attempt 2:

```
! This time I'll make sure I don't fall off the end of the
! list by stopping if I find ItemSought or reach a node whose
! link field is null.

Found = .FALSE.
CurrPtr => List
DO
    IF (Found .OR. .NOT. ASSOCIATED(CurrPtr%Next)) EXIT
    IF (CurrPtr%Data == ItemSought) THEN
       Found = .TRUE.
    ELSE
       CurrPtr => CurrPtr%Next
    END IF
END DO
```

Although this avoids the problem of moving beyond the end of the list, it will fail to locate the desired item (that is, set `Found` to `.TRUE.`) if this item is the last one in the list. When `CurrPtr` reaches the last node, `CurrPtr%Next` is null, and repetition is terminated without examining the `Data` component of this last node.

Attempt 3:

```
! Now I see how to fix the last try.

Found = .FALSE.
CurrPtr => List
DO
   IF (CurrPtr%Data == ItemSought) THEN
      Found = .TRUE.
   ELSE
      CurrPtr => CurrPtr%Next
   END IF
   IF (Found .OR. .NOT. ASSOCIATED(CurrPtr)) EXIT
END DO
```

This is close, but there is still one case in which it fails, namely, when the list is empty. One correct solution is to use a pretest loop to control the repetition:

Attempt 4:

```
Found = .FALSE.
CurrPtr => List
DO
   IF (Found .OR. .NOT. ASSOCIATED(CurrPtr)) EXIT
   IF (CurrPtr%Data == ItemSought) THEN
      Found = .TRUE.
   ELSE
      CurrPtr => CurrPtr%Next
   END IF
END DO
```

If the item is found in the list, then `Found` will be set to `.TRUE.` and repetition will be terminated. If it is not in the list, `CurrPtr` will eventually become null and repetition will terminate.

■ *You can't get water from an empty well.* Don't try to access elements in an empty list; this case usually requires special consideration. For example, if `List` is null, then initializing `CurrPtr` to `List` and attempting to access `CurrPtr%Data` or `CurrPtr%Next` is an error. (Go back now and reconsider Attempts 2 and 3 if you did not see when they might fail.)

- *Don't burn bridges before you cross them.* Be careful that you change links in the correct order, or you may lose access to a node or to many nodes! For example, in the following attempt to insert a new node at the beginning of a linked list,

```
List => NewNodePtr
NewNodePtr%Next = List
```

the statements are not in correct order. As soon as the first statement is executed, `List` points to the new node, and access to the remaining nodes in the list (those formerly pointed to by `List`) is lost. The second statement then simply sets the link field of the new node to point to itself:

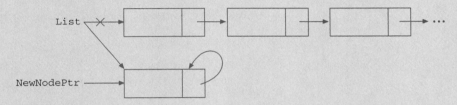

The correct sequence is first to connect the new node to the list and then to reset `List`:

```
NewNodePtr%Next => List
List => NewNodePtr
```

PROGRAMMING PROBLEMS

Section 13.4

1. Write a program to test the function in Exercise 21 of Section 13.4.
2. Write a program to test the function in Exercise 22 of Section 13.4.
3. Write a program to test the function in Exercise 23 of Section 13.4.
4. Write a program to test the subprogram in Exercise 24 of Section 13.4.
5. Write a program to test the function in Exercise 25 of Section 13.4.
6. Write a program to test the subprogram in Exercise 26 of Section 13.4.
7. Write a program to test the subprogram in Exercise 27 of Section 13.4.
8. Write a program to test the subprogram in Exercise 28 of Section 13.4.
9. Write a program to test the subprogram in Exercise 29 of Section 13.4.
10. Write a program to test the subprogram in Exercise 30 of Section 13.4.
11. Write a program to test the subprogram in Exercise 31 of Section 13.4.
12. Declarations like those for linked lists can be used to define a *linked stack*:

```
TYPE StackNode
   type :: Data
   TYPE(StackType), POINTER :: Next
END TYPE StackNode

TYPE(StackNode), POINTER :: Stack
```

The value of `Stack` will be a pointer to the top of the stack. For example, a linked stack of integers might be pictured as

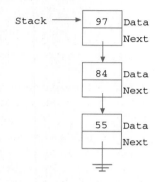

(a) Describe how an element would be popped from this linked stack. Include a picture of the modified stack.

(b) Assuming that this linked stack has been modified as in part (a), describe how the integer 77 would be pushed onto the linked stack. Include a picture of the modified stack.

(c) Modify the Internet address program in Figure 13.1 to use a linked stack.

13. One method for finding the base-*b* representation of a positive integer given in base-10 notation is to divide the number repeatedly by *b* until a quotient of zero results. The successive remainders are the digits from right to left of the base-*b* representation. For example, the binary representation of 26 is 11010, as the following computation shows:

$$
\begin{array}{r}
0 \ \text{R} \ 1 \\
2\overline{)1} \ \text{R} \ 1 \\
2\overline{)3} \ \text{R} \ 0 \\
2\overline{)6} \ \text{R} \ 1 \\
2\overline{)13} \ \text{R} \ 0 \\
2\overline{)26}
\end{array}
$$

Write a program to convert numbers to other bases using a linked stack to store the remainders (see Problem 12).

14. Like stacks, queues also can be implemented as linked lists. For *linked queues*, we might use two pointers, `FrontPtr`, which points to the node at the front of

the queue, and `RearPtr`, which points to the node at the rear. For example, a linked queue containing the integers 573, −29, and 616 in this order, might be pictured as

(a) Describe how an element would be removed from this linked queue. Include a picture of the modified queue.

(b) Assuming that this linked queue has been modified as in part (a), describe how the integer 127 would be added to the linked queue. Include a picture of the modified queue.

(c) Write appropriate declarations for a linked queue.

(d) Write a subprogram for the basic queue operations of adding an element to a queue and removing an element from the queue.

15. Suppose that jobs entering a computer system are assigned a job number and a priority from 0 through 9. The numbers of jobs awaiting execution by the system are kept in a *priority queue*. A job entered into this queue is placed ahead of all jobs of lower priority but after all those of equal or higher priority. Write a program to read one of the letters R (remove), A (add), or L (list). For R, remove the first item in the queue; for A, read a job number and priority and then add it to the priority queue in the manner just described; and for L, list all the job numbers in the queue. Maintain the priority queue as a linked list.

16. A limited number of complimentary copies of new CAD/CAM software will be released tomorrow. Requests are to be filled in the order in which they are received. Write a program that reads the names and addresses of the persons requesting this software, together with the number of copies requested, and stores these in a linked list. The program should then produce a list of names, addresses, and the number of requests that can be filled.

17. Modify the program in Problem 16 so that multiple requests from the same person are not allowed.

18. Write a program to read student records from `STUDENT.DAT` (see Appendix B) and construct five linked lists of records containing a student's name, number, and cumulative GPA, one list for each class. Each list is to be an ordered linked list in which the names are in alphabetical order. After the lists have been constructed, print each of them with appropriate headings.

19. Write a menu-driven program that allows at least the following options:

GET   Read student records from `STUDENT.DAT` (see Appendix B) and store them in five linked lists, one for each class, with each list ordered so that the student numbers are in ascending order.

INS   Insert the record for a new student, keeping the list sorted.

RET   Retrieve and display the record for a specified student.

UPD   Update the information in the record for a specified student.
DEL   Delete the record for some student.
LIS   List the records (or perhaps selected items in the records) in order.
        This option should allow the following suboptions:
            List for all students
            List for only a specified class
            List for students with GPAs above/below a specified value
            List for a given major
            List for a given gender
SAV   Save the updated list of records by writing them to a new file.

20. A *polynomial of degree n* has the form

$$a_0 + a_1 x + a_2 x^2 + \cdots + a_n x^n$$

where $a_0, a_1, \ldots, a_n$ are numeric constants called the *coefficients* of the polynomial and $a_n \neq 0$. For example,

$$1 + 3x - 7x^3 + 5x^4$$

is a polynomial of degree 4 with integer coefficients 1, 3, 0, −7, and 5.

(a) Develop an ordered linked list that can represent any such polynomial. Let each node store a nonzero coefficient and the corresponding exponent.

(b) Write a program to read the nonzero coefficients and exponents of a polynomial, construct its linked representation, and print the polynomial using the usual mathematical format with x^n written as $x \uparrow n$ or $x\wedge n$. The program should then read values for x and evaluate the polynomial for each of them.

21. Write a program that reads the nonzero coefficients and exponents of two polynomials, possibly of different degrees, stores them in linked lists (as described in Problem 20), and then calculates and displays their sum and product.

22. The Cawker City Candy Company maintains two warehouses, one in Chicago and one in Detroit, each of which stocks a large number of different items. Write a program that first reads the product numbers of items stored in the Chicago warehouse and stores them in a linked list Chicago, and then repeats this for the items stored in the Detroit warehouse, storing these product numbers in a linked list Detroit. The program should then find and display the *intersection* of these two lists of numbers, that is, the collection of product numbers common to both lists. Do not assume that the lists have the same number of elements.

23. Repeat Problem 22, but find and display the *union* of the two lists, that is, the collection of product numbers that are elements of at least one of the lists.

24. *Directed graphs* and their representations using adjacency matrices were described in Programming Problem 14 of Chapter 9.

(a) Develop a representation of a directed graph by using an array of pointers (one for each vertex) to linked lists containing the vertices that can be reached directly (following a single directed arc) from the vertex corresponding to the subscript.

(b) Draw a diagram showing the linked representation for the following directed graph:

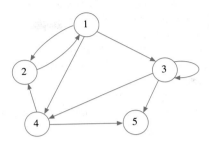

(c) Write a program to read the numbers (or names) of the vertices of a directed graph and ordered pairs of vertices representing the directed arcs, construct the linked representation for the digraph, and then use it to display the adjacency matrix.

25. In Chapter 9 we represented matrices by two-dimensional arrays. But for a *sparse matrix*, that is, one with only a few nonzero entries, this is not an efficient representation.

(a) Develop a representation for a sparse matrix by using one ordered linked list for each row and an array of pointers to the first nodes in these lists. Do not store zero entries of the matrix. (*Hint*: Store a matrix entry and the number of the column in which it appears.)

(b) Write a program to read the nonzero entries of a sparse matrix and their locations in the matrix, and construct its linked representation. Then print the matrix in the usual table format with all entries (including 0s) displayed.

26. Extend the program of Problem 25 to read two sparse matrices and calculate their sum and product (see Section 9.6).

Section 13.5

27. Write a program to process a BST whose nodes contain characters. Allow the user to select from the following menu of options:

    I followed by a character: To insert that character into the BST
    S followed by a character: To search for that character in the BST
    TI: For inorder traversal of the BST
    TP: For preorder traversal of the BST
    TR: For postorder traversal of the BST
    QU: To quit

28. Write a program that uses a binary tree as described in Section 13.5 to decode messages in Morse code.

29. In a *doubly* or *symmetrically linked list*, each node has two link fields, one containing a pointer to the predecessor of that node and the other containing a pointer to its successor. It might be pictured as follows:

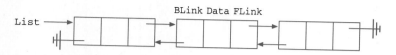

It is especially useful when it is necessary to traverse a linked list or a part of it in either direction.

(a) Write the necessary type declarations for such a doubly linked list.

(b) Write a subprogram for traversing the list from left to right.

(c) Write a subprogram for traversing the list from right to left.

(d) Write a subprogram for inserting an item (1) after or (2) before some other given element in a doubly linked list.

(e) Write a subprogram to delete an item from a doubly linked list.

30. Another application of multiply linked lists is to maintain a list sorted in two or more different ways. For example, consider the following multiply linked list having two links per node:

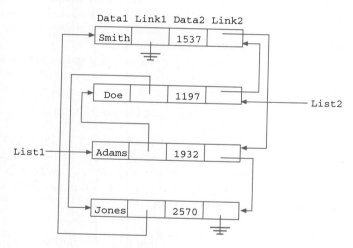

If this list is traversed and the data fields are displayed by using `List1` to point to the first node and following the pointers in the field `Link1`, the names will be in alphabetical order:

Adams 1932
Doe   1197
Jones 2570
Smith 1537

A traversal using `List2` to point to the first node and following pointers in the field `Link2` gives the identification numbers in ascending order:

Doe   1197
Smith   1537
Adams 1932
Jones   2570

This list is logically ordered, therefore, in two different ways. Write a program to read the first 10 records from `USERS.DAT` (see Appendix B) and store them in a multiply linked list that is logically sorted so that the user identification numbers are in ascending order and the resources used to date are in descending order. Traverse the list and display the records so that the identification numbers are in ascending order. Then traverse the list and display the records so that the resources used to date are in descending order.

31. In Problem 20, a linked list representation for a polynomial in x,

$$P(x) = a_0 + a_1x + a_2x^2 + \cdots + a_nx^n$$

was described. A *polynomial in two variables* x and y can be viewed as a polynomial in one variable y, with coefficients that are polynomials in x; that is, it has the form

$$P(x,y) = A_0(x) + A_1(x)y + \cdots + A_{m-1}(x)y^{m-1} + A_m(x)y^m$$

where each $A_i(x)$ is a polynomial in x. For example,

$$6 + 8x^4 + y^2 - 3xy^2 + 4x^5y^2 + 5x^2y^3 + 7x^5y^3$$

can be rewritten as

$$(6 + 8x^4) + (1 - 3x + 4x^5)y^2 + (5x^2 + 7x^5)y^3$$

A multiply linked representation for such polynomials is obtained by representing each term of the form $A_k(x)y^k$ by a node that stores the exponent of y and two links, one containing a pointer to a linked list representing the polynomial $A_k(x)$ and the other a pointer to the next term. For example, the first term in the preceding example can be represented as

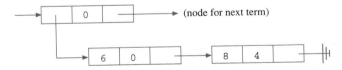

(a) Draw a multiply linked representation for

$$P(x, y) = 1 + 4x + x^2 + 9y + 2xy + xy^4 + 6x^2y^4 - 7xy^5 + 5x^7y^5 + 3x^9y^5$$

(b) Write a program to read triples of the form

(coefficient, x-exponent, y-exponent)

for a polynomial in x and y and construct its linked representation. Then read values for x and y and evaluate the polynomial.

(c) Modify the program in part (b) so that the exponents of x and the exponents of y need not be read in increasing order.

Section 13.6

32. Use the subroutine of Exercise 10 in Section 13.6 in a program that encodes a message entered by the user.

33. (Project)   Write a program to compress a text file using a Huffman code and to decompress a file generated using this code. The program should first read through the text file and determine the number of occurrences of each character in the file and the total number of characters in the file. The weight of each character will be the frequency count for that character. The program should then use these weights to construct the Huffman codes for the characters in the file. It should then read the file again and encode it using these Huffman codes and generate a file containing this encoded data. Compute the compression ratio, which is the number of bits in the compressed file divided by the total number of bits in the original file (eight times the number of characters in the file). The program should also provide the option of decompressing a file that was encoded using this Huffman code.

A

ASCII and EBCDIC

ASCII and EBCDIC Codes of Printable Characters

Decimal	Binary	Octal	Hexadecimal	ASCII	EBCDIC
32	00100000	040	20	SP (Space)	
33	00100001	041	21	!	
34	00100010	042	22	"	
35	00100011	043	23	#	
36	00100100	044	24	$	
37	00100101	045	25	%	
38	00100110	046	26	&	
39	00100111	047	27	' (Apostrophe)	
40	00101000	050	28	(	
41	00101001	051	29	)	
42	00101010	052	2A	*	
43	00101011	053	2B	+	
44	00101100	054	2C	, (Comma)	
45	00101101	055	2D	− (Hyphen)	
46	00101110	056	2E	. (Period)	
47	00101111	057	2F	/	
48	00110000	060	30	0	
49	00110001	061	31	1	
50	00110010	062	32	2	
51	00110011	063	33	3	
52	00110100	064	34	4	
53	00110101	065	35	5	
54	00110110	066	36	6	
55	00110111	067	37	7	
56	00111000	070	38	8	
57	00111001	071	39	9	
58	00111010	072	3A	:	
59	00111011	073	3B	;	
60	00111100	074	3C	<	
61	00111101	075	3D	=	
62	00111110	076	3E	>	
63	00111111	077	3F	?	
64	01000000	100	40	@	SP (Space)
65	01000001	101	41	A	
66	01000010	102	42	B	
67	01000011	103	43	C	
68	01000100	104	44	D	
69	01000101	105	45	E	
70	01000110	106	46	F	
71	01000111	107	47	G	
72	01001000	110	48	H	
73	01001001	111	49	I	

ASCII and EBCDIC Codes of Printable Characters *(cont.)*

Decimal	Binary	Octal	Hexadecimal	ASCII	EBCDIC
74	01001010	112	4A	J	¢
75	01001011	113	4B	K	. (Period)
76	01001100	114	4C	L	<
77	01001101	115	4D	M	(
78	01001110	116	4E	N	+
79	01001111	117	4F	O	|
80	01010000	120	50	P	&
81	01010001	121	51	Q	
82	01010010	122	52	R	
83	01010011	123	53	S	
84	01010100	124	54	T	
85	01010101	125	55	U	
86	01010110	126	56	V	
87	01010111	127	57	W	
88	01011000	130	58	X	
89	01011001	131	59	Y	
90	01011010	132	5A	Z	!
91	01011011	133	5B	[	$
92	01011100	134	5C	\	*
93	01011101	135	5D	]	)
94	01011110	136	5E	^	;
95	01011111	137	5F	_ (Underscore)	¬ (Negation)
96	01100000	140	60	`	- (Hyphen)
97	01100001	141	61	a	/
98	01100010	142	62	b	
99	01100011	143	63	c	
100	01100100	144	64	d	
101	01100101	145	65	e	
102	01100110	146	66	f	
103	01100111	147	67	g	
104	01101000	150	68	h	
105	01101001	151	69	i	
106	01101010	152	6A	j	^
107	01101011	153	6B	k	, (Comma)
108	01101100	154	6C	l	%
109	01101101	155	6D	m	_ (Underscore)
110	01101110	156	6E	n	>
111	01101111	157	6F	o	?
112	01110000	160	70	p	
113	01110001	161	71	q	
114	01110010	162	72	r	
115	01110011	163	73	s	

ASCII and EBCDIC Codes of Printable Characters *(cont.)*

Decimal	Binary	Octal	Hexadecimal	ASCII	EBCDIC
116	01110100	164	74	t	
117	01110101	165	75	u	
118	01110110	166	76	v	
119	01110111	167	77	w	
120	01111000	170	78	x	
121	01111001	171	79	y	
122	01111010	172	7A	z	:
123	01111011	173	7B	{	#
124	01111100	174	7C	|	@
125	01111101	175	7D	}	' (Apostrophe)
126	01111110	176	7E	~	=
127	01111111	177	7F		"
128	10000000	200	80		
129	10000001	201	81		a
130	10000010	202	82		b
131	10000011	203	83		c
132	10000100	204	84		d
133	10000101	205	85		e
134	10000110	206	86		f
135	10000111	207	87		g
136	10001000	210	88		h
137	10001001	211	89		i
.	.	.	.		.
.	.	.	.		.
.	.	.	.		.
145	10010001	221	91		j
146	10010010	222	92		k
147	10010011	223	93		l
148	10010100	224	94		m
149	10010101	225	95		n
150	10010110	226	96		o
151	10010111	227	97		p
152	10011000	230	98		q
153	10011001	231	99		r
.	.	.	.		.
.	.	.	.		.
.	.	.	.		.
161	10100001	241	A1		~
162	10100010	242	A2		s
163	10100011	243	A3		t
164	10100100	244	A4		u
165	10100101	245	A5		v
166	10100110	246	A6		w
167	10100111	247	A7		x
168	10101000	250	A8		y
169	10101001	251	A9		z

ASCII and EBCDIC Codes of Printable Characters *(cont.)*

Decimal	Binary	Octal	Hexadecimal	ASCII	EBCDIC
.	.	.	.		.
.	.	.	.		.
.	.	.	.		.
192	11000000	300	C0		{
193	11000001	301	C1		A
194	11000010	302	C2		B
195	11000011	303	C3		C
196	11000100	304	C4		D
197	11000101	305	C5		E
198	11000110	306	C6		F
199	11000111	307	C7		G
200	11001000	310	C8		H
201	11001001	311	C9		I
.	.	.	.		.
.	.	.	.		.
.	.	.	.		.
208	11010000	320	D0		}
209	11010001	321	D1		J
210	11010010	322	D2		K
211	11010011	323	D3		L
212	11010100	324	D4		M
213	11010101	325	D5		N
214	11010110	326	D6		O
215	11010111	327	D7		P
216	11011000	330	D8		Q
217	11011001	331	D9		R
.	.	.	.		.
.	.	.	.		.
.	.	.	.		.
224	11100000	340	E0		\
225	11100001	341	E1		
226	11100010	342	E2		S
227	11100011	343	E3		T
228	11100100	344	E4		U
229	11100101	345	E5		V
230	11100110	346	E6		W
231	11100111	347	E7		X
232	11101000	350	E8		Y
233	11101001	351	E9		Z
.	.	.	.		.
.	.	.	.		.
.	.	.	.		.
240	11110000	360	F0		0
241	11110001	361	F1		1
242	11110010	362	F2		2
243	11110011	363	F3		3
244	11110100	364	F4		4

ASCII and EBCDIC Codes of Printable Characters *(cont.)*

Decimal	Binary	Octal	Hexadecimal	ASCII	EBCDIC
245	11110101	365	F5		5
246	11110110	366	F6		6
247	11110111	367	F7		7
248	11111000	370	F8		8
249	11111001	371	F9		9
.	.	.	.		.
.	.	.	.		.
.	.	.	.		.
255	11111111	377	FF		

ASCII Codes of Control Characters

Decimal	Binary	Octal	Hexadecimal	Character
0	00000000	000	00	NUL (Null)
1	00000001	001	01	SOH (Start of heading)
2	00000010	002	02	STX (End of heading and start of text)
3	00000011	003	03	ETX (End of text)
4	00000100	004	04	EOT (End of transmission)
5	00000101	005	05	ENQ (Enquiry—to request identification)
6	00000110	006	06	ACK (Acknowledge)
7	00000111	007	07	BEL (Ring bell)
8	00001000	010	08	BS (Backspace)
9	00001001	011	09	HT (Horizontal tab)
10	00001010	012	0A	LF (Line feed)
11	00001011	013	0B	VT (Vertical tab)
12	00001100	014	0C	FF (Form feed)
13	00001101	015	0D	CR (Carriage return)
14	00001110	016	0E	SO (Shift out—begin non-ASCII bit string)
15	00001111	017	0F	SI (Shift in—end non-ASCII bit string)
16	00010000	020	10	DLE (Data link escape—controls data transmission)
17	00010001	021	11	DC1 (Device control 1)
18	00010010	022	12	DC2 (Device control 2)
19	00010011	023	13	DC3 (Device control 3)
20	00010100	024	14	DC4 (Device control 4)
21	00010101	025	15	NAK (Negative acknowledge)
22	00010110	026	16	SYN (Synchronous idle)
23	00010111	027	17	ETB (End of transmission block)
24	00011000	030	18	CAN (Cancel—ignore previous transmission)

ASCII Codes of Control Characters *(cont.)*

Decimal	Binary	Octal	Hexadecimal	Character
25	00011001	031	19	EM (End of medium)
26	00011010	032	1A	SUB (Substitute a character for another)
27	00011011	033	1B	ESC (Escape)
28	00011100	034	1C	FS (File separator)
29	00011101	035	1D	GS (Group separator)
30	00011110	036	1E	RS (Record separator)
31	00011111	037	1F	US (Unit separator)
.	.	.	.	.
.	.	.	.	.
.	.	.	.	.
127	01111111	177	7F	DEL (Delete)

EBCDIC Codes of Control Characters

Decimal	Binary	Octal	Hexadecimal	Character
0	00000000	000	00	NUL (Null)
1	00000001	001	01	SOH (Start of heading)
2	00000010	002	02	STX (End of heading and start of text)
3	00000011	003	03	ETX (End of text)
4	00000100	004	04	PF (Punch off)
5	00000101	005	05	HT (Horizontal tab)
6	00000110	006	06	LC (Lower case)
7	00000111	007	07	DEL (Delete)
10	00001010	012	0A	SMM (Repeat)
11	00001011	013	0B	VT (Vertical tab)
12	00001100	014	0C	FF (Form feed)
13	00001101	015	0D	CR (Carriage return)
14	00001110	016	0E	SO (Shift out—begin non-ASCII bit string)
15	00001111	017	0F	SI (Shift in—end non-ASCII bit string)
16	00010000	020	10	DLE (Data link escape—controls data transmission)
17	00010001	021	11	DC1 (Device control 1)
18	00010010	022	12	DC2 (Device control 2)
19	00010011	023	13	DC3 (Device control 3)
20	00010100	024	14	RES (Restore)
21	00010101	025	15	NL (Newline)
22	00010110	026	16	BS (Backspace)
23	00010111	027	17	IL (Idle)
24	00011000	030	18	CAN (Cancel—ignore previous transmission)

EBCDIC Codes of Control Characters *(cont.)*

Decimal	Binary	Octal	Hexadecimal	Character
25	00011001	031	19	EM (End of medium)
26	00011010	032	1A	CC (Unit backspace)
28	00011100	034	1C	IFS (Interchange file separator)
29	00011101	035	1D	IGS (Interchange group separator)
30	00011110	036	1E	IRS (Interchange record separator)
31	00011111	037	1F	IUS (Interchange unit separator)
32	00100000	040	20	DS (Digit select)
33	00100001	041	21	SOS (Start of significance)
34	00100010	042	22	FS (File separator)
36	00100100	044	24	BYP (Bypass)
37	00100101	045	25	LF (Line feed)
38	00100110	046	26	ETB (End of transmission block)
39	00100111	047	27	ESC (Escape)
42	00101010	052	2A	SM (Start message)
45	00101101	055	2D	ENQ (Enquiry—to request identification)
46	00101110	056	2E	ACK (Acknowledge)
47	00101111	057	2F	BEL (Ring bell)
50	00110010	062	32	SYN (Synchronous idle)
52	00110100	064	34	PN (Punch on)
53	00110101	065	35	RS (Record separator)
54	00110110	066	36	UC (Upper case)
55	00110111	067	37	EOT (End of transmission)
60	00111100	074	3C	DC4 (Device control 4)
61	00111101	075	3D	NAK (Negative acknowledge)
63	00111111	077	3F	SUB (Substitute a character for another)

B

Sample Files

This appendix contains the following sample data files that may prove useful with some of the exercises in the text: INVENTOR.DAT, STUDENT.DAT, USERS.DAT, INUPDATE.DAT, STUPDATE.DAT, USUPDATE.DAT, and LSQUARES.DAT. Descriptions of these files and sample listings follow.

An Inventory File

INVENTOR.DAT

Columns	Contents
1–4	Item number
5–28	Item name
29–33	Unit price (no decimal point, but three digits before and two after the decimal point are assumed)
34–36	Reorder point
37–39	Number currently in stock
40–42	Desired inventory level

The file is sorted so that the item numbers of the records are in increasing order.

    INVENTOR.DAT

```
1011TELEPHOTO POCKET CAMERA   5495 15 20 25
1012MINI POCKET CAMERA        2495 15 12 20
1021POL. ONE-STEP CAMERA      4995 10 20 20
1022SONAR 1-STEP CAMERA      18995 12 13 15
1023PRONTO CAMERA             7495  5 15 15
10318MM ZOOM MOVIE CAMERA    27999 10  9 15
1032SOUND/ZOOM 8MM CAMERA    31055 10 15 15
104135MM SLR XG-7 MINO. CAM.38900 12 10 20
104235MM SLR AE-1 PENT. CAM.34995 12 11 20
104335MM SLR ME CAN. CAM.   31990 12 20 20
104435MM HI-MATIC CAMERA     11995 12 13 20
104535MM COMPACT CAMERA       8999 12 20 20
1511ZOOM MOVIE PROJECTOR     12995  5  7 10
1512ZOOM-SOUND PROJECTOR     23999  5  9 15
1521AUTO CAROUSEL PROJECTOR  21999  5 10 10
1522CAR. SLIDE PROJECTOR     11495  5  4 10
2011POCKET STROBE             1495  5  4 15
2012STROBE SX-10              4855 10 12 20
2013ELEC.FLASH SX-10          2899 15 10 20
```

INVENTOR.DAT *(cont.)*

```
2013ELEC.FLASH SX-10        2899 15 10 20
3011TELE CONVERTER          3299 15 13 30
301228MM WIDE-ANGLE LENS    9799 15 14 25
3013135MM TELEPHOTO LENS    8795 15 13 25
301435-105 MM ZOOM LENS    26795  5  8 10
301580-200 MM ZOOM LENS    25795  5  7 10
3111HEAVY-DUTY TRIPOD       6750  5  4 10
3112LIGHTWEIGHT TRIPOD      1995  5 10 10
351135MM ENLARGER KIT      15999  5 10 10
401140X40 DELUXE SCREEN     3598  5  4 15
401250X50 DELUXE SCREEN     4498  5 10 10
5011120-SLIDE TRAY           429 25 17 40
5012100-SLIDE TRAY           295 25 33 40
5021SLIDE VIEWER             625 15 12 25
5031MOVIE EDITOR            5595 10 12 20
6011CONDENSER MICROPHONE    5995  5 10 10
6111AA ALKALINE BATTERY      891 00 80200
7011GADGET BAG              1979 20 19 35
8011135-24 COLOR FILM        149 50 45100
8021110-12 COLOR FILM         99 50 60100
8022110-24 COLOR FILM        145 50 42100
8023110-12 B/W FILM           59 25 37 75
8024110-24 B/W FILM           95 25 43 75
8031126-12 COLOR FILM         89 50 44100
8032126-12 B/W FILM           59 25 27 50
80418MM FILM CASSETTE        689 50 39100
804216MM FILM CASETTE       1189 50 73100
9111COMBINATION CAMERA KIT 95999 10  8 15
```

AN INVENTORY-UPDATE FILE

INUPDATE.DAT

Columns	Contents
1–7	Order number (three letters followed by four digits)
8–11	Item number (same as those used in INVENTOR.DAT)
12	Transaction code (S = sold, R = returned)
13–15	Number of items sold or returned

The file is sorted so that item numbers are in increasing order. (Some items in INVENTOR.DAT may not have update records; others may have more than one.)

INUPDATE.DAT

CCI75431012S	2	BTP53963013S	1
LTB34291012S	7	GFL49133013S	8
DJS67621021S	9	EHQ75103013S	7
NQT18501022S	1	QQL64723013S	5
WYP64251023S	4	SVC65113014S	4
YOK22101023R	2	XJQ93913014S	4
QGM31441023S	1	ONO52513111S	3
NPQ86851031S	5	CXC77803111S	1
MAP81021031S	13	VGT81693112S	8
JRJ63351031S	1	IMK58613511S	2
UWR93861032S	3	QHR19443511S	1
TJY19131032S	11	ZPK62114011S	2
YHA94641041S	5	VDZ29704012S	6
SYT74931041S	3	BOJ90695011S	6
FHJ16571042S	7	MNL70295011S	9
OJQ12211043S	8	MRG87035021S	10
UOX77141043S	2	DEM92895021S	1
ERZ21471043S	7	BXL16515031S	2
MYW25401044S	1	VAF87336111S	65
UKS35871045S	2	UYI03687011S	2
AAN37591045S	2	VIZ68798011S	16
WZT41711045S	12	GXX90938011S	19
TYR94751511S	1	HHO56058021S	41
FRQ41841511S	1	BOL23248021S	49
TAV36041512S	2	PAG92898023S	15
DCW93631522S	1	MDF55578023S	17
EXN39641522R	1	IQK33888024S	12
OIN55241522S	1	OTB13418024S	28
EOJ82181522S	1	SVF56748031S	24
YFK06832011S	2	ZDP94848031S	15
PPX47432012S	4	OSY81778032S	15
DBR17092013S	4	GJQ01858032S	8
JOM54082013S	3	VHW01898041S	20
PKN06712013S	1	WEU92258041S	6
LBD83913011S	9	YJO37558041S	8
DNL63263012S	9		

A Student File

STUDENT.DAT

Columns	Contents
1–5	Student number
6–20	Student's last name
21–35	Student's first name
36	Student's middle initial
37–59	Address
60–66	Phone number
67	Gender (M or F)
68	Class level (1, 2, 3, 4, or 5 for special)
69–72	Major (four-letter abbreviation)
73–75	Total credits earned to date (an integer)
76–78	Cumulative GPA (no decimal point, but one digit before and two after the decimal point are assumed)

The file is sorted so that the student numbers are in increasing order.

STUDENT.DAT

```
10103Johnson          James          LWaupun, Wisconsin       7345229M1ENGR 15315
10104Andrews          Peter          JGrand Rapids, Michigan 9493301M2CPSC 42278
10110Peters           Andrew         JLynden, Washington      3239550M5ART  63205
10113Vandenvander     Vannessa       VFremont, Michigan       5509237F4HIST110374
10126Aristotle        Alice          AChino, California       3330861F3PHIL 78310
10144Lucky            Lucy           LGrandville, Michigan    7745424F5HIST 66229
10179Euler            Lennie         LThree Rivers, Michigan 6290017M1MATH 15383
10191Nakamura         Toky           OChicago, Illinois       4249665F1SOCI 12195
10226Freud            Fred           ELynden, Washington      8340115M1PSYC 15185
10272Spearshake       William        WGrand Rapids, Michigan 2410744M5ENGL102295
10274Tchaikovsky      Wolfgang       AByron Center, Michigan 8845115M3MUSC 79275
10284Orange           Dutch          VGraafschaap, Michigan   3141660M2ENGR 42298
10297Caesar           Julie          SDenver, Colorado        4470338F4HIST117325
10298Psycho           Prunella       EDe Motte, Indiana       5384609F4PSYC120299
10301Bull             Sitting        UGallup, New Mexico      6632997M1EDUC 14195
10302Custer           General        GBadlands, South Dakota 5552992M3HIST 40195
10303Fahrenheit       Felicia        OSheboygan, Wisconsin    5154997F2CHEM 40385
10304Deutsch          Sprechen       ZSparta, Michigan        8861201F5GERM 14305
10307Mendelssohn      Mozart         WPeoria, Illinois        2410744M3MUSC 76287
10310Augusta          Ada            BLakewood, California    7172339F2CPSC 46383
```

STUDENT.DAT *(cont.)*

```
10319Gauss          Carl       FYorktown, Pennsylvania 3385494M2MATH 41400
10323Kronecker      Leo        PTraverse City, Michigan6763991M3MATH 77275
10330Issacson       Jacob      ASilver Springs, Md     4847932M5RELI 25299
10331Issacson       Esau       BSilver Springs, Md     4847932M5RELI 25298
10339Dewey          Johanna    ASalt Lake City, Utah   6841129F2EDUC 41383
10348Virus          Vera       WSaginaw, Michigan      6634401F4CPSC115325
10355Zylstra        Zelda      ADowns, Kansas          7514008F1ENGL 16195
10377Porgy          Bess       NColumbus, Ohio         4841771F2MUSC 44278
10389Newmann        Alfred     ECheyenne, Wyoming      7712399M4EDUC115099
10395Medes          Archie     LWhitinsville, Ma       9294401M3ENGR 80310
10406Macdonald      Ronald     BSeattle, Washington    5582911M1CPSC 15299
10415Aardvark       Anthony    AGrandville, Michigan   5325912M2ENGR 43279
10422Gestalt        Gloria     GWheaton, Illinois      6631212F2PSYC 42248
10431GoToDijkstra   Edgar      GCawker City, Kansas    6349971M1CPSC 15400
10448Rembrandt      Roberta    ESioux Center, Iowa     2408113F1ART  77220
10458Shoemaker      Imelda     MHonolulu, Hawaii       9193001F1POLS 15315
10467Marx           Karl       ZHawthorne, New Jersey  5513915M3ECON 78275
10470Scrooge        Ebenezer   TTroy, Michigan         8134001M4SOCI118325
10482Nightingale    Florence   KRochester, New York    7175118F1NURS 15315
10490Gazelle        Gwendolyn  DChino, California       3132446F2P E  43278
10501Pasteur        Louise     AWindow Rock, Arizona   4245170F1BIOL 16310
10519Elba           Able       MBozeman, Montana       8183226M3SPEE 77340
10511Lewis          Clark      NNew Era, Michigan      6461125M4GEOG114337
10515Mouse          Michael    EBoise, Idaho           5132771M5EDUC 87199
10523Pavlov         Tiffany    TFarmington, Michigan   9421753F1BIOL 13177
10530Chicita        Juanita    AOklahoma City, Ok      3714377F5ENGL 95266
10538Busch          Arch       ESt Louis, Missouri     8354112M3ENGR 74275
10547Fault          Paige      DPetoskey, Michigan     4543116F5CPSC 55295
10553Santamaria     Nina       PPlymouth, Massachusetts2351881F1HIST 15177
10560Shyster        Samuel     DEverglades, Florida    4421885M1SOCI 13195
10582Yewliss        Cal        CRudyard, Michigan      3451220M3MATH 76299
10590Atanasoff      Eniac      CSpringfield, Illinois  6142449F1CPSC 14188
10597Rockne         Rocky      KPortland, Oregon       4631744M4P E 116198
10610Roosevelt      Rose       YSpring Lake, Michigan  9491221F5E SC135295
10623Xerxes         Art        ICincinatti, Ohio       3701228M4GREE119325
10629Leibniz        Gottfried  WBoulder, Colorado      5140228M1MATH 13195
10633Vespucci       Vera       DRipon, California      4341883F5GEOG 89229
10648Principal      Pamela     PAlbany, New York       7145513F1EDUC 14175
10652Cicero         Marsha     MRapid City, Sd         3335910F3LATI 77287
10657Weerd          Dewey      LDetroit, Michigan      4841962M4PHIL115299
10663Hochschule     Hortense   CLincoln, Nebraska      7120111F5EDUC100270
10668Einstein       Alfred     MNewark, New Jersey     3710225M2ENGR 41278
10675Fibonacci      Leonard    ONashville, Tennessee   4921107M4MATH115325
10682Angelo         Mike       LAustin, Texas          5132201M4ART  117374
10688Pascal         Blaze      RBrooklyn, New York     7412993M1CPSC 15198
```

A Student-Update File

STUPDATE.DAT

Columns	Contents
1–5	Student number (Same as those used in STUDENT.DAT)
6–12	Name of course #1 (e.g., CPSC141)
13–14	Letter grade received for course #1 (e.g., A–, B+, Cb)
15	Credits received for course #1
16–22	Name of course #2
23–24	Letter grade received for course #2
25	Credits received for course #2
26–32	Name of course #3
33–34	Letter grade received for course #3
35	Credits received for course #3
36–42	Name of course #4
43–44	Letter grade received for course #4
45	Credits received for course #4
46–52	Name of course #5
53–54	Letter grade received for course #5
55	Credits received for course #5

The file is sorted so that the student numbers are in increasing order. There is one update record for each student in STUDENT.DAT.

STUPDATE.DAT

```
10103ENGL176C 4EDUC268B 4EDUC330B+3P E 281C 3ENGR317D 4
10104CPSC271D+4E SC208D-3PHIL340B+2CPSC146D+4ENGL432D+4
10110ART 520D 3E SC259F 1ENGL151D+4MUSC257B 4PSYC486C 4
10113HIST498F 3P E 317C+4MUSC139B-3PHIL165D 3GEOG222C 3
10126PHIL367C-4EDUC420C-3EDUC473C 3EDUC224D-3GERM257F 4
10144HIST559C+3MATH357D 3CPSC323C-2P E 246D-4MUSC379D+4
10179MATH169C-4CHEM163C+4MUSC436A-3MATH366D-2BIOL213A-4
10191SOCI177F 4POLS106A 4EDUC495A-3ENGR418B+2ENGR355A 4
10226PSYC116B 3GERM323B-4ART 350A 4HIST269B+4EDUC214C+3
10272ENGL558A-4EDUC169D+3PSYC483B+4ENGR335B+2BIOL228B 4
10274MUSC351B 4PSYC209C-4ENGR400F 1E SC392A 4SOCI394B-3
10284ENGR292D 4PSYC172C 4EDUC140B 4MATH274F 4MUSC101D+4
10297HIST464F 1HIST205F 1ENGR444F 1MATH269F 1EDUC163F 1
10298PSYC452B 3MATH170C+4EDUC344C-2GREE138C-2SPEE303A-3
10301EDUC197A 4P E 372B 3ENGR218D 4MATH309C 4E SC405C-4
```

STUPDATE.DAT *(cont.)*

```
10302CHEM283F 1P E 440A 2MATH399A-3HIST455C-4MATH387C-3
10303HIST111D-3ART151 C+3ENGL100C-3PSYC151D+3PE104  A-1
10304GERM526C-2CHEM243C 4POLS331B-4EDUC398A 3ENGR479D+4
10307MUSC323B+3MATH485C 4HIST232B+4EDUC180A 3ENGL130B+4
10310CPSC264B 2POLS227D+3ENGR467D-3MATH494D-4ART 420C+4
10319MATH276B 2E SC434A 3HIST197B-4GERM489B-2ART 137C-3
10323MATH377D-4EDUC210D 4MATH385D-4ENGR433C 2HIST338A-4
10330HIST546C+3E SC440B+3GREE472C+3BIOL186B 4GEOG434C+2
10331HIST546C 3E SC440B+3GREE472C 3BIOL186B+4GEOG434C+2
10339EDUC283B 3CPSC150B 3ENGR120D 4CPSC122F 4ART 216B 4
10348CPSC411C-3HIST480C+4PSYC459B 4BIOL299B+4ECON276B+3
10355ENGL130C-3CPSC282C+4CPSC181A-4CPSC146C-4SOCI113F 1
10377SOCI213D+3PSYC158D 4MUSC188C 3PSYC281D-4ENGR339B+4
10389EDUC414D+4PSYC115C-2PSYC152D-4ART 366D-3ENGR366F 4
10395ENGR396B 4HIST102F 3ENGL111A 4PSYC210D-2GREE128A 4
10406CPSC160C+4CPSC233C 1LATI494C+3ENGL115C-3MATH181A 3
10415ENGR287C 4EDUC166B-4EDUC106A-3P E 190F 3MATH171B-3
10422PSYC275A-4MATH497A 4EDUC340F 1GERM403C-4MATH245D+4
10431CPSC187D-4CPSC426F 4ENGR476B-4BIOL148B+3CPSC220F 3
10448ART 171D+3CPSC239C-3SOCI499B-4HIST113D+3PSYC116C 4
10458POLS171F 1CPSC187C+4CHEM150B 2PHIL438D-4PHIL254D 4
10467ECON335D-3E SC471B+4MATH457C+3MATH207C 2BIOL429D 4
10470MUSC415C+3POLS177C 3CPSC480A 4PSYC437B 3SOCI276D 4
10482ENGL158D-4EDUC475B 3HIST172B-2P E 316F 4ENGR294A-3
10490P E 239F 4ENGL348F 3LATI246F 4CPSC350F 4MATH114F 1
10501BIOL125F 4CPSC412F 3E SC279F 4ENGR153F 2ART 293F 1
10519SPEE386B+4HIST479C 4PSYC249B-2GREE204B-4P E 421A 1
10511E SC416B 3MATH316D-4MATH287C 2MATH499A-4E SC288D 3
10515EDUC563D+3PHIL373D-3ART 318B 4HIST451F 1ART 476C+3
10523BIOL183D-2HIST296D+4HIST380B+4ENGR216C 4MATH412B-2
10530ENGL559F 1EDUC457D+4CPSC306A 3ENGR171B+1CPSC380A 4
10538ENGR328A-4ENGR336C 3EDUC418D+3PHIL437B+4CPSC475D 4
10547CPSC537A-4ART 386D 4HIST292D-4ENGR467A-4P E 464B+4
10553HIST170A-4SOCI496D-3PHIL136B+4CPSC371D-4CPSC160A-1
10560SOCI153D+3MATH438D+4CPSC378C 4BIOL266F 3EDUC278D+3
10582MATH388A-3P E 311B 3ECON143D 4MATH304C+3P E 428C+4
10590CPSC134B-3E SC114B+3CPSC492C 4ENGL121C 4ENGR403A-4
10597P E 423A-3BIOL189D+3PHIL122D-4ENGL194C-4SOCI113D+3
10610E SC594C-3PHIL344F 4CPSC189B+2ENGR411D-3MATH241A 4
10623GREE412B-4ENGL415D-3ENGL234D-4MATH275F 1SOCI124B+3
10629MATH137D 2MATH481F 3E SC445F 1MATH339D 4ART 219B+4
10633GEOG573B 4ENGL149C+4EDUC113B+4ENGR458C-2HIST446D+4
10648EDUC132D+4MUSC103D-4ENGL263C 4ENGL134B+4E SC392A 3
10652LATI363F 3BIOL425F 1CPSC267C 4EDUC127C+3MATH338B 4
```

STUPDATE.DAT *(cont.)*

```
10657PHIL429F 1ART 412D-4MUSC473B-4SOCI447C-4MATH237D+2
10663EDUC580B-4ENGR351B+4SOCI283D 4ART 340C 4PSYC133D+3
10668ENGR274B+4SOCI438C 1P E 327C 4BIOL158A 4EDUC457A-4
10675MATH457A 4ENGR114C 4CPSC218C 3E SC433C-3PSYC243C+1
10682ART 483D+3GERM432C 3ENGL103B+4MUSC169C-3SOCI381C-2
10688CPSC182F 1HIST371C+4PSYC408F 1MUSC214B+4MATH151C 3
```

A Users File

USERS.DAT

Columns	Contents
1–15	User's last name
16–30	User's first name
31–35	Identification number
36–43	Password
44–47	Resource limit (in dollars)
48–52	Resources used to date (no decimal point, but three digits before and two after the decimal point are assumed)

The file is sorted so that the identification numbers of the records are in increasing order.

    USERS.DAT

```
Babbage         Charles      10101ADA'S#1  75038081
Newton          Isaac        10102apple4u  65059884
Leibniz         Gottfried    10103Calculus 25019374
Fahrenheit      Freda        10104freeze32 25017793
Celsius         Christine    10105freeze0  85019191
Tower           Lean         10106Piza/__  35022395
VanderVan       Henry        10107Dutch#1  75016859
Freeloader      Freddie      10108RedSkelt 450 7661
Alexander       Alvin        10109DaGreat  65040504
Mouse           Michael      10110()ears()  50 4257
Lukasewicz      Zzzyk        10111hsiloP   350 7350
Christmas       Mary         10112NoelNoel 850 3328
Sinke           CJ           10113TRAINS#1 75032753
Nijhoff         Laran        10114Kansas#1 55038203
```

USERS.DAT *(cont.)*

```
Liestma          Stan        10115Saab-PU  550 2882
Zwier            Apollos     10116PJPJPJPJ 95025618
Jaeger           Tim         10117bike4fun 45033701
VanZwalenberg    Jorge       10118sphinx/\ 35024948
Jester           Courtney    10119laff_8^) 45028116
McDonald         Ronald      101201/4pound 250 3500
Nederlander      Benaut      10121DI====KE 650 3836
Haybailer        Homer       101224Hforall 850 3732
Spear            William     10123Shake_it 25024673
Romeo            Juliet      10124XOXOXOXO 15010019
Greek            Jimmy       10125BET$1000 250    3
Virus            Vera        10126sicko8^( 750 6735
Beech            Rocky       10127(shell)  55039200
Engel            Angel       10128{wings}  150 1639
Abner            Lil         10129DaisyMae 950 8957
Tracy            Dick        10130TessTrue 85046695
McGee            Fibber      10131&Mollie  75033212
Bell             Alexander   10132R%I%N%G% 85033743
Cobb             Tyrus       20101slide__   50 3281
George           Ruth        20102Babe!O!O 25010934
Descartes        Ronald      20103b4-horse 35026993
Euclid           Ian         20104geometry 95018393
Daniels          Ezekiel     20105[[lion]] 35012869
Tarzan           Tom         20106U-Jane   15010031
Habbakuk         Jonah       20107(_)whale 350 6363
Colombus         Chris       20108NAmerica 85020224
Byrd             Richard     20109North|    55016849
Bunyan           Paul        20110Babe_OX   55033347
Chaucer          Jeff        20111PoetNoEt 950 3702
Stotle           Ari         20112T_F_T_F  75033774
Harrison         Ben         20113USPres    55026297
James            Jesse       20114Colt_45  250 5881
Scott            Francine    20115O_Say_UC 35016811
Phillips         Phyllis     2011666-gas-  65032222
Doll             Barbara     20117KenXOXOX 350 2634
Finn             Huck        20118Tom_Sawy 350 2286
Sawyer           Tom         20119Huck_Fin 95046030
Newmann          Alfred      20120MAD_mad  45011600
Simon            Simple      20121says...  55048605
Schmidt          Messer      20122aeroflot 250 3531
Luther           Calvin      20124Reform!! 77766666
Yale             Harvard     20125Iv-v-v-y 15012770
```

A User-Update File

USUPDATE.DAT

Columns	Contents
1–5	Account number
6	Blank
7–10	Resources used (no decimal point, but three digits before and two after the decimal point are assumed)

The file is sorted so that the account numbers are in increasing order.

USUPDATE.DAT

10101	732	10122	3402
10101	2133	10122	222
11003	3502	10122	328
10105	555	10123	3409
10105	329	10130	45
10105	89	10130	89
10105	1053	10130	328
10109	8934	10132	4412
10116	1234	10132	1210
10116	583	20101	1122
10116	1563	20101	534
10117	5023	20101	1001
10117	9823	20101	634
10118	4523	20111	1164
10118	234	20111	154
10118	8993	20111	3226
10120	2331	20111	9923
10122	345	20121	5545
10122	679	20121	6423
10122	78	20121	3328

A Least-Squares File

LSQUARES.DAT

This is a text file in which each line contains a pair of real numbers representing the x-coordinate and the y-coordinate of a point.

LSQUARES.DAT

2.18	1.06		5.63	8.58
7.46	12.04		8.94	15.27
5.75	8.68		7.34	11.48
3.62	4.18		6.55	9.92
3.59	3.87		4.89	7.07
7.5	12.32		9.59	15.82
7.49	11.74		1.81	0.45
7.62	12.07		0.99	-0.71
7.39	12.17		4.82	6.91
1.88	0.58		9.68	16.24
6.31	10.09		1.21	-0.22
2.53	2.04		4.54	5.64
5.44	8.25		1.48	0.3
1.21	-0.76		6.58	9.8
9.07	15.5		3.05	3.56
3.95	5.0		6.19	9.62
9.63	17.01		6.47	9.83
9.75	16.91		8.13	10.75
9.99	16.67		7.31	11.73
3.61	4.69		0.33	-1.93
9.06	15.0		5.12	7.41
5.03	6.62		5.23	7.73
4.45	6.12		7.14	11.02
4.54	5.89		1.27	-0.21
0.92	-1.02		2.51	1.59
0.82	-1.5		5.26	7.86
2.62	2.1		4.74	6.19
5.66	8.53		2.1	2.12
8.05	13.05		5.27	7.73
8.99	14.85		2.85	2.63
5.12	7.03		1.99	1.09
3.85	4.43		8.91	15.03
6.08	9.21		2.19	1.21
1.42	0		1.6	-0.05
2.58	2.38		8.93	15.12
5.99	9.42		3.19	3.56
0.63	-1.63		3.37	3.64
9.98	17.25			

C

Program Composition

PROGRAM, FUNCTION, SUBROUTINE, MODULE or BLOCK DATA Statement		
USE Statements		
	IMPLICIT NONE	
	PARAMETER Statements	IMPLICIT Statements
FORMAT and ENTRY Statements	PARAMETER and DATA Statements	Derived Type Definitions, Interface Blocks, Type Declaration Statements, Statement Function Statements, and Specification Statements,
	DATA Statements	Executable Constructs
CONTAINS Statement		
Internal Subprograms or Module Subprograms		
END Statement		

This diagram indicates the correct placement of the various types of Fortran statements in a program unit. Statements that are separated by vertical lines may be interspersed. Statements separated by horizontal lines must appear in the order shown; they may not be interspersed. Comments may be appear anywhere in the program unit.

D

Intrinsic Procedures

The following table lists all of the standard intrinsic functions and subroutines in Fortran 90. Underlined arguments are optional. Detailed descriptions of these procedures follow the table.

Name	Description
ABS(A)	Absolute value of A
ACHAR(I)	Ith character in ASCII collating sequence
ACOS(X)	Arccosine of X
ADJUSTL(STRING)	Adjust STRING to the left
ADJUSTR(STRING)	Adjust STRING to the right
AIMAG(Z)	Imaginary part of complex value Z
AINT(A, KIND)	Truncate A to an integer value
ALL(MASK, DIM)	Check if all elements of MASK are true
ALLOCATE(ARRAY)	Check if ARRAY is allocated
ANINT(A, KIND)	Nearest integer to A
ANY(MASK, DIM)	Check if any element of MASK is true
ASIN(X)	Arcsine of X
ASSOCIATED(POINTER, TARGET)	Check if POINTER is associated with TARGET
ATAN(X)	Arctangent of X
ATAN2(Y, X)	Arctangent of Y / X
BIT_SIZE(I)	Maximum number of bits in integer I
BTEST(I, POS)	Checks if bit in position POS of I is 1
CEILING(A)	Least integer $\geq$ A
CHAR(I, KIND)	Character in Ith position of collating sequence
CMPLX(X, Y, KIND)	Conversion to COMPLEX type
CONJG(Z)	Complex conjugate of Z
COS(X)	Cosine of X
COSH(X)	Hyperbolic cosine of X
COUNT(MASK, DIM)	Number of true elements in array MASK
CSHIFT(ARRAY, SHIFT, DIM)	Circular shift of array elements
DATE_AND_TIME(DATE, TIME, & ZONE, VALUES)	Subroutine that returns current date and time
DBLE(A)	Convert A to double-precision real
DIGITS(X)	Number of significant digits in X
DIM(X, Y)	Larger of X $-$ Y and 0
DOT_PRODUCT(VECTOR_A, & VECTOR_B)	Dot product of two vectors
DPROD(X, Y)	Double-precision product of X and Y
EOSHIFT(ARRAY, SHIFT, & BOUNDARY, DIM)	End-off shift of array elements
EPSILON(X)	Number almost negligible compared to 1.0
EXP(X)	e^X
EXPONENT(X)	Exponent part of X
FLOOR(A)	Greatest integer $\leq$ A
FRACTION(X)	Fractional part of X

(cont.)

Name	Description
HUGE(X)	Largest value for numbers of same type as X
IACHAR(C)	Position of C in ASCII collating sequence
IAND(I, J)	Bitwise logical AND of I and J
IBCLR(I, POS)	Clears bit POS of I, setting it to 0
IBITS(I, POS, LEN)	Extracts a sequence of bits from I
IBSET(I, POS)	Sets bit POS of I to 1
ICHAR(C)	Position of C in machine's collating sequence
IEOR(I, J)	Bitwise exclusive OR of I and J
INDEX(STRING, SUBSTRING, & BACK)	Position of SUBSTRING in STRING
INT(A, KIND)	Convert A to integer type
IOR(I, J)	Bitwise inclusive OR of I and J
ISHFT(I, SHIFT)	Bit shift of I
ISHFTC(I, SHIFT, SIZE)	Circular bit shift of I
KIND(X)	Kind type parameter of X
LBOUND(ARRAY, DIM)	Lower bounds of ARRAY
LEN(STRING)	Length of STRING
LEN_TRIM(STRING)	Length of STRING without trailing blanks
LGE(STRING_A, STRING_B)	Test if STRING_A $\geq$ STRING_B, using ASCII
LGT(STRING_A, STRING_B)	Test if STRING_A $>$ STRING_B, using ASCII
LLE(STRING_A, STRING_B)	Test if STRING_A $\leq$ STRING_B, using ASCII
LLT(STRING_A, STRING_B)	Test if STRING_A $<$ STRING_B, using ASCII
LOG(X)	Natural logarithm of X
LOG10(X)	Common (base-10) logarithm of X
LOGICAL(L, KIND)	Converts between logical kinds
MATMUL(MATRIX_A, MATRIX_B)	Matrix multiplication
MAX(A1, A2, A3, ...)	Maximum value
MAXEXPONENT(X)	Maximum exponent
MAXLOC(ARRAY, MASK)	Location of maximum array element
MAXVAL(ARRAY, DIM, MASK)	Maximum array elements
MERGE(TSOURCE, FSOURCE, MASK)	Select from TSOURCE or FSOURCE
MIN(A1, A2, A3, ...)	Minimum value
MINEXPONENT(X)	Minimum exponent
MINLOC(ARRAY, MASK)	Location of minimum array element
MINVAL(ARRAY, DIM, MASK)	Minimum array elements
MOD(A, P)	Remainder when A is divided by P
MODULO(A, P)	A modulo P
MVBITS(FROM, FROMPOS, LEN, & TO, TOPOS)	Subroutine that copies bits

(cont.)

Name	Description
NEAREST(X, S)	Machine number nearest to X in direction of S
NINT(A, _KIND_)	Nearest integer to A
NOT(I)	Logical complement
PACK(ARRAY, MASK, _VECTOR_)	Pack array elements
PRECISION(X)	Decimal precision of X
PRESENT(A)	Checks if optional argument A is present
PRODUCT(ARRAY, _DIM_, _MASK_)	Product of array elements
RADIX(X)	Base of model of numbers like X
RANDOM_NUMBER(HARVEST)	Subroutine that generates random numbers
RANDOM_SEED(_SIZE_, _PUT_, _GET_)	Subroutine to (re)start random number generator
RANGE(X)	Decimal exponent range for X
REAL(A, _KIND_)	Convert A to real type
REPEAT(STRING, NCOPIES)	Concatenates copies of STRING
RESHAPE(SOURCE, SHAPE, _PAD_, & ORDER)	Reshape an array
RRSPACING(X)	Reciprocal of relative spacing of numbers near X
SCALE(X, I)	$X * b^I$, where b = RADIX(X)
SCAN(STRING, SET, _BACK_)	Search STRING for a character in SET
SELECTED_INT_KIND(R)	Kind of type parameter for an integer type
SELECTED_REAL_KIND(_P_, _R_)	Kind of type parameter for a real type
SET_EXPONENT(X, I)	Set exponent of a model number
SHAPE(SOURCE)	Shape of an array
SIGN(A, B)	$|A| \times$ (sign of B)
SIN(X)	Sine of X
SINH(X)	Hyperbolic sine of X
SIZE(ARRAY, _DIM_)	Size of ARRAY
SPACING(X)	Absolute spacing of model numbers near X
SPREAD(SOURCE, DIM, NCOPIES)	Array formed by copying array SOURCE
SQRT(X)	Square root of X
SUM(ARRAY, _DIM_, _MASK_)	Sum of array elements
SYSTEM_CLOCK(COUNT, & COUNT_RATE, COUNT_MAX)	Subroutine that returns data from real-time clock
TAN(X)	Tangent of X
TANH(X)	Hyperbolic tangent of X
TINY(X)	Smallest possible value for values like X
TRANSFER(SOURCE, MOLD, _SIZE_)	Transfer a bitwise value to a different type
TRIM(STRING)	Strip trailing blanks from STRING
UBOUND(ARRAY, _DIM_)	Upper bounds of ARRAY
UNPACK(VECTOR, MASK, FIELD)	Unpack array elements
VERIFY(STRING, SET, _BACK_)	Check if SET contains all characters in STRING

In the following detailed descriptions of Fortran 90's intrinsic procedures, we will assume the following:

- Arguments of all functions are INTENT(IN); for subroutines, the INTENT attribute of each argument is given.
- Optional arguments are underlined.
- In specific name descriptions of the form *specific-name* $(X \rightarrow Y)$, X denotes the argument type and Y the result type (DP = double precision, I = integer, R = real, C = complex, and Char = character).

Also, each procedure is classified as one of the following:

- *Elemental procedures* are described here for scalar arguments, but they may also be applied to array arguments by applying them to each element individually. When there are two or more arguments, the arrays must all have the same shape. Also, not all of the array arguments can correspond to optional formal arguments, since the compiler must be able to establish the rank of the array. For an elemental function with an array argument, the result returned is an array of the same shape as the argument. For an elemental subroutine with an array argument, each INTENT(OUT) or INTENT(INOUT) argument must be an array, each element of which results by applying the subroutine to corresponding element of each array argument. There is only one intrinsic elemental subroutine (MVBITS).
- *Inquiry functions* return a value that depends on properties of a principal argument (such as its type and/or kind) rather than on the value of the argument; this value need not even be defined.
- *Transformational functions* are neither elemental nor inquiry functions. They usually have at least one array argument and return an array that depends on the elements in the actual array arguments.
- *Subroutines* perform a variety of tasks. There are five intrinsic subroutines: DATE_AND_TIME, MVBITS, RANDOM_NUMBER, RANDOM_SEED, and SYSTEM_CLOCK, of which only MVBITS is elemental.

ABS(A)

Returns the absolute value of A.
Argument type: A is any numeric type.
Result type: Same type as A, but real if A is complex
Class: Elemental function
Specific names: ABS $(R \rightarrow R)$, CABS $(C \rightarrow R)$, DABS $(DP \rightarrow DP)$, IABS $(I \rightarrow I)$

ACHAR(I)

Returns the character in position I of the ASCII collating sequence.
Argument type: I is an integer, with $0 \leq I \leq 255$.

Result type: Character of length 1

Class: Elemental function

ACOS(X)

Returns the angle in $[0, \pi]$ (in radians) whose cosine is X.

Argument type: X is real, with $|X| \leq 1.0$.

Result type: Same type as X

Class: Elemental function

Specific names: ACOS (R → R), DACOS (DP → DP)

ADJUSTL(STRING)

Returns the string obtained by adjusting STRING to the left, removing leading
blanks and adding trailing blanks.

Argument type: Character

Result type: Same type as STRING

Class: Elemental function

ADJUSTR(STRING)

Returns the string obtained by adjusting STRING to the right, removing trailing
blanks and adding leading blanks.

Argument type: Character

Result type: Same type as STRING

Class: Elemental function

AIMAG(Z)

Returns the imaginary part of Z.

Argument type: Z is complex.

Result type: Real

Class: Elemental function

Specific names: AIMAG (C → R)

AINT(A, KIND)

Returns the real value obtained by truncating the fractional part of A.

Argument type: A is real; KIND (optional) is integer.

Result type: Real

Class: Elemental function

Specific names: AINT (R → R), DINT (DP → DP)

ALL(MASK, _DIM_)

Determines whether all values in MASK (if DIM is omitted or rank(MASK) = 1) or all values along dimension DIM (if DIM is present and rank(MASK) > 1) are true.

Argument type: MASK is a logical array, DIM (optional) is an integer with $1 \leq$ DIM $\leq$ rank(MASK).

Result type: If DIM is omitted or rank(MASK) = 1: a logical scalar.

If DIM is present and rank(MASK) > 1: a logical array with rank = rank(MASK) − 1 and having the same shape as MASK with dimension DIM omitted.

Class: Transformational function

Example: For $A = \begin{bmatrix} 11 & 22 & 33 \\ 44 & 55 & 66 \end{bmatrix}$ and $B = \begin{bmatrix} 40 & 45 & 50 \\ 55 & 60 & 65 \end{bmatrix}$:

ALL(A < B) returns false.

ALL(A < B, DIM = 1) returns (true, true, false) (checking columns).

ALL(A < B, DIM = 2) returns (true, false) (checking rows).

ALLOCATED(ARRAY)

Returns true if allocatable ARRAY is currently allocated, false if not.

Argument type: Allocatable array of any type

Result type: Logical

Class: Inquiry function

ANINT(A, _KIND_)

Returns the real value that is the integer nearest to A: AINT(A + 0.5) if A > 0, and AINT(A - 0.5) otherwise.

Argument type: A is real; KIND (optional) is integer.

Result type: Real

Class: Elemental function

Specific names: ANINT (R → R), DNINT (DP → DP)

ANY(MASK, _DIM_)

Like ALL(MASK, DIM) but determines whether any value in MASK (if DIM is omitted or rank(MASK) = 1) or any value along dimension DIM (if DIM is present and rank(MASK) > 1) is true.

Example: For $A = \begin{bmatrix} 11 & 55 & 22 \\ 66 & 44 & 33 \end{bmatrix}$ and $B = \begin{bmatrix} 15 & 20 & 25 \\ 30 & 35 & 40 \end{bmatrix}$:

ANY (A < B) returns true.

ANY (A < B, DIM = 1) returns (true, false, true) (checking columns).

ANY (A < B, DIM = 2) returns (true, true) (checking rows).

ASIN(X)

Returns the angle in $[-\pi/2, \pi/2]$ (in radians) whose sine is X.

Argument type: X is real with $|X| \leq 1.0$.

Result type: Same type as X

Class: Elemental function

Specific names: ASIN $(R \rightarrow R)$, DASIN $(DP \rightarrow DP)$

ASSOCIATED(POINTER, TARGET)

If TARGET is omitted: Returns true if POINTER is associated with a target and false otherwise.

If TARGET is present and is a target: Returns true if POINTER is associated with TARGET and false otherwise.

If TARGET is present and is a pointer: Returns true if POINTER and TARGET are associated with the same target and false otherwise; also returns false if both are disassociated.

Argument type: POINTER is a pointer to any type and must not be undefined; TARGET (optional) is a pointer that cannot be undefined or is a target.

Result type: Logical

Class: Inquiry function

ATAN(X)

Returns the angle in $(-\pi/2, \pi/2)$ (in radians) whose tangent is X.

Argument type: X is real.

Result type: Same type as X

Class: Elemental function

Specific names: ATAN $(R \rightarrow R)$, DATAN $(DP \rightarrow DP)$

ATAN2(Y, X)

Returns the angle in $(-\pi, \pi]$ (in radians) whose tangent is Y/X if $X \neq 0$, positive if $Y > 0$, negative if $Y < 0$. ATAN2 (0, X) is 0.0 if $X > 0$, π if $X < 0$; ATAN2 (Y, 0) is $-\pi/2$ if $Y < 0$, $\pi/2$ if $Y > 0$.

Argument type: X and Y are real and not both 0.

Result type: Same type as X and Y

Class: Elemental function

Specific names: ATAN2 (R → R), DATAN2 (DP → DP)

BIT_SIZE(I)

Returns number of bits in an integer type.

Argument type: Integer (argument may be undefined since only its type is examined)

Result type: Integer

Class: Inquiry function

BTEST(I, POS)

Returns true if bit in position POS of I is 1, false if it is 0.

Argument type: I and POS are integers with $0 \le POS < BITSIZE(I)$

Result type: Logical

Class: Elemental function

CEILING(A)

Returns the least integer $\ge$ A.

Argument type: Real

Result type: Integer

Class: Elemental function

CHAR(I, KIND)

Returns the character in position I of the collating sequence associated with the specified kind.

Argument type: I and KIND (optional) are integers with $0 \le I \le$ number of characters in collating sequence of the specified kind.

Result type: Character of length 1

Class: Elemental function

Specific name: CHAR (I → Char)

CMPLX(X, Y, KIND)

Returns a complex value with real part REAL(X, KIND) and imaginary part REAL(Y, KIND). If X is not complex and Y is omitted, the result is the same as if Y were 0. If X is complex and Y is omitted, the result is the same as if Y were AIMAG(X).

Argument type: X is integer, real, or complex; Y (optional) is integer or real and must be omitted if X is complex; KIND (optional) is integer.

Result type: Complex
Class: Elemental function

CONJG(Z)

Returns the conjugate of the complex number Z.
Argument type: Z is complex.
Result type: Complex
Class: Elemental function
Specific name: CONJG (C → C)

COS(X)

Returns the cosine of X (radians).
Argument type: X is real or complex.
Result type: Same type as X
Class: Elemental function
Specific names: COS (R → R), CCOS (C → C), DCOS (DP → DP)

COSH(X)

Returns the hyperbolic cosine of X.
Argument type: X is real.
Result type: Same type as X
Class: Elemental function
Specific names: COSH (R → R), DCOSH (DP → DP)

COUNT(MASK, DIM)

Counts the number of true values in MASK (if DIM is omitted or rank(MASK) = 1) or the number of true values along dimension DIM (if DIM is present and rank(MASK) > 1).

Argument type: MASK is a logical array, DIM (optional) is an integer with $1 \leq$ DIM $\leq$ rank(MASK).

Result type: If DIM is omitted or rank(MASK) = 1: an integer scalar.

If DIM is present and rank(MASK) > 1: an integer array with rank = rank(MASK) − 1 and having the same shape as MASK with dimension DIM omitted.

Class: Transformational function

Example: For $A = \begin{bmatrix} 11 & 55 & 22 \\ 66 & 44 & 33 \end{bmatrix}$ and $B = \begin{bmatrix} 15 & 20 & 25 \\ 30 & 35 & 40 \end{bmatrix}$:

COUNT(A < B) returns 3.

COUNT(A < B, DIM = 1) returns (1, 0, 2) (checking columns).

COUNT(A < B, DIM = 2) returns (2, 1) (checking rows).

CSHIFT(ARRAY, SHIFT, DIM)

Returns array obtained by shifting the elements of all vectors along dimension DIM (1 if omitted) of ARRAY by the amounts specified in SHIFT (toward the beginning of the vector if SHIFT > 0, and toward the end of the vector if SHIFT < 0). The shift is circular so that elements shifted out at one end of a vector are shifted in at the other end.

Argument type: ARRAY is an array of any type; SHIFT is an integer scalar or an integer array with rank = rank(ARRAY) − 1 and having the same shape as ARRAY with dimension DIM omitted; it must be a scalar if rank(ARRAY) = 1; DIM (optional) is an integer with $1 \leq$ DIM $\leq$ rank(ARRAY) and with default value 1.

Result type: Same type and shape as ARRAY

Class: Transformational function

Example: For A $= \begin{bmatrix} a & b & c & d \\ e & f & g & h \\ i & j & k & l \end{bmatrix}$:

CSHIFT(A, SHIFT = (/0,-1,1,0/), DIM = 1)

returns $\begin{bmatrix} a & j & g & d \\ e & b & k & h \\ i & f & c & l \end{bmatrix}$.

CSHIFT(A, SHIFT = (/-1,2,1/), DIM = 2)

returns $\begin{bmatrix} d & a & b & c \\ g & h & e & f \\ j & k & l & i \end{bmatrix}$.

DATE_AND_TIME(DATE, TIME, ZONE, VALUES)

Subroutine that returns the current date and time. The values assigned to the arguments will be

DATE: CCYYMMDD, where CC, YY, MM, and DD are the century, year, month, and day, respectively; set to blanks if no date is available

TIME: hhmmss.sss, where hh, mm, and ss.sss are the hours, minutes, and seconds, respectively; set to blanks if no clock is available

ZONE: ±hhmm, where hh (hours) and mm (minutes) are the time difference with respect to Coordinate Universal Time (UTC, also called Greenwich Mean Time); set to blanks if no clock is available

VALUES: an array of 8 integers:

VALUES(1): Year
VALUES(2): Month number (1 to 12)
VALUES(3): Day of the month
VALUES(4): Time difference with respect to UTC in minutes
VALUES(5): Hour (0 to 23)
VALUES(6): Minute (0 to 59)
VALUES(7): Second (0 to 60)
VALUES(8): Milliseconds (0 to 999)

Array element will be set to -HUGE(0) if the information is not available.

Argument type: All are INTENT(OUT); DATE (optional) is character with length ≥ 8; TIME (optional) is character with length ≥ 10; ZONE (optional) is character with length ≥ 5; VALUES (optional) is a one-dimensional integer array of size 8.

Class: Subroutine

DBLE(A)

Returns value obtained by converting A to double-precision real type.

Argument type: Integer, real, or complex

Result type: Double-precision real

Class: Elemental function

DIGITS(X)

Returns the number of significant digits for numbers that have the same type and kind as X when X is represented using the mathematical model for integer data, $X = \pm (f_1 f_2 \cdots f_p)_{\text{base } b}$, or the mathematical model for real data, $X = \pm b^e \times (0.f_1 f_2 \cdots f_p)_{\text{base } b}$.

Argument type: Integer or real; may be an array

Result type: Integer

Class: Inquiry function

DIM(X, Y)

Returns $X - Y$ if $X > Y$ and 0 otherwise.

Argument type: X may be integer or real; Y must have the same type and kind as X.

Result type: Same as X

Class: Elemental function

Specific names: IDIM (I → I), DIM (R → R), DDIM (DP → DP)

DOT_PRODUCT (VECTOR_A, VECTOR_B)

Returns dot product of VECTOR_A and VECTOR_B.

Argument type: One-dimensional arrays with integer, real, complex, or logical elements

Result type: A scalar whose type is the same as that of the arguments

Class: Transformational function

DPROD (X, Y)

Returns double-precision product of X and Y.

Argument type: X and Y are real.

Result type: Double-precision real

Class: Elemental function

Specific name: DPROD (R → D)

EOSHIFT (ARRAY, SHIFT, BOUNDARY, DIM)

Like CSHIFT (ARRAY, SHIFT, DIM), but uses an end-off shift—elements shifted off at one end are lost—and copies of BOUNDARY's elements are shifted in at the other end.

Argument type: ARRAY, SHIFT, and DIM (optional) are as described for CSHIFT; BOUNDARY (optional) has the same type as ARRAY and may be a scalar or an array with rank = rank(ARRAY) − 1 having the same shape as ARRAY with dimension DIM omitted; if it is a scalar, this value is used in all shifts; if it is omitted, the default values used are a blank for character type, .FALSE. for logical type, 0 for integer type, 0.0 for real type, and (0.0, 0.0) for complex type.

Result type: Same type and shape as ARRAY

Class: Transformational function

Examples: For $A = \begin{bmatrix} a & b & c & d \\ e & f & g & h \\ i & j & k & l \end{bmatrix}$ and B = [? # * &]:

$$\text{EOSHIFT(A, (/0,-1,1,0/), B, 1) returns} \begin{bmatrix} a & \# & g & d \\ e & b & k & h \\ i & f & * & l \end{bmatrix}$$

$$\text{EOSHIFT}(A, \quad (/-1,2,1/), \quad 2) \text{ returns} \begin{bmatrix} a & b & c \\ g & h & \\ j & k & l \end{bmatrix}$$

EPSILON(X)

Returns a positive number that is almost negligible compared to 1.0 for numbers of the same type and kind as X.

Argument type: Real; may be an array

Result type: Same as X

Class: Inquiry function

EXP(X)

Returns e^X. Same type as X.

Argument type: X is real or complex.

Result type: Same as X

Class: Elemental function

Specific names: EXP (R $\rightarrow$ R), CEXP (C $\rightarrow$ C), DEXP (DP $\rightarrow$ DP)

EXPONENT(X)

Returns 0 if X is 0.0; if X is nonzero, it returns the exponent e when X is represented using the model for real data (see DIGITS(X)).

Argument type: Real

Result type: Integer

Class: Elemental function

FLOOR(A)

Returns the greatest integer $\leq$ A.

Argument type: Real

Result type: Integer

Class: Elemental function

FRACTION(X)

Returns the fractional part of the model representation of X (see DIGITS(X)).

Argument type: Real

Result type: Same as X

Class: Elemental function

HUGE(X)

Returns the largest number for numbers having the same type and kind as X.
Argument type: Integer or real
Result type: Same as X
Class: Inquiry function

IACHAR(C)

Returns the position of C in the ASCII collating sequence.
Argument type: Character of length 1
Result type: Integer
Class: Elemental function

IAND(I, J)

Returns the value obtained by performing a bitwise AND on I and J.
Argument type: I is integer; J has the same type and kind as I.
Result type: Same as I
Class: Elemental function

IBCLR(I, POS)

Returns the value obtained by clearing the bit in position POS of I to zero; bits
are numbered 0 to BIT_SIZE(I) − 1, from right to left.
Argument type: I and POS are integers with $0 \le POS < BIT\_SIZE(I)$.
Result type: Same as I
Class: Elemental function

IBITS(I, POS, LEN)

Returns the value obtained by extracting LEN consecutive bits from I, beginning
at position POS, and setting leftmost bits to 0; bits are numbered 0 to
BIT_SIZE(I) − 1, from right to left.
Argument type: I, POS, and LEN are integers with $LEN \ge 0$ and $0 \le POS +
LEN \le BIT_SIZE(I)$.
Result type: Same as I
Class: Elemental function

IBSET(I, POS)

Like IBCLR(I, POS), but sets the bit in position POS of I to one.

ICHAR(C)

Like IACHAR(C), but returns the position of C in the machine's collating sequence.

Specific name: ICHAR (Char → I); may not be passed as an argument

IEOR(I, J)

Returns the value obtained by performing a bitwise exclusive OR on I and J.
Argument type: I is integer; J has the same type and kind as I.
Result type: Same as I
Class: Elemental function

INDEX(STRING, SUBSTRING, BACK)

Returns the starting position of the first occurrence of SUBSTRING in STRING if BACK is omitted or has the value .FALSE., the starting position of the last occurrence of SUBSTRING in STRING if BACK has the value .TRUE., and 0 if SUBSTRING is not found in STRING.
Argument type: STRING is character; SUBSTRING is the same type and kind as STRING; BACK (optional) is logical.
Result type: Integer
Class: Elemental function

INT(A, KIND)

Returns the integer value obtained by truncating the fractional part of A.
Argument type: A is real; KIND (optional) is integer.
Result type: Integer
Class: Elemental function
Specific names: INT (R → I), DINT (DP → I), IFIX (R → I); may not be passed as an argument

IOR(I, J)

Like IEOR(I, J), but performs an inclusive OR on I and J.

ISHFT(I, SHIFT)

Returns the value obtained by shifting I by SHIFT positions, to the left if SHIFT < 0, to the right if SHIFT > 0. Bits shifted out are lost, and vacated bits are filled with 0s.
Argument type: I and SHIFT are integers with |SHIFT| ≤ BIT_SIZE(I).
Result type: Same as I
Class: Elemental function

ISHFTC(I, SHIFT, SIZE)

Returns the value obtained by circularly shifting the rightmost SIZE bits of I by SHIFT positions, to the left if SHIFT $<$ 0, to the right if SHIFT $>$ 0. Bits shifted off one end are inserted at the other end. If SIZE is omitted, the entire bit string is shifted.

Argument type: I, SHIFT, and SIZE (optional) are integers with $|$SHIFT$| \leq$ SIZE and 0 $<$ SIZE $\leq$ BIT_SIZE(I).

Result type: Same as I

Class: Elemental function

KIND(X)

Returns the kind value of X.

Argument type: Any intrinsic type

Result type: Integer

Class: Inquiry function

LBOUND(ARRAY, DIM)

Returns the lower bound (a scalar) for subscript DIM of ARRAY, or if DIM is omitted, an array containing the lower bound of each dimension of ARRAY. If ARRAY is an array section or expression that is not an entire array, each lower bound will be returned as 1.

Argument type: ARRAY may be of any type, size, and shape, but cannot be an allocatable array or a disassociated pointer; DIM (optional) is an integer with $1 \leq$ DIM $\leq$ rank(ARRAY).

Result type: Integer scalar if DIM is present; otherwise, a one-dimensional integer array

Class: Elemental function

Examples: For A declared by REAL, DIMENSION(5, -5:5, 0:10):

LBOUND(A) returns an array containing 1, -5, 0.

LBOUND(A, DIM = 2) returns the scalar -5.

LBOUND(A(:, 0:5, 4:6)) returns an array containing 1, 1, 1.

LEN(STRING)

Returns the length of STRING.

Argument type: Character; it may be an array.

Result type: Integer

Class: Inquiry function

Specific name: LEN (Char $\rightarrow$ I); may not be passed as an argument

LEN_TRIM(STRING)

Returns the length of STRING, not counting trailing blanks.

Argument type: Character

Result type: Integer

Class: Elemental function

LGE(STRING_A, STRING_B)

Checks if STRING_A is lexically greater than or equal to STRING_B. Returns true if STRING_A and STRING_B are the same or STRING_A follows STRING_B in the ASCII collating sequence and false otherwise. If the strings have different lengths, the comparison is made as though the shorter string was padded with enough blanks on the right to make the lengths of the strings agree.

Argument type: Character

Result type: Logical

Class: Elemental function

Specific name: LGE (Char → L); may not be passed as an argument

LGT(STRING_A, STRING_B)

As with LGE(STRING_A, STRING_B), but checks if STRING_A is lexically greater than STRING_B.

LLE(STRING_A, STRING_B)

As with LGE(STRING_A, STRING_B), but checks if STRING_A is lexically less than or equal to STRING_B.

LLT(STRING_A, STRING_B)

As with LGT(STRING_A, STRING_B), but checks if STRING_A is lexically less than STRING_B.

LOG(X)

Returns the natural logarithm of X.

Argument type: X is real and positive or complex and nonzero with imaginary part in $(-\pi, \pi]$.

Result type: Same type as X

Class: Elemental function

Specific names: ALOG (R → R), CLOG (C → C), DLOG (DP → DP)

LOG10(X)

Returns the common (base-10) logarithm of X.

Argument type: X is real and positive.

Result type: Same type as X

Class: Elemental function

Specific names: ALOG10 (R → R), DLOG10 (DP → DP)

LOGICAL(L, KIND)

Returns the value obtained by converting L to the specified KIND.

Argument type: L is logical; KIND (optional) is integer.

Result type: Logical of the specified kind

Class: Elemental function

MATMUL(MATRIX_A, MATRIX_B)

Returns the matrix product MATRIX_A × MATRIX_B of numerical or logical matrices. For numeric matrices, the (I, J) element of the product is

SUM((I-th row of MATRIX_A) * (J-th column of MATRIX_B))

and for logical matrices, the (I, J) element of the product is

ANY((I-th row of MATRIX_A) .AND. (J-th column of MATRIX_B))

Argument type: MATRIX_A is a one- or two-dimensional array of numeric or logical type; MATRIX_B is a one- or two-dimensional array of numeric or logical type, but it must be numeric if MATRIX_A is numeric.

Result type: An array whose type depends on the types of MATRIX_A and MATRIX_B

Class: Transformational function

MAX(A1, A2, A3, ...)

Returns maximum value of A1, A2, A3, ...

Argument type: There must be at least two arguments, and they must all be integer or all real and must have the same kind.

Result type: Same as arguments

Class: Elemental function

Specific names: AMAX0 (I → R), AMAX1 (R → R), DMAX1 (DP → DP), MAX0 (I → I), MAX1 (R → I); may not be passed as an argument

MAXEXPONENT(X)

Returns the maximum exponent for numbers that have the same type and kind as X, when X is represented using the standard model for real data (see DIGITS(X)).

Argument type: Real; it may be an array.

Result type: Integer

Class: Inquiry function

MAXLOC(ARRAY, MASK)

Returns the location of the first element of ARRAY having the maximum value of all elements determined by MASK, or in the entire array if MASK is omitted.

Argument type: ARRAY is an array of integer or real type; MASK (optional) is a logical array having the same shape as ARRAY.

Result type: A one-dimensional integer array with size equal to rank(ARRAY); its entries are the subscripts where the maximum was found.

Class: Transformational function

Example: For $A = \begin{bmatrix} 11 & 55 & 44 \\ 66 & 22 & 33 \end{bmatrix}$:

MAXLOC(A) returns the array containing 2, 1 (row 2, column 1).

MAXLOC(A, MASK = A < 50) returns the array containing 1, 3 (row 1, column 3).

MAXVAL(ARRAY, DIM, MASK)

Returns an array of elements of ARRAY whose values are the maximum values of all elements in ARRAY along each vector specified by DIM that correspond to true elements of MASK. If all elements of MASK are false (or ARRAY has size 0), the negative number of largest magnitude of the type and kind of ARRAY is returned. If MASK is omitted, the entire array is examined; if DIM is omitted, the entire array is examined and a scalar is returned.

Argument type: ARRAY is an array of integer or real type; DIM (optional) is an integer with $1 \le DIM \le$ rank(ARRAY); MASK (optional) is a logical array having the same shape as ARRAY.

Result type: A one-dimensional integer array with size equal to rank(ARRAY) − 1 and of the same type as ARRAY or a scalar if DIM is missing or ARRAY is one-dimensional

Class: Transformational function

Example: For $A = \begin{bmatrix} 11 & 55 & 44 \\ 66 & 22 & 33 \end{bmatrix}$:

MAXVAL(A) returns the scalar 66.

MAXVAL(A, MASK = A < 40) returns the scalar 33.

MAXVAL(A, DIM = 1) returns the array containing 66, 55, 44 (largest value in each column).

MAXVAL(A, DIM = 2) returns the array containing 55, 66 (largest value in each row).

MAXVAL(A, DIM = 2, MASK = A < 40) returns the array containing 11, 33 (largest value in each row that is less than 40).

MERGE(TSOURCE, FSOURCE, MASK)

Returns the scalar or array formed by selecting from TSOURCE when MASK is true and from FSOURCE when MASK is false.

Argument type: TSOURCE can be of any type; FSOURCE must have the same type and shape as TSOURCE.

Result type: Same as TSOURCE and FSOURCE

Class: Elemental function

Examples: For $TTAB = \begin{bmatrix} 11 & 55 & 22 \\ 66 & 44 & 33 \end{bmatrix}$, $FTAB = \begin{bmatrix} 15 & 20 & 25 \\ 30 & 35 & 40 \end{bmatrix}$,

$MASK = \begin{bmatrix} T & F & F \\ F & T & T \end{bmatrix}$:

MERGE(TTAB, FTAB, MASK) returns $\begin{bmatrix} 11 & 20 & 25 \\ 30 & 44 & 33 \end{bmatrix}$.

RATE = MERGE(100, 200, R1 < R2) assigns 100 to RATE if R1 is less than R2 and assigns 200 to RATE otherwise.

MIN(A1, A2, A3, ...)

Returns minimum value of A1, A2, A3, ...

Argument type: There must be at least two arguments, and they must all be integer or all real and must have the same kind.

Result type: Same as arguments

Class: Elemental function

Specific names: AMIN0 (I → R), AMIN1 (R → R), DMIN1 (DP → DP), MIN0 (I → I), MIN1 (R → I); may not be passed as an argument

MINEXPONENT(X)

Like MAXEXPONENT(X), but returns the minimum exponent.

MINLOC(ARRAY, MASK)

Like MAXLOC(ARRAY, MASK), but locates a minimum element.

MINVAL(ARRAY, DIM, MASK)

Like MAXVAL(ARRAY, DIM, MASK), but finds minimum values.

MOD(A, P)

Returns the remainder when A is divided by P: A - INT(A/P) * P.

Argument type: A is integer or real; P is the same type and kind as A.

Result type: Same as A

Class: Elemental function

Specific names: MOD (I → I), AMOD (R → R), DMOD (DP → DP)

MODULO(A, P)

Returns A modulo P. For A an integer, returns value R such that A = P*Q + R, with Q an integer, P and R of the same sign, and $0 \leq |R| < |P|$. For A real, returns A - FLOOR(A/P)*P.

Argument type: A is integer or real; P is the same type and kind as A and P is nonzero.

Result type: Same as A

Class: Elemental function

Examples: MODULO(9,4) returns 1, MODULO(-9,4) returns 3, MODULO(9,-4) returns -3, MODULO(9.0,4.0) returns 1.0.

MVBITS(FROM, FROMPOS, LEN, TO, TOPOS)

Subroutine that copies LEN bits from FROM beginning at bit FROMPOS to position TOPOS of TO; no other bits of TO are changed. The bits of an integer I are numbered 0 to BIT_SIZE(I) - 1, from right to left.

Argument type: FROM, FROMPOS, and LEN are INTENT(IN) arguments of integer type, with LEN $\geq$ 0 and $0 \leq$ FROMPOS + LEN $\leq$ BIT_SIZE(FROM) - 1; TO is an INTENT(INOUT) argument of integer type; TOPOS is an INTENT(IN) argument of integer type, with $0 \leq$ TOPOS + LEN $\leq$ BIT_SIZE(TO) - 1.

Class: Elemental subroutine

Example: For TO = 11 (= $00...001011_2$), CALL MVBITS(16,3,2,TO,1) copies the two bits 10 in positions 3 and 4 of 16 (= $00...010000_2$) to positions 1 and 2 of TO, changing its value to 13 (= $00...001101_2$).

NEAREST(X, S)

Returns the nearest machine-representable number different from X in the direction indicated by the sign of S (toward $+\infty$ or toward $-\infty$).

Argument type: X and S are real with S $\neq$ 0.

Result type: Same as X

Class: Elemental function

NINT(A, KIND)

Returns integer of the specified kind (if any) nearest to A.

Argument type: A is real and KIND (optional) is integer.

Result type: Integer of the specified kind (if any)

Class: Elemental function

Specific names: NINT (R $\rightarrow$ I), IDNINT (DP $\rightarrow$ I)

NOT(I)

Returns the value obtained by complementing each bit of I ($0 \rightarrow 1$, $1 \rightarrow 0$).

Argument type: Integer

Result type: Same as I

Class: Elemental function

PACK(ARRAY, MASK, VECTOR)

Returns a one-dimensional array containing the elements of ARRAY for which the corresponding element of MASK is true, padding with elements of VECTOR (if any) if there are not enough elements selected by MASK.

Argument type: ARRAY is of any type; MASK is an array of logical type having the same shape as ARRAY or is a logical scalar; VECTOR (optional) is a one-dimensional array having the same type elements as ARRAY.

Result type: A one-dimensional array having the same type elements as ARRAY; its size is the size of VECTOR if VECTOR is present, and otherwise it is the number of true elements in MASK or the number of elements in ARRAY if MASK is a scalar with value .TRUE..

Class: Transformational function

Examples: For A $= \begin{bmatrix} 11 & 55 & -22 \\ 66 & -44 & 33 \end{bmatrix}$:

PACK(ARRAY, MASK = A >= 0, VECTOR = (/0,0,0,0,0,0/)) returns the one-dimensional array containing 11, 66, 55, 33, 0, 0.

PACK(ARRAY, MASK = A >= 0) returns the one-dimensional array containing 11, 66, 55, 33.

PRECISION(X)

Returns the decimal precision of real numbers having the same kind as X.

Argument type: Real or complex

Result type: Integer

Class: Inquiry function

PRESENT(A)

Returns true if an actual argument was passed to the optional formal argument A of the procedure containing this reference to function PRESENT, and false otherwise.

Argument type: A is the name of an optional formal argument in the procedure containing this reference to PRESENT.

Result type: Logical

Class: Inquiry function

PRODUCT(ARRAY, DIM, MASK)

Returns the product of all the elements of ARRAY along dimension DIM (if present—else all array elements) that correspond to true elements of MASK; if MASK is omitted, all array elements along dimension DIM are multiplied. If all elements of MASK are false or ARRAY has size 0, 1 is returned. If DIM is omitted or ARRAY is one-dimensional, value returned is a scalar.

Argument type: ARRAY is an array of numeric type; DIM (optional) is an integer with $1 \leq$ DIM $\leq$ rank(ARRAY); MASK (optional) is a logical array having the same shape as ARRAY or a logical scalar.

Result type: A one-dimensional integer array with size equal to rank(ARRAY) − 1 and of same type as ARRAY if DIM is present; a scalar if DIM is missing or ARRAY is one-dimensional

Class: Transformational function

Example: For $A = \begin{bmatrix} 1 & 5 & -2 \\ 6 & -4 & 3 \end{bmatrix}$:

PRODUCT(A) returns the scalar 720.

PRODUCT(A, MASK = A > 0) returns the scalar 90.

PRODUCT(A, DIM = 1) returns the array containing 6, −20, −6 (column products).

PRODUCT(A, DIM = 2) returns the array containing −10, −72 (row products).

PRODUCT(A, DIM = 2, MASK = A > 0) returns the array containing 5, 18 (products of row elements greater than 0).

RADIX(X)

Returns the base of the mathematical model for values of the same type and kind as X (see DIGITS(X)).

Argument type: Integer or real

Result type: Integer

Class: Inquiry function

RANDOM_NUMBER(HARVEST)

Subroutine that returns values for HARVEST that are pseudorandom numbers selected from the uniform distribution over the interval [0, 1).

Argument type: HARVEST is an INTENT(OUT) argument of type real that may be either a scalar or an array variable.

Class: Subroutine

RANDOM_SEED(SIZE, PUT, GET)

Subroutine that restarts the pseudorandom number generator if no arguments are present or queries it if there is exactly one argument. If SIZE is present, it is set to the number of integers used to hold the value of the seed; if PUT is present, it is used for the seed; if GET is present, it is set to the current value of the seed.

Argument type: SIZE is an INTENT(OUT) argument of integer type; PUT and GET are one-dimensional integer arrays of size = SIZE; PUT is INTENT(IN) and GET is INTENT(OUT).

Class: Subroutine

RANGE(X)

Returns the decimal exponent range in the model for integer or real numbers having the same kind as X (see DIGITS(X)).

Argument type: Real or complex

Result type: Integer

Class: Inquiry function

REAL(A, KIND)

Returns the real value of the specified kind obtained by converting A to this type.

Argument type: Integer, real, or complex

Result type: Real

Class: Elemental function

Specific names: REAL (I $\rightarrow$ R), FLOAT (I $\rightarrow$ R), SNGL (DP $\rightarrow$ R); may not be passed as an argument.

REPEAT(STRING, NCOPIES)

Returns the string formed by concatenating NCOPIES copies of STRING.

Argument type: STRING is character and NCOPIES is a nonnegative integer.

Result type: Character

Class: Transformational function

RESHAPE(SOURCE, SHAPE, PAD, ORDER)

Returns the array having shape SHAPE constructed by placing the elements of SOURCE into the array using the subscript order given by ORDER (or in the usual array-element order if ORDER is omitted), filling any extra values with elements of PAD.

Argument type: SOURCE is an array of any type; SHAPE is a one-dimensional integer array with up to seven elements that specify the shape of the result; PAD (optional) is an array of the same type as SOURCE; if it is omitted, the size of the result cannot exceed the size of SOURCE; ORDER (optional) is a one-dimensional array whose elements are a permutation of (1, 2, ..., SIZE(SHAPE)).

Result type: Array with shape SHAPE and whose elements have the same type as those of SOURCE

Class: Transformational function

Examples: For $A = \begin{bmatrix} a & b & c & d \\ e & f & g & h \\ i & j & k & l \end{bmatrix}$:

RESHAPE(A, SHAPE = (/2,6/)) returns $\begin{bmatrix} a & i & f & c & k & h \\ e & b & j & g & d & l \end{bmatrix}$.

RESHAPE(A, SHAPE = (/2,6/), ORDER = (/2,1/))

returns $\begin{bmatrix} a & b & c & d & e & f \\ g & h & i & j & k & l \end{bmatrix}$.

RESHAPE(A, SHAPE = (/5,3/), ORDER = (/2,1/), &

PAD = (/"A","B","C","D","E"/)) returns $\begin{bmatrix} a & e & i \\ b & f & j \\ c & g & k \\ d & h & l \\ A & B & C \end{bmatrix}$.

RRSPACING(X)

Returns the reciprocal of the relative spacing of the model numbers near X (see DIGITS(X)); this value is

ABS(FRACTION(X)) * FLOAT(RADIX(X))$^{\text{DIGITS(X)}}$.

Argument type: Real

Result type: Same as X

Class: Elemental function

SCALE(X, I)

Returns the scaled value $X \times b^I$, where $b = \text{RADIX}(X)$.

Argument type: X is real; I is integer.

Result type: Same as X

Class: Elemental function

SCAN(STRING, SET, BACK)

Returns location of leftmost character of STRING that is in SET if BACK is .FALSE. or is omitted; the rightmost such character if BACK is .TRUE.; 0 if no such character is found.

Argument type: STRING is of character type; SET is the same type as STRING; BACK (optional) is logical.

Result type: Integer

Class: Elemental function

SELECTED_INT_KIND(R)

Returns the kind type parameter for an integer type with values between -10^R to 10^R, -1 if no such type is available. If there is more than one such kind, the value returned is for the smallest decimal exponent range.

Argument type: Integer

Result type: Integer

Class: Transformational function

SELECTED_REAL_KIND(P, R)

Returns the kind type parameter for a real type whose values have precision of at least P digits (see PRECISION(X)) and a decimal exponent range of at least R (see RANGE(X)), -1 if the precision is not available, -2 if the exponent range is not available, and -3 if neither is available. If there is more than one such kind, the value returned is the smallest kind number for the smallest decimal precision.

Argument type: P (optional) and R (optional) are integers.

Result type: Integer

Class: Transformational function

SET_EXPONENT(X, I)

Returns a real number that, in the real data model (see DIGITS(X)), has the same fractional part as the fractional part of X but whose exponent part is I.

Argument type: X is real; I is integer.

Result type: Same as X

Class: Elemental function

SHAPE(SOURCE)

Returns a one-dimensional integer array whose elements are the extents of the dimensions of SOURCE.

Argument type: SOURCE is an array or scalar of any type, but it must not be an assumed-size array, a nonallocated allocatable array, or a disassociated pointer.

Result type: One-dimensional integer array

Class: Inquiry function

SIGN(A, B)

Returns absolute value of A times the sign of B.

Argument type: A is integer or real; B is the same type and kind as A.

Result type: Same as A

Class: Elemental function

Specific names: ISIGN (I $\rightarrow$ I), SIGN (R $\rightarrow$ R), DSIGN (DP $\rightarrow$ DP)

SIN(X)

Returns the sine of X (radians).

Argument type: Real or complex

Result type: Same as X

Class: Elemental function

Specific names: SIN (R $\rightarrow$ R), CSIN (C $\rightarrow$ C), DSIN (DP $\rightarrow$ DP)

SINH(X)

Returns the hyperbolic sine of X.

Argument type: Real

Result type: Same as X

Class: Elemental function

Specific names: SINH (R $\rightarrow$ R), DSINH (DP $\rightarrow$ DP)

SIZE(ARRAY, <u>DIM</u>)

Returns the extent of ARRAY along dimension DIM or the number of elements in ARRAY if DIM is omitted.

Argument type: ARRAY is an array of any type, but it must not be a nonallocated allocatable array or a disassociated pointer; DIM (optional) is an integer with $1 \le$ DIM $\le$ rank(ARRAY); it must be present and less than rank(ARRAY) if ARRAY is an assumed-size array.

Result type: Integer

Class: Transformational function

SPACING(X)

Returns the absolute spacing of the model numbers near X (see DIGITS(X)); this value is $(RADIX(X))^{EXPONENT(X) - DIGITS(X)}$ for nonzero X, and TINY(X) if X is 0.

Argument type: Real

Result type: Same as X

Class: Elemental function

SPREAD(SOURCE, DIM, NCOPIES)

Returns an array with rank = rank(SOURCE) + 1 constructed by copying SOURCE NCOPIES times along dimension DIM.

Argument type: SOURCE is an array or scalar of any type; DIM is an integer with $1 \le$ DIM $\le$ rank(SOURCE) + 1; NCOPIES is an integer.

Result type: Array whose elements have the same type as those of SOURCE

Class: Transformational function

Examples: For A $=$ (/ a b c d /):

$$
\text{SPREAD(A, DIM = 2, NCOPIES = 3) returns} \begin{bmatrix} a & a & a \\ b & b & b \\ c & c & c \\ d & d & d \end{bmatrix}.
$$

$$
\text{SPREAD(A, DIM = 1, NCOPIES = 3) returns} \begin{bmatrix} a & b & c & d \\ a & b & c & d \\ a & b & c & d \end{bmatrix}.
$$

SQRT(X)

Returns the square root of X; for X complex, result has the form $x + yi$ with $x \ge 0$ or $0 + yi$ with $y \ge 0$.

Argument type: X is real and nonnegative or complex and nonzero with imaginary part in $(-\pi, \pi]$.

Result type: Same as X

Class: Elemental function

Specific names: SQRT (R → R), CSQRT (C → C), DSQRT (DP → DP)

Class: Elemental function

SUM(ARRAY, DIM, MASK)

Like PRODUCT(ARRAY, DIM, MASK), but sums elements of ARRAY; also, it returns 0 if all elements of MASK are false or ARRAY has size 0.

Example: For $A = \begin{bmatrix} 1 & 5 & -2 \\ 6 & -4 & 3 \end{bmatrix}$:

SUM(A) returns the scalar 9.

SUM(A, MASK = A > 0) returns the scalar 15.

SUM(A, DIM = 1) returns the array containing 7, 1, 1 (column sums).

SUM(A, DIM = 2) returns the array containing 4, 5 (row sums).

SUM(A, DIM = 2, MASK = A > 0) returns the array containing 6, 9 (sums of row elements greater than 0).

SYSTEM_CLOCK(COUNT, COUNT_RATE, COUNT_MAX)

Returns data from a real-time clock. COUNT is set to some processor-dependent value based on the current value of the system clock; this value is incremented by 1 for each clock count until COUNT_MAX is reached and will then be reset to 0; it is HUGE(0) if there is no clock. COUNT_RATE is set to the number of clock counts per second, or 0 if there is no clock; COUNT_MAX is set to the maximum value that COUNT may have.

Argument type: All are INTENT(OUT) arguments of type integer.

Class: Subroutine

TAN(X)

Returns the tangent of X (radians).

Argument type: Real or complex

Result type: Same as X

Class: Elemental function

Specific names: TAN (R → R), DTAN (DP → DP)

TANH(X)

Returns the hyperbolic tangent of X.

Argument type: Real

Result type: Same as X

Class: Elemental function

Specific names: TANH $(R \to R)$, DTANH $(DP \to DP)$

TINY(X)

Returns the smallest possible positive value for numbers of the same type and kind as X.

Argument type: Real; may be an array or a scalar

Result type: Same as X

Class: Inquiry function

TRANSFER(SOURCE, MOLD, SIZE)

Returns a value with physical representation identical to that of SOURCE but interpreted with the type and kind of MOLD; SIZE is the number of elements in the result. It is truncated if the specified size is too small and has an undefined trailing part if it is too large.

Argument type: SOURCE is an array or scalar of any type; MOLD is a scalar or an array and may be of any type; SIZE (optional) is an integer.

Result type: Same type as MOLD. It is a scalar if MOLD is a scalar and SIZE is omitted; it is a one-dimensional array otherwise of size SIZE, or if SIZE is omitted, having the smallest size required to hold SOURCE.

Class: Transformational function

Examples: For

```
REAL, DIMENSION(3) :: A = (/ 1.0, 2.0, 3.0 /)
COMPLEX :: Z
```

TRANSFER(A, Z) returns the complex scalar (1.0, 2.0).

TRANSFER(A, Z, SIZE = 2) returns a one-dimensional complex array whose elements are (1.0, 2.0) and (3.0, undefined).

TRIM(STRING)

Returns the string obtained from STRING by removing all trailing blanks.

Argument type: Character

Result type: Same as STRING but with length reduced by the number of trailing blanks in STRING

Class: Transformational function

UBOUND(ARRAY, <u>DIM</u>)

Like LBOUND(ARRAY, <u>DIM</u>), but returns upper bounds.

UNPACK(VECTOR, MASK, FIELD)

Returns an array obtained by unpacking the elements of VECTOR, using MASK to determine where to place these elements. The result contains an element of VECTOR in each position for which the corresponding element of MASK is true, and an element of FIELD otherwise.

Argument type: VECTOR is a one-dimensional array of any data type; MASK is a logical array; FIELD is an array having the same shape as MASK and same type of elements as VECTOR.

Result type: Same shape as MASK and same type of elements as VECTOR.

Class: Transformational function

Examples: For V = (/ 11, 22, 33 /), M = $\begin{bmatrix} T & F & F \\ F & T & T \end{bmatrix}$, F = $\begin{bmatrix} -1 & -2 & -3 \\ -4 & -5 & -6 \end{bmatrix}$:

UNPACK(V, MASK = M, FIELD = F) returns $\begin{bmatrix} 11 & -2 & -3 \\ -4 & 22 & 33 \end{bmatrix}$.

UNPACK(V, MASK = M, FIELD = 0) returns $\begin{bmatrix} 11 & 0 & 0 \\ 0 & 22 & 33 \end{bmatrix}$.

VERIFY(STRING, SET, <u>BACK</u>)

Checks if SET contains all the characters in STRING; returns location of left-most character of STRING that is not in SET if BACK is .FALSE. or is omitted; the rightmost such character if BACK is .TRUE.; 0 if each character in STRING is in SET or STRING is empty.

Argument type: STRING is of character type; SET is the same type as STRING; BACK (optional) is logical.

Result type: Integer

Class: Elemental function

E

Obsolescent and Redundant Features

Fortran 90 is upwardly compatible with FORTRAN 77, which means that all of the features of FORTRAN 77 are present in Fortran 90. Consequently, any valid FORTRAN 77 program is a valid program in Fortran 90.

There are, however, some features of Fortran 77 for which there are better alternatives in Fortran 90. Some of these features have been designated in the standard as *obsolescent*, which means that they are recommended for removal from the language in the next revision. Other features have not been yet been declared to be obsolescent but they are considered to be *redundant* because of the availability of newer and better alternatives in Fortran 90. In this appendix, we describe the obsolescent features and then several of the redundant features. Use of these features is discouraged.

OBSOLESCENT FEATURES

The Arithmetic **IF** Statement. The **arithmetic IF statement** has the form

```
IF (expression) n₁, n₂, n₃
```

where the expression enclosed in parentheses is an arithmetic expression and n_1, n_2, and n_3 are labels of executable statements, not necessarily distinct. When this statement is executed, the value of the expression is calculated, and execution continues with statement n_1 if this value is negative, with statement n_2 if it is zero, and with statement n_3 if it is positive. For example, consider the arithmetic IF statement

```
IF (X ** 2 - 10.5) 10, 15, 20
```

If X has the value 3.1, statement 10 will be executed next.

The **ASSIGN** and Assigned **GO TO** Statements. A statement label can be assigned to the integer variable by an **ASSIGN statement** of the form

```
ASSIGN statement-label  TO integer-variable
```

If the *statement-label* is that of a FORMAT statement, then *integer-variable* may be used as a format specifier in a formatted input/output statement. If it labels an executable statement, then *integer-variable* may be used in an **assigned GO TO statement** to select the statement to be executed next. It has the form

```
GO TO integer-variable
```

or

```
GO TO integer-variable, (n₁, . . ., nₖ)
```

where $n_1, \ldots, n_k$ are labels of executable statements. The comma following the integer variable in the second form is optional. This statement causes execution to continue with the statement whose label has been assigned to *integer-variable*.

In the second form of the assigned GO TO statement, at the time of execution a check is made to determine whether the statement label assigned to the integer variable is in the list $n_1, \ldots, n_k$. If it is not, an error message results. In the first form of the assigned GO TO statement, no such validation of the value of the integer variable takes place; if it is out of range, execution continues with the next executable statement in the program.

Alternate Returns. It is possible to return from a subroutine at some point other than the normal return point (the first executable statement following the CALL statement). This can be accomplished as follows:

1. In the CALL statement, specify the alternate points of return by using arguments of the form *n , where n denotes a statement label indicating the statement to be executed upon return from the subprogram.

2. Use asterisks (*) as the corresponding formal arguments in the SUBROUTINE statement.

3. Use a statement in the subroutine of the form

```
RETURN k
```

where k is an integer expression whose value indicates which of the alternate returns is to be used.
The following example illustrates:

```
PROGRAM Main_Program
   ⋮
  CALL Subr(A, B, C, *30, *40)
  20 D = A * B
   ⋮
  30 D = A + B
   ⋮
  40 D = A - B
   ⋮
END Main_Program

SUBROUTINE Subr(X, Y, Term, *, *)
   ⋮
  IF (Term < 0) RETURN 1
  IF (Term > 0) RETURN 2
END SUBROUTINE Subr
```

The return to the main program from the subroutine SUBR is to statement 30 if the value of TERM is less than 0, to statement 40 if it is greater than zero, and to statement 20 (normal return) if it is equal to zero.

PAUSE Statement. In some cases, it may be desirable to interrupt program execution and then either terminate or continue it after examining some of the results produced. A **PAUSE statement** may be used for this purpose. This statement has the form

```
PAUSE
```

or

```
PAUSE constant
```

where *constant* is an integer or a character constant that is displayed when execution is interrupted; the exact message (if any) depends on the compiler.

When the PAUSE statement is encountered, execution of the program is interrupted, but it may be resumed by using an appropriate command. Execution resumes with the first executable statement following the PAUSE statement that caused execution to be suspended. The action required to resume execution depends on the system.

DO Loops. DO loops in FORTRAN 77 have the form

```
DO n control-var = initial-value, limit, step-size
    statement-sequence
n terminating-statement
```

where *n* is the label of the last statement in the DO loop. This commonly is a **CONTINUE statement**, but it can also be other Fortran statements (with certain exceptions). In the case of nested loops, the same statement can be used to terminate both loops; for example,

```
    DO 10 I = 1, 3
        DO 10 J = 1, 4
            PRINT *, I + J
 10 CONTINUE
```

or simply

```
    DO 10 I = 1, 3
        DO 10 J = 1, 4
 10 PRINT *, I + J
```

The control variable, initial value, limit, and step size in a DO loop are usually integers. They are, however, also allowed to be of real or double-precision type.

REDUNDANT FEATURES

Source Form. Earlier versions of Fortran do not allow the free-form style of writing programs. Rather, programs have a fixed-form layout in which statement labels have to appear in the first five columns (i.e., character positions) of a line and a statement itself must appear in columns 7–72; columns 73 on are ignored by the compiler. Comments are indicated by placing a C or an asterisk (*) in column 1, and column 6 is reserved for a continuation indicator (any character other than a blank or 0).

Data Types and Declarations

- In addition to the INTEGER, REAL, and COMPLEX numeric data types, a DOUBLE PRECISION type may be used for double-precision real values.
- Type specification statements may have the form

      type-name list-of-variables

- Array declarations have the form

      type-name(dim) list-of-array-variables

   or the **DIMENSION statement** may be used:

      type-name list-of-array-variables
      DIMENSION array-variable₁(dim), . . .

   where dim specifies the extent(s) of the array as described in Chapters 8 and 9.

IMPLICIT Statement. The usual Fortran naming convention is that unless otherwise specified, all variable names beginning with I, J, K, L, M, or N are integer and all other variables are real. This naming convention can be modified with an **IMPLICIT statement** of the form

      IMPLICIT type₁ (a₁, a₂, ...), type₂ (b₁, b₂, ...), ...

where each a_i, b_i, ... is a letter or a pair of letters separated by a hyphen (–), and each $type_i$ is a type identifier. The effect of this statement is to declare that all variables whose names begin with one of the letters a_1, a_2, ... are $type_1$ variables, all those whose names begin with one of the letters b_1, b_2, ... are $type_2$ variables, and so on.

PARAMETER Statement. Named constants can be declared by means of a **PARAMETER statement** of the form

```
PARAMETER (param₁ = const₁, ..., paramₙ = constₙ)
```

DATA Statement. Variables can be initialized using a **DATA statement** of the form

```
DATA list₁/data₁/, list₂/data₂/, ..., listₙ/dataₙ/
```

where each $list_i$ is a list of variables separated by commas, and each $data_i$ is a list of constants, separated by commas, used to initialize the variables in $list_i$; for example,

```
REAL :: W, X, Y, Z
DATA W, X, Y, Z /1.0, 2.5, 7.73, -2.956/
```

The DATA statement could also be written as

```
DATA W /1.0/, X, Y /2.5, 7.73/, Z /-2.956/
```

or in a variety of other forms.

A list of n variables may all be initialized with the same value by preceding the value with $n*$, where n is an integer constant; for example,

```
INTEGER :: M, N
REAL :: A, B, C, D, Zeta
DATA Zeta, M, N, A, B, C, D /1.23578E-10, 2*3, 4*3.14/
```

Arrays may also be initialized in a DATA statement; for example,

```
INTEGER, PARAMETER :: Limit = 10
REAL, DIMENSION(Limit) ::  Alpha
DATA Alpha /Limit*0.0/
```

initialize each of the 10 elements of Alpha to 0.0. Implied DO loops may also be used; for example, the preceding declarations could also be written as

```
INTEGER, PARAMETER :: Limit = 10
REAL, DIMENSION(Limit) ::  Alpha
DATA (Alpha(I), I = 1, Limit) /Limit*0.0/
```

The **GO TO** Statement. The **GO TO statement** has the form

```
GO TO n
```

where n is a label of an executable statement. When this statement is executed, execution will continue with the statement whose label is n_i.

The Computed GO TO Statement. The **computed GO TO statement** has the form

```
GO TO (n₁, n₂, . . ., nₖ), integer-expression
```

where n_1, n_2, ..., n_k are labels of executable statements, not necessarily distinct, and the comma preceding the integer expression is optional. When this statement is executed, the value of the expression is computed. If this value is the integer i, execution will continue with the statement whose label is n_i.

DO-WHILE Loops. **DO-WHILE loops** have the form

```
DO WHILE(logical-expression)
   statement-sequence
END DO
```

The body of the loop is executed so long as the logical expression is true; when it becomes false, execution continues with the statement following the END DO. This statement is equivalent to a (preferred) DO loop of the form

```
DO
   IF (logical-expression) EXIT
   statement-sequence
END DO
```

DO-WHILE loops were not a part of standard FORTRAN 77, but they do appear in many versions of it. They are provided in Fortran 90.

Scale Factors. To permit more general usage of the E, F, G, and D format descriptors, they may be preceded by scale factors of the form

```
nP
```

where n is an integer constant. In the case of output, a descriptor of the form

```
nPFw.d
```

causes the displayed value to be multiplied by 10^n. For the E (and D) descriptor,

```
nPEw.d      or      nPEw.dEe
```

causes the fractional part of the displayed value to be multiplied by 10^n and the exponent to be decreased by n. For the G descriptor, a scale factor has an effect only if the value being output is in a range that causes it to be displayed in E form. In this case, the effect of the scale factor is the same as that described for the E descriptor.

In the case of input, scale factors may be used with the descriptors for real data in much the same manner as they were for output. The only difference is that if a real value is input in E form, the scale factor has no effect.

The H Descriptor. Character constants can be displayed by including them in the list of descriptors of a format specifier; for example,

```
(1X, "For", I5, " samples, the average is", F8.2)
```

Strings may also be displayed by using a Hollerith descriptor of the form

```
nHstring
```

where *n* is the number of characters in *string*. Thus, the preceding format specifier could also be written

```
(1X, 3HFor, I5, 24H samples, the average is, F8.2)
```

Statement Functions. A statement function can be used when the function can be defined by means of a single expression that does not change from one execution of the program to another. A statement function is defined by a single statement of the form

```
name(formal-argument-list) = expression
```

where *expression* may contain constants, variables, formulas, or references to library functions, to previously defined statement functions, or to functions defined by subprograms, but no references to the function being defined. Statement functions must appear in the program unit in which the functions are referenced, and they must be placed at the end of the specification part.

The ENTRY Statement. The normal entry point of a subprogram is the first executable statement following the FUNCTION or SUBROUTINE statement. In some cases, some other entry may be convenient. For example, it may be necessary to assign values to certain variables the first time a subprogram is referenced but not on subsequent references.

Multiple entry points are introduced in subprograms by using **ENTRY statements** of the form

```
ENTRY name(argument-list)
```

where *name* is the name of the entry point and *argument-list* is similar to the argument list in a FUNCTION or SUBROUTINE statement; for example,

```
FUNCTION Quad(X)
  REAL :: Quad, A, B, C, Poly
  REAL, INTENT(IN) :: X

  READ *, A, B, C

  ENTRY Poly(X)
  Quad = A * X ** 2 + B * X + C
  SAVE A, B, C
END FUNCTION Quad
```

The first reference to this function in the main program would be with a statement such as

```
Value = Quad(Z)
```

which would cause values for A, B, and C in the subprogram to be read and the function evaluated at Z. Subsequent references to this function might be by a statement such as

```
Y = Poly(Z)
```

The **COMMON** Statement. The **COMMON statement** is used to establish common memory areas in which this data can be stored and accessed *directly* by different program units. One form establishes a common region to which no name is assigned and which is thus called **blank** or **unnamed common**:

```
COMMON list-of-variables
```

When COMMON statements are used in different program units, the first item in each list is allocated the first memory location in blank common. These items are thus **associated**, because they refer to the same memory location. Successive items in the list are similarly associated because they are allocated successive memory locations in the common region.

Restrictions apply to items that are allocated memory locations in blank common:

1. Associated items must be of the same type.
2. If they are of character type, they should be of the same length.
3. They may not be initialized in DATA statements (a BLOCK DATA subprogram can be used for this purpose).
4. They may not be used as formal arguments in the subprogram in which the COMMON statement appears.
5. Numeric and character variables (or arrays) may not both be allocated memory locations from blank common.

To illustrate, suppose that one program unit contains the statements

```
REAL :: A, B
INTEGER :: M, N
COMMON A, B, M, N
```

These four variables are allocated memory locations in the common region in the following order:

Variable	Blank Common Location
A	#1
B	#2
M	#3
N	#4

If another program unit contains the statements

```
REAL :: W, X
INTEGER :: I, J
COMMON W, X, I, J
```

then W, X, I, and J are also allocated the first four memory locations in the common region:

Variable	Blank Common Location
W	#1
X	#2
I	#3
J	#4

It follows that these eight variables are then associated in the following manner:

Variable	Blank Common Location	Variable
A	#1	W
B	#2	X
M	#3	I
N	#4	J

Sometimes it may be preferable to share one set of variables among some program units and to share another set among other program units. This is possible by using a form of the COMMON statement that establishes common regions that are **named**:

```
COMMON /name1/ list1 /name2/ list2 . . .
```

For example, suppose that the variables A, B, L, and M are to be shared by the main program and a subroutine Gamma, and the variables A, B, N1, N2, N3 are to be shared by the main program and the subroutine Beta. The following program scheme would be appropriate:

```
PROGRAM Named_Common
   REAL :: A, B
   INTEGER :: L, M, N1, N2, N3
   COMMON /First/ A, B /Second/ L, M /Third/ N1, N2, N3
      ⋮
END PROGRAM Named_Common

SUBROUTINE Gamma
   REAL :: A, B
   INTEGER :: L, M
   COMMON /First/ A, B /Second/ L, M
      ⋮
END SUBROUTINE Gamma

SUBROUTINE Beta
   REAL :: A, B
   INTEGER :: N1, N2, N3
   COMMON /First/ A, B /Third/ N1, N2, N3
      ⋮
END SUBROUTINE Beta
```

A COMMON statement may also be used to associate two or more arrays with a single array. If the statements

```
REAL :: A(3,3), Const(3)
COMMON A, Const
```

appear in one program unit and

```
REAL :: Aug(3,4)
COMMON Aug
```

appear in another, the following associations will be established:

Array Element	Blank Common Location	Array Element
A(1,1)	#1	Aug(1,1)
A(2,1)	#2	Aug(2,1)
A(3,1)	#3	Aug(3,1)
A(1,2)	#4	Aug(1,2)
A(2,2)	#5	Aug(2,2)
A(3,2)	#6	Aug(3,2)
A(1,3)	#7	Aug(1,3)
A(2,3)	#8	Aug(2,3)
A(3,3)	#9	Aug(3,3)
Const(1)	#10	Aug(1,4)
Const(2)	#11	Aug(2,4)
Const(3)	#12	Aug(3,4)

Numeric and character type variables may not be allocated memory locations from the same common region. Named common regions, however, are separate regions. Consequently, numeric variables may be allocated to one named region and character variables to another, with both regions established in the same COMMON statement.

Block Data Subprograms. Items that are allocated memory locations in blank common may not be initialized in DATA statements. However, items allocated memory locations from a named common region may be initialized in a DATA statement, provided that this initialization is done in a special kind of subprogram called a **block data subprogram.**

The first statement of a block data subprogram is

```
BLOCK DATA
```

or

```
BLOCK DATA name
```

A program may have more than one block data subprogram, but at most one of these may be unnamed. A *block data subprogram contains no executable statements*, only comments and specification statements. The last statement must be an END statement.

A block data subprogram initializes items in named common regions by listing these items in COMMON statements and specifying their values in DATA statements. Suppose, for example, that variables A and B and the array List are allocated memory locations in common region Block_1 and that character variable Code and the character array Name are allocated locations in common region Block_2. The following block data subprogram could be used to initialize A, B, List(1), ..., List(5), Code, and the entire array Name:

```
BLOCK DATA
   INTEGER, PARAMETER :: M = 20,  N = 50
   REAL :: A, B
   INTEGER :: List(M)
   CHARACTER(10) Code, Name(N)
   COMMON /Block_1/ A, B, List/Block_2/ Code, Name
   DATA A, B, (List(I), I  = 1, 5) /2.5, 3.5, 5*0/
   DATA CODE, NAME /'&', N*' '/
END
```

The **EQUIVALENCE** Statement. The **EQUIVALENCE statement** makes it possible to associate variables and arrays in the *same* program unit so that they refer to the same memory locations. This statement is of the form

```
EQUIVALENCE (list₁), (list₂), . . .
```

where each of $list_1$, $list_2$, ... is a list of variables, arrays, array elements, or substring names separated by commas, which are to be allocated the same memory locations. Each of the sets of items that constitute one of the lists in parentheses is said to be an *equivalence class*. As an illustration, consider the statements

```
INTEGER :: M1, M2, Num
REAL :: X, Y, Alpha(4), Beta(4)
EQUIVALENCE (X, Y), (M1, M2, Num), (Alpha, Beta)
```

The variables and elements of the arrays that appear in the EQUIVALENCE statement are allocated in the following manner:

$$X \leftrightarrow Y$$

$$M1 \leftrightarrow M2 \leftrightarrow NUM$$

$$ALPHA(1) \leftrightarrow BETA(1)$$

$$ALPHA(2) \leftrightarrow BETA(2)$$

$$ALPHA(3) \leftrightarrow BETA(3)$$

$$ALPHA(4) \leftrightarrow BETA(4)$$

Because associated variables refer to the same memory locations, changing the value of one of these variables also changes the value of all variables in the same equivalence class.

The following rules govern the use of EQUIVALENCE statements:

1. Two (or more) items may not be equivalenced if they *both* (or all) appear in a COMMON statement(s) in the same program unit.

2. Formal arguments may not be equivalenced.

3. Items of character type may be equivalenced only with other items of character type. Numeric items of different types may be equivalenced, but extreme care must be exercised because of the different internal representations used for different numeric types.

F

Internal Representation

We noted in Section 1.2 that a binary scheme having only the two binary digits 0 and 1 is used to represent information in a computer. These binary digits, called *bits*, are organized into groups of 8 called *bytes*, and bytes in turn are grouped together into *words*. Common word sizes are 16 bits (= 2 bytes) and 32 bits (= 4 bytes). Each byte or word has an *address* that can be used to access it, making it possible to store information in and retrieve information from that byte or word. To understand how this is done, we must know something about the binary number system.

NUMBER SYSTEMS

The number system that we are accustomed to using is a **decimal** or **base-10** number system, which uses the digits 0, 1, 2, 3, 4, 5, 6, 7, 8, and 9. The significance of these digits in a numeral depends on the positions that they occupy in that numeral. For example, in the numeral

$$485$$

the digit 4 is interpreted as

$$4 \text{ hundreds}$$

and the digit 8 as

$$8 \text{ tens}$$

and the digit 5 as

$$5 \text{ ones}$$

Thus, the numeral 485 represents the number four hundred eighty-five and can be written in **expanded form** as

$$(4 \times 100) + (8 \times 10) + (5 \times 1)$$

or

$$(4 \times 10^2) + (8 \times 10^1) + (5 \times 10^0)$$

The digits that appear in the various positions of a decimal (base-10) numeral thus are coefficients of powers of 10.

Similar positional number systems can be devised using numbers other than 10 as a base. The **binary** number system uses 2 as the base and has only two digits, 0 and 1. As in a decimal system, the significance of the bits in a binary numeral is determined by their positions in that numeral. For example, the binary numeral

$$101$$

can be written in expanded form (using decimal notation) as

$$(1 \times 2^2) + (0 \times 2^1) + (1 \times 2^0)$$

that is, the binary numeral 101 has the decimal value

$$4 + 0 + 1 = 5$$

Similarly, the binary numeral 111010 has the decimal value

$$(1 \times 2^5) + (1 \times 2^4) + (1 \times 2^3) + (0 \times 2^2) + (1 \times 2^1) + (0 \times 2^0)$$

$$= 32 + 16 + 8 + 0 + 2 + 0$$

$$= 58$$

When necessary, to avoid confusion about which base is being used, it is customary to write the base as a subscript for nondecimal numerals. Using this convention, we could indicate that 5 and 58 have the binary representations just given by writing

$$5 = 101_2$$

and

$$58 = 111010_2$$

Two other nondecimal numeration systems are important in the consideration of computer systems: **octal** and **hexadecimal.** The octal system is a base-8 system and uses the eight digits 0, 1, 2, 3, 4, 5, 6, and 7. In an octal numeral such as

$$1703_8$$

the digits are coefficients of powers of 8; this numeral is therefore an abbreviation for the expanded form

$$(1 \times 8^3) + (7 \times 8^2) + (0 \times 8^1) + (3 \times 8^0)$$

and thus has the decimal value

$$512 + 448 + 0 + 3 = 963$$

A hexadecimal system uses a base of 16 and the digits 0, 1, 2, 3, 4, 5, 6, 7, 8, 9, A (10), B (11), C (12), D (13), E (14), and F (15). The hexadecimal numeral

$$5E4_{16}$$

has the expanded form

$$(5 \times 16^2) + (14 \times 16^1) + (4 \times 16^0)$$

which has the decimal value

$$1280 + 224 + 4 = 1508$$

Table F.1 shows the decimal, binary, octal, and hexadecimal representations for the first 31 nonnegative integers.

Table F1   Numeric Representation

Decimal	Binary	Octal	Hexadecimal
0	0	0	0
1	1	1	1
2	10	2	2
3	11	3	3
4	100	4	4
5	101	5	5
6	110	6	6
7	111	7	7
8	1000	10	8
9	1001	11	9
10	1010	12	A
11	1011	13	B
12	1100	14	C
13	1101	15	D
14	1110	16	E
15	1111	17	F
16	10000	20	10
17	10001	21	11
18	10010	22	12
19	10011	23	13
20	10100	24	14
21	10101	25	15
22	10110	26	16
23	10111	27	17
24	11000	30	18
25	11001	31	19
26	11010	32	1A
27	11011	33	1B
28	11100	34	1C
29	11101	35	1D
30	11110	36	1E
31	11111	37	1F

DATA STORAGE

Integers.   When an integer value must be stored in the computer's memory, the binary representation of that value is typically stored in one word of memory. To illustrate, consider a computer whose word size is 16, and suppose that the integer value 58 is to be stored. A memory word is selected, and a sequence of 16 bits formed from the binary representation 111010 of 58 is stored there:

Memory

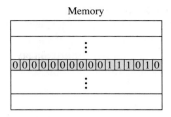

Negative integers must also be stored in a binary form in which the sign of the integer is part of the representation. There are several ways that this can be done, but one of the most common is the **two's complement** representation. In this scheme, positive integers are represented in binary form, as just described, with the leftmost bit set to 0 to indicate that the value is positive. The representation of a negative integer $-n$ is obtained by first finding the binary representation of n, complementing it—that is, changing each 0 to 1 and each 1 to 0, and then adding 1 to the result. For example, the two's complement representation of -58 using a string of 16 bits is obtained as follows:

1. Represent 58 by a 16-bit binary numeral:

$$0000000000111010$$

2. Complement this bit string:

$$1111111111000101$$

3. Add 1:

$$1111111111000110$$

Note that the leftmost bit in this two's complement representation of a negative integer is always 1, indicating that the number is negative.

Since integers are stored in a single word of memory, the word size of a computer determines the range of the integers that can be stored internally. For example, the largest positive integer that can be stored in a 16-bit word is

$$0111111111111111_2 = 2^{15} - 1 = 32767$$

and the smallest negative integer is

$$1000000000000000_2 = -2^{15} = -32768$$

The range of integers that can be represented using a 32-bit word is

$$10000000000000000000000000000000_2 = -2^{31} = -2147483648$$

through

$$01111111111111111111111111111111_2 = 2^{31} - 1 = 2147483647$$

Representation of an integer outside the allowed range would require more bits than can be stored in a single word, a phenomenon known as **overflow.** This limitation may be partially overcome by using more than one word to store an integer. Although this enlarges the range of integers that can be stored exactly, it does not resolve the problem of overflow; the range of representable integers is still finite.

Real Numbers. Numbers that contain decimal points are called **real numbers** or **floating-point numbers.** In the decimal representation of such numbers, each digit is the coefficient of some power of 10. Digits to the left of the decimal point are coefficients of nonnegative powers of 10, and those to the right are coefficients of negative powers of 10. For example, the decimal numeral 56.317 can be written in expanded form as

$$(5 \times 10^1) + (6 \times 10^0) + (3 \times 10^{-1}) + (1 \times 10^{-2}) + (7 \times 10^{-3})$$

or, equivalently, as

$$(5 \times 10) + (6 \times 1) + \left(3 \times \frac{1}{10}\right) + \left(1 \times \frac{1}{100}\right) + \left(7 \times \frac{1}{1000}\right)$$

Digits in the binary representation of a real number are coefficients of powers of two. Those to the left of the **binary point** are coefficients of nonnegative powers of two, and those to the right are coefficients of negative powers of two. For example, the expanded form of 110.101 is

$$(1 \times 2^2) + (1 \times 2^1) + (0 \times 2^0) + (1 \times 2^{-1}) + (0 \times 2^{-2}) + (1 \times 2^{-3})$$

and thus has the decimal value

$$4 + 2 + 0 + \frac{1}{2} + 0 + \frac{1}{8} = 6.625$$

There is some variation in the schemes used for storing real numbers in computer memory, but one common method is the following. The binary representation

$$110.101_2$$

of the real number 6.625 can also be written equivalently as

$$0.110101_2 \times 2^3$$

Typically, one part of a memory word (or words) is used to store a fixed number of bits of the **mantissa** or **fractional part**, 0.110101_2, and another part to store the **exponent**, $3 = 11_2$. For example, if the leftmost 24 bits in a 32-bit word are used for the mantissa and the remaining 8 bits for the exponent, 6.625 can be stored as

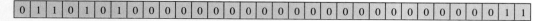

mantissa   exponent

where the first bit in each part is reserved for the sign.[1]

Because the binary representation of the exponent may require more than the available number of bits, we see that the **overflow** problem discussed in connection with the integer representation will also occur in storing a real number whose exponent is too large. A negative exponent that is too small to be stored causes an **underflow**. (See Section 2.11.) Also, there obviously are some real numbers whose mantissas have more than the allotted number of bits; consequently, some of these bits will be lost when storing such numbers. In fact, most real numbers do not have finite binary representations and thus cannot be stored exactly in any computer. For example, the binary representation of the real number 0.7 is

$$(0.10110011001100110\ldots)_2$$

where the block 0110 is repeated indefinitely. If only the first 24 bits are stored and all remaining bits are truncated, the stored representation of 0.7 will be

$$(0.101100110011001100110011)_2$$

which has the decimal value 0.6999999284744263. If the binary representation is rounded to 24 bits, the stored representation for 0.7 will be

$$(0.101100110011001100110010)_2$$

which has the decimal value 0.7000000476837159. In either case, the stored value is not exactly 0.7. This error, called **roundoff error**, can be reduced, but not eliminated, by using a larger number of bits to store the binary representation of real numbers.

Logical and Character Values

Computers store and process not only numeric data but also logical or boolean data (false or true), character data, and other types of nonnumeric information. Storing logical values is easy: false can be encoded as 0, true as 1, and these bits stored.

The schemes used for the internal representation of character data are based on the assignment of a numeric code to each of the characters in the character set. Several standard coding schemes have been developed, such as ASCII (American Standard Code for Information Interchange) and EBCDIC (Extended Binary Coded Decimal Interchange Code). A complete table of ASCII and EBCDIC codes for all characters is given in Appendix A.

Characters are represented internally using these binary codes. A byte can thus store the binary representation of one character. For example, the character string HI can be stored in two bytes with the code for H in the first byte and the code for I in the second byte; with ASCII code, the result is as follows:

---

[1] In most computers, exponents are stored using *biased notation* so that it is easier to compare exponents. In biased notation, a bias 2^{n-1} is added to the exponent, where n is the number of bits used to store the exponent. Thus for a 32-bit word with 8 bits for the exponent, the bias would be $2^7 = 128 = 10000000$. For the real value 6.625, the exponent would be stored as 10000011.

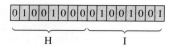

Memory words of size 32 (bits) are usually divided into four bytes and thus can store four characters. Character strings whose length exceeds the number of bytes in a word are usually stored in adjacent words of memory.

Exercises F

1. Convert each of the following binary numerals to base 10:
   (a) 1001
   (b) 110010
   (c) 1000000
   (d) 111111111111111 (fifteen 1s)
   (e) 1.1
   (f) 1010.10101

2. Convert each of the following octal numerals to base 10:
   (a) 123
   (b) 2705
   (c) 10000
   (d) 77777
   (e) 7.2
   (f) 123.45

3. Convert each of the following hexadecimal numerals to base 10:
   (a) 12
   (b) 1AB
   (c) ABC
   (d) FFF
   (e) 8.C
   (f) AB.CD

4. Converting from octal representation to binary representation is easy, as we need only replace each octal digit with its three-bit binary equivalent. For example, to convert 617_8 to binary, replace 6 with 110, 1 with 001, and 7 with 111, to obtain 110001111_2. Convert each of the octal numerals in Exercise 2 to binary numerals.

5. Imitating the conversion scheme in Exercise 4, convert each of the hexadecimal numerals in Exercise 3 to binary numerals.

6. To convert a binary numeral to octal, place the digits in groups of three, starting from the binary point, or from the right end if there is no binary point, and replace each group with the corresponding octal digit. For example, $10101111_2 = 010\ 101\ 111_2 = 257_8$. Convert each of the binary numerals in Exercise 1 to octal numerals.

7. Imitating the conversion scheme in Exercise 6, convert each of the binary numerals in Exercise 1 to hexadecimal numerals.

8. One method for finding the **base-b** representation of a whole number given in base-10 notation is to divide the number repeatedly by b until a quotient of zero results. The successive remainders are the digits from right to left of the base-b representation. For example, the binary representation of 26 is 11010_2, as the following computation shows:

$$\begin{array}{r} 0 \text{ R1} \\ 2\overline{)1} \text{ R1} \\ 2\overline{)3} \text{ R0} \\ 2\overline{)6} \text{ R1} \\ 2\overline{)13} \text{ R0} \\ 2\overline{)26} \end{array}$$

Convert each of the following base-10 numerals to (i) binary, (ii) octal, and (iii) hexadecimal:

(a) 27   (b) 99   (c) 314   (d) 5280

9. To convert a decimal fraction to its base-b equivalent, repeatedly multiply the fractional part of the number by b. The integer parts are the digits from left to right of the base-b representation. For example, the decimal numeral 0.6875 corresponds to the binary numeral 0.1011_2, as the following computation shows:

	.6875
	× 2
1	.375
	× 2
0	.75
	× 2
1	.5
	× 2
1	.0

Convert the following base-10 numerals to (i) binary, (ii) octal, (iii) hexadecimal:

(a) 0.5   (b) 0.25   (c) 0.625
(d) 16.0625   (e) 8.828125

10. Even though the base-10 representation of a fraction may terminate, its representation in some other base need not terminate. For example, the following computation shows that the binary representation of 0.7 is $(0.10110011001100110011001100110\ldots)_2$, where the block of bits 0110 is repeated indefinitely. This representation is commonly written as $0.1\overline{0110}_2$.

	.7
	× 2
1	.4
	× 2
0	.8
	× 2
1	.6
	× 2
1	.2
	× 2
0	.4

Convert the following base-10 numerals to (i) binary, (ii) octal, (iii) hexadecimal:
   (a) 0.3   (b) 0.6   (c) 0.05   (d) $0.\overline{3} = 0.33333 \ldots = 1/3$

11. Find the decimal value of each of the following 16-bit integers, assuming a two's complement representation:
    (a) 0000000001000000   (b) 1111111111111110
    (c) 1111111110111111   (d) 0000000011111111
    (e) 1111111100000000   (f) 1000000000000001

12. Find the 16-bit two's complement representation for each of the following integers:
    (a) 255   (b) $1K \ (= 2^{10})$
    (c) -255 (d) -256
    (e) -34567_8 (f) $-3ABC_{16}$

13. Assuming a 24-bit mantissa and an 8-bit exponent, and assuming that two's complement representation is used for each, indicate how each of the following real numbers would be stored in a 32-bit word if extra bits in the mantissa are (i) truncated or (ii) rounded:
    (a) 0.375   (b) 37.375
    (c) 0.03125   (d) 63.84375
    (e) 0.1   (f) 0.01

14. Using the tables for ASCII and EBCDIC in Appendix A, indicate how each of the following character strings would be stored in two-byte words using (i) ASCII or (ii) EBCDIC:
    (a) TO   (b) FOUR
    (c) AMOUNT   (d) ETC.
    (e) J.DOE   (f) A#*4−C

G

Answers
to Quick Quizzes

Quick Quiz 1.2

1. (a) mechanical devices for calculation
   (b) stored program for automatic control of a process
2. D, E, R, O, V, Q, I, H, T, P, W, M, F, U, B, S, G, A, J, K, C, L, N

Quick Quiz 1.4

1. problem analysis and specification
   data organization and algorithm design
   program coding
   execution and testing
   maintenance
2. input and output
3. sequence, selection, and repetition
4. false
5. flowchart
6. syntax
7. top-down design or divide-and-conquer strategy
8. syntax errors
   run-time errors
   logical errors
9. (a) Input: temperature on Celsius scale
       Output: corresponding temperature on Fahrenheit scale

   This algorithm converts a temperature on the Celsius scale to the corresponding temperature on the Fahrenheit scale.

   1. Enter Celsius.
   2. Calculate Fahrenheit = 1.8 * Celsius + 32.
   3. Display Fahrenheit.

   (b)

```
PROGRAM Temperature
!-------------------------------------------------------------
! Program to convert a temperature of Celsius degrees to
! corresponding temperature on the Fahrenheit scale.
! Variables used are:
!   Celsius     : temperature on the Celsius scale
!   Fahrenheit : temperature on the Fahrenheit scale
```

Quick Quiz 1.4 *(cont.)*

```
!
! Input : Celsius
! Output: Fahrenheit
!-------------------------------------------------------------
  REAL :: Celsius, Fahrenheit

  ! Get the Celsius temperature
  PRINT *, "Enter the temperature in degrees Celsius:"
  READ *, Celsius

  ! Compute the corresponding Fahrenheit temperature
  Fahrenheit= 1.8 * Celsius + 32.0

  ! Display Fahrenheit
  PRINT *, "Fahrenheit temperature is: ", Fahrenheit

END PROGRAM Temperature
```

Quick Quiz 2.2

1. integer
   real
   complex
   logical
   character

2. program heading
   specification part
   execution part
   subprogram part
   END PROGRAM statement

3. apostrophes ('), double quotes (")

4. a letter

5. 31

6. legal

7. not legal: the character - is not legal in an identifier

8. not legal: identifier must begin with a letter

9. legal

Quick Quiz 2.2 *(cont.)*

10. legal

11. not legal: the character . is not legal in an identifier

12. not legal: the character / is not legal in an identifier

13. not legal: the character $ is not legal in an identifier

14. integer

15. none: comma not allowed in numeric constant

16. real

17. real

18. real

19. character

20. none: doesn't begin with a digit or a sign and is not enclosed in quotes

21. none: apostrophes within strings must be doubled, or enclose string with "

22. character

23. none : $ not allowed in numeric constant

24. real

25. none: doesn't begin with a digit or sign and is not enclosed in quotes

26. integer

27. none: + not allowed in numeric constant

28. character

29. `INTEGER :: Mu`

30. `REAL :: Time, Distance`

31. `CHARACTER(20) :: Name1, Name2, Name3*10`

32. `REAL, PARAMETER :: Gravity = 32`

33. `REAL, PARAMETER :: Mars = 1.2E12, Earth = 1.5E10`

34. `CHARACTER(4), PARAMETER :: Department = "CHEM"`
    `INTEGER, PARAMETER :: CourseNumber = 141`

35. `REAL :: Rate1 = 1.25, Rate2 = 2.33`

36. `CHARACTER(4) :: Department = "ENGR"`
    `INTEGER :: Course1 = 141, Course2 = 142`

37. `INTEGER :: Limit_1 = 10, Limit_2 = 20, Limit_3 = 20, &`
    `            Limit_4 = 30`

Quick Quiz 2.3

1. 1
2. 2.6
3. 2
4. 5
5. 11
6. 25
7. 12.25
8. 36.0
9. 2
10. 3.0
11. 11.0
12. 1
13. 12.25
14. 5.1
15. 4.0
16. 6.25
17. 3.0
18. `10 + 5 * B + 4 * A * C`
19. `SQRT(A + 3 * B ** 2)`

Quick Quiz 2.4

1. valid
2. not valid: variable must be on the left of =
3. valid
4. not valid: variable must be on the left of =
5. valid: but not recommended because it is a mixed-mode assignment
6. not valid: `"1"` is a character constant
7. valid
8. not valid: multiple assignments are not legal
9. 12.25

Quick Quiz 2.4 *(cont.)*

10. 6.1

11. 6

12. 10

13. 5.0

14. 1

15. not valid: 1 is a numeric constant

16. `"1"`

17. `"OneT"`

18. `"12bb"` (where b̸ is a blank)

19. `Distance = Rate * Time`

20. `C = SQRT(A**2 + B**2)`

21. `Count = Count + 1`

Quick Quiz 2.6

1. Any characters following an exclamation mark (!)—except within a string constant—and running to the end of the line form a comment.

2. Executable statements specify actions to be taken during the execution of the program. Nonexecutable statements provide information that is used during compilation of a program.

3. true

4. false

5. false

6. false

7. true

8. a blank line

9. `37.0 7`
   `X = 1.74 I = 29`
   `4.23`
   `15`

Quick Quiz 3.1

1. `.TRUE.` `.FALSE.`
2. `<, <=, >, >=, ==, /=`
3. `.NOT.,` `.AND.,` `.OR.,` `.EQV.,` `.NEQV.`
4. `.FALSE.`
5. `.TRUE.`
6. `.FALSE.`
7. `.FALSE.`
8. `.TRUE.`
9. `.TRUE.`
10. `.TRUE.`
11. `.TRUE.`
12. Invalid; should be `(0 <= COUNT) .AND. (COUNT <= 5)`
13. `.TRUE.`
14. `X /= 0`
15. `-10 < X .AND. X < 10` or simply, `ABS(X) < 10`
16. `(X > 0 .AND. Y > 0) .OR. (X < 0 .AND. Y < 0)` or simply, `X * Y > 0`

Quick Quiz 3.5

1. legal
2. not legal: logical expression should be enclosed in parentheses
3. legal
4. not legal: logical operator is `==`
5. not legal: logical expression is not correct
6. legal
7. 6
8. 5
9. 6
10. 10
11. 10
12. 10

Quick Quiz 3.5 *(cont.)*

13. Excellent
14. Excellent
15. Good
16. Fair
17. Bad
18. `IF ((Number < 0) .OR. (Number > 100)) PRINT *, "Out of range"`
19.
```
IF (X <= 1.5) THEN
   N = 1
ELSE IF (X < 2.5) THEN
   N = 2
ELSE
   N = 3
END IF
```

Quick Quiz 3.7

1. 198
2. -2
3. default
4. 123
5. 456
6. no output produced
7. not a legal CASE construct—selector may not be real

Quick Quiz 3.9

1. false
2. false
3. false

Quick Quiz 3.9 *(cont.)*

4. false

5. false

6. false

7. true

8. false

9. true

10. true

11. `LOGICAL :: Larger`
    `Larger = A > B`

12. `LOGICAL :: FreshPerson, UpperclassPerson`
    `FreshPerson = Class == 1`
    `UpperclassPerson = .NOT. FreshPerson`

Quick Quiz 4.1

1. (a) *repetition controlled by a counter* in which the body of the loop is executed once for each value of some control variable in a specified range of values

   (b) *repetition controlled by a logical expression* in which the decision to continue or to terminate repetition is determined by the value of some logical expression

2. `Hello`
   `Hello`
   `Hello`
   `Hello`
   `Hello`

3. `Hello`
   `Hello`
   `Hello`

4. `1  2`
   `2  3`
   `3  4`
   `4  5`
   `5  6`
   `6  7`

Quick Quiz 4.1 *(cont.)*

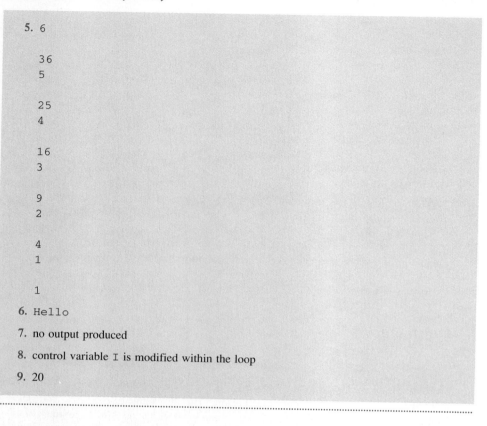

5. 6

   36
   5

   25
   4

   16
   3

   9
   2

   4
   1

   1

6. Hello

7. no output produced

8. control variable I is modified within the loop

9. 20

Quick Quiz 4.5

1. In a pretest loop, the logical expression that controls the repetition is evaluated *before* the body of the loop is executed. In a posttest loop, the termination test is made *after* the body of the loop is executed.

2. false

3. true

4. syntax errors, run-time errors, and logical errors

5. run-time

6. syntax

7. logical

Quick Quiz 4.5 *(cont.)*

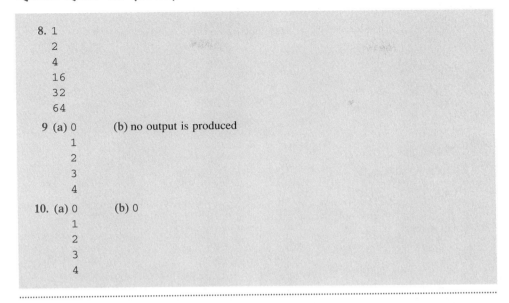

8. 1
   2
   4
   16
   32
   64

9 (a) 0   (b) no output is produced
      1
      2
      3
      4

10. (a) 0   (b) 0
       1
       2
       3
       4

Quick Quiz 5.3

1. false

2. true

3. false

4. false

5. false

6. false

7. true

8. slash

9. right

10. 1

11. ƀIƀ =987ƀƀXƀ=ƀ234.560THEƀEND

12. ƀƀƀ987ƀƀƀƀƀ234.6
    ƀƀƀ-44ƀƀƀƀƀƀ-1.0

13. ƀƀƀƀƀƀƀ235.
    ƀ987ƀƀƀƀƀƀƀƀ-44

14. 99, 876, 123.45, 6.0 (other answers are possible)

Quick Quiz 5.3 *(cont.)*

15. ␢99876123.45␢␢␢␢␢␢6 (other answers are possible)
16. ␢99␢123.45␢␢␢␢␢876␢␢␢␢␢␢6
17. ␢99876123456
18. 9912345
    87660

Quick Quiz 5.5

1. unit number
2. FORMAT
3. WRITE(*, *) Answer
4. false
5. OPEN(UNIT = 15, FILE = "QUIZ", STATUS = "OLD")
6. READ (15, '(T6, I3)') Score
7. true
8. true
9. false
10. REWIND

Quick Quiz 6.1

1. functions and subroutines
2. heading, specification part, execution part, and END FUNCTION statement
3. formal arguments
4. REAL
5. as an internal subprogram, a module subprogram, or an external subprogram
6. scope
7. true
8. actual
9. 6

Quick Quiz 6.1 *(cont.)*

10. true
11. false
12.
```
FUNCTION F(X)

    REAL :: F
    REAL, INTENT(IN) :: X

    F = X**2 * SIN(X)

END FUNCTION F
```

Quick Quiz 6.7

1. recursion
2. Its definition consists of two parts:
   (1) An *anchor* or *base case*, in which the value of the function is specified for one or more values of the argument(s)
   (2) An *inductive* or *recursive step*, in which the function's value for the current value of the argument(s) is defined in terms of previously defined function values and/or argument values
3. RECURSIVE
4. RESULT
5. true
6. 15
7. 0
8. 0

Quick Quiz 7.1

1. functions and subroutines
2. heading, specification part, execution part, and END SUBROUTINE statement
3. formal arguments

Quick Quiz 7.1 *(cont.)*

4. (1) Functions are designed to return a single value to the program unit that references them. Subroutines often return more than one value, or they may return no value at all but simply perform some task such as displaying a list of instructions to the user.

   (2) Functions return values via function names; subroutines return values via arguments.

   (3) A function is referenced by using its name in an expression, whereas a subroutine is referenced by a `CALL` statement.

5. cannot be used: `Calculate` must be referenced with a `CALL` statement.

6. cannot be used: `Number_2` is an `INTENT(INOUT)` argument, so the corresponding actual argument must be a variable.

7. cannot be used: incorrect number of arguments

8. can be used

9. cannot be used: incorrect number of arguments

10. cannot be used: type mismatch in second and third arguments

11. `String =batbatelk`

Quick Quiz 7.6

1. true

2. false

3. `EXTERNAL`

4. the number of arguments, the type of each argument, and the type of the value returned by the function

5.
```
INTERFACE
   FUNCTION F(X, Y, N)
     REAL :: F
     REAL, INTENT(IN) :: X, Y
     INTEGER, INTENT(IN) :: N
   END FUNCTION F
END INTERFACE
```

Quick Quiz 8.2

1. direct
2. subscripted
3. subscript or index
4. one-dimensional
5. false
6. true
7. true
8. false
9. false
10. correct
11. not correct
12. not correct
13. not correct
14. NUMBER(1) = 3
    NUMBER(2) = 4
    NUMBER(3) = 7
    NUMBER(4) = 8
    NUMBER(5) = 11
15. NUMBER(1) = 2
    NUMBER(2) = 4
    NUMBER(3) = 8
    NUMBER(4) = 16
    NUMBER(5) = 32
16. X_Value(1) = 0.5
    X_Value(2) = 1.0
    X_Value(3) = 1.5
    X_Value(4) = 2.0
    X_Value(5) = 2.5
17. NUMBER(1) = 1
    NUMBER(2) = 2
    NUMBER(3) = 3
    NUMBER(4) = 3
    NUMBER(5) = 3

Quick Quiz 8.4

1. true
2. 1, 4, 9, 16, 25, 36
3. 22, 33, 44
4. 11, 33, 55
5. 11, 66, 22, 44, 33, 55
6. 14, 34, 60, 92, 130, 174
7. 3, 3, 3, 3, 3, 3
8. not legal: `F` and `A(1:4)` do not have the same size.
9. 12, 26, 42, 60, 30, 30
10. true
11. `Animal = ape rat cat`

Quick Quiz 9.2

1. false
2. true
3. columnwise
4. columnwise
5. 3
6. 2
7. 3
8. no value assigned
9. the `READ` statement in Question 7
10. 3
11. false
12. 2, 3
13. true
14. 4
15. no
16. yes
17. no

Quick Quiz 9.2 *(cont.)*

18. yes
19. yes
20. yes

Quick Quiz 9.3

1. true

2. $\begin{bmatrix} 10 & 30 & 50 \\ 20 & 40 & 60 \end{bmatrix}$

3. $\begin{bmatrix} 1 & 16 \\ 4 & 25 \\ 9 & 36 \end{bmatrix}$

4. $\begin{bmatrix} 40 & 60 \end{bmatrix}$

5. $\begin{bmatrix} 1 & 16 \\ 9 & 36 \end{bmatrix}$

6. $\begin{bmatrix} 1 & 16 \\ 9 & 36 \\ 4 & 25 \end{bmatrix}$

7. $\begin{bmatrix} 20 & 60 & 100 \\ 40 & 80 & 120 \end{bmatrix}$

8. not legal: A and B do not have the same shape.

9. $\begin{bmatrix} 100 & 900 & 2500 \\ 400 & 1600 & 3600 \end{bmatrix}$

10. $\begin{bmatrix} 3 & 3 & 3 \\ 3 & 3 & 3 \end{bmatrix}$

11. $\begin{bmatrix} 11 & 31 & 49 \\ 21 & 39 & 59 \end{bmatrix}$

12. $\begin{bmatrix} 1 & 0 & 0 \\ 0 & 1 & 0 \\ 0 & 0 & 1 \end{bmatrix}$

Quick Quiz 9.3 *(cont.)*

13. $\begin{bmatrix} 1 & 1 & 1 \\ 1 & 1 & 1 \\ 1 & 1 & 1 \end{bmatrix}$

14. $\begin{bmatrix} 1 & 2 & 3 \\ 2 & 4 & 6 \\ 3 & 6 & 9 \end{bmatrix}$

Quick Quiz 10.3

1. derived, structure
2. false
3. the component selector %
4. nested structure
5. true
6. ```
TYPE Date
   CHARACTER(8) :: Month
   INTEGER :: Number, Year
END TYPE Date
```
7. ```
Day = Date("July", 4, 1776)
```
8. ```
READ *, Day%Month, Day%Day, Day%Year
```
9. ```
TYPE InventoryInfo
   CHARACTER(20) :: Name
   INTEGER :: StockNumber
   TYPE(Date) :: Received
END TYPE InventoryInfo
```
10. ```
Item = InventoryInfo("Camera", 12384, &
         Date("December", 10, 1995))
```
11. ```
READ *, Item%Name, Item%StockNumber, &
         Item%Received%Month, Item%Received%Day, &
         Item%Received%Year
```

Quick Quiz 11.4

1. false
2. SELECTED_INT_KIND(15)
3. true
4. SELECTED_REAL_KIND(12, 40)
5. false
6. true
7. false
8. $(-10.0, 11.0)$
9. false
10. true
11. false
12. $15 + 5i$
13. $1 + i$
14. $50 + 37i$
15. $(62 + 5i)/53$
16. $\sqrt{73}$
17. $(-1.0, 7.0)$
18. $(2.0, -1.0)$
19. $(1.5, 2.1)$
20. 2.0
21. $(1.5, 0)$
22. (1.5, 2.5)
23. ƀ1.5ƀ2.5

Quick Quiz 11.7

1. false
2. true
3. false
4. false
5. true

Quick Quiz 11.7 *(cont.)*

6. true

7. false

8. 2

9. 1

10. 1

11. "12345   "

12. " 1 2 3 4"

13. "1212121212"

14. .TRUE.

15. "A"

16. Bↄↄↄↄↄ

17. kanga

18. ThreeCPO

19. warts

Quick Quiz 12.3

1. To access a particular record in a sequential file, all of the preceding records must first be accessed. Each record in a direct access file can be accessed directly, usually by using a record number.

2. OPEN (UNIT = 12, FILE = "TESTDATA", &
        STATUS = "OLD", IOSTAT = OpenStatus)

3. OPEN (UNIT = 10, FILE = "NEWDATA", ACCESS = "DIRECT", &
        RECL = 30, STATUS = "NEW", IOSTAT = OpenStatus)

4. READ(10, '(I5)', REC = 100) IdNumber

5. Files in which information is represented in internal binary form. They are used for files that are to be read and processed only by the computer and not displayed to the user.

6. Given file

        F: 4 1 7 3 6 2 5

   Split:

        F1: |4|36|
        F2: |17|25|

Quick Quiz 12.3 *(cont.)*

Merge:

F: | 1 4 7 | 2 3 5 6 |

Split:

F1: | 1 4 7 |
F2: | 2 3 5 6 |

Merge:

F: | 1 2 3 4 5 6 7 |

Quick Quiz 13.1

1. The sizes of static data structures are fixed once memory is allocated, but dynamic data structures expand or contract as required during execution.

2. nodes

3. An element of the list and a link or pointer that indicates the location of the node containing the successor of this list element.

4. Items can be inserted into or deleted from a linked list without shifting list elements as is necessary in the array-based implementation of a list.

5. null

Quick Quiz 13.4

```
1. INTEGER, POINTER :: P1
2. TYPE Point
      REAL :: XCoord, YCoord
   END TYPE Point
   TYPE(Point), POINTER :: P2
3. ALLOCATE(P1)
   P1 = -1234
4. ALLOCATE(P2)
   P2%XCoord = 3.15
   P2%YCoord = 12.9
```

Quick Quiz 13.4 *(cont.)*

5. undefined, associated, disassociated

6. IF (.NOT. ASSOCIATED(P1)) PRINT *, "Not associated"

7. NULLIFY

8. DEALLOCATE

9. false (P1 and P2 do not have the same type.)

10. 1
    1 3
    6 3
    3 5
    7 7
    9 9

Index of Programming Problems

Chapter 4

Chapter 5

Chapter 6

Chapter 10

Chapter 11

Chapter 12

Chapter 13

Priority queues (Problem 15, p. 947)
Constructing linked lists (Problems 16–19, p. 947)
Processing polynomials using linked lists (Problems 20 and 21, p. 948)
Finding the union and intersection of linked lists (Problems 22 and 23, p. 948)
Using linked lists to represent directed graphs (Problem 24, p. 948)
Processing sparse matrices using linked lists (Problems 25 and 26, p. 949)
Processing binary search trees using linked lists (Problem 27, p. 949)
Decoding Morse code using binary search trees (Problem 28, p. 949)
Doubly linked lists (Problem 29, p. 950)
Multiply linked lists (Problem 30, p. 950)
Processing polynomials in two variables using linked lists (Problem 31, p. 951)

Index

Essential Lahey Fortran 90 (Elf90)

Elf90 is a Fortran language system for students interested in learning and writing programs using the modern features of Fortran 90. Elf90 enforces structured, modular coding. It removes redundant features while preserving the strengths of the Fortran language.

- Essential (the best!) Features of Fortran 90
- Windows-Based Editor
- 350-Page Users Guide and Language Reference
- Elf90 Language-Specific Error Messages
- Detailed Error and Warning Messages
- Programs up to 4GB
- Free Technical Support
- Debugger

Educational Price
US$79!
Regularly $195

Send me Essential Lahey Fortran 90 for only $79!

Name _____

School _____

Instructor _____

Address _____

City _____ State ____ Zip ____

Country _____

Phone (___) _____

Email _____

☐ Check Enclosed ☐ MasterCard
☐ Discover   ☐ VISA

Credit Card #: _____

Exp. Date: ____ - ____

Signature _____

Essential Lahey Fortran 90	US$79.00
Shipping Charges:	
Within the Continental U.S.	US$7.50
International and Alaska/Hawaii	US$25.00
Subtotal	US$____
NV Residents add 7% Sales Tax	US$____
TOTAL	US$____

LIMITED TIME OFFER!

Lahey
Computer Systems, Inc.

Fortran is our forte

(800) 548-4778
(702) 831-2500
Fax: (702) 831-8123

sales@lahey.com
http://www.lahey.com

865 Tahoe Blvd.
P.O. Box 6091
Incline Village NV 89450
USA

FTN90 Student Edition now only $99!

Congratulations! As an owner of BOOK-TITLE by AUTHOR you are entitled to a copy of our Student Edition of FTN90.

The Salford FTN90 Compiler

FTN90 was the worlds first Fortran 90 compiler available on the IBM PC and compatibles. FTN90 is a full ISO implementation of the Fortran 90 language.

FTN90 is supplied with an easy to use source level debugger with features such as single stepping, breakpointing, display of variables and arrays. All of the features that you would expect with a professional development tool. FTN90 also utilises Salford Software's unique dynamic checking system. By using a simple compile time switch you have the extra debugging power of automatic array bounds checking, pointer association etc.

Run-time Libraries

All Salford compilers are shipped with a library of over 250 routines supporting graphics, operating system access, bit field manipulation, sorting etc.

Windows Programming

Using the Salford ClearWin+ library in conjunction with FTN90 you can add a *true* windows interface to your Fortran applications in a fraction of the time required when using other methods. ClearWin+ uses format codes to describe the layout of your windows interface. The same codes also control the operation of the interface and its interaction with your program. Your program variables are automatically updated as the objects within the window are manipulated by the user.

Which Operating System

The DOS extended edition of FTN90 allows access to a full two gigabytes of memory under DOS or a DOS box under Windows 3.x or Windows 95.

The Win32 edition of FTN90 runs under Windows and Windows NT in native 32-bit mode.

System Requirements

FTN90 will run on almost any modern IBM PC or compatible which has a 386 (or higher) processor. The DOS extended compiler requires either DOS 5.0 or higher. The Win32 compiler requires either Windows 95 or Windows NT.

Both the DOS and Win32 development systems require 10 Mbytes or more of free disk space.

Documentation

This edition of the compiler is shipped with:

- FTN90 compiler for DOS or Win32
- Run-time library of over 250 routines
- ClearWin+ Windows programming library
- page compiler user guide
- ClearWin+ help file (full manual text)

How Do I Order?

Simply complete the order form on the reverse side and return to Salford Software Ltd.

FTN90 Student Edition Order Form

I would like to order the following:

_____ copies of the Student edition of FTN90 for DOS / Win32* @ $99 $ _____

Add VAT @ 17.5% for UK and EEC orders $ _____

Shipping charge @ $20 per copy $ _____

Total $ _____

Name: _____

Job Title: _____

Organisation: _____

Address: _____

_____

Post/Zip Code: _____

Telephone: _____

Fax: _____

I understand that the Student Edition of FTN90 is for personal educational use only.

Signature: _____

Please debit my Visa/ Master/ American Express* card.

Card holder's Name: _____

Address: _____

_____

_____

Card Number: _____

Expiry Date: _____

Please send me further information on the following:

☐ FTN90 Full Commercial Licence
☐ FTN90 Site Licence
☐ Other Salford Products

Delete as appropriate

Salford Software Ltd ● Adelphi House ● Adelphi Street ● Salford ● M3 6EN ● United Kingdom
Tel: +44 (0) 161 834 2454 ● Fax: +44 (0) 161 834 2148 ● http://www.salford.ac.uk/ssl/ss.html

Examples, Applications, and Sample Programs

Chapter 1

Radioactive decay (pp. 16–23)

Chapter 2

Velocity of a projectile (pp. 66–72, 93, 115–116)
Temperature conversion (pp. 76–81, 116–117)
Circuits with parallel resistors (pp. 82–85)
Acid dilution (pp. 85–91)

Chapter 3

Quadratic equations (pp. 131–134)
Effect of roundoff error (pp, 134–136)
Pollution index classification (pp. 136–141, 148, 151, 178–179)
Pay calculation (pp. 142–146)
Fluid flow in a pipe (pp. 151–156)
Logical circuits (pp. 161–165)

Chapter 4

Calculating depreciation (pp. 181–182, 191–197)
Mean time to failure (pp. 182, 205–213, 252–253)
Damped vibration curve (pp. 185–187)
List of products of two numbers (pp. 187–189)
Summation of integers (pp. 197–200, 201–205)
Temperature conversions (pp. 213–216)
Range of noise levels (in decibels) (pp. 216–223)
Least-squares line (pp. 230–236)

Chapter 5

Table of computed values (pp. 269–271, 312–313)
Time, temperature, pressure, and volume readings (pp. 292–300)

Chapter 6

Voltages across a capacitor (pp. 319–321, 331)
Pollution index classification (pp. 323–324)
Poisson probability (pp. 325–329)
Beam deflection (pp. 334–344)
Root finding—Newton's method (pp. 344–348)
Numerical integration—trapezoidal method (pp. 348–352, 370–373, 388–390)
Differential equations—Euler's method (pp. 352–356)
Differential equations—Runge–Kutta method (p. 356)
Road construction (pp. 357–361)
Counting paths in a street network (recursively) (pp. 390–391)

Chapter 7

Displaying an angle in degrees (pp. 395–398)
Displaying an angle in degrees–minutes–seconds format (pp. 398–402)
Conversion of polar coordinates to rectangular coordinates (pp. 402–406, 453–454, 468–469)
Designing a coin dispenser (pp. 410–416)
Using random numbers in a dice-roll simulation (pp. 417–421)
Normal distribution (pp. 421–422)